John Keay

In a long and distinguished writing career, John Keay's most recent works have been on south and south-east Asia, most notably *Last Post: The End of Empire*, *India: A History* and the bestselling *The Great Arc*. He is married to the author Julia Keay and together they compiled the *Collins Encyclopaedia of Scotland*. They have four children and live in the Highlands.

Sowing the Wind

The Mismanagement of the Middle East 1900–1960

JOHN KEAY

'For they have sown the wind,
and they shall reap the whirlwind.'
Hosea 8:7

JOHN MURRAY

First published in Great Britain in 2003
by John Murray (Publishers)
A division of Hodder Headline

Paperback edition 2004

2 4 6 8 10 9 7 5 3 1

ISBN 0 7195 6171X

Printed and bound in Great Britain by Clays Ltd, St Ives plc.

John Murray (Publishers)
338 Euston Road
London
NW1 3BH

For Sam

Contents

Contents

Illustrations

Illustrations

The author and publisher would like to thank the following for permission to reproduce illustrations: page 1 (above), *Illustrated London News* Picture Library; 1 (below) and 11, Popperfoto; 2, 4 (above and below), 5, 8, 18, 19, 20, 21 (above and below), 27 (above) and 32 (above and below), Trustees of the Imperial War Museum, London; 3, 16 (above and below) and 29 (below), © Topham Picturepoint; 6, 7, 15 and 25, AKG London; 9, 12 (below), 13 and 31, © Hulton Archive; 10, 17, 22, 24, 26 and 27 (below), from Walid Khalidi, *Beyond the Diaspora* (Institute for Palestine Studies, Washington DC, 1984); 12 (above), Mary Evans Picture Library; 14, John Murray Archive; 28 and 29, Associated Press; and 30, © Bettmann/CORBIS.

Author's Note and Acknowledgements

Written as the winds of war were again whirling about the Middle East, this book was informed by concern, rising to alarm. I wish I could say that it was also the distillation of a lifetime's scholarly involvement, but this is not the case. It is the product of numerous visits to the Middle East, of earlier writings and broadcasts about the Arab world, and a lot of reading. But I speak neither Arabic nor Hebrew. I am neither Jewish nor Muslim. I first came to the subject cold and unconfident. Like a traveller in a strange land, I tried to convince myself that an inquisitive eye and an open mind were sufficient unto themselves. Narrative crammed with dramatic events and eloquent personae would surely contain its own commentary, so making the modern Middle East intelligible to writer and reader alike. More desperately I cast about for reassurance.

This was provided during the writing by my wife Julia, editor Gail Pirkis and agent Bruce Hunter, and during the editing by the scholar Basim Musallam and the Arabist and author Tim Mackintosh-Smith. Between them they frustrated my best efforts to reform the orthography of the English and Arabic languages, and redeemed the book from a host of obscurities and howlers. They also found the gentle phrases to lull a troubled mind. Thanks are inadequate. I owe you.

Additionally Bikram Grewal and Alpana Khare in Dehra Dun, and Pam McVeigh and Tim Williams at Les Guis extended the unobtrusive hospitality – serious food, shady veranda, dreamy vistas –

essential to meticulous research. Thanks to you all. Thanks, too, to Michael Allcock for his recollections of the larger-than-life Miles Copeland and to William Rubinstein for his paper on 'The Secret of Leopold Amery'.

Finally no thanks (because it is their job) but hearty congratulations to the staffs of the London, British, SOAS, RGS, Scottish National and Mitchell libraries for their unfailing courtesy. To me you are all just faces; to you I'm another champing reader or long overdue borrower. But without your cataloguing, your shelving and your forbearance, books like this would not get written. Across the issue desk I salute you.

Maps

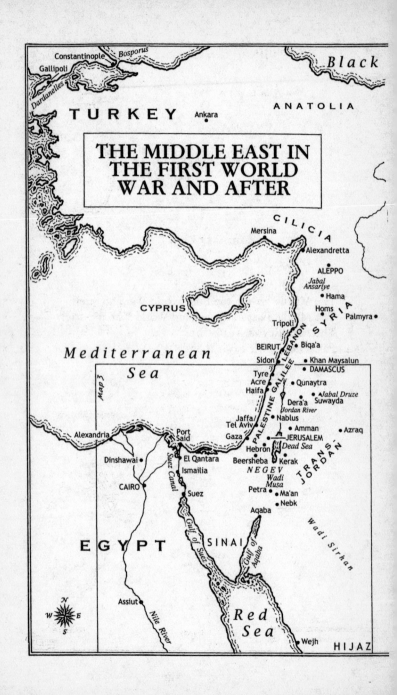

THE MIDDLE EAST IN
THE FIRST WORLD
WAR AND AFTER

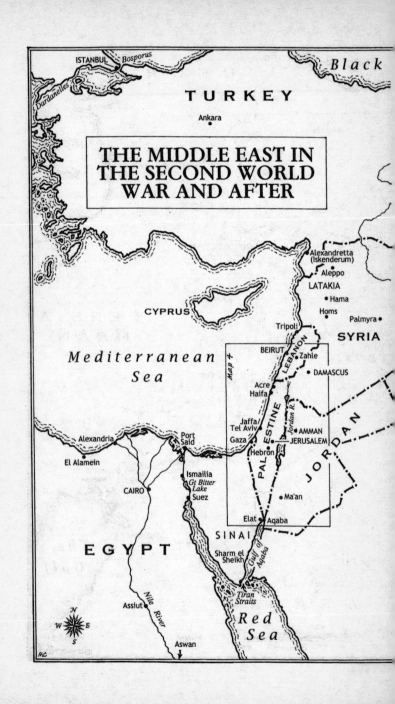

THE MIDDLE EAST IN THE SECOND WORLD WAR AND AFTER

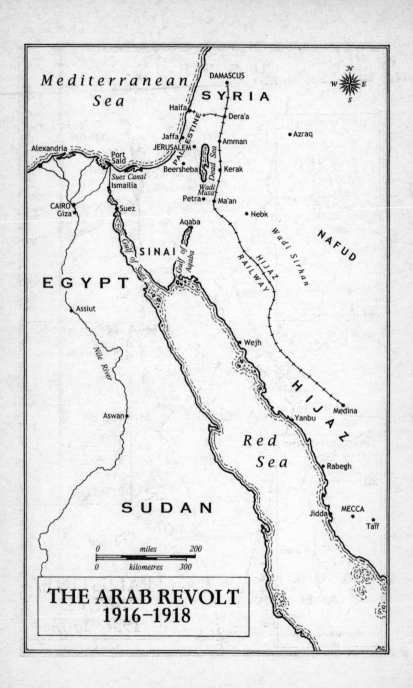

Mediterranean Sea

DAMASCUS

S Y R I A

Haifa

Dera'a

Jaffa

JERUSALEM

Amman

• Azraq

Dead Sea

Alexandria

Port Said

Beersheba

Kerak

Suez Canal

Ismailia

Wadi Musa

CAIRO

Giza

Suez

Petra

Ma'an

• Nebk

Wadi Sirhan

N A F U D

Aqaba

S I N A I

Gulf of Aqaba

Gulf of Suez

HIJAZ RAILWAY

E G Y P T

• Assiut

Nile River

Wejh

H I J A Z

Medina

• Aswan

Yanbu

Red Sea

Rabegh

S U D A N

MECCA

Jidda

Taïf

0   *miles*   200

0   *kilometres*   300

**THE ARAB REVOLT
1916–1918**

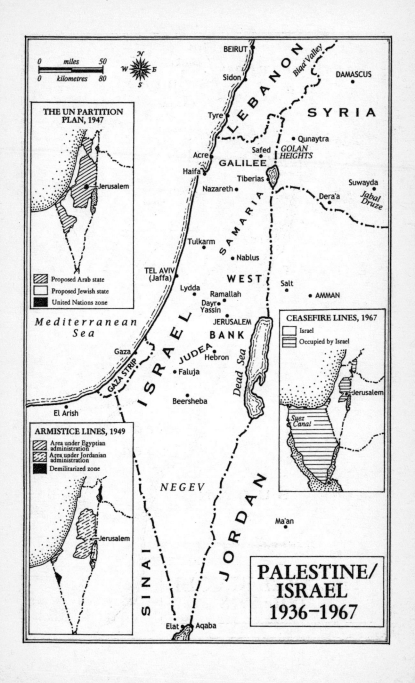

PALESTINE/
ISRAEL
1936–1967

THE UN PARTITION
PLAN, 1947

Proposed Arab state
Proposed Jewish state
United Nations zone

Jerusalem

CEASEFIRE LINES, 1967

Israel
Occupied by Israel

Jerusalem

Suez
Canal

ARMISTICE LINES, 1949

Area under Egyptian
administration
Area under Jordanian
administration
Demilitarized zone

Jerusalem

miles 50
kilometres 80

N
W   E
S

BEIRUT
Sidon
Biqa' Valley
DAMASCUS

LEBANON   SYRIA

Tyre
Quanytra
Safed   GOLAN
Acre   HEIGHTS
Haifa   GALILEE
Tiberias   Suwayda
Nazareth   Dera'a   Jabal
Druze

SAMARIA

Tulkarm
Nablus

TEL AVIV   WEST
(Jaffa)   Salt
Lydda   Ramallah   AMMAN
Dayr
Yassin   JERUSALEM
BANK

*Mediterranean
Sea*

JUDEA
Gaza   Hebron
Faluja

El Arish   Beersheba

Dead Sea

NEGEV

Ma'an

SINAI   JORDAN

Elat   Aqaba

Introduction

THERE IS NO accepted definition of the region we call 'the Middle East'. History has tended to shift it around to suit its own convenience, like a movie set. Afghanistan and Azerbaijan have sometimes been included, sometimes not; likewise Sudan and Libya. Traditionally those countries bordering the eastern Mediterranean – Turkey and the Levant region of Syria, Lebanon and Palestine – belonged not to the Middle East but the Near East, a construction that also included neighbouring bits of Europe, like Greece and the Balkans. Elsewhere the Near East and Middle East overlapped and could be confused. Egypt might be awarded to either, or to neither; it depended on whether, as part of Africa, it could also be part of an East that was otherwise Asian.

Overflying the lands between the Mediterranean and the Gulf, one is struck by their monotony. Their colour is that of a camel-hair coat, their texture as brittle as biscuit. From 30,000 feet the region looks to have a distinct physical identity, whatever we choose to call it. But this impression is misleading. The Middle East is no more one big sand bowl than the Far East is one big rice bowl. Its considerable deserts are contradicted by the most productive of deltas, and its extensive plains are interrupted by snow-scabbed mountains and rent by that deep depression in which the Dead Sea is breathlessly expiring. Elsewhere olive groves and orchards, palm groves and marshes fringe the oaten wastes. Seen at close quarters the Middle East defies the notion of a prevailing terrain.

Nor does its coastal outline afford a recognizable perimeter. Unlike the pear-drop which is South America, or India's triangle, the Middle East lacks an obvious configuration. On the maps, instead of a distinctive shape outlined in ocean, it appears as an undifferentiated chunk of intercontinental torso, severed with no regard for geography, and presenting the punch-bag profile of a Henry Moore sculpture. The indentations at lower right are those made by the Gulf and the Red Sea. They appear to be extending fingered greetings from the Indian Ocean. But the Atlantic, here represented by the blunt extremities of the Mediterranean and the Black Sea, makes no effort to reciprocate. It is as if creation's plan for an east–west waterway linking Europe and Asia had at the last minute been rejected in favour of a north–south land-bridge linking Anatolia and Africa.

The oceanic handshake between East and West remained unconsummated until the Suez Canal was cut in the 1860s. This channel, while serving the interests of world trade, did nothing to further a regional identity. Africa, insulated by the Canal, became detached from Asia; Arabia, its overland routes rendered redundant by maritime intercourse, became a dead end; and the region as a whole, once conceived as a barrier across which transit had to be negotiated, could now be counted a corridor through which passage might be commanded.

Even supposing that a physical definition of the region were possible, it would be flatly denied by its human component. The ethnology of the Middle East is as complicated and controversial as one would expect of a continental isthmus. No less heterodox are its belief systems. Jews, Christians and Muslims all account parts of the Middle East, and sometimes the same parts, as peculiarly 'holy land'. Islam has long been the prevailing religion and Arabic the prevailing language, but neither is exclusive to the region. Arabic is also spoken throughout much of North Africa, and there are far more Muslims outside the Middle East than within it. The human geography is no more revealing than the physical geography.

In fact 'the Middle East' has never been a geographical expression; it has always and essentially been an economic and political one. As noted elsewhere in this book, the term is of fairly recent provenance; it was coined in the West; and it reflects Western perceptions in that it defines the region in terms of what the Western powers considered its characteristic uses and abuses. These varied during the early twentieth century, the uses being often strategic and the abuses always requiring foreign intervention. Today the relevant criteria might be summed up as 'oil and turmoil'. Popularly, anywhere between Tunis and Tehran which pumps crude and provokes headlines is consigned to 'the Middle East'. Conversely, countries within this area which at any given moment are doing neither tend to be excused from 'the Middle East'.

I, too, have subscribed to this conceit. In no less arbitrary fashion, I have interpreted the term 'Middle East' to suit the theme of this book. Hence large parts of the region, notably Turkey, are ignored completely; others, like Iran, appear only when their affairs become subject to decisive Western direction. For this is not a history of the Middle East but an account of how it was manipulated and managed, or mismanaged, by the Western powers.

Relations with the tiny shaykhdoms of the Gulf, the colony of Aden and the Imamate of Yemen ought, nevertheless, to be included. They are not because it would be distracting to do so. The West's involvement in these peripheral entities predates the period under consideration. It had little bearing on relations with the rest of the region and was largely conducted not from the West but from what was then British-ruled India.

This book is more concerned with the hard core of the region, with Egypt and that eastward arc of unrest, sometimes known as the Fertile Crescent, that embraces Jordan, Israel/Palestine, Lebanon, Syria and Iraq. It sounds a more daunting list than it is. Were all outstanding hostilities resolved, border formalities simplified and roads unblocked, one might breakfast beside the Mediterranean in the Lebanese capital of Beirut, drive up to the Syrian capital of Damascus for lunch, race south to Jordan's Amman for tea, make Jerusalem for an early dinner, and be back beside the Mediterranean for a stroll before bed in Tel Aviv. From Damascus an extra day's drive would bring you to Baghdad in Iraq. From Jerusalem a similar excursion would take you across the sands of Sinai to the Suez Canal and the fleshpots of Cairo. The core of the Middle East is not big. It might be squeezed into the British Isles or a state the size of Florida. It is, in effect, of eminently manageable size.

A bit of squeezing is permissible because only a fraction of the land area is actually populated. The rest was, and still is, uninhabitable desert. Explorers, swaying along on their camels, invariably likened the desert to a sea in which the cultivated areas were reckoned islands. Strung across 2,000 miles of sand, the islands formed an archipelago; and in this archipelago two islands, one at each end, stood out by reason of their fertility, antiquity and density of population.

The more westerly was Egypt's Shatt al-Nil, the delta of the river Nile; it was also the more favoured and much the more populous. Its eastern equivalent, Iraq's Shatt al-Arab, comprised the lands along the lower reaches of the Tigris and the Euphrates; less obliging rivers in a less temperate land, they nevertheless supported a population of several million and boasted a record of spawning early civilizations (Sumerian, Akkadian and so on) that was rivalled only by that of the Nile itself. For five thousand years before Alexander the Great of Macedon set out to conquer the world, the axis of exchange and enmity in the Middle East followed the continental land-bridge between these twin poles of human precosity.

There are no other rivers in the Middle East with a comparable capacity for easy and extensive irrigation. The rest of the archipelago depends heavily on climatic caprice. Rain clouds forming over the Mediterranean fitfully water the north–south Levant coast and the mountains that run parallel to it through Syria, Lebanon and Israel/Palestine. The coastal plain and the mountains themselves bristle with settlements, while the seaport cities of Tripoli, Beirut, Haifa and Tel Aviv/Jaffa are matched inland by an equivalent string of desert-port cities stretching from Aleppo down through Damascus to Amman. This Levantine world is the plenteous horn of the Fertile Crescent, with citrus groves in the south giving way to peach and apricot orchards in the north. Further north and east, cotton and cereals are grown to advantage in the Syrian Jazirah which, by way of the upper Euphrates, links the Mediterranean horn of the Crescent to its Iraqi extremity, a flatter land of abundant but featureless fields and tousled date palms.

Within and below the arc of this Fertile Crescent, and for thousands of miles to the south of it, all is desert. Oases, like Syria's Palmyra or Jordan's Azraq, owe their importance simply to their rarity and hence their attraction to caravan traders, highway builders and pipeline layers. Arabic, a language as steeped in humour as in faith, has no illusions about the desert. One adage tells of how, when God created the Sudan, He laughed; another of how, when He created Arabia, He wasn't thinking. When He created the jewel that is Lebanon, the Lebanese were frankly amazed. What had they done, they asked, to deserve a land so well endowed with spreading cedars, golden beaches and cool mountain breezes? Ah, said God, but wait until you see who I am giving you as neighbours.

As a cockpit of contention the region has no rival. It has long been so, and always for the same reason. Since Alexander of Macedon made a point of securing the Nile before embarking on his oriental conquests, no imperium has ventured to claim world dominion without asserting its authority over the Middle East. Romans, Arabs, Mongols and Turks successively pitched on the region as a pivot of empire; where Alexander led, Napoleon would follow, with Nelson hard astern. Zealots and dynasts, no less than imperialists and super-powers, could ill afford to ignore the acknowledged 'crossroads of the world'. And when in time their fortunes waned, each left by the wayside a trail of endeavour and destruction paved in stone, pre-served in word forms and belief systems, or treasured in blood lines. So strewn is the Middle East with this detritus of conquest that a powerful case for further intervention might be mounted on the grounds of historical precedent alone.

But the region had attractions other than as a stamping-ground for armies. Through its crossroads rare commodities were funnelled and from its hinterland highly prized produce and livestock were corralled. Long before anyone realized that energy could be derived from igniting the oil that lay untapped beneath those biscuit wastes, other novelties – preservatives, unguents, gems and delicacies – were transhipped, hauled and transhipped again across the Arabian penin-sula from the Indian Ocean to the desert-ports of the interior, then on to the seaports of the Mediterranean.

This east–west 'spice-trade' was probably the most remunerative in the medieval world, but it was matched and, following the late fifteenth-century discovery of the sea-route round Africa, eclipsed by a no less lucrative west–east trade, principally in bloodstock. From the Gulf, reported Marco Polo in the thirteenth century, ten thousand horses a year were being shipped to just one small Tamil kingdom at the tip of India. Comprising Arabian thoroughbreds and hardy Central Asian chargers, these shipments provided the motive force which, until the nineteenth century, powered the armies of the East. 'Horse-power' was as vital an energy source in its day as oil is now, and the trade was so valuable that, according to a Portuguese traveller in the sixteenth century, even those mounts that arrived in India dead were always paid for. Such was the fear, then as since, of an embargo on deliveries from the Gulf.

And then as since, compounding its centrality, parts of the Middle East exercised on the hearts and minds of much of mankind a unique and deeper attraction, one out of all proportion to the region's assets and amenities. For here met not just Asia and Africa, or West and East, but Creation and Creator. God himself had chosen the Middle East in which to confront His people. Here were His Word revealed, His commandments received, His miracles performed; here trod His prophets, His law-givers, His Son: and here, like swallows returning to the barn of their hatching, flocked His followers in prayer and pilgrimage.

The flood of Muslim pilgrims who made the annual *hajj* to Mecca and Medina in the Hijaz region of what is today Saudi Arabia paid handsomely for their piety. They represented a major source of income to the region, and like all Muslims they looked on it as peculiarly their own. Like the language in which the Prophet had once preached, the lands in which He had once lived were endowed with an exclusive sanctity, one that transcended geography, commanded reverence and must be defended.

The stream of Christians who came to explore their own 'Holy Land', and the trickle of Jews who, hankering after the same small land of their ancient provenance, occasionally returned to it, contributed less to the local economy. But both looked on the lands beside the Jordan river with equally zealous and proprietary eyes. Nearly a thousand years before twentieth-century Zionists would tirelessly lobby and recruit among the Jews of Europe and America for a 'promised' homeland in *Eretz Israel*, popes and clerics were similarly cajoling the Christian kingdoms of Europe into recruiting, financing and fighting for their own 'return' to the 'Holy Land'. The Crusaders themselves often had less reputable motives, but their sponsors, the Norman kingdoms and the Holy Roman Empire, heeded arguments based on moral pressure, biblical prophecy, strategic advantage, humanitarian concern and hard cash – just as would Lloyd George and Britain's Gentile Zionists, just as would Harry Truman and the Democratic Party.

Spun out over five centuries and latterly as much concerned with the fate of the Byzantine empire as of Palestine, the Crusades ultimately stalled. Wider horizons offering softer targets for Christian endeavour and greater opportunities for financial reward beckoned. A New World waited in the Americas and newly accessible lands in Africa and the Indies. The Christian powers, their own backyard menaced by the ascendant Ottoman Turks and their ranks then rent by the Reformation, mothballed their designs on the 'Holy Land', conceded its political hegemony to the Ottomans, and took to the high seas. New worlds, new resources, new inventions and new thinking soon challenged the pontifications and orthodoxies of revelation. Church and state questioned their mutual relationship; nature and science indicted the dogmatism of religion; observation and deduction were the new chapter and verse. Islam, a romanticizable irrelevance to enlightened minds and no longer Christianity's main challenger, could be disregarded, the Islamic world bypassed. The Middle East was consigned to the Middle Ages.

Enlightenment was to empire as the glove to the fist. It softened the blow of aggression and made it almost respectable. Trade might follow the flag but reason and enquiry legitimized it. From the sixteenth to the eighteenth century expansionist blows administered to the soft underbelly of the Afro-Asian landmass by the Portuguese, Dutch, British and French awakened in each notions of a global empire based on the profits of trade, the benefits of civilization and command of the oceans. No oceans met in the Middle East. But the awareness that in Egypt they nearly did, and the possibility that they might yet be made to do so, quickened Western interest.

Egypt, the granary as well as the pivot of past empires, appealed particularly to the young Napoleon. Its Red Sea frontage offered access to the Arabian Sea and the incipient Indian empire of his British foe, its northern shores commanded the eastern Mediterranean, and its great river beckoned adventurers into the heart of Africa. In 1798 Napoleonic troops stormed ashore near the port of Alexandria. A second army of antiquarians, agriculturists and scholars came hard on their heels. The military occupation, the first by a non-Islamic power since the Crusades, was controversial. By the British it would be hotly contested, swiftly terminated and, within a century, faithfully emulated.

The assumption that the Middle East was a fit subject for study and improvement was less controversial. While Egypt was back under Egyptian rule, the Canal was triumphantly cut. But its engineer was a Frenchman, its financing was organized in Paris and London, and the Egyptian government's shares would be quickly acquired by the British. Of the dignitaries who attended its grand opening in 1869, most came from Europe. The inrush of water from the Mediterranean seemed symbolic; so did the foreign flags which, flown from ships unseen below the Canal's embankments, were soon forging across the desert.

By 1882, when the British occupation began, all Egypt was already gouged by the inroads of Western capital. Its culture was being appropriated, its economy managed, its politics manipulated. But as the twentieth century dawned, this level of intervention had yet to be extended to the rest of the Middle East. For those biscuit wastes still under Ottoman rule the implications of the Canal and its security had still to be appreciated. The demands of the internal combustion engine and of Zionism, let alone the latter's endorsement by the Western powers, were quite unanticipated. And the new Crusaders, in or out of uniform, had yet to acquire an intensity of purpose, yet to evolve a sanction for their presence, yet to provoke an effective response.

Part One

1900–1918

I

Straws in the Wind

THE DOVES OF DINSHAWAI

BEFORE HIGH DAMS confused its flow, the River Nile disdained the deserts of Egypt. Like an arm upraised out of Africa, it seemed intent only on reaching the Mediterranean coast. Not until past the pyramids and north of Cairo did it finally splay its fingers in that generous gesture of triumph and fulfilment that is the Nile delta. Here, amid willow-fringed waterways plopping with kingfishers, irrigation was made easy. Ducts and sluices had proliferated as a sedentary society guddled in the silt-laden waters and explored the potential of hydraulic agriculture. Six thousand years ago what we choose to call civilization, cradled like the infant Moses in his basket, bobbed into history on the bosom of the lower Nile.

Later the delta became one of the world's most intensively farmed tracts supporting one of the world's most densely packed populations. Pockets of scrub and pasture shrank to extinction; an erstwhile paradise for wildlife had by the early twentieth century become one great farmscape. It was no place for the sportsman. Wildfowl on jealously guarded waters provided a winter bag for the Egyptian sovereign and his colonial cronies. For lesser mortals, and especially during the long summer months, there were only doves and pigeons.

Whirling round the mud-built villages in close coveys, these birds were not as wild as the purist would have wished. The pigeons fed on the fellahin's crops and the fellahin fed on the pigeons' offspring. Their meat augmented a diet short on protein while their colourful presence animated hard, drab lives. They were not fair game; and the party of eager young shots – five British officers *en route* to Alexandria – who descended on the village of Dinshawai, sixty miles north of Cairo, one boiling June morning in 1906 should certainly have asked permission to shoot. They did so, but whether it was given is disputed; so is much else about the so-called 'Dinshawai incident'. But authorized or not, the guns opened fire. Feathers flew and a few birds dropped, but the shoot had hardly got underway when, for no clear reason, a nearby threshing ground suddenly went up in flames.

For the by now incensed villagers of Dinshawai this was the final outrage. With staves and hoes they belaboured the strangers. Then a gun went off. A woman fell, apparently dead; others were peppered with shot. 'For a moment, the crowd surged back,' recalled Lieutenant Standish Smithwick, an Irishman like several of his colleagues, 'and then it seemed as if all hell was let loose.'[1]

As pale skins bruised and British bones were broken, an escape attempt was mounted. Though badly beaten, the sportsmen ran through the fields in the midday sun, heading back to camp for help. Before they reached it, two were overtaken and dragged back to the village; and a Captain Bull was left for dead. He had been felled by a brick that may have fractured his skull, though medical opinion later held that he had died as much from sunstroke as from concussion. More certainly, an Egyptian peasant, who may have been trying to revive him, was clubbed to death by Bull's regimental comrades as they rushed to his aid. Meanwhile, back at the barn, the local police had restrained the irate villagers and rescued the bloodied sportsmen, all of whom would eventually recover.

Although the details of this fracas have been hotly disputed ever since, it is clear that only one of the British shooting party understood Arabic and none of the villagers knew English. Among the occupying British forces in Egypt the docility of the *fellahin*, or peasantry, had long been axiomatic. There was no reason to expect trouble at Dinshawai; nor was there ever found any firm evidence of premeditation on the part of the villagers. The attack seemed to have been as arbitrary and accidental as the burning of the barn and the discharge of the shot-gun. It all looked, in short, like a terrible misunderstanding.

That was not how the subsequent tribunal chose to see it and not how posterity came to regard it. Convened under a draconian piece of legislation that had scarcely ever been invoked, the Special Tribunal comprised three Britons and one pro-British Egyptian under the chairmanship of a Coptic Christian. Its justice was summary and there could be no appeal. Fifty-two villagers were accused. The tribunal took just thirty minutes to examine them all; and their British victims supposedly identified an improbable twenty-one of them.

Of these, twenty were found guilty. Four were sentenced to hang, and sixteen were given terms of imprisonment ranging from a year to life, plus fifty lashes. It was all over within that same suffocating month of June 1906. The hangings and the floggings were carried out immediately and in the nearby desert. Indeed, the gallows had been erected before the trial was over. 'One man was hanged and left hanging while two others were being whipped,' reported a newsman, 'another was then hanged and two more whipped' – and so on, as the doves wheeled overhead and the villagers of Dinshawai looked on.[2] From the village itself came the loud wails of the womenfolk; 'save for this,' noted the reporter, 'all was strangely quiet'.[3]

Later protests from luminaries such as the playwright George Bernard Shaw and the novelist Pierre Loti went unheeded. The *Manchester Guardian* took up the case and Egyptian nationalism briefly rejoiced in a rare display of British sympathy.[4] In the House of Commons questions concentrated on the justice, or otherwise, of the sentences. But in Egypt it was the wisdom of enforcing such sentences that troubled the British community; for as one of its members reported, 'the Egyptian public was stupefied by the infliction of such terrible penalties . . . [and] local British opinion was disposed to believe that nothing would contribute more to the development of latent hostility against the Occupying Power than actions of the type adopted at Dinshawai'.[5]

In the Black Book of empire the Dinshawai incident would rank as 'Egypt's Amritsar', a reference to the 1919 massacre of several hundred Panjabis by an unrepentant British officer that radicalized India's independence struggle. The Amritsar scandal was compounded in that the Englishman responsible was never brought to justice; indeed he was idolized by certain sections of the British press. Likewise, no enquiry was ever held into the proceedings of the Dinshawai tribunal and no official action was taken against its personnel. Egyptians were outraged. The doves of the delta came to symbolize the peaceful *fellahin* mown down by the brutality of the British occupation. A first chapter had been written in the mythology of Egypt's anti-colonial struggle. Mustafa Kamel, the leading critic of British rule, welcomed a million new converts to the nationalist cause.[6] The Arabic press took up the cry, poets elevated the protests over the 'incident' into a veritable *intifada*, and popular ballads told of how:

> They fell upon Dinshawai
>> And spared neither man nor his brother.
> Slowly they hanged the one
>> And slowly they flogged the other.[7]

The one Egyptian judge who had sat on the tribunal, as also the Public Prosecutor, would be dogged by pigeon slurs for the rest of his days; and when, four years later, the Copt who had chaired the proceedings was assassinated, it was supposedly on account of his part in the infamous 'incident'. (He was called, incidentally, Butros Ghali, a name that his grandson would do much to rehabilitate as Secretary-General of the United Nations.) More to the point, Dinshawai became an acknowledged watershed in Anglo-Egyptian relations; the *fellahin* had made common cause with the educated classes, and a cherished British belief about the loyalty of the peasantry had exploded in their face.[8] Since the myth that the British were protecting the *fellahin* was also the most commonly cited reason for the British presence in Egypt, grave indeed were the implications.

During the preceding decades Lord Cromer, Britain's long-serving proconsul in Egypt, had re-established order in the country, restored the Egyptian economy and set up an effective administration while revolutionizing agriculture and offering some genuine security to the downtrodden *fellahin*. Yet when, soon after Dinshawai, Cromer bade farewell to Egypt, not a tear was shed nor a salutation raised. 'He drove to the station', wrote an observer, 'through streets lined by troops armed with ball cartridge, amid a silence chillier than ice.'[9] The 'incident', according to Cromer's one-time assistant and successor, was 'our worst-managed . . . since the beginning of our occupation'.[10] It had discredited one of imperialism's greatest works and prejudiced any chance of continued Anglo-Egyptian collaboration.

Although not the first show of Egyptian discontent with the British presence, it was the first sign that resentment of this presence was a prerogative neither of the country's traditional leadership nor of those more radical groups who might wish to challenge this leadership – students, religious spokesmen, 'nationalist' agitators. On the contrary, the hostility was evidently 'of the people', welling up on the rising waters of the Nile with imperceptible but potentially devastating effect.

In retrospect, Dinshawai can be seen to foreshadow a new and insistent phenomenon. During the first years of the twentieth century other straws in the wind, harbingers of the troubled times ahead, were detectable. But Dinshawai was as the wind itself. Expressions of popular disquiet and eruptions of popular revolt emanating from the unconsidered and unrepresented masses would come to constitute a veritable climate change. In the Middle East, as elsewhere, the new century would be 'the People's Century'. Any regime, whether foreign or indigenous, would need to recognize and adapt to this new political meteorology; and if the colonial powers signally failed to do so, they would not be the only ones.

ATTENDING THE OTTOMAN

Even so, in 1906 Egypt's predicament was untypical of the Middle East as a whole, and Dinshawai looked like an aberration. The country had been occupied by British forces since 1882 when, at the request of the Khedive (the Ottoman Sultan's 'viceroy' in Egypt), they had intervened to suppress a populist uprising. Led by Ahmed Arabi, a colonel in the Egyptian army, this revolt had allied discontent among army officers to agrarian unrest and profound resentment of foreign influence in the internal affairs of the country. The same elements would coalesce in another revolution, seventy years later, under the leadership of Colonel Gamal Abd al-Nasser. On both occasions the colonels served as agents of a revolutionary tendency that was both widely endorsed and, though provoked by the extravagance and misgovernment of the sovereign, decidedly national; for, aside from whether the khedives (or, later, kings) could be deemed Egyptian (all were descended from the nineteenth-century Turkish-Albanian adventurer Muhammad Ali), the monarchy seemed to be dancing to a tune called by the European powers. Long before the British occupation, Europe's financiers had inveigled Egypt into a debtor's straitjacket, Europe's strategists had habitually treated the country as an imperial corridor, and Europe's statesmen had exacted privileges that enabled over 90,000 foreigners to dominate Egypt's bureaucracy and exploit its economy while remaining immune from its taxation and protected from its law courts.

This state of affairs dated back to the commercial and judicial concessions (known as 'Capitulations') that European merchants in the Ottoman territories had been steadily accumulating since the sixteenth century. Napoleon's 1798 invasion of Egypt, though principally intended to distract the British and menace their Indian links, had been encouraged by French mercantile interests and had set a precedent for armed intervention on their behalf by the European powers. The Napoleonic occupation had been short-lived, but French investment had subsequently flourished and the French language and French culture had been generally adopted by Egypt's ruling classes. Students who could afford it were sent to study in France. Business and government were conducted in French. The Suez Canal, opened in 1869, was a French initiative.

But in 1882 it was the British who rose to the challenge posed by Arabi's revolt. By then it was they who had most to lose. Lancashire's textile mills had become heavily dependent on Egypt's raw cotton, British manufacturers looked on Egypt as a promising market, and of the shipping that passed through the Suez Canal (itself half-owned by the British since 1875) 80 per cent was British.

The strategic importance of the Canal could scarcely be exaggerated. It was ironic that a global empire that prided itself on ruling the waves should be hostage to a ditch across the Sinai desert; but by this artery the imperial heart in Asia pumped blood to the imperial head in London, and by this thread the empire was articulated. Across the generations British imperial strategists might agonize over Afghanistan or bicker about the Gulf, but they unfailingly concurred on the importance of the Canal. Arabi, like Nasser later on, had to be challenged; and in 1882, unlike 1956, no rival power could stay the British. The Egyptian forces were duly crushed; the British occupation had begun.

Elsewhere, though, the twentieth century dawned on a Middle East which, apart from some deep-fried British treaty ports in the Gulf and a coaling station at Aden, was unacquainted with the realities of European colonialism. Nor was there any reason to anticipate them. When Miss Gertrude Bell, a 31-year-old Englishwoman of intimidating intellect and inexhaustible epistles, chose Jerusalem as the appropriate place from which to see in the new century, she found nothing political to report. Her letters of December 1899–January 1900 record the difficulties of mastering Arabic and applaud the pale sunshine that terminated a wet Christmas. On New Year's Day she wrote to her step-mother for a grey felt sun-hat: 'it must be a *regular Terai shape* and broad-rimmed';[11] she was very particular about such things. Ten days later she noted rumours about the relief of Ladysmith, with relief. But the new year received scarcely a nod; nor did the old; and despite her top-level diplomatic contacts, Miss Bell betrayed not the faintest premonition that on the Middle East the palely dawning twentieth century would have peculiar designs.

With a view to travel Miss Bell was also hiring guides and buying a horse. As yet there were no motorable roads anywhere between the eastern Mediterranean and the Gulf, and the only railways were stubs of track like that by which she had transferred from the port of Jaffa, still innocent of the Tel Aviv that would engross it, to Jerusalem. Beyond the holy city, the bare hills and the barren deserts, the stony fields and the dusty plains which now form the states of Palestine/Israel, Lebanon, Syria, Jordan and Iraq were just an undifferentiated chunk of the Ottoman empire.

Though overwhelmingly Arab in population, these lands had been under the rule of the Turkish Ottoman sultans in Constantinople for the last four hundred years. Nominally they looked likely to remain so for the foreseeable future. Decrepit in the Balkans, Turkey was already characterized as 'the sick man of Europe'; a similar diagnosis applied in North Africa where during the nineteenth century Algeria, then Tunisia, had passed from Ottoman rule to the French, as had Egypt to the British. But in Asia the Ottoman patient's ailments were less obvious, and under Sultan Abd al-Hamid II (reigned 1876–1909) convalescence was on the cards. With German help the Ottoman army was remodelled on European lines, education was promoted and industry encouraged.

A flurry of constitutional reforms fared less well. Eagerly adopted, but quickly aborted when the constraints of parliamentary scrutiny became apparent, the reforms were then boldly appropriated by the so-called 'Young Turks' of the Committee of Union and Progress

(CUP). An outlawed organization in 1900, the CUP would steadily win over sections of the Ottoman army and in 1908 successfully stage a revolution. Convalescence was proving traumatic.

More consoling to the Ottoman invalid was the solicitude of his doctors. Indeed their anxiety to keep him alive was his best guarantee of survival. Such were the jealousies of the British, French, Germans and Russians that any projected assault on Ottoman territory by one power, or any advantage gained there, instantly brought the other powers rushing to Constantinople's bedside. Dismembering what remained of the Turkish empire might appeal to all, but it was in the interest of none. When the Sultan plaintively insisted that 'I will not agree to vivisection', the powers approved; the life-support system must continue.

Technically even British-occupied Egypt was still part of the Ottoman empire. The Khedive supposedly ruled on behalf of the Sultan, and the British supposedly occupied on behalf of the Khedive in the name of the Sultan. Lord Cromer might run the show but officially he was neither a viceroy nor a governor, just 'Agent and Consul-General'. Indeed, in diplomatic parlance, Egypt never would become a British colony. Punted experimentally round the touchline of empire, it would pass from occupied status to protected status to treaty status without any theoretical diminution of its parlous sovereignty and without much practical concern for the consent of the Egyptian people. If in 1900 it was anyone's colony, it was technically Constantinople's, just like the rest of the Middle East.

But as plots gave way to counter-plots and rumour begat report, speculation about the future of the Ottoman lands became an industry. Constantinople buzzed with intrigue. Here the rival legations paraded their finest talents while top-hatted concessionaires flexed their cheque books. The Bosporus churned with mysterious deals and improbable alliances. Further afield, in Baghdad and Damascus, Beirut and Jerusalem, itinerant antiquarians and earnest Bible scholars lent an all too innocent ear to the political gossip. Explorers incognito pounced on *terra incognita* in the sands of Arabia, supposedly oblivious of the desert's contentious status on the fringe of Ottoman territory. Likewise, off-duty British officers heading home from India chose eccentric routes through Mesopotamia and took an unexpected interest in the tribal groupings they encountered.

In Paris, St Petersburg and Berlin, as well as London, their often unsolicited reports and route-maps accumulated. Particular note was taken of disaffected minorities, dissident factions, natural resources, trading prospects and transportation potential. Long before the Cold War, before even the Russian Revolution, the Middle East was a hotbed of intelligence-gathering and crypto-diplomacy. What Miles Copeland, a genial American go-between and *agent provocateur* in the early 1950s, would call 'The Game of Nations' was already under way. Copeland's informants – 'agents of various nationalities, mostly archaeologists and missionaries of odd sects, administered by retired college professors and a miscellany of businessmen' – were operative long before the 1950s.[12] For all her girlish exuberance and dazzling erudition, Gertrude Bell was just such a one. From Jerusalem in 1900 she trekked to the monumental splendours of Petra and Palmyra as a tourist. By 1909 she was back in Syria in the role of archaeological surveyor; in 1913 she probed deep into Arabia as an explorer; in 1915 she was officially appointed as a political counsellor in Iraq; and by 1923 she would be that country's king-maker.

To the political officers of the colonial future a knowledge of Arabic, a taste for travel, and a range of contacts would be valuable qualifications. Among the British, Hogarth, Lawrence, Philby, Wilson, Sykes and many others would follow Miss Bell's example and turn their pre-1914 rambles in the Ottoman empire to good professional account. The Germans and the French were no less thorough in this groundwork. German travellers concentrated on Anatolia and the northern Arab lands, the French on Lebanon and Syria whose Christian minorities, especially the Maronites of Mount Lebanon, were grateful for past favours, including an 1861 landing by French troops on their behalf.

Some vague division of European interests was thus already discernible; and a methodology of map-making, intelligence-gathering and mutual surveillance was generally accepted. Less obvious were the two explosive elements which, igniting Western interest in the region, would turn a parched tale of colonial misappropriation into a fiery epic of disastrous confrontation, so making of the Middle East that journalist's delight, 'the global flash-point of the twentieth century'. For even in 1900 frock-coated diplomats and wind-dusted travellers were not the only ones casting stolen glances at the Ottoman territories. From a distance oil prospectors scanned the desert sands with mounting interest. Meanwhile a homeless people yearned for redemption in a promised, if pre-empted, land.

GRACIOUS UNTO SION

Among the remedies formulated for the ailing Ottoman empire was a proposal from a Viennese journalist that was submitted to Sultan Abd al-Hamid II in 1901. The journalist was Theodor Herzl, a Hungarian Jew who four years earlier had organized the first Zionist Congress held in Basle, Switzerland. With 'the creation in Palestine of a home for the Jewish people' as its sole, momentous object and with the inspirational Herzl as its leader, a World Zionist Organization had been established amid a millennial rapture that would become part of Zionism's abiding mythology.

Some Jews had already made their home in Palestine. Late nineteenth-century pogroms and persecutions, most notoriously in the Russian 'Pale' (an arc of territory stretching from Lithuania to Ukraine), had compelled the four million Jews concentrated there to re-examine the Jewish condition. If the Jews were a people, they must be a nation; and how did a nation protect its people and express its identity if not as a territorial state? Most eastern European Jews considered emigration, and many determined that it should not be just another wandering between persecution and discrimination. Only a Jewish state could guarantee Jewish rights; and in the idea of a redemptive return to the 'promised' land of biblical Israel, whence they had been 'exiled' two thousand years before, a 'chosen people' saw the God-given solution to its present plight.

The ardour generated by this idea of 'reclaiming Mount Zion' did not deter emigration elsewhere, especially to the United States where two million European Jews arrived between 1881 and 1914. About 150,000 reached Britain in the same period. Palestine, on the other hand, received, by the most optimistic calculation, only 35,000 Jewish immigrants, an average of about a thousand a year and 'an insignificant fraction of the . . . mass migration'.[13] The Ottoman empire discouraged Jewish settlement within its territories because it shared none of Christendom's guilt about the Jewish condition and because an influx of Jews might provoke, indeed was already provoking, unrest among its mainly Muslim subjects. Except in Anatolia, these subjects were predominantly Arabs, at least 600,000 of whom lived and mostly farmed the land in the southern half of Syria, a region that was sometimes known as Palestine and that was almost identical with the biblical Israel.

Land, in fact, was already at the heart of the problem. For Zionists the idea of renouncing the ghettos of the gentile world in order to return to Zion was closely bound up with that of renouncing urban, ledger-bound pursuits in order to return to agriculture and hard productive labour. Farming settlements run on co-operative lines were very much part of the redemptive ideal; and thus the difficulties of acquiring land were as much a brake on immigration as the hostility of the Ottoman government.

Herzl hoped to change this by appealing direct to Sultan Abd al-Hamid II. He had tried this approach in 1896, before the formation of the World Zionist Organization. 'I cannot sell even a foot of land,' replied the Sultan on that occasion, 'for it does not belong to me but to my people.' Rebuffed, Herzl was not discouraged; he was very rarely discouraged. The Sultan had suggested that he wait and that 'the Jews save their billions'; for 'when my empire is partitioned, they may get Palestine for nothing'.[14] This and other suggestions Herzl took to mean that the door was, at least, still ajar. The prospect of Jewish capital helping to rid the Ottoman empire of its financial liabilities (a loan of £2 million was mentioned) in return for concessions which might yet, thought Herzl, assist Jewish settlement in Palestine had not been totally rejected; his self-appointed role as spokesman for the Jewish people had apparently been accepted; and the channel of communication remained open.

Hence in 1901 and again in 1902 Herzl returned to Constantinople, now on behalf of the World Zionist Organization. Its Congress had accepted that it was premature to demand a fully fledged Jewish state and unrealistic to expect the Sultan, or anyone else, to concede an existing province for that purpose. Instead a formula had been adopted whereby the Zionists publicly sought only a *heimstatte*, a home or homeland, that would be secured to them by law. But even this formula did not reassure the Sultan. He continued to oppose any settlement in Palestine and he became increasingly doubtful of the Zionists' ability to raise the large sums that Herzl dangled before him. The negotiations came to nothing. In the autumn of 1902 Herzl faced about and began looking to London for the support he had failed to win in Constantinople.

Again he compromised and again he was disappointed. Palestine was as yet beyond the gift of the British and full statehood was out of the question; but perhaps a temporary homeland, a staging-post, could be found within British-controlled territory in the vicinity of Palestine. Cyprus was canvassed and so was El Arish in Egyptian Sinai. But the Colonial Secretary Joseph Chamberlain ruled out the former while Lord Cromer eventually objected to the latter; Egypt, three years before the Dinshawai incident, already had enough problems without compounding them by encouraging Jewish settlement.

Both Englishmen were, though, sympathetic; and Chamberlain actually came up with an alternative suggestion for a Jewish homeland in East Africa. Again it failed. The British settlers there soon raised objections, and an exploratory commission from the Zionist Congress came away disappointed. 'What with elephants by day and lions by night, together with an encounter with Masai warriors in full war regalia, they decided that Kenya was no place for Russian Jewry,' recalled a passionate British Zionist who happened to be stationed in Kenya at the time.[15] Meanwhile, in 1904, Herzl's premature death had deprived the movement of its most effective emissary, and in 1905 the Zionist Congress reaffirmed that Palestine, and only Palestine, could be the subject of Zionist endeavour.

On the credit side, it was noted that the British had shown a genuine interest in the Zionist ideal and a willingness to co-operate, if only to stem the tide of Jewish immigration into Britain. Another 'stake had been driven in', as Herzl had liked to put it, and the stake might yet guy a tabernacle. Meanwhile a trickle of fugitive settlers continued to make their way to Ottoman Palestine.

By 1914 the Jewish population in Palestine had crept up to an estimated 60,000–80,000. But that still represented only slightly over a tenth of the total Palestinian population; and Jerusalem, with the largest Jewish complement, was still neither a predominantly Jewish city nor significantly more Jewish than other Middle Eastern cities. Gertrude Bell, during her centennial residence there, never mentioned the Jewish community; Jews would figure in her diaries only after she settled in her adopted home beside the Tigris. For, perversely, much the largest concentration of Jews in the Middle East, about 80,000, lived not in Jerusalem but in Baghdad. They had been there for centuries; like other minorities under Ottoman rule, they had generally enjoyed protection and considerable autonomy; and they cared nothing for Zionism. Soon they would actually oppose Zionist ambitions in Palestine as prejudicial to good relations with their Muslim neighbours.

But not yet. While Europe, the cold catalyst of Zionist sentiment, already acknowledged the force of the Zionist argument, the peoples of the Middle East appreciated neither the uncompromising nature of the Zionist vision, nor the support that it could mobilize, nor the challenge that it would pose.

KEROSENE AND 'THE MIDDLE EAST'

Much the same could be said of petroleum in the early 1900s. To the uninformed it, too, looked irrelevant. Despite oil's established importance to one corner of what was then considered 'the Middle East', in 1900 only prophets foresaw its potential as an energy source and only dreamers imagined that from the vast Perso-Arabian deserts there might yet come something more desirable than dates.

True, in 1892, after much argument over the safety of inflammable cargoes in confined waters, the first oil-carrying 'steamer-tankers' had begun to pass through the Suez Canal. They carried, curiously, not Arab oil extracted with American collaboration but Russian oil handled by Jewish enterprise. And the tankers were passing through the Canal in what now seems like the wrong direction. Loading took place at the port of Batum in Georgia at the eastern extremity of the Black Sea. Thence the tankers headed through the Bosporus to the Mediterranean and through the Suez Canal to the Indian Ocean. Their destination was more often the crowded townships of the Far East than the industrialized cities of the West.

It was early days in the oil business. At the turn of the century, mechanized industry had yet to discover its appetite for petroleum products; shipping, including oil tankers, still relied on coal-fired steam-power, and the first automobiles were as likely to be spluttering along on coal-gas as gasoline. To most people oil meant not power but light, and perhaps a little warmth. It was refined at source into highly flammable kerosene (paraffin, petrolin), it retailed in cans, and it was burnt principally in lamps. With electricity still a fairground novelty and gaslight an urban luxury, it was by kerosene that most of the world worked and played after dark.

The largest producer-nation was the United States whose Pennsylvania wells, mostly controlled by John D. Rockefeller's Standard Oil, supplied about half the world, including western Europe. Stiff overseas competition only materialized in the 1890s, and although the new supply originated mainly in what imperial strategists were soon pleased to call 'the Middle East', this was not today's Middle East.

Not inappropriately the concept of a 'Middle East' was of American provenance, like petroleum. Alfred Thayer Mahan, the naval strategist who persuaded Theodore Roosevelt to re-equip the US Navy, coined the phrase in 1902. Previously global planners had felt no need for an intermediary zone between the 'Near East' (the eastern Mediterranean and beyond) and the 'Far East' (India and beyond). Mahan, however, in an influential article on Britain's naval strategy for the *National Review*, emphasized the importance of containing both Russian expansion in Persia and German influence in Turkey by establishing a strong naval presence in the Gulf, the axis of his 'Middle East'. The London *Times* heartily endorsed this view and Valentine Chirol, its foreign editor (as well as Gertrude Bell's loyalest correspondent), rattled off twenty articles on the subject. In 1903 they were reprinted in a book, *The Middle East Question and Some Problems of Indian Defence*. With the loss of its inverted commas, the Middle East had finally shed its experimental aspect. But it remained imprecise and, in British thinking at least, had slipped east towards India. Briefly its node was Persia itself, and it included a Persian hinterland that stretched from Afghanistan and Uzbekistan in the east to the Gulf and Mesopotamia in the west. It also extended north to the countries of the Caucasus mountains and the Caspian Sea.

It was beside the last, at Baku in Azerbaijan, that oil had begun to gush in the 1890s. But the strike defied the received idea of an oil bonanza in that it took no one by surprise. Arguably Azerbaijan's oilfields had been the first in the world to be commercially exploited. Eruptions of gas and seepages of oil had been reported by travellers as far back as Marco Polo in the thirteenth century, and their yield had been locally utilized since at least the eighteenth century.

By the time Azerbaijan was annexed by Tsarist Russia in the early nineteenth century the difficulties of refining this viscous leakage into something that produced light, as well as smoke, had been partially overcome. But to do this on a commercial scale, to ensure a plentiful and dependable supply, and to overcome the problems of bulk transport in a region backward even by Russian standards had to await the late nineteenth-century initiatives of two notable families, the Swedish-Jewish Nobels and the German-Jewish Rothschilds.

In jealous competition both these family conglomerates obtained concessions in Azerbaijan and set about modernizing the refining process and boosting production. The transportation problem was solved by railways, then by a pipeline from Baku on the land-locked Caspian to Batum on the Black Sea with its Mediterranean access to the world's oceans. In association with the Nobels an east London merchant, Marcus Samuel, developed the first bulk tankers and negotiated their use of the Suez Canal. By 1900 Baku's output was rivalling that of Pennsylvania as around the world the Rothschilds and the Nobels were locked in cut-throat competition with the Rockefellers' Standard Oil.

But Baku's sudden prominence in the turn-of-the-century oil wars would be short-lived. Haphazard drilling and appalling working conditions brought a fall in yield just when industrial, political and ethnic turmoil in the Russian Caucasus discouraged further investment. Marcus Samuel's Shell Transport and Trading Company, plus the Rothschilds' Russian production interests, would both soon merge with the Royal Dutch Company to form a conglomerate that was no longer dependent on Azerbaijan's yield.

This first Middle Eastern oil boom is nevertheless memorable, if only for the unlikely assortment of interests that profited from it. From a clandestine printing press in Baku the revolutionary writings of one Vladimir Ilyich Lenin, in exile in Switzerland from 1900 until 1905, were secretly disseminated throughout his native Russia using the oil companies' distribution network. Meanwhile in Batum a young Georgian labour leader was organizing protests and strikes before drumming up 'unlimited distrust of the oil industrialists' in Baku itself. 'There in Baku,' wrote the man who later called himself Josef Stalin, 'I . . . became a journeyman for the revolution.'[16] Fifty years later, in a Cold War context, few would recall this early confrontation between socialist struggle and 'Middle East' oil. The ideology of communism would not be quite as alien to the wider Middle East as its mid-century opponents would pretend.

As for the industrialists, it was to a Paris branch of the same Rothschild family that Zionists like Herzl looked for the financial backing required to establish Jewish settlements in Palestine; and it was to Baron Lionel Rothschild of the family's London cousins that the ground-breaking Balfour Declaration, committing the British government to support Jewish settlement in Palestine, would eventually be addressed.

OIL OUT OF THE EARTH

In such driven company, William Knox D'Arcy, the man credited with being 'the founder of the [current] oil industry of the Middle East', seems not to belong.[17] D'Arcy had no financial pedigree and no family collateral. He simply liked a flutter. As a young man, he had emigrated from England to Australia where he bet heavily on the horses and gambled on a gold mine. The mine came good; D'Arcy returned to England to live like a lord. When, therefore, in the year 1900 he was approached by a Persian general about investing in Persian oil, he had every reason to say no. He was the wrong side of fifty, lately married to a scintillating actress, and devoted to the turf. Nor, with two country estates, a London town-house and a string of racehorses, was he hard up. On the contrary, the gold mine was living up to its proverbial expectations.

But to an inveterate gambler with money to burn, the Persian deal proved irresistible. Just like the Ottoman Sultan, the Shah of Persia had debts; and D'Arcy, unlike Herzl, definitely had the money to relieve them. In return for D'Arcy's financial input, Kitabgi, the Shah's general, was offering to obtain a vast and exclusive concession. It would be for sixty years and would cover most of Persia, a country that was already suspected of possessing oil reserves. A further bonus was that D'Arcy could count on the backing of the British government and of its satellite government in India. Both saw the scheme as an excellent way of extending British interests in Persia, which they regarded as a buffer region between an encroaching Russia and a vulnerable India. Although not anxious to become directly involved, neither were they prepared to see the venture fail.

This D'Arcy conceived to be his trump card. By the end of 1903, after two years of fruitless prospecting just inside the Persian frontier to the north of Baghdad, oil in commercial quantities had yet to be found and D'Arcy was overdrawn. Fortunately the Admiralty were already toying with the idea of converting the British navy to oil-fired combustion and were therefore casting about for a reliable, British-owned source of crude. As someone engaged in just such a search, D'Arcy was encouraged to approach his government for a loan. He did so, but was refused. His bank also refused; so did Standard Oil and so did Baron Alphonse of the French Rothschilds. Meanwhile costs continued to spiral and D'Arcy was obliged to sell shares in his gold mine. In early 1904 one of his Persian boreholes struck oil. He breathed again; with buoyant step he resumed the search for backers. A few weeks later the well dried up. It looked like the end of the road. Either D'Arcy was going under or his concession was going elsewhere.

It seems to have been the threat of its going to France via the Rothschilds, plus the resultant loss of British leverage in Persia, as much as a mischievous Russian plan to redirect Baku's oil to the Gulf, that finally persuaded the British government to intervene. With a bit of arm-twisting in respect of oil purchases by India and the navy, the government prevailed on the mainly Scottish directors of the Burmah Oil company to throw their considerable weight behind D'Arcy's Persian venture. The Indian government also chipped in with a guard of twenty cavalry from the Bengal Lancers. They were dispatched to the region under the command of Lieutenant A.T. Wilson, a daredevil empire-builder of startling physique and undoubted promise. Officially Wilson was supposed to guard the British consulate in nearby Ahwaz, unofficially to protect the D'Arcy Exploration Company's prospectors from hostile tribes, and in practice to keep order among the Company's roistering roughnecks, some Canadian, others Azeri.

But D'Arcy was still not out of the woods, still not sure of oil. In 1906 George Reynolds, his indefatigable manager in Persia, moved the rigs south to Masjid-i-Suleiman in the skirts of the Zagros mountains. It was 'the last throw of the concessionary dice'.[18] Like Baku, the new location had a reputation for seepages and emissions and, despite the immense difficulties of operating in such an out-of-the-way place, Reynolds seemed confident. The well-heeled lairds of Burmah Oil were less so. Their penny-pinching complaints drove Reynolds to distraction and by 1907 they were ready to pull the plug.

In 1908 they actually telegraphed him to wind up the operation. Reynolds refused, insisting that such a directive needed to be in writing. A letter to that effect was on its way when in the early hours of a suffocating May night the Masjid-i-Suleiman site erupted.

Lieutenant A.T. Wilson was asleep under the stars; as befitted a man of iron, he habitually disdained a tent and declined a bed. It was just after 4 a.m. when his rigid slumbers were interrupted. Men were screaming, there was a strong smell of gas, and high above the rig, towering one hundred feet into the night sky, waved a gushing plume of oil. 'It smother[ed] the drillers and their devoted Persian staff who were nearly suffocated by the accompanying gas,' reported Wilson.[19] He took it for a sign. Reaching for the Bible that never left his side, he scribbled a cable to his superior in Mohammerah (now Khorramshahr): 'See Psalm 104 verse 15 third sentence and Psalm 114 verse 8 second sentence.' *Oil out of the earth to make him a cheerful countenance . . .* ; it said it all. You could count on the Bible. Wilson read little else and for quick-fire scriptural repartee he knew no rival.

There was still much uncertainty, still much to be done before Persian oil became a commercial success. New sites would be tried, new wells opened, and a 138-mile pipeline constructed down to a new refinery at Abadan, an island in the Shatt al-Arab (the waterway through which the Tigris and the Euphrates disgorge into the Gulf). D'Arcy did indeed get rich again, but he lost his remaining interest in the concession syndicate with Burmah Oil when it concluded a distribution deal with a Royal Dutch/Shell subsidiary while reserving its output of fuel oil for the newly formed Anglo-Persian Oil Company(APOC).

D'Arcy remained on the board of APOC until his death in 1917. But for its first six years APOC too staggered towards financial ruin. Then in 1914 the persuasive talents of an old and incorrigible First Sea Lord, Admiral John 'Jacky' Fisher, and of a young and bombastic First Lord of the Admiralty, Mr Winston Churchill, combined to convince the British government that ships sailed faster on oil and that safeguarding a reliable oil supply must therefore be a national priority. In the nick of time, the British government poured in £2.2 million and gave APOC a 20-year contract to supply the Royal Navy. It also took a 51 per cent share in the company which thus joined the Suez Canal in the London government's Middle Eastern portfolio.

D'Arcy's find had established that the Middle East contained one of the world's few proven oil reserves, but it was this switch in marine fuel, plus the new technology of internal combustion, that now made the region of such paramount interest to the British empire. Back in May 1908, as the first oil gushed into the night sky, Lieutenant A.T. Wilson had correctly guessed the consequences. As he wrote to his father:

> It will provide all our ships east of Suez with fuel; it will strengthen British influence in these parts. It will make us less dependent on foreign-owned oil fields; it will be some reward for those who have ventured such great sums . . . The only disadvantage is personal to myself – it will prolong my stay here.[20]

Wilson, or 'A.T.' as he became known – partly to distinguish him from other Wilsons, partly because he was not the sort to encourage familiar use of his 'Arnold Talbot' – had nothing against Persia. In fact he had mastered the language and he rejoiced in the country's wide open spaces, liking nothing better than to ride a hundred miles a day, swim a couple of rivers and dine with the tribesmen at nightfall.

He was wrong only in imagining that a prolonged stay in Persia would be bad for his career prospects as an Indian army officer. On the contrary, a first-hand knowledge of a region as strategically critical, thanks to APOC's refinery and pipeline, as the head of the Gulf would be a decided advantage. The outbreak of the First World War would bring his urgent recall to the Shatt al-Arab and, by 1917, A.T. would be a power in the land then known as Mesopotamia (and now as Iraq). Indeed, in what the British troops would inevitably call 'Mess-pot', Wilson would be despot. Dictatorially and prodigiously would he labour to assure for the British empire its most significant territorial acquisition since the completion of the conquest of India.

But it was not to be. Between the youthful Wilson and his nineteenth-century notions of empire-building would stand the frail but impeccably connected and infuriatingly knowledgeable Miss Gertrude Bell. Debate over the nature of European colonial rule in the Middle East would be encapsulated in their bitter and highly personal confrontation; and from the triumph of Bell and other luminaries whose imperialism was fashionably disguised in the flowing robes of Arabism, European relations with the Middle East would be plunged into a charade of dissimulation and ambiguity that would last for forty years.

2

Getting up Steam

RAILWAY MANIA

IN THE SUMMER of 1908, as the first Persian oil gushed from the strike at Masjid-i-Suleiman, Abd al-Hamid II's roller-coaster of a reign as Ottoman sultan lurched to its climax. In April work had been completed on the Hijaz railway, the most ambitious project of his thirty years in power. Loudly promoted by the Sultan himself, the Hijaz railway had been funded to a considerable extent by the subscriptions of the Muslim faithful. In connecting Damascus, where other lines converged from Beirut and Aleppo, to the holy cities of Mecca and Medina in the Hijaz (then within Ottoman territory, now in Saudi Arabia) it would transform the obligatory *hajj* (pilgrimage) from an arduous and costly desert trek lasting two to three months to an inexpensive train-ride lasting as many days.

By such beneficence did Abd al-Hamid aim to enhance his status throughout the Islamic world as Caliph, a title implying both temporal and spiritual authority over all Muslims; and according to the British ambassador in Constantinople, in this Abd al-Hamid had succeeded admirably. Thanks to the Hijaz line, the Sultan-Caliph had finally won 'the blind obedience of his subjects', reported the ambassador, and so 'reconciled them to a despotism more absolute than has perhaps ever been known in the whole course of history'.[1]

Or so it seemed. But Britain's man-on-the-spot was not to know that getting things spectacularly wrong would be the unfailing lot of foreign diplomats in the twentieth-century Middle East. Barely three months after the opening of the railway, confounding both ambassador and Sultan, this most awesome of despotisms abruptly crumpled when officers and officials belonging to the outlawed Committee of Union and Progress staged their revolution in Constantinople. In reality no one had been blindly reconciled to Ottoman absolutism, not the Turks, 'Young' or old, nor the Arabs, Armenians and Kurds who constituted the bulk of the Sultan's Asian subjects. Rather did the railway anticipate what the revolution would confirm: that by 1908 Ottoman rule had reached the end of the line.

The railway had been built with some financial assistance and much technical supervision from imperial Germany. The Kaiser himself had approved the ashlar fortress, with its booking-hall of truly imperial dimensions, that was the Hijaz railway's grand Damascus terminus. Thence, beyond the shaded platforms, the several tracks shimmered in the glare before shrinking to a single line which, embanked, embridged and culverted, was borne south above the sands of what are now Syria, Jordan and Saudi Arabia for 900 miles. Observers likened it to a causeway across the desert, or a breakwater against the ebb and flow of tribal conflicts. Telegraph poles marched beside it, and its few stations, their water-towers doubling as watch-towers, corresponded less to existing settlements and more to the operational requirements of the locomotives and the strategic requirements of the empire. Amman, for instance, would grow from a station to a barracks and only then to a town and a city. With trouble threatening in both Yemen and Arabia, and with the Hijaz itself far from secure, the line was as much about moving troops as pilgrims. It hinted at Abd al-Hamid's endangered authority as sultan quite as much as it proclaimed his desired supremacy as Islam's caliph.

It also had the unfortunate effect of provoking the British in Egypt. Turkish troops passing down the line were within 200 miles of the Suez Canal, most of those miles being across the little-known Negev and Sinai deserts. In 1906 an Ottoman reoccupation of Aqaba fort on the south-eastern side of the Sinai peninsula had prompted a British panic that saw the Royal Navy steaming into the Gulf of Aqaba, and Constantinople buckling under a bombardment of protests. A frontier had subsequently been agreed that awarded much of Sinai to Egypt, although not Aqaba itself. The newly acquired area had then been mapped. But the Negev desert between it and the railway remained a challenge to British strategists and, as the risk of a European war increased, this wedge of southern Palestine so close to the Canal was deemed ripe for investigation. Suddenly its desert, conveniently identified as the biblical 'wilderness of Zin', was suspected of hiding sites of exceptional historical interest; by late 1913 archaeological surveyors were carefully criss-crossing its billowing sands, digging little but mapping hard.

Several of these scholars might have been seen to don uniforms when they returned to Cairo to report on progress; and some had already gained previous experience of similar work in eastern Syria. For the Damascus–Medina Hijaz line was in fact the least of Britain's railway worries in the Ottoman empire; and whereas to imperial observers the Hijaz looked like a strategic *cul-de-sac*, Baghdad and the Gulf very definitely did not.

In 1913 Lieutenant Hubert Young, a stocky British artillery officer with some basic Arabic and a taste for political work, obtained permission to return to his regiment in India by an overland route through the Ottoman territories. He landed at Beirut and proceeded east by train, zigzagging up to Damascus and then north to Aleppo. There he was pleasantly surprised to learn that a new stretch of track was open to Jerablus on the upper Euphrates. He bought a ticket as much out of curiosity as anything else.

The line in question was a section of the notorious Baghdad railway, notorious from a British point of view because it, too, was being built by German engineers and because it threatened to overturn the decades of patient diplomacy that had established Britain's exclusive control of the Gulf. By linking Turkey with Baghdad and then, by river-steamer or railway, with Basra on the Shatt al-Arab and possibly Kuwait on the Gulf itself, it would introduce a most unwelcome rivalry on India's Persian doorstep. Worse still, with a large German military mission already established in Ottoman Turkey, it could, in the event of war, enable German or Turkish troops to be whisked to within a few miles of the Abadan refinery, APOC's pipeline and Masjid-i-Suleiman's oilfield. Further afield, the railway would upset the Anglo-Russian understanding over spheres of interest in an unstable Persia (as adumbrated by Valentine Chirol of *The*

Times), it would threaten India's vulnerable sea links (as foreseen by Alfred Thayer Mahan of the US Navy), and, if the Sultan-Caliph was involved, it might excite Islamic loyalties in India itself.

Lieutenant Young was well aware of all this, and he knew, too, of the safeguards for British control of the Baghdad–Basra link that were currently being explored in London. He was, nevertheless, relieved to find that the new line was making only fitful progress, and he was reassured to discover that this progress was being carefully monitored. At Jerablus a labour force of Turks and Kurds under German direction was hard at work constructing a bridge across the Euphrates within sight of Carchemish, an ancient mound whose Greek and Hittite treasures had attracted a British archaeological team. The excavations were under the direction of D.G. Hogarth, a bearded academic from the Ashmolean Museum in Oxford who was an authority on the modern, as well as the ancient, Middle East and was much consulted by travellers there, including Gertrude Bell. Less obviously, Hogarth was in contact with, and possibly already in the employ of, Naval Intelligence, then Britain's senior espionage outfit.

Hogarth happened to be absent when Young trudged over to the site headquarters; operations had closed down for the summer and everyone had dispersed. Young could find no one about except 'a quiet little man called Lawrence who was for some reason living there alone'.[2] Earlier Gertrude Bell, passing close to the Euphrates, had also noticed this Lawrence. 'An interesting boy,' she grandly opined, 'he is going to make a traveller.'[3] Evidently 'this remarkable creature', as Young called him, liked to be alone and, far from fraternizing with his German neighbours beside the river, went out of his way to antagonize them. They reciprocated, accusing him of both spying and stirring up trouble among their workforce. But the local Arabs liked him well enough; 'they all thought him mad but they could not resist his absolute fearlessness'.

Like the Arabs, Young was taken with Lawrence's daredevil charm. He stayed with him for a week. Together they quaffed coffee from tiny Hittite cups, practised their marksmanship, pottered about in the river and talked endlessly. Thomas Edward Lawrence was then 25 years old, although 'he looked about sixteen'. A brilliant Oxford pupil, he had been selected – or recruited – by Hogarth following a summer of improbable escapades as he tramped round the Crusader

castles of Syria. He was fair, scruffy, self-absorbed and small. In fact
he was so small that even Bell, no giant herself, habitually described
him as 'an imp'. He looked less than his 5 feet 3½ inches because of
an elongated head, which seemed to belong on a much bigger body,
plus a fondness for trousers that stopped short of the ankles, as if he
might conceivably have outgrown them. His voice was thin, his
laugh high-pitched, and he had a disconcerting habit of smiling –
some said sniggering – at some private insight. Practical jokes he
loved, although, like most practical jokers, not if they were at his own
expense. Leonard Woolley, who had been standing in for Hogarth
as director of operations at Carchemish, reckoned ridicule so upset
him because of 'his knowing that other people found it hard to
take him seriously'. 'It *was* hard', added Woolley, for 'he was not on
the surface of things impressive'.[4]

Lawrence's less obvious handicaps included his illegitimate birth
and his choice of companions. Although the easy-going Young
seems not to have been aware of either and was disconcerted only by
Lawrence's contempt for regular soldiers like himself, Woolley, who
knew him better, was puzzled by his preference for a particularly
handsome Arab boy and worried about the innuendo to which this
companionship had given rise. It was another example of Lawrence's
naïvety, what Woolley called 'his essential immaturity'. 'The charge
[of homosexuality]', Woolley huffed, 'was quite unfounded . . . He
was in no sense a pervert; in fact he had a remarkably clean mind.'[5]

Both Young and Woolley wondered, though, about his taste in
clothes. 'He liked to shock,' wrote the latter, an observation confirmed by almost everyone who knew Lawrence. 'In the evening he
would put on . . . a white and gold embroidered Arab waistcoat and
a magnificent cloak of gold and silver thread, a sixty-pound garment
which he had picked up cheaply from a thief in the Aleppo market.'
His hair, so long that 'it got into his mouth at mealtimes', was then
neatly brushed, and thus attired, with a copy of Homer to hand, he
exuded an air of sleek seraglio luxury. When alone, he wore Arab
dress by day, too. With his give-away features wrapped in a *keffiyeh,* he
wandered abroad 'storing his phenomenal memory with scraps of
local knowledge which came in very useful later on'. Woolley confessed that he himself 'had not the insight to see then the genius that
was in him'; but on Young, Lawrence made a deep impression. As
the Lieutenant moved on, heading north for the river Tigris, he had

no doubt that he had just encountered one of the bravest men in the British empire.

Reaching the Tigris, Young found another section of the Baghdad railway under construction. He toyed with the idea of a train ride but preferred the greater luxury of a houseboat. It was actually more a 'hut-raft', buoyed by inflated goatskins. On its semi-submerged decking he cooked porridge, hoisted a Union Jack and, donning his solar topi, the indispensable sun-helmet of British Indian official-dom, sat back to enjoy the view. Gently borne on oily eddies, the hut pirouetted downstream to Mosul and then Baghdad. He took ship to Basra and by November 1913 was back in India. He little thought that he would ever hear again from Lawrence, little thought that he would ever revisit Mesopotamia, and had not the faintest premoni-tion that, except for the ubiquitous Miss Bell (who would partly follow his route in reverse in early 1914), he was the last Britisher to enjoy uncontested passage on either of Mesopotamia's great rivers.

Nor were his superiors any more prescient when he reported his arrival at Simla. British Indian Intelligence, though surprised by his itinerary, declined the offer of a report and turned a deaf ear to the details. 'This shows', wrote Young, a man of modest sentiment and refreshing normality compared to his fellow British Arabists,

> how little it was foreseen that exactly a year later an Indian expeditionary force would be waiting at Bahrein for the declaration of war with [Ottoman] Turkey before proceeding to the Shatt al Arab to occupy Fao and possibly Basrah. Still less was it foreseen that this operation would lead three years later to the British occupation of Baghdad itself.

THE AWAKENING ARAB

In those set-piece essays on the reasons for the First World War the Middle East features more as a condition than as a cause. Egypt apart, most of the region was still under Ottoman rule in 1914, and when the world's worst war broke out in Europe in July/August of that year, it was not certain that the Ottoman forces would become involved or, if they did, which side they would favour. The issue remained unresolved until November when, in part due to the British government's earlier knee-jerk seizure of two warships ordered by the Ottoman government and already paid for by public subscription, Constantinople finally aligned with Germany and Austria-Hungary.

But that the war would anyway have a profound impact on the Middle East and open the door to European penetration seemed likely. The concert of powers which had traditionally orchestrated the Ottoman empire's survival were screeching in discord. The integrity of the empire's territories, lately eroded in Africa by the Italian seizure of Libyan Tripoli and in Europe by Balkan turmoil, would surely be prejudiced in Asia. Whatever Constantinople decided, whoever she sided with, and whether they won or lost, there would be a price to pay.

The Allies, initially Russia, France and Britain, were able to reconcile themselves to an assault on their erstwhile patient by emphasizing that it was not the chaotic old Ottoman empire that they were fighting but a new, militaristic and German-loving usurper known as Turkey. Nor was this just propaganda. The 1908 revolution by the reform-minded officers of the Committee of Union and Progress had reduced the Sultan to a figurehead, and the same Young Turks of the CUP were now attempting to transform his sprawling empire into a strong, centralized and Turk-dominated state.

This exercise provided an early lesson in the difficulty of ideological transplants. A construct like the nation-state, forged through centuries of conflict and consolidation among linguistically distinct peoples in western Europe, could not be replicated elsewhere simply by a dollop of representational reform and a squirt of nationalistic rhetoric. The Ottoman territories were too vast, their peoples too varied, and the local and communal autonomy that they had traditionally enjoyed under Ottoman rule too precious. Nationalism as proclaimed by the Young Turks was essentially Turkish nationalism, yet Turks accounted for only a third of the empire's subjects. Another sixth consisted of Kurds, Armenians, Greeks, Albanians, Jews and Circassians; and the great majority, nearly half the total, were Arabs.

Not unreasonably the Arabs of Beirut, Damascus and Baghdad had at first joined their Turkish brethren in hailing the CUP's 1908 revolution as a brave new dawn. Censorship was lifted, political prisoners freed, and the Sultan's army of informers disbanded. 'Like a carnival queen,' recalled George Antonius, a 17-year-old student at the time, 'Liberty made her entry from round the corner and bowed, scattering her favours by the armful.'[6] Turk and Arab, Christian and Muslim scrabbled to retrieve them. The revolution promised constitutional liberties and promoted patriotic nationalism. But just as the nationalism, in so far as it was Turkish, soon proved divisive, so the liberties, in so far as they applied to non-Turks, were swiftly curtailed. Arab expectations of a more proportional say in government, of a guarantee that military service would be local, and of an educational role for the Arabic language were rudely disappointed. Lady Liberty stood revealed as a sham, what Antonius called 'a paper imitation'.

Antonius himself was of Christian Arab parents who had migrated from Lebanon to Alexandria in Egypt. It was a trail that educated but disaffected Arabs from the Ottoman territories often took, British-occupied Egypt being laxer in matters of censorship and asylum. During and after the war Antonius would play an important, if largely secret, role in Anglo-Arab and American-Arab relations. But he is principally remembered for a book, *The Arab Awakening* published in 1938, which would do rather more for Arab nationalism then T.E. Lawrence's *Seven Pillars of Wisdom*. Both works have attracted criticism, with Lawrence accused of fabrication, Antonius merely of an unscholarly partisanship. Of that he would not have been ashamed; for were anyone deserving of such a grandiose tag, it should have been 'Antonius of Arabia', not 'Lawrence'.

Where Antonius broke new ground was in alerting the world to the pedigree and parameters of a sporadic but, since the 1860s, sustained Arab national movement in parts of the Ottoman empire. It had begun with a revival of Arabic literature and language that generated a succession of literary and scientific societies from Cairo to Constantinople; and it had found enthusiastic support among young Arabs studying or working abroad, especially in Paris where Najib Azuri founded an Arab *ligue,* launched a review called *L'Indépendance Arabe,* and published a book on the same subject. But it was most notable in Syria/Lebanon where schools and colleges run by Christian missionary interests offered a liberal European syllabus, promoted a spirit of enquiry and provided printing and publishing facilities. Principal among these establishments was the Syrian Protestant College founded by American Presbyterians in Beirut in 1866 (and later to become the American University of Beirut). It was not surprising that many of those who participated in this early revival were Arabs who belonged to the various Christian persuasions.

The revival became a movement, according to Antonius, when, responding to Ottoman repression, Arab writers began addressing political issues and airing ideas for constitutional reform and greater autonomy. And the movement edged towards revolt when further repression at the hands of the Young Turks forced the several Arab nationalist societies to go underground or give way to other clandestine associations with more subversive objectives. Among the latter were al-Fata, a civilian organization, and al-Ahd, whose undisclosed membership comprised Arab officers serving in the Ottoman army, most of them from Iraq.

In charting this progression, Antonius convincingly demonstrated that Arab nationalism predated its First World War discovery by British agents like Lawrence and Bell, predated even the CUP's 1908 revolution, and was a genuine 'awakening' by a long-suffering and widely dispersed people. Parallels with another long-suffering and widely dispersed people he did not draw. But just as Zionists in eastern Europe had turned to tradition, to their scriptures and history, in formulating a plan of national redemption, so had Arabs in late nineteenth-century Beirut and Damascus. They recalled their forebears' central role in the spread of Islam, revived the memory of the Caliphate as an Arab (rather than Ottoman) institution, and emphasized the glorious legacy of the Arabic language as a literary and scientific medium.

A reminder that Arabic was also the sacred language of the Quran would have been superfluous. But Antonius was at pains to show that Arab identity, although deeply in debt to Islam, was not coterminous with it. He was, after all, a Christian himself. Nor was ethnicity a determinant of Arabness, although a study of the Arab diaspora that had accompanied Islam's early triumph did indeed provide a clue to 'the most decisive' Arab criterion; for Arabs, according to Antonius, were ultimately all those 'whose mother tongue is Arabic'.[7]

As well as giving modern Arab nationalism a historical pedigree, he thereby also gave it a geographical context. Contrary to French opinion, which scoffed at the idea of, for instance, Algerians being Arabs, and contrary to British insistence that Egyptians were not Arabs and never – not excluding even Nasser – would be, Antonius blithely mapped out the concept of an inclusive 'Arab world'. It stretched unbroken from Arabic-speaking Morocco to Arabic-speaking Oman – from the Atlantic to the Gulf – and from Sudan to Kuwait. It was not the same as Dar-ul-Islam, the more familiar 'Islamic world', since it excluded Persia, India and other countries with a large Muslim population where Arabic was not the mother tongue of the faithful. Yet it was just as socially fragmented as the Islamic world, just as politically unintegrated.

How this sprawling community with a shared language, howsoever rich in cultural, historical and religious appeal, might be effectively represented in a world dominated by tight and assertive little nation-states was anyone's guess. Turkish/Ottoman repression, European colonialism and Zionist immigration provided specific grievances, but they were not shared by all Arabs. A pan-Arab cause was needed; and in the ambitious claims about to be made by, and for, the Hashemite *sharifs* of Mecca the British would pretend to have found it. But the greater question of establishing a congenial political framework for the Arab world remained. It would take the best part of the century to resolve. It was still open in the minds of Arab leaders from Nuri al-Said to Nasser and Saddam Husayn. And it could hardly fail to attract the attention of outsiders with an interest in creating a world order, or disorder, advantageous to themselves.

THE HASHEMITE CONNECTION

By 1914 the British and French governments were well aware that disaffection was rife among the Ottoman empire's Asian subjects. Travellers in Syria, such as Bell and Young, had reported on 'a growing movement towards independence' and had passed on the comments of interested parties. Typical was an observation relayed by Hubert Young and attributed to the leader of the Druze, an independently minded sect established in the mountains of Syria: 'These past two years have seen the Turks driven out of Tripoli by the Italians,' Young was told, 'and out of Macedonia and Thrace by the Balkan Powers. Would to God there were some power to drive them out of the Jabal [Druze] and all the Arab countries.'[8]

Meanwhile Syrian exiles in Egypt had provided some casual contacts between British officialdom and Arab nationalism. But it was not until early 1914, when Abdullah, the second son of *sharif* Husayn of Mecca, passed through Cairo, that there came a more direct appeal, 'the ultimate impact of which upon the war and the destinies of the Near and Middle East is not even yet,' wrote Ronald Storrs twenty-five years later, 'fully calculable'.[9]

To Storrs, acting for Lord Kitchener, Cromer's successor-but-one as Britain's 'Consul-General' in Egypt, had fallen the pleasure of dealing with the young and evasive Abdullah. 'He appeared to have something to say but somehow did not reach the point of saying it,' noted Storrs. Instead the Englishman was treated to stirring tales from Arabian antiquity and a fine rendering of 'the Seven Suspended Odes of Pre-Islamic Poetry'. As a collector of orientalia and a connoisseur of all things recherché and exquisite, Storrs was profoundly impressed. The hours slipped by; the Khedive's best coffee (they were meeting in the Egyptian ruler's Abdin palace) kept coming. But what did Abdullah want? The son of the desert proceeded to intone the 'Lament of Antar ibn Shaddad'. His memory was truly astonishing; Storrs was so transfixed that he nearly missed the mention of machine-guns. A dozen, half a dozen, would do. Purely for defence, of course. But against whom? 'Pressed further, [Abdullah] added that the defence would be against attack from the Turks.'[10] So that was it. Abdullah was probing British reaction to the possibility of his father in Mecca defying Constantinople's authority.

In the matter of machine-guns Storrs had no choice but to decline. The war had not yet started and the Ottoman empire was still considered a friendly power. Yet the encounter was one that stuck in the memory, partly because of Abdullah's beguiling ways but mostly because of the *sharif* of Mecca's unique position in the Islamic world. If anyone could offer a legitimate Arab challenge to Turkish supremacy, it was a *sharif*. A considerable clan with claims to pre-eminence in the Hijaz that predated Islam, the *sharifs* were revered by virtue of their senior descent from the Prophet and were acknowledged by pious tradition as the hereditary guardians of the holy cities of Mecca and Medina. Under Ottoman rule one of their number was traditionally selected as the Grand Sharif, or Amir, of Mecca with responsibility not only for the holy places but also for the reception and management of the *hajj,* a function both lucrative and prestigious. As the clan grew, this honour had become confined to one of the several sharifian branches – the descendants of Hashem, who were thus known as 'Hashemites'. Husayn, an able but enigmatic icon who had spent much of his life as the Sultan's guest/hostage in Constantinople, was the current Hashemite incumbent as Amir; and Abdullah was the second and most politically minded of his four remarkable sons.

The family's position was, however, far from secure. There were other sharifian claimants to Mecca; Husayn's disloyalty was already suspected in Constantinople; some of his *hajj* perquisites were threatened by a proposed extension of the Hijaz railway from Medina to Mecca; and to the east, in the deserts of central Arabia, a sandstorm was brewing as warrior-fanatics, fired by the puritanical teachings of Abd al-Wahhab, an eighteenth-century reformer, pressed the claims of their champion, Ibn Saud of Riyadh. The Saudis and the Hashemites, although equally Arab and equally wary of the Turks, were bitterly divided over doctrinal issues, tribal allegiances and territorial claims. Their forces had clashed in 1910 and continued, sporadically, to do so. Any British support afforded to the one could easily alienate the other. As reported by Captain W.H. Shakespear, a British political officer who paid several visits to Ibn Saud in the pre-war years, the consequences of an anti-Turk *jihad* led by Husayn of Mecca were 'unforeseeable and incalculable'. It would 'raise the whole Arab world' but its outcome for British relations with other Arab leaders, particularly Ibn Saud, would need 'to be constantly kept in mind'.[11]

Five months after the Abdullah–Storrs meetings, with the war in Europe now under way and Ottoman involvement becoming increasingly likely, the Hashemite game began to look worth the Saudi candle. It was Lord Kitchener, now elevated from the consul-generalship in Cairo to Secretary of State for War in London, who revived the question. In a cable of 24 September 1914 he asked Storrs to contact Abdullah and find out whether, should German influence in Constantinople prevail, 'he and his father and the Arabs of the Hijaz would be with us or against us'. Another cable, dated 31 October, indicated that war with Ottoman Turkey was now imminent and promised, in return for the assistance of 'the Arab nation', its immunity from British intervention and its protection against the enemy.

In the light of the first telegram, this 'Arab nation' presumably meant just the Arabs of the Hijaz. But a curious paragraph in the second telegram hinted otherwise.

It may be [concluded the Secretary of State for War, archly] that an Arab of true race will assume the Khalifate [Caliphate] at Mecca or Medina, and so good may come by the help of God out of all the evil which is now occur-ring. It would be well if your Highness could convey to your followers and devotees who are found throughout the world in every country the good tidings of the freedom of the Arabs and the rising of the sun over Arabia.[12]

The imperious Kitchener was not a man to waste his words. He may not have realized precisely what the office of caliph implied. (Its Christian equivalent was not so much pope, as Kitchener seemed to imagine, but Holy Roman emperor.) And he may not, therefore, have appreciated that the promotion of a caliphal candidate by a Christian power was nonsensical, if not insulting. But he was right in imagining that it was a prize fit to be dangled before the *sharif*. Husayn was impressed. Having been awarded a 'nation' and guaranteed an immun-ity tantamount to independence in one paragraph, he was in the next being invited to lay claim to supremacy over the entire Islamic world.

Clearly the British placed a high value on his support. To discover how high, and to bolster his position in the face of mounting evi-dence of Constantinople's plans to relieve him of power, Husayn entered into an exchange of letters with Sir Henry McMahon, Kitchener's successor in Egypt. The correspondence would last for six months, from July 1915 to January 1916. It would prove suffi-ciently conclusive to trigger the Arab Revolt, sometimes described as the most romantic campaign of the First World War and certainly the most romanticized. And thanks to the Revolt, the fate of the Ottoman empire in the Middle East would be heavily prejudiced, the 'quiet little man called Lawrence' would be catapulted to stardom, and thrones for Husayn and three of his sons would even-tually be won. But, as will be seen, the Husayn–McMahon corre-spondence was otherwise far from conclusive. Its wording is often unclear and its status is still disputed. The only thing that can be said for certain is that the Hashemite interpretation of it would rarely coincide with that of the British government.

OPENING SALVOES

No great need for urgency can excuse the uncertainties of this exchange of letters. Husayn and his sons were not yet ready to con-front Turkish authority in the Hijaz and they required time to reach an understanding with the clandestine Arab nationalist groups in Syria. Meanwhile the British and their allies appeared to be managing quite well without an Arab revolt. Indeed the first six months of the war in the Middle East looked as if they might be the last six months.

Deadlocked in the trenches of the Western Front, in the east the Allies had eagerly sought a signal success against the new but supposedly weaker Turkish foe. Kitchener was receptive to Russian requests for any action that would divert Turkish attention from the Caucasus and the Black Sea, while the pushy young Churchill, as First Lord of the Admiralty, saw an opportunity for both naval heroics and strategic advantage in a quick triumph in the eastern Mediterranean. The favoured option was a landing at Alexandretta (Iskenderun), a deep-water port west of Aleppo in the right-angle between the Levantine and Anatolian coasts. It was an idea that would be revived in 1916 but rejected on both occasions, partly because the advantage to be gained scarcely justified the number of troops required, and partly because objections were raised by the French; they had significant interests in Syria and they were not happy for it to become a purely British bridgehead. Besides they trusted that, ere long, the privilege of its conquest might be their own.

In its stead, with misplaced audacity, Churchill and Admiral Fisher persuaded their Cabinet colleagues to go straight for the Turkish capital. A massive naval bombardment of the straits known as the Dardanelles (which gave access to Constantinople, the Bosporus and the Black Sea) would be followed by an Allied landing on their European shoreline, otherwise known as the Gallipoli peninsula. The bombardment got under way early in 1915. The troops meanwhile, many of them from Australia and New Zealand, assembled in Egypt where the havoc they wreaked in the red-light districts of Cairo left a deeper impression on Egyptian sensibilities than their heroics at Gallipoli. So did the military's expectations of Egyptian supplies, baggage animals and charitable donations to the war effort. It was easy for the British to overlook the fact that Egypt was not technically British territory and that Egyptians were not therefore at war with anyone, less easy for the Egyptians to overlook the fact that they were being treated as if it was, and they were. Resentment mounted; around the well-remembered graves at Dinshawai a wind-blown dune of more generalized grievances steadily accumulated.

Elsewhere, a Turkish offensive in Sinai directed against the Suez

Canal was easily repulsed in February 1915. No less easily a British-led expeditionary force from India, sailing from the Gulf into the Shatt al-Arab, overwhelmed the port of Basra and secured the Anglo-Persian Oil Company's installations. There, many thought, it should have stayed. But despite misgivings, especially in India, about deploying a sea-borne force equipped for estuarine defence as the spearhead of a major landward offensive, the Indian expedition was ordered forward into Mesopotamia. Any residue of strategic logic was thereafter confounded by tactical necessity. So open and feature-less is the countryside between the Tigris and the Euphrates that 'a single heron, reposing on one leg . . . looks as tall as a wireless aerial'.[13] In such terrain the security of the port of Basra could only be guaranteed by occupying the entire Basra province, which in turn meant encroaching into the neighbouring province of Baghdad, which in turn meant advancing on Baghdad itself.

To administer these occupied territories and mobilize their resources and revenue for the campaign in hand, Sir Percy Cox, an urbane and persuasive mandarin with long experience of the Gulf, was installed as Chief Political Officer. Cox, burdened by other responsibilities, wisely chose the workaholic A.T. Wilson, he of the Bible tags and the spartan regime who had witnessed the first Persian oil strike, as his assistant and then deputy. On a recent voyage home, A.T. had elected to save himself the fare by travelling as a stoker. For sixteen hours a day in temperatures of around 40 degrees Celsius he had out-shovelled every other stoker on board; then, landing at Marseille, he had bicycled the remaining 500 miles to his home in Worcester. Exploding with energy and still only 31, this moustachi-oed Hercules would now be the chief executive of Britain's embryonic administration in Mesopotamia with Cox as its silver-haired chairman.

They were soon joined by others of that select band who could claim some pre-war experience of the 'Land between the Rivers'. As the British Indian Expeditionary Force forged up the Tigris, Hubert Young, on the strength of his close acquaintance with that river and its 'hut-rafts', was summoned from regimental duties to serve under Wilson. With him from India came Harry St John Bridger Philby, a robust polyglot of limited means and alarmingly progressive ideas who would soon succeed Captain Shakespear, killed in early 1915, as Britain's contact with Ibn Saud. Likewise Gertrude Bell, currently cataloguing losses on the Western Front while she nursed a badly broken heart. She was plucked from her mid-life crisis by the Director of Naval Intelligence and sent post-haste to Cairo, then Basra. 'When the call came it was as though everything that had gone before was but preparation for this moment,' writes her biographer.[14]

The call had come in November 1915, just as Young and Philby took up their administrative duties in Basra and just as, upriver, the Expeditionary Force gathered itself for a final push on Baghdad. 'Baghdad by Christmas' was the call. In a war as yet unremarkable for triumphs, the capture of the city of 'One Thousand and One Nights' was being billed as the first great victory. But thereby hung a tale.

KUT AND THRUST

Three hundred miles from Basra, considerably more by the twists and turns of the Tigris, and way beyond the ability of the Expeditionary Force's toy-town flotilla of river-steamers to provide effective support, Major-General Charles Townshend's 6th Division suffered its first reverse. On 23 November at Ctesiphon, an ancient site from whose massive arch the minarets of Baghdad were already visible, Townshend's approximately 10,000 active troops encountered a well-entrenched Turkish army estimated at 20,000. It was not quite a defeat; the Turks also suffered heavy losses and both armies withdrew. But the Turks were being reinforced while Townshend's division was too weakened to risk another battle. He had earlier insisted that two divisions would be needed to take Baghdad and he was encouraged to hear that more troops were being sent.

Such assurances would soon become excruciatingly familiar. To await these vital reinforcements, he withdrew downriver to the provisions and better security offered by the little town of Kut al-Amara. This week-long manoeuvre under heavy fire was conducted with skill and bravery, although 'oddly, the first sight that greeted the troops was a gibbet'.[15] Oddly, it would also be the last. Kut was rapidly fortified – it helped that it had river on three sides – and there, like a nesting duck on a mudbank, Townshend made his stand.

It is a mud plain [and] from this plain rise villages of mud and cities of mud. The rivers flow with liquid mud. The air is composed of mud refined into a gas. The people are mud-coloured; they wear mud-coloured clothes, and their national hat is nothing more than a formalised mud-pie.

So wrote Robert Byron of Mesopotamia in September. On 3 December when Townshend's men limped into Kut, the mud was cold and covered in hoar frost; the rain came as sleet on an icy gale. His troops, mostly Indian and many from around Bombay, had no experience of such conditions and were woefully clothed. Their reluctance, on religious grounds, to eat horseflesh also meant that they were the first to suffer from malnutrition. As the days became weeks, the flour ration dwindled from 20 ounces per day to 4, and as the weeks became months, the town's population of rats, cats and dogs disappeared into shrunken bellies. Incessant sniping and shelling would account for 537 deaths; another 488 died of wounds because it had not been thought necessary to provide the division with a decent field-hospital; and 721 died of disease and malnutrition.

In the conduct of operations Townshend could scarcely be faulted. It so happened that he knew about sieges and had himself been a central figure in the last great stand made by the Indian army, that in the fortress of Chitral in the Hindu Kush in 1895. In fact, he had since become such an authority on history's great sieges that people could not but wonder whether he had not, perhaps, invited this one. But such suspicions apart, he behaved admirably, resolute against the enemy, ruthless in dealing with deserters, and candid to a fault with his men. The only serious criticism would arise over his part in the fate of Kut's civilian population.

To his credit, Townshend had initially planned to eject the local townsfolk, thus saving them from untold hardship. He was over-ruled by the high command in Basra who thought them safer inside Kut than out. They were, of course, predominantly Arabs, albeit settled ones. But in wartime Mesopotamia, all Arabs were regarded as enemy. As yet British India, unlike British Egypt, had no confidence in an Arab nationalist movement in the Arabian peninsula, nor did it have any expectation of Arabs there revolting against the Turks. In fact, Delhi would determinedly dismiss the idea of any Arab accommodation, denying the pretensions of the Hashemite *sharifs* and thereby provoking a major feud with Cairo. But it did so with reason. India had the largest Muslim population in the world;

Britain's Indian Army relied disproportionately on Muslim recruitment; and Indian Muslims recognized the Ottoman Sultan as Caliph. If under British command they fought fellow-Muslims, it was emphatically not to set up a rival caliph in Mecca but, as British propaganda explained, to free the existing caliph from the clutches of the godless Young Turks who had usurped his authority.

In the course of Townshend's march up the Tigris, and even more so as relief force after relief force endeavoured to reach him, the British had developed a hearty respect for their Turkish opponents. Turks might be incapable of marching in step but their marksmanship was good while their spadesmanship, so crucial in a land devoid of cover, was truly exceptional. In a flurry of earth and shovels an entire battalion could disappear into fresh trenches before the attackers' eyes. It was like watching a crab sink in soft sand. But the Arabs were very different. They were the scavengers of the campaign. Some fought alongside the Turks but most merely scouted for them while helping themselves to easy spoils. They hung about on the horizon, swooped on the wounded, picked off stragglers, and committed unspeakable atrocities. They fought, in fact, as desert guerrillas, harassing the British on behalf of the Turks just as, on the other side of the Arabian peninsula, they would soon be harassing the Turks on behalf of the British, a white-robed Englishman in their midst.

In early 1916 Lawrence was in Cairo, hobnobbing with Professor Hogarth and other luminaries as they devised a regime of liaison and intelligence for their just-sanctioned Arab Bureau. As to why, in March, he too received the call to proceed to Basra, little is recorded. He would later explain that it had something to do with the Russian capture of the Turkish town of Erzerum and that, at the time, he and his Arabist colleagues 'had hopes of Mesopotamia'.[16] Perhaps a proclamation about the British negotiations with the Hashemite *sharif* could be used to rally Arab opinion in Mesopotamia against the Turks; and perhaps Townshend could yet be saved by some consequent Arab diversion. But this looks suspiciously like hindsight. The Tigris/Euphrates tribes were less in awe of Mecca's *sharif* than they were of Ibn Saud's blood-curdling fanatics; and with neither of these Arab groupings did Lawrence as yet have any more credibility than he did with the high-ranking Kitchener-lookalikes of the Expedition's high command. Besides, as he admits, it was much too late.

'How Kut holds out still I can barely guess,' wrote Gertrude Bell on 16 April.[17] She was one of the few in Basra who had welcomed Lawrence when he and Aubrey Herbert, an English MP with excellent Turkish contacts, passed through *en route* to Kut. It was not just that a diminutive civilian as smirking and effeminate as Lawrence was anathema to most army officers; his mission, as now revealed, was even more distasteful. For it transpired that he and Herbert were going not to save Kut but to surrender it. The last of three major attempts to relieve Townshend had failed in March. So too, in early April, had an ambitious scheme – perhaps the first ever – to supply the besieged by air; and so too, in late April, had a last-gasp effort to run the blockade on the river with an armour-plated steamer. The food was finished; after nearly five months of unimaginable horror, Kut was doomed and 'the death of an army' imminent. Its only chance lay with Lawrence and Herbert who, to the disgust of all save the besieged, had been empowered to try bribing the Turks. An offer of £1 million had been sanctioned in return for the safe passage of Townshend and his men out of Kut and down the river.

Halil Pasha, the Turkish commander, ignored the suggestion. The offer was upped to £2 million and he brusquely turned it down. There was some agreement about an exchange of wounded, but when Herbert entered a plea for clemency on behalf of Kut's Arab population, this too was rejected. Halil Pasha abruptly closed the meeting by looking at his watch. 'At this moment,' he announced, 'my army is entering Kut.'[18] It was 29 April. The siege had lasted for 147 days, longer than Ladysmith (1899), longer even than Plevna (1877). With professional satisfaction, Townshend had toasted each of these milestones as they passed.

In Turkish captivity he and his fellow-officers would be treated well. But of their approximately 10,000 British and Indian troops less than 6,000 would survive the forced marches and the hard labour of detention. As for the Arabs of Kut, no figures are available. Perhaps there were 10,000, and some, surely, were spared. But before the British were marched out of Kut, all those who had had any dealings with them during the siege were already being hunted down. A firing squad was busy in the town's *serai*, and a veritable forest of makeshift gibbets lined the river-bank.

To any who held honour dear, this betrayal was the real shame of Kut. Militarily, compared to the much greater débâcle at Gallipoli (whence withdrawal had taken place in March), the fall of Kut rated as a reverse rather than a defeat. A Mesopotamia Commission quickly pinpointed the failures, and in the following February (1917) Kut was successfully retaken before the greatly augmented Expeditionary Force marched again on Baghdad. But the fate of Kut's civilians still rankled. And however dim were the prospects for Anglo-Arab collaboration in Mesopotamia, they faded further as a result. 'Tales of the treatment meted out by the Turks to the Arabs of Kut', wrote the plain-speaking Young when in August he was appointed Political Officer of a Euphrates district, 'had already reached Nasiriyah . . . and it was not to be wondered at if the Euphrates tribes hesitated to throw in their lot with a new master who might at any moment disappear, leaving them to the mercy of their own legal rulers.'[19]

Nor was it to be wondered at that Anglo-Arab relations in Mesopotamia suffered from chronic distrust and that India-hands like A.T. Wilson were confirmed in their view that some form of direct British rule was essential as well as inevitable. A concession, like substituting the Arabic 'Iraq' for the Greek 'Mesopotamia', was in order; but as for independence, 'it never entered my head', wrote Young in April 1917 just after Baghdad was finally taken. 'The country was so obviously unready for self-government that no one on the spot could possibly have advocated anything at that stage but the substitution of British for Turkish control.'[20] Even Gertrude Bell, as yet working amicably with A.T., wrote in similar vein to Valentine Chirol. 'The stronger the hold we are able to keep here, the better the inhabitants will be pleased . . . they can't conceive an independent Arab government. Nor, I confess, can I.'[21] Yet in Cairo, McMahon's letters, Lawrence's chatter and the politicking of the Arab Bureau were indeed promising just such independence with little more than supervisory responsibilities and strategic safeguards reserved for the British.

Returning downriver from his abortive mission to Kut, Lawrence had again been cold-shouldered by the British Indian establishment in Basra. 'Suffering from a passion of contempt for the regular army . . . he was not very popular in Mesopotamia,' recalled Young with loyal understatement.[22] Even a new uniform won him no friends. Lawrence, though as innocent as he was contemptuous of army discipline, had been given the acting rank of an army captain; likewise

Professor Hogarth, now at the Arab Bureau, had been metamor-phosed into a lieutenant-commander of the Royal Navy (not because of his beard but because of his links with Naval Intelligence); and Bell, for the same reason, would no doubt have discarded her Paris gowns for a WRNS uniform, had such a service then existed. It was all part of the accreditation process necessary to turn the spying aca-demics of peace-time into what Lawrence called 'a band of brothers' for wartime service.

Lawrence's return to Cairo in May 1916, and the outbreak of the Hashemites' Arab Revolt in June, heralded a more convincing phase in this transformation. Next time they met, Hubert Young would not find himself the only officer willing to shake the hand of the now 'Lawrence of Arabia'. Young was, though, alone in fondly imagining that, had Lawrence visited Basra under more favourable circum-stances, the impending tug-of-war between Cairo and Delhi over the fate of the Middle East might have been avoided. 'If only he [Lawrence] and A.T. Wilson had met on this occasion [that is, after Kut] and got to know each other well, all might have been different; but they did not meet.'[23] It was probably just as well. Given person-alities as poles apart as their respective statures, and given the con-tempt that each would show for all the other held sacred, a meeting of minds between the two great exponents of British policy in the Arab world was never likely.

3

Something Connected with a Camel

THE HUSAYN–MCMAHON CORRESPONDENCE

Estimates vary, but it seems that in the formulation of British policy in the Middle East during the First World War around twenty separate government and military departments were involved at any one time. London's War Cabinet, Admiralty, War Office, India Office and Foreign Office competed both with one another, as was their wont, and with a similar spread of bureaucracies in India, plus a lesser cluster in Egypt (Cairo) and the Sudan. Further input came from the staff of the three major expeditionary forces, one in Mesopotamia and two in Egypt (at Ismailia for the Sinai front and at Alexandria for the Mediterranean), and from the various naval and political establishments in the Red Sea, Aden, the Gulf and Mesopotamia/Iraq. Interdepartmental committees, though designed to override the conflicts of interest that arose, also unwittingly contributed their mite to this muddle.

Small wonder then that Britannia, with her knickers so twisted, progressed unsteadily. Open disagreements as between Cairo and Basra/Baghdad or India and London merely hinted at the deeper jealousies and conflicts within each of these headquarters. Small wonder, too, that British commitments made in one area could only with difficulty, if at all, be squared with those made in another. The well-known contradictions between the Anglo-Arab understanding implied in the

Husayn–McMahon correspondence and the Anglo-French agreement known as Sykes-Picot or the Anglo-Zionist undertaking contained in the Balfour Declaration would prove symptomatic rather than exhaustive. And small wonder, finally, that resourceful operators found it easy to play off one department against another while pursuing their own agendas in defiance of both.

But this bureaucratic proliferation, so damaging to British good faith, would prove a godsend to scholars. More departments generate more paper, and more paper means more historical debate. A selective trawl through the spring-loaded box-files and the ribbon-tied folders in the record offices may be relied on to provide textual support for any one of a surprising range of views. With the First World War and its immediate aftermath acknowledged as the genesis of the Middle East's subsequent conflicts, scholars have flocked to these hoppers to pick and to peck voraciously. New finds are always possible and crucial documents yet yield to meticulous scrutiny. In the case of the pro-Zionist declaration made by His Majesty's Government (but usually credited to Arthur James Balfour, its signatory), every one of its 68 typewritten words, plus its three commas and its missing full stop, have been subjected to the sort of forensic examination usually reserved for libel matters or biblical exegesis.

Perhaps the English language, and the French, lend themselves to this minute inspection, as if words were diamonds whose worth and import can be gauged beyond question by squinted biopsy. Arabic, on the other hand, may be less susceptible to such analysis. According to a 1930s pundit writing in the *Journal of the Royal Central Asian Society*, every Arabic word has five meanings: '1, the original meaning; 2, the opposite of the original meaning; 3, something poetical and nothing to do with the first two; 4, something connected with a camel; and 5, something too obscene to be translated.'[1] All of which, though surely a grotesque Orientalist calumny, suggests that, in the case of a document in Arabic, shades of meaning and the spirit of intention conveyed by the wording may be as relevant as the literal meaning of the individual words. Add to this the formidable barrier of translation, plus a tendency to withhold sensitive matter for communication by word of mouth alone, and the enigma of the Husayn–McMahon correspondence may be appreciated.

There were ten letters in the exchange, five from each party. Some are lost, others do not survive in their original form, and the sole draft of one of them only emerged when it was found behind a filing cabinet in Ronald Storrs's Cairo office. They cover a wide range of subject matter, but attention has largely focused on what they have to say about the *sharif* Husayn's conditions for raising the standard of revolt and the extent to which these requirements were conceded by Agent and Consul-General McMahon.

The most obvious requirement, recognition of the authority of the Hashemite *sharif* to speak for the 'Arab nation', was implicit. Kitchener had as good as conceded it in his earlier dealings through Abdullah; and with Faysal, Husayn's third son, now bolstering his father's position by enlisting the support of al-Fata and al-Ahd, the most effective of the clandestine Arab nationalist groupings in Syria, the British were happy to deal exclusively with Husayn and those who claimed to represent him. But recognition of the *sharif*'s right to speak for the 'Arab nation' did not mean recognition of his right to rule over it. Kitchener's original idea of Husayn making a bid for the Caliphate lost favour as India raised objections and Hogarth pointed out the significance of the Caliph as a supreme ruler. When Husayn adopted the title 'king of the Arabs', the British would firmly reject it. Instead he would just be acknowledged as the more geographically restricted 'king of the Hijaz'.

To Husayn the geography was important. By way of a manifesto he endorsed a document, known as the Damascus Protocol (because it had been drawn up by Arab nationalists in Syria), that registered an Arab claim to the great parallelogram of territories bounded by the Red Sea, Egypt, the Mediterranean, Turkish Armenia and the Gulf. Within these parameters lay the Arab lands to which the British must agree to grant post-war independence as the price of an Arab revolt. It was an ambitous demand, awarding only Aden to the European powers, and McMahon duly prevaricated.

Husayn was having none of it. A wounded reproach and a further insistence persuaded McMahon to draft the crucial letter, no. 4 in the series, of 24 October 1915. This conceded Husayn's suggested boundaries with one reservation: that the coastal districts of Mersina and Alexandretta (both now in Turkey) and 'portions of Syria lying to the west of the districts of Damascus, Homs, Hama and Aleppo' be excluded as not 'purely Arab'. Precisely how far south these 'portions of Syria' extended, especially the 'district of Damascus', and whether they included Palestine, has been hotly debated ever since.

Did McMahon mean to extract Palestine from the Arab demand, so making its future status a legitimate subject for Anglo-French debate and Zionist lobbying? Or is this a preposterous reading of the geography? If the criterion for exclusion was the 'purity' of its Arabness, was Palestine more Arab or less Arab than, say, Lebanon (which clearly was excluded)? And was McMahon being intentionally vague or just inept? As for Husayn's interpretation of this wording, it scarcely matters. He rejected McMahon's reservation, insisted that no portions of Syria should be excluded, but suggested that agreement could wait until after the war was won.

Husayn therefore seemed to have conceded nothing in the way of territory. But he failed to appreciate that the geography was something of a red herring, and he almost certainly underestimated McMahon. So too, to be fair, did most of McMahon's colleagues. He was seen as a stop-gap appointee, a night-watchman plucked from India to occupy the Cairo Residency while Kitchener was away in London winning the war. Few appreciated his shrewdness: nor did they quite realize that, much as Townshend was to sieges, Henry McMahon was to boundaries. Frontiers, borders, buffers and their subtle shades of autonomy were his speciality. He had been involved in the 1893 demarcation of the Durand Line which now divides Pakistan from Afghanistan, had just come from chairing the 1914 Simla conference which divided an Inner Tibet from an Outer, and is well remembered in India to this day for the controversial McMahon Line which still demarcates the Sino-Indian frontier in the eastern Himalayas.

Thus the imprecise wording of his letter no. 4 was probably deliberate. More significant, though, was its spirit which, while appearing to concede much, in fact gave away little. For it went on to sandwich the desired promise of British recognition of 'the independence of the Arabs' between several fat clauses which so prejudiced the nature of this independence that Arab rule anywhere could only be a travesty. In the Ottoman provinces of Baghdad and Basra (most of present-day Iraq) the Arabs were to recognize that the 'position and interests' of Great Britain would necessitate 'special administrative arrangements'. In the Hijaz Great Britain was to be the sole guarantor of the holy places 'against all external aggression'. And in areas where Britain had 'existing treaties with Arab chiefs' – so most of Arabia and the Gulf – these treaties were to stand. Moreover, Britain was everywhere to have the privilege of advising and assisting in the establishment 'of what may appear to be the most suitable forms of government' – which looked suspiciously like a blanket power of veto. Finally, and most alarmingly of all, Britain's promise of Arab 'independence' did not apply to the unspecified regions in which her ally France might have 'interests'. Husayn firmly rejected only this last proviso. But as will appear, McMahon could not admit the rejection, and like those contentious 'portions of Syria', the matter remained open.

As well as territorial assurances Husayn needed cash, arms, provisions and logistical support. All these were more readily forthcoming. Storrs would estimate that the Arab Revolt cost Britain £11 million. Lawrence says £10 million; his saddle-bags were often so weighted down with gold that harsher critics would delight in calling him Britain's bagman. So great was this demand for cash that the Egyptian treasury, whence it was drawn, was unable to keep up with the supply and the Hashemites had sometimes to make do with Indian rupees. Likewise, rifles, machine-guns, ammunition, explosives, uniforms, wireless sets, camels and eventually vehicles were poured into the revolt. British naval support was crucial in the early stages; aerial reconnaissance and bombardment came into their own in the later stages. For all the brave talk of the Arab nation winning its independence, it would be British cash that underwrote Arab cohesion just as it would be British munitions that undermined Turkish resistance.

Only in artillery were the Turks superior, a doubtful advantage in the impossible terrain of the Hijaz and one that would be largely offset if mountain guns could be obtained. Just such a battery happened to be stationed near Suez on Egypt's Sinai front. But it was comprised of Algerian gunners under French command. And as Lawrence would discover, French participation in the Anglo-Hashemite adventure came with strings attached.

THE SYKES-PICOT AGREEMENT

The 'interests' of France in the Middle East were embodied in an agreement that was being negotiated simultaneously with the Anglo-Hashemite exchange of letters. McMahon in Cairo was aware of these negotiations but not directly involved in them. They were mainly handled in London by Sir Mark Sykes on the British side and François Georges-Picot on the French, neither of whom initially took much cognizance of Arab opinion, although Sykes warmly supported the Anglo-Hashemite alliance. An older perspective of great power rivalry in the Ottoman empire prevailed. Sykes had once been attached to the British legation in Constantinople and Georges-Picot had served as French consul in Beirut. Theirs would be a conventional agreement between imperial powers, reasonably clear in its language, positively stark in its presumption, and 'quite alien to those modern notions of nationality' that the British in Cairo had been confronting since the Dinshawai Incident and that would soon be enshrined in the League of Nations covenant.[2]

At issue in the Anglo-French negotiations was the long foreseen dismemberment of the Ottoman territories, plans for which had become urgent when in early 1915 St Petersburg insisted that the Bosporus and adjacent territories be awarded to Russia in any post-victory settlement. France, hard-pressed at home and least able to divert troops to what then seemed more promising theatres in the Middle East, sought to secure comparable gains by diplomacy. She therefore made any agreement with Russia contingent on recognition of her own interests in the region. Britain then followed suit. As the Prime Minister H.H. Asquith nicely put it, 'if . . . we were to leave the other nations to scramble for Turkey without taking anything for ourselves, we should not be doing our duty'.[3]

French claims centred on Cilicia (the Turkish region around Alexandretta) and 'Syria', a rather vague term that could apply to the entire Levant coast and all the lands immediately behind it, including modern Syria, Lebanon, Palestine/Israel and Jordan. Here, as well as a historical attachment reaching back to the Crusades, France had an accepted role as protector of the local Christian communities and considerable investment in banking, railways and education. Georges-Picot, 'the scion of a colonialist dynasty' and a firm believer in France's *mission historique et civilisatrice* in the Middle East, therefore demanded all of this 'Syria', plus Cilicia.[4] He was willing, and possibly eager, to compromise only to the extent that in the less favoured interior of the region he would accept some form of indirect rule rather than the direct colonial administration envisaged for the coastal districts.

Had an Arab been invited to observe these Anglo-French negotiations he would not have been impressed. While McMahon in Cairo
had proffered Husayn the brimming cup of independence but had
then drunk all but the dregs, Georges-Picot in London was proposing to offer an empty cup to which dregs just might be added. The
French stance would convince the British of France's incorrigible
annexationalism; the British stance would convince the French of
Albion's incorrigible duplicity. It was an old refrain, familiar to native
audiences from Madras to Shanghai. And however different the
approach of the colonial powers, for those on the receiving end it
amounted to much the same thing.

In this case there was even unanimity on the French idea of a land-
locked and largely desert area of indirect control fringing the more
favoured areas of direct control. Sykes, an ebullient figure who reckoned the Ottoman territories vast enough to satisfy all conceivable
claimants, saw this as a chance to accommodate Husayn's territorial
demands as diluted by McMahon's administrative reservations. Since
indirect control left room for some form of indigenous sovereignty,
areas so designated could double as Husayn's 'independent' Arab
entity. The idea was so appealing that Sykes happily adopted a similar
partition of British spoils.

A map attached to the final agreement said it all. Mesopotamia/
Iraq, comprising the Ottoman provinces of Basra and Baghdad, was
coloured red. This would be the 'British Sphere' of direct control. It
was flanked by a much larger area stretching across the Middle East
from northern Persia to Egypt which was merely outlined in red,
marked as 'B', and which the legend identified as the 'Independent
Arab State' within the 'British Sphere of Influence'. Similarly, there
was a solid blue area covering the Levant coast from Acre northwards and extending deep into Turkey. This would be the 'French
Sphere'. It, too, was flanked to the east and south by a larger area
outlined in blue, abutting 'B' and designated 'A', which stretched
from Damascus, Homs and Hama to Mosul on the Tigris. This was
the 'Independent Arab State' within the 'French Sphere of
Influence'.

Additionally there was a small brown area. It comprised Palestine
and was designated as an 'International Sphere'. Close inspection
also revealed in its midst an enclave of red around the port of Haifa.
The British had insisted on sole control of the port in recognition of

their plans to build a railway thence to Mesopotamia, so connecting the Mediterranean with the Gulf. But this, and the whole idea of Palestine being under international control, represented an untidy compromise. Both parties were planning to reject it almost before the brown wash had dried on the map. In fact the whole Sykes-Picot agreement, stitched together at speed to preserve the Allied *entente cordiale* in a region where it was clearly fraying, would be unravelling for the rest of the war. In the Middle East Indo-imperialists like A.T. Wilson no less than Anglo-Arabists like T.E. Lawrence would bitterly resent it. And anyway, events swiftly overtook it. Within a month of its May 1916 signature, Lord Kitchener, the inspiration behind both McMahon's letters and Sykes's negotiations, was dead. He drowned during a gale in the North Sea when, *en route* to Russia, his ship struck a German mine. On the following day, 6 June, under a cloudless Meccan sky, *sharif* Husayn's Arab Revolt got under way.

THE ARAB BUREAU

At about the same time 'Captain' T.E. Lawrence returned to Cairo after his abortive mission to extricate Townshend from Kut. At odds with his military superiors in Egypt as well as in Mesopotamia, his first priority was to get himself attached to a new agency – definitely not an 'organization' – called the Arab Bureau. The Bureau was another brainchild of Mark Sykes who, on a fact-finding tour prior to the French negotiations, had been horrified at how British policy in the Middle East was hamstrung by bureaucratic complexity; nothing like it, he claimed, had been known since 'the ancient constitution of Poland'.[5] Sykes, a mimic and a brilliant caricaturist, thought in bold emphatic strokes; he grasped at solutions rather than grappled with problems. The solution in this case was yet another department, based in Cairo, nominally under Foreign Office control but working closely with the Admiralty and the military, and acting as a clearing-house for all political intelligence and propaganda concerning the Middle East. It was to be staffed by a galaxy of the most dazzling Arabists, all highly educated, liberal by the standards of the day, and many of them articulate to the point of artistry. As the 'Arab Bureau' the new agency had been approved in January 1916 and had submitted its first report in May.

This was too late for it to be involved in either the Husayn–McMahon correspondence or the Sykes-Picot negotiations. In fact, despite a considerable output of reports, bulletins and handbooks on every conceivable subject, the Arab Bureau is notable less for its activities and more for the ideas and personnel that were associated with it. Its staff was small, typically about fifteen. They were comfortably housed in Cairo's Grand Continental Hotel with offices next door in the even grander Savoy Hotel. There, despite a bustle and bell-ringing that reminded Aubrey Herbert of an oriental railway station, they cultivated a mystique of omniscience suggestive of the Oxford common rooms with which many of them were familiar. Professor/Commander Hogarth, as the Bureau's director, lined the walls with books on Middle Eastern subjects; pipe-smoke and Arabic drifted in the stifling air. There was little to suggest the 'band of wild men' on which Lawrence insists.

'We called ourselves "Intrusive" as a band; for we meant to break into the accepted halls of English foreign policy, and build a new people in the East,' writes Lawrence with typical bravado; '. . . we who believed we held an indication of the future, set out to bend England's efforts towards fostering the new Arabic world in hither Asia.'[6] This emphasis on influencing policies, rather than co-ordinating them, plus the need for secrecy common to all intelligence units, endowed the Bureau and its pro-Arab policies with a suspect, if not sinister, aura. Nor was it always easy to say exactly who was working for the Bureau, or what precisely they were up to. Of the six men singled out by Lawrence as providing the Bureau's leadership, Sykes in London soon found himself at odds with his creation, while Storrs and Clayton in Cairo (the first the influential Oriental Secretary to Kitchener and McMahon, the second the Head of Military Intelligence) were the Bureau's patrons rather than its operatives. Among its permanent staff, Hogarth was Director of Operations for just nine months in 1916; Kinahan Cornwallis, his American-born successor, lasted until 1919 but little is known of his activities until after he left the Bureau; and George Lloyd, the sixth of Lawrence's 'wild men', was neither very wild nor much of an Arabist. He came from the Lloyd's banking family, was valued for 'his knowledge of money', and 'did not stay very long with us'.[7]

To those in the field, the Bureau's great attraction was the latitude and independence from local political control that secondment afforded. Its two most famous recruits much appreciated this, although they responded quite differently. Gertrude Bell, representing the Bureau in Basra and Baghdad, prepared some elegant and admired reports, mostly on the Euphrates tribes. She also found the Bureau an admirable bolt-hole in which to shelter from A.T. Wilson's interventionist energies. Yet she prejudiced the Bureau's hopes of an influential role in Mesopotamia by idolizing Cox, the Chief Political Officer, who was a staunch critic of Bureau interference; and if she was supposed to wrench Mesopotamia from Delhi's authority to that of Cairo, she failed dismally. The wrench would come, but not until after the war, by when Wilson had had the satisfaction of disbanding the local branch of the Bureau and Bell had secured a more strategic position on Cox's staff.

Then there was Lawrence. The Bureau's informality suited such an independent spirit admirably. Before he had been officially transferred to it, he made his first trip to Arabia under the Bureau's auspices; six months later he would launch into his most famous exploit without troubling to seek its approval; and thereafter he was pretty much a law unto himself, undoubtedly the Bureau's star but a star that the wise men in Cairo found themselves following rather than directing as it soared out of reach. Lawrence had been drawn to the Bureau by the scintillating company that it offered and the ambitions for Arab resurgence that it promoted. But soon it was the Bureau that was being drawn to Lawrence; his dreams became its policies and their realization its principal responsibility.

LAUNCHING A LEGEND

Lawrence's first taste of Arabia came in the autumn of 1916 when he took ship down the Red Sea from Suez to Jidda. He managed this by attaching himself to the fastidious Storrs who was heading for a rendezvous with Abdullah, the *sharif*'s second son who had once regaled Storrs with tales from Arab antiquity while asking for machine-guns. 'Storrs' intolerant brain', says Lawrence, 'seldom stooped to company';[8] but he apparently made an exception for 'little Lawrence, my super-cerebral companion'[9] and during the two-day voyage treated him to a symposium on Debussy and Wagner. Arrived at Jidda, Storrs renewed his friendship with Abdullah, introduced

Lawrence to his first Hashemite, and tried to discover why the Arab Revolt was going so badly.

The first great disappointment had been the lack of Arab support. The *sharif* had suggested that he had only to hoist his standard in Mecca and Arabs as far away as Damascus would rise in revolt, while Arab divisions within the Ottoman army would mutiny and Arab tribes from all over Arabia would come rushing to his aid. In fact, when in June he had hoisted the standard, nothing much happened at all. An erratic shuttle service from British Sudan ferried arms and cash across the Red Sea while the Royal Navy helped secure the Hijaz ports, including Jidda. But during the Revolt's first five months all the Hashemites had themselves achieved was the retention of Mecca and the capture of Taïf, its nearby summer retreat. If anything, they were losing ground and becoming more dependent on British naval support. Nowhere outside the Hijaz had the Revolt triggered an Arab rising; and a recent defeat before the walls of Medina, 300 miles north of Mecca, meant that the *sharif*'s forces were now bottled up in the southern Hijaz and of no conceivable use to the British Expeditionary Force confronting the Turks east of the Suez Canal in Sinai.

Medina, the second of Islam's holy cities and the railhead of the Hijaz line from Damascus, looked to be the key to the situation. Here the Turkish garrison, 2,000 strong, well provided with artillery and easily reinforced by rail, presented a formidable barrier to any advance. But unless Medina was addressed, there seemed little to prevent other Turkish troops in the Hijaz from going on the offensive. Even now a force was closing for an attack on Rabegh, a port north of Jidda on the Medina–Mecca road. Abdullah wanted British troops to help defend Rabegh; otherwise, he told Storrs, the victorious Turks would roll on to Mecca where, in a last-ditch resistance, the *sharif* himself would die rather than surrender. Courtesy of the Hijaz's only telephone line, a call to the *sharif*, telephone number 'Mecca 1', confirmed his willingness to do just that.

But Lawrence, whom Storrs had introduced as an expert on military matters, objected. Landing foreign troops anywhere near the holy cities would probably outrage Muslim opinion and would certainly outrage India's hypersensitive British bureaucrats. Worse still, it would make it impossible to fend off French participation in the Revolt. At the time 'the only real soldier in the Hijaz' according to Lawrence was

Lieutenant-Colonel Edouard Brémond, 'the great bearded chief of the French Military Mission'.[10] Brémond had reached Jidda a month ahead of Lawrence while his 1,000-man Mission, including Algerian gunners, was still at Suez. In fact it was awaiting directions to provide just the support that Abdullah was demanding. Lawrence, however, was deeply suspicious. He distrusted French ambitions in the region and, like most of his Bureau colleagues, regarded the Sykes-Picot agreement as a betrayal of the Anglo-Arab understanding and something that must therefore in due course be reversed.

Brémond, if Lawrence is to be believed, soon confirmed his worst suspicions. In the course of a blazing row, the Frenchman admitted that his mission was not about promoting the Revolt but about preventing its spread to Syria, where it could only complicate the eventual imposition of French rule. By bringing his infidel force into the Hijaz, Brémond appreciated that the *sharif* would be discredited. That was the whole point. With the *sharif* revealed as a puppet of the Christian powers, the Syrians would promptly forget about him while the Bedouin levies on whom he currently relied would slink back to their tents in disgust. The Hashemites in the Hijaz would thus find themselves totally reliant on Allied troops for the survival of their wretched little kingdom; and Syria would thus be preserved for its manifestly French destiny.

But if this was indeed Brémond's master plan, Lawrence was not yet aware of it when Abdullah first asked for British troops. He knew only that British troops must also mean French troops, and that no British troops might mean only French troops. The latter, a distinct possibility given the reluctance of the British high command to spare any units from Sinai, had to be avoided at all costs. Hinting instead, therefore, at more explosives, an Egyptian gun battery and even aerial support, Lawrence insisted first on an inspection of the critical situation at Rabegh plus a meeting with Faysal, the *sharif*'s third son who was actually opposing the Turkish advance. Another phone-call from Jidda to Mecca, and some eloquent arm-twisting by Storrs, wrung a grudging permission from *sharif* Husayn. Two days later Storrs and Lawrence sailed back up the coast and anchored off Rabegh. There Lawrence was put ashore. 'I can still see him,' Storrs would recall, 'waving grateful hands as we left him there – left him to walk from that moment into the pages of history.'[11]

INSIDE THE DREAM PALACE

'Little Lawrence', 'the bumptious ass' with 'the daredevil attitude', was immediately swallowed up by a combination of Arabia's timeless immensity and a legend, no less enduring, of his own making. After the first of many gruelling camel treks, some downright gruesome and all memorably chronicled in his *Seven Pillars of Wisdom,* he located Faysal. Instantly he recognized in this resolute but fiery 'man of moods' those qualities of charismatic, almost hieratic, leadership that he reckoned essential to the Revolt.

Faysal reciprocated and seems to have seen something similar in Lawrence. He gave him the fleetest of camels, dressed him in the whitest of silken robes with the costliest of gold-spun head-ropes, and permitted him the pick of his wildest Bedouin followers as personal companions. In time the Englishman might go anywhere, speak with anyone, attempt anything. As he visited other Hashemite units, Lawrence began to take the measure of the thing ('the bigness of the Revolt impresses me')[12] and of its supporters ('mobile . . . reckless . . . impossible to make an organised force out of them').[13] He developed ideas about how such troops could best be used and how the spark of revolt could be spread by maximizing minor triumphs. He advised on deployment and took part in operations, principally blowing up the railway. When Rabegh was secured without British or French troops, he supported an advance up the coast to Wejh, another port. The Royal Navy captured the place before Lawrence and Faysal arrived. But the tables had been turned. The initiative now lay with the Arabs; and with another 200 miles of the Hijaz railway track exposed to flanking attack as a result of this advance, the Revolt was, as it were, back on the rails. By March 1917, as they planned their next big move, Lawrence and Faysal were as one. Brémond was left fuming on the sidelines.

Lawrence's attachment to Faysal would also sideline the more acute but easy-going Abdullah, ignore the enigmatic *sharif* Husayn, and be equalled only by his devotion to the Arab cause. Faysal, on the other hand, appreciated Lawrence as a military adviser and a guarantor of Britain's cash and arms shipments, while overlooking his inexperience, his comparatively junior rank and his desperate need for an essentially personal form of recognition. Each man was undoubtedly gratified by the other's regard, and while the war lasted, neither would disappoint. The reckoning would come later.

In the introduction to *Seven Pillars*, Lawrence wrote memorably of the early days of the Revolt, how 'it felt like morning, and the freshness of a world-to-be intoxicated us'.

> I meant to make a new nation, to restore to the world a lost influence, to give twenty million of Semites [that is, Arabs] the foundation on which to build a dream-palace of their national thoughts. So high an aim called out the inherent nobility of their minds and made them play a generous part in events . . .[14]

Even when, later, he considered the Arabs betrayed, he would still hope that his actions had contributed to a new world order 'in which the dominant races will forget their brute achievements, and white and red and yellow and brown and black will stand up together without side-glances in the service of the world'.

As ever, it was magnificently phrased but it was not the whole story. The psychological contradictions that so delight Lawrence's biographers extended well beyond his complex personality. Already, in an annotation made by Lawrence at the time, a different sort of ambivalence is evident. It appears in his personal copy of a 'Report on Faysal's Operations' which he wrote on the spot on 30 October 1916 and which was printed two weeks later in the Bureau's confidential *Arab Bulletin*. The report ended by saying that, however inexperienced the Hashemites, he no longer doubted their ability to form a government. Then came the following hand-written note:

> They [the Arab leaders] are weak in material resources and always will be, for their world is agricultural and pastoral and can never be very rich or very strong. If it were otherwise we would have had to weigh more deeply the advisability of creating in the Near East a new power with such ex-uberant national sentiment. As it is, their military weakness which for the moment incommodes us should henceforward ensure us advantages immeasurably greater than the money, arms and ammunition we are now called upon to spare.[15]

Another report of the same month clarifies the kind of client state that Lawrence and the Arab Bureau envisaged for their new allies. Sykes had already designed a flag for this state; Lawrence himself had advised on its new postage stamps and had had them printed. All the trappings of a nation-state were to be made available. But it would not be a nation-state as understood in Europe.

> For their idea of nationality is the independence of tribes and parishes; their idea of national union is episodic, combined, resistance to an intruder. Constructive politics, an organized state, and an extensive empire, are not only beyond their capacity but anathema to their instincts ... Unless we or our allies make an efficient Arab empire, there will never be more than a discordant mosaic of provincial administrations.[16]

For all the fine words about building a new Arab nation, Lawrence was as intent as Brémond on creating a post-war Middle East that would be easily manageable in his own nation's interest. Syria, in Lawrence's reckoning, was no more a suitable subject for sovereign independence than Arabia. It was 'by nature a vassal country [and] by habit a country of agitations and rebellions'; it spawned only 'discordant kingdoms with areas and populations at best the size of Yorkshire and at worst of Rutland'.[17] The only hope of an effective Arab state was if the British or French chose to create one. But they would not; for a loose confederation of ineffectual states would serve their interests better. Nor was Mesopotamia/Iraq an exception. Lawrence would later write, not with shame but pride, of having there been instrumental in establishing 'our first brown dominion'. He was proud because he thus frustrated the formation of 'our first brown colony'.[18] But the idea of its being 'no one's brown anything' seems never to have occurred to him.

The differences between the British and the French, or between the Arab Bureau in Cairo and the Indo-British administration in Iraq, were as to means, not ends. All were convinced that some form of tutelage was essential and would long remain so. The Arabs were supposedly incapable of managing their own affairs without it, and the Europeans were supposedly entitled to supply it. If conjuring up that 'dream-palace' of a sovereign and consolidated Arab state would help to sustain the Revolt, then so be it. 'It has suited me, as I believe it has suited all of us, to give the leaders of the Arab Movement this impression,' wrote Reginald Wingate, the Governor-General of the Sudan and an early supporter of the Revolt; as Commander-in-Chief of the Egyptian army, Wingate was also Clayton of the Bureau's immediate superior. 'We are sufficiently covered by the correspondence which has taken place [the Husayn–McMahon letters] to show that we are acting in good faith as far as we have gone.'[19] But the 'good faith' was largely specious consolation and the 'impression' given to the leaders of the Revolt was clearly meant to mislead.

The 'dream-palace', in effect, was all dream and no palace. Lawrence wore his Arab outfit for effect, like fancy-dress, and Storrs cultivated his impeccable Arabic for its pleasing virtuosity, like an academic hobby. It was a fine thing to speak better Arabic than the Arabs, to ride a camel harder, suffer thirst more stoically, render their Revolt more effective, and articulate their liberation more fluently. Britain could be proud of its Arabists. But there was neither sense nor virtue in identifying with the Arabs to the extent of condoning their political presumption. The Bedouin, even in Lawrence's piercing blue eyes, were uncouth and unmanageable; settled Arabs he was loth to consider Arabs at all; and as for the educated, Westernized classes, they were the worst of all. The sight of an Arab in European-style 'spring-sided boots' gave Storrs apoplexy and sent Sykes rushing to his sketch pad. 'Europeanized youth', 'native Christians' like George Antonius, and 'nationalist hot-heads' were abominations who offended British conceits about both class distinction and racial privilege. Their manners were appalling yet they were precisely the people who, given a chance, would be running the 'dream-palace'. It was unthinkable.

THE AQABA AFFAIR

To his considerable credit, Lawrence himself was perfectly candid about 'the fraud' (his word) in which he was involved. If we may believe his later *Seven Pillars of Wisdom*, at moments of idleness or indecision it troubled him most, 'and the knowledge of this axe I was secretly grinding destroyed all my assurance'.[20] One such crisis of confidence seems to have occurred at the remote camping ground of Nebk in June 1917.

Six weeks earlier Lawrence had parted from Faysal and his troops at Wejh and made a vast detour through the desert interior. Seemingly every prophet needs his forty days in the wilderness. It was a necessary, as well as a fitting, prelude to his greatest exploit, and it heralded his entry into the wider arena of the Allied advance on

Syria; for the object of this great swing through the Arabian desert was to bring him out at the head of the Red Sea above the port of Aqaba which, if it could be taken by surprise, would place the Arab forces on the flank of the British in Sinai.

The desert trek, the longest and most awesome Lawrence ever made, was led by *sharif* Nasir from Medina, a cousin of the Mecca *sharifs,* and by Auda Abu Tayi, the legendary chief of the Howeitat tribe. They proved excellent company but the terrain, an infinity of petrification, was the most savage in the world. As they climbed inland, the painted canyons, garish as wigwams, opened on to grim and distant escarpments. Hard white sand, pocked with craters, seared their sight and a fiery wind shredded their faces. There were perilous meadows deeply laid with shifting pebbles, and nightmare forests of black basaltic blocks. The gullies flowed with streams of volcanic lava; a rifle barrel was like magma to the touch. As a writer as well as a traveller, Lawrence was in his element.

In this lunar furnace, they rose with the moon and at dawn paused to get their bearings, then pressed on again until the pounding of the sun hammered them into submission. Camels died, men were lost, water-skins ran dry. But *sharif* Nasir marshalled their progress and Auda knew the ground. They fringed the dunes of the *nafud*, the great sand-sea of central Arabia, and bore north into the long carto-graphical scratch that is Wadi Sirhan. Here was water of sorts, a plague of snakes, and a hint of the Howeitat's sparse summer grazing. The ordeal was over. Auda's tribesmen feasted them royally; and at Nebk they halted to raise the tribes ahead with bribes of gold, to recruit fighting men and to lay their plans.

Two Syrians in the party were all for ignoring Aqaba and pressing on northwards for Damascus. Lawrence insisted on Aqaba. But he let the Syrians go; in fact their optimism so excited him that, while Nasir and Auda assembled the troops, he too slipped away on a mys-terious reconnaissance into Syria. The mystery was entirely of his own making. He says so little of why or where he went in 'the north country' that many doubt whether he went at all. 'A rash adventure suited my abandoned mood,' he says in his book. The mood, a product of exhaustion as much as exhilaration, evidently obscured the adventure. Rather than substantiate this possibly fraudulent trip, he bared his soul about the greater 'fraud' which was his political imposture.

Although ignorant at the time of their precise wording, Lawrence, unlike Wingate, could see no way of reconciling the Husayn–McMahon correspondence with the Sykes-Picot accord. The Anglo-French carve-up foreshadowed in the latter flatly contradicted the promise of 'independence', however qualified, contained in the former. His personal contempt for Arab statehood, though adding a further dimension to the 'fraud', was not relevant in this context, and in *Seven Pillars* he does not mention it. He appears to agonize solely over the conflict between what he knew was British policy and what his companions must be led to think was British policy. Yet the double imposture surely deepened the agony. 'Instead of being proud of what we did together, I was continually and bitterly ashamed.' Then he added in parenthesis: 'did ever second lieutenant [his captaincy, like his uniform, was temporarily in abeyance] so lie abroad for his betters?'[21]

From Nebk, the raiding party, now 300 strong, completed their desert circuit by swinging west and south, back towards the railway and the coast. Dynamited wells confirmed that the Turks were aware of their presence. To throw them off the scent, Lawrence made another northerly foray, bypassing Amman to attempt a railway raid near Dera'a (just beyond Jordan's present-day frontier with Syria). On his return they formed up again to close on Aqaba. The town of Ma'an with its large Turkish garrison was left alone. So was Wadi Musa, down which the buses now roll through a canyon of hotels to the rock-parting for Petra.

South of Ma'an the ground fell away. Vistas opened below them and the air grew moist with a hint of salt. Only a couple of Turk-manned outposts now barred their progress to the sea. But then word came that a long column of both infantry and artillery had just taken up position at the first of these posts. So their position was known; surprise was no longer on their side. 'We had lost command . . . of the Aqaba road without a shot being fired.'[22] Two months of hardship and several hundredweight of gold looked to have been squandered on a mirage.

Back at Nebk, in revenge for the impossible dilemma in which British policy had placed him, Lawrence had 'vowed to make the Arab Revolt the engine of its own success . . . [and] to lead it so madly in the final victory that expediency should counsel to the [European] Powers a fair settlement of the Arabs' moral claims'.[23]

The arrogance of this gamble would not have reassured his Arab companions; and with final victory still but a distant dream, the whole idea reeks of hindsight and creative liberty. But if ever there was a time for leading madly, this was it. An instant attack was ordered.

Surrounding the Turkish troops as they slept, the Arabs poured in rifle fire, but to little effect. More desperate measures were called for. The final onslaught, a mad rush of men and camels at breakneck speed, was not led by Lawrence, only provoked by him; he had merely to impugn Auda's prowess with a few well-chosen taunts to launch the Howeitat on their do-or-die charge. Lawrence joined in, although, as he cheerfully admits, not gloriously. For at the crucial moment his famed marksmanship betrayed him. Firing from a crazily rocking saddle he succeeded only in shooting his own camel through the head. The beast crumpled beneath him, and the seven-stone bundle of raiment and rhetoric that was about to be hailed as 'Lawrence of Arabia' fizzed through the air like a shuttlecock. A hard landing concussed him; when he came round, the battle was won. It was the only critical encounter of the whole Aqaba raid, and he had missed it.

Two days later, Aqaba was his. Its elaborate defences, its rock-cut galleries and walled gun emplacements, all faced the sea whence Royal Naval poundings invariably came. There were no landward defences; attack from the interior had never been contemplated. The garrison sensibly surrendered, and the Arab forces celebrated with a mass dip in the sea. Leaving them to savour victory, if not much else (for they were desperately short of food), Lawrence rode hard for Suez. A ship-load of provisions and gold must be dispatched immediately; and there were glad tidings to be carried to the outside world.

Sinai's 150-mile breadth was crossed in an impressive 49 hours. Added to all his other excursions since Nebk, it made a distance of 1,400 miles in four weeks, a feat of camel-riding unequalled before or since by any stranger to the desert. Allied to such feats, the capture of Aqaba on 6 July 1917 brought Lawrence lasting celebrity. It did not change the course of the war; neither Lawrence's subsequent exploits nor Faysal's growing forces ever would. But Aqaba changed the British perception of the Arab Revolt and this was in large part due to Lawrence and his burgeoning legend. With the Arabs established on their Sinai flank, the British of the Egyptian Expeditionary

Force awoke to the possibilities of turning the Turkish position in Palestine, and with Lawrence as liaison, they realized that the Arabs could play a useful role in this strategy.

To this end, advisers, instructors, auxiliaries and experts were soon pouring into Aqaba along with all the machinery of contemporary warfare; an airstrip was marked out and the sands were churned with tracks and tyres; henceforth Lawrence and his wild Bedouin companions would as often drive as ride. Faysal moved his headquarters north to Aqaba. The flow of gold became a spate. It was as if the British too were determined 'to make the Arab Revolt the engine of its own success' and so provoke 'a fair settlement of the Arabs' moral claims'. Whatever that meant, it was a handy formula for pursuing the war to a successful conclusion with consciences untroubled.

4

A Tale of Two Cities

1917 AND ALL THAT

ANOTHER GOOD REASON for Lawrence's 49-hour camel marathon across the Sinai peninsula was to keep ahead of the news about Aqaba. It was not enough just to have captured the place; to make that feat peculiarly his own and to savour its reception by his countrymen he needed to be there when the news broke. In similar fashion, years later, he would sneak into shows about 'Lawrence of Arabia', unobserved but acutely attuned to the audience's reaction.

On reaching Suez, he found a hotel, took a bath, and said little. Next morning he boarded the first train north. This connected with the Port Said–Cairo express at Ismailia. The express puffed into the station and, as if to order, there clambered from its Pullman car a stiff-backed bevy of high-ranking staff officers. The dignitaries paced the platform, silencing the hubbub as they passed and freezing the uniformed crowds in rigid salutes. Only Lawrence fidgeted and stared. His Arab dress and weathered features conferred a delicious anonymity. No less delicious were the certainty of discovery and the jaw-dropping revelations that would follow.

Sure enough, one of the staff officers met his impudent gaze, enquired who he was, and was rewarded with the first news of Aqaba's fall. 'It excited him,' noted a laconic Lawrence. He pretended to be more intrigued by 'a very large and superior general' whom alone among the top brass on the platform he did not recognize. This, he was told, was Edmund Allenby, lately appointed to the command of the British Egyptian Expeditionary Force. Moreover the general, unlike his predecessor, enjoyed the confidence of the Prime Minister and had been directed to use all means to drive the Turks out of Palestine.

Here, then, was the man on whom would depend the Arab Revolt's chances of collaborating in the conquest of Syria/Palestine, so becoming 'the engine of its own success' and winning some form of Arab 'independence'. Lawrence looked on the General and saw only a rubicund hulk; to one popularly known as 'The Bull', his own puny stature, let alone his outrageous garb, must have appeared as the proverbial red rag. Yet when summoned, two days later in Cairo, to render a full report on the Revolt, he sidled into the august presence still perversely swathed in Arab dress. Seeing the 'little barefooted silk-skirted man', the General should have pawed the ground, an overpowering scent of charlatan in his flaring nostrils. Perhaps he did, but Lawrence just sat and talked. He talked non-stop, explaining the origins of the Revolt, how Faysal's forces operated, where they had broken out of the Hijaz, what support they needed, and how effective they could be as desert guerrillas in the badlands east of the Jordan river.

Allenby appeared to listen, although it was hard to tell because he asked no questions. When Lawrence had finished, he simply said he would do what he could, 'and that ended it'. The chances for one of wartime's most improbable partnerships looked unpromising. Lawrence had yet to learn that 'what Allenby could do was', as he put it, 'enough for his very greediest servant'.[1]

Allenby's appointment, and the priority now being given to the hitherto static Sinai front between British-protected Egypt and the Ottoman territories, reflected a host of other changes. In fact there were so many major developments in the course of 1917 that, except in terms of the unremitting slaughter on Europe's Western Front, the post-1917 war looked like a different struggle to that pre-1917.

Britain, for instance, was under new leadership. In December 1916 Asquith's government had resigned and the more dynamic David Lloyd George had taken over as Prime Minister with Arthur James Balfour, a languid ex-premier, as Foreign Secretary. Decisions were taken by a small War Cabinet which included the imperially minded Lords Curzon and Milner, men who appreciated that the war, while threatening Britain's empire, might also strengthen it. More specifically Lloyd George, unlike Asquith, believed that the Middle East presented those opportunities for psychological and political advantage that were so woefully lacking on the Western Front; he therefore thought it worth diverting the resources necessary to realize them. As a Bible-bred Nonconformist the new Prime Minister was also much interested in the fate of the Holy Land.

France, after a succession of wartime ministries that differed little one from another, followed suit; in November 1917 Georges Clemenceau took over as premier. A die-hard fighter of 76, Clemenceau shared a radical past with Lloyd George, plus dictatorial tendencies and an unshakeable determination to press the war with Germany to its conclusion. But the two men differed markedly over colonial policy. Lloyd George has been called 'the first British Prime Minister who wanted to acquire territory in the Middle East' and Clemenceau 'the only French politician who did not want to do so'.[2] Neither statement defies qualification, and both men were more pragmatists than ideologues. But that Lloyd George's forward policies in the Middle East would encourage him to seek a larger share in the colonial cake-cutting envisaged by the Sykes-Picot agreement, and that Clemenceau might be willing to compromise on aspects of this agreement, was widely anticipated.

Such revision also looked likely in the light of another, more dramatic change of government which was convulsing the third member of the wartime *entente*; 1917 was Russia's year of revolutions. Back in early 1916 General Townshend, while scanning the military horizon from the makeshift ramparts of Kut, had taken heart from the news that Russian troops had reached Erzerum in what is now eastern Turkey. With the British relief efforts from Basra being continually rebuffed, Townshend saw this rapid Russian advance from the Caucasus as opening an alternative prospect of succour. Turkish troops might be siphoned off from Mesopotamia to oppose the Russians; perhaps the siege would be lifted. Glasses were raised in the officers' mess and the news was quickly communicated to Kut's staunch but starving defenders. It seemed at the time that, with British operations slithering in the sands of Sinai or stuck in the Mesopotamian mud, Russia alone was making good in the Ottoman territories.

But winning ways abroad were crippling the primitive Tsarist economy and exposing profound domestic turmoil. Strikes, mass demonstrations and military mutinies ushered in one revolution when in February/March 1917 the Tsar abdicated; Lenin's return from exile, with some well-calculated assistance from Berlin, and the subseqent Bolshevik takeover of October/November constituted another. Meanwhile the Russian advance in Anatolia faltered. To the Russian people the war had long since become a scapegoat for their woes; and to Lenin it had always been an irrelevance to the proletariat's struggle. Disengagement quickly followed, the terms being finally contained in the March 1918 treaty of Brest-Litovsk.

To spite the Tsar's erstwhile allies, Russia's new rulers were also quick to make public the terms of the Sykes-Picot agreement, a copy of which was held in St Petersburg. Although supposedly secret, the existence of the agreement was already widely suspected and its drift known to a select few, probably including the *sharif* Husayn. Publication of its precise terms was nevertheless an embarrassment to the Allies, particularly when the Turkish leadership variously used it to discredit the British in the eyes of the Hashemites, to disparage the Hashemites in the eyes of other Arab nationalists, and to rally pro-Turkish support within Syria by exposing French designs on the country. The gravity of the situation may be judged from the hasty disclaimers that were being prepared by the Arab Bureau in Cairo.[3] *Sharif* Husayn would be assured that Sykes-Picot did 'not constitute an actually concluded agreement', only a record of 'provisional exchanges and conversations'. Moreover it would 'not be pressed by the surviving parties' since the success of the Arab Revolt and the withdrawal of Russia had 'created an altogether different situation'.[4]

In this contention, as well as wishful thinking and some downright dissimulation, there lurked a germ of logic . It was, after all, Russian demands that had originally prompted the Sykes-Picot agreement; it had been framed in the light of Russia's expected gains in the Ottoman lands; and it had been signed as part of a tripartite pact that included Russia. With Russia's withdrawal from the war and all its spoils, the agreement invited revision just as the cake invited re-cutting. This was especially the case with that brown area on the accompanying map which comprised most of Palestine. It had been designated an 'International Zone' largely in deference to Russia's traditional rights as protector of Palestine's several Christian

Orthodox communities. But without Russian participation, did 'international' mean simply 'Anglo-French'? And was such a co-dominion desirable between two such jealous allies? If nothing else, politically as well militarily, Palestine was being promoted to front-line status.

As Russia dropped out of the war, the United States had, as it were, dropped in. President Woodrow Wilson's declaration of hostil-ities in April 1917 was a reluctant response to the sinking of US ships by German submarines. As such, its curiously unilateral intent was understandable; the President declined the status of an ally and refused to become identified with the wider war aims of the European Allies. On the other hand it soon transpired that America's own war aims were anything but unilateral; for the President's high-minded idealism – his 'doctrinarian (*sic*) genius' as a dismissive A.T. Wilson called it – was not content simply to oppose Allied aims on the grounds that they were acquisitive; it also transcended them by insisting on a world-wide moratorium on all territorial transactions. The goal was simply, if ambitiously, peace, peace among nations, not anyone's particular peace and not any particular nations, but univer-sal peace for all nations – plus, most famously, a 'world . . . made safe for democracy'.

The US declaration of war also differed from that of the Allies in that it applied only to the Kaiser's Germany. Austria-Hungary would indeed later be accorded enemy status, but the Ottoman empire was never included among America's foes and so American forces never served in the Middle East. This precluded neither American involve-ment nor American interest. Some individual Americans joined the British forces specifically to fight in the East, most notably Kermit Roosevelt, the endearingly romantic second son of ex-President Theodore Roosevelt. As a captain in a motorized unit of lightly armed Rolls-Royces, young Roosevelt cruised the desert south of Baghdad, won the Military Cross, and in Cairo in 1918 met a subdued but still silkily resplendent Lawrence. Thirty years later Kermit Roosevelt's son, also Kermit or 'Kim', together with cousin Archie Roosevelt, were to revive the family's swashbuckling ways in the region to more telling effect.

In Cairo Kermit senior also encountered William Yale who had been the Jerusalem representative of Standard Oil's kerosene empire until 1917. Yale had then transferred to US government service as an official observer in the region, and seldom can the State Department have been better informed. His copious contacts resulted in some of the most perceptive reports of the period. Impartial and prescient, they have since inspired much historical revision, although it may be doubted whether they were fully appreciated at the time.

Nor, of course, did America's non-combatant status mean non-participation in plans for the Ottoman empire's future. Thanks to Yale, the President suspected, and soon knew, that Britain and France entertained imperialist ambitions in the area which, to the President's way of thinking, could only perpetuate the great power rivalries that had spawned the war in the first place. America, on the other hand, was fighting neither for territorial gain nor for political advantage but for an end to all such destabilizing ambitions. In the White House an acutely liberal conscience needed to be assuaged, and in the American Midwest, isolationist if not positively pro-German constituents needed to be mollified; as so often, high-minded principles fed on grass-roots exigencies.

Wilson's famous Fourteen Points as outlined in January 1918 included one that demanded an end to all secret treaties, like Sykes-Picot, and another, no. 12, that dealt solely with the Ottoman territories. This asserted that all 'nationalities' currently under Turkish rule 'should be assured . . . an absolutely unmolested opportunity of autonomous development'; which, as refined by subsequent pronouncements, seemed to mean the freedom for the Ottoman territories to decide for themselves on all questions of sovereignty, territory, economic concessions and external relations.

Thus, courtesy of the USA, did a new and revolutionary rhetoric enter the debate on the post-war settlement. Even the Husayn–McMahon correspondence as understood by the *sharif* did not go so far. As for Sykes-Picot, it was now such an embarrassment that the same President who denounced all secret agreements was soon wishing this one had stayed secret. London and Paris shuffled awkwardly: Sykes-Picot, it was repeated, was not set in stone; a more liberal gloss could be put on its wording. Paying lip-service to the President's ideals was the least that nations so heavily indebted to America could do. The British even claimed to have anticipated the new thinking in pronouncements like that issued after the capture of Baghdad in March 1917. Drafted in London by the busy Mark Sykes, this claimed that the British forces came as 'liberators' to help 'the

Arab race' regain its former glory; it also invited popular participation 'through your nobles and elders and representatives . . . in the management of your civil affairs'. But while toying with the vocabulary of freedom and representation, it made no concessions to autonomy, let alone self-determination. The European powers mouthed the US lyrics; but to the new music they remained tone-deaf.

Only in the Middle East itself did the President's message receive unequivocal support. The Fourteen Points were widely reported and no. 12 instantly became a mantra dear to every nationalist. It was repeated verbatim not just by those who subscribed to a pan-Arab identity (as espoused by the Hashemite Revolt and subsequently defined by Antonius), but also by those whose sense of community was more restricted. For where Sykes supposed the region to be composed of 'races', President Wilson supposed 'nationalities'; and such entities being as yet hard to discern, 'nationalities' came to be equated with the various geographic, ethnic and sectarian particularisms that Ottoman rule had accommodated within its administrative system of provinces (*wilayet*), sub-provinces (*sanjak*) and minorities (*millet*).

In Syria and Iraq, not to mention Egypt, powerful and assertive élites took heart. So did the leaders of embattled communities like the Armenians, Kurds, Druze and Maronites. Seemingly a man could be a Druze, a Syrian and an Arab, for example, all at the same time. 'Nationality' was evidently a many-layered thing. The obvious question, then, was which was the lucky layer to which all this US-made sovereign discretion applied. In terms of that search for a congenial political framework for the Arab world, such pronouncements merely raised the stakes. It might even be argued that Wilson's Fourteen Points, while honourably promoting self-determination as an antidote to the colonial affliction, unwittingly induced a fever on which the neo-colonial affliction would thrive.

THE BALFOUR DECLARATION

Another community that aspired to be a 'nationality' and therefore welcomed American support for self-determination was the Jewish one in Palestine. Variously estimated at 60,000 to 80,000, of whom about half were first-generation settlers, Palestine's Jews belied their modest numbers in that they were but the tip of the now world-wide Zionist iceberg. The weakness of their case for consideration as a rather insignificant Ottoman entity was more than offset by that strong moral claim on the Christian world's conscience, and this was itself now upheld by much of the world-wide Jewish community and promoted by an international apparatus of powerful patrons, wealthy benefactors and very persuasive negotiators.

In the Balfour Declaration of November 1917, another product of that watershed year, Zionism would win the recognition of the British government, and then that of the USA and the Allies. By many Christians as well as Jews the support conveyed by the Declaration was seen as just reward for a scripturally sanctioned and morally appealing cause, plus some highly effective lobbying. The Zionist Congress, founded by Theodor Herzl, was unable to meet because of the war; but Nahum Sokolow in France and Italy, Louis Brandeis in the USA and, above all, Chaim Weizmann in England pursued the negotiations with a rare single-mindedness. Together they pulled off a political master-stroke matched for its extra-governmental orchestration only by that which, thirty years later, would secure American and UN support for an Israeli state.

Their stories have been much told. That of Weizmann, the emi-grant from Russia to Manchester whose attainments as a chemist won him offficial gratitude and whose friendship with Simon Marks and Marcus Sieff of the retailers Marks and Spencer led to contacts with the *Manchester Guardian* which in turn led on to Whitehall, Sykes, Lloyd George and Balfour, is as extraordinary and persuasive as was Weizmann himself. But politics, especially wartime politics, having little to do with sentiment, a satisfactory explanation as to why the British government chose to adopt the fateful initiative remains elusive. 'Nobody knows why the Balfour Declaration was made,' according to Christopher Sykes.[5] As an admirable historian and the son of Mark Sykes, principal British architect of the Declaration (as of so much else), he should have known if anyone did. Other histor-ians have traced the British championship of Zionism to man-oeuvres designed to bring the United States into the war, to a last-ditch effort to stop Russia dropping out of the war, and to a pre-emptive strike to deny Zionist support going to Germany.

Alternatively the reason may lurk in the Middle East itself. The war there would provide the British with an occasion for gratifying

Zionist ambitions; more controversially, Allied designs on the Middle East look to have provided the imperative for doing so. If only on the grounds of synchronism, some such linkage might be suspected. Serious negotiations with the Zionists only began in 1917 and thereafter marched in step with the Allied advance into Palestine, acquiring greater urgency as the military momentum increased. Just as Weizmann's first meeting with Sykes coincided with the first British attempt to move east from Sinai, so the Declaration itself was issued just as Allenby drew near to Jerusalem.

This was surely no coincidence. So close a connection lends weight to the idea that, by the British, the Declaration was seen as a device for ensuring that that brown 'International Zone' into which their troops were now encroaching should become a red British zone in the post-war settlement. If, on the one hand, Palestine was to be isolated from Arab claims for an 'independent' Arab state (or states) as per Husayn–McMahon, and if, on the other, it was also to stay detached from French claims to a Greater Syria as per Sykes–Picot, some internationally respectable grounds for its exception had to be found. In this context the rights of a Palestine-based people who, according to their representatives, were agreeable to British rule, even insistent on it, could not have been more welcome. Recognition of Jewish claims also accorded with Wilsonian ideas on self-determination. And the *quid pro quo* of an open-ended British declaration in favour of Jewish settlement looked like an insignificant price to pay.

Kermit Roosevelt later likened the Declaration's 'deliberate ambiguities' to 'the poetical obscurity of the Delphic Oracle'.[6] At the time, few foresaw its long-term implications or feared its binding character. It attracted little contemporary comment in the British press. It was not dissimilar to other commitments made, for instance, to the Armenians. The exigencies of war dictated such accommodations. But thus, almost casually, was laid beneath the central pier of a region habitually likened to a continental bridge, the heaviest of all the many charges that would eventually explode to devastating effect.

Subsequently the Balfour Declaration would become, from a British point of view, 'one of the greatest mistakes in our imperial history'.[7] Some, like Gertrude Bell, had doubts about its imperial utility at the time; from Baghdad, between indenting for summer stockings, then winter boots, she registered her disgust, called it 'artificial', and wished it 'the ill-success it deserves'.[8] But not so Lawrence and some of the other Arab Bureau members who were closer to the situation in Egypt. To them it was precisely the imperial perspective which commended the Balfour Declaration.

Prior to 1917, the mainly British Egyptian Expeditionary Force had been pinned down in Sinai for two years, unable to advance and barely able to secure the Suez Canal. With headquarters at Ismailia on the waterway's west bank, it was asked whether the Expeditionary Force was actually defending the Canal or just taking cover behind it. Two attempts in early 1917 to break through the Turkish lines to Gaza disproved this idea and provided evidence of Lloyd George's forward intent. But both failed, the second dismally. Meanwhile, in between these two forays, the British Indian Expeditionary Force in Mesopotamia had made good with its long-awaited capture of Baghdad. Comparisons between the two Middle Eastern fronts were proving invidious and had raised profound questions about imperial deployment.

The ease with which the Turks had been able to stretch a hand to the imperial jugular of Suez, keep it there, and so pin down 100,000 badly needed troops while (as will appear) also destabilizing the situation in Egypt argued strongly for some strategic rethinking. A desert strip like Sinai was evidently no protection against an assault spearheaded by motorized transport and trailing railway tracks along which support and supplies could be maintained. What was needed in future, therefore, was a strong British position east of the Canal with its own port facilities and communications, an equivalent to the tracery of roads, railways and bases to the west of the Canal in Egypt. Such a nexus could only be located in Palestine.

Likewise, the probability of Mesopotamia/Iraq remaining under some form of British rule argued for direct links between it and the Mediterranean; and assuming French rule in Lebanon and Syria, it was again only Palestine which offered the necessary Mediterranean frontage, plus a desert contiguity with Iraq. A Haifa–Baghdad railway had long been envisaged as a speedier alternative to the sea voyage through the Canal, the Red Sea and round the Arabian peninsula into the Gulf. More recently the potential of a trans-Mesopotamian air link from Cairo to India, and even of an oil pipeline from the Shatt al-Arab to the Mediterranean, had been mooted. Aviation being then a matter of short hops between frequent refuelling points, the air link was no more feasible than the pipeline without a continuous belt of British territory which must include Palestine.

Timely, then, was the success that would attend Allenby's Palestine offensive in the autumn of 1917; and timely, indeed, was the undertaking, simultaneously negotiated, that provided a possible basis for British retention of Palestine in the post-war settlement. Addressed to Lord Rothschild of the Zionist Federation in Britain, signed by Balfour, and dated 2 November 1917, the famous Declaration conveyed British government approval for 'the establishment in Palestine of a national home for the Jewish people'.

It also promised His Majesty's Government's 'best endeavours to facilitate the achievement of this object' provided 'nothing shall be done which may prejudice the civil and religious rights of existing non-Jewish communities in Palestine'. The failure to specify that these 'non-Jewish communities' constituted the vast majority of Palestine's population, that they were overwhelmingly Arab, and that they were entitled to political (as well as 'civil and religious') rights could be interpreted as clearing a path towards the creation of a Jewish state. Lloyd George, a Zionist by biblical conviction, seems to have cheerfully agreed with Weizmann that 'a national home' was just a euphemism for 'a state'; and Weizmann himself would soon be talking unguardedly of Palestine becoming 'as Jewish as England is English or America is American'. But equally, a wording that implicitly denied the existence of any existing political community in Palestine and determinedly ignored its specifically Arab nature could be interpreted as a necessary clearing of the path for some form of British protection.

INTO JERUSALEM

Allenby's military breakthrough in the autumn of 1917 began with a flanking cavalry movement across the Negev desert to the south of the main Turkish lines radiating from the Gaza coast. Its objective was Beersheba, and the danger of its being cut off by Turkish forces from the south had been greatly reduced by the capture of Aqaba, plus continued Hashemite raids on the Hijaz railway to the east. On

27 October Beersheba's garrison was duly taken by surprise; the Turkish position was turned. Ahead the road to Hebron led on to Jerusalem. But a first attempt to reach the holy city failed. So did a raid, conducted by Lawrence and his Bedouin friends, against a spur of the Hijaz railway which spiralled down from Dera'a in Syria to the Jordan river and by which the Turkish forces in Gaza were supplied.

It was not a good period for the Arab Revolt. Despite the addition of vehicles, planes and those long-awaited French mountain guns under the command of a Corsican called Pisani, Faysal's men were unable to dislodge the large Turkish garrison in Ma'an and barely able to hold on to Aqaba and their forward base at Wadi Musa. Meanwhile the formation of two regular brigades to supplement the tribal levies on whom Faysal had hitherto relied was taking longer than expected.

The new units were comprised mainly of prisoners and deserters from the Turkish forces, all being Arabs and most of them Iraqis; in fact at least four of them would later become prime ministers of Iraq. As trained Ottoman soldiers who faced execution for treachery if recaptured, their commitment to the Arab cause was absolute, and they duly became the backbone of Faysal's army. 'Without them the Revolt would have been ineffective and would probably have collapsed,' noted Alec Kirkbride, a gangly 20-year-old lieutenant who, on the strength of colloquial Arabic learnt while at school in Alexandria, had been temporarily attached to Faysal's forces. The Bedouin mercenaries and levies with whom Lawrence preferred to consort were, by contrast, unreliable and useless in battle. Their principal virtue was as hit-and-run scavengers who lived off the desert. They also, thought Kirkbride, 'looked very picturesque'.[9]

By December 1917 a more 'bullish' Allenby was gearing up for another push on Jerusalem. The Turkish forces, obliged now to fight on two fronts, had begun falling back from Gaza, and the long-awaited British advance up the coast to Jaffa (Tel Aviv) had at last materialized. As if by way of reward, the inland prong of 'the Bull's' charge defied the wintry conditions to carry the Turkish positions along the Hebron road. By 9 December 1917 an undefended Jerusalem was in sight.

Nobly the Turks had elected not to contest a city so central to three of the world's great religions. 'It had often gone down in blood and ruin', wrote General Wavell, one of Allenby's subordinates (and later his biographer, and later still his Second World War counter-part), but 'this time its surrender had an air of comedy'. With a nice appreciation of the proper conduct on such occasions, the mayor of the city had ventured forth clutching a white flag, actually a bedsheet, and the keys to the city's gates. His gesture went unappreciated. Oddly for a city whose every stone was reputed sacred to someone and whose status was to be so hotly contested for the next ninety years, there were no takers. Two cockney NCOs who had lost their way while foraging for supplies doubtless told the mayor what he could do with his keys, a bored sergeant on outpost duty indicated that accepting surrenders was not his job, and some artillery officers busy with their guns were too preoccupied with the range of the Turkish rearguard to engage in ceremonial. 'None of these felt them-selves equal to so historic occasion', says Wavell; and it was not until the beflagged, and now flagging, mayor was brought to the attention of a divisional commander that his duty was finally discharged.[10] Sadly, to this comedy of errors there was an unhappy sequel. The chill night air left the mayor with a bad cold. It quickly developed into pneumonia, and three weeks later he was dead.

Meanwhile Allenby had made amends for the botched surrender by staging a ceremonial entry. Flanked by representatives of the small French and Italian contingents under his command – a recognition that this was supposed to be an Allied triumph – and trailed by assorted civilians and staff officers including Lawrence on behalf of Arab aspirations and Georges-Picot on behalf of French interests, Allenby stalked through the city's Jaffa Gate. The solemn procession on foot, very different from that which would follow in Damascus, was meant to show respect for the holy city and to silence those who, to the consternation of Allenby's Muslim contingents (Arab, Indian and Egyptian), insisted on drawing comparisons with the Crusades. But in this it predictably failed. To Christians it seemed peculiarly appropriate that, from a war against evil, so bright a sign of divine favour should shine forth. France applauded the triumph of *Le Croix contre Le Croissant* and in England the church bells rang. Lloyd George could not resist exulting over Christendom's repossession of the holy places. Weizmann offered effusive congratulations. 'The Bull', of course, was lionized.

'And tomorrow, my dear General,' Georges-Picot is supposed to have announced beneath the Jaffa Gate, ' we will take steps to set up an administration in this city.' Whether his 'we' meant just France, or Britain and France, was not clear. Nor did Allenby enquire. Appreciating the impossibility of reconciling Britain's conflicting promises to the Arabs, the French and the Zionists, he snubbed Georges-Picot, refused to publish the Balfour Declaration, and rejected a plan, reported by William Yale, for Faysal to make his own ceremonial entry into the city. Instead he ordained that Palestine should remain under military rule until military considerations should permit otherwise. This would prove to be a long time, nearly three years. Military requirements would change with the Armistice, but not vanish; and the peace settlement would take nearly as long as the war. Unsurprisingly the French, the Arabs, the Americans and even the Zionists would grow increasingly suspicious of British intentions.

From Jerusalem a further advance to Damascus was delayed first by the winter, then by the recall to Europe's Western Front of most of Allenby's British troops. The offensive would not be renewed until the autumn of 1918. In the meantime Faysal's forces would move up to Allenby's front line while, from Cairo, the Arab Bureau frantically tried to reconcile its Hashemite clients to the unsettling implications of the Balfour Declaration.

'When the news of the Declaration reached King Husayn [that is, the *sharif*] he was greatly disturbed,' recalled George Antonius. Now 27, the future author of *The Arab Awakening* had found employment under the British, and in January 1918 accompanied Professor/ Commander Hogarth on a mission of reassurance to Jidda. Like most other Britons, Hogarth saw the peoples of the Middle East in terms of race. Lawrence, his protégé since Oxford days, was probably expressing Hogarth's views in the early chapters of his *Seven Pillars* with their many references to the 'Semites'. As the descendants of the biblical Shem and as members of a single language group, the Semites supposedly included both the Arabs and the Jews. To Lawrence and Hogarth, therefore, Jew and Arab were not separate and incompatible races but 'cousins' whom history and religion had mischievously parted. Reuniting them was an exciting prospect. The Arabs of Palestine had the land; the Jews had the know-how and capital to develop it. It was a pairing that could supposedly bring benefit to both.

Husayn may have been intrigued by all this, but he was not reassured until Hogarth promised that Jewish settlement in Palestine would not be allowed to infringe 'the political and economic freedom of the Arab people'. This was definitely an improvement on the Declaration's reservation about Palestine's unspecified 'non-Jewish communities' having merely 'civil and religious rights'. George Antonius made a special note of it at the time and Lord Curzon later confirmed it. In the contrast between the Declaration's wording and that now being offered by Hogarth 'lay the difference', wrote Antonius in 1938, 'between a peaceful and willing Arab-Jew cooperation in Palestine and the abominable duel of the last twenty years'– or, indeed, seventy years. On this basis Husayn apparently accepted the idea of Jewish settlement and then bestirred himself to convince his sons and the Arab world in general.[11]

A Zionist commission from London, which included Weizmann, provided some further reassurance. It reached Cairo in March 1918 and Palestine in April. Public disavowals of any Zionist pretensions to supreme power were noted, and the idea of Arab-Jewish collaboration stirred some interest. The commission trod warily among the thorns of Arab antipathy, reserving its wrath for the barbed wire of a British military administration that was doing nothing to publicize or promote the terms of the Balfour Declaration. Weizmann blamed Ronald Storrs, previously Cairo's ultra-refined Oriental Secretary whose 'intolerant brain seldom stooped to company'. Now installed as Governor of Jerusalem in remote succession, as the mischief-making Philby would put it, to Pontius Pilate, Storrs seemed to be doing the Jews fewer favours than Pilate and, according to Weizmann, had just sat through an Arab diatribe against Jewry without turning a hair.

Storrs, whose balding head had few hairs left to turn, contested this accusation and insisted that he was, in fact, a Zionist by conviction. But with Allenby adamant that a military administration's job was simply to maintain the status quo, there was not much either Storrs or Weizmann could do about the situation. After all, the war was far from won, half of Palestine was still in Turkish hands, and the French as well as the Arabs still nursed a prior claim to the country. Weizmann, though, remained bitterly critical of what he termed this 'Arab-run' British administration. In May he wrote to Balfour in uncharacteristically blunt language about 'treacherous Arabs . . . who scream as often as [they] can and blackmail as much as [they] can'. Given the democratic principle – or what Weizmann contemptuously called the operation of 'brutal numbers' – there would surely 'be an Arab Palestine if there were an Arab people in Palestine'. But according to Weizmann, there was not. There were only peasants who were 400 years behind the times plus 'the effendi', a species of Turcophile Arab who was by nature 'dishonest, uneducated, greedy, and as unpatriotic as he is inefficient'.[12]

Happily, on a further mission of reassurance to Faysal at Aqaba, Weizmann was more his old diplomatic self. Although Faysal refused to pledge his support for Zionist settlement, he was persuaded to agree that this aspect of the Zionist programme was 'not incapable of realisation'. In general, the *sharif* and his sons, now heavily dependent on the British, were more easily swayed than Arab opinion in Palestine. There the issue of land transfers to Jews continued to exercise Arab suspicions just as that of language, and the official preference for Arabic, exercised Jewish suspicions. To counter British delicacy about Arab interests Weizmann would like to have seen a Jewish legion fighting alongside the Allies. He had earlier proposed such a unit but had been defeated by qualms among both Zionist Jews and anti-Zionist Jews. Meanwhile, to his chagrin, Faysal's Arab legion was about to come of age.

ON TO DAMASCUS

Arab operations in 1918 were observed by Hubert Young, the level-headed Indian army officer who had once rafted down the Tigris, and subsequently served as a political officer in Mesopotamia and who, now a major, suddenly found himself posted to Aqaba. The posting had been requested by the also now Major Lawrence himself. Apparently Lawrence had been asked to suggest who could take over as British liaison officer with the Arab forces, should he meet the untimely end which his exploits seemed to invite. He had replied, as he now confessed to Young, that no one could; but pressed again, 'I said I could only think of Gertrude Bell or yourself and they seemed to think you would be better for this particular job than she would.' Young somehow took this as a compliment and happily imagined himself performing 'Lawrentian stunts' and winning Lawrentian fame, perhaps as 'Young of Syria'. Lawrence encouraged him: it was all terrific fun, he said, and there was 'plenty of honour and glory to be picked up without any great difficulty'.[13]

But the glamour eluded Young, and to a tidy mind used to the clockwork discipline of Britain's Indian Army, the Arab forces seemed a hopeless shambles. Faysal's new model army numbered only 3,000 and, though keen enough and well armed, its deployment was continually being frustrated by vacillating counsels from above, usually emanating from either Faysal himself or Zayd, his half-brother and deputy. Orders were countermanded, supplies were re-allocated and transport was requisitioned, all without notice or reason. Lawrence, who might have composed such differences, was never there; busy living his own legend, he disappeared into the unknown and reappeared only when it suited him. Young protested in no uncertain terms and, as witnessed by the young Kirkbride, violent rows ensued. Apoplectic, the understudy no longer thought much of 'Lawrentian stunts'.

At the time Young was trying to organize a move from Wadi Musa and Aqaba (in the extreme south of modern Jordan) to a new operational base 300 miles to the north-east at the desert oasis of Azraq (in the extreme north). Nowadays a fly-blown and oil-stained way-station where sanctions-busting convoys of battered Iraqi tankers join the curtained limousines cruising from Riyadh to Amman, Azraq was then a pristine location boasting little more than a sheet of water, the jumbled shelter of a black and haunted fortress, and the security of its desert isolation. It was, though, crucial if the Arab army was to be of any use in Allenby's final advance. Lying due east of both Amman and Jerusalem, its occupation would firmly establish the Arabs on the right flank of Allenby's now north-facing lines, thereby affording desert protection and offering opportunities for forward diversions and sabotage. It would also expose to Arab attack another 200 miles of the Hijaz railway, including the garrison at Amman and the important junction of Dera'a. And, best of all, it was within striking distance of Damascus, to enter which capital as one of the victorious Allies had long been the dream of Faysal, Lawrence and their Arab following.

But Azraq was devoid of supplies, even grazing. Through the heat of August–September 1918 Hubert Young laboured prodigiously to organize the daily camel and mule trains needed to maintain an army two weeks away across enemy territory in the back of beyond. It was a magnificent achievement, disparaged by Lawrence but decisive in the successes that followed. Sadly it completely exhausted the conscientious Young. No lover of camels, he made one ride too many on an ill-fitting saddle and was invalided down to Aqaba with abdominal damage. His active role in the war, though not in the peace, was over.

Thanks to his elaborate arrangements, to the dedication of the numerous other British officers who were attached to Faysal's army, and to the loan of an Imperial Camel Corps detachment plus the air cover provided by the men of the Flying Corps, thanks too to the heroics of those Algerian gunners under Captain Pisani (whose help, says Young, was habitually 'minimised . . . for political reasons'), thanks to the authority and courage of Faysal's mainly Iraqi staff, and only then thanks to the wayward genius of Lawrence and his Bedouin following, the Arab forces were able to perform their greatest service.

This took the form of a series of carefully timed engagements around Dera'a whereby the three railway lines, which there converged, were all simultaneously cut just as Allenby launched his great northward offensive. The disruption of all communications between Palestine and Syria was partly a needful precaution, partly a diversionary tactic; for on this occasion it was the landward prong of Allenby's offensive that was the feint, and the coastal assault that was the main thrust. Although an overwhelming superiority in numbers never left much doubt of success, both moves succeeded more rapidly than expected. While in the west the infantry poured north into Galilee and southern Lebanon, in the east Faysal's forces captured whole stretches of railway and completely surrounded Dera'a. They withdrew only to admit a British division, and then, accompanied by a squadron of Australian cavalry, they raced north for the honour of capturing Damascus.

Who would capture what, and especially who would first enter the historic city whence Arab rule had once spread to three continents, had become a matter of some importance. Had the mayor of Damascus ventured forth, like his counterpart of Jerusalem, with a white flag and a set of keys he would have found takers galore. For in June 1918 yet another strand had been added to the tangled cat's cradle of British commitments on the future of the Middle East.

As well as rewarding the Hashemites, placating the French, satisfying the Americans and supporting the Zionists, the British government was now seemingly prepared to recognize Arab sovereignty and independence in those 'areas emancipated from Turkish control by the action of the Arabs themselves during the present war'. In other words, there was to be a 'rights of conquest' element in the final settlement. The claims of the Arabs, and possibly others, were to be judged not simply on the basis of existing agreements, like that supposedly contained in the Husayn–McMahon correspondence, but also in accordance with military realities. How much territory and how many cities the Arabs were able to overrun would help to determine how much they might be able to retain.

This competitive and potentially divisive principle had been enunciated, along with other novelties, in an important document known as 'The Declaration to the Seven'. During the previous summer, while the Zionist commission was touring the region, a memorial had been submitted to the British authorities in Cairo by seven Arabs who were concerned about British intentions in the light of the Balfour Declaration and the now public Sykes-Picot agreement. The Declaration to the Seven, dated 11 June 1918, was the British government's response. Although neither the memorial nor the declaration mentioned the names of the seven Arabs, George Antonius would later reveal them: all were Syrian exiles in Egypt who belonged to the newly formed Party of Syrian Unity. Additionally, the American William Yale observed that all had links to a British agent who was often referred to as 'Ozzy'. This seems to have been both code-name and nickname, its bearer otherwise labouring under the genuine but wildly improbable appellative of Main Swete Oswald Walrond.

A close associate and agent of Lord Milner, the British Secretary of State for War, M.S.O. Walrond had been cultivating the Syrian Seven for some months. Yale describes him as 'encouraging them to think in terms of an Arab State or Confederacy of States' and, to that end, 'supplying them with such materials as the constitution of the United States, of the Federal Republic of Switzerland and other such documents'.[14] Moreover Walrond may well have had a hand in actually drafting the Seven's memorial; he certainly took delivery of it, forwarded it to London, and then addressed the Seven when announcing London's response. He was also a member of the Arab Bureau, although Lawrence, for one, strongly disapproved of his activities. His Syrian memorialists, according to Lawrence, were just 'an unauthorised committee of seven Gothamites' (Gotham being a proverbial village of idiots).[15] Like most nationalists from that chron-

ically discordant 'vassal country' of Syria, they were the most paro-
chial of 'effendis', a class for whom Lawrence had no greater regard
than did Weizmann.

But in Lawrence's contempt for this initiative – which he might
otherwise have been expected to welcome in that it recognized Arab
rights of conquest – lay the real nub of the matter. For, by implication, the Declaration to the Seven completely bypassed his
Hashemite protégés, made no mention of the valiant Faysal or the
revered *sharif* Husayn, dropped all references to 'the Arab race' and
'the Arab kingdom', and awarded the sovereign independence of territories liberated by the Arabs to 'the Arabs inhabiting these areas'.
In other words, the Declaration appeared to renege on commitments
made to the monarchical Hashemites and to substitute as likely
beneficiaries the peoples of Syria. These, naturally, were precisely
those whom the petty 'Gothamites' of the Party of Syrian Unity
claimed to represent.

The Declaration to the Seven may thus be read as a first triumph
for those particularist sub-Arab interests, in this case Syrian, that had
been galvanized by President Wilson's talk of 'nationalities' and self-
determination. It may also be seen as the first salvo in a two-year duel
between Hashemite ambitions to a sovereignty that embraced Syria,
and Syrian hopes of a more popular sovereignty exclusive to Syria;
for it was precisely with a view to creating a Syrian Arab state, devoid
of the feudal, dynastic and religious conservatism of the Hashemites,
that the Seven had been poring over those republican constitutions
of Switzerland and the United States. And finally, by the French
especially, the Declaration to the Seven would be seen as the first of
many Macchiavellian schemes devised by the British in Cairo to frustrate French claims by promoting a puppet Arab nationalism amenable to British pressure.

These French suspicions were now heightened by the unseemly
dash for Damascus. Dearly would Georges-Picot have liked to see
French troops entering the city first. But a man described by Yale as
'vain . . . weak . . . jealous of his own position and of the prestige of
France' was never likely to win any favours from Allenby and was
getting little support even from Clemenceau.[16] Apart from the presence of token units like that of Pisani and his Algerian gunners, in
1918 Clemenceau needed every available Frenchman for the defence
of France.

Yet, little noted, there was in fact a French contingent in the vanguard of the advance on Damascus. Commanded by a Capitaine Pinchon, it was attached to the corps of Australian cavalry and Indian infantry that had moved north from Dera'a with the Arabs; and on the afternoon of 30 September 1918 it was about to enter the suburbs of the city.

But at this point the whole advance was mysteriously halted, much to the disgust of the French and the Australians. According to Lawrence, the latter 'saw the campaign as a point-to-point with Damascus [as] the [winning] post'. Lawrence disapproved, and therefore welcomed Allenby's directive that 'no troops may enter Damascus without express orders'.[17] Evidently Allenby 'hoped that we [the Arab army] would be present at the entry'. To the Arabs the city was very much more than a trophy; and Allenby may also have looked to the Arab forces to reassure the local population that the invaders came as liberators and were not to be resisted. Accordingly, writes Lawrence, while French, Indians and Australians cooled their heels in the hills, 'one night was given to us [the Arabs] to make the Damascenes receive the British army as their allies'.

So 'the point-to-point' race as conceived by the Australians had, in fact, been fixed. Bedouin detachments entered the city that evening; and when Lawrence drove into town next morning, the city was already in Arab hands with the red, white, green and black flag of the Hashemites fluttering from the city hall. For Lawrence and his Arab companions Allenby had indeed 'done what he could'; but it was perhaps rather more than he should. For ensuring that the Arabs won the race meant ensuring that the French, if they managed to enforce the Sykes-Picot agreement, would find a prickly British ally already installed on their patch.

Nasir, Lawrence's sharifial companion on the long ride to Aqaba, galloped into the city centre first, 'a privilege of his fifty battles' says Lawrence, forgetting that the avoidance of anything remotely amounting to a battle had been both his aim and his achievement. Resplendent as ever in white and gold, he himself followed in an armoured Rolls-Royce.

The way was packed with people lined solid on the side-walks, in the road, at the windows and on the balconies and house-tops. Many were crying, a few cheered faintly, some bolder ones cried out our names; but mostly they looked and looked, joy shining in their eyes. A movement like a long sigh from gate to heart of the city, marked our progress.[18]

Yet all was not quite so rosy. That Damascene sigh may have been one of despair, so confused were the populace as to who exactly their new masters were. And as for the Damascene delirium, it looks more like a bit of Lawrentian licence. The Revolt needed a crowning triumph; his book needed a resounding climax. Damascus had to provide them. But Kirkbride, arriving soon after with some of Faysal's regulars, noticed only Damascene indifference. 'There were no cheers or other signs of joy, which one might have expected from a population supposed to be in the process of liberation . . . I was rather pained at the lack of popular enthusiasm'.[19]

Moreover, it soon transpired that the Arabs had in fact been forestalled. Earlier that morning of 1 October the first regular troops to stage an entry and receive an official welcome had been a brigade of Australian cavalry. They had been taking a short-cut to their ordained positions astride the road north to Homs; and they had since passed on out of the city in that direction. But what they had found was that Damascus already had an Arab government operating in the name of the *sharif*. It had been set up two days before, and was headed by Amir Said al-Jazairi, one of two brothers who had once enjoyed Faysal's confidence. This transitional government had taken over with the approval of the departing Turks and had installed itself in the governor's offices. There it had welcomed the Australians, and there it now prepared to receive Lawrence as he drew up outside.

Lawrence detested the Jazairi brothers. He considered them religious fanatics and he may have suspected them of being French agents. Either way, they were not the people to be seen handing a Hashemite on to the throne; that was Britain's role, and it was important that she be seen to perform it, both for her own prestige and for that of her Arab protégés. Nor were the Jazairis welcome as Hashemite counsellors whose influence might rival Britain's own. Indeed, they must go, immediately. 'In my capacity as deputy for Faysal,' recalled Lawrence, 'I pronounced their civil government abolished.' There followed a scuffle. A knife was drawn and Lawrence's Bedouin allies bayed for blood. He resisted the temptation to indulge them; but within hours the Jazairi brothers were outlawed on suspicion of incitement and within weeks one was shot down and the other arrested. Thus did the colonial powers' involvement in the affairs of Syria begin with the overthrow of a government. And thus would it continue, *ad nauseam*.

Damascus, meanwhile, had ceased to celebrate, if it ever had. Faysal's Bedouin, plus some more recent Druze allies, had gone on the rampage. Turkish stragglers were being butchered before they could surrender, and the city's famous souks were being pillaged. On the morning of 1 October Lawrence had asked the Australian commander to keep his troops out of the city. On the morning of the 2nd he was frantically asking him to bring them in. A stroll in the streets with young Kirkbride as bodyguard had resulted in three dead Syrians, all shot by Kirkbride's revolver as they refused Lawrence's command to stop molesting Turks and turned their weapons on the living legend himself.

The Australians rode in later that day and quickly restored order. British and Indian troops followed; so did Pisani, the cheery Corsican with his Algerian gunners. By now the people of Damascus must have been wondering what further surprises their gold encircling hills could possibly hold.

On the 3rd there arrived Allenby by road and Faysal by train. To preserve the façade of a military occupation empowered, as in Jerusalem, only to maintain the status quo, Faysal's forces were officially gazetted as Allied belligerents, a formality which had hitherto been neglected, and Faysal himself was then appointed military commander responsible under Allenby for an area of occupation. The area in question was designated as that east of the Jordan from Aqaba to Damascus. This excluded Palestine and the coastal districts of Lebanon/Syria but roughly corresponded to the ground over which the Arabs had actually operated.

Faysal took the appointment to be a temporary expedient until he or his father was confirmed as sovereign. The *sharif*'s flags continued to fly over the city in contravention of the supposedly Allied status quo, and others began to appear in places not included under his official command, like Beirut. Frantic French protests resulted in the removal of the Beirut flags, an action that heralded the next phase of the struggle for Syria. Faysal, however, continued to confuse his official command on behalf of the Allies with his effective rule on behalf of the *sharif,* and the British did little to dissuade him.

From his room in the Victoria Hotel (aptly named, but only after the event) Lawrence looked on his work, saw it was good, and declared it complete. 'When Damascus fell, the Eastern war – probably the whole war – drew to an end.' Allenby's advance rolled on, largely unopposed, to Homs, Hama, Tripoli and then Aleppo. A last engagement was fought outside Aleppo on 26 October; four days later the Turkish armistice was announced, and two weeks later that in Europe followed. Lawrence had made only one request of Allenby when they met in victory at Damascus: that he be given immediate leave. The request was reluctantly granted. He left on 4 October, 'and then at once I knew how much I was sorry'.[20]

So ends Lawrence's *Seven Pillars of Wisdom*. The note of contrition is not explained. It might have been over what he had achieved and the 'fraud' it had involved. But writing at least five years after the events, it could also have been over the disillusionment, both personal and political, that followed.

Part Two

1918–1936

5

Cairo Rose

IN 1914, AS Armageddon engulfed Europe, H.G. Wells had published a book with the upbeat title of *The War that Will End War*. The phrase subsequently acquired a far wider currency than the book and entered popular usage as 'the war to end all war'. That the war in question had proved to be nothing of the sort was, of course, what gave the tag its ironic resonance.

Nearer the truth was the corollary of a 'peace to end all peace'. So comprehensively did the settlement that followed the First World War preclude goodwill among nations that scarcely a year in the next twenty passed without more war, and then came the Second World War. Indeed, with a two-year gap beween the Armistice and the peace settlement, and another two-year gap between the settlement and its acceptance (notably by Turkey), it was not unlikely that the 'peace to end all peace' would be shattered well before it was fully implemented.

In the Middle East especially, events would race ahead of the arrangements that were supposedly being designed to contain them. Egypt would issue a bombshell ultimatum within hours of the Armistice, Syria would scarcely draw breath between one war and the next, Iraq would not be far behind, and Arabia, although not actually on the peace agenda, would contrive an early conflict of its own. Complaints about the unconscionable delay in the settlement, and about the uncertainties that resulted, were heard from all over the region, from British and French administrators as much as from Arab and Zionist activists. Meanwhile the negotiators, convening amid the comforts of Paris and Versailles, then London, Sèvres, San Remo and Lausanne, seemed oblivious to the urgency of the situation. In the later notion of peace being an interminable 'process' there is little new; and then, as latterly, the fault did not lie entirely with the peacemakers.

In November 1918 the Armistice brought from the victorious Anglo-French allies yet another declaration. Drafted by the ever-ready pen of Mark Sykes and directed specifically to the peoples of Iraq and Syria, it promised 'the setting up of national governments and administrations that shall derive their authority from the free exercise of the initiative and choice of the indigenous population'. In fact, it made the same point twice, in case there be any confusion:

> Far from wishing to impose on the populations of these regions any particular institutions, [the British and French governments] are only concerned to ensure, by their support and by adequate assistance, the working of governments and administrations freely chosen by [the people] themselves.[1]

These sentiments were obviously congenial to American opinion; and outraged annexationists, like A.T. Wilson and François Georges-Picot, would assume that they were intended mainly for transatlantic consumption. Arabs, on the other hand, took the new declaration as a solemn Allied undertaking. Like the Declaration to the Seven, its tone was encouraging. Even if, on French insistence, there was no sign of the magic word 'independence', it did for once carry French, as well as British, endorsement. If it also guaranteed America's participation in the peace negotiations, that too was good news. Hopes ran high when in November 1918 Faysal headed for the Paris peace conference to register the Arab bid.

At the conference the various delegations and observers represented a wide array of interested parties including subject nations, like India, who had contributed to the Allied victory, and putative nations, like the Zionists, Armenians and Maronites, who sought recognition and redress as a result of it. On both grounds, Egypt had as good a case for representation as any. She had not been a belligerent but had contributed handsomely to the war effort. Moreover, for thirty years she had repeatedly been assured by Cromer and his successors that the British presence in Egypt was a temporary necessity, to be reviewed as soon as conditions allowed. Accordingly, on 13 November 1918, forty-eight hours after the signing of the Armistice in Europe, a three-man 'delegation' (*wafd*) of Egyptian politicians presented itself at the offices of Britain's senior representative in Cairo. They were there, they explained, to lodge a demand for immediate negotiations on independence, for an end to wartime's martial law, and for a chance to present their case at the peace conference.

The delegation was received by Sir Reginald Wingate, McMahon's successor as Britain's 'High Commissioner in Egypt'. His title had changed from the 'Consul and Agent-General' of Cromer's day to reflect an important alteration in Egypt's status that had come about as a result of the 1914 declaration of war on the Ottoman empire. Since it made no sense for Britain's rights in Egypt to rest on its status as the agent of a hostile power, a new arrangement had become necessary, and from 'the veiled protectorate', as the occupation was known, the veil had been torn; Ottoman suzerainty over Egypt ('just a figure of speech for the past half century', according to Ronald Storrs) had been formally rejected, and the Khedive, who represented it, retitled.

At the time, with Turkish/Ottoman forces closing on the Suez Canal, London had seen this as a chance not only to remove the veil but also to appropriate the lady. Orders were accordingly issued for a proclamation annexing Egypt as a colony of the British crown. However, British officials in Cairo had protested; annexation might be seen as typical of the high-handed rapacity which the Allies claimed to be opposing; it was also guaranteed to alienate Egyptians just when their co-operation was most needed. Waging war on the Caliph of all Islam was risky enough; it was partly to guard against a pro-Caliphal Muslim backlash in Egypt that Kitchener had briefly encouraged *sharif* Husayn to proclaim himself Caliph. But to provoke political discontent, as well as religious resentment, would have been to invite that near-disastrous combination of popular and nationalist outrage which had followed the Dinshawai incident.

On reflection, therefore, annexation had not looked such a good idea; the London directive had been withdrawn and, in its stead, a

straightforward British protectorate had been declared. It was justified in terms of military expediency; it was to last for the duration of
the war; and since a protectorate assumed the sovereignty of the protected subject under the suzerainty of the protecting power, Egypt
had continued to enjoy the appearance of self-rule, with Egyptian
ministers forming Egyptian governments and working through an
Egyptian bureaucracy. British advisers readily offered advice that
could not easily be ignored, but technically Egypt never became a
British colony. It therefore remained a responsibility of the British
Foreign Office, whose representative thenceforth had enjoyed the
super-ambassadorial status of High Commissioner.

That had left the question of what to do with the Khedive.
Fortunately Khedive Abbas II had been easily disposed of. He had
been in Constantinople when war broke out and, throwing in his lot
with the Turks, he stayed there. The British had therefore deemed his
office forfeit and turned to his aged uncle, Prince Husayn Kamel. As
the senior descendant of the great Muhammad Ali, legitimacy was on
the Prince's side and, since he could hardly be a khedive without
Ottoman sanction, he had a good case for assuming the title of
'king'. Storrs, then still Oriental Secretary in Cairo, had objected. On
the specious grounds that, since Husayn Kamel's suzerain was the
King of England, he too could not be a king, Storrs suggested he be
'Sultan of Egypt'. Husayn Kamel demurred and took matters to the
wire, but eventually he had agreed.

During the new Sultan's long inaugural procession through the
heart of Cairo, Storrs had reckoned his own chances of assassination
at 'twenty or thirty per cent' and Husayn Kamel's very much higher.
The crowds were certainly not ecstatic, but although the Sultan
would be the target of two later attempts on his life, the induction
had gone off without trouble. So had that of the Sultan's young
brother, Prince Ahmed Fuad, who succeeded to the throne when
Husayn Kamel died in 1917. Again there was talk of annexation,
this time from Cairo where Wingate and his political adviser
Gilbert Clayton, both supporters of Arab 'independence', deemed
Egyptians deserving only of direct colonial rule. Too much attention, according to Clayton, had been paid to 'the aspirations of the
small and interested ruling class of Egypt' and not enough to the
desires of the 'submissive and amenable masses' for whom 'a just
and efficient rule' was all that mattered.[2] On this occasion, though, it

had been the Foreign Office in London that objected. Annexation would horrify the Americans, outrage the French and unsettle the Arabs. The protectorate must stay.

As the war wore on and the new sultanate began flexing its political muscle, it had become apparent that it was not British sponsorship of their Sultan that rankled with Egyptians; nor was it the British protectorate. What, according to Storrs, 'exasperated Egyptians beyond endurance' was the fact that 'nations they considered unbreeched barbarians [that is, the *sharif*'s trouserless Arab Bedouin] in the Hijaz and elsewhere were being granted the complete independence denied to Egypt'.[3]

Such sentiments certainly figured in the minds of the three Egyptian politicians who confronted Wingate at the High Commission in Cairo in November 1918. The delegation, or *wafd*, was led by Saad Zaghlul, an ageing but charismatic sphinx with inscrutable gaze and unshakeable will who had been minister of education back in Cromer's day. 'He possesses all the qualities necessary to serve his country,' Cromer had noted; honest, capable and courageous, 'he should go far'.[4] But unanticipated by Cromer, it was Zaghlul's grasp of populist rhetoric that had since gone far, reaching out beyond the narrow intrigues of Cairo's political élite to establish a network of nationalist protest among the very masses whom Clayton had thought most receptive to British rule. With the legislature in abeyance and with Zaghlul a fierce critic of the existing government, Wingate had no obligation to heed Zaghlul's demands. But he recognized that the delegation was indeed representative of grass-roots Egyptian opinion and urged the Foreign Office to invite its members to London.

The suggestion was refused. So too was a copycat demand for an all-party delegation made by Husayn Rushdi, the Egyptian prime minister. Rushdi then resigned, and on 8 March 1919, in an attempt to isolate the source of the trouble, Zaghlul and his delegation were summarily arrested. The order for their arrest, and their immediate deportation to Malta, was couriered to military headquarters by a young chancery official called Lawrence Grafftey-Smith. 'I might have done better to throw it in the Nile,' he later wrote.

To the *wafd*'s supporters Zaghlul's arrest was as a torch to the stubble. Students at the Islamic university of al-Azhar proclaimed a revolution, civil servants downed pens, workers went on strike, and as the street protests got out of hand, property was ransacked and persons waylaid. Egyptian mothers and daughters joined in the demonstrations; schoolchildren chanted incessantly. As well as anti-British and pro-Zaghlul slogans, 'Long Live Wilson' was heard, and also 'Long Live *Ismuay*'. Wilson was the US President but the identity of '*Ismuay*' was a mystery. Then someone realized that the chant-leader, unable to recall the name of the US representative in Cairo, had sung out the Arabic equivalent of 'What's-his-name'.

With an insensitivity bred of wartime priorities, the British had unwittingly reconstituted that explosive combination of nationalist pride and popular protest which had followed the Dinshawai incident. In fact, according to Grafftey-Smith, 'the long-hoarded photographs of the poor Dinshawai dead, swinging by the neck in 1906, were brought out of hiding, reproduced by the thousand, and circulated as being yesterday's news'.[5] Well publicized, too, was an unguarded British comment to the effect that any Egyptian flare-up could be easily extinguished merely by spitting on it. But as the protests and the violence spread like wildfire, upriver and down, not even water-cannon would have doused them. Within a week the whole country was at a standstill, the death toll was climbing, and outlying British communities were under siege. To historically minded officials it looked like the most serious internal challenge to the British empire since India's 1857 Great Rebellion.

EDGING TOWARDS INDEPENDENCE

Zaghlul and his *wafdist* supporters were in little doubt as to why the British, while 'liberating' other Arabs, seemed intent only on colonizing the Egyptians. Egypt, unlike Arabia, was a colony worth having. As well as being the crossroads of the British empire it had the nearest thing to a developed economy in Africa or the Middle East. By 1919 its population exceeded 12 million, which was more than those of Iraq, Syria/Palestine and the Arabian peninsula combined. Its physical and financial infrastructures were among the most elaborate outside Europe. Its cotton, sugar and tobacco industries were part of the global economy. And thanks to recent irrigation projects, its agriculture was sufficiently productive to yield a substantial revenue as well as exportable cash crops. In short, after a century of modernization and investment, the Egyptian economy generated the sort of returns that made the country well worth the expense of whatever administrative and policing arrangements were necessary to retain it.

In March 1919, as the troops were called out on to the streets to quell the pro-*wafd* riots, Cairo particularly looked worth fighting for. To home-bound passengers from the liners of P&O or Messageries Maritimes, the city was where the East ended and the West began. It was where, after the year-round summers of Singapore or Saigon, the seasons started again, the trees shed their leaves, and European fashions mattered. 'I have never seen Cairo gayer,' wrote Kermit Roosevelt on his way back from Iraq in 1918, 'the dances were as pleasant as any that could be given in London.'[6] Combining English amenities with Indian prices, Cairo was also where the fever-ridden bearers of the white man's burden met its rosy-cheeked beneficiaries – rich adventurers safari-ing into Africa, the adventurous rich cruising up the Nile.

As a place from which to watch the world go by, the open-air terrace of Cairo's Shepheard's Hotel was said to have no rival. Here tassled fezzes greeted solar topis, peaked caps toasted pill-box kepis, and skullcaps attended top hats while bushwhacking wide-awakes bent over their beer. The shops, like the hotels, were internationally famous; a building boom was transforming the pre-war boulevards into asphalt canyons choked with sidewalk salesmen, cooking fumes and, as of early 1919, club-toting mobs. When the trains and trams were not on strike, vast new suburbs in Heliopolis, Helouan and Maadi daily disgorged commuters into the region's only real conurbation.

Disturbances permitting, transit passengers from the Far East entrained at Suez for a few days in Cairo and then rejoined their ships at Port Said, the Mediterranean terminus of the Canal and 'well known as the wickedest town in the world', 'a sink of iniquity', 'a hell on earth', 'a notorious centre for the White Slave traffic' and any other epithet that the colonial letter-writer thought sufficiently mouth-watering for his stay-at-home siblings.[7] Leave-taking Europeans from Egypt, on the other hand, usually sailed from Alexandria. Once the city of Cleopatra, Alexandria now boasted the trappings of a Riviera resort, plus a vast dockyard, major industries and one of the most cosmopolitan populations in the world. The novelist E.M. Forster described the city as scarcely Egyptian at all. In 1915, 'in a slightly heroic frame of mind', Forster had forsaken his considerable celebrity to serve with the Red Cross as a medical orderly in Alexandria. There he tended the Gallipoli wounded, had a homo-erotic affair with a tram conductor, and wrote a city guidebook. In it, a thousand years of Arab rule merited less than a sentence and all the Islamic architecture was left to the pen of his collaborator, the ubiquitous George Antonius. The book was nevertheless a gem, as rare as it was finely crafted. In 1941 a copy would come into the possession of Lawrence Durrell, drawing him to the city, to the revision of Forster's guide, and to the collection of material for his own *Alexandria Quartet*.[8]

In Durrell's *Quartet*, as in Forster's guide, it is as if the entire *demi-monde* of the Levant were attracted to Alexandria, like bath-water to its Mediterranean plug-hole. Artists, spy-masters, deviants and dreamers, all of exotic descent and louche demeanour, circulate among seedy colonial stereotypes and a few token Copts. But Egypt's 12 million Muslims, toiling outside in the fields, swarming from the dockyard gates, are strangely invisible. The *fellah's* turban was similarly absent from the terrace at Shepheard's Hotel. It was undeniable that Egypt had done well out of the war. Cotton prices had trebled; military demand had boosted local industry; the pimps, liquor merchants and curio sellers could scarcely believe their good fortune; investment was at unprecedented levels; and the balance of payments showed a healthy surplus. If political squabbles appeared to have been suspended for the course of the war, it was only partly because of martial law restrictions, not at all because of any sympathetic concern for the Allies' predicament, and mostly because of the contentment afforded by this economic bonanza.

But while Egypt had never had it so good, most Egyptians had never had it so bad. The contracts, the concessions and the kickbacks went either to the Sultan's cronies, their business and landowning rivals, or the cosmopolitan gentlemen who summered in Durrell's Alexandrian salons and wintered amid the potted palms of Cairo's sporting clubs. Further afield, in the mud-built villages and ramshackle towns of the Delta or along the dust-laden byways of the upper Nile, the war was less popular. In spite of wartime restrictions on the acreage dedicated to cotton, foodstuffs failed to meet the increased demand, prices doubled, and the poorer *fellahin* went hungry. Technically Egypt was not at war and there was no requisitioning or conscription. In practice the strong demand for military transport denuded the land of camels, donkeys and fodder, while some 125,000 *fellahin* were 'compulsorily volunteered' for military labour by their landlord-creditors. As Grafftey-Smith put it, 'while we were winning the war, we were losing the *fellahin*'.[9] Hundreds died on active service, and of the thousands who absconded or were destitute, many drifted towards the cities, resorted to crime and thuggery, and lent eager ears to Zaghlul's passionate oratory.

Nor, for once, did this have much to do with population growth. In fact, in 1918 a suddenly soaring death rate actually exceeded the birth rate as Egypt's population recorded its only twentieth-century decline. Thomas Russell, who commanded the Cairo police during the 1919 uprising, noted a possible cause. *A propos* the poor physique of his recent recruits, he supposed that it must have something to do with 'the deterioration of the standard of health in the villages'.[10]

Despite their 'poorer fighting quality', the police gave a good account of themselves. During a *wafdist* riot in Cairo's Saiyida Zaynab Square, when the sight of the gallant Russell on his prancing white horse failed to cow the mob, the police fired on their compatriots without question, killing five. Outside the cities, pacification was entrusted to the military; suspicious gatherings were first bombed or strafed from the air. But it was mid-April before a relieving force reached Aswan on the upper Nile. By then Egyptian fatalities had reached about a thousand, including 47 who were judicially executed. British deaths were more precisely recorded; there were 40, most of them unspeakably brutal. 'The great train massacre' of 8 March would be especially remembered, partly because the 6.50 from Assiut was so boldly hijacked by the perpetrators and partly because its eight British passengers, armed only with empty soda-water bottles, were so mercilessly 'sticked and stoned', then bludgeoned and slashed, then mutilated and dismembered. Their crime, according to a spokesman for the mob, was that of being Englishmen 'who seized our grain and camels, our money, who orphaned our children, who fired at al-Azhar and the mosque of Hussein'.[11]

But if the police and the army wielded the stick, the High Commission proffered the carrot. Wingate, who happened to be in London at the time of the outbreak, had been summarily replaced, and in his stead there arrived in Cairo as the new High Commissioner the much-fêted and about to be ennobled Edmund Allenby. It was late March and the army was already on top of the 'revolution'. Allenby carefully assessed the situation and, within a week, was ready with his master-plan. As during the advance into Palestine, he eschewed confrontation in favour of a flanking movement; but in politics, belying his 'bullish' reputation and to the consternation of his colleagues, Allenby's idea of outflanking meant wholesale concessions. Zaghlul and his colleagues were to be released immediately from their confinement in Malta, and an enquiry into the causes of the trouble was to follow. London blanched. But Allenby, purple, refused to budge; the 'Malta Martyrs' walked free.

While Egypt erupted with joy at this unexpected triumph, Zaghlul and his colleagues proceeded straight to Paris, there to engage in lobbying the peace delegates while cold-shouldering the British. Meanwhile the promised enquiry was constituted in the form of a high-level mission from London headed by Lord Milner, who like Zaghlul had once served in Egypt under Cromer. As well as investigating the recent disorders, the Milner Mission was to report on what reforms 'under the protectorate' might be conducive to peace, prosperity and the development of self-governing institutions.

Needless to say, this was not quite the 'independence' that Zaghlul had in mind. When the Milner Mission finally reached Egypt in December 1919, the euphoria over Zaghlul's release had long since evaporated and a boycott was in place; no one outside the charmed circles of the Sultan and the governing élite dared even to correspond with Milner or any of his five very senior colleagues. The Mission's attempts at direct contact prompted only strikes and protests; and with its competence limited to winning Egyptian acquiescence in the existing protectorate, it lagged well behind even Allenby's expectations. Clearly its only chance of securing agreement lay in establishing contact with Zaghlul himself; and since Zaghlul would not come to Egypt or be seen to recognize the Mission, there followed what was in effect a 'two-track process'. While the Mission went through the motions of enquiry and consultation in Egypt, Milner's trusted sleuth, the mysterious 'Ozzy' Walrond, mastermind of the Declaration to the Seven, was put on to Zaghlul's case in Paris. There he trailed the Egyptian leader and his colleagues round the *arrondissements*, hinting at compromise and unauthorized concessions.

Meanwhile Zaghlul's hopes of the Paris peace conference had already been dented when, soon after his arrival, the British had won from the US a grudging recognition of the imperatives that necessitated their protectorate over Egypt. Zaghlul, nevertheless, persevered. For, as France's leftist press readily advertised, he rested his case not on international commitments, like Faysal with his portfolio of assorted declarations and correspondence, but on his well-demonstrated authority as the undisputed champion of the Egyptian people.

Zaghlul's *wafd*, a 'delegation' in the process of being transformed into a political party so now more properly the Wafd, was like India's National Congress, itself originally an annual gathering that was undergoing a similar transformation. At the time, both organizations represented an unfamiliar but formidable national consensus that transcended the traditional religious, regional and social divisions of their respective societies. Copts, for instance, were prominent among Zaghlul's supporters just as Indian Muslims were among Gandhi's. Post-war expectations of Indian self-rule had been disappointed and, just as now in Egypt, violent protests had followed. In fact the 1919–20 Milner Mission to Egypt faithfully mirrored that of 1917–19 to India under Edwin Montagu and Lord Chelmsford.

But there the similarities ended. Egypt was not India. When in 1921 Montagu and Chelmsford presented their report, Congress would welcome its proposed reforms and Gandhi would insist on a vote of thanks. But when in the same year Milner presented his Egyptian report, Zaghlul would contrive to have it rejected. He could afford to; for whereas the British were in India by rights of conquest and treaty which precluded any legal necessity of further endorsement, they were in Egypt merely as the protecting power, a status which assumed not just Egyptian acquiescence but Egyptian agreement. India, in short, was part of the British empire; Egypt was not, and as Milner firmly admitted, it never had been. Since the Khedive/Sultan had not actually asked for protection, in legal terms it was doubtful whether it was even a protectorate. And, anyway, protectorate status merely confused the issue. Protectorates over small and vulnerable entities, like the Malay states, made a certain sense; over one of the oldest nations in the world whose 12 million members now clearly rejected such protection, it was a nonsense. As Clayton, with his eyes opened by the March 1919 'revolution', had written to Gertrude Bell in Baghdad, the only things tht needed protection in Egypt were Britain's interests, like 'the Suez Canal, the Nile waters, the army and the police'.[12]

The idea of abandoning the protectorate, and so conceding independence while retaining rights in respect of specific British interests, now began to gain ground. Allenby had never seen much future for the protectorate, Milner dropped all reference to it in a January 1920 explanation of his Mission, and Walrond in Paris, either persuaded by his own enthusiasm or misled by Zaghlul's colleagues, reported that the Wafd would welcome direct negotiations on such a basis. These took place in London in the summer of 1920 after the Milner Mission had returned from Egypt. But Zaghlul, far from graciously accepting independence, immediately began to question the residual rights that the British proposed to retain. Again, he could afford to; for such rights would require Egyptian agreement in the form of a treaty between an independent Egypt and Great Britain. He was also wise to; for as envisaged by the British, the protection of their special interests would consitute a substantial diminution of Egypt's independence.

Negotiations thus degenerated into complex squabbles about which rights the British would retain in Egypt. When Zaghlul failed to endorse the final British offer, further concessions were made to induce one of his rivals to sign on behalf of Egypt. Installing such a dignitary as Egyptian prime minister was a mere formality; Allenby leant on the Sultan, and the Sultan duly made the appointment. But preventing the incumbent from resigning when it came to signing a treaty that spelled his political death proved almost impossible. It also raised the question of who was actually competent to sign; and that in turn came to be seen as dependent on what sort of constitution Egypt would eventually adopt. There was, indeed, no end in sight.

In April 1921 Zaghlul returned to Egypt to a tumultuous reception which reportedly saw crowds line the railway all the way from Alexandria to Cairo. Nine months later, refusing to desist from incitement, he was re-arrested and packed off into exile again. Meanwhile the strikes and the protests barely ceased; terrorist incidents, usually involving an Egyptian bomb and a British subject, increased; and in Alexandria there was a short but bloody battle in which the expatriate community suffered nearly as many casualties as the Egyptians.

In the end it was the now Field Marshal Lord Allenby who blew the whistle. Making it a resignation issue, he demanded that the treaty be shelved and that the protectorate be ended with an unconditional grant of independence; items affecting British interests were

Cairo Rose

simply to be listed as reserved until such time as an agreement could be negotiated. Failing this, Allenby predicted the need for repressive measures leading to an annexation 'which would greatly increase our difficulties'. He was evidently unaware that, according to Grafftey-Smith, 'not a few people at home had long favoured annexation'.[13] They included Winston Churchill, now back in the British cabinet; as a convinced imperialist, Churchill was much puzzled about why annexation was undesirable or how it could entail greater difficulties.

Allenby's ultimatum had very nearly misfired. He was lucky to get away with a stern rebuke. Curzon, playing for time, cabled him for an explanation of his 'violent metamorphosis'. Allenby, aware of the urgency, came to London in person. There he waited throughout February 1922 as the government agonized and three more British officers succumbed to Egyptian assassins. 'You have waited five weeks,' Lloyd George told him when 'the Bull's' patience finally snapped, 'wait five minutes more.' Allenby paced the vestibule. Such was his stature that his resignation would trigger chaos in Egypt; in London it could even bring down Lloyd George's fragile coalition government. For so persuasive an argument, five minutes sufficed. The objections were withdrawn, 'the Bull' charged out, and on 28 February 1922 Allenby declared Egypt independent.

THE ELUSIVE EGYPTIAN TREATY

Unilateral declarations of independence are usually made by the subject people; this one had been made by the suzerain power. It was welcomed only by Sultan Fuad, who now became King Fuad. There were no popular celebrations; there was not much to celebrate. British martial law became Egyptian martial law, Zaghlul was still in exile, and he was anyway insisting that a unilateral declaration could not regulate a bilateral relationship. The unconvincing provenance of Egypt's independence was, though, appropriate; for in terminating one anomaly – the protectorate – it only replaced it with another – the 'semi-protectorate' (as Allenby's 'independence' has been called).[14] A prefix and a hyphen were scarcely a sea-change. Contrary to the doomsday predictions of British imperialists, the empire had not begun its piecemeal displenishment, since it could hardly be said to have relinquished a territory that had never been part of it. And contrary to the smug editorials of the anti-imperialists, British influence in Egypt would remain almost as firmly entrenched and substantial as ever.

The first of the twentieth century's many acts of independence was thus its least convincing; and unfortunately it set a precedent for others, most notably in Syria and Iraq. Encouraged by the example of Egypt, the British and the French would come to see 'independence' not as 'non-dependence' but as 'diminished dependence', a qualified and possibly transitional form of colonial control but not an absolute negation of that relationshp. Between the 'parent' country and its 'offspring', bonds of responsibility and gratitude were presumed to extend into the indefinite future. The ex-dependency was deemed to value the colonial dispensation under which it had been introduced to administrative efficiency, law and order, impartial justice, speedy communications, modern production methods, the global economy and the concourse of nations. In return the ex-colonial power claimed privileged insights by dint of experience, and exclusive rights by dint of the inevitable treaty. It expected a free hand in protecting its investments and promoting its interests, both of which were presumed to be of mutual benefit. It also expected recognition of its unique role as the new nation's arbiter of conflicts, preferred place of refuge, parent culture, major trading partner, chief aid-donor, exclusive munitions-supplier, source of know-how and manufactures, exemplar of justice, adjudicator of elections and guiding spirit in foreign affairs. In effect, the ex-colonial power expected to retain rights of management.

In Allenby's declaration of Egyptian independence the four matters reserved for a subsequent Anglo-Egyptian treaty were succinctly stated as:

a. the security of the communications of the British empire in Egypt;
b. the defence of Egypt against all foreign aggression or interference, direct or indirect;
c. the protection of foreign interests in Egypt and the protection of minorities; and
d. the Sudan.

The first related principally to the Suez Canal and was self-explanatory. In the second, had the word 'protection' been used instead of 'defence', its import would have been clearer. Protectorate or not, Egypt was to remain under British protection; British forces would stay on Egyptian soil and British diplomacy would render Egypt's hard-won right to foreign representation a travesty. The third point, about foreign interests in Egypt, related to those Ottoman Capitulations that conferred extraterritorial privileges on members of the large foreign community in Egypt. Under the protectorate the Egyptian government had been responsible for complying with the terms of the Capitulations and fending off any objections raised by the capitulatory powers. Britain now proposed to take over this responsibility. She would thus gain opportunities for legitimate interference in the Egyptian government's handling of several hundred thousand influential Egyptian residents; and this arrangement would also reduce the scrutiny of Egyptian affairs hitherto exercised by the other capitulatory powers. Elsewhere in the ex-Ottoman territories such scrutiny would be replaced by that of the League of Nations under the emerging mandate system. But Egypt could not be placed under a mandate; it was independent.

Finally, the Sudan. This vast but sparsely populated territory, now the largest state in Africa, which commanded the upper reaches of the Nile, had been conquered by Egypt in the early nineteenth century and conquered again by Egyptian troops under Kitchener on behalf of the Khedive in 1898. The Sudan was thus occupied by Egypt at a time when Egypt itself was occupied by the British. This posed a legal conundrum which had been solved by declaring the country an Anglo-Egyptian 'condominium'. In Khartoum, the capital, the British and Egyptian flags had flown side by side ever since, and while British administrators were responsible for civil administration, Egyptian troops had continued to provide the occupying force. Their commander-in-chief, or *sirdar*, was also the Governor-General of the Sudan. But since, under both the occupation of Egypt and the protectorate, the Egyptain army was always commanded and partly officered by the British, the *sirdar*/Governor-General was actually a Briton.

The end of the British protectorate over Egypt obviously endangered this whole precarious construction. Egyptians assumed that the Sudan would revert to Egypt; they had conquered it, their troops still occupied it, and to the extent that the Sudan had an upriver call on the waters of the Nile, their economy depended on it. Immediately after Allenby's declaration, Sultan Fuad not only became king, he also demanded he be recognized as king of both 'Egypt and the Sudan'. Allenby objected, and Fuad was silenced. But thereafter no Egyptian politician could afford to be seen to negotiate for anything less than complete Egyptian sovereignty in the Sudan.

The British, though, also had a case. It was they who ran the Sudan, who had invested in it, and who were its peoples' best guarantee of not being submerged in a greater Egypt. Their corps of administrators was highly regarded, and for the British empire the country had some strategic relevance as part of a 'Cape-to-Cairo' corridor for projected rail, telegraph and air links. Its status was therefore very much 'reserved' and on a par with that of the Canal.

All four reserved subjects necessitated the continued presence of a considerable number of British troops on Egyptian soil and of British warships in Egyptian waters. Zaghlul's rejection of the declaration of independence had to this extent been prescient, as well as logical. British forces would in fact remain in Egypt for another thirty years; and the treaty itself would not materialize for another fourteen years. But this delay, the result of mutual intransigence, reinforced British notions of the influence they might continue to wield. No treaty meant no definition of what they could or could not do; and until the treaty was signed, the 'semi-protectorate' might be considered only semi-operative. In this interim various issues, like the debate over Egypt's new constitution, the increasingly autocratic tendencies of King Fuad, and the intense competition between the throne, the Wafd and other less intractable political parties, combined to provide the British with practice in the murky arts of informal imperialism.

Allenby would not have seen it that way. He could be difficult, downright alarming and plain wrong, but he was too honest for duplicity. When he intervened to rein in the King's ambitions and secure the adoption of a liberal constitution (modelled on that of Belgium), he did so in the firm belief that a representative government under a constitutional monarch was the best possible model. That it was unsuited to Egypt – as Lord Lloyd, his ultra-imperialist successor, would claim and as Gamal Abd al-Nasser would confirm – was beside the point. It was what most Egyptians wanted, it was duly adopted by an overwhelming majority of their representatives, and even Zaghlul, for once, concurred.

With the ending of martial law in July 1923, Zaghlul returned to Egypt, and in the elections of the following January his Wafd won a massive majority. As the new prime minister, Zaghlul's first duty would normally have been to pay a courtesy call on the High Commissioner. Allenby pre-empted either compliance or refusal by ensuring that he was the first to call on Zaghlul. The protocol had been reversed, but the primacy of the British relationship had been preserved.

Coincidentally, Britain's first Labour prime minister was just taking office in the person of James Ramsay MacDonald. The Labour Party in opposition habitually decried imperial ventures, and MacDonald already knew and respected Zaghlul. But when, in September 1924, the Egyptian leader accepted an invitation to come to London for negotiations on the long-awaited treaty, the chances of success already looked remote. Rejecting the four 'reserved' items as a basis for the talks, demanding the removal of all British forces as a precondition, and doing nothing to prevent sporadic attacks on British interests by those who claimed to be his supporters, Zaghlul came to collect, not to negotiate. Unsurprisingly the talks came to nothing.

As over the Milner Mission's report in 1921, Zaghlul, according to British observers, thus missed another historic opportunity to resolve Anglo-Egyptian differences. Grafftey-Smith in Cairo put it down to his 'schizophrenia'; Zaghlul wanted the support of the British and personally got on well with them, but he was constrained by his more rabid followers and his own obstinacy. Later writers detected other flaws in his personality. Writing in the 1950s John Marlowe diagnosed a fatal lack of statesmanship. 'He was incapable of seeing Egyptian politics except in terms of struggle' and, more revealingly, 'was not interested in the results of independence, which was to him not a means to an end, but an end in itself.'[15]

Whatever one thinks of independence as 'a means to an end', Zaghlul's point was that Egypt did not yet enjoy independence. Nor would she until British 'rights' were retracted, British forces removed, and the Sudan returned to Egypt. The last two of these grievances were epitomized in that august office of Egyptian-*sirdar*-cum-Sudan-Governor-General, whose current incumbent was General Sir Lee Stack.

Stack came down to Cairo for consultations with Allenby in November 1924. Waves of radical Egyptian protest had lately been rushing up the Nile like a tidal bore, provoking sympathetic demonstrations in the northern Sudan and triggering mutinies among the occupying Egyptian troops. The British suspected Egyptian agitators and Stack wanted them restrained.

Meanwhile Cairo was back on the boil. Zaghlul was engaged in a row with the King and was on the point of being forced to resign. 'A monster demonstration' even by Cairo standards gathered outside the Abdin palace and screamed for 'Saad [Zaghlul's retention] or Revolution'. Three days later, on 19 November 1924, Lee Stack was being driven back to the High Commission when his car was stopped and boarded. There were seven assailants. One sprayed the passengers with bullets while the others let off a bomb. The chauffeur, though critically wounded, managed to restart the car and drive on to the Residency. Allenby was in the middle of lunch as the bodies were brought in. It was discovered that the Governor-*sirdar* was still breathing, and he was laid on a sofa in Allenby's study. But he died the next day.

Short of assassinating Allenby himself, no greater outrage was conceivable. 'This tragedy struck the streets of Cairo to silence,' wrote Lawrence Grafftey-Smith, who was now on Allenby's staff. 'People tiptoed about their business, apprehensive of they knew not what British retribution.' Zaghlul raced to the deathbed as soon as he heard the news. There an overwrought Allenby made no secret of whom he held responsible. It was Zaghlul whose rhetoric had singled out the anomaly of a British Governor-*sirdar* as inconsistent with Egypt's national dignity, and it was Zaghlul who had so lamentably failed to restrain or condemn previous 'terrorist' activities.

The Egyptian leader scarcely needed to be told; his response, if any, is not known. Now into his seventies, he was genuinely upset by the murder and seems to have been dogged by remorse over it ever after. 'The very aspect of life [became] hateful to him . . .', wrote Husayn Heikal, a contemporary and friend, 'he kept repeating; the bullet that killed the *sirdar* was aimed at my own heart. He wondered incessantly; who killed the *sirdar*, and why.'[16] He was also painfully aware of the political consequences of the murder. 'This is a death-blow for me,' he told a Reuter's correspondent.

It was a death blow for Allenby too. With Lee Stack a close colleague and a guest in his house, the High Commissioner's distress was acutely personal. His draconian response, jotted on some scrap paper

while the Governor-*sirdar* breathed his last, and delivered in person
that afternoon to the Egyptian parliament, was phrased as an ultimatum but, innocent of all reason, successfully concealed his grief
beneath the rantings of a famously explosive temper. Apologies were
demanded, punishment of the perpetrators insisted on, demonstrations banned, a £500,000 fine imposed, an end to objections over the
modification of the Capitulations announced, the immediate withdrawal of Egyptian troops from the Sudan ordered, and an unlimited
extension of Sudanese irrigation authorized, thereby threatening agriculture on the lower Nile and bringing 'British vengeance into every
small-holding in Egypt', according to Grafftey-Smith.[17]

As if to shatter any Egyptian windows still intact after this explosion, an additional note announced the formation of a Sudan
Defence Force answerable only to the British-run Sudan government, the reinstatement of certain British advisers in the Egyptian
government, and a wholly favourable resolution of the wrangling
over redundancy settlements for those Britons who had retired from
Egyptian service. Only then did Allenby rest from his labours and
peruse a cable from London in response to a draft of his proposed
ultimatum. He had previously chosen to ignore it; and if this was
because he suspected censure, he was right. Some of his demands
were repudiated, while the idea of opportunistically scraping them all
into a reprisals package was condemned as unseemly and vindictive.
The cable, in fact, was what Allenby always called 'a BOO telegram',
and for once he offered no 'BOO-BOO' response. From now on his
credit was undermined and his days, like Zaghlul's, were numbered.

Zaghlul resigned immediately. He retired to a house out by the
pyramids, made one further bid for power in 1926, and died in 1927.
Allenby soldiered on for eighteen months. His ultimatum had had
some effect. A British naval landing in Alexandria (which was
designed to enforce it), plus a police reign of terror as Stack's assassins were hunted down, combined to cow the Wafd: and thus did a
calm of sorts follow the storm. He resigned in 1925 when the new
Conservative government betrayed its lack of confidence in him.
Alert to his virtues as well as his faults, the Egyptian press regretted
his going, and his send-off was warm, even 'spectacular'.

Perhaps this also had something to do with the man who replaced
him, the much sharper and much less sympathetic George Lloyd. 'I
know Lloyd George', said an Egyptian official, 'but who is this

George Lloyd?' 'Ah, but the very same man,' he was told, 'only he is coming arse-first.'[18] He was in fact the George Lloyd of the Lloyds Bank family who had served with the Arab Bureau but, according to Lawrence, knew no Arabic and 'did not stay with us very long'. As a firm believer in both the mission and the merits of British imperialism, he was expected by many to restore the protectorate, even to try again for annexation. He did not oblige, but neither did he attempt to press negotiations on the four reserved subjects, agreement on which would, in effect, have ratified Allenby's declaration of independence. Instead he concentrated on cutting down to size any Egyptian politician who looked likely to inherit Zaghlul's mantle of leadership.

The first such candidate was King Fuad, whose attempt to change the electoral law so as to produce a legislature that he could more readily influence was quickly scotched. Next came Zaghlul himself on the crest of another Wafd triumph in the 1926 elections. A British warship again steamed into Alexandria and the Wafd was persuaded to drop his candidature for the premiership. Yet another Royal Naval intervention, the third in three years, was necessary in 1927 when the Egyptian government attempted to end British control of the Egyptian army. 'We have magnitude without position; power without authority; responsibility without control,' complained Lloyd.[19] To a dedicated servant of empire the state of Anglo-Egyptian relations was as unsatisfactory as it was to the Egyptians. Yet Grafftey-Smith hints at the High Commissioner's adept manipulation of both palace and parliament. With George Antonius, 'the Lebanese historian', acting as his confidential go-between, and with warships at his elbow, Lloyd was no more disempowered than he was demeaned.

In the summer of 1927 King Fuad and his prime minister made a state visit to London. Without apparently informing Lloyd, the Foreign Office grasped the occasion to resurrect the memory of the long-overdue Anglo-Egyptian treaty. Agreement was actually reached and the draft treaty was approved by the British Cabinet. But as Lloyd could have told them, there was no hope of the treaty being endorsed in Egypt. In 1928 it was roundly rejected by the Egyptian parliament.

A similar initiative was aborted in 1930 when, anticipating future wrangles, the Sudan for the first time eclipsed the Canal as the most contentious of the four reserved subjects. Not until 1936 would a treaty finally materialize. By then a beaming young Farouq had succeeded the deceased King Fuad; in Europe Adolf Hitler was busily overseeing Germany's rearmament; and from neighbouring Libya, Benito Mussolini's troops were encircling the Sudan as they overran Abyssinia (Ethiopia).

'This [Mussolini's advance] was a development of decisive importance,' noted Grafftey-Smith, 'all Eyptian leaders saw a bright red light [and] were eager to crowd round the conference table.'[20] Forming a united front, they asked as one for a resumption of the treaty negotiations. With the new Rome–Berlin axis threatening to sever the Mediterranean, the conclusion of the Anglo-Egyptian treaty was more about survival than sovereignty. Rather than redressing a dismal past, it addressed an even grimmer future.

6

Uncharted Territory

WHY MOSUL?

PIONEER AVIATORS LIKED to fly low and keep an eye on the ground. Like early mariners hugging the coastline, they navigated the skies by observing landmarks. In the summer of 1921, as a preliminary to establishing a Mediterranean-to-Gulf air mail service, two convoys of vehicles set out across the Syrian desert, one heading west from Ramadi near Baghdad and the other heading east from Amman in what is now Jordan. Their task was to establish a chain of landing-strips, each about thirty miles apart, while scoring the intervening desert with their tyre tracks. Drums of fuel were deposited beside the landing-strips for emergency use; and the tyre tracks, later accentuated by ploughing, were designed to serve as navigational corridors. By carefully following the line of these furrows, the postman-pilot could make the desert crossing in daylight without getting lost or landing other than at the marked strips (where, in difficulty, he might easily be located). Fuel drums dumped in the middle of nowhere sometimes proved irresistible to passing Bedouin marksmen, but once this problem had been overcome by constructing bunkers fitted with padlocks, the system worked well.[1]

Clear skies and lunar landscapes suited the infancy of aviation. As wartime reconnaissance gave way to peace-time surveillance, aeroplanes looked to have a promising future in the Middle East. Britain's

Royal Air Force, established as a separate service in 1918, reckoned that in the desert it had found the perfect training-ground. Winston Churchill was already convinced that the region could be policed more cheaply and effectively by an airborne strike-force than by an army of occupation. Aircraft being less conspicuous and objectionable than ground troops, the new coercive capacity in the skies also accorded nicely with the new political thinking about an unobtrusive, or informal, imperialism, one in which the obvious forms of hegemony might be conceded so long as the substance was retained.

Of its nature, this new thinking was itself uncharted territory. Across the labyrinthine landscape of conflicting promises, hidden priorities and unwritten deals which characterized the First World War peace process, the landmarks were scarce and understated. But like those tyre tracks across the desert, events in Egypt provided contemporaries with some direction and a few points of reference. Saad Zaghlul's populist appeal, for instance, and his defiance of the 'protecting' power were closely observed throughout the Arab world and especially in Syria. The Wafd's techniques of mass mobilization and protest were noted, and the apparent concessions wrung from the Milner Mission and Allenby were applauded. Just as, earlier, Egyptian nationalists had demanded the independence on offer to trouserless tribesmen in the service of the Hashemites, so now Syrian, Palestinian and Iraqi nationalists readily claimed, either for themselves or for Arabs in general, the freedoms that Egyptians appeared to be acquiring.

In similar fashion British officialdom was ever mindful of Egypt. Its riots were what they hoped to avoid in Mesopotamia and Palestine; and there would be many injunctions like that issued to A.T. Wilson, Britain's hyperactive 'Acting' Civil Commissioner in Baghdad, that unless he found employment for influential Arabs 'we will have another Egypt on our hands'.[2] But if Egyptian troubles were a salutary warning, Egyptian precedents were often cited in the search for a political solution. Cromer's 'occupation' initially recommended itself to the India Office as a useful formula for the British administration of Mesopotamia, although A.T. Wilson preferred the wartime Egyptian 'protectorate'. Lawrence, on the other hand, and all those connected with the Arab Bureau dismissed Wilson as an Anglo-Indian dinosaur and condemned both schemes as extravagant and reactionary throwbacks to the nineteenth century. They favoured something supposedly more progressive and cited the treaty-dependent 'independence' on offer in Egypt.

All, however, eventually agreed on one thing: an amir or king was a useful idea. The British had a natural preference for royalty and, more to the point, Egypt had alerted them to the advantages of a head of state who, whether khedive, sultan or king, owed title, throne and succession to the British. Kings were internationally acceptable as symbols of a nation's sovereign independence, yet they could also be agents of the colonial power and so symbols of a nation's subjection. In 1919 the French and the Americans saw Faysal as just such a cuckoo, fattening on British subsidies in Damascus; likewise his brother Abdullah, for whom a nest would soon be found in Amman; and likewise their father the *sharif,* whose Hijazi status, as precarious as Colonel Brémond had once foretold, led the mischievous Sykes to dub him 'the marmoset of Mecca'. When, during the long post-war wrangles, Lawrence and his Arab Bureau colleagues argued in favour of these Hashemite dispositions, they spoke of obligations incurred in the Husayn–McMahon correspondence, of keeping faith with the Arabs, and of British honour being at stake; and no doubt they were sincere; but, acknowledged or not, British obligations and British honour also had a way of coinciding with British interests.

These interests, whose protection generated such controversy but whose pursuit was so sparingly acknowledged, were arguably more germane to the peace negotiations of 1918–22 than were the commitments made during the course of the war (Husayn–McMahon, Sykes-Picot, Balfour's Declaration, Wilson's Fourteen Points). On 1 December 1918, amid the victory celebrations, the French premier Clemenceau joined the Prime Minister Lloyd George in London. They basked in the applause of the flag-waving crowds and then retired to the French embassy to strike the first deal of the post-war settlement in the Middle East. This ignored Arab demands for independence, made no mention of Zionist settlement, and flouted American strictures against secret diplomacy and the dictatorial disposal of ex-Ottoman 'nationalities'. 'After we reached the Embassy,' recalled Lloyd George, '[Clemenceau] asked me what it was I especially wanted from the French. I instantly replied that I wanted Mosul attached to Irak [*sic*], and Palestine from Beersheba to Dan.'[3] 'You shall have it,' said Clemenceau of Mosul; 'you shall have it,' said he of Palestine; and to this purely verbal agreement Clemenceau would remain true throughout the increasingly acrimonious negotiations that followed.

What Clemenceau was promised in return is not recorded. France's priorities lay in Europe and it was there that Clemenceau most needed British support. But as regards the Middle East he probably understood that, by making exception for Mosul and Palestine, the rest of the Sykes-Picot carve-up would stand and that French claims in Syria and neighbouring Cilicia (now in Turkey) would therefore be respected. He may also have received the assurance that the distinction in Syria between the coastal sphere of direct French control and the inland sphere of indirect French influence would not be insisted on. That, after all, was the assumption on which the British were working in Mesopotamia/Iraq; and that, after much further argument, would indeed be the eventual outcome in Syria. Faysal's fledgling rule in Damascus would be short-lived.

But what of Mosul and Palestine? Why were they Lloyd George's priorities? Palestine, as noted, afforded protection to the Suez Canal, plus opportunities for imperial links by air, rail and pipeline between the British-dominated Gulf and the British-dominated Mediterranean. There might too, it was supposed, be fringe benefits resulting from the championship of Zionist settlement and the command of the Holy Land. That Palestine's Zionists would be other than grateful, or Palestine's Arabs other than manageable, occurred to few at the time, and troubled fewer. British administrators prided themselves on their fairmindedness; their empire accommodated many other disputatious peoples; and with the British presence in Palestine sanctioned by the League of Nations, right would be on their side. Palestine, in short, was desirable in itself; and because of the Canal, it was absolutely imperative that no other power become established there.

But Mosul? An unprepossessing town on the upper Tigris, nearer to the Black Sea than the Gulf, Mosul also gave its name to the erstwhile Ottoman province (or *wilayet*) in which it was located. The province marched with Persia; it was extremely rugged and, thanks to its large Kurdish population, had a reputation for being ungovernable. Many must have wondered that Lloyd George even knew of its existence. In 1916 Sykes had conceded most of it to Georges-Picot without any apparent qualms. In fact, Sykes was rather pleased to have interposed a finger of French control between the sphere claimed by the British in Mesopotamia and that then expected to fall to Russia in Anatolia. His concern was purely strategic; oil, it seems, played no part in his thinking. But it was indeed oil, and the near-certainty that Mosul contained the next major Middle Eastern deposits, that had elevated this obscure Ottoman *wilayet* to the top of Lloyd George's list of post-war desiderata.

MESOPOTAMIA'S OIL

For the British presence in Egypt and Palestine, the Suez Canal provided the unassailable imperative. The waterway's importance, deemed too obvious for emphasis in the early twentieth century, would by mid-century be too axiomatic for examination. Whether occupied, protected or secured by treaty, Egypt's French-built Canal was enshrined as an incontestably British concern. Necessity had become the mother of convention; the scene was already set for the Suez crisis of the 1950s.

Elsewhere in the Middle East, it was oil that provided the great imperative for Western intervention. But whereas in the second half of the century the region's colossal output of crude would warrant a chorus of international concern, in the first half petroleum priorities were acknowledged much more discreetly. As later with uranium, known reserves were few, the technology was advanced, and the necessary investment was considerable. So were the political implications. Clearly, it was most unfortunate that oil had not been found in western Europe, whose industrial economies so badly needed it; and clearly its abundance beneath territories whose peoples had no idea how to extract, refine, distribute or use it, argued strongly for foreign involvement. But cut-throat international competition for oilfields, the corporate scramble for drilling concessions, and the strategic debates about pipelines could not easily be reconciled with the colonial powers' espousal of 'a sacred trust' that was altogether burdensome to the 'white man'. Accessible oil and responsible imperialism did not mix. Petroleum anxieties, although the stuff of statesmen's nightmares, were therefore publicly denied and rarely made the headlines until mid-century, by when the Middle East's staggering reserves were fully appreciated.

The 1906 Dinshawai 'Incident', in which four villagers were hanged (*above*) and others flogged, exposed British claims to be protecting the Egyptian peasantry. The miscarriage of justice and the draconian sentences inflamed nationalist sympathies and inspired the demand for Egyptian independence voiced by Sa'ad Zaghlul (*right*) and his Wafd.

(Left) For the British troops in the trenches of Kut al-Amara dawn prayers were in vain. In 1916, following the First World War's longest siege, Turkish forces here secured the surrender of an entire division, so halting the West's first invasion of what later became Iraq.

(Below) In 1917 the shame of defeat at Kut al-Amara was redeemed when British Indian forces entered Baghdad. Under various guises British influence in Iraq would last for the next forty-one years.

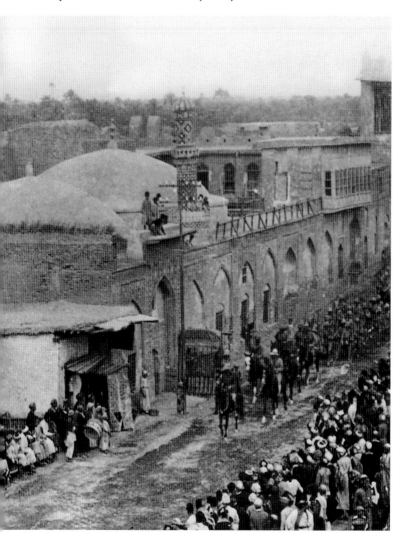

The Hijaz railway – and especially the bridges near Dera'a in Syria (*above*) – was a prime target for the elusive Arab patrols (*below*) operating against the Turks in the First World War. As part of the Arab Revolt, such actions afforded T. E. Lawrence scope for some famous heroics. But misunderstandings about the basis of Allied-Arab collaboration would confound the post-war settlement.

Out of Arab dress, T. E. 'Lawrence of Arabia' (*left*) was 'not on the surface of things impressive'. Like other members of the Cairo-based Arab Bureau, including his patron D. G. Hogarth (*centre*), he was awarded military rank and uniform only as a wartime necessity.

When the Turkish forces withdrew from Jerusalem in late 1917, the city's mayor (*with walking stick*) sallied forth with a white flag. But he found no takers for the keys to what would become the century's most contested real estate. The surrender was finally accepted by two unenthusiastic British officers.

While proclaiming the Allied occupation of Jerusalem in December 1917, General Edmund Allenby carefully avoided any Christian triumphalism. In Britain and France less guarded statements recalled the Crusades and hailed a victory of *le Croix contre le Croissant*.

Ronald Storrs (*left*), military governor of Jerusalem 'in distant succession to Pontius Pilate', welcomes Muslim pilgrims during the 1918 Nebi Musa pilgrimage. Two years later the same festival was soured by the first serious clashes as Arabs attacked Jews in what Storrs called 'an agony of fear and hatred'.

Allenby (*left*), promoted to Field Marshal, returned to the Middle East in 1919 as High Commissioner in Egypt. During Allenby's six years in Cairo, King Faysal (*right*) was removed from the throne of Syria by the French and rewarded with that of Iraq by the British.

George Antonius put the case for Arab independence as adviser to the King-Crane Commission and, later, to Mufti Hajj Amin al-Husayni. Antonius' book, *The Arab Awakening*, was even more influential and became the Bible of Arab nationalism.

In 1922 Amir Abdullah (*third from right*) welcomed to Amman T. E. Lawrence (*second from left*) and Sir Herbert Samuel, High Commissioner in Palestine (*centre*). In discussions over the status of Abdullah's just-created Transjordan, Lawrence carried the day and Transjordan survived to become the modern Jordan.

(*Above*) 'It was my picnic and I did it beautifully.' Gertrude Bell (*centre*) both claimed and deserved much of the credit for installing Faysal (*second from right*) as King of Iraq in 1921. Under Faysal and his descendants oil-rich Iraq would provide a classic example of the informal and remunerative imperialism which best suited Britain in the inter-war years.

(*Below*) Kermit Roosevelt (*second from left*) was one of the few Americans to fight in the Middle East in the First World War. The son of President Theodore Roosevelt, he was the father of Kermit ('Kim') Roosevelt who would abet the 1952 Nasserist coup in Egypt and mastermind the 1953 countercoup in Iran.

(*Above*) Winston Churchill (*centre*) chaired the 1921 Cairo Conference which would offer to Faysal the throne of Iraq and to Abdullah the territory of Transjordan. Churchill is here flanked by Samuel, High Commissioner of Palestine, and the silver-haired Sir Percy Cox, High Commissioner of Iraq. Behind Cox stands Lawrence, with Hubert Young on the extreme right and A. T. Wilson on the extreme left. Wishing she weren't, Gertrude Bell is positioned beside Wilson.

As travel-writer, explorer and Arabist, Freya Stark criss-crossed the Middle East in the 1930s, propagandized there in the early years of the Second World War, and was one of those detained in the 'siege' of the British embassy in Baghdad in 1941.

Rosita Forbes, more by her presence than her books, glamorized the Middle East in the inter-war years. Storrs was fooled by her disguise, Grafftey-Smith beguiled by her conversation, and Glubb terrified by her *décolletage*. Philby planned to explore the Empty Quarter with her.

The one-armed
General Gouraud
entered Damascus
(*left*) following his
1920 defeat of Syria's
citizen army at Khan
Maysalun. French
rule in Syria ushered
in a fragmentation of
the country which
was challenged in the
Great Revolt of
1925–7. The French
responded by
bombing Damascus
(*below*).

The end of the First World War had found Britain still dependent on the United States for 80 per cent of its oil requirement. Admiral 'Jacky' Fisher's insistence on converting the ships of the Royal Navy to oil combustion had been handsomely vindicated on the high seas, but Winston Churchill's hopes of securing an adequate supply of the new fuel by buying into D'Arcy's Anglo-Persian Oil Company had not been realized. From APOC's Abadan refinery in the Shatt al-Arab the oil had merely oozed, like the tide across the mud-flats; by 1918 APOC's, and the Middle East's, total output was just 2 per cent of US production.

APOC foresaw better times ahead. Production was increasing, and the Gulf region was now acknowledged as possessing one of the old world's few known reserves. Even American companies like Standard Oil were showing an interest. But with the demand from Britain's automobiles, industry and aviation increasing exponentially, APOC could hardly hope to meet it. Post-war governments would therefore become obsessed with gaining access to, and control over, other substantial oil sources. In London a Petroleum Executive had been set up in 1917 to co-ordinate British oil policy, and in 1918 a Petroleum Imperial Policy Committee (PIPCo) began investigating 'what steps should be taken to secure control of as much as possible of the world supply of natural petroleum'.[4]

There were two ways of achieving this, according to PIPCo. Another existing oil company could, like APOC, be acquired; or another new oilfield could be developed for the British market. The first involved only control of a company, the second control of territory; and between these alternatives British governments would vacillate, occasionally preferring commercial control without territorial responsibilities, as in Persia, but more often preferring territorial control while inviting commercial collaboration. Either way, possible candidates were already identifiable. As a corporate target, the obvious choice was the Royal Dutch-Shell conglomerate, some of whose several subsidiaries already had British directors. And as a potential new oilfield, the obvious area was east of the upper Tigris around the town of Kirkuk. Adjacent to APOC's Persian fields, this 'Mesopotamian' oilfield betrayed a similar geology, had already yielded encouraging results in preliminary surveys, and lay just 80 miles north of Baghdad in the Ottoman *wilayet* of Mosul.

- Creation of "IRAQ"

Happily Royal Dutch-Shell, through one of its subsidiaries, was already deeply interested in Mesopotamian oil. Might not, then, its non-British and mostly Dutch directorate be willing to accommodate British notions of control in return for a major share of the Mesopotamian concession? It was the sort of trade-off with which the oil companies were familiar, and it in no way conflicted with the industry's few principles. But to the beauty of this solution there were insuperable objections. For one thing, Royal Dutch-Shell was reluctant to co-operate and, for another, a consortium known as the Turkish Petroleum Company considered that it had already been granted the Mesopotamian concession.

On the other hand, controlling the territory rather than the company also posed problems; for Mosul itself was not actually under British control when the Armistice was signed. At the time it was still in Turkish-controlled territory; and although the Armistice awarded all of so-called 'Mesopotamia' to the Allies, it was not obvious that Mosul was comprehended by this term. The Arab *wilayets* of Baghdad and Basra certainly constituted 'Mesopotamia', but Mosul, with its Kurdish hinterland, was anyone's guess. After all, 'Mesopotamia' was a Greek word, beloved of classicists but politically imprecise and quite unknown to Turks, Arabs or Kurds.

A rapid British advance, covered by some decidedly specious argument, forced the protesting Turks out of Mosul town four days after hostilities were supposed to have ceased. Meanwhile A.T. Wilson found a way round the semantic difficulty: Mosul was declared part of 'Iraq'. As he would explain, 'Iraq' was simply 'a geographical expression which, in order to avoid the vague connotations of "Mesopotamia", we employed after the Armistice to denote the three *wilayets* [Baghdad and Basra plus Mosul]'.[5] The new word had an ancient pedigree and supposedly denoted either the 'banks' of the two great rivers or a dividing 'ridge' somewhere in the Syrian desert. Either way, it could just about be taken to include the province of Mosul; and its Arabic provenance further commended it. Middle Eastern topography could be most obliging. In a region submerged under several overlays of cartographic nomenclature – Hebrew ('Israel'), Greek ('Mesopotamia'), Latin ('Syria'), Arabic ('Palestine') and medieval French ('Levant') – an ancient name for a new territorial package was rarely lacking.

It remained only to square French claims to the Mosul region as per Sykes-Picot – which was where Lloyd George came in – and to sort out the concessionary claims of the Turkish Petroleum Company. The latter represented a complication rather than a major obstacle. Like other large commercial concerns set up under the Ottoman dispensation, the Turkish Petroleum Company was not actually Turkish. Its main participant, the National Bank of Turkey, was a British-run institution with headquarters in the City of London. Moreover, the Bank had long been trying to dispose of its share, and had actually done so in March 1914 to APOC. Arguably, the Turkish Petroleum Company's only remaining Turkish dimension lay in the Byzantine ramifications of its composite shareholding. When in June 1914 it had secured from Constantinople a promise of the Mesopotamian concession, 47½ per cent of its shares were held by APOC, 47½ per cent were split between a Shell subsidiary and a German bank, and 5 per cent were held by Calouste Gulbenkian, the Armenian who had originally set up the company.

The German bank was now disqualified by the outcome of the war. Its holding eventually passed to the French as part of the compensation package for surrendering their political claim to Mosul. But this deal, which included provision for a pipeline to the Mediterranean and other peripheral arrangements, took two years and seven draft agreements to materialize, and even then no drilling commenced. French attempts to maximize their involvement were more than matched by British intransigence; and American disapproval increasingly overshadowed both. President Wilson's Fourteen Points – and the League of Nations Covenant in which they were embodied by the Versailles treaty – proclaimed an 'open-door' policy in the ex-Ottoman territories. In commerce as in diplomacy there were to be no secret deals, no exclusive rights, no preferential access. Why then, Americans asked, were other nations, like their own, being shut out of the Mesopotamian concession?

In 1927 drilling was at last started. The reserves appeared abundant and the door could be inched ajar; two American companies, Standard Oil of New Jersey and Socony-Vacuum, were admitted to the Turkish Petroleum Company in 1929. In the same year the company was renamed the Iraq Petroleum Company. The door then slammed shut. Through APOC the British retained their lion's share.

If the potential of Mesopotamian oil had ignited British ambitions in Iraq, the actuality of oil production would henceforth sustain them (although 'it has always been rather bad manners to say so', notes Peter Sluglett, the author of the best account of Iraq in the 1920s).[6] Contemporary British statements to the contrary abound, yet their shrill wording suggests desperation more than conviction. 'The idea that H[is] M[ajesty's] G[overnment] would have gone through all the difficulties they have gone through, faced all the expenses and burdened themselves with all the military risks and exactions in order to secure some advantage in regard to some oil-fields . . . is . . . too absurd for acceptance,' declared Churchill in the House of Commons in December 1920.[7] 'Oil had not the remotest connexion with my attitude, or with that of His Majesty's Government, over Mosul,' chimed in Lord Curzon in a letter to *The Times* of 1924; it echoed his disclaimer of the previous year that 'the exact amount of influence' exercised by oil on the British stand over Mosul was precisely 'nil'. So there.

Obviously Curzon had not seen the Admiralty memo of just five weeks earlier in which he was reminded that 'from a strategical point of view, the essential point is that Great Britain should control the territories on which the oilfields are situated'.[8] This unequivocal advice, and Curzon's denials, related not to the Mosul negotiations with France of 1918–20 but to the Mosul negotiations with Turkey of 1922–5. Seemingly 'the Mosul question' just would not go away; no sooner had Paris been bought off than Ankara stepped forward. Now under Mustapha Kemal 'Atatürk', a resurgent Turkey – having been given ample time and provocation to resurge – had rejected the peace terms of the 1920 Sèvres treaty as agreed with the Ottoman government and had proceeded to inflict what the American William Yale called 'the first defeat of European imperialism in the Near East'.[9] This involved rooting out of Anatolia a Greek invasion force backed by the Allies. Meanwhile Atatürk's troops were successfully denying much of Cilicia to the French; and now he was disputing the British contention about Mosul being part of Iraq.

By this time the League of Nations had awarded the mandate for Iraq to Britain (at the San Remo conference of 1920, as will appear). It therefore fell to Curzon at the Lausanne conference of 1923 to respond to the Turkish challenge over Mosul. In long sentences crafted into masterful paragraphs, Curzon spoke as lesser men

wrote, enunciating the British point of view with a bloodless
cogency. Mosul was essential to Iraq because its mountains afforded
the country its only 'natural' northern frontier. Conversely, any frontier which excluded Mosul must slice across the open Tigris plain
and be totally indefensible. (That just such a frontier, slicing across
the Nile valley, was implicit in the division of Egypt and the Sudan,
no one thought to mention.) Additionally, Mosul contained significant Kurdish and Assyrian minorities. The Assyrians, though few,
were Christian; and the Kurds, though Muslim, were numerous.
Both must therefore be afforded protection and some degree of
autonomy; and such safeguards could only be guaranteed if Mosul
were incorporated within a country under the supervision of a
League of Nations mandate, like Iraq. Yet again, Mosul's population
was predominantly Sunni Muslim, while an Iraq comprising only the
Baghdad and Basra *wilayets* would be overwhelmingly Shi'a.
Incorporating Mosul into Iraq would redress this sectarian imbalance and produce something closer to the parity that was supposed
to be conducive to national stability.

And so on. The case for rejecting Turkey's claim was overwhelming. Oil, though in the back of everybody's mind, proved as superfluous to the argument as Curzon claimed it was irrelevant. For with the
French and the Dutch already involved in the Turkish Petroleum
Company, and the Americans and the Italians not finally excluded, a
League of Nations dominated by these very nations must obviously
award Mosul to its mandated territory of Iraq, just as the British
wanted.

There was, though, genuine uncertainty about the actual line of
Mosul's, and so Iraq's, northern frontier. British and Turkish claims
on this score could not be reconciled at Lausanne; nor would Turkey
accept a subsequent League of Nations decision in favour of the
British alignment. Only when, in December 1925, the Court of
International Justice in The Hague finally threw out the Turkish
claim did Ankara bow to the inevitable.

And so, seven years after the end of the war, the extent of the
largest of the ex-Ottoman territories was at last settled, and Iraq
assumed its now familiar configuration. 'In the Near East,' wrote an
acid William Yale of this settlement, 'the League of Nations was
doing splendidly. The great and powerful were obtaining what they
wished, under law, without violence or threat of war.'[10]

AN IMPERIAL DINOSAUR

Against so chaotic a background of peacemaking delays, territorial uncertainties, escalating rivalries, suspect agendas and a complicit League of Nations, the modern Middle East was born. It was an inauspicious beginning. 'The great and powerful' were indeed having it all their own way, although Yale was deceiving himself about the absence of coercion. Violence was, in fact, a constant of the situation; and if it stopped short of war, this was only because survivors of the Great War were reluctant to apply a term of such hideous memory to conflicts which, however bloody, were at least contained.

One such conflict would occasion a death-toll generally estimated at around 10,000, plus some of the worst retaliatory bombing and burning of civilian targets yet witnessed. It occurred in Iraq during the late summer of 1920, but at the time it was overshadowed by events in Syria and has since been buried beneath the historiographical mountain thrown up by the confict in Palestine. (Contrary even to informed opinion, there were in fact about twice as many participants, and twice as many casualties, in the three-month Iraqi revolt of 1920 as there would be in the three-year Palestinian revolt of 1936–9.)

But so little does the Iraqi affair feature in popular history that it has no accepted designation in English. General Sir Aylmer Haldane, under whom RAF pilots and British and Indian troops suppressed it, subsequently wrote a book which he called *The Insurrection in Mesopotamia*. Others have preferred 'Iraq' to 'Mesopotamia' and used words like 'revolution', 'uprising' or 'rebellion'. Yet A.T. Wilson, a stickler for these things and still Acting Civil Commissioner in Iraq, mentions specific War Office instructions not to refer to their Iraqi opponents as 'rebels'. They might only be termed 'anarchists – or some similar expression not conveying the suggestion that allegiance is due from Arabs to Great Britain'. A.T. was unhappy about this. Quoting first the *Oxford English Dictionary*, then chapter and verse of the Manual of Military Law, he demonstrated that 'rebellion' covered resistance to any legally constituted authority. He agreed, however, to desist from 'rebel' and settled instead for 'insurgent'. Later he changed his mind. Citing Macaulay, Wordsworth, Milton and Aristotle, all on the same page, he decided that the 1920 affair had been something altogether worse. 'Neither in its nature . . . nor in its results was the rising of 1920 a revolution; it was a tragedy.'[11]

For A.T. himself it would certainly be a tragedy, both politically and personally. His administration in Iraq would lie in tatters, his prodigious energies wasted and his hitherto brilliant career discredited. Still only 36 and widely regarded as the ablest administrator of his generation, he would be quickly relieved of office and would never again serve in a political capacity. Even his detractors were appalled at the loss. But his biographer rightly calls him a 'late Victorian'[12] and there is no denying that A.T. was out of sympathy with the times. Educated at Clifton, the most empire-minded of English public schools (where his father was headmaster and whence he had gone straight to India), he believed implicitly in that imperialist euphemism, the *pax Britannica,* and saw himself as one of a dedicated band duty-bound to its ideals.

> Curzon, at his best, was our spokesman [he would write] and Kipling, at his noblest, our inspiration . . . We read the lives of John Nicholson, [Henry] Lawrence and [Frederick] Roberts, and the works of Sir Willam Hunter, whilst we toiled at our own ponderous Gazetteers, like willing slaves making bricks for builders yet to come.[13]

John Nicholson and Henry Lawrence had been part of a small and much-mythologized band of British officials who in the mid-nineteenth century had restored order in the war-torn Panjab while establishing a higly personalized and generally benevolent British administration. Evidently A.T. saw himself as similarly engaged in Iraq. Here, too, was a land of immense potential reduced to scarcity and impotence by centuries of neglect and strife. The irrigation systems must be restored and extended, maps made, rivers dredged, railways built, tribes settled, justice administered, taxes collected, budgets balanced. If Iraq was to pay its way, Mosul's oil was absolutely vital; the province must be included in Iraq and the concessionary arrangements with the oil companies must include the best possible terms for the government of Iraq. There must also be special provision for Kurdish autonomy and a role for the Assyrians. Then there were education, public health, posts and telegraph, judicial reform, land tenure, livestock improvement. Under the direction of any but a self-confessed imperialist, Wilson's dynamism might have passed for 'nation-building'.

Aided by an eager following of devoted young assistants, A.T. in Baghdad hurled himself into the administrative fray. From as far away as Basra, Hubert Young felt the blast of 'his boundless energy and phenomenal memory'. 'I always knew when I had got through to the great A.T. himself from the masterful rattle of the receiver as he snatched it from the telephone.' When not leaping from an RAF cockpit, like a compressed jack-in-the-box, to surprise some unsuspecting official in the back of beyond, he laboured long at his desk, flailing through stacks of paperwork 'like a threshing machine', says Young. For the dispatch of dispatches, as for the quotation of quotations, he comfortably broke all known records. He seemed impervious to the health risks and the climate. Chain-smoking through the day and catnapping on the office floor at night, he slaved away at his baking of bricks for the 'builders yet to come' much as he had once shovelled coal as a Red Sea stoker.[14]

Gertrude Bell, though old enough to be his mother, was genuinely impressed by such a tower of smouldering strength and, until the final months, happily served as his Oriental Secretary. Together they did the rounds of the Paris peace conference in March 1919, emphasizing the need for firm British direction in Iraq, explaining the country's requirements, and meeting, among many, Faysal and Lawrence. Flanked by this berobed pair, Bell was ecstatic; her 'little Lawrence' held forth 'admirably' on the increasingly fraught relationship between Damascus and the French, and 'his charm, simplicity and sincerity convinced his listeners'.[15] Not, however, A.T. Feeling like a Gulliver among skirted Lilliputians, A.T. found Lawrence as objectionable as ever. He 'seems to have done immense harm, and our difficulties with the French in Syria seem to be mainly due to his actions and advice,' he wrote.[16] It was the irresponsible encouragement of Arab aspirations by Lawrence, Hogarth and Co., plus the well-meaning but misguided intervention of President Wilson, that were delaying the peace settlement and igniting nationalist expectations. Stability and reconstruction should be the priorities, thought A.T.; political representation could come later.

When the Arab Bureau, which A.T. regarded as Lawrence's Cairo fan club, was finally wound up, he positively crowed. 'The Arab Bureau died unregretted in 1920 having helped to induce [the British] government to adopt a policy which brought disaster to the people of Syria, disillusionment to the Arabs of Palestine, and ruin to the Hejaz.'[17] To this catalogue of impending woes 'tragedy' in Iraq should most certainly have been added. For if A.T. was especially critical of Lawrence and his dealings over Syria, it was because the troubles that were about to overwhelm Iraq seemed to emanate from Lawrence and from Syria. As he later wrote with the full benefit of hindsight, plus an unusual lack of quotations:

> If a political weather forecast on conventional lines had been constructed in the beginning of December 1919 . . . it would have shown a deep depression, originating in Syria, moving steadily [eastwards] from Damascus . . . causing grave atmospheric disturbances and much material damage.

A.T.'s metereological map also showed pressure falling at Baghdad, Karbala and Najaf, 'all three well known storm centres' in Iraq, and much thunder and lightning elsewhere, 'the air being surcharged with electricity owing to the absence of lightning conductors'.[18] In other words an almighty storm was brewing over Iraq; it was coming from Syria; and without lightning conductors – by which he meant cautionary statements of Britain's intention to retain direct control of Iraq by all available means – there was little he could do about it.

THE ROAD TO DAMASCUS

In early 1919, when Anglo-Iraqi relations were still being conducted to the clink of teacups as Gertrude Bell interviewed visiting shaykhs at 'Chastity Chase' (the irreverent name for her riverside home in Baghdad), Franco-Syrian relations were already echoing to the rattle of French sabres and the roar of Syrian protest. Faysal's men were still ensconced in Damascus where, at the time of the 1918 Armistice, Lawrence and Allenby had left them as part of the Allies' military administration. Under Hashemite leadership and British protection, Arab nationalism appeared to have triumphed in Damascus, and Syria's political life revived. The secret societies and clubs which had spearheaded nationalist sentiment under Ottoman rule now spawned a variety of political parties.

Some of these parties supported *sharif* Husayn's leadership in the creation of an independent pan-Arab state (or confederation of states), while others concentrated on the consolidation and independence of Greater Syria, or 'Syria within its natural boundaries'. All, however, demanded the complete liberation of 'South Syria', otherwise Palestine, which was still under British occupation, and 'West Syria', otherwise the Levantine coast stretching from what is now south Lebanon right up to Alexandretta. But here French officials had already taken up their duties under Allenby's Allied administration. The French navy was in evidence in Beirut, French troops, largely from North Africa, were beginning to arrive, and the French government was reasonably confident that, supported by the Maronite Christians of Mount Lebanon, its rule in these coastal regions would be established as per the Sykes-Picot agreement.

By the same agreement, inland Syria, including Damascus, Homs, Hama and Aleppo, should have been preparing to admit French advisers. Yet there stood Faysal's administration, denying the validity of Sykes-Picot, installing its own officials and augmenting its armed forces, all under the umbrella of British occupation and courtesy of the substantial British subsidy that Faysal still enjoyed. French overtures were being rejected; and as minor clashes flared over disputed assets and enclaves, Syrian agitation against the French appeared to go unchecked.

Meanwhile in Paris Faysal himself, with Lawrence determined to act as his interpreter and adviser, lingered at the peace conference. Faysal was there ostensibly to represent the interests of the Hijaz (since his father, the *sharif* Husayn, was regarded as one of the wartime allies, his state, according to the British, had a right to representation). But the French were profoundly suspicious of Faysal's presence, and with good reason. For he was insisting that, while the British must honour the promise of Arab independence made by McMahon, the other nations must honour the pledges of self-determination sponsored by President Wilson and enshrined in the Anglo-French declaration of November 1918 (the one about 'governments freely chosen by the people' that had so distressed A.T. Wilson). Either way, according to Faysal, there was no role for France in Syria.

Lawrence's well-known Francophobia only made matters worse. He frankly intended to 'biff France out of Syria', as he put it; and he saw Faysal as the fist to do just that. Others saw Faysal as merely the glove; the fist was British. Among these cynics was Colonel Georges

Catroux who had succeeded Brémond in charge of the French military mission to the Hijaz and who would soon be summoned to Syria:

> By this treaty [the Husayn–McMahon correspondence], *concluded without reference to her ally France,* Great Britain . . . intended to shape to her advantage the future of the Middle East, and through the medium of her client, the Hashemite family transmuted into a sovereign dynasty, to reserve for herself a monopoly of political and economic influence, [that being] the eternal objective of her eastern policy.[19]

Some such Machiavellian plan may indeed have lurked in the recesses of the deep minds at the Arab Bureau. But it was not official British policy. Lloyd George had his understanding with Clemenceau over Mosul and Palestine; and Mesopotamia's oil and Egypt's Canal must come first. He could not afford to jettison this agreement for a Syria where the British had no major interests, or for Syrians whose demands in respect of Palestine were as objectionable to British ears as those in respect of the rest of Syria were to the French. Faysal, in other words, must deal with the French direct and could not expect British support in attempts to evade French claims to an interest in the whole of Syria.

There remained, though, America's hostility to any arrangements, whether Franco-British or Franco-Hashemite, that did not take account of the wishes of the people involved. A clause in the League of Nations Covenant relating to the ex-Ottoman territories specifically stated that the wishes of those 'communities' whose 'stage of development' qualified them for 'provisional independence' must be 'a principal consideration in the selection of the Mandatory'. The 'Mandatory' was the power that would be appointed under a League of Nations 'mandate' to oversee such an evolved community's 'well-being and development' in accordance with its wishes; and Syria being just such a 'community', this pledge of self-determination was music to Faysal's ears. In fact he was initially inclined to represent it as conferring on the Syrians, and himself as their assumed representative in Paris, the right to choose their own mandatory. With France, Britain and the US all supposedly lining up as contenders for the mandate, he would be able to take his pick; and in this 'judgement of Paris' the prize, needless to say, was unlikely to go to 'Miss France'.

But Faysal was wrong about the likely contenders; Miss France was in fact the only one. And he was wrong in assuming that, if there were a choice, it was his to make; it was up to the Syrian people. How, though, were the wishes of the Syrian people to be ascertained? Dr Howard Bliss, president of the Syrian Protestant College of Beirut and an immensely respected American Arabist, was advising President Wilson in Paris, and it was he who proposed that an Inter-Allied Commission of Enquiry be dispatched to the region to canvass opinion. Lord Curzon declared it 'the most absurd and inappropriate idea in the world'[20] and so it soon seemed. The commission was supposed to have Italian, French, British and American representatives; but the Italians showed no interest, the French objected on the grounds that the enquiry's witnesses would be influenced by the continued British occupation, and the British, nervous of what the commission might make of Palestinian opinion, decided not to go ahead without the French. That left just the Americans. They went ahead regardless. Dr Henry C. King and Mr Charles R. Crane duly accepted the assignment and were in the Middle East by June 1919.

King was president of Ohio's Oberlin College and also a director of the YMCA; Crane, a maverick millionaire whose fortune derived from the manufacture of sanitary ware, had travelled widely in Russia and the Far East. According to President Wilson, they were 'particularly qualified to go to Syria because they knew nothing about it'[21] – that, and the fact that Crane just happened to have been the major contributor to Wilson's presidential campaign. William Yale, the acerbic US observer in Cairo, was deputed to assist them, and it was probably he who secured the engagement of George Antonius as interpreter and go-between.

What with Crane's crude anti-Semitism and Antonius's reasoned Arabism, the findings of the King-Crane Commission were to some extent predictable. On 10 July they cabled news of 'intense [Syrian] desire for unity . . . and early independence . . . strong expressions of national feeling . . . [and] determined repulsion to French Mandate'.[22] If there had to be a mandate, the only mandatory acceptable to the Syrians was seemingly the United States, or just possibly Great Britain. All of which sounded partisan, although the members of the commission had been nothing if not thorough. Their tour lasted six weeks, they visited 36 towns, and they studied 1,863 petitions. Their final report, submitted to the American peace delegation in August 1919, deserved better than the blank indifference with which it was received. President Wilson probably never read it, it was withheld from the San Remo and Sèvres conferences, and it only saw the light of day when, three years later, as a historical curiosity, the New York *Editor and Publisher* printed an abbreviated version.

Events had overtaken King-Crane. In June, while the commission was in Palestine, President Wilson had sailed home to seek ratification for the Versailles treaty, plus approval from the American public for possible US mandates in Turkey and Armenia. But the necessary lobbying effort for this package induced a stroke and partial paralysis of the President's faculties. This in turn boded ill for the outcome in Washington and so paralysed the peace process in Europe. Dust gathered on the King-Crane report because its sole sponsor was in no position to endorse it. When in April 1920 the US Senate capped its rejection of both the Versailles treaty and US membership of the League of Nations by declining all mandates, America was out of the peace process and out of Middle Eastern involvement for the foreseeable future. It would take another world war to bring her back in.

Stripped of their last champion, the Arabs were now face-to-face with the European powers. The King-Crane Commission had turned out to be yet another betrayal. Worse still, like a tree whose fruit dangles just out of reach, it had encouraged exertions that were fraught with danger. In anticipation of the commission's visit to Damascus, Faysal had bowed to party pressure to hold elections to a General Syrian Congress. Delegates were returned not just from Faysal's East Syria but also from French-administered West Syria (that is, Lebanon and the coastal region) and the British-administered South (that is, Palestine). Meeting in July 1919 this congress promptly passed resolutions demanding independence for all Syria and Iraq, while rejecting Sykes-Picot, the Balfour Declaration, any form of French assistance, and any but the most benevolent mandatory tutelage. Certainly it left the King-Crane Commission in no doubt as to the wishes of the Syrian people; but it also made any Syrian accommodation with the French virtually impossible.

Within a month of the Syrian resolutions, others were adopted in Europe. Lloyd George, caving in to a combination of French pressure and the urgent need for post-war economies, signalled his decision to withdraw all British troops from Cilicia and Syria (excluding

Palestine and the east bank of the Jordan). Arab troops would take over entirely in Faysal's East Syria, French troops in West Syria and Cilicia. The deadline was set for November. At Beirut and Tripoli French reinforcements began disembarking in October. They were soon joined by the magnificent General Henri Gouraud as Commander-in-Chief and High Commissioner.

Faysal's Damascus, its territory at last rid of all foreign troops as a result of the British withdrawal, might have been expected to celebrate. But in fact Faysal was desperate and his adoptive country destabilized and bankrupted by the British decision. Rarely can a subject nation have so heartily regretted the withdrawal of a colonial power. The British pull-out, accompanied by a halving of the British subsidy, was seen as yet another betrayal; and this 'Evacuation Crisis' duly became a milestone in Syria's independence struggle. For with the British departure, there also went the umbrella of Allied occupation. Greater Syria, now divided between French and Arab zones (not to mention British-occupied Palestine), was effectively partitioned. Moreover, the departure of much the largest peace-keeping force in the region removed the main obstacle to French designs on the rest of Syria. The French press argued that, if Lloyd George expected a mandate for the whole of Iraq, France could settle for no less a comprehensive mandate throughout Greater Syria. And the British withdrawal seemed to signal acceptance of such a settlement.

Faysal, in Europe again (September 1919 – January 1920), desperately made a final bid for an understanding with the French. But in the disputed Biqa' valley his Arab forces clashed with the French; in Mecca the *sharif* Husayn disowned Faysal's negotiations; and when Faysal returned to Damascus with a deal that was tantamount to accepting the French mandate, over 100,000 marched through the city in protest. A radical Syrian national consciousness, suspicious alike of the French, the Hijazi Hashemites and their mainly Iraqi advisers, had begun to assert itself. The political parties were losing ground to popular committees based on the commercial, religious and familial organizations of the cities. Directed by a Higher National Defence Committee under shaykh Kamil al-Qassab (once one of the Cairo-based Syrian 'Seven' to whom Ozzy Walrond had delivered the British 'Declaration' of early 1918), this protest network organized enormous demonstrations, mobilized opinion, and pressured the government. Women helped with the raising of

funds and even volunteered for the new militias. Journalists, writers
and theatre groups assisted in the propaganda; schoolchildren joined
the marches. As Damascus seethed with politicized ferment, observers unfamiliar with the Cairo demonstrations were reminded of the
French Revolution. A petition boldly entitled 'The Nation Dictates
Its Wishes to the Syrian Congress' was typical of many. Mass politics
had reached Syria.[23]

In this atmosphere of militancy, any moderation was treason.
'Independence is taken, not conferred,' chimed in Faysal, anticipating Ho Chi Minh as he sought to match the radical rhetoric. Plans for
an accountable parliamentary democracy were now being drawn up
by the fiery shaykh Kamil al-Qassab; and with a view to uniting all
interests, Faysal was not excluded. He was invited to accept the role
of 'constitutional King of United Syria', and did so. On 8 March 1920
a deputation from the Syrian General Congress collected him from
his Damascus residence and processed to Martyrs' Square in the city
centre. A solemn proclamation of independence was read and Faysal
was sworn in amid general rejoicing. By way of addendum, and as if
not to waste the occasion, the Iraqi contingent in Faysal's service,
having formed their own congress, then staged an encore.
Proclaiming the independence and integrity of Iraq, they installed *in
absentia* Abdullah, Faysal's brother, as Amir of Iraq.

These proceedings won no friends in either Paris or London.
Curzon, on behalf of both, protested and declared the Syrian congress illegal. Since it looked as if Faysal had thrown in his lot with the
'extremists', his subsequent attempts to mend bridges with France
and Britain were treated as suspect. A month later, as though by way
of Anglo-French revenge, the San Remo conference awarded the
mandates for Iraq and Palestine to Britain, and that for Syria, including Faysal's kingdom, to France. The die was cast. Damascus again
erupted with demonstrations. Conscription was introduced and
there were more clashes in disputed areas like the Biqa'.

The French, meanwhile, had temporarily extricated themselves
from Cilicia by coming to terms with Kemalist Turkey. That freed
more troops for Syria; General Gouraud duly deployed them for an
advance on Damascus. Minus an arm (which he had lost at Gallipoli),
standing straight as a flagstaff, and with a *tricolore* visage (blue eyes,
white beard, ruddy complexion), the General was the very embodiment of patriotism. As a devout Catholic he also believed passionately

in France's historic role in the Middle East as protector of the Christian communities of the Levant. But he played by the book. Faysal's regime in Damascus had not been recognized by the League of Nations; France's mandate had. Forcible occupation might negate the spirit of the League's Covenant but it was consonant with the terms of the mandatory's obligations. Right was on his side. He issued several ultimata; and Faysal's responses being either inadequate, late or lost, he was yet willing to delay. But Paris was not. On instructions from the Quai d'Orsay, Gouraud ordered the advance.

The result was a foregone conclusion. Faysal and his mainly Iraqi commanders from the Arab Revolt appreciated this and declined to mobilize. But the popular committees and their ill-armed militias, a few Bedouin levies and the Syrian defence minister with some small sections of the regular army sallied forth to Khan Maysalun, an outpost twenty miles from Damascus on the road up from Beirut. There Syria's inexperienced *citoyens* were routed by regular forces comprising mainly Moroccan *chasseurs*, Algerian gunners and Senegalese infantry; 'an incredible mixture of races' according to Pierre Lyautey (nephew of the great Maréchal Lyautey), 'united under the same flag, our flag, on 24 July 1920, on the road to Damascus'.[24] But Arab lives were lost not just to Africans but to artillery, aircraft and tanks. How many died is unknown. Perhaps there were 4,000 Syrians and perhaps there were 400 casualties. Gouraud's men lost 24, none French.

Damascus was occupied the next day, and the rest of Faysal's kingdom soon shared its fate. Much partitioned and rarely peaceful, Syria would remain under French control for the next quarter of a century. More immediately, there was no role for Faysal. The French were not averse to tame sovereigns, and in Indo-China they would sponsor an emperor. But Faysal was not simply King of Syria; he was Britain's King of Syria, and that disqualified him. Quickly packed aboard a train at the Hijaz railway station, he and his family chugged south, retracing the track that had led his forces to victory just two years previously. From Dera'a, the scene of the Arab Revolt's greatest triumph, he travelled under British auspices to Haifa, then Egypt and Europe. Ronald Storrs reported that on the platform at al-Qantara station, 'he awaited his train sitting on his luggage'. While paying what he supposed would be his last respects, Storrs got close enough to see that 'the tears stood in his eyes and he was wounded to the soul'.[25]

7

Three Wee Kings of Orient Are

WITNESSING THE TURMOIL in neighbouring Syria, the British in Iraq could be forgiven a sense of quiet satisfaction. Throughout the inter-war period Anglo-French rivalry would gorge on the contrasting fortunes of their mandated territories, and if the British in Iraq gloated over French difficulties in Syria, then no less would the French in Syria gloat over British difficulties in Palestine. Conversely, an embattled French Damascus could always pin the blame on Jerusalem, as it soon would. And a disturbed British Baghdad could point the finger at Damascus, as it already was. It was all very convenient, as well as confusing.

Immediately post-war, Iraq's British administration had been less anxious about the direction of events in Syria and more concerned about the lack of direction in Iraq itself. Because of the delay in concluding a peace treaty with Turkey – partly the result of Turkish resurgence, partly of uncertainty about US involvement, and partly of British obstinacy over Mosul – Iraq's incubation was prolonged and fraught with indecision. A.T. Wilson's status as the eternally 'Acting' Civil Commissioner, first in the long-running military administration, then in a provisional mandatory one, was itself indicative. The older and much respected Sir Percy Cox was always about to relieve him, but like the Messiah-to-come, he never quite did, preferring his current assignment in Persia. Meanwhile, although A.T. cabled frequently and drafted incessantly, London declined to issue any clear statement of British policy towards Iraq or to authorize any political moves which might suggest that it had one. For to anticipate the outcome of the peace negotiations might be to their prejudice, especially in relation to Mosul and its oil; and with even the configuration of the new Iraqi state undetermined, any allocation of authority would be premature.

Yet A.T., with the busy Miss Bell by his side, was not to be totally deflected; 1919, after all, was the year of commissions. With Montagu consulting local opinion in India, King-Crane about to do so in Syria, and Milner in Egypt, A.T. received orders to proceed with what he termed a 'plebiscite' in Iraq. No doubt he had looked the word up in his *Oxford English Dictionary*. It sounded daringly populist, yet it could mean no more than 'a public expression . . . without binding force . . . of the wishes of a community'. That was A.T.'s reading, anyway. A plebiscite less plebs, it was conducted through informal discussion between his political officers and 'the better sort' of Iraqis.

Views were sought on three questions: did Iraqis want a single Arab state under British tutelage which would include Mosul? If so, did they want 'a titular Arab head' placed over it? And if so, who would they like? The results showed a politic 'yes' to the first, a doubtful 'no' to the second, and a wary 'don't know' to the third. In effect, they were wholly predictable. But the exercise had served its purpose. Lawrence and his Arabist friends could not now claim that Iraq was hankering after a Hashemite ruler like Syria's. And the Americans could not now claim that the British in Iraq were totally ignoring that Anglo-French declaration about ensuring 'governments and administrations freely chosen by the people'. According to William Yale, it was thanks to A.T.'s plebiscite that the King-Crane Commission decided there was no need for it to visit Iraq since the Iraqis had already demonstrated their preference for a British mandate.[1]

Armed with these 'returns', plus a long paper by Gertrude Bell entitled 'Self-Determination in Iraq', A.T. Wilson and his Oriental Secretary had, as noted, set off for Paris in early 1919. Bell went ahead by sea; A.T. followed by air, eventually. There were three forced landings, one for running repairs in the desert near Palmyra, another because of engine failure in a field above Lake Tiberias (where the plane was abandoned), and a third when the replacement aircraft ran out of fuel and 'we went on our nose' in soft ground at Tulkarm. But it was, as he proudly made clear, only the second attempt ever to cross the Syrian desert by plane.[2] Not for another two years would the RAF set about their directional furrowing of the desert.

Paris, of course, settled nothing. But Bell, impressed by what Lawrence told them of Faysal's regime in Syria and of the calibre of his Iraqi followers, made a detour to Damascus on her way back east and there seemingly underwent her own conversion. In her paper on 'Self-Determination' she had quoted at length the sentiments of Baghdad's *naqib* (hereditary governor) in favour of a British occupation of Iraq that would be long and assertive. Like the *naqib* and like A.T., she too deplored the liberal sentiments of the 1918 Anglo-French declaration and the plebiscite that it had necessitated; 'more sound and fury . . . heart-burnings and intrigue' could scarcely have been aroused, she wrote; they had positively encouraged nationalist dissent; it was all most unfortunate.[3]

But in October her report on Faysal's Syria, as she found it just before the evacuation of British troops and the eruption of popular protest, took a very different line. Her eyes opened by the discovery that Faysal's rule was moderately effective as well as acceptable to both the Arabs and the British, she now insisted that 'indigenous governments and administrations' were the only solution throughout the ex-Ottoman territories.[4] She had also talked with some of Faysal's Iraqi followers (including most of those future Iraqi premiers who had taken part in the Arab Revolt) and was fully persuaded of their determination and capacity to man a regime in Baghdad that would match that in Damascus.

A.T. Wilson, of course, was horrified and firmly contradicted her: the assumption that the immediate installation of an Arab government in Iraq would be either responsible, practicable or popular was, he declared, 'erroneous'; Mosul's Kurds would not stand for it and were already up in arms; the Arab tribes would come out in revolt; the Jews and Christians would be terrified; and the Shi'a Muslim majority would never accept rule by the politically dominant Sunni Muslim minority. Any state cobbled together from disparate and ill-governed *wilayets* of the ex-Ottoman empire needed a long and strenuous induction into the ranks of nationhood. He was already setting up municipal councils and (purely advisory) divisional councils, some of whose members would be elected; this was all part of the educative process; but the premature election of an entire Arab government with executive powers could only result in 'the antithesis of democratic Government'.[5]

Bell, unconvinced, prevaricated. Her apostasy had undoubtedly been influenced by Lawrence, who maintained that France could still be dissuaded from overthrowing Faysal's Arab state in Damascus if only the British would make way for an equivalent Arab state in Baghdad. But she now justified her support for Iraqi autonomy simply on the grounds that there was no other choice. A.T.'s paternal and gradualist approach involved a large and indefinite military presence which the British taxpayer would not countenance; its unashamed imperialism was no longer internationally acceptable; and its uncertain adoption was creating even greater problems in the management of Iraq than those which might arise from installing an Arab government.

Judged by events, moreover, Bell was right. In December 1919, as British troops were being dramatically reduced in Iraq and evacuated from Syria, confusion over the Iraqi-Syrian border on the upper Euphrates resulted in what the British considered to be an incursion of Faysal's forces into the Dayr al-Zor district. The invaders were led by a local chief wearing a false nose, the original having been lost to some disease, and they consisted mainly of tribesmen, although the incursion did appear to have the backing of some of Faysal's Iraqi officials. A British political officer was taken hostage, Dayr was occupied, a *jihad* or holy war was declared, and even the RAF failed to dislodge the intruders.

The British were on weak ground both politically (Dayr had originally been occupied on behalf of the Damascus government to preclude a Turkish claim) and militarily (it was 400 miles from Baghdad). But the ineffectual British response was construed as a victory by Arab opinion. Anti-British sentiment in Iraq was immensely encouraged, and the upper Euphrates henceforth became a bridgehead for Iraqi nationalists infiltrating from Syria as well as a launch-pad for their long-range propaganda.

Simultaneously in the Kurdish districts of the Mosul *wilayet* there were almost continual disturbances. Several British political officers were murdered; and in the rugged terrain retaliation proved difficult as well as costly and provocative. Chronic divisions among the Kurdish leaders and uncertainty about the future frontier, plus a general resistance to any form of administrative control, were more to blame than any sympathy for Iraqi nationalism. But another partial British withdrawal again suggested weakness and encouraged defiance.

In March news that Faysal had been proclaimed king in Damascus provoked further excitement. The copycat adoption of his brother Abdullah as 'Amir of Iraq' aroused less enthusiasm; apart from those in Faysal's employ, few Iraqi Arabs as yet felt any attachment to the *sharif* and his Hijazi family, nor did they accept Hashemite claims to represent them. But the emergence of an independent Arab kingdom in Damascus, one which was defying the French in Syria and the British on the margins of Iraq, was much more significant. Coupled with the evidence of Turkish revival under Atatürk, it seemed to suggest that infidel rule was far from inevitable. The stream of Iraqi exiles, mostly ex-Ottoman officials and officers returning from the nationalist ferment in Turkey and Syria and eager for office and influence in their homeland, confirmed this opinion and also added to British anxieties by providing a channel for funds and a focus for dissent.

'On the whole events have defeated me,' wrote A.T. Wilson somewhat prematurely on 19 March 1920. He was referring not to events in Iraq but to those in the wider Middle East, and particularly to 'our failure to make good . . . in Egypt, Turkey and Syria'.[6] With the international current running strongly against his schemes for a British-built Iraq, he likened his situation to that of King Canute, nonplussed by the insurgent tide. The British press was giving him a hard time; the arrival as commander-in-chief of General Sir Aylmer Haldane, a semi-retired, semi-invalid officer with instructions to make further troop reductions, was not reassuring; and he was becoming increasingly suspicious of Gertrude Bell's activities. Any colleague – and now critic – who spent as much time as she closeted with members of the Iraqi élite and corresponding direct with policy-makers in London must be a liability. In vain he suggested a holiday, then urged Cox in Persia to engineer her recall.

April saw the completion of a report that he had commissioned on Iraq's constitutional future; it was quickly followed by the award to Britain of the mandate for Iraq (at the San Remo conference). But neither document brought the dividends he anticipated, and their coincidence led to some telegraphic confusion, with proposals based on the one crossing with those based on the other. The constitutional report, while recommending an amir (or king), a council of state and a legislative assembly, enjoined an indefinite delay in their implementation. It therefore won A.T.'s approval. He wanted to publish it, hoping that its liberal sentiments would help to lull the growing ferment. But publication was expressly forbidden; the mandate, he was told, must become operative first, and this must wait because, although awarded, its actual terms had still to be agreed.

But this time A.T. did not wait, and he announced the good tidings of the mandate regardless. Itching to impart something official to the Iraqis, he issued a communiqué which said much about the responsibilities of the mandatory and practically nothing about the rights of the mandated. 'Reconstruction is not the work of a day,' he warned, and he then rambled on about how 'the guardian rejoices over the growth of his ward into sane and independent manhood'. This went down badly in London and worse in Baghdad. As the only gloss available, it created a deep distrust of the mandate, which now became as much a target of Iraqi hostility as the mandatory. A.T. ducked behind his dictionary; the word 'mandate' was 'most unfortunate', he thought; its connotation of 'the power and authority to command' was what was upsetting the Arabs.[7]

THE TRAGEDY OF 1920

By mid-May Baghdad was warming up. 'The temperature just touches 100 F,' wrote Gertrude Bell; but her new pony was 'as clever as can be' and 'A.T. is being very pleasant'.[8] Not so Sir Aylmer Haldane. Ignoring unanimous advice to the contrary, the General removed his staff to the cooler climes of a remote mountain retreat on the Persian frontier, and himself joined them there after a short visit to Persia. Such complacency (Bell called it 'desertion') also appalled A.T., especially since some of Faysal's troops from Dayr al-Zor had just struck at a British outpost in the Mosul province. Three British officers and eighteen other ranks had been killed before order was restored and other vulnerable outposts withdrawn. This again sent the wrong message to Iraqi nationalists. Meanwhile British protests were lodged with the Arab government in Damascus. Although Faysal disclaimed all responsibility for the raid (as he had earlier over the Dayr incursion), A.T. was not slow to point out that the perpetrators had served in his army, and that their war chests and weapons originated in his British subsidy.

With this incursion repelled and with Kurdistan quiet for once, the troubles in the north-west of the country seemed to be subsiding. They were immediately replaced by an eruption in the south-east. It so happened that in 1920 the month-long fast of Ramadan coincided with the infernal heat of May/June, a conjuncture which Bell and Wilson rightly feared as certain to inflame religious sensibilities. Bell had also detected an ominous closing of Islamic ranks as Sunni and Shi'a draped their shared hostility to the mandate in the green flag of *jihad*.

From the holy Shi'ite cities of Najaf and Karbala there came the expected defiance. But what seems to have been anticipated by no one was the response that this drew from the mainly Shi'ite tribes, some settled, some nomadic, in adjacent districts along the middle and lower Euphrates. Here, it has been suggested, Islamic incitement and nationalist propaganda may have been but sparks to a high-octane vapour of resentment emanating from changes in land tax and tenure. These dated back to late Ottoman times; but it was probably the administrative zealotry of A.T. and his political officers which, taking precedent for practice, first ensured their stern and impartial operation. Revenue was demanded, and fines and detention were imposed for non-payment, all on the basis of land registrations and assessments that had never been accepted, that implied fundamental social changes, and that most tribal leaders and cultivators had hitherto evaded. In other words, the Euphrates tribes were for the first time being confronted by the realities of direct government control.[9]

This being the case, A.T. could reasonably contend, as he did, that some resistance was an unavoidable consequence of the measures necessary to convert Iraq into an integrated, stable and governable entity. It was not a view which found much sympathy at the time; but given the country's subsequent record of unrepresentative government under an enfeebled monarchy and then a ruthless dictatorship, it has since enjoyed something of a revival. Reviewing Iraq's highly artificial inception, some have wondered whether the integration of

Sunni and Shi'a, Arab and Kurd, nomad and cultivator, should not indeed have been given a higher priority. And perhaps the creation of a strong Iraq under a short-lived British colonial regime would have been a better beginning than the creation of a weak Iraq under long-lasting British influence. Even to some Arabs, the name of Arnold Talbot Wilson is no longer anathema.

But A.T. also contended that the administration must be well supported by the military and that resistance must be quickly isolated and firmly quelled. Because of troop reductions, and because of General Haldane's lassitude, this was not possible in the summer of 1920. In fact British military activities, far from discouraging other outbreaks, were initially so inadequate and disastrous as positively to invite them. As the towns and villages strung along the Euphrates to the south of Baghdad either capitulated to the 'insurgents' or came under siege, detachments of troops were rushed to the rescue and then themselves became cut off. It was like the fire station that catches fire while the firemen are attending an emergency.

There were no pitched battles; as Lawrence had demonstrated, Arab tactics did not lend themselves to battles. But in countless lesser skirmishes and ambushes, the British lost over 400 mostly Indian troops with a further 600 missing in action or captured, while Arab losses probably topped 8,500. Ten thousand is the fatality total given by Haldane and Lawrence, and the latter put the cost of the 'insurrection' to the British taxpayer at £40 million, four times that of his wartime Arab Revolt. Wildly critical of the whole affair and especially of A.T.'s supposed responsibility for it, Lawrence bombarded the British press with denunciations and portrayed the Iraqis as being engaged in a freedom struggle that was but a continuation of his own Revolt. Their hit-and-run tactics were certainly familiar. As well as waylaying troop trains, the Iraqis sometimes first marooned them by removing long sections of track both upline and down. It was this practice which provoked the novel sight of trains attempting to make their escape across the desert by lifting rails from behind in order to lay them in front, like crossing a swamp on a couple of planks.

By such laborious means in early August was the garrison at Diwaniya evacuated to Hilla along the main Basra–Baghdad line in an epic of railway lore. The distance was only sixty miles, but what with the constant attentions of the enemy and the continual lifting and laying of track, it took an agonizing eleven days. Retrieving various stranded relief and repair trains *en route*, the Diwaniya 'special', when it finally drew into Hilla, stretched for well over a mile and consisted of six locomotives hauling 251 assorted carriages and wagons, all riddled with bullets. Haldane, now back at his post in Baghdad, described this episode as the most anxious in his entire military career, including the four years he had spent on the Western Front.

Encouraged by such spectacles of British retreat, the revolt spread way beyond the Euphrates. British installations were destroyed, British communities isolated and British rule repudiated throughout much of Iraq. Only firm military control of Baghdad, Basra and the middle Tigris denied the 'insurrection' a wholly national dimension. But the co-ordination supposedly supplied by ex-Ottoman officers, like those in Faysal's employ, was not always effective, and there was no point at which the entire country was in arms simultaneously. Nor was there any moment when the 60,000–100,000 British and Indian troops were simultaneously engaged.

From a British perspective the worst time was undoubtedly those anxious days in early August. It was also then that news arrived from Damascus of the battle at Khan Maysalun and the ousting of 'King' Faysal. Defeat for Syria's Arab nationalists should have been welcome news to those fighting Iraq's Arab nationalists, especially since the former were deeply implicated in the latter's struggle. Yet Bell, true to her new colours, was horrified. 'Damnable' she called the Syrian situation, and she was disappointed that Faysal himself did not take the field against the French. She saw no contradiction in booing French operations against the Hashemite kingdom in Syria while cheering British operations against the Hashemite-backed Iraqis.

A.T. was more guarded. Unlike Lawrence he did not suffer from Francophobia, and he may have sympathized with French contempt for the terms of the League of Nations Covenant. He too would have liked to ignore the liberal sentiments of the mandate and impose a form of direct colonial rule. But this option was now being rapidly foreclosed; and it was certainly not a subject for discussion with his Oriental Secretary. The uneasy Wilson-Bell relationship had broken down completely just as the 'insurrection' began. 'An appalling scene' resulted when in June Bell admitted to having let slip to one of her Arab friends 'a bit of information', presumably classified.

Worse followed when in July Haldane revealed that his complacency stemmed from unauthorized assurances given by Bell that the 'revolt' had already peaked. 'You've done more harm here than anyone,' growled A.T. after the first of these revelations. His attempts to have her removed were no longer a secret; and at the height of the 'revolt' the two most influential figures in the administration were barely on speaking terms.

Bell was unrepentant: 'I know really what's at the bottom of it,' she confided, 'I've been right and he has been wrong.'[10] She was right because she had divined the likely drift of British government policy and had correctly judged that A.T. had no hope of changing it. Events, in the shape of the 'insurrection', were indeed defeating him. His experiment in direct British rule was now deemed a fiasco and its cost, reckoned at over £2 million a month, was a totally unacceptable burden. That he had achieved the impossible in getting Iraqis of all persuasions to unite against his administration was no consolation.

In truth, for A.T., the last of the imperial dinosaurs, though barely in his prime and never more tireless than during the 1920 'tragedy', the writing had been on the wall for months. Friendly advice had been ignored, opaque official warnings dismissed, Arabist spite deflected. His repeated requests for the polished and much more diplomatic Cox to return to Baghdad had stemmed from the knowledge that Cox had originally secured his appointment, supported his policies, and had a much better chance than he of getting London to endorse them. But when in June 1920 he was at last authorized to announce that Cox was indeed to return, it was clear that the Messiah would be coming not to applaud his stewardship but to supersede it. For Cox, like Bell, had read the writing on the wall and had got the message.

Seemingly A.T. only did so as the wall itself came crashing down under 'insurgent' pressure. Congratulations on his 'magnificent work' of the past two and a half years and the award of a knighthood, both accepted signs of imminent betrayal, should have alerted him. In fact they merely emboldened him. In mid-June he told London that more troops were essential and that, notwithstanding the mandate, the British must either govern Iraq or get out altogether. 'If they thought they could shut me up by giving me a K[nighthood] they are much mistaken,' he told a friend.[11] Hubert Young, once his admirer and now advising Curzon at the Foreign Office, took his 'govern or go' ultimatum 'as tantamount to resignation and thought [it] should be accepted as such'.[12] Instead, on 23 June the announcement of Cox's return was coupled with a proclamation from London which called for the establishment of a council of state and the election of a general national assembly.

Whether A.T. liked it or not, an Arab government was on the way. There was to be no little India in Iraq, no pink Mesopotamian link in the globe-encircling empire, no jewel of Araby in the imperial crown. 'Kipling at his noblest' would pen not a verse about the stalwart Arab; nor was 'Curzon at his best' when, sick and overworked, he endorsed criticisms of A.T.'s obstructive conduct.

A month later, in the midst of the 'revolt', A.T. greeted the news of Khan Maysalun and Faysal's ejection from Damascus by proposing that the ex-king of Syria be offered the throne of Iraq. It looked as if he too had performed a volte-face and joined the pro-Hashemite camp; Lawrence and Bell must have been dumbfounded. But, in fact, A.T. reasoned simply that the chastened Faysal, now painfully aware that no Arab government could function without British support, was just the man to endorse his own ideas of a strong British military presence and an efficient British-staffed administration. In other words, it was Faysal who had changed, not he. Additionally, he reasoned that, at a time of mounting panic in Baghdad, the announcement of such an offer would take the sting out of the insurrection. But, as usual, A.T. was ordered to say nothing; and once again, by his reckoning, an opportunity was lost through indecision.

That this was in fact precisely the solution which Bell and Cox (who finally arrived in Baghdad in October) would pursue would be little consolation. By then, thanks to massive reinforcements from India, the 'insurrection' was on its last legs and the insurgents were being rounded up, disarmed and sentenced. Additionally their flocks and herds were being confiscated, their villages burned and their encampments bombed, all with a vindictive ferocity fully commensurate with the scale of the 'revolt'. It was the only part of the military operations that A.T. heartily applauded. But he did so from a distance; for by late October, humiliated if not humbled, he was enjoying some well-earned leave back where his Middle Eastern career had begun, in the Persian hills around Masjid-i-Suleiman. As the leave turned out to be indefinite, he pounded the hillsides ever harder, brushing up on his endurance skills before returning to England.

He would need them. His critics were waiting for him in both Fleet Street and Whitehall. It was no fun 'to see the work of years arbitrarily destroyed . . . hopes dashed to the ground . . . subordinates vilified . . . and [to be] described as parasites battening upon a distressed and resentful country'.[13] Nor was he pleased to find his personal integrity a matter of public debate when he took up a post with the Anglo-Persian Oil Company as manager of their operations in the Middle East. A volley of aphorisms, mostly in Latin, were presumed to have discomfited his critics; and a trip to Switzerland worked wonders. 'I went in for winter sports whole-heartedly,' he says; on his return, he met the young widow who would soon become Lady Wilson.

A.T. featured once more in Middle Eastern affairs of state when on behalf of APOC, in March 1921, he again rubbed shoulders with Lawrence and Bell at the 1921 Cairo conference. But he took no part in its political deliberations. His official career was over. He would later champion other unfashionable causes as a somewhat unpredictable Member of Parliament; and in 1939 he would sign up with RAF's Bomber Command. He died, aged 55 and probably the only knight of the realm serving as a rear-gunner, when his plane was shot down over Dunkirk in May 1940.

THE GENESIS OF JORDAN

The 1921 Cairo conference was Winston Churchill's big idea. With the British exchequer demanding substantial economies and the British press aghast at events in Iraq, Lloyd George had bowed to the pressure for change with sweeping bureaucratic and personnel moves. The existing division of responsibilities between the India, Foreign and War Offices was rightly supposed to have contributed to London's indecisive and sometimes contradictory responses to A.T.'s initiatives, as well as to other Middle Eastern alarms. It was decided, therefore, that British responsibilities in the now mandated territories of Iraq and Palestine should be concentrated in a new Middle Eastern department constituted within the Colonial Office. At the same time Winston Churchill was appointed to head the Colonial Office as Secretary of State.

Churchill co-opted, among others, T.E. Lawrence and Hubert Young on to his advisory staff and immediately launched into a complete reappraisal of British commitments in the region. Militarily he was convinced that the mandatory's obligation to defend its mandated territory and support the civil power could be largely, and most cheaply, discharged from the air. Troop numbers were therefore to be slashed and their role taken over by the RAF. Politically, he likewise favoured cost-cutting settlements that would assuage Arab expectations without prejudicing British interests or abandoning ultimate British control. It was these arrangements, plus the RAF deployment, that were to be finalized with those responsible for implementing them at the conference that he called in Cairo in March 1921.

Falling in the lull in Egyptian affairs between the Milner Mission's report and Saad Zaghlul's tumultuous return, Churchill's conference was a busy but relaxed affair. It lasted two weeks and the schedule allowed for a group camel ride round the pyramids, plus several photo sessions. In the team line-up, Churchill sits in the middle flanked by Sir Herbert Samuel, High Commissioner for Palestine, and Sir Percy Cox, now High Commissioner for Iraq. Beside Cox sits General Haldane, and behind them stands a mincing Lawrence. In the wings Hubert Young sports a Churchillian bow-tie, A.T. Wilson amply fills his new businessman's suit, and Gertrude Bell models a Paris hat and a dead fox. Wilson and Bell stand side by side, frigidly. 'We had a cordial meeting,' reported Bell, 'but I've not seen him to talk to and don't much want to.'[14] At their feet, as if in allegory, a large dog tangles with a leopard on a leash.

Cox and Bell brought good tidings from Baghdad. With Bell's 'Chastity Chase' operating as the hub of a vast network of political intrigue, she and 'Jack' Philby, Cox's choice as political adviser, had sifted through Iraq's notables and cobbled together a provisional government consisting of a Council of Ministers, each with his British adviser. As well as directing the administration of the country, this Council had drafted an electoral law which was to lead to the installation of a representative national assembly which would in turn select a head of state.

At least, that was Philby's understanding; and, being a man with opinions as robust as his physique, Philby had no doubt who would emerge as the crucial head of state. It would be the formidable Saiyid Talib, son of the *naqib* of Basra, whose popularity rested on a record of British-imposed exile that rivalled that of Zaghlul and yet whose co-operation with the British during the 'revolt' had been partly responsible for stifling opposition in Baghdad and Basra. All, even A.T., conceded Talib's ability. Indeed, the Iraqi's only handicap was such an abundance of political skills that he might just make a success of Iraq's first government.

Philby thought, somewhat naïvely, that this was the whole point of the exercise. As 'adviser' to Talib in the latter's capacity as Minister for the Interior in the provisional Council of Ministers, Philby genuinely admired him and strongly urged his suit as the future prime minister or president. But not so his colleagues. 'Bell hated Saiyid Talib like poison,' says Philby, 'while . . . Cox mistrusted him and on the whole disliked him.'[15] Moreover Bell, in particular, had her own candidate in mind; and it was no small joy for her to discover in Cairo that Churchill and his advisers had fixed on the same man. Ex-king Faysal of Syria was already slated as next-king Faysal of Iraq.

Lawrence had been the prime mover in this scheme. He was still wedded to the idea of honouring the McMahon understanding, at least in part; he considered that Faysal, his old comrade-in-arms, had been badly betrayed by the British in Syria; and he saw Iraq as a chance to make all good. Additionally, although Faysal's installation would not 'biff France out of Syria', it would certainly be one in the eye for the French. To less rabid Francophobes, however, French hostility to the British adoption of France's Syrian foe was a matter for concern. The subject was tactfully raised with the French government and Faysal was given to understand that a condition of his British sponsorship in Iraq would be that he abandon all claims to Syria and all active support of Syria's nationalists. Faysal apparently agreed.

There were a couple of other problems. It will be remembered that in Damascus, when Faysal was joyously proclaimed king by the Syrians exactly a year earlier, Faysal's elder brother Abdullah was simultaneously acclaimed *in absentia* as ruler of Iraq. Abdullah had been in the Hijaz at the time, angling for the extension of his father's (the *sharif* Husayn's) kingdom at the expense of Ibn Saud. Very correctly Faysal himself now insisted that he could not usurp Abdullah's selection as king of Iraq without the latter's agreement, and that this would be best obtained by awarding Abdullah a similarly royal role elsewhere – say, in Palestine.

Three Wee Kings of Orient Are

Abdullah had long been an enigma to the British. Smaller even than Lawrence, much rounder, and lacking that dignified demeanour that so impressed the British in Faysal, he was yet far from a nonentity. Pre-war he had represented the Hijaz in the Constantinople parliament and he was well-informed about international affairs. He played a fair game of chess and it was he who had originally impressed Ronald Storrs with his knowledge of Arabian lore and his need for British guns. The war he had spent mainly outside the walls of Medina, theoretically besieging its garrison of 7,000 Turks but, in reality, merely preventing them from interfering with the Arab Revolt, while at the same time he actively contested the widening influence of Ibn Saud of Riyadh amongst the adjacent tribes. The British had complained that that was not why they had armed and subsidized him; but Abdullah had stuck to his guns. Beneath an affability bordering on buffoonery, there evidently lurked a resolve comparable with Faysal's.

Two months after the end of the war, Medina had belatedly surrendered. Abdullah promptly went on the offensive against Ibn Saud. It was a bad mistake, and the results were catastrophic. In May 1919 Abdullah's forces were taken by surprise and suffered heavy casualties. He himself, slightly wounded, suffered far more from the indignity of having to flee across the desert in a nightshirt. The 'Shaykh-let', the pint-size Shaykh, as the Saudis called him, became the laughing-stock of Arabia. Known as the Battle of Turaba, this encounter proved to be 'a turning point in Abdullah's life and in the history of Arabia', according to Mary Wilson, his perceptive biographer.[16] The Saudis would henceforth have the upper hand in their Arabian vendetta with the Hashemites, a matter of growing concern to the British who were subsidizing both. And more immediately Abdullah must look elsewhere for an outlet for his political ambitions.

Specifically he began to look north, towards the British and Syria/Palestine. Gathering up his shattered forces, in September 1920 Abdullah left Mecca and, travelling in the footsteps of Lawrence and the Arab Revolt, reached Ma'an in November. There, like Lawrence prior to the attack on Aqaba, he cast about for tribal support. He also made contact with influential Syrian exiles from French rule as he let it be known that he planned to march on Damascus. At the request of, among others, Shaykh Kamil al-Qassab – he who had led the Damascus communes in the heady days before the French invasion – Abdullah continued on up the Hijaz railway to Amman, then a village of about 2,000 souls. He arrived there in March 1921, just as Churchill was convening his Cairo conference.

What to do about this loose cannon – he actually had six machine-guns – on the far side of the Jordan had been troubling the British. It was unthinkable that he be allowed to mount an attack, however quixotic, on the French in Syria from territory which was included in the Palestine mandate and so was a British responsibility. The international repercussions would be horrific. Equally, given Palestine's strategic importance to the British and their commitment to Zionist settlement there, it was unthinkable that he be invited to try his hand as king in Jerusalem. Yet something had to be found for him. How else could the more trusted Faysal be foisted on Iraq?

It was this thinking, roughly, which gave birth to the least plausible of the post-Ottoman successor states. For the solution of what to do about Abdullah was, typically, as little as possible. Abdullah was to stay put; the loose cannon was to be allowed to bed down in the sands to the east of the Jordan; and an apparently worthless tract of declivity and desert, with no cities, no towns worthy of the name, no obvious resources, and a population of only 200,000, most of them expatriates and nomads, was to be detached from mandated Palestine and declared the putative Amirate of 'Transjordania'.

Where Egypt had a river, and Iraq two rivers, Transjordania had a railway line. But Sultan Abd al-Hamid's 400 miles of metre-gauge track, with stations, although the spine of the country and its sole commercial asset, had been so often mined that it was barely functional. If a state, let alone a nation, was ever to materialize along its length, it was not down to the railway engineers but the country's only other symbol of territorial integrity, the roly-poly Hashemite with the disastrous military record. For Abdullah was indeed now invited by the British to assume the role of Transjordania's Amir and to make what he might of this unfancied wilderness. He was given six months to do so. The arrangement, he was told, was less expedient than experiment. Transjordania was on probation. Abdullah, while keeping out of international trouble, must sell the idea of a state to his assorted subjects within twenty-six weeks; otherwise the place must be relinquished in the condition in which he had found it. Crown and country were on sale or return.

Such was the genesis of what is now Jordan. Its political viability, even its value to the British, had yet to be proven; its international status had yet to be determined; and its frontiers had yet to be demarcated. A child of political expediency, it had neither an economic nor a geographical rationale.[17] Without even a residence there, Abdullah spent the first years of his 'reign' either in a tent or as a lodger in the homes of his sympathizers. From Amman to Salt to Ajlun and back to Amman he drifted in search of a capital. For an income, military support and political advice he was entirely dependent on the British.

Seemingly he only accepted the situation because he still had hopes of a throne in either Jerusalem or Damascus. Churchill did not entirely disabuse him; in the fullness of time, he implied, anything could happen. But all that mattered immediately was installing Abdullah in a cheap and inconspicuous billet so that Faysal would go to Iraq.

GOD SAVE THE KING

Faysal's Iraqi destiny was the central plank of the Cairo settlement, and much thought was given to its actual implementation. But this, too, presented problems. For as well as an accommodation with Abdullah, Faysal was demanding that his candidature for the throne of Iraq be underwritten by British support exercised so discreetly as in no way to prejudice his royal prerogatives or alienate nationalist opinion. In other words, his acceptance by the Iraqis depended on British leverage, yet admitting as much could easily result in his rejection by the Iraqis. The British, too, understood the need for this delicate balance, although they saw it slightly differently. Faysal must appear to be Iraq's choice rather than theirs, certainly; but on the other hand, he must not become so emboldened by Iraqi endorsement as to imagine that he could challenge his British sponsors. As in any form of puppetry, the strings needed to be strong enough to withstand all manner of antics yet so fine as to remain invisible to the audience.

Sailing back to Baghdad from Cairo, Gertrude Bell relished the challenge and could barely contain her excitement. The conference had been 'wonderful', Churchill 'admirable'. As she told Colonel

Frank Balfour, a close friend whose London advocacy of Faysal had carried much weight with Churchill:

> When we get our Amir out [to Baghdad] he will need a great deal of help and guidance, and it would be more than I could bear not to be there to give whatever help I can. Oh Frank, it's going to be interesting! If we bring it off we shall make a quite new thing which will serve as an example – let's hope not as a warning.[18]

The cautionary note was prompted by the challenge being mounted by Philby's protégé, Saiyid Talib. The Council of Ministers was by now under Talib's control and could not therefore be relied on to ask for Faysal as king. Similarly, there was no guarantee that an elected national assembly would ask for Faysal; for by the time such a body was constituted, Talib would be even more firmly entrenched and the sobering effect of General Haldane's recent punitive operations would have worn off.

In the management of public opinion Talib was proving more than a match for the British. As Minister of the Interior, he scotched the launch of a pro-Hashemite newspaper in Baghdad. Fears that he might interfere in the telegraph office meant that the flood of Iraqi telegrams imploring Husayn to send his son to Iraq lost much of their spontaneous effect by having to be dispatched through the British High Commission (where many had doubtless been drafted). 'All this shows how impossible it is to conduct "free elections" while one party is in high office', sighed Bell in words quite innocent of irony. Talib was using the influence of his ministerial office to frustrate that of the British High Commission. He was calling the British bluff, in other words; and for this he must go.

Two weeks after their return from Cairo, Bell and Cox made their move. At a Baghdad dinner party attended by Bell's informants, Talib had reportedly complained about 'undue influence' in the forthcoming elections and suggested that, if this was the case, certain friendly shaykhs 'with 30,000 rifles' would want to know why. Bell took this for 'an incitement to rebellion', 'as bad as anything which was said by the men who roused the country last year', and 'not far from a declaration of *jihad*'. She reported the matter to Cox on 17 April. That afternoon Talib was arrested. In an extraordinary breach of Arab etiquette, he was apprehended just as he was leaving a tea party at the High Commissioner's residence to which he had been invited by Cox's wife. There was no hearing, no trial. Bundled down-river by special launch, at Fao on the Gulf he was packed aboard a ship to another indefinite exile, this time in Ceylon.

Bell was delighted. 'Talib was capable of anything', she believed, 'and almost certain to attempt the assassination of Faysal.' Patting Cox on the back for his firm handling of 'a delicate political problem', she then took a last swipe at A.T. for having let Talib return from his wartime exile in the first place. 'It's the final unravelling of the harm that A.T. Wilson did,' she wrote, ingenuously adding, 'for no one knows what he promised Talib when he brought him [back].'[19]

But if promises had indeed been made, they more likely came from Philby. As Talib's man, Philby had been told nothing of the arrest and had been carefully prevented from interfering. In fact he believed that his telephone line had been intentionally cut on the crucial day. When, livid with rage, he eventually confronted Cox, he was mollified only by an assurance that he himself might now step into Talib's ministerial shoes. Taking this to mean that it was up to him to prevent 'undue influence', he broke off contact with Bell, once his friend and champion, and continued to do all in his power to frustrate his government's policy of manufacturing a constituency for Faysal. Bell found it 'very provoking'. In her demonology Philby had become another A.T.; like Talib, he too must go.[20]

Philby thought otherwise. Confident that Iraq's national assembly, when elected, would refuse to appoint Faysal, he stayed on. The news, in May, that Faysal was in fact already on his way to Iraq, indeed aboard a British warship, meant that 'the Cairo cat was now out of the bag', as he put it.[21] Lest the Iraqis had not got the message about Britain's preference, Churchill then issued a statement that his govern-ment would 'place no obstacles in the way of [Faysal's] candidature'. Philby, of course, disapproved; for what did this benign attitude to Faysal imply about British feelings towards the other candidates? But he took comfort when Faysal's landward progress up to Baghdad proved anything but royal. Despite official receptions, guards of honour and organized festivities, the jubilant Iraqi crowds stayed away. Even Cox could muster no more than a 'cordial' to describe the welcome. As for Faysal, he felt himself betrayed yet again. Contrary to what he had been led to believe, the Iraqis were not clamouring for his rule; nor, if Philby was anything to go by, were the British.

Philby had accompanied Faysal from Basra to Baghdad as Cox's representative. In the course of the three-day journey by special train, he had taken it upon himself to explain that, however much the British government might wish to see Faysal as king, it was the job of British officials like himself to show impartiality, ensure that the elections were free and fair, and uphold whatever decision Iraq's elected representatives reached about their head of state. Faysal reported this lecture to Cox in some alarm; Cox then asked Philby to explain himself; and Philby finally dug his own grave. For as he explained, anything less than strict impartiality could only mean that the elections were to be 'rigged'; and if so, how could he remain at his post? He would rather resign immediately. Cox, to whom such plain speaking was the height of bad manners, thanked him – ostensibly for his candour, actually for his resignation – and that was that. Like A.T., Philby betook himself to Persia on indefinite leave.

Bell ascribed Philby's behaviour to 'republican' (or antimonarchist) principles and a contempt for the Hashemites. Yet his next appointment would be as political adviser to Amir Abdullah in Transjordania, and his ultimate loyalties would be found to lie with that most absolute of monarchies, the Saudi kingdom in Riyadh. The rift in the British ranks had nothing to do with ideology. It was just that, while Bell liked to be right, Philby preferred to be righteous. A slave neither to his socialist sympathies nor to any supposed republicanism, he was simply pugnacious in any worthwhile cause that he made his own.

The way was now clear for what was called 'the Hashemite solution'. Realizing, like Philby, that an elected assembly would almost certainly choose one of its own rather than Britain's hand-picked exotic, Cox postponed the elections and so in effect dispensed with the principle of an elected head of state. Instead, the existing British-appointed Council of Ministers, cowed by Talib's removal, was invited to take the initiative and ask for Faysal as king. Then Cox, as if bowing to popular pressure, invited the Iraqi people to endorse the Council's decision in a single-issue referendum. Sometimes described as another 'plebiscite', the referendum carried no more conviction than had A.T. Wilson's exercise. All other contenders were removed, it was conducted under British scrutiny, and it produced the inevitable result. Faysal's candidature won a reported 96 per cent of the vote.

Three Wee Kings of Orient Are

This represented a remarkable turn-around. In 1919 A.T.'s plebis-cite had supposedly produced a 'no' to any sort of amir; in 1920 the utterance of pro-Hashemite slogans had actually been accounted treason; and now in 1921 a Hashemite amir, indeed king, was sud-denly revealed as the almost unanimous choice of all the 'better sort' of Iraqis. Either the electorate was extraordinarily volatile or the results had indeed been rigged. As yet popularity ratings of over 90 per cent were not recognized as the exclusive prerogative of unloved dictatorships. But Philby rightly declared that for Iraq this was not a happy introduction to the democratic process. Nor, in retrospect, was it an encouraging precedent.

A month later, on 23 August, the ex-king of Syria was duly crowned King Faysal of Iraq. The preparations did not go without a hitch. When Faysal discovered that his speech of acceptance included an acknowledgement of the High Commissioner's superior authority, he threatened to pull out and only proceeded once the offending words had been removed. 'It was all a mistake,' explained Bell.

Because of the dust and the heat, the enthronement ceremony was held at the unlikely hour of 6 a.m. In the middle of a bare and well-secured courtyard Faysal, flanked by Cox and Haldane, sat beneath the dawning sky on a timber dais strewn with carpets. Opposite, offi-cers, officials and wives were ranged on hard chairs. It had all the dignity of a school concert. As if it were, Bell in the front row managed to catch Faysal's eye and 'gave him a wave of encourage-ment'. The proclamation was duly read, the Hashemite flag was raised and, for want of an Iraqi national anthem, the band played 'God Save the King'. Then guns fired a salute, Faysal made his speech, and everyone went home for breakfast.

BELL'S 'BIG THING'

It was not God but the British who would save the King – just as they had made him, just as they had made Iraq. 'Now look,' Bell had pleaded with Valentine Chirol of *The Times* just before the corona-tion, 'for once, for once in the world, we are giving a corner of the East a fair and honest chance to get its house straight. If we succeed, it is not unlikely that we will modify the whole relationship between England and Asia. It's a big thing we are doing . . . ' This echoed her 'new thing which will serve as an example' of the previous May; and once again she was infuriatingly right.

Now in her mid-fifties, Gertrude Bell was enjoying her finest hour. More than anyone, the slight lady with the long nose and the big hats could claim the Iraqi monarchy as her personal creation. Lawrence knew no more of Iraq than Churchill, Cox was completely dependent on her advice and contacts, and Faysal looked to her as his champion and go-between. A busy-bodying gossip and an intellectual and social snob, she would not have been greatly loved whatever her gender. Yet she was indeed admired, and not just because she was a woman in an aggressively male society. Her arrogance was well-founded. She did know more about what was going on in Iraq than any of her contemporaries, and she did have the intelligence to interpret this information and the influence to get others to act on it. She was wholeheartedly engaged on 'a big thing' of considerable consequence, and although its transaction was not quite as 'fair and honest' as she pretended, being right about it was her business.

For, unthinkable as it had been in the dark days of the 1920 'revolt', Iraq would eventually realize Bell's hopes and, after a few more fraught exchanges, emerge as Britain's showpiece in the Middle East. The first among the occupied ex-Ottoman territories to achieve lasting self-government under an Arab sovereign, it would promptly embark on a fast track to treaty-dependent independence, thus completing in one decade a constitutional obstacle course that took Egypt nearly five. By the 1930s optimistic commentators would be hailing the country as a model of enlightened self-government and a monument to the liberal thinking and innovative genius of Cox and Bell. Iraq's apparent emancipation would afford not only a damning indictment of France's authoritarian rule in Syria but also proof of Britain's good faith elsewhere – in Palestine, were that unhappy country only to co-operate, or in slow-moving Egypt.

Iraq's constitutional progress further differed from Egypt's in the order of things. For here the bitter medicine of a one-sided treaty with the colonial power was not administered after the heady sherbet of independence, as in Egypt, but before it. The treaty idea, 'a magnificent move' according to Bell, came from Cox, and had first been aired even before the enthronement. Since both Faysal and the Iraqis continued to object to the provisions of the League of Nations mandate, Cox had proposed to render these provisions more palatable by incorporating some, and superseding the rest, in a bilateral Anglo-Iraqi treaty. Faysal, naturally, wanted to know the exact terms of this treaty before he accepted the throne. But Cox insisted that the terms had to be negotiated, and negotiations could only start after he had ascended the throne.

Against his better judgement Faysal concurred. But when the negotiations did open in late 1921, they promptly ran into difficulties. To obtain approval from the League's supervisory Mandates Commission (and to avoid further antagonizing the French in Syria), Britain's representative told the League of Nations Commission in Geneva that the proposed change was essentially cosmetic. The mandate, he said, would 'remain the operative document' and the treaty would 'merely regulate' it, not supersede it. But this was the opposite of what Faysal had been told; it was precisely as a substitute for the mandate that he had welcomed the treaty, and he expected it to include words to that effect. By now betrayed more often than he could remember, Faysal made no attempt to hide his displeasure. The 'minor hurricane' with which, according to Bell, he greeted the Geneva text ended his honeymoon with the British and marked the beginning of an obscure and tempestuous three years.

Throughout this period the treaty hung in the balance. Faysal's approval, when at last extracted, was conditional on ratification by Iraq's elected assembly, which itself awaited the long-delayed elections. For these, electoral lists had to be prepared and an easily managed system of indirect representation introduced. Then the assembly had to be convened, the treaty submitted, and a favourable vote secured. At every stage of this process objections were raised by disenchanted individuals and interests who often made common cause with Iraq's perennial dissidents – the Kurds, the Shi'a religious establishment and the tribes.

External factors compounded the confusion and further highlighted the lack of national consensus. In the north, Turkish intrigues in Kurdistan intensified as Ankara endeavoured to frustrate that long-running British demand for the incorporation into Iraq of the whole Mosul province (including, of course, its oil). Meanwhile in the south Ibn Saud's 1921 conquest of his central Arabian rivals in Haïl brought refugee tribesmen fleeing across the Iraqi border with the Saudis' fanatical followers in hot pursuit. Here in the southern desert, as in Kurdistan, the Royal Air Force got more practice than it had dared hope for. Anticipating a much later solution to the Kurdish problem, Churchill even proposed the use of chemical weapons as he wondered whether 'some kind of asphyxiating bombs to cause disablement of some kind' might not be the answer.[22] The more conventional bombing of Kurdish villages and strafing of Bedouin encampments brought from critics in the House of Commons such adjectives as 'barbarous' and 'Hunnish'.[23]

But without this British military support, Faysal's regime could scarcely have survived. Lieutenant John Bagot Glubb, at the start of a long and distinguished Arabian career, had reached Iraq too late in 1920 to be involved in suppressing the 'revolt' yet nevertheless found himself almost continuously in action. For instance in 1923, as the army officer responsible for directing RAF strikes in a sector south of the Euphrates, he took part in a notorious two-day bombing raid from Samawa that resulted in 144 killed plus uncounted wounded. This was sufficiently bad for the ultra-discreet Glubb to suppress the casualty figures in his published narrative. And what made it especially 'regrettable' was that the 'aerial action' had been undertaken simply to enforce the payment of taxes.[24] Yet to Gertrude Bell it rated as 'our latest success'. As noted by Elie Kedourie, once the *enfant terrible* of Middle Eastern studies, such heavy-handed tactics when employed by A.T. Wilson had been deemed 'tyrannical excess' but when used on Faysal's behalf were warmly applauded as being 'in the interests of order and security'.[25]

Unsurprisingly opposition, whether from tribesmen on the fringes of Iraq or from the more politically articulate classes in the cities, was in fact directed as much at Faysal as at the British. That, of course, from a British point of view was one of the benefits of having set him on the throne. But briefly in 1922, as Faysal continued to refuse the detested treaty, it seemed that, like Talib, he too might just call the British bluff. An exasperated Cox damned him as 'crooked and insincere'; Bell, so long his passionate supporter, settled for 'vain and feeble and timid' and cursed his 'double-dealing'; there was even talk of replacing him. But at the height of the crisis Faysal shrewdly went down with appendicitis. During his long convalescence, his plenipotentiary, who was Bell's old friend the ever-pliable *naqib* of Baghdad, signed the treaty on the dotted line.

Thereafter Faysal, though unpredictable and often obstructive, ceased to contest the treaty. But this made the elections and the treaty's passage through the resultant assembly no easier. Since most of those who supported Faysal had known previous employment under the Sunni Ottomans, Faysal's governments had a decidedly Sunni complexion. This was deeply resented by the slightly more numerous but less enfranchised Shi'a who duly adopted the treaty negotiations as a suitable battlefield. In 1923 their protests and *fatwas* against both the treaty and the elections (which were to lead to its ratification) resulted in the deportation of the principal Shi'ite divine, whereupon other clerics joined him in a mass exodus to Persia. Although most eventually returned, confessional relations did not improve, and never would. The price of Faysal's adherence to his British sponsors, and of the British preference for an obligated Sunni oligarchy rather than an unmanageable democracy, was the permanent alienation of Iraq's largest community.

The long-awaited assembly, known as the Chamber of Deputies, finally convened in 1924. By then Great Britain had had two changes of government, Iraq at least as many, and the treaty itself had been modified. A protocol had been added to the effect that its terms were to remain in force for only four years from whenever peace was signed with Turkey (and Mosul thereby secured to Iraq). Yet despite this concession and much blatant arm-twisting, the treaty was ratified only by a slim majority of a bare quorum of the not truly representative Chamber.

Moreover the treaty's four-year term would prove a doubtful Iraqi gain since it soon became apparent that the country had no chance of satisfying the other stipulations of the treaty within that period. These included the payment of a crippling contribution to the pre-war Ottoman debt owing to the European powers, further hefty payments to Britain for assets transferred and expenditures incurred as a result of the British presence, and the creation of an Iraqi army capable of defending the country against external aggression and ensuring internal order. Another treaty would be needed in 1930 and, although Iraq would indeed achieve qualified independence in 1932, the military requirement would ensure the presence of British forces, including RAF bases, for another two decades.

Gertrude Bell did not live to see her life's work realized. With her supposed ability to control Faysal exposed by the treaty row of 1922, and with her influence curtailed by the departure of Cox in 1923, she ceased to pull the strings of power and became increasingly sidelined.

She stayed on in Baghdad as creator of its archaeological museum and director of Iraq's antiquities. But her health deteriorated and her political irrelevance rankled. Two days before her fifty-eighth birthday, on 12 July 1926, she died in her sleep after taking an overdose of barbiturates. Her letters, now travelling home by airmail, offer no explanation for her suicide, and none has been convincingly adduced from other sources.

Her last years saw the final round in the interminable squabble over Mosul's oil, the incorporation of Mosul into Iraq, and the settlement of Iraq's northern frontier. The League of Nations, foreseeing a special need for the protection of Mosul's Kurdish population, insisted on a 25-year term for the mandate as part of this settlement. Only if in the interim Iraq achieved independence by meeting the criteria for becoming a member of the League could this be changed. But Bell had anticipated just such a move. Writing to her father in January 1926, she dismissed the 25-year term as quite irrelevant. 'If we go on as fast as we've gone for the last two years, Iraq will be a member of the League before five or six years have passed, and our direct responsibility will have ceased.'[26]

She was right, as usual. Iraq joined the League six and a half years later. But this would by no means end British involvement, as she well knew. Rather was it a sign that the British were so satisfied with her 'big thing' – especially the advantages that they had secured and 'the machinery of constraints'[27] that they had imposed – that close supervision and 'direct responsibility' were no longer necessary. Informal empire was working 'admirably', as she would have put it; and long would it continue to do so. For Iraq, the first Middle Eastern state to achieve a heavily qualified independence, would be one of the last to break free from the post-colonial relationship. Long after the Second World War, even after Suez, British armed forces were still assisting Iraq, and Britain's stranglehold on the economy continued. Until the revolution of 1958 it was to London, rather than to the Iraqi people, that the Sunni-Hashemite governing clique looked for support.

Perhaps the proprietorial indulgence exemplified by Bell's maternalism worked a little too well. Comparatively blessed with resources, surrounded by the playthings of sovereignty, and yet increasingly conscious of its more street-wise neighbours, Iraq clung to Britain's threadbare skirts too long. The reaction, when it eventually came, would be angry and violent.

8

Stifling Syria

INTERRUPTING A CAREER in Egypt that would span thirty years, Lawrence Grafftey-Smith spent 1920–2 as British vice-consul in Jidda, the diplomatic capital and principal Red Sea port of *sharif* Husayn's kingdom of the Hijaz. The fresh-faced young Englishman, who in 1919 had been tempted to throw into the Nile the order for Saad Zaghlul's arrest, got on better than most with king-*sharif* Husayn and delighted in the old man's somewhat demanding company. But he failed to persuade him to come to terms with Ibn Saud of Riyadh who, following victory over the night-shirted Abdullah at Turaba, was pressing ever harder on the kingdom of the Hijaz; and he was greatly mystified by the fact that Husayn, during his interminable reflections on British perfidy, 'never once mentioned the name of Lawrence'. Nor did anyone else in Jidda. 'I had come to the Hijaz expecting to find a legend,' wrote Grafftey-Smith, 'and there was only silence.' Barely two years after the Arab Revolt, 'Lawrence was not a subject of conversation.'[1]

Just as the Black Hole is notorious everywhere but Calcutta, so Lawrence was a legend everywhere but Arabia. Courtesy of the lectures and press briefings given by his self-appointed publicist (the American Lowell Thomas), 'the uncrowned King of Arabia', as one British paper called him, had become an international celebrity. And thanks to his prominence at the Paris and Cairo conferences, he was also the recognized conscience of the British government on all matters Arab.

It was therefore cause for congratulation when, in a 1922 draft for his *Seven Pillars of Wisdom*, Lawrence at last felt able to 'put on record my conviction that England is out of the Arab affair with clean hands'.[2] The recent installation of Faysal as king of Iraq and of Abdullah as amir of Transjordania, together with the continued British support of Husayn as king of the Hijaz, could be taken, thought Lawrence, as full and final settlement of those wartime promises originally made by McMahon.

His one regret was that Syria had eluded the Arabs and fallen to the French. But even this need not be regarded as irrevocable. Till her dying day Gertrude Bell would argue that, since Faysal's dazzling success in Iraq must soon lead the Syrians to re-adopt him, a union of Arab states under Hashemite leadership would yet come to pass.[3] Lawrence, on the other hand, confidently predicted that it would be the French who would change tack. Shamed because Churchill's Iraqi settlement had 'set honesty before expediency' (as Lawrence saw it), France would eventually feel morally obliged to offer the Syrians a government which was just as much Arab as that in Iraq.

But he was wrong; the French would feel nothing of the sort. And so, for once, was Bell; for the Syrians, whatever they thought of Iraq, were pining not for the collaborationist Faysal but for their own endangered identity. In 1921–2, while the British were determinedly aggregating ex-Ottoman provinces to create a monolithic Iraq, the French were no less determinedly atomizing ex-Ottoman provinces to create a scatter of communal Levantine statelets. Indeed, by the time the mandates were confirmed in 1923, the component territories of what Arabs regarded as geographical Syria, or 'Syria within its natural borders', had been so parcelled and packaged as to constitute another Balkanization. Besides the British-mandated territory of Palestine, itself now divided into Palestine and Transjordania, French-mandated Syria had been cropped of Lebanon (plus much additional territory that was awarded to Lebanon), and the remainder had then been chopped into five administrative entities – the so-called 'states' of Aleppo, Damascus, Alexandretta, (the mainly Druze) Jabal Druze, and (the mainly Alawi) Jabal Ansariya.

This dicing and paring could be seen to follow the recipe for administrative croutons favoured by the French in West Africa and Indo-China. Similarly an incorporated Iraq looked to conform to the all-inclusive soup, an *administrone* even, favoured by the British in India. Yet, oddly, two years earlier at the end of the war, national tastes had been exactly the opposite. Then it had been the French who championed *la Syrie intégrale* while the British argued for its partition. The main concern of the British was, of course, to detach Palestine, but they had also toyed with the idea of an autonomous Kurdish state in Iraq; and east of the Jordan in what would eventually become Abdullah's Transjordania they had contemplated a whole chain of Arab states.

According to Alex Kirkbride, the lanky subaltern who had been Lawrence's bodyguard when he first entered Damascus, these trans-Jordan states were more than administrative doodles and actually aspired to a brief autonomy. In 1920 Kirkbride himself was dispatched as political midwife to the most southerly of them and there took up residence in a Crusader castle whence he peered over what were once Sodom and Gomorrah down to the Dead Sea. The castle was that of Kerak, but for a name for the new state he returned to the Bible. After consultation with the local tribes, he reports, 'we decided to call the new administration the "National Government of Moab" and to form a Council of Elders who would, in fact, be the cabinet'. At the cabinet's insistence, Kirkbride himself was elected president; and so, aged 23, 'I became head of a more or less independent republic.'

Meanwhile Kirkbride's brother Alan, who was even younger, was playing a similar role in a neighbouring state based on Amman. By way of diplomatic intercourse the siblings bandied obscure biblical taunts, like 'Moab is my washpot'; and much time was spent snipping up small squares of paper which, gummed on one side and hand-printed with 'the National Seal' on the other, served as Moab's postage stamps. The fun lasted for nine months. Then Abdullah and his men disembarked from one of the Hijaz line's rare trains, Churchill decided that the incomers should stay put, and 'so the National Government of Moab passed away quite painlessly, as did the other autonomous administrations [in Trans-Jordan]'.[4]

Apart from a mutual antipathy which seemingly obliged the French and the British to do exactly the opposite of one another,

France's initial espousal of a united Syria had been designed to strengthen her chances of being awarded the mandate by deflecting the hostility of Syrian nationalists towards the Palestine-grabbing British. The mandate having been secured and the Syrians proving as implacable as ever, French policy changed. By April 1920 the idea of any accommodation with Syrian nationalism had been abandoned in favour of crushing it; and as well as the July assault on Faysal's Damascus, one obvious way of achieving this was by isolating the main centres of nationalist resistance through a policy of administrative fragmentation.

The first and only beneficiary of this disastrous initiative would be Lebanon. Yet the creation of this state had as much to do with the character and priorities of French colonial policy as with the challenge of Arab nationalism. For although to President Wilson British colonialism and French colonialism appeared equally acquisitive and so indistinguishable, the two countries in fact differed fundamentally in their attitudes to overseas empire and in the mechanics of colonial policy-making.

To the British their global empire was a source of immense pride which almost transcended purely national sentiment. The romance of empire had long since captured the popular imagination, and although the Liberal and Labour parties, when in opposition, criticized imperial ventures and condemned the expenditure involved, in government they hesitated to reverse them. Likewise Whitehall's warring departments might differ over the details of implementation, but they were nevertheless agreed that imperial policy belonged at the heart of government and that the support of the Royal Navy, the protection of the arteries of empire, and the upkeep of India and its army were indisputable priorities.

No such consensus existed in France; and here imperialism and colonialism were not interchangeable terms. Maréchal Lyautey might try to interest his countrymen in the British model with cries like 'Colonial empire, let's not be afraid of the words';[5] but to the French, empire had an essentially European context and, although projected further afield, was not supposed to prejudice France's essentially European interests. Her far-flung colonies, on the other hand, however exotic and romantically appealing, remained politically peripheral, economically irrelevant and primarily the concern of special interest groups like the Catholic Church, the armed forces and various cultural and commercial lobbies. Obviously these interests rejoiced when in Paris the sun of empire shone brightest. But they rarely basked in official favour for long and their pet interests could not be said to lie at the heart of government. London was the capital of a global empire, Paris just the capital of France, albeit a France some of whose would-be citizens happened to be stuck in the limbo of gallicization which was France Outremer.

The territories which comprised this 'Overseas France', often acquired through unauthorized initiatives and retained in the face of official indifference, were the poor relations of metropolitan France and commanded little popular attention. Indeed it has been argued that during this final phase of colonial expansion they eluded even official attention as 'French governments lost control of imperial policy-making even in their own capital'.[6] The initiative passed to the *parti colonial*, which was a term of convenience for several pressure groups of like-minded activists rather than a political organization. Also known as 'the dinner party', the colonial party's existence was most evident in the popularity of banquets organized by associations for the promotion of a particular colony or colonial product. That this *parti colonial* nevertheless managed to win support for policies like those pursued in Syria, and to control their direction, was largely thanks to the chronic fragility of France's inter-war governments. Between 1920 and 1940 the premiership alone changed hands thirty-three times.

Additionally, as of 1918, new overseas responsibilities were seen as some reward for wartime sacrifices and as evidence of the revival of France's international prestige. General Gouraud, the mutilated war hero resplendent with his Croix de Guerre at the head of a new French administration in the Levant, epitomized this spirit. The British might sneer at the idea of France benefiting from conquests and sacrifices in the Middle East that had been overwhelmingly their own (and India's, Australia's, and so on). But in Europe, France had borne more than her fair share of the tragedy in the trenches; and in the Middle East her military contingent, though minuscule, had invariably distinguished itself. The American William Yale was not alone in believing that, but for a good publicist and an unlimited supply of gold, it could well have been 'Brémond of Arabia' rather than Lawrence.[7]

Gouraud, Brémond and his successor in the Hijaz, Georges Catroux (who in 1920 became Gouraud's *délégué* in Damascus), had all previously served in North Africa and had there been much influenced by Maréchal Louis-Hubert Lyautey, incomparably the greatest of France's twentieth-century empire-builders. Lyautey's 1912 addition of Morocco to a colonial hand that already included Algeria and Tunisia had not only strengthened France's North African suit but also confirmed the Mediterranean littoral as the axis of France Outremer. And just as, to the British, considerations of Indian policy and especially the sensibilities of India's Muslims were important factors in their dealings with Muslims in the Middle East, so North Africa and its overwhelmingly Muslim population influenced French policy in the Levant. Syrian nationalism, when not perceived as an Anglo-Hashemite plot concocted to deny France her rights, was construed as fundamentally Islamic. Mention of *jihad* was taken much more seriously than in, say, Iraq; and, lest such *Arabo-Mussulmane* excitement spread west to her North African colonies, France felt obliged to take whatever measures were necessary for its prompt suppression in Syria.

Had it not been for French reticence back in the 1880s, Egypt might have been added to Paris's hand, thus completing a full house of North African colonies (save only Libya). But the French government of the day, which included a young Clemenceau, had declined to join the British in their Egyptian adventure and the opportunity had passed. Ever since, Egypt's abiding cultural and commercial ties with France had provided a reminder of what might have been. Latterly the resurrection of the same anti-colonial Clemenceau as chairman of the Paris peace conference threatened the awful prospect of history repeating itself. Fears about missing this second chance of extending French influence into the eastern Mediterranean had guided Georges-Picot's prickly relationship with Allenby and now loomed large in the thinking of his close associate in the *parti colonial*, Robert de Caix. With Gouraud a splendid mascot but a doubtful administrator, it was de Caix as his Secretary-General in the Levant, plus Catroux as his representative in Damascus, who would be principally responsible for formulating and implementing policy during the first years of the mandate.

In that the mandate mentioned both Syria and Lebanon, the separate existence of an entity called Lebanon, as of one called Palestine, was already presumed. In fact, ever since the 1860s the district of Mount Lebanon, an enclave of olive groves and stony terraces populated predominantly by Maronite Christians who looked to France as their protector, had enjoyed an autonomous status in direct subordination to Constantinople. This autonomy had been abolished by the Turks only in 1915, and its desired restitution in some form had brought a Lebanese delegation to the Paris peace conference in 1919.

Initially the idea of extending any recognition to Lebanon had not appealed to the Allies, despite Maronite eagerness to accept French tutelage. But when, after the British forces left Faysal in control in Damascus, it looked as if Syria was being partitioned anyway, the French attended more closely to Lebanese protestations and welcomed the opportunity to champion within geographical Syria a pro-French constituency to whom rule from Muslim-dominated Damascus was anathema.

The case for Mount Lebanon's autonomy, whether judged historically or in terms of the 'wishes of the community', was thus a strong one. For economic and administrative reasons it also made sense for the Mount to remain in some kind of federal arrangement with the rest of the Syria and under the same mandatory dispensation. But de Caix and others in the colonial party saw in the pro-French disposition of the Lebanese Maronites a much greater opportunity. Some Lebanese representatives were demanding autonomy not just for the few hundred square miles of Mount Lebanon but for the few thousand adjacent square miles of Syria which, they claimed, had once been under Lebanese rule and where Maronites and other Christian sects were still well represented. This 'Greater Lebanon' held a much stronger appeal for the French, who encouraged its supporters by indicating that they would grant autonomy only to a *Liban* which was *Grand* and not just the *Mont*.

Obviously *le Grand Liban* was a more viable economic and strategic proposition. As well as the Mount, it was deemed to include the largely Shi'ite Biqa' valley to the east, the largely Sunni district of Tripoli to the north, the roughly half-Muslim, half-Christian district of Tyre and Sidon to the south, and the similarly composed port-city of Beirut. It thus embraced over a hundred miles of prime Mediterranean coastline, plus an agriculturally rich hinterland about fifty miles deep. It was both the most desirable chunk of *Syrie intégrale* and, to any power with a navy, the most readily defensible. As Catroux would put it, Greater Lebanon was conceived by the

French as a redoubt and 'erected into a solid rampart of our establishment in the Levant'.[8] Similarly, the creation of a state pandering to Alawi separatism in Jabal Ansariya (Alawis, or Nussayris, adhered to a variant form of Islam) was designed to continue this rampart to the north. Beirut became Gouraud's headquarters and the administrative capital of the entire French mandate. And whatever happened in the Syrian interior, French domination of the Levantine littoral was assured. Another card was thus added to Paris's Mediterranean hand.

Even the mathematics of the new Greater Lebanon had a certain logic which, though perverse in principle and of disastrous significance for the state's future, was congenial enough to the mandatory. For as a result of this expansion of Lebanon, the Maronites no longer enjoyed an absolute majority. The French could not therefore be accused of exclusively favouring fellow-Christians when they created the new state. By the same token, the Maronites were now even more dependent on French protection and amenable to French direction. Better still from a French point of view, since the Maronites would be obliged to share whatever power was on offer with Muslims and other Christians, these too would acquire a stake in Lebanon's statehood and especially in the offices and emoluments that it provided.

On the other hand, in the confessional Babel of *Grand Liban* (Albert Hourani, citing a 1932 census, lists ten Christian sects and five Muslim)[9] the Maronites (numbering 226,000) were still the largest single community. When pushed into an alliance with the other Christian sects (totalling 166,000), they could still deliver a majority that just exceeded the total number of Muslims (383,000). *Grand Liban* could therefore be counted on to continue resisting Damascus's demands for the country's reincorporation into a united and predominantly Muslim Syria.

Such then was the new Lebanon as prefigured in the mandate and eagerly espoused by the mandatory. It became a reality in August 1920, six weeks after Khan Maysalun and the French capture of Damascus. Gouraud published the necessary decree; it was endorsed by a Lebanese assembly; and the new state duly accepted the French mandate. Damascus was not consulted. Syrian and Arab nationalists did object but, dispersed to Palestine and Egypt following the fall of Damascus, they were easily ignored.

Stifling Syria

Two months later, similar decrees were issued in respect of the — new states of Damascus and Aleppo, with Jabal Druze and Jabal Ansariya following in 1921–2. To these dispositions there was some internal resistance but none of it very effective. In the Aleppo countryside, groups opposed to the French represented Turkish interests as much as Arab; they were heavily dependent on Kemalist support, and lost ground as soon as this was removed.

Damascus remained quiet until 1922. Then protests and demonstrations flared during a follow-up visit by the American Charles Crane, once of the King-Crane Commission. The visit took place at a time when the Mandates Commission in Geneva was doubtful whether France's fragmentation of Syria had popular support and — when expatriate Syrians, especially in America, were insisting that it definitely did not. Crane's visit, though, was unofficial. He had come at the request of a grouping of Syrian nationalists known as the 'Iron Hand' and was the guest of their leader, Dr Abd al-Rahman Shahbandar; and it was Shahbandar, foreign minister during Faysal's short-lived rule in Damascus, who was the principal casualty of the crack-down that followed Crane's departure. Found with a cheque from the American for £1,000 on his person, he was put on trial and sentenced to 20 years' detention in an offshore penal colony. Already hailed as the 'Zaghlul of Syria', he, like Zaghlul, was not destined to serve his full term.[10]

Georges Catroux, Gouraud's delegate in Damascus, deemed this affair 'localized' and 'feeble'; yet he took it as a warning that the main threat to French security was to be expected from outside Syria. Two months later his suspicions were confirmed when Gouraud himself became the target of an assassination squad from Transjordania.[11] For the genial Catroux, this was a much more serious *incident*. A dapper colonel with a neatly trimmed moustache, Catroux worshipped God, Gouraud and France – in that order. The battle-scarred Gouraud was his ideal, his patron, *le grand colonial* and the epitome of a God-fearing patriot. That this sacred person should be nearly assassinated while under his, Catroux's, protection was an almost unbearable shame.

The ambush had occurred during a visit to Qunaytra in the Hauran, south-east of Damascus. Catroux had arranged a convoy of cars, the first of which, an open-topped sedan with three rows of seats, flew the High Commissioner's flag. The assassins, therefore, had no difficulty in identifying the vehicle. But, as it approached, they wrongly assumed that Gouraud must be the French officer sitting in the front beside the driver. In fact this was an Arabic-speaking lieutenant who was there as interpreter; he was hit several times and died immediately. Catroux, behind him, was unscathed; and behind Catroux, Haqqi al-Azm, the French-appointed Governor of Damascus, was only slightly wounded. General Gouraud, sitting beside al-Azm, was hit three times. The bullets all tore into the right sleeve of his uniform. But Catroux, in telling the story, was so out-raged by this sacrilege that he forgot to explain that the General felt nothing, his right arm being the one that had been blown away at Gallipoli.[12] Rarely can an amputee have been so grateful for his disability.

As would happen after General Stack's assassination in Cairo in 1924, a protracted witch-hunt of the culprits ensued. Since the plot had clearly originated among Syrian exiles in British-mandated Transjordania, there was, according to *The Times* correspondent, 'considerable and very natural Anglophobe criticism both in French Syria and France'.[13] Amir Abdullah's expressed ignorance of the affair was probably genuine; but the results of an investigation by Philby, the new British representative in Amman, did not reassure the French. Of the names on their list of suspects, Philby reported, several were women or children, some had been dead for years, and the rest were not and never had been in Transjordania.[14] Flying in the face of much evidence to the contrary, such breezy denials merely heightened the rancour. The French would continue to regard Transjordania as *un foyer d'intrigues et d'enterprises* directed at their man-dated territories. And according to Catroux, this policy of cross-border interference accorded with the subversive but undeclared agenda of the British government.[15]

HEEDLESS ENTHUSIASM

Catroux, while loth to criticize Gouraud in any way, claims to have had reservations about the fragmentation of Syria. He accepted the logic of 'divide and rule' and loyally implemented the policy in respect of the Damascus state and the neighbouring Jabal Druze. But he also appreciated the hostility that it provoked, and he

Stifling Syria

reported as much. He was therefore gratified when in 1922 Gouraud and de Caix came up with a scheme of Syrian federation.

This linked only the states of Damascus, Aleppo and Jabal Ansariya, whose recently established representative councils were invited to send delegations to a federal assembly. But their separate existence as autonomous states was not abolished; in fact it was the new Federation that went first. In late 1924, after only two years, it was dissolved by Gouraud's successor, General Weygand, in favour of a full union of the Damascus and Aleppo states. These two now became the unitary state of 'Syria' with Damascus as its capital. Meanwhile Jabal Ansariya reverted to separate status; Greater Lebanon and the Jabal Druze remained separate; and the northern district around Alexandretta, whose international status was still disputed by Turkey, comprised another de facto state. In 1925, when this whole confection blew up in her face, France's mandated territory was still divided five ways.

Fragmented or federated, and perpetually in transition, Syria was being governed to distraction. Catroux claims to have been mindful of the example of Cromer who 'with a few high officials and a modest title' had directed Egyptian affairs 'discreetly and effectively'.[16] Gouraud and Weygand looked more to Lyautey's model in Morocco which, like that adopted in Nigeria by Sir Frederick Lugard (himself now a member of the Mandates Commission in Geneva), espoused indirect rule through indigenous institutions under loose colonial supervision. In each case, the attraction was that ruling through others meant a minimum of intervention and expense. Yet in Syria and Lebanon the reality proved quite otherwise: intervention was pervasive, the expense excessive.

The Levant, in truth, was a very different proposition from these African models. Ottoman weakness, Turkish repression and Arab revival had generated organizational skills, political sophistication and close links between the cities and the countryside. Faysal's nearly two years in Damascus, while whetting the appetites of the land-owning élite for office, had also roused the religious and commercial classes and politicized the souks and the suburbs. By any standard, Syria did indeed belong among those 'communities' (as the League's Covenant had put it) whose 'existence as independent nations [could] be provisionally recognized'. On the other hand, colonial control, howsoever represented in the mandate, could only be seen as retrograde, destructive and insulting.

1918–1936

The exercise of the mandate thus posed a greater challenge than in, say, Iraq, and severely taxed French ingenuity. The creation of communal statelets did initially siphon off some resistance and make containment more feasible. But as well as aggravating pan-Syrian resentment, this fragmentation created its own problems. For the individual packaging of so many mini-states meant administrative duplication, indeed quintuplication. Equipping each state with the *délégués*, *fonctionnaires* and *conseillers techniques* reckoned essential for effective French control, and providing a network of advisers and informants at local level, resulted in an enormous bureaucratic burden which France, lacking a high-powered colonial élite, could ill provide, and which Syria/Lebanon, devastated by war and famine, could ill afford.

Other colonial initiatives were also counter-productive. Land reforms designed to reduce the political influence of the great land-owning families and to free arable ground for cash crops, like cotton, necessitated cadastral surveys whose expense outweighed the questionable social benefits of the reforms. The Syrian pound, now tied to the French franc, plummeted in value, local industries languished, popular national assets (like the Syrian section of the Hijaz railway) passed into French hands, and traditional trade links (like those between Aleppo and Anatolia) were severed by the regional carve-up.

In education, communications and public works the advantages of French rule were no easier to discern. Yet Syrians might still have been reconciled to the mandate had France been more obviously committed to the mandatory's main function – that of advising and assisting in the creation of all that pertained to an independent Syria. Various councils and assemblies were indeed set up, their members either nominated or indirectly elected. But neither legislative nor executive power was actually conceded to them. All decisions were made by the High Commissioner or his *délégués*, all implementation required the authorization of the appropriate *conseillers*. Catroux's notion of the mandate as a dynamic exercise in 'Franco-Syrian co-operation' which, predominantly 'Franco' at first, would become progressively more 'Syrian' in time, was never elaborated into a staged transfer of responsibilities, nor was it given a timetable. Yet without such evidence of good faith it carried no conviction. Moreover such 'co-operation' was consonant with the mandate only if that was what the Syrians desired. But clearly they did not.

druze

Stifling Syria

Rather did they look elsewhere and cite with approval the sovereignty, self-rule and freedom of political expression on offer in Iraq and Egypt. Their own situation was barely comparable. In early 1924 Dr Shahbandar, though now released, was still in exile; so were many of his fellow-nationalists. Martial law was in force. The country was still partitioned. And progress towards independence was imperceptible.

All this, plus worsening economic hardship, provided a powerful stimulus to armed resistance. Like Iraq in the summer of 1920, Syria in the summer of 1925 was poised to rise against the mandatory in spectacular fashion. To nationalist historians, this 'Great Revolt' would be the touchstone of Syrian nationalism and the turning-point in her struggle for freedom. Yet here, as in Iraq, the uprising had an irritatingly fortuitous origin in which Syrian nationalism played no great part. For it began not among the politicized classes in the cities but among the much-disparaged Druze, a marginal and dissenting community generally reckoned among the most feudalized and backward in the country.

The Druze numbered about 130,000. Two-thirds inhabited the black sierras of the Jabal Druze, a desert massif on the border with Transjordania, which thus constituted a distinct ethnic and geographical entity; others lived in the neighbouring Hauran and in Lebanon. Their esoteric beliefs, although as impenetrable and closely guarded as their mountain fastnesses, had long intrigued scholars and were generally taken as a deviant form of Islam. Organized into clans under the hereditary leadership of one or two powerful families, their factionalism was also notorious; and so was their military prowess. Ottoman rule had respected both and refrained from unnecessary interference in the Jabal. But some Druze had joined the Arab Revolt and participated in Faysal's nationalist government. Subsequently the task of persuading them to accept France's mandatory tutelage had fallen to Catroux, who took considerable pride in engineering a settlement acceptable to most, albeit at the expense of separate statehood, considerable autonomy, the alienation of a branch of the all-powerful al-Atrash family, and 'several hundred thousand gold francs'.[17]

Catroux's pacification held good until July 1922. Then the arrest in Druze territory of one of the suspects in the Gouraud assassination attempt provoked the already disaffected Sultan al-Atrash to stage a retaliatory ambush of the convoy that was escorting the prisoner to justice. The French responded by bombing Sultan's home; and for the next nine months, as Sultan al-Atrash flitted between the Jabal and neighbouring Transjordania, his followers kept up a desultory guerrilla war.

In the midst of this affair there arrived as the French High Commissioner's representative in Jabal Druze a Captain Gabriel Carbillet. Young and of limited experience, all of it in the *brousse* of West Africa, Captain Carbillet saw the Jabal Druze as an exceptional career opportunity and quickly made his mark. In July 1923, with the feuding al-Atrash family unable to agree on a governor for the state, Carbillet himself accepted the appointment and thus, like Alex Kirkbride in Moab, became 'the head of a more or less independent republic'. This was contrary to Catroux's settlement, which stated that only a Druze could be governor, and a decidedly backward step in terms of the mandate. But it seemed to be what the Druze patriarchs wanted, and Captain Carbillet, afire with good intentions, rose heroically to the occasion.

A British officer who met Carbillet in 1925 described him as 'a rugged-looking individual with a long unkempt beard'; indeed, after two years in the Jabal, he had 'become almost a Druze himself'.[18] Doubtless the hirsute Captain knew of 'Lawrence of Arabia' and sought a Gallic equivalence as 'Carbillet of the Druze'. But if Lawrence provided the romantic inspiration, it was A.T. Wilson whom, for energy, enterprise and unswerving conviction, Carbillet more obviously resembled. Thanks to his industry, the basalt-strewn slopes of the Druze mountains were soon echoing to the thump of picks and the grating of shovels as irrigation channels and motor roads were carved through the country. The streets of Suwayda, the capital, were paved, schools were built, public sanitation improved. Carbillet's zeal was unstoppable. He reformed the judicial system, set up a court of appeals, tackled feudal land holdings by offering property rights to the peasantry, held elections and founded Suwayda's still extant museum.

The museum was not a complete irrelevance. Antiquities had been awarded a high priority in the mandate, the longest of whose twenty often imprecise articles dealt with the subject in excruciating detail. While Carbillet scoured his mountains for Roman treasures, Bell was founding Baghdad's great treasure-house of Mesopotamian artefacts.

Stifling Syria

But if, as she claims, the Iraqis were decidedly cool towards their pre-Islamic heritage, then the Druze were positively indifferent. Providing desirable accommodation for redundant statuary seemed to them as perverse as building motor roads in a country without motors. As Stephen Longrigg, a historian and contemporary, nicely puts it, 'that such a programme, carried out with heedless enthusiasm, must bewilder rather than please the inhabitants . . . was little appreciated'.[19]

Bewildered and ungrateful, the Druze were also growing angry. Carbillet's public works required peasant labour, most of it forced. And the landowning families were being taxed as never before just when their influence was being eroded by the land reforms. Yet the Captain, with that blinkered ardour of the heavily bearded, pushed on regardless. Autocratic and dictatorial, he brooked no protest. Druze participation in his great experiment dwindled to a surly compliance as 'arbitrary and even capricious' punishments were meted out for the pettiest offences. The reputation of the Jabal as the great success story of the French mandate was being won at a price that was not acceptable to any section of Druze society.

In May 1925 Carbillet came down from his mountains for some well-earned leave. The Druze patriarchs, for once pooling their grievances, had just sent a delegation to protest to the new High Commissioner in Beirut; it barely secured a hearing and was sent home with an unequivocal endorsement of young Carbillet ringing in its ears. But the Captain's leave opened the way for some discreet enquiries; and his temporary replacement duly reported new stirrings by the implacable Sultan al-Atrash, widespread disquiet and the possibility of imminent revolt. So did a second investigation, the report of the first having been deemed unsatisfactory. Whether the High Commissioner then acted on these warnings, or whether he acted despite them, is unclear. But his next meeting with three al-Atrash chiefs in Damascus in July turned out to be a trap. Invited to dinner, the three were summarily arrested, thereby uniting the rest of the clan and further antagonizing the Druze nation. Within a week the now all-powerful Sultan al-Atrash raised the standard of revolt. Aircraft buzzing the mountains were fired on; a detachment of French colonial troops was ambushed; and the French garrison in Suwayda was besieged.

The 'heedless enthusiasm' of Carbillet was now being eclipsed by the chronic ineptitude of the new High Commissioner. This was

General Maurice Sarrail, who had just succeeded the more accommodating General Maxime Weygand. Sarrail, a cantankerous septuagenarian whose impeccably secularist credentials had blinded France's new leftist ministry to his failings of judgement and temper, had already managed to alienate France's strongest constituency, the Lebanese Maronites. He now capped this by encouraging her strongest opponent, the formidable Dr Shahbandar.

Allowed to return to Damascus in 1924, Shahbandar organized a new People's Party which was soon clamouring for the reintegration of geographical Syria. It sent delegates to Geneva to protest against any constitutional settlement that recognized the French carve-up of the country; and in April a spectacularly inappropriate visit to Damascus by the now Lord Balfour (of Britain's eponymous Declaration) reminded Syrians of Palestine's forced defection and rekindled their opposition to Zionism. Outside Damascus's great Umayyad mosque crowds fought with gendarmes, as Balfour was whisked away under military escort to Beirut and safety. Incredibly, it seems that the French authorities indulged this protest, believing it more embarrassing to the British than subversive of their own authority.

THE GREAT REVOLT

Whether, after the anti-Carbillet rising, Dr Shahbandar and the nationalists would make common cause with Sultan al-Atrash and his Druze remained unclear. But it became highly likely when on the night of 2 August a French column, 3,000 strong, wound its way into the Jabal Druze *en route* to the relief of Suwayda and there was smartly surprised and overwhelmed by Sultan al-Atrash's mounted cohorts. French losses were put as high as 800, although the actual fatalities came to less than fifty and few of those were French by birth. Morale, not firepower, was the decisive factor. A Madagascan contingent fled *en masse*, provoking its French colonel to suicide; and the numerous Syrian levies, most of whom were in fact recruits from Syria's refugee communities of Armenians and Circassians, simply melted into the night. It was nevertheless a signal defeat, eloquent alike of French military weakness after recent troop reductions and of the Druze's ability to mount a concerted action. General Roger

Michaud, who commanded the column, promptly resigned; Sultan al-Atrash, with 2,000 captured rifles to distribute, augmented his forces.

When news of this engagement reached Damascus, Shahbandar's People's Party went into closed session. Two weeks later contact was made with Sultan al-Atrash and an agreement emerged whereby Damascus would rise against the French if and when the Druze forces reached it. They attempted to do so in late August but were held back five miles from the city. Simultaneously the French moved against the nationalist leadership, apprehending some and dispersing others; Shahbandar was one of those who escaped to the Jabal Druze. The city was thus deprived of popular leadership on the eve of the revolt. It did not immediately recover, but the revolt prospered without it.

From the Jabal Druze waves of defiance radiated outwards across the Hauran, around Damascus and Mount Hermon, and on to the Lebanon and Aleppo. Bands of marauding Druze were joined by Bedouin tribesmen, fleeing townsfolk and starving peasants. Some fought for gain, others for political freedom, many just for survival, and most, perhaps, for a combination of all three. As in 1920 in Iraq, it was a national uprising in so far as much of the country was at some point affected, with road and railway communications interrupted, administration at a standstill, and large tracts of countryside deemed unsafe. It was equally a nationalist rising to the extent that the Druze and the People's Party proclaimed a Syrian national government, fought under the flag of Faysal's ex-kingdom, and adopted a programme that called for Syrian unity, independence and liberation from French rule.

The French response, like that of the British in Iraq in 1920, relied heavily on air strikes until reinforcements could arrive. Suwayda, though relieved in September, was soon abandoned again, and the Jabal remained under Druze control until well into 1926. Elsewhere the military crackdown lasted into the following year, much longer than in Iraq, although this was partly because of the doubtful quality of the available colonial troops. The brutality of the Armenian and Circassian mercenaries in France's Syrian Legion would be long remembered and, inflated by desertions, French losses were heavy. Syrian casualties, much heavier, probably fell short of the 10,000 fatalities recorded in Iraq.

— damascus bombed

Yet Syria's 'Great Revolt' acquired a much greater notoriety. It made the headlines of the world's press, brought widespread condemnation of France's repressive tactics, provoked much heart-searching in Paris, and alarmed the Permanent Mandates Commission in Geneva. For in the closer confines of the Levant the insurgents soon threatened the main population centres, thus provoking draconian and very public reprisals; and they gained a foothold in at least two major cities.

The first was Hama, 300 miles north of Damascus. On 4 October 1925 Fawzi al-Qawuqji, an officer of Turcoman extraction who had served many masters including the Ottoman Sultan, Faysal's Arab Revolt and now France's Syrian Legion, defected yet again and led his men, plus some local Bedouin, in a takeover of Syria's fourth largest city. Qawuqji's rising had been orchestrated with the Druze and the nationalist leadership, although they took no direct part in it. Administrative and other buildings associated with French rule were sacked; and many of Hama's residents, including its conservative religious establishment, supported the insurgents. But the occupation had lasted only two days when, heavily bombed from the air, the devastated city was recaptured by French reinforcements from Aleppo. Qawuqji escaped. He continued to defy the French in and around the city for another eighteen months and eventually found sanctuary in Iraq. Thence he would ride again, to considerable effect, at the head of the 1936–9 Arab Revolt in Palestine and, after another ten-year interval, as commander of the Syrian-based Palestine Liberation (or Salvation) Army in the 1947–8 war that marked the birth of Israel.

Hama's stand, though fleeting, was not in vain. Two weeks later, on 18 October, Damascus itself at last erupted. The pattern of events was similar, with insurgent forces (Druze, nationalist and Bedouin) being welcomed by disaffected elements in the city, gaining control of several quarters, and singling out for attack the symbols of French rule and the properties of collaborationist families. The French response also ran dismally true to form with a massive bombardment by tanks, artillery and aircraft. It lasted 42 hours; and this being as crowded a city as any in the Middle East, the damage was extensive, the casualties high, and the victims almost entirely civilian. An official French estimate gave 150 fatalities; one provided by the Damascus Municipality gave nearly 1,500.[20]

Foreign observers, including the city's small diplomatic contingent, were horrified. That what was reputedly the world's oldest city could be indiscriminately bombed and shelled in the name of one of the world's most civilized peoples simply beggared belief. In the heat of the First World War, Baghdad, Jerusalem and Damascus itself had all changed hands with no more than occasional rifle fire within their revered precincts. Yet here, outwith the sanction of war, the champions of liberty, equality and fraternity were dealing death to the innocent and destruction to the hallowed on a battlefield scale, while supposedly discharging a sacred trust on behalf of the League of Nations and operating within the consensual constraints of one of its mandates.

Apart from evacuating French troops from the target areas and alerting French residents, no warning of the shelling of Damascus seems to have been given and no declaration of martial law made. Sarrail claimed that only immediate bombardment would clear the bazaars of insurgents, put a stop to the widespread looting, and reassure the city's Christian and Jewish minorities. This it did, but only to the extent that the insurgents, their ranks now swelled by homeless Damascenes, repaired to the city's outlying districts and to the cover of its extensive hinterland of orchards and gardens. Thence for the next six months, through the chill of winter and until the harvesting of the apricots, armed raids on the southern Maydan area of the city were carried out. Despite frequent patrols and the ring-fencing of the central districts with barbed wire, it took further French bombardments in February and May 1926 to clear this area. From adjacent villages the insurgents were only flushed during the following summer after a long war of attrition among the fruit trees. Further afield, resistance continued well into 1927.

By then General Sarrail had departed and new political initiatives were afoot. The General's supposed presence in Damascus had prompted the insurgents to make an early attack on his residence, and this may have panicked him. He had clearly misread the situation throughout, under-reacting in the Jabal Druze and then over-reacting outside it. Prised from the protection of his leftist supporters in France, he had been recalled in disgrace in November 1925. The man who replaced him as Syria/Lebanon's High Commissioner was for the first time a civilian. Forceful methods having evidently failed, France was about to try negotiation.

THE TREATY THAT NEVER WAS

Henri de Jouvenel, a newspaper editor and politician, enjoyed the respect of the Mandates Commission and looked to be a conciliatory choice as the new High Commissioner. He quickly lived up to his liberal credentials in respect of Lebanon, if not Syria. Short-circuiting the laborious process of electing a constituent assembly, he empowered the existing Representative Council to act as such and to draw up Lebanon's first constitution. Its text may actually have been drafted in Paris rather than Beirut, but with the Maronites and other Christians anxiously closing ranks in the face of Druze incursions, it was adopted with little modification. On 24 May 1926 the Lebanese Republic was proclaimed.

The timing conformed with the mandate, which called for 'an organic law' to be framed within three years of the mandate's becoming operative in 1923. But the terms scarcely conformed with its directive to 'take into account the rights, interests and wishes of all the population inhabiting the said territory'. In so far as they could be established, the wishes of Lebanon's Muslims, nearly half the population, were against any Lebanese constitution and in favour of the country reverting to Syria. Although their rights and interests were to be protected under a system of communal representation, this was little consolation to those who opposed the whole concept of *Grand Liban* and deplored alienation from Greater Syria, both of which principles were enshrined and legalized in the new constitution. Protests were made, but the publications that carried them were closed down and the protesters arrested.

Nor, of course, was the new Lebanese constitution, either as adopted in 1926 or as revised in 1927, that of a sovereign independent state. The mandate remained. Foreign relations continued to be a French prerogative, as did relations with the other Syrian states; France reserved the right to dissolve parliament and veto its legislation; French troops were to remain on Lebanese soil; and the mandatory retained a large measure of control over the economy by reserving to itself *les intérêts communs*. These 'interests' embraced subjects 'common' to the whole Levant and not easily apportioned between its constituent states, such as the railways, the postal service and, especially, the customs and excise duties that constituted the main source of revenue. Political fragmentation was thus revealed as

- continued struggle for independence
- fractured Syrian leadership

providing an excellent pretext for continued French supervision. In effect, 'dividing' not only facilitated 'ruling': it necessitated it.

The Lebanon settlement, presented to the anxious Mandates Commission by de Jouvenel in person, did reassure that body. But it cut no ice with still insurgent nationalists in Syria. In talks with various bodies claiming to represent nationalist opinion, de Jouvenel and (following his 1926 resignation) his successor Henri Ponsot therefore dangled the prospect of constitutional progress in 'Syria' (that is, the Aleppo-Damascus state) similar to that in Lebanon.

In the course of these discussions, there emerged the idea of a Franco-Syrian treaty. Modelled on the hotly disputed Anglo-Egyptian and Anglo-Iraqi treaties, such an agreement would, it was hoped, gratify nationalist aspirations by recognizing Syrian 'independence' while also affirming and endorsing the rights reserved to France that might undermine that 'independence'. But, although there were Syrians willing to explore these ideas, nationalists who had fled the country or were still under arms continued to demand complete French withdrawal, a reunification of geographical Syria including all or most of Lebanon, a blanket amnesty, a national army and all else that pertained to full and genuine independence.

Ponsot, the new High Commissioner, had a Quai d'Orsay background and approached this apparent deadlock with diplomatic circumspection. Events favoured such temporizing. During late 1926 and early 1927 the last embers of the Great Revolt were being snuffed out. The pacified Jabal Druze was receding into its wonted isolation; a provisional government in Damascus was attempting, under close French supervision, to muster some moderate support; and the task of reconstruction could begin.

At the same time, a split opened up in the ranks of the exiled Syrian nationalist leadership, now located mainly in Cairo. As well as playing into the hands of the French, this split is significant in that it anticipated some of the divisions that would bedevil Arab policy-making for the rest of the century. The battle lines were not clearly drawn and, as with later nationalist leaderships in exile (including that of the Palestinians), they thrived on personal vendettas and quarrels over funding. But ideological differences over the centrality, or otherwise, of Islam in the freedom struggle were well represented, as were political divergencies between those Arabs who looked for support to the Turks and Ibn Saud and those, on the other hand, who respected the claims of the Hashemites and their British sponsors.

Differences relating specifically to geographical Syria revolved around the attitude to be taken to Lebanese aspirations and the priority to be given to reclaiming Palestine. Thus while one faction, which included Dr Shahbandar and his People's Party, was essentially secular and favoured co-operation with the Hashemites, good relations with the British, concessions to Lebanese autonomy and minimal involvement with Palestinian grievances, the other emphasized its Islamic credentials, shunned non-Islamic collaborators and took a less compromising position on Lebanon and Palestine.[21]

Ponsot and his advisers, including Catroux who had briefly returned to the Levant, skilfully exploited this split by fanning mutual jealousies to discredit both factions. Meanwhile some leaders were permitted to return to Syria, thus isolating and marginalizing those, like Shahbandar and Sultan al-Atrash, whom the French still considered beyond accommodation. The returnees made common cause with those nationalists who had remained in Syria; and together they set the pace of nationalist politics during the early 1930s as what became known as the National Bloc. This was a broad-based front like the Egyptian Wafd which, while continuing to pursue independence for a reintegrated Syria, was prepared to do so through negotiation with a French administration supposedly chastened and more conciliatory as a result of the revolt. From a Syrian point of view, instant independence through armed insurrection was clearly no longer a possibility. The National Bloc adopted a more pragmatic approach, working within the constraints of the mandate while seizing on the idea of electing a constituent assembly and of negotiating a Franco-Syrian treaty as possible stepping-stones on the path to reintegration and independence.

The path would prove long and confusing with many a cul-de-sac. Elections were held in April 1928 and, despite much massaging by the French and their allies, returned a constituent assembly in which the emerging National Bloc was well represented and better organized than any of its rivals. When the assembly duly drew up a constitution that affirmed the integrity of geographical Syria (including Palestine, Lebanon and the two Jabals) and also insisted on a national army and control of foreign affairs, Paris was horrified. Portraying acceptance as tantamount to handing France's hard-won triumph in the revolt to the insurgents, the colonial lobbies prevailed on the Quai d'Orsay and Ponsot to suspend and then prorogue the assembly.

That was in 1929. Demonstrations and strikes ensued. A year later Ponsot unilaterally imposed a constitution of his own, devoid of the contentious clauses in the assembly's draft. Similar settlements were made in the two Jabals, which remained distinct states. Needless to say, the new constitution found no favour in nationalist circles and prompted further protests and strikes. Its only redeeming feature was that it was not to come into operation until elections could be held for the Chamber of Deputies (or parliament) that it envisaged. It also seemed to leave open the possibility that French rights and reservations might be sidelined, as in Egypt, for separate negotiation in the projected Franco-Syrian treaty.

In the 1930s, for nationalists in Syria, as in Egypt, the treaty and the acceptability or otherwise of its terms came to overshadow the question of the constitution. Elections to the new parliament went ahead in 1932, not without violence and postponements. The National Bloc continued to make the running although it just failed to win a majority. Its consequent indifference to the new chamber turned to boycott when it emerged that the terms of the proposed Franco-Syrian treaty were to apply only to the current state of Syria. In other words, Lebanon, Jabal Druze and Jabal Ansariya were to remain parts of a mandatory regime, and only the truncated Syria (once the Aleppo and Damascus states) was to have a treaty regime. In effect the treaty, like the Lebanese and Syrian constitutions, would uphold the fragmentation of the country; and this being unacceptable even to moderate opinion, it stood no chance of acceptance. Amid more tumult and surrounded by troops, the new parliament, like the constituent assembly before it, was prorogued in 1933.

An uneasy lull ensued. Despite a decade of mandatory tutelage, Syria looked to be no nearer its promised independence. With a configuration that was unacceptable, a constitution that was imposed and a parliament that was suspended, its progress seemed to be stalled amid institutional mirages. It was especially galling because at the time, in Geneva, a sovereign Iraq was taking its seat in the League of Nations and, in Cairo, Egypt was finally addressing the treaty that would dot the 'i' and cross the 't' of its own 'independent' status.

Yet in 1936, influenced by Egypt's decision, a Franco-Syrian treaty was actually signed. In fact there were two treaties, the other being Franco-Lebanese; and very promising they looked. A general strike and another burst of riots and arrests in Damascus had just threatened a second revolt. To forestall it, a Syrian delegation was invited to Paris with the promise of a more acceptable treaty; and by chance the ensuing talks happened to coincide with an election in France that brought to power Léon Blum's Socialist-Communist coalition, the Popular Front.

Suddenly France's colonial party found itself without friends in government, and the Syrians found French intransigence crumbling. A treaty similar to that concluded by the British with Iraq was quickly signed. It foresaw Syria's admission to the League of Nations within three years and, crucially, conceded arrangements for the incorporation of Jabal Druze and Jabal Ansariya into the Syrian state. The parallel Lebanese treaty pre-empted the possibility of that country's incorporation into Syria or of the renegotiation of its boundaries. But this apart, Syria's nationalists seemed finally to have triumphed. The Syrian delegation returned to a rapturous reception in Aleppo and Damascus; and in the November elections the National Bloc was swept to power. A month later Syria's first nationalist government unanimously ratified the treaty. Bedecked with the national flag, the mirage looked at last to have substance.

But appearances were deceptive, for no such ratification was forthcoming from Paris. The treaty was indeed just another *trompe l'œil*, another glimpse of what might have been. France's Popular Front government lasted only a year, during which time it never enjoyed sufficient support to risk submitting the treaty to parliament. Blum was then succeeded by Edouard Baladier, a Radical Socialist, whose party was neither radical nor socialist. On the contrary, it aspired 'to defend [France's] endangered colonial empire, the security of French territory, [and] French communications in the eastern Mediterranean'.[22] Ratifying a treaty that would diminish such things was out of the question.

The colonial party, with its various vested interests in the Levant, had triumphed again. Moreover it now enjoyed the support of military strategists suddenly exercised about the French position throughout the Mediterranean. The threat of a new war with Germany had helped to expedite the Anglo-Egyptian treaty.

The same threat effectively aborted its Franco-Syrian equivalent. Seemingly France had learnt little from its nearly two decades in the Levant. Syria would face the approaching conflict in that condition of chronic disarray for which French policy was largely responsible.

9

Stranger than History

SPRINGTIME IN PALESTINE

IN THE INTER-WAR years, while Egyptians, Iraqis and Syrians chal-lenged colonial rule and approached its obstacle course of consti-tutions and treaties with an increasingly confident stride, it was otherwise with the people of Palestine. Uniquely among ex-subjects of the Ottoman empire, they were seen as less deserving of consid-eration than the landscape in which they lived; indeed they were reckoned almost incidental to it. Zionists can be criticized for por-traying Palestine as a wilderness awaiting settlement, as 'a land without people for a people without land'. But this conceit was not peculiar to Zionism; it was also shared to some degree by all those of European descent and Christian upbringing; and it was from the tilth of this alien consensus, so objectionable to Arabs and congenial to Zionists, that the seeds of future conflict would greenly sprout.

The Balfour Declaration had assumed that, although Palestine did indeed have existing inhabitants, they possessed only 'civil and reli-gious rights'. In 1918 'Commander' Hogarth, supported by Curzon, had hastened to reassure the Hashemites that this wording did not preclude 'the political and economic freedom of the Arab people' as per previous British commitments. But the League of Nations mandate would ignore this gloss and adopt exactly the same wording as the Declaration. By implication the 90 per cent of Palestine's

*— non-Jews had no
national identity*

population who were not Jewish therefore possessed no national
identity and no political rights. Neither alone nor as part of some
other existing entity were they reckoned a putative nation.

Accordingly the Palestine mandate, unlike those for Iraq and
Syria/Lebanon, made no provision for an 'organic' (that is, constitutional) law and no mention of any 'measures to facilitate the progressive development of an independent state'. The overwhelming
majority of Palestinians were acknowledged only as 'existing non-
Jewish communities', a perverse phrasing that ignored their shared
past, their common language and their predominant faith while
implying confessional deviancy and a lack of social cohesion.

Palestine, regardless of its proximity to the Suez Canal, whatever
its mandatory status, and with or without Zionism, was a place apart.
Filastin to the Arabs and Israel to the Jews, it was to most Christians
not a country at all but an imagined landscape. A sliver of sacred
geography, a cradle of history, a source of literary allusion and an
article of faith, it was pre-eminently a Land (with a capital L) so Holy
(with a capital H) that in respect of its inhabitants the norms of
nationality and government need not apply.

Describing it as 'an Arab province no larger than Wales' was like
calling the Koh-i-Nur diamond 'a piece of crystallised carbon about
the size of a pigeon's egg', according to Philip Graves, Palestine correspondent of the London *Times*. Such a description, though scientifically correct, was 'essentially false and barren' because it entirely
missed the point.[1] Palestine was no more just an Arab province than
the diamond was just a shiny stone. It could 'never be regarded as a
country on the same footing as the other Arab countries', insisted
Lord Milner, because 'you cannot ignore all history and tradition in
the matter . . . [or] the fact that this is the cradle of two of the great
religions of the world'.[2]

School atlases awarded it a page to itself; the preferred colour
was pale yellow, and most of the place-names were printed in gothic
script and did not correspond well to the current topography. Nor
did it have any definite borders. In legislating for such hallowed
ground, it was understood that account must be taken of such
things as antiquarian concern, biblical sentiment, devotional traditions and international opinion. Anomalies and contradictions
would inevitably arise in its administration, regardless of the expectations of its existing inhabitants or of what Graves, echoing Lloyd

George, called the 'daring and romantic experiment' of Zionist settlement.

'Palestine, as you know, is full of uncertainties,' confirmed Sir Henry Gurney two decades later when British rule was drawing to a chaotic close. 'The first thing you have to do here in Jerusalem is to find out in which particular century anyone else is living.' He was writing to a friend and the year was 1947, 'but the Jews are in 5707 and the Arabs have it that it's 1366'. When recently a witness had appeared before the United Nations Special Commission on Palestine (UNSCOP) armed with a map which purported to show the distribution of the population in 3000 BC, 'the committee was visibly impressed and no official comment was offered on this piece of factual evidence'.

Day-to-day, Gurney's administration (he would be the last Chief Secretary of British-mandated Palestine) had to cope with three official languages (English, Arabic and Hebrew), which meant that 'a large part of the population are more or less continuously engaged in translating'. Language policy was laid down in the mandate, and so were plenty of holidays, including every Friday (for the Muslims), Saturday (for the Jews) and Sunday (for the Christians). 'The authorities hope', added Gurney, 'that the Palestine problem will be solved before anyone else accustomed to holidays on Monday or Thursday wants to come here.'

Such patronizing humour was matched only by the Chief Secretary's utter and very British imperturbability. As Mrs Golda Meir would complain, 'no one in that position had any right to be unruffled. He ought to have been pacing his room day and night trying to find a solution to the Jewish problem.' Seemingly Palestine brought out both the best and the worst in the British character. Having devised and embraced irreconcilable commitments of devastating consequence, the British stood back, knowing that the problems were insoluble but expecting sympathetic applause for their generally impartial and good-humoured handling of them.

Thus, according to Gurney's glossary, 'law and order' was to the Arabs 'a term not widely known' and to the Jews 'a state of affairs when any number of bullets travel at any time in the direction of the Arabs'. Similarly, 'dissidents' were 'people over whom it is useful to be able to say that you have no control'. He claimed to be quoting from the rule book of 'The Sodom and Gomorrah Golfing Society', an esteemed organization down whose grassless fairways beside the

—MANDATE WAS OF INDEFINITE
duration

Dead Sea members, accompanied by an armed escort, competed for a trophy in the shape of Lot's wife. Originally modelled from a block of salt, the trophy had quickly eroded and been re-carved in marble, which 'gave rise to rumours that the British had no intention of leaving Palestine anyhow'.[3]

The rumours were not unfounded. Palestine's mandate, unlike all the others, was of indefinite duration; so were the problems it posed; and only Great Britain showed willing to shoulder them. The problems, after all, had been devised by the British; and their reasons for doing so held good. Occupying Palestine in order to deny it to any other power had appeared to be the only way of safeguarding the Suez Canal and other imperial communications, a precaution that proved handsomely vindicated in 1941–2; and it was principally to ensure that this British occupation would be authorized in the post-First World War settlement that they had endorsed the Jewish national home – or what Ronald Storrs all too presciently called 'a little loyal Ulster in the heart of a fundamentally hostile Arabia'.[4] They could hardly complain if this commitment, so 'daring' as well as 'romantic', involved them in controversy and rancour. Perhaps unrest even suited them, for anything less might lead the League of Nations to consider setting a date for the termination of the mandate.

A low level of resistance, comfortably contained, was thus possibly desirable and certainly predictable. Prior to 1920, it took the innocuous form of Zionist protests over the pro-Arab sentiments of Allenby's military administration and Arab protests against the Zionist demands thus advertised, as well as against the Balfour Declaration in general and the partition of Greater Syria. At the time the military administration, dominated by Arab Bureau champions such as Ronald Storrs (Governor of Jerusalem, 1917–20) and Gilbert Clayton (Chief Political Officer, 1917–19), regarded the promotion of Zionist objectives as being none of its business and productive only of Arab alarm at a time when maintaining peace and the political status quo was the priority. Clayton objected to British pronouncements of support for Zionism, General Sir Arthur Money (Chief Administrator in Palestine, 1918–19) urged that the Balfour Declaration be dropped altogether, and Colonel B.H. Waters-Taylor (Chief of Staff in Palestine, 1919–20) actively intrigued with the then Arab administration in Damascus for the acceptance of Hashemite sovereignty over Palestine.

Zionists naturally construed all this as prevarication over the Balfour commitment, and so highly provocative. In London they prevailed on the British government to remind its officials in Palestine that promoting Zionist interests was already official British policy; and in Palestine they openly challenged the administration with, for instance, a November 1918 procession through Jerusalem to mark the first anniversary of the Balfour Declaration. It was followed in December by a Zionist conference in Jaffa which demanded that Palestine 'be recognised as the Jewish homeland in the affairs of which the Jewish people as a whole shall have a determining voice', adding for good measure that the country's name should be *Eretz Israel* ('The Land of Israel'), and its flag the Jewish flag.[5]

Such claims naturally provoked the Arab majority. Not without encouragement from some British officers as well as from Damascus, Muslim-Christian associations were formed to articulate Arab demands, the first Palestine Arab Congress met (November 1919), resolutions in favour of Syrian unity and the rejection of Zionism were adopted, and more protests were registered with the British authorities. Each side accused the other of amassing weapons, forming militias and planning violence. The violence nearly erupted in April 1919 during the usual coincidence of the Christian Easter, the Jewish Passover and the annual Muslim procession to Nebi Musa (Moses's tomb) that formed up in Jerusalem. But partly thanks to the moderation shown by both Faysal and Dr Weizmann, and partly to the mollifying effect of a League of Nations Commission of Enquiry (which, as the King-Crane Commission, took depositions during the summer of 1919), the situation remained under control.

Disturbances were largely confined to border raids in Galilee, where Palestine's northern frontier with Faysal's Syria was undefined and in dispute. Indeed, compared with the Wafd-led revolution in Egypt or the growing turmoil in Iraq and Syria, Palestine entered 1920 with the distinction of having seemingly enjoyed 'eighteen months of peace'. So said Jerusalem's Governor, who in February 1920 thought it a good moment to take a holiday. With his sister and a friend, the dilettante Storrs motored north from Jerusalem to Haifa, whose British chief introduced his guests to the mysteries of poker, and on to Tiberias and Nablus. There the travellers were brought to an abrupt standstill. Roads were blocked and telephones were down. All British troops were either cut off or confined to barracks. The country had been taken by surprise, in fact completely overwhelmed, by an unforeseen disaster in the shape of the worst snowstorm in years.

Storrs and company abandoned their car and continued back to Jerusalem on horseback. It was 'one of the most dramatically beautiful journeys imaginable'. The snowfields, solemn and deserted under a darkened sky, reminded him of an El Greco landscape. When he strayed from the track, the drifts closed over his head 'as though I had suddenly and in silence been swallowed into the earth'. For the next two weeks protest and counter-protest were muffled as a peaceful Palestine lay hushed beneath its dazzling blanket of white.[6]

March 1920 came in with news of ferment in Damascus: the Syrian General Congress had proclaimed Faysal king of Greater Syria (including Palestine). Arab demonstrations in Jerusalem duly hailed the event and demanded British recognition of Faysal's authority over Palestine. The military administration, mindful of the previous year's Nebi Musa anxieties, braced itself for another anxious Easter. But on 4 April, Easter Sunday, the Nebi Musa celebrants were not expected to reach the city's Jaffa Gate until the afternoon. Storrs therefore 'made what were then considered adequate dispositions' before taking his parents, who were staying with him, to Matins at St George's Cathedral. His father was the distinguished Dean of Rochester, he himself a lover of liturgy; besides, it was Easter. He left word with a member of his staff to alert him if the Nebi Musa festivities ran ahead of schedule.

This injunction was forgotten. It was not until Storrs was sauntering back to his residence after the service that news of fatalities at the Jaffa Gate was whispered to him by his orderly. 'It was as though he had thrust a sword into my heart,' Storrs recalled. The Nebi Musa celebrants had arrived early and had responded to speeches by their leaders with cries of support for Faysal and contempt for the Zionists. Who or what actually triggered the first lunge is unclear, but with the locally recruited police proving at best ineffectual, Arabs quickly set about Jews and rampaged through the Old City for the next four days. The intervention of armed Zionist units served only to escalate the situation; and as ever, the victims were mostly the innocent. Unarmed Palestinian Jews and Jewesses, long resident in the Old City and bitterly opposed to Zionist pretensions, found their worst fears confirmed as they suffered for the assertions of their newly arrived and more politicized brethren.

Storrs wrung his hands in despair. '[A]ll the carefully built relations of mutual understanding between British, Arabs and Jews seemed to flare away in an agony of fear and hatred,' he would write. But nine dead (five Jews and four Arabs), plus over 200 wounded, belied any notion of mutual understanding, prior or subsequent. Colleagues in the military administration, who had warned that British commitments to Zionism were incompatible with those made to the Arabs, appeared vindicated. Storrs, like his superiors in London, looked elsewhere for an explanation. If only he had been told sooner, his account implies, if only the police had been better officered.[7] Seeking tactical solutions for a strategic nonsense was typical of the pragmatism on which the British so prided themselves.

Inevitably it was the makeshift military administration that took the blame. Its handling of the situation brought widespread criticism which the subsequent trials of the supposed miscreants, plus its refusal to publish the report of an official enquiry, did little to dissipate. 'It cannot be said', reported Graves, 'that well-informed neutrals were much impressed by [the military court's] proceedings or by its findings.'[8] A hefty sentence (later commuted) on Vladimir Jabotinsky, organizer of the armed Zionist militia (Haganah), confirmed Jewish suspicions that the military authorities were discriminating against Zionism. Similar sentences against Arab leaders, including the young Hajj Amin al-Husayni, convinced Arab opinion that the British remained committed to Zionism. Storrs himself was vilified by each side for his supposed favour to the other. He took this as a compliment to his impartiality; indeed Lloyd George reassured him that 'if either . . . side stops complaining [about you], you'll be dismissed'.[9] But though personally consoling, this was politically defeatist. Trusted by both sides, the British might yet have advanced some basis for an accommodation; trusted by neither, they could only hold the line.

London now favoured the replacement of the military administration with a civilian one. This decision nicely coincided with the San Remo conference of April 1920 at which it was confirmed that the Palestine mandate would indeed be awarded to Britain. Both the mandate, with its affirmation of the Balfour Declaration, and the selection of Sir Herbert Samuel as High Commissioner and head of

the new civilian government represented triumphs for Zionism and
a rebuff to Arab opinion. As High Commissioner, Storrs himself had
looked to many to be the obvious choice. But despite the objections
of Curzon and Allenby, Lloyd George preferred Samuel, an ex-
Cabinet minister and an administrator of frigid genius untainted by
association with the military administration. He was also by birth a
Jew and, unlike most other British Jews (including his cousin Sir
Edwin Montagu at the India Office), by conviction a declared
Zionist. In fact he had played a significant part in the adoption of the
Balfour Declaration and had lately championed Zionist protests
against the conduct of the military administration. With his appointment as the first High Commissioner, the name of Samuel, according to Storrs, joined those of Herzl, Weizmann and Balfour among
'the Big Four' of Zionist founders.

Arriving at Jaffa in late June 1920, Samuel also epitomized the
ambiguity of an idealistic Zionism nestling up to a worldly imperialism. '[T]he first Jewish ruler in Palestine since Simon Bar Cochba',[10]
he came ashore not with some Messianic fanfare from on high but in
the stern of a launch beneath an ensign of the Royal Navy, a vision of
imperial glory in the white drill, spiked helmet, gold braid and purple
sash (with Empire Star) of that most mundane of contemporary
deities, a British colonial governor. Storrs received him and then
introduced him to the assembled Zionist leaders. Even to a gentile, it
was a moment of profound import. The Jews, 'almost faint with happiness', were 'moving as if in the glory and freshness of a dream
come true'.

'I was acutely conscious', added Storrs, 'that I was walking in
something stranger than history – the past summoned back and
made to live again.' How could one not be excited by prophecy in the
process of fulfilment, or by the dawn of what he called the century's
first 'Great Adventure'? Not to spoil the moment, he said nothing of
the assassination threats, nothing of the armoured car that would
precede Samuel's convoy to Lydda, nor of the camouflaged train that
would take them on to a less than enthusiastic reception in
Jerusalem, nor of the little Browning pistol, 'loaded and cocked', that
he clutched in his left hand throughout.[11]

Although Storrs would serve Samuel loyally, he too thought the
appointment highly provocative, indeed 'madness'.[12] The announcement of the mandate was no less provocative. Though now awarded,

its wording had not at this point been determined. It was known that it endorsed the Balfour Declaration, and Samuel quickly confirmed this; but until its terms were published, there was much to play for. Zionists looked for reassurance that 'facilitating' a national home for the Jewish people would mean that the British would be internationally obligated to support Jewish immigration, the Jewish acquisition of land, the promotion of Hebrew and other matters conducive to the speedy creation of a Jewish state. In Palestine they pressed the new administration on these issues as they had the old, but with considerably greater success; and in Paris their draft for the mandate would be so substantially adopted by the British delegation as to give rise to accusations of an 'Anglo-Zionist conspiracy'.[13]

Likewise, to Palestine's anxious Arab majority the wording of the mandate looked to be a crucial test of their national aspirations. Within a month of Samuel's arrival in Jerusalem, Faysal had been forced to flee Damascus following the French victory at Khan Maysalun. This challenged the existing basis of Palestinian protest. For with Faysal in exile and Syrian nationalism in disarray, Palestinians could no longer pin their hopes on Damascus and the British promises of Arab independence made to the Hashemites. Nor could they now rely on Syria for funds, arms and diplomatic support. The pan-Syrian foundations of Palestinian politics had been undercut, and feuds ensued as different nationalist groupings cast about for an alternative framework of protest.

To most Palestinian Arabs, the League's Covenant, with its talk of self-determination and a tutelage leading to independence, now looked a more promising basis for progress than the disputed claims of the dispossessed Faysal. Palestine, rather than 'south Syria', became the focus of national aspirations, and Palestinian Arabs, both Muslim and Christian, sought to emphasize their national credentials by responsible engagement in civic and economic activities. By belying the idea that they comprised merely marginal and dysfunctional 'non-Jewish communities', they hoped for recognition in the text of the mandate and an assurance of progress towards statehood.

All of which provided a welcome breathing space for the new administration. Soon after his arrival a delighted Samuel reported to Weizmann that the country was so quiet 'you could hear a pin drop'.[14] Reassured, he pressed ahead with arrangements to facilitate Jewish immigration and land acquisition. The Vale of Esdraelon, a vast swathe of Galilee and the most significant purchase of the entire mandatory period, changed hands almost immediately and would soon become a showplace of Jewish agricultural settlement. Immigrants, mostly from Russia and eastern Europe, began pouring in at the rate of 8,000–9,000 a year.

In accordance with the norms of a civilian administration, Samuel also set up an advisory council consisting of both official and appointed members and promised further 'self-governing institutions'. The Zionists, whose international Zionist Commission already enjoyed quasi-official status in Palestine, added a local 'Constituent Assembly'; and the Arabs followed suit with a permanent 'Arab Executive' nominated by the annual Palestinian Arab Congress. Both bodies would be officially recognized, but the latter later and less readily than the former. For the Arab Executive was pledged to unequivocal rejection of the Balfour Declaration and the abrogation of all measures so far introduced to promote Zionism. To this effect it lobbied Churchill when, after the April 1921 Cairo conference, he came to Palestine to meet and vet Abdullah as amir of Transjordania. A month later the Arab Executive dispatched the first of several delegations to London. Meanwhile growing disillusionment throughout Palestinian society, rather than any premeditated programme of direct action, erupted in more violence.

THE CLOCK THAT STOPPED

Easter in Jerusalem had passed off quietly in 1921. But a week later, May Day saw a small and unauthorized display of proletarian solidarity by Bolshevist Jews in Tel Aviv (still just a Zionist enclave on the outskirts of the mainly Arab port of Jaffa). At the time, the influence of communist doctrine among immigrant Jews from Russia was much exaggerated and roundly deplored by Arabs, Britons and most Zionists alike. And it was in fact a counter-demonstration by moderate Jewish socialists that clashed with the Tel Aviv Bolsheviks on May Day. The police successfully separated these warring leftists. Meanwhile a large crowd of disapproving Arabs gathered and then, according to Philip Graves, 'suddenly, so to speak, exploded and attacked both [groups]'.[15]

The ensuing 'Jaffa riots' followed the pattern of the 1920 Nebi Musa outbreak in Jerusalem. Arabs massacred Jews, including the inmates of a property used to house newly arrived immigrants; the Jewish militia exacted their own reprisals; the police performed dismally and actually aided the rioters; and it was three days before British troops had regained control. Unlike the 1920 Jerusalem riot, though, the trouble then spread and briefly threatened a general revolt. North to Tulkarm and south to Ramleh, Jewish settlements were attacked and plundered. To defend them, the British deployed more troops and called in aircraft. Although the crisis was over within a week, the damage was great and the shock profound. Of the 48 Arab fatalities, most had fallen to British bullets; of the 47 Jewish fatalities, most to Arab assassins.

Samuel, a sober bureaucrat possessed, says Storrs, of a 'supposed incapacity for feeling either anger or joy',[16] was genuinely horrified. General Congreve, in command of the British troops, began reviving the concerns of his military predecessors and foretelling 'a state of insurrection' unless his forces were substantially augmented (unthinkable in the light of Churchill's cost-cutting brief); otherwise, only 'an alteration of policy' in respect of the Balfour Declaration would save the day. Samuel seemed to draw the same conclusion. He announced a suspension of all Jewish immigration, proposed that his advisory assembly acquire a representative character with some of its members being chosen through elections (in which the Arab majority would surely prevail), and sought further to reassure Arab opinion with a speech that appeared to emasculate the Balfour Declaration. Only 'some [Jews] within the limits which are fixed by the numbers and interests of the present population' would be admitted to Palestine; 'a national home' was just a home for the Jewish people and did not mean a state in which Jews would rule over Arabs; and the British would never impose upon the people of Palestine 'a policy which that people had reason to think was contrary to their religious, their political, and their economic rights'.[17]

Arab opinion was mildly impressed. Although rejecting these concessions as falling far short of its demands (principally complete annulment of the Balfour Declaration, rejection of the Zionist Commission, and the establishment of a Palestinian state), the Arab Executive now concentrated on its diplomatic offensive and disowned extremists (like those responsible for another anti-Jewish affray in Jerusalem in November 1921). But to Lloyd George and to Churchill, Samuel's 'concessions' looked more like weakness from a man unaccustomed to pressure; and to the Zionists they represented the rankest treachery by one of their very own. Last year's Messiah was suddenly revealed as this year's Lucifer. The Zionist Commission recognized in Samuel's apparent apostasy 'its gravest crisis'. Weizmann, tirelessly orchestrating the flow of funds and support on both sides of the Atlantic, toyed with the idea of having Samuel replaced. And the London *Jewish Chronicle* reported 'one of the blackest instances of political betrayal recorded throughout all history'.[18]

Early resumption of a limited flow of immigrants reassured no one. As of 1922 the principle of immigrant numbers being regulated in accordance with the labour needs and social provisions of Palestine's expanding economy became official British policy. Since the British ultimately determined this 'absorptive capacity', they exercised responsibility for Palestine's most contentious issue; and any immigration being unacceptable to the Arabs, while any restriction of it was unacceptable to the Zionists, they were assured of general obloquy. On the other hand, regulating the stopcock of immigration gave them political leverage and was wholly compatible with notions of a lasting regime of British management.

Samuel, now shunned and distrusted by both sides, laboured to give this regime a fig-leaf of popular legitimacy. In an attempt to introduce some form of representation, an elected advisory council, then an elected legislative assembly, were proposed. Both were fiascos. The Jews, being a minority, rightly feared the elective principle; but it was the Arabs, critical of the limited powers and uneven representation on offer and aware that participation would lend legitimacy to British rule (and so imply acceptance of the Balfour commitment), who obligingly boycotted the elections, so aborting the institutions.

The same thing happened with a proposal to blunt Arab criticism of the Zionist Commission's influence by setting up an equivalent 'Arab Agency' with similar access to government. Again the Zionists were deeply suspicious but had only to wait for the Arabs themselves to reject the idea. Thereafter official attempts to engage the people of Palestine in the country's government flagged. Jews and Arabs were left to regulate the affairs of their own communities, and for the next twenty-five years Palestine as a whole would be ruled by a British-run bureaucracy unaccountable to any institution representative of Palestinian opinion. Instead of the constitutional progress so proudly advertised in Iraq and Egypt, instead of the blow-for-blow trading of concessions for reservations and constitutions for treaties, in Palestine the British had in effect thrown in the towel at the end of round one.

The wording of the mandate, as prompted by the Zionists, drafted by the British and accepted with little modification by the League in July 1922, confirmed this failure. 'Self-governing institutions' were mentioned, but after, and as if contingent on, the mandatory's duty to 'secure the establishment of the Jewish national home'. That Palestine was now to be 'the' national home, as opposed to Balfour's 'a' national home, signified rather more than this casual nod to autonomy. Here, as in the other twenty-seven articles, the word 'Arab' was nowhere to be found. Yet 'Jewish', and 'Jew' made a dozen appearances. 'The historical connexion of the Jewish people with Palestine', albeit 2,000 years ago, was accepted as the basis for 'reconstituting their national home'; official recognition of the Zionist Organization as a consultative body entitled to advise the administration was specifically accorded; and Jewish immigration leading to 'close settlement by Jews on the land' and their development of all natural resources, public works, services and utilities was carefully spelled out. As for the 'existing non-Jewish communities', they were vouchsafed no historical links with the country and no special representation. Their purely 'civil and religious rights' had merely to be safeguarded; they were not specified and they were not to be promoted.

The contention that Britain's mandatory duty was simply to administer the country while enabling the Jews to build their national home was the result, therefore, not of Zionist wishful thinking or aggressive intent but of a reasoned reading of the document. And although public denial was often necessary, privately many British statesmen admitted the further contention that a Jewish national home must mean a genuine state in which the Jewish people would be politically, economically and one day demographically pre-eminent. Whatever they thought of Samuel and his successors, Zionists had few complaints about the intent of the mandate. Their task was to hold the British to it. Meanwhile the Arabs would endeavour to persuade the British otherwise by demonstrating that it was unworkable as well as unjust. And as for the British, they had merely to keep the peace and so justify their indefinite presence.

In this they were for a while moderately successful. Despite strikes, riots and occasional massacres, the first twelve years of British rule in Palestine witnessed nothing like the Iraqi 'insurrection' of 1920 or the Syrian 'Great Revolt' of 1925. Fatalities for the period barely reached three figures, let alone five; no cities were bombarded, few villages burnt, and communications rarely interrupted. The press was reasonably free, civil rights largely respected. In 1925 Arthur James Balfour paid his one and only visit to Palestine, in connection with the opening of Jerusalem's Hebrew University. Another highly controversial 'coming', it was ardently desired by the Jews, but 'conspued', says Storrs, by the Arabs and dreaded by the police. Yet it passed off with no incident of note.

The tone of the visit was set in the customs shed at Jaffa where the disembarking VIP was supposedly accosted by an officer asking 'And have you anything else to declare, Mr Balfour?'[19] Security throughout was necessarily tight, and 'scores of abusive telegrams' were delivered to Ronald Storrs's Jerusalem office, there to be quickly destroyed; the visit, Storrs noted, had 'put back the clock of reconciliation by at least a year'. Ever the optimist, Storrs assumed the clock was actually working. In reality it had already stopped, and the expectations of Jews and Arabs were now as irreconcilable as the high walls of the Old City's narrow alleys down which Balfour blithely strolled, unmolested, to the Church of the Holy Sepulchre. He would find a much livelier reception awaiting him in French-ruled Damascus. And smuggled thence to the safety of a liner moored in the harbour of Beirut, he would spend the last days of his trip 'guarded from a hostile shore by the circling of a French torpedo-destroyer'.[20] From this tale of three cities, Storrs and his colleagues derived much satisfaction. Palestine was no paradise, but thanks to its peculiar mandate it looked to be an endurable limbo.

EAST OF THE JORDAN

Another peculiarity of the Palestine mandate was that its terms did not necessarily apply to all of Palestine. Tucked away near the end of the published text, Article 25 advised the mandatory that he might, if he chose, ignore most of its injunctions and make whatever arrangements he considered suitable in 'all the territories lying between the

Jordan [river] and the eastern boundary of Palestine'. These were of course the largely desert lands, otherwise known as Transjordania, which Churchill had just entrusted to Abdullah on a 'sale or return' basis. It was in recognition of this settlement that Article 25 had been inserted, and it was because of the settlement's provisional nature that the mandate's terms might here be either 'postponed' or permanently 'withheld'. Subject to the general responsibilities of any mandatory, the British had, in effect, a free hand in Transjordania.

Except for the Jordan river, the boundaries of the exempted territories were as yet undetermined; but it was already obvious that this trans-Jordanian Palestine greatly exceeded in terms of area (though not much else) the cis-Jordanian Palestine to which the mandate applied in full. Paradoxically, therefore, the largest, least populated part of mandated Palestine, and that most obviously in need of development, was under no obligation to accommodate Jewish immigrants, nor admit their 'close settlement of the land', nor benefit from their investment, nor host their 'national home'. To disinterested parties it seemed perverse. If anywhere could be called a 'land without people' awaiting 'a people without land', it was not little (cis-Jordanian) Palestine (with a population of 750,000) but this large and unfrequented (Palestinian) trans-Jordania (with a mere 220,000). Here lay the desert which might be made to bloom, here the unwanted acres whose progressive settlement need antagonize no one.

It was a nonsense even to one of the interested parties. Although cis-Jordanian Palestine was the essence of *Eretz Israel*, Zionists were alert to the potential of Transjordania and questioned the mandatory's right to exclude them from it. In advance of the Cairo conference Weizmann had warned that Transjordania was economically and strategically essential to the Jewish home and that it had formed 'from earliest times an integral and vital part of Palestine'; for 'here the tribes of Reuben, Gad and Manasseh first pitched their tents and pastured their flocks',[21] he explained. Israelite grazing grounds as attested by the Book of Numbers might seem a tenuous basis for territorial claims in the twentieth century, but such was the 'historical connection' between the Jews and an undifferentiated Palestine as acknowledged in the mandate. Additionally, under Article 5, the mandatory was strictly forbidden to cede, lease or place under the control of a foreign power any part of this undifferentiated Palestine, including

Transjordania

Transjordania. So if, courtesy of Article 25, he was in fact entitled to do just that, the mandate was clearly self-contradictory.

The British government disagreed. The mandate was well known to be based on the Balfour Declaration which envisaged a Palestine without any territories east of the Jordan; that such territories had in fact been included in the mandate did not mean that they too were automatically intended for the Jewish national home. Transjordania had always been considered as Arab territory. And it was simply for convenience that it had found its way into the Palestine mandate at all.

In the 1916 Sykes-Picot agreement, Transjordania had been shown as destined for Arab rule within the sphere of indirect British influence. In 1917–18 it had been liberated from the Turks by Lawrence and the Arab Revolt. It had then come under the Allied military administration of Faysal in Damascus; and it had subsequently formed part of Faysal's short-lived Syrian Arab kingdom. The 1920 imposition of French rule in Damascus meant a reversion to the Sykes-Picot division, with Transjordania being detached from Syria and reaffirmed as within the British sphere of influence. Faysal could legitimately have retired there after his flight from Damascus. He was dissuaded from doing so by British sensitivity to French objections and by the prospect of better things in Iraq. This resulted in a Transjordanian vacuum which the British briefly filled with a number of putative Arab states, like Kirkbride's 'National Government of Moab'. Then out of the Hijaz rolled Abdullah in search of a kingdom; and from London came Churchill, bearing crowns.

Advised by Lawrence, Churchill saw provisional British support of Abdullah as going some way towards fulfilling obligations to the Arabs as per Husayn–McMahon while keeping open all options as to the long-term future of Transjordania. Consonant with the territorial contouring envisaged by Sykes-Picot, Transjordania was also projected as an area of indirect British influence fringing and framing an area under direct British rule, that is Palestine. From Palestine Abdullah was to be indirectly influenced; and Palestine's High Commissioner was duly made responsible for British relations with Transjordania. It remained only to legitimize this situation by ensuring Transjordania's inclusion in the Palestine mandate while at the same time providing for its exclusion, if desired, from any injunctions that would prejudice its development as an Arab state, like those for the Jewish national home. Hence the need for Article 25.

— Zionists don't claim transjordan

But other considerations of a less honourable nature were not thereby precluded. Alec Kirkbride, writing of his days as head of the National Government of Moab, would insist that in 1920 when the mandate was actually announced, it was the British intention that Transjordania should 'serve as a reserve of land for use in the resettlement of Arabs once the National Home for the Jews in Palestine . . . had become an accomplished fact'.[22] This was an explosive admission by Kirkbride. A greatly respected figure writing long after the event, he must have been aware that any suggestion of a masterplan for the transplantation of Palestine's Arabs was political dynamite which would expose the British to accusations of the rankest duplicity. He vaguely implies, although in no way does he insist, that with the installation of Abdullah this plan was dropped; and if some such thinking was indeed current, it would explain why moderate Zionists, like Weizmann, quickly ceased their criticisms of Article 25. The pastures of Reuben, Gad and Manasseh were thus left to be occasionally touted as the answer to Palestine's overcrowding but consistently claimed only by the wilder apostles of Zionist irredentism.

Other British requirements in relation to Transjordania were less controversial. To ensure a British-controlled corridor from the Mediterranean to the Gulf – an imperial axis along which airplanes might hop and oil pipelines and railway tracks be laid – London insisted on Abdullah's amirate being territorially contiguous with Iraq. This would be achieved by welding on to Transjordania a long eastward flange of desert, interposed between French Syria and Ibn Saud's Arabia.

This border, fringing the wastes of the *nafud*, looked straightforward, being uncomplicated by either human settlement or geographical features and for the most part a matter of ruling straight lines on an agreed map. But as of 1924 it would become fraught with strategic significance; for in that year Ibn Saud's encroachments into northern and western Arabia would climax with an invasion of the neighbouring Hijaz. There Abdullah's father, the *sharif* Husayn, still ruled; and father and son being equally implicated in Arabian intrigues, Ibn Saud would regard both as hostile.

This international crisis for the Hashemites would cap a domestic one involving Abdullah and the British. Indeed Abdullah's relations with the British had been in a state of crisis ever since Churchill had installed him. Still hoping for a kingdom in Syria, he had initially surrounded himself with displaced Syrian nationalists. The British distrusted these men as ardent anti-Zionists, the Transjordanians detested them as urbanized parasites, and the French condemned them as a Syrian government-in-exile and the instigators of the assassination attempt on General Gouraud. Abdullah was unmoved.

Indeed, with eyes firmly fixed on Damascus, he seemed to take little interest in Transjordania itself and soon confessed that he had had enough of 'this wilderness'. His British subsidy was being squandered on his tribal dependants, and his government was a joke. The six months 'on approval' had been a disaster. In 1922 Lawrence was therefore sent to Amman to wind up the experiment and repossess the country. But on reflection Lawrence, ever a law unto himself, did no such thing. Discerning another chance to spite the French, uphold the Hashemites and honour the memory of his Arab Revolt, he advised that Abdullah be retained and greater support be afforded him.

It was to this end that the pugnacious and pro-Arab Philby was summoned from his Baghdad disgrace to be Britain's representative in Amman. With something of the proprietary pride of a Captain 'Carbillet of the Druze', Philby set about creating in Transjordania 'a self-governing entity' to which, Churchill assured him, 'the Zionist clauses of the mandate would on no account apply'. Syrian nationalists were sent packing, the French were greatly reassured, and Samuel's authority as High Commissioner for Transjordania was vigorously contested. Abdullah warmed to his new champion and, according to Philby, 'we got on famously from the beginning'.[23] But as in Iraq, Philby held no brief for the Hashemites. To his way of thinking, a 'self-governing entity' did not mean a Hashemite autocracy. In creating an Arab Transjordania it was more important to promote fiscal regularity, constitutional rule and democratic representation, all of which were disagreeable novelties to Abdullah.

A visit to London in 1922 brought an increase in Abdullah's subsidy to £150,000 a year (much of which went towards the cost of his British advisers) plus, in 1923, the first written recognition of 'an independent government in Trans-Jordan under His Highness the Amir Abdullah ibn Husayn'. Abdullah was delighted. At last he was officially 'His Highness' and the country had become the more pithy 'Trans-Jordan', thereby ending possible confusion between the Hashemite's 'Transjordania' and Count Dracula's Transylvania. But the recognition was contingent on the establishment of 'constitutional' government and on the conclusion of a satisfactory 'agreement' between Great Britain and Transjordan. In both cases the British, as judge and jury, would not easily be convinced. Abdullah was thus as obligated to his sponsor as ever; and a decidedly fictional aura continued to cling to his country's 'independence', if not to its name. His biographer compares Transjordan's status to that of the British mini-dependencies in the Gulf. While elsewhere concessions were being won by mass protest and negotiation, in Transjordan and the Gulf shaykhdoms they were simply 'rewards for good behaviour'.[24]

Earlier in 1922 an incursion by Ibn Saud's forces in the south-east of the country, plus a tribal rising in the north, had provided practical reminders of Abdullah's abject dependence on British support. Their salutary effect, however, was negated by the arrival in Amman in early 1924 of his father, the now septuagenarian *sharif* Husayn, King of the Hijaz. He was closely followed by three trains hauled by expiring locomotives and carrying track-laying troops. They were the first to complete the run from Medina for eight years.

Philby assumed that Husayn had come to reclaim the line and just possibly, like Lawrence, to reclaim the whole country. The districts of Aqaba and Ma'an in the south of what is today Jordan had been under Husayn's Hijaz administration since 1916, and the *sharif* seemed to imagine that the rest of Transjordan was merely vassal territory temporarily in Abdullah's care until the reopening of the railway. Moreover father and son were on the worst of terms. Husayn was particularly jealous of Abdullah's deference to the British, rather than to himself, and of his taking orders from a Zionist-led government in Jerusalem, rather than from his own *sharif*-led government in Mecca.

Abdullah, not unhappy to take a back seat, dutifully deferred to his visitor, who settled in for an indefinite stay. Indeed 'the marmoset of Mecca', so venerable in appearance yet unpredictable in temper, seemed bent on recreating the heady days of the Arab Revolt; for when in March news came from Turkey of the deposition of the last Ottoman caliph, it was calmly announced that Husayn would himself now assume that prestigious title.

Whether this move was intended to bolster the Hashemites' flagging claims to be the champions of Arab nationalism or whether it was supposed to remind the British of Husayn's once vaunted Islamic credentials is unclear. Either way, it failed. Husayn and the Hijaz, like Abdullah and Transjordan, badly needed British military support – plus the reinstatement of their British subsidy – if they were to withstand the challenge to the kingdom from Ibn Saud of Riyadh. But the price of British support, as revealed during negotiations in which Lawrence, Clayton, Philby, Antonius, Graffey-Smith and just about everyone else had a hand, was the *sharif*'s endorsement of the Palestine mandate (and so of the Balfour Declaration) plus what Husayn considered a demeaning treaty with Ibn Saud. Caliphal claims only made things worse; for Palestinian opinion was thereby inflamed and the Saudi king greatly provoked. Clearly, reasoned the British, Husayn was a liability and must be winkled out of Transjordan as quickly as possible; indeed he could take his son with him unless the latter came to a proper understanding of where lay his and Transjordan's only salvation.

Alec Kirkbride, urgently extricated from a desk job in Jerusalem, was given the unenviable task of inviting Husayn to leave. Swapping cap for *keffyeh*, Kirkbride crossed the Jordan in some trepidation and approached the *sharif* with the utmost caution, making little of the troops at his disposal and much of a reconditioned locomotive for the royal train. Husayn hesitated, then with a beatific smile signified his concurrence. He insisted only that Kirkbride accompany him and his several hundred retainers to Ma'an for a grand, if poignant, send-off.

> The locomotive was preceded by a flat truck mounting a machine-gun and other machine-guns were carried at intervals on the roof of the trucks. Hardly a picture of a beloved monarch returning to his people. We all paid our final respects to the King and watched the train puff out of sight. No one realised at the time that we were seeing the last train which was to pass over the line between Ma'an and Medina.[25]

It was the last train because four months later Ibn Saud launched his offensive against the Hijaz, and the line became a casualty of the fighting. So did Husayn's kingdom. Aided only by some White Russian pilots flying antiquated Italian aircraft, the Hashemite forces crumbled before the onslaught of Ibn Saud's fanatical Wahhabi followers. Mecca fell in October, Husayn then abdicated, and next year his kingdom of Hijaz disappeared into what, save for the Yemen, Aden and the Gulf states, now became an all-Saudi Arabia.

Back in Amman Abdullah had also succumbed, but in this case to a British ultimatum demanding tighter financial supervision and military inspection in Transjordan, the expulsion of various Arab nationalists, and an extradition treaty with Syria. Indirect influence was giving way to direct management of the minutiae of Transjordanian affairs.[26]

Philby would have approved. But he too had moved on, not without prompting. After defying the British High Commissioner in Palestine once too often and having been too indulgent of Husayn's presence, he was for a second time relieved of his post. Ironically his ultimate destination would prove to be the Hijaz where, despite British orders to the contrary, he renewed friendships dating back to his Iraqi days with Ibn Saud, the new ruler of the Hijaz, and with Saiyid Talib, the man whom he had supported as head of state in Baghdad. In Jidda, Philby tried his hand at business as the Saudi kingdom's supplier of Sunlight Soap, Standard Oil kerosene and Ford automobiles. Later he would move to Riyadh as one of Ibn Saud's confidants, adopt Islam, acquire an Arab wife and family, and explore much of central Arabia, all the while somehow retaining the affections of Dora, his long-suffering English wife, and of their son Kim, notorious for a later and greater defection to Moscow.

The events of 1924–5, while inviting tighter British management of Transjordan, had nevertheless demonstrated that country's utility to the British and even the convenience of retaining Abdullah. As Ibn Saud's forces moved further into the Hijaz in 1925, British armoured units swept south to Ma'an and Aqaba, which districts (the first including Wadi Musa and Petra, the second affording access to the Red Sea) were then added to Abdullah's amirate. A tranche of Transjordanian territory was thus interposed between the now Saudi Hijaz and British-controlled Sinai.

Sinai flanked the Suez Canal; Palestine proper still simmered with anti-Zionist resentment; and to the north Syria was now plunged in revolt. All were therefore supposedly vulnerable to the uncompromising doctrines of Ibn Saud's militantly Islamic followers. Only Transjordan barred their path. How better to control this desert rampart of the colonialized Levant than through a soft and compliant Arab regime headed by a British puppet who was trapped between his Hashemite hatred of the Saudis and his subjection to a pro-Zionist administration in Jerusalem?

With the political temperature rising in Palestine, and constitutional progress there at a standstill, it was no longer thought desirable to allow for possible integration of the Transjordanian territories with their cis-Jordanian parent. Indeed Churchill's casual creation of a separate state began to look like a master stroke. While in Damascus battles raged, and in Cairo and Jerusalem police were thick on the streets, in Amman protest scarcely stirred. In fact Transjordan, with its population swollen by Hijazi, Druze and Syrian exiles, looked to be a promising ground for military recruitment. In 1926 the British augmented Transjordan's existing Arab Legion with a Trans-Jordanian Frontier Force (TJFF). Both units were armed and officered by the British, although the Legion owed allegiance to Abdullah while the new TJFF was part of the British imperial forces.

The TJFF was intended for tribal control and frontier defence in the eastern deserts of Transjordan. But it was first called into action under very different conditions when in 1929 it was ordered west, across the Jordan into Palestine. There it was to assist in suppressing the first wave of a new and escalating tide of violence. Reversing the mandate's conception of Transjordan as a Palestinian dependency, a precedent was thus set for Transjordanian intervention in Palestinian affairs. Like its amir, the country was emerging from an embarrassing political infancy into an adulthood as an eager and active agent in Palestine's future.

BEWAILING THE WALL

The 1929 Palestine riots, in which over a hundred Jews would be massacred by Arabs and a like number of Arabs gunned down by the security forces, had flared over the placing of some outdoor furniture on a sun-drenched pavement beside a high stone wall in Jerusalem's Old City. The furniture comprised benches, folding chairs and sometimes a screen or a lectern, all unremarkable, easily moved and paltry encumbrances in what was a pedestrian area. But just as Palestine was not simply 'another Arab country', or Jerusalem another city, so the wall was not simply a wall and the furniture not just an amenity.

Jews believed that the wall's lowest courses of stonework were archaeological survivals of the outer 'Western Wall' of the temple of King Herod and, as such, the only tangible relic of the ancient kingdom of Israel. At this hallowed place of pilgrimage, prayer and painful remembrance (hence the 'Wailing Wall'), orthodox Jews had been assembling for centuries. They had also for some years been bringing with them temporary pews and other props appropriate to their devotions.

Muslims objected. Erratically in Ottoman times but insistently during the 1920s, they opposed this furnishing of the site. The wall, plus the surrounding area, belonged to a Muslim foundation; the Jews' right to assemble there had only customary sanction and no basis in written law. In the light of the failure of several recent attempts by Jewish benefactors to purchase the whole area, Muslims were readily persuaded that custom was now being finessed. Seating, lecterns to read from, screens to separate the sexes and awnings to provide shade were seen as an escalation of existing practice that could only presage claims to a permanency of occupation.

This was unacceptable on religious as well as legal grounds. The area which the wall flanked and supported, although known to the Jews as the 'Temple Mount', was to Muslims Haram al-Sharif, the 'Noble Sanctuary'. It was the third holiest place in the Islamic world, a site visited by the Prophet on his celestial steed as recorded in the Quran, and subsequently endowed with both the gleaming Dome of the Rock and the extensive complex, immediately above the Wall, of the al-Aqsa mosque. Indeed, according to later tradition, it was to this self-same section of wall that Buraq, the Prophet's horse, had been tethered before finally prancing heavenwards.

The British, after careful consideration, were inclined to admit Muslim objections to the encroachments at the base of the Wall, and cautioned the Jews accordingly. On several occasions in the 1920s the police removed offending benches and turned back advancing chairs. The mandatory's intention was to preserve the status quo in respect of all Palestine's holy places; and in this instance the status quo seemed a fair reflection of the actual situation. For as might be generally said of Palestine at the time, the Jewish element in this topographical controversy was the less impressive of the two. A section of outer wall, between whose massive stones written prayers could be stuffed, was less convincing than the great Muslim structures above it, less holy because unassociated with a divine intermediary (like the Prophet), and less proof against archaeological sophistry.

But it was precisely because of the Wall's near-miraculous archaeology, its chronological primacy and its undoubted rarity that to Jews of every persuasion it was so precious and to Zionist Jews, bent on reconstituting the ancient polity to which the Wall belonged, so very emotive. They therefore persevered. The benches kept reappearing, bigger crowds brought more chairs, and for Yom Kippur in 1928 a screen was erected to separate the sexes.

When Edward Keith-Roach, Storrs's successor as District Commissioner for the city, remarked on this development while paying a courtesy call at the Haram al-Sharif, his interest was noted. A strong Muslim protest was promptly registered, a British demand for the screen's removal was delivered, and a Jewish official undertook to comply. Next day the screen was still there. Keith-Roach, ignoring the disturbance which must be involved, had the police dismantle it. A conscientious official schooled in the rough-and-ready Sudan administration, he knew not to shirk responsibility and was confident that 'nothing more would be heard of the matter'.[27]

He was wrong. The police action brought a storm of condemnation not just from Palestine's Zionists but from Jews world-wide. Meanwhile Palestinian Muslims had adopted the defence of the Haram al-Sharif as a defining issue and were canvassing support from Muslim communities throughout Asia against this perceived threat to Islam's holy places. Huge campaigns were mounted, funds raised and demonstrations organized. To the dismay of the British Foreign Office, Palestine and its administration were for the first time being subjected to international scrutiny, and the British to diplomatic pressure, from New Delhi to New York.

Meanwhile in Jerusalem the vicious cycle of provocation and protest gathered momentum. Some building operations adjacent to the al-Aqsa mosque, plus a new access which turned the cul-de-sac into a labourers' thoroughfare, gave intense annoyance to worshipping Jews below. The works were legitimate, but that only made them more aggravating; and it was likewise with the Muslim call to prayer which so often seemed to coincide with Jewish devotions. Both sides bombarded the administration with appeals. Their newspapers printed threat and counter-threat; calls for restraint by their respective leaderships were reckoned half-hearted and had little effect.

The furore was a gift to militants and revisionists. Hajj Amin al-Husayni, the wispy young firebrand who was convicted over the 1920 Nebi Musa riot, had since secured a pardon, ingratiated himself with the British, been installed by them as Grand Mufti of Jerusalem and now headed the British-sponsored Supreme Muslim Council. With the dignity, funds and patronage of his combined offices, he had become the recognized head of the Muslim community and 'the most powerful political figure in Arab Palestine'.[28] Those British, including Samuel, who had rated his abilities so highly, were evidently right. But if by promoting Hajj Amin al-Husayni they imagined that he must be beholden to them and compromised in the eyes of his rivals, they were sorely mistaken both as to the character of the man and the cohesion of the Arab leadership. The administration's creature emerged as its most uncompromising critic, and he easily divided the Arab Executive.

For both of these manoeuvres, the Wall was the perfect platform. A religious issue at the heart of Jerusalem, it accorded precisely with the Mufti's exclusive competence. In the tall turban and flowing robes of a Muslim doctor of divinity, he rose majestically to the occasion, castigating the administration for any hint of compromise on the legal aspect while outdoing all rivals in his alarmist anti-Jewish rhetoric.

Extreme Zionists, though less well-placed, were also alert to the situation. Impatient of Weizmann's gradualism and British ambivalence, disciples of Vladimir Jabotinsky and other revisionist leaders were eager for an immediate and extensive Jewish state rather than an eventual and restricted 'national home'. They dismissed any concessions to the Arab majority as appeasement and blatant infringements of the mandate. For according to Jabotinsky, the Jews were entitled to operate 'a colonisation regime' dedicated to opening up territory on both sides of the Jordan for the settlement of 'millions'. His motivation was essentially secular and his followers were not well-represented in Jerusalem; but neither could they remain indifferent when the very foundations of the ancient Israelite state were being called into question.

On 14 August 1929 some 3,000 peaceful Orthodox Jews held a prayer vigil at the Wall and were there joined next day by several hundred youths, mostly from Tel Aviv. The new arrivals belonged to a militant wing of pro-Jabotinsky nationalists, and they had not come

— Jews incite riot
— muslims massacre innocents

to pray. They marched to the Wall, raised the Jewish flag, saluted it in ——
silence, then sang the Jewish national anthem and shouted regi-
mented slogans demanding ownership of the Wall and vowing to
defend it at all costs.

This was a direct political challenge, ungraced by devotional
fervour; and as with the building works, the demonstration was all
the more provocative of Muslim sentiment for having been officially
authorized. On 16 August, a Friday, Muslims attending the al-Aqsa
mosque staged a counter-demonstration at the Wall, demolishing
evidence of Jewish worship and burning prayer sheets, including
those pious petitions stuffed into the Wall's crevices. There followed
a week of outraged Jewish protests, of scuffles in which a Jewish boy
was killed while retrieving his football from an Arab garden, and of
frantic negotiations by the acting British High Commissioner.
Nothing, however, was decided.

By the following Thursday, 22 August, the city was awash with
armed Muslims from outlying villages come to defend the Haram
and contest any further Jewish challenge. On the 23rd, undeterred by
the absence of such a challenge and unwilling to let slip the chance of
pre-empting it, they went on the rampage. The riot became a mas- ——
sacre of Jews; and the massacre, embellished with rape and other
atrocities, was repeated among the defenceless Jewish communities
of Hebron, Safed and elsewhere.

Once again the victims were for the most part long-established ——
Jewish familes, ambivalent about Zionism and unprotected by the
guns and militias of the rural Zionist settlements. And once again the
authorities were initially unequal to the occasion. Palestinian police
were no longer deployed in sectarian riots and regular troops had
been withdrawn, leaving only some 300 British constables plus an
armoured-car unit for the whole country. Hence the urgent appeal
for British reinforcements from Transjordan and Egypt. They
arrived in a matter of days, but by then the worst was over.

To men like Keith-Roach it was self-evident that in this instance
the motivation behind the massacres must be sectarian rather than
political. Other British officials, accustomed to refereeing Hindu–
Muslim clashes over devotional details of mind-numbing inconse-
quence in India, were reassured. The carnage of August 1929 became
simply the 'Wailing Wall Riots', an unfortunate consequence of 'the
screen nonsense'.[29] The inevitable commission of enquiry, headed by

Sir Walter Shaw, was empowered only to investigate the immediate cause of the trouble and make recommendations designed to prevent its recurrence. It was not necessary to look into the political background; nor was it desirable. The new Labour government in London led by Ramsay MacDonald, although less enamoured of the Balfour Declaration than its predecessor, was not prepared to jeopardize the British position in Palestine by abandoning Zionism. Pretending to be stretched upon the rack of the mandate, the government advised Shaw not to question its terms but to grin and bear it.

Yet as embodied in a White Paper of 1930, the Shaw Report (and that of a subsidiary commission investigating Palestine's economic prospects with a view to maximizing its 'absorptive capacity' for immigration) did make recommendations of considerable political importance. Although never implemented, they were aired at a time when policy could still be informed more by Palestine's plight than by the external exigencies of Nazi persecution and world war. And as such they represented what Christopher Sykes (whose father Mark, he of Sykes-Picot and the Balfour Declaration, had died in 1919) would call 'the last cross-roads in the history of mandated Palestine'.[30] The slow erosion of these proposals would help to stay the violence for another five years. But the final 1935 repudiation of their suggestion for a revived legislative assembly triggered the civil protests and military operations of the climactic Palestine Revolt of 1936–9.

'THE LAST CROSS-ROADS'

Sir John Chancellor, High Commissioner from 1928 to 1931, had been on leave during the Wall crisis. He had returned in haste and quickly antagonized Muslims by implying that they were responsible for the trouble, then Jews by saying that he had meant no such thing. Rightly, though, he does seem to have realized that there was much more to the grievances of both sides than differences over furniture and faith. Adopting an issue of such volatile consequence, but little political promise, had been an act of desperation. The problem over the Wall, he reasoned, would never have arisen (and would soon be quietly resolved by an independent award) had not both Zionists and Arabs felt their very existence endangered.

Stranger than History

Zionism was indeed witnessing one of its 'gravest crises'. In the late 1920s the flow of immigrants, as of funds, had faltered, then slowed to a trickle. After allowing for an increased rate of emigration out of the country, another sign of disillusionment, Palestine's Jewish population had actually declined in 1928. Meanwhile Weizmann's efforts to rally international Jewry to the Zionist cause appeared to be making little progress, and the advent of the Labour government in London left him without that ready ministerial access to the counsels of the mandatory afforded by Lloyd George and Churchill.

Zionism's prospects would soon improve, but its salvation was not yet evident, nor was it clear whence it would come. The recent transformation of Palestine's Zionist Executive into the world-wide Jewish Agency looked on paper more like a compromise with un-Zionized Jews than the long-desired means of involving and mobilizing international, and especially American, Jewry. US investment in Palestine was in fact declining as the world recession bit; and the sympathy of Americans for the plight of the Jews was being eclipsed by concern for their own countrymen lining up outside the soup kitchens.

Accordingly, in 1929 Washington imposed severe restrictions on immigration to the US, thus denying migrant European Jews access to what was still their favoured destination. In its stead the flow, which thanks to Nazi persecution was about to become a flood, was diverted elsewhere, especially to Palestine. In the mid-1930s Jewish immigration to Palestine rocketed, peaking at over 60,000 in 1935, nearly ten times the annual average for the 1920s. It was accompanied by a surge in investment and rapid development. Zion's crisis was over. Unconsciously, and purely for domestic reasons, the US government had rendered to Zionism a decisive service. It would be the first of many.

But none of this was anticipated in the critical years of 1928–9. Zionism was then fighting for its life, and the Wall controversy had come as a godsend to galvanize flagging hopes. It was likewise for Palestinian nationalism. Arabs were aware of the current decline in Jewish immigration but they were more concerned about the effects, now being felt, of the 100,000 Jewish immigrants who had already arrived since the Balfour Declaration, and of the land sales that had more than doubled Jewish holdings in the same period.[31] When land changed hands, many of those Arabs who actually worked it lost their livelihoods and their homes. Sometimes there was compensation but rarely was there alternative land or any but menial employment. The Histadrut, the Jewish labour union, enacted Zionist policy in insisting that only Jewish labour be employed in Jewish enterprises. How else were immigrants to be encouraged and a brave new society of self-reliant communes created? Arabs were unwelcome not just because they were Arabs but because Arab society, dominated by absentee landlords and a few all-powerful families, was irreconcilable with the all-caring, self-sacrificing, state-run enterprises of the Zionist ideal.

The distress which resulted from this policy alerted the hitherto unpoliticized Arab peasant to the very real threat of Zionism. As an ideology it had not commanded his attention; as a design for his dispossession and destitution it became an obsession. But neither the distress of the few nor the alarm of the many seemed to be appreciated by the Arab leadership. Some of those Arab leaders who attended the Palestinian Arab Congresses or sat on bodies like the Arab Executive were actually implicated in land sales to Jews; few of them, as landowners themselves, were accustomed to think positively of peasant grievances; and all were more preoccupied with the nationalist agenda and the bitter feuds to which it gave rise. Popular anger as evinced over the Wall came as a revelation. The club-wielding peasants who swarmed into Jerusalem in August 1929 felt economically threatened, and leaders like Hajj Amin al-Husayni perceived political advantage; but all were united in defence of Islam. Religion transcended all other concerns and united all levels of Muslim Arab society.

The defence of the Haram was, of course, more than just a pretext. Sectarian paranoia had long pervaded Palestinian society; and Islam had long been central to Palestinian Arab nationalism, especially in its relations with Damascus and Cairo. But for the Arab leadership the affair chiefly exposed the potential of mass action as a negotiating weapon, even an ultimate sanction. And for High Commissioner Chancellor it prompted the inescapable conclusion that Shaw's commission of enquiry must address issues arising from the mandate itself, like the physical dispossession and political alienation of peoples in his charge.

Tacitly the British government seems to have approved this sabotaging of its instructions and to have agreed to give Chancellor a

— no land available for dispossessed
Arab peasants.

chance.[32] The High Commissioner had already sounded out Arab opinion and was aware of a report from Philby, who had passed through Damascus and Jerusalem in October 1929. Although a Labour man and on good terms with the new Colonial Secretary, Philby had no authority to negotiate but simply indulged his passion for promoting representative Arab government. He talked to several Arab leaders and became convinced that, despite their demands for full self-government, they would actually 'meet the British government half way'[33] and settle for a representative assembly within the framework of the mandate.

Chancellor related this suggestion to the aborted 1922 proposal for a partially elected Legislative Assembly, or Council. Further negotiations on it were conducted through the ubiquitous George Antonius, lately of the Palestine Education Service, now closely associated with the Mufti, and enjoying the financial support of his old friend Charles Crane of the King-Crane Commission. Antonius endorsed the proposal, and the Legislative Council duly figured in the Shaw Report and was tabled in the 1930 White Paper.

If Arabs were intrigued by this, they were quietly jubilant over the economic proposals that accompanied the White Paper. Sir John Hope Simpson, who compiled this subsidiary report, had lately served as a specialist in population transfer and resettlement. As such, he frowned on what he found in Palestine, confirming the plight of the Arab peasantry, urging stricter control of land sales, condemning the Zionist boycott of Arab labour, and pleading for a well-funded and 'methodical scheme of agricultural development'. This scheme, if implemented (a big 'if', given the world-wide recession), might eventually allow for the settlement of another 20,000 immigrant families. But without it, the 'absorptive capacity' of the country (which 'should take into account the effect of immigration on Arab employment') was, by implication, nil. The Shaw report agreed: 'only by the adoption of such a policy [that is, a development programme] will additional Jewish agricultural settlement be possible'.[34] Meanwhile immigration would obviously have to be curtailed. It looked, in short, as if a British government had at last grasped the nettle in the thicket of Arab grievances.

But nettles sting, sometimes in unexpected places. In making his report Hope Simpson had been emphatic about there being no surplus land in Palestine available for dispossessed Arabs or new

Jewish immigrants. Zionists sought to contest this and, mindful of the wide open spaces across the Jordan, redirected attention to Abdullah's Transjordan.

It so happened that the British, by way of rewarding Abdullah for his military co-operation over the 'Wailing Wall riots', had enabled him to become a large Transjordanian landowner in his own right and so ease his always straitened financial circumstances. Much of the land Abdullah thus acquired, though tax-exempt, yielded little income; but as already discovered by some of his fellow-countrymen, its development potential to Zionist investors might be considerable. Contacts were therefore made, and although Abdullah refrained from actually leasing anything, he did in 1932–3 conclude a deal in which an option to lease a substantial tract of land in Transjordan was taken up by the Jewish Agency in return for an annual payment to the Amir.

Money for old rope, it must have seemed to Abdullah; but it was the British who had supplied the rope and Abdullah who now obligingly hanged himself with it.[35] For as news of the deal leaked out, his denials neither reassured critics in Transjordan nor impressed Palestinian Arabs. Not for the last time, Abdullah was thus fatally compromised in the eyes of Palestinian nationalism just when worsening Anglo-Palestinian relations might have enabled him to play his long-cherished role as Arab champion and intermediary with the British.

A White Paper is not law, merely a report of government intent for the information of Parliament. In the case of the 1930 White Paper which incorporated the Shaw and Hope Simpson reports, this was just as well. Parliament did not like it; nor did the British press; nor, needless to say, did the Zionists. Howls of protest came not just from Palestine but from all over the world. Weizmann made a public announcement of his immediate resignation as chairman of the Jewish Agency and of the Zionist Organization. Other British and American Jews followed suit. Conservative politicians roundly denounced the Paper's terms, while their legal experts declared it a breach of the mandate. Lloyd George likewise fulminated about its 'breaking the word of England'. Even some Labour MPs joined the chorus of criticism.

Although heading a minority government, Ramsay MacDonald might yet, by making the White Paper an issue of confidence, have

[handwritten marginalia: "Jews don't want Legislative Council as long as they are minority"]

[handwritten marginalia: "support of Jews despite 'White paper'"]

secured approval. But taking fright at this reaction and anxious over the response of the Mandates Commission, he now so compromised the proposals as to render them ineffective. In a letter, billed as a 'clarification', to Weizmann of February 1931 (the 'MacDonald Black Letter' in Arab historiography) he affirmed support of the Balfour Declaration, declared that there would be no change in policy, repudiated the suggestion that Jewish immigration must now be dependent on full Arab employment, and confirmed that Jewish enterprises might continue to employ only Jewish labour. The Shaw Report, in short, had been shorn.

Not mentioned in this retraction, however, was Sir John Chancellor's idea of reviving the 1922 proposal for a Legislative Council. It therefore remained on the table, a sad left-over of the original banquet but a crumb to comfort Arab indignation. It stayed there for the next three years. Possible permutations of the representative element in the Assembly's composition had to be studied with due regard to Muslim, Christian and Jewish sensibilities; the Council's competence, or lack of it, in respect of immigration and other contentious issues had to be thrashed out; and according to Chancellor's successor as High Commissioner, it was best to proceed first with self-governing institutions at municipal level. These took time to organize but, following elections in 1934, proved a modest success, with Arabs and Jews actually working together on some town councils. Meanwhile the Legislative Council proposals went back and forth between the High Commissioner's office, the Colonial Office, the Permanent Mandates Commission, the Zionist Executive and the Arab leadership.

Opinion was fairly equally divided. The Zionists would have nothing to do with the idea; so long as Jews remained a minority in Palestine, representative government must be prejudicial to the establishment of the national home; they would support such proposals only if confident that the Arabs would reject them. The Arabs were ambivalent. Publicly the more influential of the several political parties into which Arab opinion was now divided were dismissive, although privately and individually most Arab leaders were willing to consider the proposals with a view to securing more concessions. The Colonial Office felt much the same. If the proposals were implemented, it was apprehensive of the parliamentary and international consequences; if not implemented, of the consequences in Palestine.

proposals dismissed

The High Commissioner shared these anxieties; but, more fearful of the Palestinian consequences of non-implementation, he remained firmly in favour of the proposals.

This carried the day. The government announced its intention to proceed, and in February 1936 the proposals were debated in the House of Lords. But as over the 1930 White Paper, it immediately became apparent that there, and in the Commons, they had little support. In fact, attitudes had considerably hardened in favour of the Zionists now that Nazi Germany had embarked on its orgy of anti-Semitism. The government therefore, having tested the water, postponed its bath. More consultation was necessary, another commission of enquiry should be set up, another Arab delegation sent to London.

In vain the High Commissioner threatened resignation, warned of 'civil disturbances' and cited the examples of Syria and Egypt. Egypt, after student riots, was at last signing the treaty that confirmed its independence; in Syria months of strikes and demonstrations had just climaxed with the French inviting a delegation to Paris to conclude the treaty with the Blum government that should have given the country independence. Hoping that a similar invitation might defuse Palestinian Arab tempers, the British government opted for an Arab delegation to London. The delegation was preparing to set off when in April 1936 a splutter of killings, mainly by Arabs of Jews, led the delegates to cancel their trip. The situation rapidly deteriorated, emergency regulations were introduced, and as the Palestine Revolt got under way, consitutional tinkering fell a casualty to the conflict.

It was not retraction of the 1930 White Paper or the 1936 Legislative Council that had provoked the Revolt. Its causes lay elsewhere – in the mandate, in the frustration born of nearly two decades of stultifying colonial rule, in the recent and overwhelming surge in Jewish immigration, in the Nazi persecutions that were prompting it, and in the international sympathy for the Jews that resulted. But just possibly elections for a Legislative Council might have pre-empted the Revolt. And just possibly acceptance and implementation of the Shaw and Hope Simpson reports might have disposed the Atlantic powers to themselves accept some responsibility for the fate of German-Polish Jewry. Without prejudicing the national home, the US and British governments might even have considered welcoming to their own spacious shores those for whom Palestine was neither the preferred place of settlement nor that which could most readily accommodate them. As it was, the proposals succumbed to party politics, and colonial government ran true to form as notoriously unresponsive. The 'last cross-roads' was allowed to slip past with no change of direction. The bus-load of dissension which was British-mandated Palestine lumbered on to disaster.

Part Three

1936–1945

10

The Arab Reawakening

PASSING WIND

To NASIRIYA DISTRICT in southern Iraq a young RAF officer called Alan MacDonald had in 1930 been posted as a 'Special Service Officer'. The job entailed collecting information about tribal movements and political activity that might be of interest to his airborne colleagues and to the desert patrols operated by 'Jack' Glubb. With the RAF being, thanks to Churchill, the senior service in Iraq, MacDonald was in effect military attaché for the district and so a notable member of local society.

As such his obligations included attendance on Nasiriya's senior shaykh to offer felicitations at the end of Ramadan. More chore than challenge, this meant wearing a uniform and wasting a morning. Without enthusiasm, MacDonald wrestled with buttons and buckles, encased his calves in puttees, attached his medals, and tramped off to the local *serai*.

Abd al-Qadir, the shaykh and civil official (*mutasarrif*), sat at the end of a long room receiving his guests. There were about thirty, all Iraqis, mostly tribal dignitaries but including a few officials like the local doctor and the judge. After salutations, each retired to one of the chairs that lined the walls. Coffee and sugared almonds did the rounds; cigarette smoke filled the room. The conversational sallies were brief and inconsequential. Mostly they sat in sweaty silence. MacDonald felt as if he was in church.

Then from one of the tribal elders there came a soft and unmistakable belch. The sound hung in the air like the cigarette smoke before dying back into the silence. No one paid any more attention to it than to the cooing of the doves outside. But MacDonald was transfixed, quivering with conjecture. To him it was as if the brotherhood of man had been called into question and as if, across the silence, East and West stood 'embattled'. The doctor, the judge and the *mutasarrif* were familiar with Western ideas of decorum. So what thoughts were 'fluttering near their hearts at this moment', he wondered? Were they despising him for being embarrassed? Or were they themselves embarrassed by their fellow-countryman? Did they warm to the foreigner in their midst for having associated them with his own unease? Or detest him for associating them with the sublimely indifferent culprit? One thing was certain, reasoned MacDonald:

> That soft unequivocal sound, venturing into the silence of our dignified and absurd assembly, exhumed truths which a week of careful debate would not have uncovered. It is a perfect comment on all the solemn Western aspirations in Asia; on the meretricious pretensions and national conceit of the Mutaserrif, the Judge and the Doctor; on my own puttees, medals and pomposity. To all these things it gives a complete answer in something less than one syllable. It has the three qualities of the perfect observation, for it is unambiguous, brief and annihilating.[1]

The same three qualities distinguish MacDonald's *Euphrates Exile*, a book possibly unique in delivering from within the system an utterly devastating critique of British involvement in the Middle East in the inter-war period.[2] During his two and a half years in Iraq MacDonald seems to have performed his duties conscientiously, yet all the while reeling in a daze of angry puzzlement. He found as much to criticize among the educated Iraqis as among his fellow-Britons, and he was not innocent of the very condescension which he so deplored. But his fundamental gripe was with official policy. It appeared to be formulated on a incredible misconception. When for the umpteenth time, in the Colonial Office, the Cabinet, or some Cairo hotel, the policy-makers gathered round the polished mahogany, their complacency seemed never to be disturbed by a simple belch-like truth: that, as he put it, 'we are loathed'. Ideals were propounded, priorities identified and intentions framed on the assumption of warm and friendly relations; but the 'horrid' fact was that, despite individual instances of Anglo-Arab camaraderie, in Iraq the British as a whole were 'unpopular, positively disliked, even hated'.[3]

Admittedly MacDonald's experience was limited to the lower Euphrates, the region whence Iraq's 1920 'insurrection' had drawn its inspiration and whose mainly Shi'ite townsmen and tribes had no love for the ruling Anglo-Sunni élite in Baghdad. Had he rubbed shoulders with Sunni partisans like Nuri al-Said and Jaafar al-Askari, men who had served with Faysal during and after the Arab Revolt and who were now happily reacquainting themselves with the fruits of office under Faysal's British-dispensed rule, he might have qualified his opinion; to them the British presence was indeed welcome, though still disliked.

On the other hand, a visit to Palestine would have confirmed MacDonald's devastating generalization. In the autumn of 1933, a series of Arab demonstrations in Jerusalem and Jaffa had for the first time been directed solely and specifically against the British administration. They were well organized and no Jews were attacked, a fact which may explain why they have sometimes been ignored in the belief that 1930–5 was a period of amity and prosperity in Palestine. But in the 1933 demonstrations twenty-six Arabs were killed by police gunfire, and the associated strikes briefly gave a foretaste of what was to follow in the 1936 Revolt. Although undoubtedly prompted by the rising tide of Jewish immigration, the trouble, according to one Arab leader, expressed 'the wrath of the Palestinian Arab Nation . . . suffering from British imperialism and the British government's violation of the rights of the owners of the country'.[4] Few Britons imagined that they were loved; but neither did they realize that to Arabs their presence had become as objectionable as that of their supposed Zionist protégés. In Palestine as in Iraq and Syria, before the Second World War as after it, the representatives of Western power were invariably 'unpopular, positively disliked, even hated'.

It could hardly be otherwise. The mandates supposed one form of Western hegemony, and independence merely supposed another. Alan MacDonald declared himself a firm believer in the principles of the mandate and had rejoiced over their consummation when in 1932 Iraq joined the League of Nations. 'I feel today happier over my nationality than I have for many a year,' he wrote.[5] But having witnessed the travesty of democratic procedures that passed for an Iraqi election, he had grave doubts about Iraq's commitment to representative government and even graver doubts about the sincerity of British support for it.

Among his colleagues the prevailing opinion favoured giving the Iraqis limited independence, in the confidence that any progress towards complete independence would be quickly aborted by some act of violence, probably sectarian. Thus the British would have a moral justification for staying on in Iraq which, according to MacDonald, was all that the more cynical or 'practically-minded' wanted. 'On every occasion when the [Iraqi] state, advised by British officials, supported by the Royal Air Force, encouraged by the British Government, succeeds in damming the threatening tide of barbarism, nearly all the "practical" Englishmen in the country groan with disappointment.'[6] As in Palestine, a certain degree of unrest was preferred. Old imperial conceits about British indispensability were thereby affirmed, careers secured and an agreeable way of life – 'comfortable house, good pay, regular meals, sleek horses, obliging servants and a most leisurely and entertaining job' – retained.

In the summer of 1933, barely a year after independence, the first 'tide of barbarism' had obligingly flooded northern Iraq in what the international press termed the 'Assyrian Massacres'. Christians from eastern Anatolia, the Assyrians had fought with the Allies against the Turks in the First World War, had lost their homeland as a result, and had sought refuge under British protection in Iraq's Mosul province. Numbering about 40,000, some had then been recruited as British auxiliaries in the locally raised Iraq Levies and had taken part in counter-insurgency work, like the suppression of the 1920 uprising. Neither this nor their faith endeared them to Muslim Iraqis; and the disbandment of the Levies became an early priority for independent Iraq.

But the protection of all minorities, and especially one as ancient, loyal and Christian as the Assyrians, was a major concern of the League of (mainly Christian) Nations and its Permanent Mandates Commission in Geneva. It was because of anxieties over Kurdish and Assyrian safety in an independent Iraq that the Commission had originally opposed the early termination of the mandate; and it had subsequently agreed to it only reluctantly and after guarantees from the Iraqis, supported by the British, that the Assyrians would be fairly treated. These guarantees now proved worthless, largely

The Arab Reawakening

because what the Iraqis and the British considered fair treatment – protected status leading to assimilation within Iraq – fell far short of the full and lasting autonomy desired by the Assyrians.

In July 1933, despairing of justice from Baghdad, a large party of armed Assyrians moved across the upper Euphrates into French Syria. The French declined to receive them; and in the confusion of disarming them and repatriating them to Iraq, fighting broke out. In this affair Arab fatalities exceeded those of the Assyrians. Baghdad was incensed. Iraqis, for once united in their determination to stamp out the supposed 'rebellion', did so by exacting ferocious reprisals on the largely defenceless Assyrian communities back in Mosul. A nationalist edge was given to this repression by the fear of British intervention on behalf of their Assyrian protégés; and with King Faysal junketing in Britain in July and on his death-bed by September, it was the young Crown Prince Ghazi who, fanning the fury, reaped much of the doubtful credit. The massacres were conducted by regular Iraqi troops as well as Kurds and Arab tribesmen. In one incident 315 Assyrians, including some women and children, were calmly mown down by machine-guns. But as is the way with most genocidal endeavours, the total casualty count is unknown.

The British had failed to prevent this disaster while unwittingly contributing to it. The RAF's presence, the Iraqi army's dependence on British advisers and arms, and the privileged position once enjoyed by the Levies undoubtedly encouraged Assyrian defiance. Yet official British policy was to support the Baghdad government and uphold its efforts at integration. In Iraq as in Geneva, the Assyrians had been betrayed, and accusations to that effect were loudly voiced. They made no difference. A few of the Levies were later re-employed by the British as guards for their airbases; but no enquiry into the massacres was held, no Iraqis were tried for their part in them, and no compensation was paid for the losses sustained by the hapless Assyrians. 'These valiant stubborn people had come to the end of their long tempestuous history,' noted the American Wiliam Yale, 'victims of the hatreds engendered by the clash between western imperialism and the rising nationalism of Near Eastern peoples.'[7] A similar fate had overcome the Armenians during and after the First World War. Who was to say that the Kurds would not be next? Or that a similar 'solution' might not be adopted in Palestine in respect either of its Jewish minority or even of its Arab majority? With such precedents to hand it was not surprising that Zionists would reject outright any suggestion of a national home, however safeguarded, within an Arab state.

Those of MacDonald's British colleagues who imagined that they were in Iraq in order to uphold the principles of the League of Nations were clearly wrong. Yale, endorsing MacDonald's candour in a later history of the region, saw the British position as designed to 'secure imperialist interests without assuming the invidious burden of colonial rule'. The Anglo-Iraqi treaty, together with its annexes, ostensibly concentrated on the country's international security, giving the British effective control of Iraq's external relations, free use of all its facilities in the event of war or the threat of war, and permanent use of certain airbases which were in effect extraterritorial enclaves. In return, as it were, the British undertook to provide the Iraqis with arms, military supplies, instructors and advisers, all to be paid for by Iraq and on the understanding that 'in view of the desirability of identity in training and methods' Iraq would not approach anyone else for similar services. Yale, writing in the 1950s, carefully examined these arrangements of the 1930 Anglo-Iraqi treaty. He did so because he thought them of particular interest to his fellow-Americans in that the same terms had since been 'adopted in modified form by the United States government in countries far beyond the confines of the Near East'.[8]

But why, mused MacDonald, was the British government so committed to Iraq's defence? What, from a British taxpayer's point of view, were the interests which must be defended? Why, in short, was he there, melting into his uniform in Nasiriya? It could only be for those two other 'unambiguous, brief and annihilating monosyllables', the air and the oil. The oil was obvious. Mosul's oilfields were within easy reach of Kemalist Turkey and, along with the neighbouring fields in Persia, too close to Bolshevist Russia to be left undefended. A military presence in Iraq was essential to the security of this vital resource. Yet ironically it was not the oilfields but the pipeline thence to the Mediterranean port of Haifa that would prove the most vulnerable part of the supply system. Completed in 1934–5, the pipeline's trans-Palestine section promptly became a prime target of the Palestine Revolt and was under threat for much of the next three years. Moreover of the three RAF bases in Iraq, that in Mosul, whence any foreign attack on the oilfields themselves might most conveniently have been repulsed, had been evacuated in 1934.

Thereafter British air-power was concentrated at Basra and at a vast new base near Lake Habbaniya to the west of Baghdad. Linked to other bases in Transjordan and Palestine by means of those directional furrows and desert landing-strips, the Iraqi installations formed part of an imperial air-route stretching from Europe and the Mediterranean to the Gulf and India. With aviation expected to play a major role in imperial defence, as well as communications, and with Iraq lying astride the empire's east–west axis, a British presence there was a strategic necessity. Once again it seemed too obvious to need emphasis. But once again realities belied the basic assumption. For all were agreed that the great object was to be able to move troops rapidly to and from India; yet in the 1920s the planes were too small to carry more than a handful of troops, while in the 1930s the technical advances that permitted larger payloads also permitted longer flights, thereby eliminating the need for the short hops on which the air-route strategy was based.

Much had been made at the time of a 1932 airlift in which a battalion was transferred from Egypt to Iraq to overawe a threatened strike by the restive Assyrian Levies prior to their 'rebellion'. But the shuttle was conducted largely by civil aircraft, like the three-engined biplanes optimistically known as 'airliners' that were operated by Imperial Airways. With a range of over 500 miles these were already offering a weekly Cairo–Karachi service. Refuelling stops at either Baghdad or Basra were normal, but they were made at civilian airports rather than military bases. It seemed, therefore, that in practice the RAF's role in Iraq, after independence as before, was more that of supporting the Iraqi government in its interminable struggles with dissidents like the Kurds and the Euphrates tribes. After independence the RAF was not supposed actually to engage these troublemakers, and indeed it seldom had to; its presence was usually enough to overawe them. In 1935, for instance, when the tribes of MacDonald's Nasiriya district rose against the government, the RAF ferried fuel and ammunition for the Iraqi forces and conducted reconnaissances for them, all of which was sufficient to convince the insurgents that British intervention was imminent and to dissuade others from joining them.[9]

So for the British presence in Iraq, oil supplies and air routes provided an imperial pretext but not, reasoned MacDonald, a logical imperative. Ultimately he and his colleagues were there, it seemed,

- IRAQ's first military coup: 1936
- IRAQI claims sovereignty over KUWAIT
1936–1945

simply to uphold the regime that permitted them to be there. Unfathomable in its intent, this dalliance was not necessarily objectionable so long as both parties were on good terms. But the discovery that in fact 'we are loathed' made it extremely dangerous. At any moment the regime might capitalize on this loathing, and what then? Iraq's first military coup came four years after independence; political trials and assassinations were soon commonplace; and within nine years sixteen cabinets had sunk without trace in the political vortex of Baghdad.[10] Constancy was a rare commodity in Iraqi politics; no treaty, least of all one with the detested British, looked likely to outlive its signatories.

Yet the first challenge came from the least expected quarter. Belying his playboy reputation, King Ghazi, Faysal's son and in 1933 his successor, built on his celebrity in suppressing the Assyrians to stand forth as 'the embodiment of the anti-British forces in the country'. 'A simple, stubborn, uncompromising nationalist', according to Said K. Aburish,[11] one of his later champions, he 'followed his feelings without giving much thought to the results'. In this carefree spirit, he set up his own palace radio station and over the airwaves preached pan-Arabism and inveighed against British policy in Palestine. Additionally, as of 1937, he promoted a claim, as popular as it was fraught with future consequence, to Iraqi sovereignty over British-protected Kuwait.

Then, as later, this claim was highly provocative. At the head of the Gulf just below the Shatt al-Arab, the shaykhdom of Kuwait had once been a constituent part of the Ottoman province of Basra. Iraq, as the successor state to three such provinces, including that of Basra, rested its legal claim on this historical precedent. Additionally, the as yet oil-less Kuwait derived its meagre revenues from pearl fishing and smuggling, the latter of which was to the economic detriment of Baghdad. Iraq and its king therefore proposed building their own Gulf port on what might be Kuwaiti territory in order to suppress this smuggling. Other minor disputes and border incursions heightened the tension. And the 'simple' Ghazi seemed oblivious to British and Kuwaiti claims that the occasional sovereignty of the defunct Ottomans had long since been superseded in international law by treaties that recognized Kuwait as a sovereign entity under British protection.

As the crisis worsened, the desirability of replacing Ghazi with a more amenable Hashemite sovereign occurred both to the British and to their closest Iraqi clients, including the wily Nuri al-Said. Whether either lifted a finger, let alone a blunt instrument, to effect this change is disputed. The official line was that towards midnight on the night of 3 April 1939, King Ghazi and two companions piled into one of the royal sports cars, raced through the palace gates on some mysterious errand, and collided with a lamp standard which then crashed down on top of them, smashing the King's skull. He died about an hour later, probably without regaining consciousness. But the freakish nature of the accident troubled contemporaries and has exercised posterity ever since. The car did not appear to have been damaged; requests for an enquiry or a post-mortem were rejected; and the readiness with which the widowed Queen recalled a royal injunction that her obligingly pro-British brother should, in the event of Ghazi's death, act as regent was, to say the least, convenient.

British satisfaction with this outcome was to be short-lived. The affair, coming just before the outbreak of the Second World War, was a gift to the Axis powers whose propaganda commanded much attention among disaffected Iraqis. Nuri al-Said's government lasted for another twelve months; but Germany's willingness to supply the Iraqi forces with the weaponry that a rearming Britain was unable to spare undermined the 1930 treaty, while early German successes in Europe raised doubts about the Allies' prospects. By 1940 a ring of young Iraqi colonels, unobligated to the British and inspired more by German militarism, were calling the political tune in Baghdad. And within a year the British would be barricading themselves behind the walls of their own embassy, mindful of Townshend at Kut as they scanned the horizon for signs of relief. Although war had finally lent some purpose to their presence in Iraq, they could no longer pretend that this presence was other than loathsome to most Iraqis.

PAN-ARABIAN

During the 1930s the oil pipeline and the air route, forged through their trans-Arabian corridor, seemed scarcely to justify the heavy price being paid by the British for their mandates in Palestine/Transjordan and Iraq. The more ambitious scheme of a direct railway linkage between the Mediterranean and the Gulf never materialized; and neither had anything resembling an east–west highway. There was, though, a bus service. Immensely popular with international travellers in the 1930s, it could be booked by the Baghdad-bound when they landed at Beirut or Haifa and tempted even tourists from their Mediterranean cruises with its promise of a desert experience independent of camels. But the buses reached Iraq not via Palestine and Transjordan but through Syria, whose terrain was flatter and firmer; for what distinguished the two-day Damascus–Baghdad run was that it had to be made almost entirely off-road.

Operated by the most memorialized fleet of omnibuses in Asia, the service was the brainchild of two brothers from Blenheim in New Zealand. Norman Nairn was the businessman, Gerald Nairn the brawny mechanic. Both had served in the Middle East during the First World War and had then stayed on, first selling cars, then operating taxis between Haifa and Beirut. In the absence of a coast road, this run was made mainly along the beach and involved, as well as tidal calculations, handling skills appropriate to sand and shingle. The same skills could be useful in the desert.

In 1923, using Buicks and Cadillacs fitted with Gerald's own balloon tyres, the Nairns won French support to pioneer a twice-weekly Damascus–Baghdad taxi service. The cars bounced along in convoy, fanning out across the desert in bow formation during the day and drawing into a circle, like covered wagons, for the overnight camp. Although occasionally waylaid by Bedouin, they were more often marooned by mechanical failure or stuck in Mesopotamia's mud. In 1924 a pontoon bridge replaced the Euphrates ferry at Ramadi. The three-day journey was cut to two, and the Nairn brothers began to be credited with having changed the course of history.

For the first time ever, the Middle East was assuming an integrated aspect. Baghdad, instead of being three weeks from Beirut by ship or camel, was now only forty-eight upholstered hours away; indeed according to the *New York Times* it was only fifteen days from the USA.[12] Amman, already linked to Jerusalem via the Allenby Bridge, soon followed suit with its own Baghdad taxi link. No longer could it be said that the region's Mediterranean front porch was unconnected to its Asiatic back yard. The desert was shrinking, the long shadows of Lebanon's cedars reaching out towards the rootbowls of Iraq's date palms.

Nor was it just a question of speedier travel. Nairn vehicles carried freight, bullion and mail as well as passengers. Closer diplomatic, economic and social links were being forged across the Arab world even as politically the constituent states into which it had been carved became more entrenched. As a correspondent of the *Near East* magazine noted in 1924, the Nairns had 'done more in the past year to unite the kingdoms of Syria and Iraq than the politicians of Europe and Arabia have been able to accomplish (or prevent, as the case may be) in a decade'.[13]

The first Nairn bus, a six-wheeler named 'The Babylon' by King Faysal, entered service in 1926. Dodging the brigandage attendant on Syria's Great Revolt, it returned a healthy profit and was soon joined by 'The Aerocar'. This was an articulated contraption consisting of a sawn-off Buick towing what looked like the wingless fuselage of an aeroplane. Robert Byron, travelling east on 'the road to Oxiana' with Christopher Sykes in 1933, likened this tender to a banana on wheels. Its windows were curtained portholes to reduce the glare and its seating wicker armchairs to ease the ride. Neither was entirely effective. At a steady forty miles an hour the Aerocar gobbled up the desert while the sun hammered remorselessly on its tin roof, rocks clattered deafeningly against its steel floor, and passenger decorum dissolved in puddles of sweat. Privacy, like personal freshness, was at a premium. At comfort stops a simple rubric of 'ladies to the left, gentlemen to the right' was observed, the only cover in the lunar wilderness being that of the bus itself. Lunch came packed in attractive boxes bearing the motto 'Service with a Smile'. 'It will be Service with a Frown if we ever operate transport in these parts,' grumbled Byron as butter-wrappers and eggshells were casually added to the desert litter.[14]

These inconveniences were largely eliminated when in 1933 on-board toilet facilities and refreshments were offered following the introduction of what probably was, as the publicity claimed, 'the biggest bus in the world'. Seventy feet long, with a mezzanine upper deck, the Marmon-Herrington was an articulated ten-wheel juggernaut, American-built like most of the Nairns' vehicles, with a 150-horsepower engine capable of desert speeds of over fifty miles per hour.[15] Its interior unashamedly mimicked the luxury of the then popular flying-boats; the thirty-eight seats all reclined into beds, and there were whirring fans, a buffet bar and smiling hostesses. Externally it dwarfed most local buildings and anticipated the road-trains of the Australian Outback. When first sighted on the horizon, it was easily mistaken for an approaching sandstorm. Emerging from this maelstrom of its own making, it crunched across the gravel flats, spurting rocks as it plunged through dried-up watercourses and scattering flocks as it thundered over the thorny scrub. Contemptuous, like its passengers, of every oriental objection, the mother of all buses bore down upon Baghdad, as impervious as the colonial ideology that it symbolized and as unstoppable as the global conflagration that was about to engulf it.

Halfway in its headlong dash towards the city of Haroun al-Rashid, the Nairns' bus made its overnight stop at god-forsaken Rutba – or to British passengers 'Rutba Wells', as if it were a displaced Tunbridge Wells. Freya Stark reckoned, somewhat fancifully, that Rutba must be the palace planted in the wilderness by Aladdin's uncle when he rubbed the lamp; two hundred miles from anywhere, 'how else can it have got there?' she wondered. Not yet the *grande dame* of many books and far-flung places, Stark was in her mid-thirties and travelling on the cheap, encumbered only by a heavy grudge against society's conventions. Although she would become something of a regular on the Damascus–Baghdad run, she scorned the comforts of 'the Nairn' for the cramped conviviality of one of the many overloaded but authentically Arab taxis that followed in the buses' wake. Her companions in 1932 were an Armenian driver, a Lebanese colonel and two large ladies from Aleppo on their way to visit their brother in Baghdad. Such was the casual traffic which the Nairns' enterprise had spawned.

To the crushed humanity in the taxis, Rutba meant relief. A water-hole, if never a leafy oasis, it had become a settlement courtesy first of the RAF, whose pioneers cleared a landing-strip, then of the pipe-line contractors, who built a pumping-station, then of the Nairns, at whose instigation a barracks-like resthouse was added to the sprawl of heavily fenced blockhouses and tents. With its few dust-laden oleanders and its promise of bug-free beds, overpriced beer and salmon mayonnaise (the salmon tinned, the sauce bottled), it left Stark feeling nearer to home than at any time since her discovery of marmalade in Jericho.[16]

Most travellers were less complimentary. At the long dining-table, beneath the notice-board and the photograph of Faysal, there would over the years sit a galaxy of celebrities. As well as exotics like Robert Byron, the Shah of Persia and Agatha Christie, through Rutba would pass almost everyone who had a hand in the Middle East in the 1930s. Hubert Young and Jack Philby, Lawrence Grafftey-Smith and Alec Kirkbride, Alan MacDonald and Jack Glubb, Nuri al-Said, Mufti Hajj Amin al-Husayni, and that ride-again hero of Hama, Fawzi al-Qawuqji – all were here and none thought much of it. A far cry from Jerusalem's King David Hotel or the Damascus Victoria, let alone Cairo's Shepheard's, it was nevertheless one of the most frequented hostelries in the East. Rosita Forbes, a better-known traveller at the time than Freya Stark (and a determinedly more attractive one), must have been a frequent visitor as she sought the sensational on behalf of her avid readers, turning imperial heads in the process. Ronald Storrs was once duped by the colloquial Arabic coming from beneath her Islamic veil into vacating the ladies' section of an Egyptian Railways waiting-room; Philby planned to run off into the Empty Quarter with her; Glubb, an innocent with women, was so disconcerted by her 'diaphanous clothing' that he had to flee the room; and Grafftey-Smith, like most, found her company a distinct improvement on her prose. Moreover, 'her beauty matched her courage', he sighed as she entranced him with the account of her attempt to reach Mecca.[17]

But for arresting glamour even Mrs Forbes was eclipsed by the identical twins who alighted at Rutba from the Marmon-Herrington in 1935. Tall and shapely, dressed alike, with peerless complexions and loose Shirley Temple tresses, the twins were accompanied by thirty-two pieces of luggage, including two cat-baskets complete with cats. Ruth and Helen Hoffman were Americans from Minnesota (the cats, also identical twin sisters, were of course Siamese); and in their usual state of high-spirited glee the Hoffman twins were venturing to Baghdad to marry an Englishman. The much envied object of their affections would meet them at the bus station. With pipe and tweeds Douglas Brooks managed a wan welcome and, exuding his customary air of unassuming authority, quietly marshalled the luggage, unfazed even by the cats.

Brooks had first spied the Hoffman girls on the train from Port Said to Cairo. But, a quintessential Englishman, having managed to change his seat to one in their compartment, he had taken five hours to come up with a conversational opening. Had the ladies, he finally ventured as the train chugged past Cheops' six-million-ton monument, by any chance seen the pyramids? From this unpromising beginning a friendship had sprung, letters had been exchanged between the Middle East and the United States, and a proposal of marriage had been accepted. By then Brooks, a civil engineer, had met Murdoch, a Scot, formed a company, and won a contract in Iraq to build an embankment on the Tigris. Journey's end for the girls would be a bungalow at Ali al-Gharbi, an unfancied spot below Kut where the aggregate brought down to the river in Brooks-Murdoch's railway wagons was transferred to Brooks-Murdoch's barges for carriage to the dam.

There, against all odds, the girls made a delightful home, filling the garden with flowers and the house with laughter, and turning the whole compound into a mini zoo. The cats gave birth, repeatedly, and their kittens were joined by a succession of gazelles, a jackal, two storks, a flock of partridges, a wild boar, a hare, several peacocks and a disapproving hawk. Children would have completed the picture but failed to arrive. Nor is it clear which of the girls had actually become Mrs Brooks. There was certainly a wedding, but no indication as to whose.[18] The Hoffman twins did nothing individually – neither travel nor marriage nor the writing of books. In *We Married an Englishman*, as in *Our Arabian Nights*, the narrative is throughout in the first person plural. Thus to the reader Ruth is as indistinguishable from Helen, and Helen from Ruth, as they appear in the accompanying photographs and as they doubtless were in real life. The adventures were always just 'ours', including the wedding.

In 1938 the entire ménage removed to Baghdad. Brooks-Murdoch, now the largest contractor in Iraq, was about to start work on a proper highway from Haifa to Baghdad and was already engaged on the completion of the Berlin–Baghdad railway, a section of which in the vicinity of the Iraqi-Syrian border was still missing. Such contracts were an important strand in the post-colonial patron-client relationship. In return for taking Iraq's oil and so providing the country with oil revenues, Britain expected a say in how those revenues were spent. To the exclusive right to supply military requirements was added preferential status in tendering for civil requirements as varied as bulldozers and bottled beer. Petro-pounds (and soon petro-dollars) were expected to benefit the industrialized economies of the West no less than the oil itself.

The girls had just returned from a trip to Amman, 'a town to which practically no one goes'. It had meant travelling on a 'native bus'. This was an experience very different from 'the Nairn', and they now followed progress on the new railway closely. Being able to 'hop aboard the Orient Express, we looked forward to reaching London in six days'. But it was not to be. The completion of the railway, originally overtaken by the First World War, was about to be overtaken by the Second.

King Ghazi's untimely end signalled the beginning of the troubles. Hostile crowds thronged Baghdad, Nuri al-Said disappeared, the British consul in Mosul was murdered, and a Mr Rand called round to tell the Hoffman twins that it was he who would be responsible for their evacuation. 'Never having heard the word "evacuate" applied to Baghdad before,' they wrote, 'we tried to be as casual as the British.'[19] Then Nuri resurfaced. The girls breathed a joint sigh of relief and went off to savour the nomadic life with a shaykh who was encamped near the new section of railway. They were still there in September 1939 when Britain declared war and the Hoffmans' *Our Arabian Nights* comes to an abrupt end.

Presumably Brooks whisked his womenfolk off to the Habbaniya air base and thence to safety. They were not among the foreigners who in 1941 took refuge in the British embassy. Nor, fortunately, was he. For without Douglas Brooks and his civil engineering expertise the force sent to relieve the embassy might never have arrived and Baghdad would have joined Dunkirk and Singapore in the catalogue of early Allied disasters.

THE PALESTINE REVOLT I

For Freya Stark the war began six months before it was declared. In early 1939 she offered to the British Foreign Office her Arabic expertise and her newly gained reputation as a traveller (she was just back from the Hadramaut in southern Arabia), then set off for Syria to kill time. Exploring Crusader castles and revisiting old friends, she collected her letters as she went along. There was no summons from the Foreign Office, but what she calls the 'letter that I desired' was waiting at Hama. In it the writer asked her to marry him; and two days later, in Aleppo, another letter told of the writer's death. It was then that her war began. For three days she wept. The sparkling landscapes were now plunged in shadow. 'Despairing in a world built with despair', she blundered through the crisis, dimly aware that it somehow mirrored that of all Europe.[20] Like Gertrude Bell fleeing heartbreak to immerse herself in Iraq in 1915, it was as if personal tragedy foreshadowed public responsibilities, bracing the spirit, stiffening the upper lip. Stark, aged 46, moderately famous and now romantically detached, would be ready for the war.

Indeed she had seen it all coming. Though English, her background was unconventional and her home was in Italy. There she had followed with dismay Mussolini's long rise to power and had rightly seen his 1935–6 invasion of Abyssinia (now Ethiopia) as a challenge to the British position in the eastern Mediterranean. 'Italy – I never doubted – would fight us if she thought she safely could,' she wrote. The Italian presence in both Libya and Abyssinia menaced the empire's sea-lanes through Suez and the Red Sea, so prompting an interest in overland alternatives like Brooks-Murdoch's proposed Haifa–Baghdad highway, and so concentrating minds wonderfully in Egypt. It jump-started the long-stalled Anglo-Egyptian treaty negotiations; it even produced a stuttering glimmer of mutual regard when, for the first and only time, the face of a British statesman appeared on a Egyptian postage stamp. Ironically the fine patrician features belonged to the then Foreign Secretary, Mr Anthony Eden. Not many countries can have so honoured their future invader.

On Palestine, too, the Italian presence in Abyssinia impinged, but with more mixed results for the British. On the one hand the new strategic threat seemed to vindicate the commitments that Britain had shouldered in order to obtain the mandate in the first place. Palestine was at last to earn its imperial keep as both a Mediterranean base and the Canal's eastern bastion. Similarly the acquisition by Transjordan of the port of Aqaba now looked like a useful insurance in the Red Sea. But, less obviously, the Italian challenge had a knock-on effect on Palestine's internal affairs. The Palestine Revolt was not in any sense prompted by Mussolini's Abyssinian adventure. The unprecedented rate of Jewish immigration in the mid-1930s, plus the retraction by the British of the 1930 White Paper and, subsequently, of its proposals for a Legislative Council, were in themselves ample provocation. Italy was merely an irritant, undermining Palestine's fragile economy and further exciting its restive Arab majority.

Because of the difficulties and delays in realizing capital assets in Europe, the recent flood of Jewish migration into Palestine had not been accompanied by sufficient funds to finance the housing and employment required for all the new arrivals. An excessive reliance on credit resulted. In 1935 street hawkers in Jerusalem were offering even kerosene 'on tick'; for a Jew 'to demand cash became almost an act of treason [betraying] a lack of faith in the future of the National Home', recalled the historian John Marlowe from personal experience.[21]

It was this bubble that the Abyssinian invasion burst. In the 1935 British elections the more hawkish Conservatives had promised to cut off Italy's oil supplies and close the Suez Canal to its Abyssinia-bound shipping. War looked imminent; and although the Conservatives, once elected, reneged on their threats, the scare was enough to cause panic in Palestine. Confidence collapsed, banks foreclosed, businesses folded, social provision was scaled down, and unemployment soared. Jews and Arabs were equally affected; but while Zionist labour policies gave priority to alleviating Jewish unemployment, Arab workers enjoyed no comparable protection and suffered disproportionately. The idea, promoted by Weizmann and endorsed by Lawrence, that Jewish investment would benefit the Arabs as well as the Jews had looked to have some substance during the boom. The bust revealed it as a sham.

Britain's reluctance to make good on its threats against the expansionist ambitions of Italian militarism did not go unnoticed either. The Mufti's followers began to parade and salute in imitation of the *Fascisti*. Meanwhile from Bari in southern Italy a radio station beamed forth in Arabic bursts of anti-British propaganda and concluded each broadcast with a juicy pornographic anecdote. This novel mix of the seditious and the salacious enjoyed a wide currency throughout the duration of the Revolt. Across the air waves, as along the bus routes, rumours, rallying cries and slogans rapidly spread through the Arab world, inspiring support and internationalizing protest.

Contrary to the normal practice of colonial exclusivity, the British would be oddly amenable to this pan-Arab involvement in the Palestinian struggle. Indeed, in defiance of the mandate, they would countenance and then encourage the efforts of other Arab governments to mediate a settlement. Palestine's revolt, in marked contrast to those in Iraq and Syria, would not be an isolated affair. Zionism had shown the way; its international appeal, its claim to represent world Jewry and its ability to mobilize overseas support naturally encouraged Palestinian Arabs to seek their own constituency outside Palestine. But international sanction for pan-Arab engagement in the Palestine problem dated only from the 1936–9 Revolt and would owe as much to the requirements of the British and the ambitions of the neighbouring Arab states as to the hopes of the Palestinian Arabs.

The Revolt is usually supposed to have begun in April 1936 when, in response to the discovery of a mysterious arms shipment, followed by several tit-for-tat killings and another massacre of Jews in Jaffa, the Arab leadership endorsed a general strike. The strike, they declared, was to end only with the establishment of representative Arab government and the halting of Jewish immigration and land purchases. Co-ordinated by a cross-party Higher Arab Committee with the Mufti Hajj Amin al-Husayni at its helm, the strike lasted for six months and defined the first phase of the Revolt. As an economic weapon it was less effective than the general strikes in Syria and Egypt on which it was modelled. Too much of Palestine's economy was already controlled by Jewish enterprise and the strike merely conceded further sectors. But it did receive widespread support, politicizing all sections of Arab society and giving to the Revolt a rationale of organized protest, plus a recognizable leadership with whom negotiations were continuously under way.

It also acted as a catalyst for more violent Arab offensives. In the cities, emergency measures quickly contained these avowedly terrorist activities. When, for instance, the old quarter of Jaffa became a fugitives' sanctuary, it was summarily demolished on the specious grounds that its narrow thoroughfares constituted a health risk. Jaffa's port, closed by the strike, was likewise consigned to oblivion, in this case thanks to British authorization for a Zionist initiative to develop port facilities at neighbouring Tel Aviv. In Jerusalem and Haifa bombs were thrown and shots exchanged before the situation was similarly brought under control. But it was a different story in rural Palestine. As the Revolt spread beyond the easy reach of the security forces, much of the country fell under the sway of local bands of insurgents. Their targets included isolated Jewish commu-

(not a sin to protect yourself — no "turn the other cheek" in Islam)

nities, British law-enforcers, and even rival Arab groups, as well as Jewish businesses and farms, government installations, and roads, railways and pipelines. In the rebels' rough justice and their savage assaults on capitalized agriculture, some observers detected a peasant's revolt, born as much of agrarian distress as of political or sectarian outrage.

But many of these rural bands were aided and armed by guerrilla volunteers from Syria, Iraq and Transjordan under the direction of Fawzi al-Qawuqji. To the British the presence of the mercurial Fawzi was a decidedly unwelcome example of pan-Arab solidarity. The hero of Hama and veteran of many earlier campaigns, Fawzi had lately been acting as a military adviser to Ibn Saud but now reappeared at the head of several hundred Iraqi and Syrian irregulars operating in the hills of Samaria. Even the Mufti, whose leadership of the Higher Arab Committee did not preclude him surreptitiously directing and funding much of this terrorist activity, resented the personal challenge posed by Fawzi's presence. When in September 1936 Fawzi's forces fought a rare battle with British regulars, downing an RAF plane in the process, the Mufti accused the self-proclaimed 'Commander-in-Chief of the Revolt in Southern Syria' (as some Arab nationalists still described Palestine) of being a British stooge and needlessly sacrificing Palestinian lives.

Fawzi replied in kind, and not without reason. The Mufti seemed to be leading a charmed existence. While his involvement in the insurgency was becoming evident to the British, while members of his family, including the young and charismatic Abd al-Qadir al-Husayni, were actively engaged in hostilities, and while lesser leaders were being summarily detained and exiled, Hajj Amin himself continued in his office as president of the Supreme Muslim Council and, with George Antonius acting as his secretary and go-between, was much consulted by the British authorities. No doubt this had something to do with the Mufti's delightful manners and serene composure which so impressed visitors like Christopher Sykes.[22] No doubt, too, there still existed among the British a residue of that ambivalence towards the Arabs which Zionists rightly sourced in the Bedouin sympathies cherished by some latter-day Lawrences and in the anti-Semitic sentiment common throughout British society. The administration as a whole was suspected of not being entirely dismayed by the assertion of Arab rights. Despite losing 37 police officers and military personnel during

1936 (as against 89 Jewish and over 200 Arab fatalities), the authorities seemed to consider their task to be more that of settling the strike than of suppressing the rebellion. Even in London the Palestine government's failure to come to grips with the rural insurgents was roundly condemned. The historian John Marlowe found the administration's indulgence towards the Mufti and his openly seditious Higher Arab Committee 'astonishing'.[23]

But there was some logic to this leniency. Wary of surrendering control to the military, and trusting that the present troubles would prove as manageable as the previous ones, the High Commissioner declined either to impose martial law or to mount operations other than those necessary to clear the roads and reclaim the pipeline and the railways. Though a lieutenant-general, High Commissioner Sir Arthur Wauchope was no warmonger. 'A tiny wizened man with long silver hair, continuously looking into space with his mouth open and head cocked to one side', he had the distracted air of a poet; he loved to garden and he was not easily swayed.[24] Succeeding Chancellor in 1931, he had already presided during one four-year term of comparative peace and modest progress. He embarked on the second determined to defend the record of the first.

This meant avoiding any major confrontation that might prejudice the continuing negotiations. The Legislative Council idea had not, it may be remembered, been formally rejected, just indefinitely retracted pending further discussions with an Arab delegation to London. The delegation was aborted by the outbreak of the Revolt and by the uncompromising demands tabled by the Higher Arab Committee. In its stead and to address the new situation, the British government proposed sending to Palestine a Royal Commission, to be led by Lord Peel. It would be the fourth such enquiry, and by no means the last, but its terms of reference were more comprehensive and its personnel more distinguished than those of its predecessors. The Zionists, mindful that past commissions had invariably meant concessions to the Arabs, opposed it, although they were not keen to be seen to do so. The Higher Arab Committee, although agreeable in principle, would co-operate with the Commission only when its own demands, especially that for a complete stoppage of Jewish immigration, had been met. And the British government, although keen to dispatch the Commission, would do so only when the Higher Arab Committee had called off the strike.

Such was the deadlock into which, at the Palestinians' request and with Wauchope's blessing, the neighbouring Arab governments boldly ventured as mediators. Abdullah of Transjordan, Ibn Saud of Arabia and Nuri al-Said (on behalf of Ghazi of Iraq) each made overtures and each was rebuffed. The Mufti shrewdly suspected that their not dissimilar proposals had first been vetted by their British ally-cum-paymaster and that their involvement was not entirely disinterested. Indeed each of them, while evincing pan-Arab sentiments and fraternal concern for the Palestinians, shared the Mufti's suspicions of the other two. Nuri al-Said made it clear that, in return for getting the Higher Arab Committee to call off its action, the Iraqi government would expect the British to involve Iraq in any settlement arising from the Royal Commission's report.[25] Abdullah, likewise, still openly cherished royal ambitions in Palestine; and Ibn Saud was well aware of both, threatening to demand the return of Aqaba and Ma'an whenever the Hashemites looked to be gaining advantage in Palestine.

The rivalry between the Hashemite king in Baghdad and his opposite number in Amman was no less bitter than that between the Saudi and the Hashemites as a whole. Each coveted Palestine; and its having been awarded to neither while it was yet denied any independent status only heightened the competition. For if, as implied by the mandate, this Cinderella of the First World War settlement was never to be invited to the League of Nations ball, who if not one of these claimants to Arab leadership was to stand up for Palestinian Arab rights and so establish a claim to Palestinian Arab loyalties?

Eventually, in October 1936, after much tedious to-ing and fro-ing, the Higher Arab Committee in Palestine bowed to a joint appeal from all three Arab sovereigns and called off the strike. A precedent was thus set for their intercession without individual advantage having been conceded to any of them. The Mufti and the Higher Arab Committee remained in control. Whether or not, from a British point of view, the intercession of the Arab states represented 'a major shift in mandatory policy' founded on a 'naïve' belief in Great Britain's ability to control future 'interference' is debatable.[26] At the time the 'interference' seemed to the British to be the only way forward if a conflagration was to be avoided. To the Mufti, on the other hand, it seemed the only way out. More British troops were arriving; martial law was about to be imposed; and in a trial of strength the Palestinians were bound to be the losers. Moreover the citrus orchards, on which many Arabs depended for seasonal work and their leaders for annual profits, were now heavy with oranges. It was time to regroup if not retreat. An amnesty for all political detainees was promised. So was the Royal Commission which, arriving within a month, was expected to address Arab political demands.

Whether in the meantime Jewish immigration was to be halted was disputed. After mutual recriminations on the subject, the number of immigrants was drastically reduced, thereby further antagonizing Zionists; but the flow was not stopped, thereby prompting the Higher Arab Committee to declare a boycott of the Royal Commission. Again the three Arab kings were called into play and again the Higher Arab Committee withdrew its boycott at their request. This evidence of the moderating influence exercised by the Arab states impressed the Royal Commission as it set about its task in the winter of 1936–7. So did the popular sympathy for the plight of the Palestinians that was being loudly voiced throughout the Arab world, impelling all Arab governments, including those of Egypt and Syria, to take cognizance of the issue whether or not they perceived advantage.

Interest was heightened by rumours, which were confirmed in its official report of July 1937, that the Royal Commission was in favour of partitioning Palestine. This was indeed 'a major shift in mandatory policy'. In submitting that the spirit of the mandate could be fulfilled only by the political division of the core territory to which it applied, Lord Peel's Royal Commission broke new ground and launched an idea which, in various forms, eventually came to be seen as the only practical solution to the 'Palestine problem'. Yet it is as well to remember that in 1937 (and arguably in 1947) the issue was not that of solving the Palestine problem but of so managing it as not to prejudice the strategic priorities that had created it. In other words, Great Britain's preoccupation in 1937 remained that of imperial defence. Through the dusty arguments for and against every solution there snaked, often unacknowledged but always incontrovertible, the Iraq Petroleum Company's pipeline and that carotid artery of empire, the Suez Canal.

Partition developed from a proposal for the 'cantonization' of Palestine on the Swiss model. This was the solution preferred by Wauchope, possibly with a 'cantonized' Palestine then being included within some form of pan-Arab federation, as proposed by the Iraqis.

J.H. Hall, Wauchope's Chief Secretary, went further along this pan-Arab road, conceding that the international boundaries created after the First World War were 'artificial', that the idea of a pan-Arab federation was gaining momentum, and that Palestine and its problem might be conveniently subsumed within it. Jewish settlement throughout the lands embraced by such an Arab federation could actually be encouraged. It would not prejudice their overwhelmingly Arab character yet it would permit unrestricted immigration at a time when mass sanctuary from Nazi persecution looked to be as much a Jewish priority as the attainment of Zion. On the other hand, and simultaneously, immigration into Palestine itself would be drastically cut, thus reassuring Palestinian Arabs.[27]

But for Zionists the 'close settlement' of Eretz Israel and its elevation to national status took precedence even over the urgent need for a place of Jewish sanctuary. They therefore opposed any scheme of federation. Dr Weizmann, the voice of British Zionism, was especially adamant on this score; and it seems to have been his inspired presentation of the Zionist case that swayed the Royal Commission in favour of outright partition. For Weizmann realized that partition represented a more significant gain for the cause of Zionism than anything since the Balfour Declaration. Crucially, it implied the acceptance by the mandatory of the principle not just of a Jewish national home, or even 'the' national home, but of a separate, sovereign Jewish state; and howsoever small, bitty and indefensible this proposed state might be, that principle was everything. 'Today, in this place,' Weizmann declared after final and conclusive discussions with the Commission's main theorist, 'we have laid the foundations of the Jewish state.'[28]

No one recorded the laying of the foundations of a Palestinian Arab state because, once again, no such entity was envisaged. There was indeed to be an 'Arab state', but it would be one consisting of Transjordan plus 'the Arab part of Palestine'. In other words Palestine, minus the areas reserved for the Jewish state and minus those retained by the British for strategic reasons (like Haifa) or religious reasons (like Jerusalem), was to be reincorporated with Transjordan. The troublesome Mufti and his Higher Arab Committee might thus be counterbalanced by the more dependable, not to say dependent, Abdullah. And wider British interests would be secured by the one-sided Anglo-Transjordanian treaty (to which

Abdullah was already committed) plus another with the new Jewish state (which its chronic vulnerability would oblige it to sign).

It soon emerged, however, that this Jewish state, however ingeniously its boundaries were drawn in order to embrace the areas of densest Jewish settlement, would still include nearly as many Arabs as Jews. The Commission therefore steeled itself to the possibility of some Arabs having to be transplanted, probably to Transjordan as Alec Kirkbride had once suspected. This was clearly an alarming prospect; and it was precisely such details that slowly discredited the whole idea of partition. Only the Higher Arab Committee rejected partition outright, being as opposed to the pretensions of the heavily compromised Abdullah as it was to the alienation of any part of Palestine. But the Zionists, while welcoming the principle of separate statehood, had reservations about the diminutive and disjointed enclaves to which it would apply. And the Iraqis, Saudis and Syrians, swayed as much by their jealousy of Abdullah as by their respect for the Palestinians' intransigence, shied away from the implications of a reunited Palestine-Transjordan.

With partition already receding, it remained only for the British government to follow suit. This it did in the light of the worsening international situation. Indeed, anxious not to alienate pan-Arab opinion on the eve of a war in which the security of its Middle Eastern position would be paramount, it had begun backing off as soon as the Commission's report was published. An Arab National Conference at Bludan in Syria in September 1937 confirmed its worst fears. Officially the conference endorsed the Higher Arab Committee's rejectionist position. It called on all Arabs to continue the struggle for Palestinian liberation and, more ominously, it warned the British government that, unless it changed its policy, 'we shall be at liberty to side with other European powers whose policies are inimical to Great Britain'.[29]

Yet for His Majesty's Government to reverse something as momentous as its own Royal Commission took time and ingenuity. Thus for more than a year the proposal remained on the table. It was not until a second commission, ostensibly designed to work out the boundaries of the two new states, obligingly found against the whole idea of partition that it could be finally withdrawn.

In the end, all that was partitioned by Peel's Royal Commission was Arab opinion. Old feuds within the Higher Arab Committee had already resurfaced, partly over partition itself but more especially with regard to Abdullah, whose ambitions were reviled by the Mufti's followers but welcomed by their rivals. Meanwhile, and in furtherance of this rivalry, old scores were being settled between the rural insurgents of 1936. Nothing had been done about disarming them during the year-long armistice, and they were now ready to renew the struggle. A secret undertaking reached at the Baludan conference ordered the resumption of 'attacks on the persons of Arabs friendly to the British authorities and on Jews'.[30] Yet two weeks later, on 26 September 1937, it was an attack on one of Palestine's most senior British administrators that launched the Revolt on its second, more serious phase.

THE PALESTINE REVOLT II

While Britain's political disillusionment with the Palestine mandate would be a long and complex process lasting from 1936 until 1947, the psychological turning-point in Anglo-Palestinian relations was abrupt and sensational. Walking to church on a sunny Sunday morning in Nazareth, the District Commissioner for Galilee and his Assistant Commissioner, accompanied by a single policeman, suddenly became aware that four Arab gunmen were closing on them from behind. At the Commissioner's suggestion they made a run for it and blundered straight into the point-blank fire of more gunmen stationed in a side alley. The Assistant Commissioner tripped and fell; he was left for dead although in fact he was unhurt. The Commissioner and the constable died instantly in a hail of bullets.

Ricocheting across the hills of Galilee and reverberating throughout Palestine, this short burst of gunfire provoked near panic among members of the British establishment. They were accustomed to the rank-and-file losses inevitable in their peacekeeping role; they were quite unprepared for an outrage against one of their very own. Lewis Andrews, Galilee's Commissioner, was the first senior member of the administration to have been killed in twenty years of British rule. Moreover there was nothing remotely accidental about the attack, as for instance with a bomb blast or a mine. Andrews, a greatly respected figure whose monitoring of Arab-Jewish land sales had implicated senior members of the Arab leadership,[31] had obviously been singled out for elimination. It was a direct challenge to the British administration and must be met as such.

At the time Wauchope, though still the High Commissioner, was on leave in Scotland. It therefore fell to his deputy to reverse his policy of reluctant engagement. In consultation with London, he outlawed the Higher Arab Committee, ordered the arrest of dozens of Arab leaders including Mufti Hajj Amin al-Husayni (who was simultaneously removed as leader of the Supreme Muslim Council), deported or excluded others, assumed emergency powers of summary trial and execution for Arabs found carrying arms, and made arrangements for the imposition of martial law. The gloves were finally being removed.

As part of the same frantic response, a telephone call was placed to Amman. There Alec Kirkbride, now 40 and no longer the bean-pole youth who had once headed the National Government of Moab, was performing the less glamorous duties of Assistant Resident. The news of Andrews's death had already reached him, challenging a famously lofty detachment. Andrews had been one of his closest friends, a professional like himself whose Australian upbringing placed him outside the charmed circle of British-educated administrators just as did Kirkbride's own schooling in Alexandria. But Kirkbride mourned in haste. The telephone call summoned him back to Palestine, in fact to Nazareth; he was to take over the Galilee and Acre district in succession to Andrews.

Comprising Palestine's northern extremity, with open borders to Syria and Lebanon, the district was regarded as the most lawless in the country; indeed orders were already circulating for the assassination of Andrews's successor, whoever he might be. From the ease of a 'town to which practically no one goes', and from the embrace of a devoted young family, Kirkbride was being plucked to what promised to be an early grave. He was given just three days to get there.

Arriving on the third day, he checked into a Nazareth hotel and took stock of the situation. To the Arabs he was an irresistible target. He stood for the policy of partition which meant much of Galilee coming under Jewish rule; and at six feet four inches he was quite unmistakable, indeed unmissable. On the other hand, to the district's 100,000 Jews, most of whom were assertive immigrants living in well-guarded settlements, he was hardly more acceptable. To them he was an Arabist who had served under Lawrence in the Arab

— dissention amongst Palestinians

Revolt and who had been consorting with the Hashemites on and off ever since. Nor was he welcomed even by his departmental personnel. The British police were traumatized by Andrews's death; their Jewish colleagues placed loyalty to their community well above that to the administration; and their Arab colleagues openly sympathized with those who were out to kill him. All of which was reflected in Kirkbride's own ambiguous feelings. Promotion was welcome, and the hills of Galilee were a naturalist's paradise; but he disliked Palestine in general, chafed at its bureaucratic administration, and deeply resented having 'to implement a policy hated by the majority of the people to which it applied'.[32]

As of October 1937 the Revolt resumed with new venom. During the worst months of 1938, all Palestine was brought to a standstill. For the reinforcements arriving from Egypt it was like entering a war zone. Every telegraph pole had been felled, every station burnt out. Along the roads, cars encased in thick steel sheeting edged through the darkness without lights; the trains pushed trolleys to which Arab detainees were handcuffed in order to discourage further mining of the track. Towns like Jaffa and Nablus were occasionally overrun, villages repeatedly burnt and bombed; even the main line to Egypt and the Jaffa–Jerusalem highway were frequently cut. But nowhere was the danger greater than in Galilee and neighbouring Samaria. There the roadless hills were a natural redoubt and their scattered settlements, Arab as well as Jewish, easy prey. The Iraq Petroleum Company's pipeline, a prime target, ran right past Nazareth; and across the Syrian and Lebanese borders poured arms, reinforcements and directives.

The directives came from the Mufti. Having eluded arrest in Jerusalem by taking sanctuary in the Haram al-Sharif, he had since escaped and was now ensconced on Kirkbride's doorstep in Lebanon. Although his condemnation of Andrews's assassination may have been sincere and his escape somewhat convenient, he now burnt his bridges with the British by his open and increasingly shrill direction of his partisans in Palestine. The leadership of his Husayni clan was being assailed from all sides. Militant *mujahidin* demanded more wholehearted support, pro-Abdullah rivals saw in his absence their chance to wrest control of Palestinian opinion, and war-weary peasants increasingly resisted rebel demands or informed on those who made them. It was not the British or the Jews who were sustaining the heaviest casualties from the new Arab offensive but other Arabs.

French hospitality towards the Mufti complicated matters still further. Until the start of the Second World War the French authorities saw no more reason to outlaw the Mufti than the British had Sultan al-Atrash, the Druze leader of the Syrian Great Revolt who had taken refuge in Transjordania. In fact Sultan al-Atrash and his co-leader of that revolt, Dr Shahbandar, continued to be on good terms with Abdullah. To the annoyance of the French, they promoted the idea of a reunited Greater Syria under Hashemite sovereignty and they supported the pro-Abdullah faction of the Palestinian leadership. This naturally led the French to look favourably on the anti-Abdullah Mufti and to ease his stay with funds and intelligence. Once again Anglo-French rivalry was feeding the flames of Arab division. Three years hence, in the midst of the global conflagration, such idle jockeying was to oblige much-needed Allied troops to be diverted to Syria to stage another dash for Damascus.

In an attempt to control the flow of arms and personnel from the north, in the spring of 1938 a barbed-wire fence, four feet wide and seven feet high, was constructed along the Palestine-Syria/Lebanon border. At the same time military roads were laboriously pushed into the lawless hill areas to the east. Kirkbride walked the length of the fence, then drove the new roads. His wife had now joined him in Nazareth, and to spare her the anxiety of his absences he usually took her along. To some they seemed to lead a charmed existence. The Commissioner, not immodestly, ascribed his survival simply to 'patience and honesty, combined with devastating frankness'.

On appeal to the High Commissioner he had been authorized to release the local Arab leadership, who had been detained *en masse* following Andrews's murder. He personally interviewed each man prior to release and asked him to conduct his struggle on constitutional lines. 'All of them promised to do so and a few actually kept their promise.' News that the order for his assassination had been rescinded was further reward; it had apparently been withdrawn 'on the grounds that they were not likely to get anyone better'. Meanwhile Jewish suspicions were lulled by exhaustive visits to every one of their settlements and by Kirkbride's willingness to enrol more Jews in the auxiliary police. Unexpectedly he identified with the leftist ideals of the more radical Zionists, and he came to admire their industry, organization and continued forbearance in the face of extreme provocation. Though the easy repartee that he enjoyed with the Arabs was lacking due to his ignorance of Hebrew, the candour of his humour was appreciated.[33]

But the killing went on, not all of it obscurely. Kirkbride's most objectionable duty was that of presiding at the hanging of convicted 'terrorists'. Over a hundred Arabs were thus executed by the British, many of them in Galilee, for no more certain involvement than the possession of a firearm. Compared to such cold judicial deaths in a dank prison yard, outrages like the July 1938 bombing of a market in Haifa or the massacre of Jews in his own Tiberias seemed less personally shaming. They nevertheless provoked the military into an all-out offensive and tested Jewish forbearance to breaking-point.

As the partition proposal, and with it any immediate prospect of a Jewish state, languished on the table – and was then put back in the drawer – militant Zionist groups, within and without the semi-authorized Haganah, began to exact revenge. At the same time, semi-officially there came to Galilee, hot in their cause, a British legend of a very different stamp from Kirkbride.

Orde Wingate has often been compared to Lawrence. He was no intellectual and he was a little taller, but still below average height, scruffy, pugnacious, eccentric and driven. Other British officers before him had espoused Zionism but none with greater zeal or less reason. 'Everyone is against the Jews, so I'm for them,' he told a fellow-officer soon after arriving in Palestine in 1936.[34] His parents, members of the fundamentalist Plymouth Brethren, had primed him on the Old Testament; Hebrew he learnt in Jerusalem while plying the Jewish Agency with confidential materials gleaned from British intelligence files. When assigned to instruct Haganah units in the field, he discarded uniform, grew a beard, and wore a cowboy holster. He saw himself as Wingate of Zion and the future commander of a Jewish army.

Kirkbride's narrative avoids all mention of him. Although Wingate's operations were wholly confined to Galilee, his was not yet a name to conjure with, and officers of more conventional stamp invariably shrank from his exhibitionist fire-raising. But Kirkbride's account of a 'most amusing' night-time encounter in Nazareth between two 'gum-shoe patrols' who mistakenly engaged one another looks like a swipe at Wingate.[35] 'Special Night Squads' were Wingate's speciality. He recruited, trained and often led them himself; and it was from just such an exchange of friendly fire that he sustained his only war wound.

Commanded by a few hand-picked British officers, the Special Night Squads were otherwise composed entirely of Jews. Wingate argued that an unconventional war must be fought by unconventional means and that nocturnal Arab raids could best be challenged by nocturnal British raiders. But British troops being in short supply and unfamiliar with the terrain, the answer was to arm and train some of those Jews who had already joined the Zionist Haganah in defence of their settlements. Wingate believed that, contrary to received opinion, Jews would make formidable fighters and that Jewish excellence in the arts of peace was no bar to excellence in the skills of war. On the contrary, in the idealism and discipline of Palestine's Jewish settlers he saw a martial potential far greater than that of those whom he dismissed as 'corrupt and slovenly' Arabs.

Such sentiments, coupled with much-embroidered accounts of the exploits of his Special Night Squads, made a deep impression on the Zionist psyche and especially on the younger post-Weizmann generation of Zionist leaders. 'You are the first soldiers of the Jewish Army', Wingate told recruits. At a time when the prospect of a Zionist state seemed to be receding and the flow of immigrants was being choked, his aggressive tactics hinted at another way forward. Demographic disadvantage could be offset by a paramilitary presence; and denied a state, Zion might yet have an army. Isolated communities took heart; Haganah units benefited from his training. Although Weizmann was occasionally embarrassed by such uncompromising fanaticism in a gentile, David Ben-Gurion and Moshe Shertok offered support, and among those who were later proud to call themselves Wingate's disciples were Menachem Begin and Moshe Dayan.

The British were more ambivalent. Wingate was well-connected, being a nephew of the Wingate who had been Governor-General of the Sudan and High Commissioner in Cairo. And he was much admired by some senior military figures who saw in his methods the genesis of later special forces, like the SAS. In Abyssinia and Burma he would eventually gain lasting fame as an exponent of unconventional warfare. But to others he was a lunatic and a liability. He ignored orders, his outspoken Zionism was a political embarrassment, and his tactics too often partook of the 'terrorism' he was supposedly combating. His successes, especially in defence of the oil pipeline, were welcome; yet deployment of Jewish guerrillas was provoking as much hostility as it quelled.[36]

It certainly did not turn the tide of the Revolt. Wingate was in the field for only six months. His Special Night Squads never numbered more than 150 men and they were disbanded soon after his departure in October 1938. Not until eight months later did Kirkbride reckon that the situation in Galilee was coming under control. Indeed exploits like Wingate's were counter-productive, according to Kirkbride; far from deterring the armed rebels they merely encouraged other Arab villagers to join them. 'The measures which ultimately extinguished the trouble had nothing to do with battle and death', insisted Kirkbride; instead they were of a sort to 'merely make life difficult and, eventually, convince the Arabs that it was not worthwhile persisting in their policy of violence'. One such measure was the introduction of identity cards and movement permits which, rigorously enforced, isolated the insurgents and cut them off from the villages on which they relied for support.[37] Another was the encouragement of Arab 'peace bands' whose anti-rebel activities were as dubious as Wingate's though much more productive of intelligence.[38]

MORE WHITE PAPER

Political overtures also helped to stem the violence. The Woodhead Commission, which was supposed to recommend boundaries for the partitioned states as proposed by Lord Peel's Royal Commission, duly failed to agree on how these boundaries could be drawn and published a report confirming the impracticability of the whole idea. That was in October 1938. In the same month an Arab-Muslim conference in Cairo reiterated the threat of Arab co-operation with Italy and Germany unless the British government satisfied Palestinian aspirations. Wingate might argue that the economic potential of the entire Arab world was only 'that of a fourth class power . . . [and its] military potential . . . very far below that', but cooler British heads were mindful of Iraq's oil, Egypt's canal, Ibn Saud's Red Sea frontage, and the Indian army's Muslim component. Jeopardizing any of these at a time of looming crisis was unthinkable.

While peace prevailed in Europe, the best rationale for a continued —— British presence in Palestine had lain in upholding Zionism; when war threatened, the only guarantee of a continued British presence lay in supporting Arab rights. It was essential therefore to assuage Arab opinion; and with partition unacceptable, this could only be achieved by dusting off those charred chestnuts of previous conflagrations – a representative legislative assembly and tighter control of Jewish immigration and land purchases.

A round-table conference, to which were invited representatives of the Arab states and international Zionism as well as the warring Palestinian factions, was convened in London in February 1939. It was largely window-dressing and achieved nothing. Arabs and Jews refused to negotiate together, and the British government had already determined its course of action. This was finessed during and after the conference and then embodied in another White Paper, that of May 1939. 'If we must offend one side, let us offend the Jews rather than the Arabs', directed the Prime Minister Neville Chamberlain in what Zionists understandably took to be another example of his penchant for ill-judged appeasement.[39]

Already Jewish protests in Palestine were less to be feared than a continuation of the Revolt; for in the event of war, Jews would have little choice but to side with those who opposed Nazism, while still disaffected Palestinian Arabs would as surely consort with the Nazis. Similarly, in the international scales, Muslim and Arab acquiescence in the war effort weighed more heavily than the likely opposition to the White Paper of international Jewry.

Yet the 1939 White Paper once again shied away from the Arab demand for full and unqualified Palestinian independence. On this score it was officially condemned by all shades of Arab opinion except Abdullah and his supporters. It did hold out the prospect, within ten years, of 'an independent Palestine State' but this state was to be one in which, through a representative assembly, Arabs and Jews would 'share authority in government in such a way that the essential interests of each are secured'. Measures designed to promote the progressive involvement of each community in the government were also outlined. But in the ten-year run-up to statehood and in the insistence on a joint state, there was nothing to please either Jews or Arabs. Moreover the ten-year delay and a likely world war might change the whole picture. How many of Palestine's population would by then be Jews and how much of the land would be in Jewish hands?

On these points, however, the White Paper offered concrete assurances that were decidedly more pro-Arab than any previous British pronouncement. Jewish immigration was to continue at the rate of 10,000 per year (plus a one-off entry for 25,000 'refugees'), but only for five years. By then the Jewish population would have reached one-third of Palestine's total and no further immigration would be permitted without Arab agreement. The open-ended commitments embodied in the Balfour Declaration and the mandate were thus to be capped, and the prospect of a Jewish-majority state was effectively ruled out. Likewise, the High Commissioner was given authority 'to prohibit and regulate transfers of land'.

Even the Mufti was not indifferent to these concessions. Had they included an amnesty for his followers and a pardon for himself, it seems possible that he would have accepted the whole package. Egypt and Iraq joined Transjordan in recommending acceptance; many members of the Higher Arab Committee (who had been released prior to the London conference) hinted privately at approval; and close advisers of the Mufti like George Antonius strove to bring about a compromise.

But when the war broke out, nothing had been decided. The White Paper had largely won over Arab opinion and thus served its immediate purpose. The British would stand by it throughout the war and endeavour to win international support for it. Freya Stark was amongst those recruited to promote it, especially in North America. Yet officially it remained anathema to the Higher Arab Committee and had even been rejected by the Mandates Commission. (A British appeal against this rejection was overtaken by the outbreak of hostilities.) Another opportunity for Anglo-Arab collaboration thus went by default, much to the chagrin of both its British sponsors and its Palestinian beneficiaries.

Once again Zionism, the main loser under the 1939 White Paper, had cause to be grateful for Arab intransigence. The restriction of immigration and land purchases, the about-turn on the Balfour commitment and the 'odious moral cruelty'[40] of denying refuge to the millions of Jews in Europe for whom Palestine was now their only refuge, brought the inevitable reaction. Illegal immigration soared and incidents of Jewish 'terrorism' increased. But the war in the Mediterranean quickly staunched the movement of migrants. It also convinced most of Palestine's Jews that, whatever they felt about the White Paper, this was not the moment to embarrass the British. 'We shall fight with the British in this war as if there was no White Paper,' declared Ben-Gurion, 'and we shall fight the White Paper as if there was no war.'[41]

Arab rejection had been timely, but it was not conclusive. To the Zionists, winning the war would indeed be all about defeating the White Paper. While most would urge enrolment in the struggle against the Nazis, others would concentrate on mobilizing Jewish opinion in the US against British policy in Palestine, and a few would directly oppose it, amassing arms and staging further acts of attrition.

Meanwhile the Mufti, declared *persona non grata* by the French as soon as war broke out, bribed his way out of Lebanon. Swathed in the costume of Muslim womanhood, he took a taxi to Rutba and then Baghdad. There he would play a principal part in the 1941 Iraqi assault on the British community. And thence he would continue his travels to Persia and so to Mussolini's Rome and Hitler's Berlin.

11

Sideshows of War

BEHIND THE LINES

THE SECOND WORLD War, unlike the First, produced few changes in the map of the Middle East. Frontiers were not redrawn and foreign interests not fundamentally redirected. The Arab political entities engineered in the aftermath of the First World War neither sheered nor fused under the stress of the Second World War. In Egypt and Iraq the British minded the machinery of their treaties more closely than ever. Syria, stripped down by French spanners, was only half-reassembled. And from a still hotly contested Palestine, the sparks continued to fly.

The war nevertheless transformed perceptions of the region. In 1940–2, with Axis armies closing on Egypt from both Greece and North Africa, the Middle East hosted an unprecedented concentration of firepower. It made the headlines as a theatre of operations. Its future as a global power base of abiding contention was anticipated. Britain's defence treaties with Egypt, Iraq and Transjordan were duly invoked, and the region came to look more like occupied territory than at any time since the First World War. Arab objections were brushed aside and nationalist resentment thereby fuelled. —

As elsewhere, in dealing with subject nations the colonial powers were compromised by their declared war aims, like the Atlantic Charter's promise of all peoples having the right to choose their own form of government. More obviously, the same colonial powers were soon fatally debilitated by the war itself. Expensive overseas involvements would henceforth be subject to the closest scrutiny; the formalities of decolonization were accelerated as a result. The church bells that would ring out for the end of the war also rang for empire's end of term. As the gates swung open, imperial lockers would be hastily cleared and colonial ties wrenched loose.

Decolonization was one thing; disengagement was another. The war handsomely demonstrated how existing linkages could be used to mobilize emerging nations on behalf of their colonial sponsors. The wisdom of retaining some kind of informal influence was thus confirmed and the work of finessing this would continue. In the Middle East such links became especially important as the region was revealed not just as a corridor to the East but as a production and distribution centre in its own right. Its yield of cotton, fruit and cereals expanded; its utility as an Allied supply base for both the Far East and the Mediterranean was demonstrated; and geo-strategists began to grasp the potential of the Gulf's unlimited energy reserves for propelling not just ships, as in the First World War, but whole economies. The USA's interest in the region was substantially rekindled, and Soviet Russia's aroused.

Reports, post 1942, of the Nazi holocaust added a moral dimension to this concern. Shamed into responding to a tragedy that transcended even the horrors of the battlefield, non-Jews as well as Jews, in the US as well as Europe, endorsed the idea of international reparation and engaged more adamantly with the Zionist adventure. British policy in Palestine was about to come in for critical appraisal from a host of new and deeply concerned interests.

Meanwhile for Churchill and Roosevelt the term 'Middle East' assumed an unprecedented immediacy. Extended west from the Gulf to the Aegean and even North Africa, the region was accorded the status of a distinct military command with its own minister, war council, and supply centre; all were located in Cairo, which city, despite its African location, became the hub of an operational theatre. Except among the diplomatic community, the nineteenth-century 'Near East' practically disappeared from everyday language. Already synonymous with international *angst,* the redefined region and its formidable problems would quickly take centre stage among the world-ordering responsibilities of the new United Nations

Organization. No longer just a dusty backyard of oriental contention between Europe's imperial dinosaurs, the Middle East was becoming a middle ground of world-wide contention between a new generation of superpowers.

The beginnings of this transformation can be traced back to 1941 and two short campaigns of such marginal significance in the great struggle then being waged from the Aegean to the Atlantic that they barely feature in histories of the war. The trouble began obscurely with an April *coup d'état* in Iraq, and it was seemingly all over three months later with an unsung victory in Syria. Yet during this short period the fate of the region, indeed the world, appeared to hang in the balance. To Freya Stark, then busily promoting Allied war aims throughout the region, the Iraqi affair was 'a turning point in the Middle Eastern war';[1] to Churchill it seemed that, thanks to these two sideshows, 'Hitler's Oriental plan' was 'blotted out'.[2]

Whether there was such a plan is beside the point. It seemed so at the time; in April 1941 anything seemed possible; and at such a bleak moment for the world's democracies, even suspect crumbs were mighty comforts. Great Britain then stood alone save for its Dominion allies. The Soviet Union was still observing its non-aggression pact with Germany; Pearl Harbor had yet to provoke the United States into action; France had fallen; and the rest of western Europe (plus much of eastern Europe) had either succumbed to the Nazis or reached an accommodation with them. Resistance to the Axis powers continued only on the European periphery – on the Atlantic seaboard, where Britain's 'finest hour' was not yet over, and in the Mediterranean. There an Italian offensive had stalled. Gibraltar and Malta held out; from Egypt the British had pushed Mussolini's invading forces back into Libyan Cyrenaica; and the Greeks had repelled another Italian probe from Albania. But these successes served only to provoke a devastating response from Berlin. Rommel was dispatched to North Africa with his feared 7th Panzers; and fifteen divisions of the German 12th Army massed in the Balkans.

Even as the radio waves crackled with news of the coup in Iraq, Rommel was recapturing Benghazi in Cyrenaica. Three days later Yugoslavia and Greece were invaded. A week after that, Rommel's tanks were across the Egyptian frontier and advancing on Alexandria. By the end of the month Greece had surrendered, Crete was a forlorn hope, and Churchill was bracing himself for the loss of the entire eastern Mediterranean. A worse moment for an unlooked-for Arab diversion behind Allied lines could scarcely have been contrived.

Yet it should hardly have come as a surprise. As a result of the hostility generated by the Revolt in Palestine and King Ghazi's mysterious death in Baghdad, the British in Iraq had become more 'unpopular, disliked and even hated' than in Alan MacDonald's day. Nor was their reason for being there any more obvious. Confirming MacDonald's investigation of the subject, a later study well describes the British in Iraq as 'a presence in search of a policy'.[3] Barricaded behind the 1930 treaty, they saw what William Yale called its 'secur[ing of] imperialist interests without the invidious burden of colonial rule' not as a transitional stage in Anglo-Iraqi relations but as the crowning achievement of their informal imperialism. An identity of interests between London and Baghdad was taken for granted; further concessions to Iraqi national pride were deemed inappropriate. The new regent Abd al-Ilah (brother-in-law of the deceased Ghazi and so uncle of his son and heir, the 6-year-old Faysal II) was proving an obliging head of state even by Hashemite standards; and Nuri al-Said, a diminutive but resourceful element in most Iraqi cabinets, remained staunchly loyal to his British patrons.

Nuri, though, met his match in the Mufti. Hajj Amin al-Husayni, preceded by his considerable celebrity as the champion of Arab rights in Palestine, and accompanied by an entourage of pro-Axis Arab activists from all over the Levant, had arrived in Baghdad in October 1939. Now white-haired and, according to Freya Stark, with 'a sort of radiance as of a just-fallen Lucifer about him',[4] he pursued his links with the Axis powers and in 1940 orchestrated an anti-British alliance between the Iraqi military and Nuri's political opponents. By 1941, says Stark, he was second only to Hitler as 'the main immediate cause of trouble'.[5]

The Iraqi military, his new allies, were represented by a quadrumvirate of colonels known as the 'Golden Square'. The army had already rescued the nation from Baghdad's squabbling politicians on a number of occasions and, with its ranks swollen by conscription and its reputation riding high after successes against the Assyrians and the Shi'ite tribes, it enjoyed much popular esteem. It was probably no less representative of national opinion than the country's 'elected' representatives. Its resentment of British policy in Palestine and of the Anglo-Iraqi treaty was widely shared. And as the British reeled before Hitler's onslaught, it was not alone in its perception of independent Iraq's interests being best served by seeking to establish relations with the Axis powers and obtain arms and support from them.

Iraq, after all, was not a belligerent in the war. Nothing in the Anglo-Iraqi treaty obliged it to be so, and neutrality was the norm throughout the Arab world. In 1939 Baghdad had officially broken off diplomatic relations with Berlin on British insistence. But when Italy had entered the war in June 1940 similar pressures for a break with Rome were resisted. Rashid Ali al-Kaylani (Gaylani, Keilani), like Nuri a perennial in Baghdad's cabinets, then headed the government. Nuri was among his ministers. But Rashid Ali, primed by the Mufti and emboldened by the support of the colonels of the Golden Square, dug in his heels over the break with Italy.

The British, unaccustomed to such defiance, looked to Nuri and the Regent to enforce compliance and sever relations with Mussolini. Ever keen to oblige, the Regent duly attempted to dismiss the Rashid Ali government. After a long and messy affair, in January 1941 he finally succeeded, albeit by sacrificing Nuri, risking civil war, and accepting a compromise ministry headed by a nominee of the Golden Square. This new ministry lasted only eight weeks. In a double-barrelled coup on 1 and 2 April Rashid Ali and the colonels, fearing that the Regent had finally prevailed on the new ministry to disperse the Golden Square and expel the Italians, brought troops into the capital and surrounded the palace.

Regent Abd al-Ilah made a run for it. Hidden under rugs and cushions in the back of a US embassy car (and then sat upon by the ambassador and his wife), he reached the sanctuary of his British supporters at the Habbaniya air base and was swiftly airlifted to Basra, then Amman and Jerusalem. There he was joined by Nuri and other loyalists. Meanwhile in Baghdad the colonels took control. Rashid Ali resumed office at the head of a 'Government of National Defence' and then replaced the Regent, recalled parliament and warned the British not to interfere. Orchestrated or not, there was general rejoicing in Baghdad.[6]

Although alarmed by the new regime's pro-Axis sympathies, the British at first sought a diplomatic solution. Kinahan Cornwallis, an old Arab Bureau hand, arrived in Baghdad as British ambassador just as the coup broke. Well briefed, he quickly condemned it as unconstitutional. But so, arguably, had been the Regent's sabotaging of the previous Rashid Ali government; it was hard to say where constitutionality lay. Moreover Freya Stark, playing Gertrude Bell to Cornwallis's Cox, interviewed George Antonius, still the Mufti's go-between, and concluded that a deal was indeed possible. London was reassured. On 18 April, as Rommel advanced in North Africa, Churchill cabled his Middle Eastern commanders that 'Libya counts first, evacuation of troops from Greece second . . . [and] Iraq can be ignored'.[7]

Stark's putative deal hinged on British recognition of Rashid Ali's new regime in return for Rashid Ali toning down his pro-Axis pronouncements, closing the Italian legation and placing a generous construction on the terms of the Anglo-Iraqi treaty. The last was important because within a week of the coup some of Britain's Indian Army troops had been ordered to Basra by sea. As at the beginning of the First World War, they were intended principally to protect the refinery at Abadan and its adjacent oilfields; and having been already *en route* to Malaya, they reached the Gulf in a matter of days. They landed unopposed, although under airborne cover, on 18 April, just as Churchill was advising that Iraq might be ignored.

Rashid Ali's government did not object because, still hopeful of British recognition, it wanted to be seen as observing the terms of the Anglo-Iraqi treaty. Since it had also been given to understand that the newly arrived troops were ultimately destined for the eastern Mediterranean and the defence of Egypt, Rashid Ali regarded them as in transit, a situation covered by the treaty. Only when it emerged that they were not in fact going anywhere did the Iraqis begin to object. Confusingly, therefore, in 1941, unlike in 1915, it was the Iraqis who were soon insisting that the Indian Army force advance upriver and the British who wanted their troops to stay put in Basra.

This misunderstanding, if such it was, came to a head with the announcement of the arrival at Basra of a second Indian Army brigade. Rashid Ali now objected strongly: the existing troops must first clear Iraq's western frontier at Rutba before the new brigade could be landed. But in the worsening climate of confrontation the Iraqi objection was brushed aside. The troops landed regardless; and on the same day, 29 April, the Iraqi High Command retaliated. Its own forces in the Baghdad district were ordered to take up positions around the RAF base at Habbaniya. Like the British and US embassies in Baghdad, behind whose gates the city's expatriate community now anxiously congregated, Habbaniya felt besieged.

The fighting started three days later, initiated by the British. Without warning, their aircraft bombed the Iraqi forces around Habbaniya, making nearly two hundred sorties in twelve hours. Elsewhere Iraqi air bases were targeted and Iraq's few aircraft largely eliminated. These attacks were followed by a ground assault from Habbaniya on 4 May which forced the encircling troops to withdraw. They took up new positions astride the road to Baghdad. Habbaniya thus remained cut off from Baghdad, where the British embassy was still under duress. Four days later unexplained aircraft were reported in Syrian air space; they proved to be German, and within a week they were strafing Habbaniya. Alarm bells rang out in Cairo and London. Iraq, quite clearly, could no longer 'be ignored'.

BULLY FOR BAGHDAD

In his history of the Second World War Churchill rather quaintly calls Habbaniya a British 'flying school'.[8] Doubtless aerial skills were honed there, but it was rather more than an aviator's kindergarten. Within a seven-mile perimeter fence defended by watch-towers, some 80 assorted aircraft, including heavy bombers, were currently on station. About 1,000 airmen manned the planes and 9,000 civilians serviced the base. In addition the base had its own garrison of 1,200 mainly Assyrian troops, plus 300 British infantrymen just flown in from Basra. It was a formidable installation, and the Iraqis' failure to shut it down now had dire consequences.

From the roof of the British embassy in Baghdad the roughly 350 interned expatriates watched the fun. Cloudless skies welcomed the incoming aircraft and, as Baghdadis dashed for cover, the city sustained the first of its twentieth-century aerial bombardments. In a familiar refrain the British insisted that only military installations were being targeted. It was surprising how many there were. From Basra as well as Habbaniya the bombers returned day after day, unloading their cargoes on the radio station, the railway terminus, the fuel depot and the landing stages, as well as the local army base, airfield, sundry anti-aircraft batteries and the usual unintended targets. 'A horrible beauty there is about a fire in a town,' wrote Freya

Stark as the eruption of the IPC's storage tanks eclipsed a fine sunset. 'The great convolutions of smoke rolled northward above the quiet houses; [the smoke was] still there in the morning.'[9]

Partly to discourage 'friendly' fire, partly to invite dropped messages, the embassy lawn had been strewn with sheets in the shape of a V. Beyond the lawn barbed wire was hastily erected across flower-beds of roses and antirrhinums. Filling sandbags for the gateways and constant patrolling among the pergolas provided further employment for the internees. Outside the walls Iraqi police, supposedly there for the embassy's protection, regulated access and discouraged escape.

But the siege, as it was inevitably called, was not exactly pressed. Bullets occasionally whistled over the walls and machine-guns greeted visiting aircraft. But no one within was hit and no attempt was made to storm the place. At the official level amicable negotiations with the Iraqi authorities were sustained throughout, while at the bottom of the garden Stark cheerfully engaged in Arabic banter with a boatload of bored policemen patrolling the river-front. Propaganda being her business, she regaled them with British successes. Six German planes downed, she claimed; forty of the RAF downed, they replied. She called Allah as witness; they roared with laughter and promised her pride of place in a policeman's harem. 'Can't help thinking', she confided in her diary, 'that the Germans must be disappointed in Iraq.'[10]

As May wore on with fiery skies, Stark watched the thermometer climb to 114 degrees Fahrenheit. The men stripped to their shorts. She wished she could do likewise but was told that their being stark naked was one thing, their seeing Stark naked quite another. The jokes grew worse; food became scarce, water and electricity fitful, the future fraught. Between monitoring outside broadcasts and organizing the defences, the embassy's sweltering inmates passed the time as the determinedly imperturbable do, with improving lectures ('Aden at War' and the surely more popular 'Iceland'), gymnastics, concerts (but no clapping lest it provoke their guards) and amateur dramatics. 'The Morale and Amusements Committee met twice daily.'[11] Tempers were occasionally tested; so too were home-made bombs constructed out of beer cans. Moscow's recognition of the Rashid Ali government came as a heavy blow; 'our neighbourhood to Oil', on the other hand, was a consolation and their best guarantee against being forgotten.

As the collective mood swung listlessly between euphoria and despair, two place-names were on everyone's lips. Neither of them was 'Kut'. The first was 'Lucknow', the city in northern India where in 1857 another British Residency had been long besieged, twice relieved, and then interminably memorialized as a defining moment in imperial lore. To Stark, as to her companions, the 'Lucknow feeling' was a source of self-conscious comfort. On the other hand the 'Lucknow spirit', heavy with vengeful thoughts of making the Iraqis pay for it, was disgraceful. Stark shuddered to share a dormitory with representatives of this hang-'em-high school and firmly championed the conciliatory Cornwallis.

The other name, even more irritating than 'Lucknow', was 'Rutba'. The way-station, where in happier times the buses stopped and the beer flowed, was reportedly recaptured several times a week. It was from across its desert border that relief was looked for, but never can a place have been so repeatedly retaken as Rutba. What sparked the reports was a mystery. News was scarce and always anodyne; in minds anxiously trained on little else, the rumours seemed to combust spontaneously. Yet they were not entirely unfounded. Across the intervening wastes an unlikely column of berobed Bedouin Arabs and bare-kneed Buckingham Palace guardsmen, plus artillery, engineers and lorries, was indeed floundering through the sands. Relief was on its way.

Churchill had changed his tune about Iraq as soon as the fighting started. On 4 May he requested – and on 6 May he ordered – General Wavell, the Commander-in-Chief of Middle East Forces, to dispatch a relieving force from Palestine. Wavell objected, having no troops to spare and no confidence in such a force safely traversing 500 miles of desert. Although absolved of responsibility for the outcome, he was firmly overruled. It was now, wrote Churchill, 'essential to do all in our power to save Habbaniya and to control the pipeline to the Mediterrean'.[12] The relief force was duly assembled and included a flying column of 2,000 men and 500 trucks that went on ahead on 9 May. This unit was largely made up of a regiment of the Household Cavalry (Royal Horse Guards and Life Guards). Minus their horses, the guardsmen had yet to adjust to motorized transport and tactics, let alone the desert. Meanwhile, ahead of them, and already attacking Rutba, was a detachment of Transjordan's Arab Legion under Major 'Jack' Glubb.

Glubb and the Arab Legion would become synonymous. After perfecting his desert tactics with the 'peacekeeping' British forces in 1920s Iraq, Glubb had resigned from the British army and entered Transjordanian service to raise and command a Desert Patrol of the Arab Legion. The Legion, once Abdullah's personal guard, was now Transjordan's gendarmerie and was destined, under Glubb's direction, to become the backbone of Transjordan's army. Unlike the British-paid Trans-Jordanian Frontier Force, it specialized in desert warfare and was recruited entirely from the Arab tribes of the country. To the British it was as yet something of an unknown quantity; and so was its shy and retiring commander. Although punctilious in supplying London with Transjordanian intelligence, Glubb seemed to identify closely with his Hashemite employer and to have 'gone native'. In Arabic he was known as Abu Hunayk (Father of the Little Lower Jaw) because much of his jawbone had been blown away in the First World War. Chinless by chance, he did not otherwise conform to the stereotype of the British officer, being also speechless, capless and abstemious; instead he wore the *keffiyeh* and lived off the desert like his long-haired legionnaires; as 'Glubb Pasha' he looked a good bet as the next aberrant Lawrence, minus the Lawrentian conceit.

Glubb's inclusion in the relief expedition resulted from his already being in the field. Before the expedition had been thought necessary, various expedients had been adopted with a view to undermining Rashid Ali's regime. A member of the American OSS, forerunner of the CIA, had attempted to pressurize the Mufti (he failed); a cell of the ultra-Zionist Irgun had been released from detention in Palestine to go and assassinate the Mufti (their leader was killed in a German air-raid on Habbaniya); and Glubb, with his first-hand knowledge of the Syria-Iraq desert, had been volunteered by Abdullah to proceed up the pipeline and infiltrate the Iraqi tribes. Riding not camels but light trucks, his 250 Bedouin legionnaires had reached Rutba only to find it well defended by Rashid Ali's police. Worse still, a mechanized force under the Arabs' ever-ready commander, Fawzi al-Qawuqji, had just arrived in the vicinity. Glubb therefore discreetly withdrew. RAF bombers were called in; and a company of armoured cars were conjured up from Palestine. Now it was Fawzi's turn to withdraw. He vanished into the desert, and on 11 May Rutba was indeed finally taken.

Next day the twenty-mile convoy carrying the guardsmen and the rest of the advance party rumbled into Rutba. Thus far they had made good progress. Kirkbride, now back in Amman as High Commissioner, had watched them pass through Transjordan, 'an amazing piece of improvisation' consisting of all manner of requisitioned vehicles, without spares 'and manned by civilian drivers who were openly rebellious'.[13] Handy tips on desert driving had been provided by a Nairn employee called Long Jack, and they had been following tracks that ran alongside the pipeline. Beyond Rutba, they must bear away from the pipeline roughly along the route pioneered by the Nairns and now in the process of being turned into a road by Brooks-Murdoch. But without the Nairns' skilled drivers, without their balloon tyres, and with much greater axle loads, the lorries were soon in difficulties. They sank to their wheel arches in the sand, the new road degenerated into occasional mounds of unscreeded rock, and the guardsmen began pining for their horses.

Water was already in short supply, and steel so hot it could only be handled with gloves. Then the first enemy aircraft appeared; a truck was hit and 'some men killed'. 'We had been discovered', noted Somerset de Chair, an enthusiastic officer with a funny name that was yet unremarkable among guards officers called Edric, Eion and Bobo. Poet, parliamentarian and now the column's Intelligence Officer, de Chair produced a breezy account of the expedition notable for personal as well as poetic licence.

Also discovered at this critical juncture was a blue saloon car. Hitherto unnoticed in the long convoy of assorted vehicles, it was found to contain 'a quiet, grey-haired civilian called Brooks'. This, of course, was Douglas Brooks of Brooks-Murdoch, the husband of the Hoffman twins and currently the builder of a bridge at Mujara, a place near Habbaniya to which he was returning. 'He was to become a valuable guide and friend, never obtruding himself but always at our elbow for consultation,' explains de Chair. Why such an obliging engineer had been labouring so long in obscurity on Iraq's behalf was beyond an Intelligence Officer's comprehension; 'but then, I reflected, it is just this sort of Englishman that makes our brand of imperialism possible'.[14] The current priority being that of making 'our brand' of heroics possible, Brooks was eagerly pumped for directions and promoted to official guide.

Glubb, meanwhile, who was being similarly importuned, welcomed the opportunity to take his Legion on ahead to reconnoitre. And thus, expertly advised, ably escorted and little troubled by the enemy, the convoy approached Habbaniya on 17 May. The desert crossing had taken barely five days; and Habbaniya had been relieved before it set off, indeed had relieved itself. De Chair, the first to enter the base, found it 'difficult to realise that I had entered a besieged settlement as the spearpoint of the relieving force';[15] he nevertheless presumed to say so.

Although another two weeks would be needed to cover the remaining fifty miles to Baghdad, that was only partly because of Iraqi resistance and principally because the Euphrates was in flood. To slow the invaders, the Iraqis had only to open the sluices and blow a few bridges. It was the RAF, pounding away at Iraqi positions, and the engineers, throwing up new bridges and improvising ferries, who ensured the final success of what de Chair cheerfully flagged as 'one of the greatest marches in history'. In fact he reckoned that it was 'the first time since Alexander the Great that an army has succeeded in crossing the desert from the shores of the Mediterranean to the banks of the Euphrates'.[16]

Such an achievement was 'not to be measured by the size of the battles nor the numbers of men engaged but rather in the surprise with which it was received', opined de Chair.[17] It was certainly a surprise to those who, in the absence of any declaration of war, still laboured under the impression that Iraq was neutral, indeed a friendly subordinate. But as noted, good news was in short supply, and Baghdad was the first city of any consequence to be captured by the British in the Second World War. In the First the conquest of Iraq had cost about 100,000 lives and taken nearly three years. In the Second it cost the British 34 lives and took thirty days. This was surprising – although less so had anyone reflected, amid the orgy of self-congratulation, that if the fall of Baghdad was a British achievement, so too had been its rising in the first place.

Probably the greatest loss of life came after the ceasefire. The Mufti, Rashid Ali and most of their military supporters had fled over the border to Persia as the British advanced. On the insistence of the ambassador, Cornwallis, the rest of the Iraqi forces were now deemed to have been deceived by their leaders but not otherwise disloyal. In a gesture of conciliation, they were therefore allowed to disperse under arms. This left a vacuum in Baghdad which the Regent Abd al-Ilah and his supporters expected to fill. Hastily dispatched from Jerusalem, they were, according to Gerald de Gaury

Sideshows of War

who accompanied them on behalf of the British Foreign Office, 'welcomed enthusiastically' by the city's dignitaries. They duly reinstalled themselves in the palace.

The British forces remained outside the city. According to de Chair, this was because the Regent felt that his chances of being well received by the Iraqis would be prejudiced by a British military presence. According to de Gaury, it was because the British commander feared the 'danger to his troops in the narrow streets'.[18] Neither explanation supports the idea of the liberators being 'enthusiastically welcomed'; and either way, on 1 and 2 June the ungarrisoned city erupted in an orgy of looting and killing.

'Mistaken idea that all is over,' noted the ever-candid Freya Stark as bloodied victims began arriving at the embassy. 'The pretence that this is an Iraqi spontaneous Restoration is just nonsense.'[19] The Regent was still unloved, the British still unwelcome, and the Iraqi people still smarting over their failure to redeem Arab fortunes, especially in Palestine. Out of this frustration, and the expectation of easy pickings in an unguarded city, there seems to have arisen the idea that the lives and livelihoods of Baghdad's large Jewish community were fair and natural game. Estimates of the fatalities during the two days of chaos vary between the official 130 and the Chief of Police's 2,000. Some were Christians, most Jews; and if few of these were Zionists, all were convenient scapegoats for the perceived injustice of British policy towards the Palestinian Arabs.

But the Baghdad massacre, unprecedented in its scale even in Palestine, was not allowed to cloud the British sense of satisfaction. Rashid Ali had supposedly been provoked into a premature revolt that had then been quashed before substantial Axis support could arrive to sustain it. Thus had one part of 'Hitler's Oriental plan' been foiled. The other part, involving Syria, was already being addressed. De Chair had supposed some leave might be in order after one of history's greatest marches but had been quickly disabused. With Glubb and his Legion, plus the guardsmen and the rest of the expedition, he was soon back in the wilderness, this time of Syria's desert, where real fighting awaited.

In Baghdad, with the riots brought under control, Anglo-Iraqi relations reverted to normal. By October 1941 Nuri al-Said was again in power and the British presence had been so substantially restored that Iraqis came to regard the next four years as 'the second British occupation'. In 1943 Iraq would even declare war on the Axis powers. Meanwhile the Mufti had repaired to Berlin and Rashid Ali eventually found sanctuary in Saudi Arabia; he did not return to Iraq until the 1958 Revolution. Some of his military colleagues had been tried, and a handful executed, immediately after the fall of Baghdad; but the real purge of the armed forces took place later at Nuri's instigation and was more about eliminating potential opposition than penalizing past demeanours. Several hundred officers were either interned or cashiered or both, among them one Tulfah Khairallah who, on his release, returned to his village near Takrit. There, still nursing a high regard for Rashid Ali's defiance and a deep dislike of the British and their Hashemite collaborators, Khairallah became a schoolmaster. In 1947 he would take under his wing as house guest, pupil and protégé the 10-year-old son of his sister, an only child named Saddam Husayn.

A RAVELLED AFFAIR IN SYRIA

The Syria into which Glubb, de Chair and their respective units advanced after the Iraq revolt was expecting them. The strike against Baghdad may have been timely, but that against Damascus was long overdue.

> For one year – June 1940 to June 1941 – Syria [had] lived on its nerves. In all the world it was the one neutral place whereof you could say with absolute certainty: 'Here will be war.' The only surprising thing was that it remained at peace for so long.[20]

As recalled by Alan Moorehead, then Middle East war correspondent for the *Daily Express*, peace had prevailed because both sides – the Allied powers and the Axis powers – believed that Syria and Lebanon could be theirs without fighting. When in June 1940 the French forces in Europe had surrendered, Marshal Pétain had withdrawn France from the war and formed a government, later based at Vichy, that was avowedly neutral. But this neutrality was prejudiced by the German occupation, by the large numbers of Frenchmen in prisoner-of-war camps, and by the hefty indemnity imposed on France. Meanwhile in London General Charles de Gaulle, with

Churchill's encouragement, had rejected the *Pétainiste* compromise and, vowing to continue the fight on behalf of 'Free France', had sought troops and support from wherever Frenchmen were still free, notably in France's colonial territories.

But de Gaulle had been disappointed. Torn between their desire to avenge defeat and their loyalty to the motherland and its legitimate government, the colonial administrations in Indo-China, North Africa and West Africa had largely chosen Pétain and *La Patrie*; only the lesser outposts in Equatoria, Chad and Cameroon opted for de Gaulle. A few, though, prevaricated, most notably Syria/Lebanon. Here the stakes were high because the Levant hosted a concentration of 50,000 French troops, mostly North African. If de Gaulle could win them over, they would give his cause real military credibility. But if they adhered to Vichy, they would pose a potential threat to the British in Palestine and might require the attention of forces that could be better employed elsewhere, like Libya.

At first the Levant administration seemed disposed to fight on alongside de Gaulle and the British. Even when officially and reluctantly it buckled to metropolitan pressure, there were high hopes that an anti-Vichy coup in Beirut might yet save the situation. One such plan failed, but in September 1940 de Gaulle and his British colleagues conjured out of the East a veritable ace of hearts: Georges Catroux, the Damascus *délégué* of the one-armed Gouraud in the early days of the mandate, and himself now a full general, indeed lately Governor-General of Indo-China, was dispatched to Cairo.

Catroux had been toppled in Saigon by a diktat from Vichy. He wanted nothing better than to turn the tables in Beirut, and such was his standing that he looked well capable of doing so. From Indo-China he had slipped away to Singapore, Glasgow and then London where his seniority and reputation led to his being fêted as a possible alternative to de Gaulle. This, needless to say, did not accord with the latter's exalted sense of his own highly personal mission. Catroux had to settle for the role of Free France's most distinguished recruit and its chief of operations in the Middle East.

Less egotistical and much more approachable than de Gaulle, Catroux got on well with the British. He arrived in Cairo unannounced and under an alias but with, according to a neighbour, much tell-tale lacquerwork, a Vietnamese valet and 'a whole tribe of cats', all Siamese except for 'the Mad Cat' (who was otherwise the formidable Madame Catroux, abbreviated).[21] The idea was that he would only declare his presence once confidential approaches had been made to his admirers among the Vichy officers in Syria. Then, when all was ready for the coup, like a *deus ex machina* he would reveal himself with a patriotic proclamation to which French Levant would rise as one. No show of force would be needed.

Unfortunately, before Catroux had even unpacked in Cairo, the plot leaked out in Beirut. His potential supporters were quickly purged and their places taken by hard-line *Pétainistes*. Catroux did not despair. He continued to bombard his fellow-officers in the Levant with propaganda and by November 1940 was again looking forward to the mass defection of their troops. 'It was not the last time that Catroux displayed an unwarranted faith in his own charisma,' writes A.B. Gaunson, a deft disentangler of this ravelled affair.[22] Hopes of a spontaneous defection were duly dashed; and with the idea of forcibly reigniting them by a show of strength, de Gaulle urged the assembly of Free France's few troops along the Palestine border. But Wavell, as over Iraq, resisted the idea of opening another front and claimed to be unable to provide even the transport for this deployment, let alone the supporting British divisions requested by Catroux.

The situation changed when in the second week of May reports began arriving from Syria that German and Italian aircraft were refuelling there on their way to Rashid Ali's Iraq. Vichy explanations about the pilots being non-combatants and their landings forced were derided. Syria's neutrality had been revealed as a sham; Wavell's caution was discredited. When towards the end of the month Catroux reported a Vichy evacuation from Syria to Lebanon, presumably to clear the former for eventual German occupation, it looked as if an immediate advance might be unopposed. The report proved baseless, but by then a joint Allied-Free French force (in fact mainly Australians, Indians and Africans and code-named, for no obvious reason, 'Exporter') was being readied in Palestine. Simultaneously orders were going out to the guardsmen and Bedouin who had lately 'liberated' Baghdad to advance thence across the Syrian desert. In Jerusalem the name of Allenby was being much invoked; Glubb was clearly cast as Lawrence; and part of the advance would again hug the Hijaz railway. Once more British and Arab sights were set on Damascus.

But therein lay the rub. History's passion for repeating itself includes more failures than successes; and just as British, French and Arabs had fallen out over Syria in 1920, so they would again in 1941. In fact, the jangle of discordant expectations and grating promises had already begun.

The deal struck between Pétain and the German High Command in 1940 had allowed Vichy France to retain her national integrity and her overseas possessions. These were crucial to French self-esteem, indeed survival, and many of the French colonial administrations that had thrown in their lot with Pétain had done so for this very reason. The British, on the other hand, were portrayed as opportunists who, having abandoned France, would now scavenge what they could of her overseas possessions. This was seemingly confirmed when a British strike aimed at pre-empting possible German use of the French fleet in the Mediterranean resulted in a heavy loss of French lives. Vichy propaganda rammed the point home; de Gaulle and his Free French were no better than renegades who would betray France's navy and colonies to perfidious Albion for an illusory freedom that was really British bondage. In the Levant, where for a quarter of a century British designs on Syria/Lebanon had been taken for granted, this argument played well. Operation Exporter, as well as being expected, was about to encounter stiff resistance.

Nor were these fears about British perfidy entirely fanciful. De Gaulle himself shared them. When Wavell had refused support for military intervention in Syria, de Gaulle suspected that the British were prevaricating over French claims to the Levant; and when Wavell provided support, de Gaulle suspected that the British had designs on the French Levant. In reality Wavell was merely juggling existing military priorities while trying to avoid new ones. But others may have been less innocent.

Edward Louis Spears, a senior British general whose many decorations included the Croix de Guerre, was known as a close friend of Churchill and a passionate supporter of all things French, including his old comrade-in-arms Charles de Gaulle. He looked to be an excellent choice as the head of Britain's mission to the Free French. Yet Spears was about to become its *bête noire*. He soon fell out with de Gaulle and, knowing nothing of the region, fell in with Cairo's well-entrenched British Arabists. As early as mid-April 1941 he had already adopted as his own a plan to 'let it be known in the Levant . . .

that de Gaulle intended when in control in Syria to grant the Arab populations their independence'.[23]

This idea of pledging Syrian independence as a means of securing Arab support for the assault on the Vichy administration had actually originated in Catroux's anti-Vichy propaganda. But, rendered into English and shuffled between departments, it had soon taken on a life of its own. Catroux had adopted it as a counterweight to similar promises emanating from the Vichy administration in Beirut. There, to offset Syrian rage over another territorial betrayal (the French surrender to Turkey of Syrian Alexandretta), the Vichy government had dusted off the unratified Franco-Syrian treaty of 1936. Catroux, in countering this move with his own offer of independence, hoped to win Syrian nationalism for the Free French. But his offer was subject to the conclusion of a mutually acceptable treaty 'like the Egyptian model' (which had taken fifteen years to materialize); it was to be an exclusively French initiative; and it had not yet been unequivocally endorsed by de Gaulle.

Spears and his Arabist allies ignored all this. Catroux's offer was represented as a blank cheque for Syrian independence with the British as its sole guarantor. In preparing the Druze and Syria's Arab tribes to stand aside when Operation Exporter got under way, officers like Glubb and Kirkbride frankly put it about that the British were coming to end the French mandate, remove the French administration, and prepare the way for full independence. De Gaulle and Catroux were scarcely mentioned, and their Free French troops were deemed little more than auxiliaries, like Glubb's Arab Legion.

If Catroux did not protest – and de Gaulle only spasmodically – it was because they still hoped for the defection of the Vichy-officered troops in the Levant. This 'Army of the Levant' was the big prize; if it accepted Free French command, Syria/Lebanon would remain under French control and all undertakings to the contrary might be ignored. Catroux continued bullish about the impact of his presence and had composed a proclamation inviting the Vichy officers to 'join me in attacking the [German] invader'; or 'at least to give me free passage to fight France's enemy'. 'Will you dare to fight us?' he asked. 'Will you shoot Catroux?'[24]

Although denied the rank of *Haut Commissionaire* because the British thought it too redolent of the mandate, as *Délégué Générale* Catroux rejoiced in a title as bristly as his eyebrows, with its five acute

— france fighting france; Vichy Damascus falls

accents neatly complementing the five gold stars on his epaulettes. Freya Stark was impressed. She had first met the General during his incognito period in Cairo. Seeing him again in Jerusalem's King David Hotel, she thought he 'looked ten years younger'. Perhaps it had something to do with having 'a war of his own in prospect', perhaps with having escaped 'the Mad Cat'. Stark, fresh from her month's confinement in the Baghdad embassy, knew how he felt. All Cairo seemed to have foregathered in Jerusalem and, on 1 June, was packing for Syria. The Levant war, she noted, 'opened next morning with an old-fashioned cavalry charge'.[25]

The charge of the Cheshire Yeomanry against some Moroccan *épahis* is said to have been the last occasion when Englishmen rode into battle on horses. It was that sort of campaign. What with Frenchmen killing Frenchmen, the British inclined to side with the Arab subjects of both, and the nationals of more than twenty other countries in four continents fighting confusingly among them, it was not an easy war to chronicle. Meanwhile out in the desert, in what a military historian calls 'one of the most picturesque battles of the Second World War'[26], the Arab Legion and the Household Cavalry locked horns with France's Foreign Legion in a desert dignified by the bleached colonnades and classical temples of Palmyra. Simultaneously but far away to the north-east and less picturesquely, the Indian Army troops who had landed at Basra in April plodded slowly along the banks of the upper Euphrates towards Aleppo.

The tactics, like the troops, were of a bygone age. The Allied forces charged rapidly north from Palestine on several fronts, so leaving their lines exposed to a devastating counter-attack. The Vichy troops had a few tanks and used them to great effect in this flanking assault. The British, on the other hand, had more planes and, having achieved air superiority as well as naval superiority, rescued the advance. Blockaded by sea and with little prospect of reinforcements by air, the Vichy regime was probably doomed from the start. But its officers, far from joining their 'Free' compatriots, or even just standing aside, fought with a pride no less fierce for being hopeless. Damascus fell much as it had in 1918, amid Arab indifference and Allied confusion: while French and Australians disputed the honour of first entering the city, a couple of American newspapermen pipped them both. On 11 July, with Beirut itself about to fall, the Vichy commander requested an armistice. So ended the campaign, five weeks after it had begun. Each side had lost more than a thousand men in what, even in the heat of a world war, contemporaries reckoned a singularly unnecessary and tragic affair.

SEDUCING THE WRONG GENERAL

But if the war in the Levant was won, the peace had still to be fought; and it was the peace that would be of most consequence for the Middle East. The Vichy army was still largely intact, its future undecided, with Catroux still hoping that in defeat it might yet prove amenable to his approaches. The political future of the Levant also hung in the balance, with Free French intentions of appropriating the mandate and harnessing the region to their cause wildly at variance with Catroux's promise of imminent independence as endorsed by the British.

The armistice, signed under farcical circumstances in a tent in Acre, only heightened the confusion. Catroux came bareheaded because a souvenir-hunter had stolen his kepi. Then, just as the signatories reached for their pens, the lights went out. An Australian wheeled in a motor-cycle, and they tried again by the light of its headlamp. This only worked if the engine was kept running. Midst choking fumes and a deafening roar the ceremony was hastily concluded but left a nasty taste.

On the insistence of the Vichy commanders, their surrender was made purely to the British. The Free French were not mentioned, and although the hatless Catroux was there, he signed only a subsidiary letter. Nor was there any mention in this Acre Convention of either the mandate or independence; by implication the whole Levant was simply handed over to the British. Vichy troops were to decide for themselves whether to stay on under Allied command or to be repatriated to France; and under a secret protocol of which Catroux was ignorant, there was to be little opportunity for the Free French to pressurize their vanquished compatriots into joining them. Vichy officers might indeed defect to de Gaulle, thereby jeopardizing their pensions and exposing their dependants in France to retaliation; or they might have a free passage home and forfeit nothing. Not surprisingly, few signed up with Free France. The Army of the Levant, for which de Gaulle had risked his scanty troops and

Catroux his cherished reputation, eventually sailed away into the Mediterranean sunset minus a mere 2,500 men.

The British claimed that, since they were not technically at war with Vichy France, indeed were anxious to keep her out of the war, repatriation must be honoured. But as de Gaulle would point out, the same troops would no doubt reappear in France's North African colonies and there have to be defeated all over again. As for the other terms agreed at Acre, they had been largely formulated by the British general who commanded the campaign and did not seem to accord with previous statements of intent. It was the Free French, not the British, who were supposed to assume control of the Levant and then grant it independence. The British were meant to be seen simply as holding the French to this commitment; and thus would they win the credit for it in Arab eyes. But as result of the Acre terms they appeared to be usurping French rights and hoovering up French colonies, just as Vichy had predicted.

General Spears was aghast and dismissed the settlement as 'quite preposterous'. De Gaulle went very much further. Armed with an ultimatum that effectively terminated the Anglo-Free French alliance, he stormed into Cairo and for three hours berated the British Minister (a newly appointed political supremo). So dire became the atmosphere that it looked as if, far from recruiting his Vichy opponents, he might be about to join them. In near-panic the British cut his wireless link to Beirut, denied him transport and debated whether 'it might be necessary to imprison de Gaulle for a time'.[27] Again the idea of replacing him with the more obliging Catroux was canvassed.

But on reflection both sides backed down; a spat over Syria could not be allowed to prejudice the whole war effort. The Acre terms were therefore reinterpreted in such a way as to mollify de Gaulle without jeopardizing Britain's wartime priorities of an Axis-free Levant and Arab docility. The only loser was logic. Under this fudge, to which both sides would formally adhere for the next three years, the British forswore any designs on the Levant but retained an overwhelming military presence there and remained committed to Syro-Lebanese independence. The Free French assumed control of the administration, police and economy; and their exclusive 'role' in the region was acknowledged. But this was somehow supposed to be compatible with a reaffirmation of Catroux's promise about sovereign independence. Catroux, like Churchill, looked to Iraq and Egypt as the ideal models. Yet such treaty-bound sovereignty was quite unacceptable to Syrian and Lebanese nationalists. They might have gulped down a diluted version in 1936 but in 1941, with the mandatory power discredited and their own position very much stronger, they declined all such potions. They had no intention of allowing a pusillanimous splinter-group of Frenchmen to make good its claim to the same detested and outdated mandate.

That this was precisely de Gaulle's intention soon became apparent. With no administrative cadre of their own, the Free French eagerly co-opted that of the Vichy French. Officials tainted in British eyes by their collaboration with the Axis powers and in Syrian eyes by their association with the mandatory regime were simply reshuffled or reconfirmed in office. Many were notoriously corrupt or incompetent; and all channelled their resentment of the British presence into an excess of officiousness. The tit-for-tat of police repression and retaliatory protest quickly resumed. More seriously, an Anglo-French clash over the Jabal Druze nearly reignited hostilities.

The Druze had responded positively to the approaches of Alec Kirkbride in early 1941 and had duly welcomed the advance of the Allied forces. In fact many Druze defected to them and were formed into a Druze Legion under British command. This was the sort of response that Catroux had hoped for in Syria; but not in the Jabal Druze. Druze relations with Transjordan's Amir Abdullah and his British sponsors had long occasioned acute French paranoia. Now, to the Free French as to their Vichy opponents, it appeared that the British were taking advantage of French weakness to encourage both Druze secession and Transjordanian ambition. If the British element in Operation Exporter was hoping to export anything, it looked to be Abdullah's long-cherished claim to the throne of Syria.

Abdullah himself certainly hoped so. But his airy expectations of acceptance in Damascus had been lately dented by the murder of Dr Shahbandar, his main supporter among the Syrian nationalist leaders, and then deflated by a pointed lack of encouragement from the British. The British were understandably cool; a Hashemite Syria would antagonize not only most Syrians but also Saudi Arabia, Iraq and even Egypt; intervention in Syria was meant to assuage Arab opinion, not provoke it.

There remained the possibility of rewarding Abdullah's loyalty by a transfer of just the Jabal Druze. Still a separate state, ill disposed to the French, not enamoured of Damascus, and contiguous to Transjordan, the Jabal looked to be gift-wrapped for Abdullah and the British. Sultan al-Atrash, the Druze hero of the 1925 Great Revolt, was still resident in Transjordan and would long remain so (he lived to nearly 100, dying in 1982). Through his kinsman Hamid al-Atrash, who was the current Amir in the Jabal, his good offices could be used to great effect. Better still, the British supposed that they possessed an asset of even more dazzling potential in the Amir Hamid's redoubtable ex-wife.

Asmahan, the heart-throb of Egyptian movie-goers, had been born Emily, of Druze parents and with the sort of looks that early gave rise to extravagant hearsay. The Amir Hamid was said to have been smitten when he visited her home to execute a contract to assassinate her high-spirited mother for conduct unbecoming in a Druze. Instead of a murder there was a marriage, quickly followed by a divorce. Ex-Amira Emily, still a teenager, then became Asmahan, the toast of Cairo's salons, a screen idol and *femme fatale* of legendary status.

According to Alec Kirkbride, it was military headquarters in Cairo who dispatched her to the Levant in early 1941; she was to assist him in his overtures to the Druze leaders. Wearing riding breeches ('she probably thought that the role of secret agent required something more glamorous than a skirt'), she arrived in Amman 'as one would expect a film actress to do; chattering and laughing vivaciously'. Glubb, invited to meet her, took one look and bolted, as he had from Rosita Forbes. Kirkbride himself was more exercised about Mrs Kirkbride and her likely reaction to his disappearing into the Jabal in such compromising company. He organized a separate car for his charge and heaved a sigh of relief when, reverting to Emily, she was reabsorbed into the bosom of Druze society. She resurfaced at the beginning of the campaign, still in trousers but now with 'a surprising form of semi-military head-dress'. Apparently she expected to lead the Anglo-Druze forces into the Jabal 'in the role of a Joan of Arc'.[28] The offer was rejected, with regrets; as Kirkbride would recall, her eyes were truly 'astounding, twice as big as those of other women and . . . of a light china blue'.[29]

Two months later General Louis Spears saw them differently. Installed in Beirut following the Syrian armistice and now bestriding the Levant as Britain's representative (in addition to his liaison role with the Free French), Spears confirmed that Asmahan's eyes were indeed 'immense', but not blue. Rather were they, he insisted, green, in fact 'green as the colour of the sea you have to cross on the way to paradise'. What prompted this fanciful insight is not known. He first met her at her wedding. More Mata Hari than Joan of Arc, she had settled in the Druze capital of Suwayda after the armistice and there, generously subsidized by the British, had for a second time successfully wooed her ex-husband, Amir Hamid. Now she was remarrying him. She wore a European outfit for the occasion but Spears would come to prefer her in Arab dress. Either way, 'she was,' he recalled, 'and will always be, one of the most beautiful women I have ever seen'. She also sang like an angel and 'bowled over British officers with the accuracy and speed of a machine gun'.[30]

Spears himself may not have received a direct hit; like most of his countrymen he suspected her of double-dealing. But he was also grateful to her. In Suwayda immediately after the armistice an extremely delicate situation had arisen when Colonel Bouvier, the Vichy commandant and a worthy successor to Captain Carbillet, had cleverly exploited the mutual suspicions of the British and the Free French. With 500 mainly Tunisian troops under his command, Bouvier had the means to ensure that the Jabal remained French, and he duly led Catroux to expect that he would declare for Free France. But word of this arrangement appeared to contradict his assurances to the British about his imminent withdrawal from the Jabal. They therefore surrounded his lines and at gunpoint ordered his Tunisians to disarm while the RAF flew low overhead. A single shot could easily have restarted the war.

Two weeks later, an even more dangerous stand-off resulted when Free French forces appeared at Suwayda demanding that the British lower their Union Jacks and hand over command. This time, on orders from Cairo, the British backed down. But on both occasions the real worry was that the Druze themselves would intervene, either to waylay Bouvier's men or to resist the Free French. That they in fact held their fire seems to have had much to do with the steadying hand of Amir Hamid, ably supported by the vivacious Emily.

The Free French having now apparently scotched all hope of the Jabal Druze being detached from French Levant, the Amira Emily turned to her British backers and in particular to General 'Mad Jack' Evetts in Damascus. He, by all accounts, did succumb to her charms;

1942 Unification of Syria
w/o palestine, Leb & Jordan

and while the romance lasted, his troops stayed put in Suwayda. But when Evetts was transferred, so were his men. The French were left in sole control.

The Amira would have done better to concentrate on Spears, whose position in Beirut seemed as unassailable as his devotion to her person. Soon redivorced by the Amir, she had frequent occasion to call on Spears for money and once for immunity from prosecution when she was stopped on the Turkish frontier with contraband, allegedly including another British officer, in the trunk of her car. More scandalously, she resurfaced in Jerusalem's King David Hotel where she 'presided over real orgies' in which she danced naked 'with specially selected British officers'. Spears knew of this only by report, of course; but such reports were too much for the Druze patriarchs. Politely alerting Spears to their intentions, they arranged a freak motoring mishap in which the ex-Amira met her untimely end in an Egyptian canal. With tragic symmetry, the contract originally taken out on the mother was thus served on the daughter.[31]

In the meantime the much-divorced Amir Hamid al-Atrash found himself elevated to ministerial rank in an all-Syrian government. The governments installed by Catroux in Syria in September and Lebanon in November 1941 were neither representative, constitutional nor, despite declarations of independence, in any sense independent. De Gaulle maintained that the mandate remained effective and, much to Spears's indignation, Catroux and his administration ensured that this was indeed the case. The only significant development was that in early 1942 the Jabal Druze and the mainly Alawi Jabal Ansariya (also known as the Latakia region) were incorporated into the new Syrian state, which thus at last assumed its current configuration. Catroux had never been keen on the fragmentation and, having just narrowly avoided the alienation of the Jabal Druze, he was now taking no chances. Hence his partial (because minus *Grand Liban*, Palestine and Transjordan) reconstitution of a unitary Syrian state, and hence the sop to Amir Hamid of a ministerial portfolio.

FREE AT LAST

The British, although indifferent to the reunification of the three French states, remained firmly committed to their ceasing to be

French. When General Spears returned to Beirut in early 1942 after collecting a knighthood, he adopted the emancipation of the Levantine Arabs as his personal crusade. The recent charade of Lebanese independence had made him feel as if his weight (plus that of the occupying 9th British Army) were 'holding down the Lebanon to be raped by Free France'. This had to stop. The damsel must be rescued, the rapist castrated, and it was hard to say which Spears relished most. A glossy and abrasive character with the sharp eye and hunched posture of a raven, he patrolled the high moral ground. He preferred fighting a cause to discharging a brief, and had the talons with which to do so. A year earlier he had been the *Gaullistes'* champion and a rabid Francophile. Now, bitterly disillusioned by their reluctance to give winning the war a higher priority than redeeming French honour, he damned the *Gaullistes* as traitors, described his old friend de Gaulle as no better than a 'Free French Führer', and espoused Arab independence with a fervour rare even among Arabists.[32]

De Gaulle heartily reciprocated this hostility; and their alliance notwithstanding, for the rest of the war the two imperial powers waged a Levantine tussle that would almost drown out the voice of indigenous protest. Spears, opening with a master-stroke, chose to call the French bluff by recognizing their client states as indeed 'independent' republics. Accredited to them (rather than to their French masters), he took their sovereignty at the face value given it by the French and pounced on every instance of French interference in their affairs. Catroux and de Gaulle interpreted this as collusion with disaffected elements and detected British treachery behind every nationalist utterance and protest strike.

In 1942 the argument revolved around the need for elections. Spears argued that only representative governments chosen by the people themselves could legitimize the new states in the eyes of the world and ensure their support for the war effort. De Gaulle retorted that, however desirable, holding elections, like terminating the mandate, was impossible under wartime conditions and while France herself was deprived of legitimate government. Spears persisted, de Gaulle demanded his recall, and Catroux ably prevaricated. In November 1942 the defeat of Rommel at El Alamein and the Anglo-American landings in French North Africa turned the tide of war in the Mediterranean. Spears pressed harder; de Gaulle at last gave ground. Reluctantly in February 1943 the French announced the restoration of constitutional government in the Levant states and the establishment of interim administrations to oversee elections in July.

The elections in Syria were held on schedule and returned a staunchly nationalist government under the presidency of Shukri al-Quwwatli, a stalwart of the pre-war National Bloc, who enjoyed British support. The French were dismayed but not surprised. They had more or less written off Syria. But Lebanon, their Mediterranean 'rampart' from which Syria might again be controlled, was a different matter. Looking to their traditionally pro-French constituency of Maronite Christians, they supposed that the nationalists could be outflanked and laboured hard to secure an agreeable result. Spears, alert to every bribe and stratagem, worked even harder; and again the French were disappointed. The delayed elections returned another nationalist government with Riad Solh, also a National Bloc stalwart, as Lebanon's prime minister.

After consultations with Damascus, which were notable for Syrian acceptance of Lebanon's right to sovereign status under a congenial nationalist leadership, it was Riad Solh who on behalf of both states threw down the gauntlet to the French. In October his government proposed abolition of the mandate plus constitutional reforms that would outlaw foreign interference and so preclude the one-sided treaty on which French hopes still rested. The proposal was approved in the Lebanese Assembly on 8 November. Three days later, in a dawn swoop by French troops, the president and most of his senior ministers were arrested, the Assembly closed down and the constitution suspended.

Only the evening before, Spears had wrung an assurance from the acting *Délégué Général* that no such action was contemplated. Incandescent with indignation, Spears now had a cause worthy of his rhetoric. His condemnations rivalled those of the incensed Lebanese themselves. For the next twelve days of frantic negotiation between London, Algiers (now home to the Free French), Cairo and Beirut, the British forces stood poised to take over the Lebanon. A general strike paralysed the country, French troops fired indiscriminately on protesters, foreign journalists had a field day, and the whole Arab world erupted in sympathy.

Spears, brandishing the threat of martial law, upheld Lebanese demands for the immediate and unconditional release and reinstatement of the government. In this he was supported by the British minister in Cairo and ultimately by his old friend Churchill. However the British Foreign Office suspected that Spears was not just upholding such demands but orchestrating them. The French were sure of it; and when on 22 November Catroux and de Gaulle finally backed down to the extent of releasing the detainees, they saved face by insisting that they did so under pressure not from the Lebanese but from the perfidious British and the unspeakable Spears.

On a tide of national rejoicing Riad Solh's government reinstated itself and confirmed its abolition of the mandate. The French did not, however, endorse this, nor rescind their orders for the suspension of the Assembly. Whether sheltering under the mandate or as part of the occupying Allied forces, they retained control of the locally recruited *Troupes Spéciales* and of the intelligence service. Their civil officials also stayed put. Although a final settlement of Franco-Syrian and Franco-Lebanese relations in the form of the inevitable treaties was urged by the British, de Gaulle was now in no hurry. France herself was biding her time. Her own liberation was drawing near and with it the prospect of readdressing the Levant from a position of much greater strength, hopefully unhampered by the presence of British troops. The only formal concession made as result of the Lebanese showdown in 1943 was the transfer to the new states of those economic *intérêts communs* (posts, customs duties, communications and so on).

The liberation of France and de Gaulle's triumphant return to Paris came in the summer of 1944. At the same time Spears was informed that his term in Beirut was coming to an end. His championship of the Levant states had now become an acknowledged embarrassment, especially so when, with the war in the west nearly won, conciliating Arab opinion was no longer the paramount consideration. 'We should discourage the throwing of stones', Churchill had told his old friend, 'since we have green-houses of our own – acres and acres of them.'[33] The British Prime Minister was thinking of Iraq, Egypt and above all Palestine; they were vulnerable because of the mounting criticism, emanating from Washington and Moscow, of the iniquities of hot-house imperialism in a more benign post-war climate. How could the British hope to defend their own mandate and their own treaties while denying to the French similar privileges of identical provenance in neighbouring countries?

Likewise Spears's ill-disguised Francophobia could no longer be indulged. The British had never denied that France had special rights in the Levant, and these might now at last be enshrined in treaties with a constitutionally legitimate French government. Spears was therefore to spend his last months in Beirut reversing the habits of a triennium. Instead of bolstering Syro-Lebanese defiance, he was to use his considerable influence to entice the Levant governments into signing away much of their hard-won independence in Iraq-style treaties. Churchill's tumultuous reception by de Gaulle in Paris in November 1944, 'one of the proudest and most moving occasions of my life', seemed to have gone to his head. Rancour and acrimony were forgotten as the two leaders toasted one another in an orgy of mutual regard. At such a moment, anything that might weaken the French government would be 'most unwise';[34] and that included provocation in the Levant.

But the Syrian and Lebanese governments had no intention of bowing to French pressure, nor of accepting an Iraq-style treaty, nor even of negotiating until the *Troupes Spéciales* had been transferred to their own command and some long-promised new rifles provided for their ill-armed police. Already fearful of the consequences of de Gaulle's installation in France, they were still more alarmed when Spears finally departed. As much fêted as Churchill in Paris, he left the Levant in December, proudly sporting the highest honours that Syria and Lebanon could award, laden with 'gifts of carpets, armour, vases, Ali Baba jars and so on', and intensely moved by the heartfelt regrets of two very anxious governments. His successor was expected to be much less sympathetic; and it was feared that the British government, after pulling out Spears, must be about to pull out its troops. Beirut and Damascus clamoured for their retention. The climax, if there was to be one, could not be long delayed.

As tension mounted throughout the Levant in the early months of 1945, the French detected a need to reinforce their own troops. The British objected on the grounds that this could be disastrous to the treaty negotiations. The French went ahead on the pretext that such troops were in fact *en route* to Indo-China. A cruiser began disembarking the first draft in Beirut on 6 May; three more battalions arrived in the middle of the month.

True to form, the Lebanese and the Syrians responded with a general strike, demonstrations and riots. True to form, French troops swept the streets with gunfire. The fighting was fiercest in Syria where the French had tanks. On 30 May, in a rerun of the worst incident in the 1925 Great Revolt, Damascus underwent heavy shelling and bombing. 'The Gaullists, like the Bourbons, seemed to have learnt nothing and forgotten nothing,' writes Gaunson.[35] In Syria alone, 400 died and thousands were wounded. It was the last demonstration of the harsh reality behind French colonial pretensions in the Levant, and what historian Philip Khoury calls 'a bitter reminder of France's quarter century of commitment to educating the people . . . in the values of Western civilisation and democracy'.[36]

The British remonstrated, threatened and, as Damascus exploded across the world's headlines, finally responded. So, in anticipation, did de Gaulle. His order for a cease-fire crossed with that from London for a military take-over. 'The British [9th] Army was ordered to move the French out of Damascus and plonk them in the Lebanon; which they did,' noted a satisfied Spears. 'Thereafter there was no further talk of a treaty between the French and the Lebanese or the French and the Syrians.'[37]

There was still the question of removing the remaining French and British troops, and in this connection Syria established a new precedent by appealing for support from Moscow and then from Washington by way of the infant United Nations Organization. Both were sympathetic but neither was eager to become embroiled; nor was it necessary. In a series of troop reductions carefully synchronized to dispel the idea that either was shepherding the other, both armies had vacated Syro-Lebanese soil by August 1946.

Despite this tactful handling, de Gaulle remained painfully conscious of France's humiliation. He continued to regard the British as overwhelmingly responsible for the 'loss' of the Levant and he now bore this grudge away into his long exile in the political wilderness. Not until nearly seventeen years later, when the British request for entry to the European Economic Community ran up against an uncompromising and apparently inexplicable *non* from the *Général* in his presidential reincarnation, were the British reminded of Spears, of their handling of the 1943 Lebanese crisis and of their 1945 military intervention in Syria.

De Gaulle, no less than Churchill, had consistently underestimated political expectations in the Arab world. If the Iraqis were rebellious, reasoned Churchill, it must be because of Nazi intrigues;

if the Syrians were obdurate, reasoned de Gaulle, it must be because Spears was encouraging them. The Anglo-Iraqi and Anglo-Egyptian treaties had been hatched in the 1920s and concluded in the 1930s. Attempting to foist something similar on the sophisticated citizenry of internationally recognized states like Syria and Lebanon in the 1940s was impractical and insulting. By the end of the war, and despite doing well out of it, the Egyptians and the Iraqis were themselves kicking hard at their treaty traces. And, beneath the umbrella of the new Arab League, they would demand that liberties just won in the Levant must be extended across the Middle East.

12

Taking Sides

CAMP FOLLOWERS

By SEA IT USUALLY took a week to get from London to the Middle East. For Hermione Ranfurly, travelling out to join her husband in February 1940, it took two days longer because her ship was delayed in Marseille by troop movements. Troops were on the move everywhere. Her husband Dan, a second lieutenant in the cavalry, had just been posted to Palestine to join the only mounted division in the British army. Being also the 7th Earl of Ranfurly, he went to war in style. His two horses accompanied him; so did his butler; and his newly wed Hermione was not the sort to be left behind. Only 26 and still unused to being a countess, she bought a ticket from an unregistered travel agent and boarded a train at Victoria station. Within forty-eight hours she was in Marseille; five days out from there she landed in Alexandria; thence she went by train to Haifa and her Dan.

Six months later, much to her disgust and despite frantic string-pulling, she was sent back to Britain following orders for the compulsory repatriation of all service wives. A special train trundled the evacuees out of Palestine. This time they were taken not to Alexandria on the Mediterranean but to the port of Suez at the Red Sea end of the Canal. There, four miles offshore, rode the *Empress of Britain,* a luxury liner lately converted for carrying troops to the

Middle East by way of South Africa. Hermione Ranfurly's voyage home, instead of one week, was expected to take six.

Through the summer of 1940 the tide of war had risen so fast that the usual route to the Middle East was already cut. It would remain so for most of the war. As Ranfurly noted in her diary, Italy's declaration of hostilities and the fall of France meant that 'the Mediterranean was a gauntlet now . . . flanked by our enemies'.[1] Only warships ventured through it. All other seaborne traffic went round Africa. Within a year of the outbreak of the war, Cairo had become as remote from London as Bombay or Singapore.

With control of the Mediterranean went the whole point of the Suez Canal. Its northern access effectively sealed, that proverbial carotid/jugular/umbilical of empire, around which strategists had traditionally constructed the whole rationale for a British presence in the Middle East, shrivelled to slimy irrelevance. Even local traffic between the Arabian Sea and the eastern corner of the Mediterranean used it only sparingly. For although Egypt remained technically neutral until 1945, British installations in Egyptian territory were a legitimate Axis target; the Canal, like the Alexandria dockyard and the Haifa refinery, was frequently bombed, and when not blocked by sunken ships, it was found that enemy aircraft had sprinkled it with mines. VIPs like de Gaulle, Churchill and Roosevelt might hop east by air through Central (and later North) Africa; but for the two million troops who would pass through Egypt during the war years, and for the billions of dollars-worth of American lend-lease armaments on which operations in the region came to depend, the only safe passage to the Middle East was its back passage – via the Atlantic and Indian oceans.

Not that that was always safe. Hermione Ranfurly's homeward voyage aboard the *Empress of Britain* would be that great liner's last. Spotted by German aircraft in the Atlantic, the ship was bombed, set ablaze and sunk 700 miles west of Ireland. Ranfurly pasted a news cutting about the disaster into her diary; weeping for lost friends, she could not but marvel at her luck. For in Cape Town, with the vague idea that it would be easier to get back to her husband and the Middle East from there than from London, she had jumped ship. It was the sort of thing one did, when one was young, fun, pretty and a countess. In South Africa a friendly bank manager lent her some money, and a nice man from Thomas Cook somehow procured her a seat on the Cape-to-Cairo flying-boat service. Hopping from lake to lake up through East Africa, her flight splashed down on the Nile in the centre of Cairo a week before the *Empress of Britain* was reported missing.

For a while she lay low. Contravening military orders was a punishable offence, even for a countess. Yet Egypt was technically independent as well as non-belligerent; if she could find work there, she could probably stay. She had a secretarial diploma, and as Louis Spears would wistfully record when he later found her working for a rival general, she was not just 'beautiful' but 'a lady of immense tact and wisdom'.[2] But initially she was *persona non grata*. No general dared employ her. Her only hope lay with someone utterly contemptuous of authority, like the now Major Orde Wingate.

'A short stocky officer . . . [with] a large head shaped like an anthill', Wingate burst, unsought and unannounced, into her bolt-hole in Cairo's Continental Hotel. Interrupting a quiet game of backgammon, he came straight to the point. He was going to Ethiopia to raise a revolt there; could she read signals? She must be ready on Tuesday; it could take six months; and would she mind being dropped in by parachute?

She wouldn't mind; she was game to be dropped in anywhere, she said, given 'the right kind of underwear'. Wingate, to whom humour of every description was incomprehensible, took this for a yes. Getting there, she could manage; it was getting back that bothered her. She wanted an official assurance that she would be readmitted to Egypt when the assignment was over. Wingate thought he could fix it and, so saying, exited as abruptly as he had entered.[3]

Since making a name for himself with his Special Night Squads in Palestine, Wingate, the most committed of Britain's gentile Zionists, had been lobbying hard in London for the formation of a Jewish army. According to the Jewish Agency, 150,000 Palestinian Jewish men and women had already volunteered for 'national' service on behalf of the 'homeland'. An army recruited from this pool could relieve the British troops in Palestine for service elsewhere; some Jewish units might even fight alongside the Allies in North Africa or Europe; its officers would be trained in Britain; and he, Wingate, would command it. What Lawrence had done for the Arabs in the First World War, Wingate might do for the Jews in the Second. Weizmann approved, indeed championed the idea. The British War

Office welcomed the prospect of more troops; and Churchill himself was all for it.

But the Colonial Office, responsible for Palestine's administration, was not; nor was the Foreign Office, which dealt with most of the other Arab states. They emphasized that the creation of a Jewish army would be construed as a major concession to Jewish statehood. Moreover, the arming of Palestine's Jewish community would be totally unacceptable to its Arab community, would almost certainly re-ignite the Palestinian Revolt, and so would ultimately necessitate more British troops in Palestine, not fewer.

In the face of these objections, action was repeatedly postponed and the proposal steadily watered down. In 1940–1 the 'Jewish army' dwindled to a 'Jewish division', then a 'Palestine regiment'. Churchill remained supportive, but he somewhat naïvely imagined that the Palestinian Arabs would be as keen as the Jews to sign up for a peace-keeping role in their homeland. This idea of allaying mutual suspicion by insisting on equal recruitment from both communities duly aroused little enthusiasm from either and resulted merely in a 'Palestine battalion' (it was otherwise the 'Palestine Buffs' because it was attached to a regiment known as The Buffs, from East Kent, presumably the nearest British recruiting-ground to Palestine).

Zionists, gentile as well as Jewish, wanted their own force with its own command structure, its own insignia and its own flag. They were less certain about the extent to which such a force should be retained in Palestine or deployed elsewhere but, either way, it would indeed be a giant step towards nationhood. As a participant in ultimate victory it might entitle Zionism to special consideration in any post-war settlement; it would certainly provide the 'homeland' with a reservoir of well-trained soldiers; and, more immediately, it would satisfy demands that the defence of one's home against foreign aggression was a fundamental right. For whereas Arabs could afford a certain detachment about the Nazi threat in the Middle East, Jews could not. As first the Italians, then the Germans, menaced Palestine's Egyptian portal, Weizmann and Wingate foresaw the imminent 'annihilation of the half-million Jews in Palestine'. 'If we have to go down, we are entitled to go down fighting', insisted Weizmann.[4]

But the debate rumbled on, waxing and waning as the Axis threat advanced and receded. Only in 1944, long after the threat had receded deep into Europe, did Churchill finally reward Weizmann's persistence with the formation of a Jewish Brigade. It had its own flag and briefly it saw service in Italy and France, but never in the Middle East. Meanwhile Orde Wingate's fiery advocacy had long since been deflected from Palestine to Ethiopia. In an attempt to dislodge the Italian presence there, his success as a guerrilla leader with the Jews during the Palestine Revolt was to be replicated with the Ethiopians. Hence his presence in Cairo in late 1940.

Hermione Ranfurly did not in the end accompany him. Wingate failed to secure the required assurances about her return to Egypt and went off without her. Six months later she cabled her congratulations; he had reinstated the Emperor Haile Selassie in Addis Ababa in April 1941. It was 'the only good news' in a quite awful month. Rommel had begun rolling back the British advance in Libya, Greece was turning into a nightmare, Rashid Ali was in revolt in Iraq, and Dan Ranfurly was 'reported missing' near Tobruk. Her diary was becoming a dirge.

Happily word soon came that the earl had not been killed, merely captured, and in the meantime his fate had produced a wave of official compassion for the distraught young countess. Work was found for her with SOE (the unsupervised and not-so-secret Special Operations Executive recently set up to promote resistance behind enemy lines) and she was at last given permission to stay on in the Middle East. Although she was subsequently employed in Palestine and Iraq, Cairo would remain her base; and as a wartime billet it could scarcely be bettered. Blacked-out London was being blitzed, Hong Kong and Singapore were soon to fall, and New York was too obviously an English escapist's refuge. But Cairo, the headquarters of Middle East Command, was in the thick of things. It was barely a hundred miles from a comprehensible battle-front yet little affected by wartime shortages, moderately safe and determinedly lively.

Arriving at the same time as Ranfurly, Alan Moorehead of the *Daily Express* had scarcely been able to believe his eyes. The streets were ablaze with lights, the bars open, the cinemas packed, and the desert parties went on until dawn. The war was 'merely a noise on the radio'.

We had French wines, grapes, melons, steaks, cigarettes, beer, whisky and abundance of all things that belonged to rich, idle peace . . . Polo continued with the same extraordinary frenzy in the roasting afternoon heat.

No one worked from one till five-thirty or six . . . Madame Badia's girls writhed in the belly dance at her cabaret near the Pont des Anglais. Grey staff cars ran back and forth over the Kasr el Nil bridge. The boatmen on the feluccas cursed and yelled and chanted . . .[5]

To Britons of means or purpose, Cairo called as never before. Besides Moorehead himself, Randolph Churchill and Richard Dimbleby were among the press corps in Egypt. Olivia Manning was the wife of the head of the British Council, Patrick Leigh Fermor and Evelyn Waugh put in brief appearances. From Alexandria Lawrence Durrell and from Cairo Robin Fedden headed whole teams of literary luminaries in an inter-city 'War of the Poets'. 'Not since Troy was there such a bash-up,' wrote Durrell to his friend Henry Miller about the exchange of obscure epigrams and defamatory verses; that other exchange out in the desert prompted suitable metaphors.[6] Far from London with its smouldering streets, its heatless homes and its stinking air-raid shelters, here was a war with sunshine and style and nonchalant heroes who danced all night and drove gaily to their death in the morning. Noël Coward came to entertain the troops; Cecil Beaton took the photographs; John Gielgud appeared as Hamlet.

Ranfurly's Cairo circle was more military and heroic: SOE operatives like Peter Fleming, the traveller whose brother Ian later wrote the James Bond books; Fitzroy Maclean, who might have been (but probably wasn't) the original James Bond; and the three Stirling brothers, one of whom, David, started the Long Range Desert Patrols from which the trouble-shooting SAS emerged. Colonel Bonner Fellers, the outspoken US military attaché to whom Ranfurly was indebted for the first news of her husband's capture, shared with her his anxieties about the North African campaign and his efforts to interest his own government in it. Although these eventually succeeded, Fellers's indiscretions were not appreciated and he was transferred to the Pacific. When, in late 1943, Ranfurly innocently asked her neighbour at dinner for news of him, she received the reply that 'Any friend of Bonner Fellers is no friend of mine'. The speaker, General Dwight D. Eisenhower, Supreme Allied Commander in the Mediterranean, then 'smartly turned his back on me again'. Ranfurly far preferred the outspoken General George Patton who clumped round her office in boots and gaiters, dispensed nylon stockings, and was 'great fun'.[7]

Less predictably she struck up a close friendship with George Antonius. Instead of following the Mufti to Berlin, Antonius had gravitated back to Cairo and there regaled his young companion with his life's story and convictions. 'He grumbled good-naturedly about the Palestine government's disapproval of him' yet refused to renounce his friendship with the Mufti; after all, they were boyhood friends; the Mufti was a great patriot; according to Antonius, he had only gone over to Hitler because he had no other choice. Then, says Ranfurly, 'we talked of [Asmahan] al-Atrash, a lovely Jabal Druze princess whose green eyes and black hair have caused a sensation here'. One day Antonius took Ranfurly to the zoo to meet Said the Hippo, 'the nicest person in Cairo'; another time, in Jerusalem, he took her to dinner to meet his estranged wife Katy. A week later Antonius was dead. The Countess of Ranfurly was one of the few Britons to attend his funeral.[8]

Also busy in Cairo was Freya Stark; 'small and rather ugly', thought Ranfurly, but 'a very brave lady with an iron will hidden under hypnotic hats'. Stark had started something called the 'Brotherhood (and Sisterhood) of Freedom' which peddled the Allies' ideals, like liberty and democracy, to ill-informed Egyptians using the trickle-down technique later (and suitably) known as 'pyramid-selling'. It sounded unpromising, and Moorehead may have been referring to the Brotherhood when he castigated British propaganda as 'childish and inept'; 'the British Empire was being hawked through the mud villages of the Delta like a dud second-hand motor car', he reported.[9] But Stark's energy knew no bounds and, after her ordeal in Baghdad, she would return there at the ambassador Cornwallis's request to launch her movement in Iraq.[10]

Her Egyptian Brotherhood – on no account to be confused with the orthodox Muslim Brotherhood (al-Ikhwan al-Muslimun) founded in Ismailia in 1929 – shared offices with an outfit headed by Lawrence Grafftey-Smith. Following dead-end diplomatic assignments in Jidda, Mosul and Albania, Grafftey-Smith was back in Cairo with his own brand of propaganda. This involved discrediting pro-Axis intelligence gatherers by feeding them rumours so implausible that they would discount more reliable information coming from the same sources. An imaginative approach to the problems of adverse publicity and espionage, it was thought to play well to both Egyptian credulity and Levantine subtlety.

- Egypt independence
- Abdin Affair

Intrigue, subterfuge and scandal gusted through Cairo like the *khamsin,* the scorching desert wind at whose dust-laden blast the doves tumbled from the city's crumbling citadel while the *boulevardiers* on the terrace of Shepheard's scurried for cover. Displaced and distant, in a neutral land that was yet an epicentre of conflict, the British and the Australians, the Free French, the dispersed Poles and Greeks, the Indians, South Africans and, as of 1942, the Americans made Cairo their own, so elevating what was already one of the world's most cosmopolitan cities into an embodiment of the whole 'free world'. All that it lacked were those very ideals for which the war was being fought and for which Stark was so energetically propagandizing, like liberty and democracy.

CRISIS IN CAIRO

It was said that Egypt was run by a triumvirate consisting of the King, the government and the ambassador (as Britain's High Commissioner had become following the ratification of Egyptian 'independence' by the 1936 Anglo-Egyptian treaty). In reality, the King reigned and the government governed while the ambassador ruled. Wartime priorities somewhat obscured this situation with all three having on occasion to fend off the claims of a specially appointed British Minister of State. Resident in Cairo as of June 1941 and entrusted with relieving the military command of non-operational responsibilities, this political supremo enjoyed Cabinet rank and thus something equivalent to prime ministerial status in British Middle Eastern circles. But with four such ministers in as many years, the incumbent seldom stayed long enough to master the intricacies of Egyptian politics and was easily outmanoeuvred, especially by the ambassador, Sir Miles Lampson.

A large, long-serving and domineering figure, it was Lampson who in 1942 provoked a seminal clash which well demonstrated the real locus of power in Egypt. Known as the Abdin affair, it would explode the notion of Egyptian 'independence', outrage nationalist opinion like nothing since the Dinshawai incident, discredit the mighty Wafd, and propel Egypt into making common cause with its Arab neighbours. Anglo-Egyptian relations at all but official level would plummet to depths from which they would never recover; and to this

— same affair the architects of Egypt's 1952 revolution would trace their politicization. Neguib tendered his resignation over it, Nasser 'almost exploded with rage'. It 'put new feelings in our hearts,' Nasser would write, '[and] taught [the officers of the Egyptian army] that there is a dignity which deserves to be defended at any price'.[11]

Dignity was much involved. Sa'ad Zaghlul had been succeeded as leader of the dominant Wafd by the experienced and austere Mustafa al-Nahas; and it was Nahas, plus Lampson as High Commissioner and Anthony Eden as British Foreign Secretary, who had secured the passage of the 1936 Anglo-Egyptian treaty. In the same year King Fuad had died and been succeeded by the inexperienced Farouq. A 17-year-old youth of still slender build and untainted ambition, Farouq was seen to symbolize Egypt's newly won independence. His popularity, however, merely fuelled his resentment of both the patronizing Lampson and the pointy-headed Nahas, each of them old enough to be his grandfather.

Lampson, according to Grafftey-Smith, had never managed the metamorphosis from High Commissioner to ambassador. He should have been replaced immediately the treaty was signed; but in 1941 'the same six-foot-five of British officialdom who had given Farouq those boring books as a child . . . still represented Great Britain' and still regarded Farouq as a delinquent; 'no sensitive young man cares to be reminded, even by his own memory, of the day a visitor knows that he has wet his trousers'.[12] Farouq, in short, detested the overbearing ambassador as much as he did the parsimonious prime minister; and like other disillusioned political players, he saw their 1936 treaty as the obvious way to discredit them.

The treaty had looked favourable enough. It confirmed Egypt's sovereign independence with the British sponsoring Egyptian membership of the League of Nations; it provided for the withdrawal of British forces; and it endorsed Egyptian rights in the Sudan. But the wording of the Sudan clause was ambiguous in that it also safeguarded the Sudan's right to determine its own relationship with Egypt (plus Britain's right to remain there to oversee this process). Likewise the withdrawal of British troops was not all that it seemed in that the necessary arrangements were scandalously protracted, were far from complete when the war broke out, and did not apply to a generous zone beside the Suez Canal. There 12,000 British troops might remain for at least another twenty years, said the treaty.

In reality, they were never reduced to anything like that figure, and until the 1950s the British 'Canal Zone' would constitute easily the largest base on foreign territory in the world. As in Iraq, Egypt's sovereignty was substantially compromised and, to that extent, its independence was impaired.

Heavily criticized on all these points, and with his own Wafd divided over them, Nahas had been persuaded to resign as prime minister in late 1937. It was a timely move. The treaty's inevitable *quid pro quo* about unrestricted British use, in the event of war, of Egyptian facilities, infrastructure, territory and air space meant that within two years the British withdrawal was reversed, and the country was obliged to host a far greater concentration of troops than in the days of its 'occupation'. In effect, most of what pertained to even compromised sovereignty and impaired independence was on hold until the war was won. Lampson pleaded military priorities and enforced the treaty; Nahas berated his successors in government and bided his time; and Farouq rattled through a succession of prime ministers heading coalition governments whose principal recommendation was that they excluded the collaborationist Nahas and his Wafd. Egypt, as Freya Stark put it, was 'quivering like a horse in a bog, with Britain's very existence shaking beneath her'.[13]

But Egypt, although not most Egyptians, was also doing well out of the war. As in the First World War, Egyptian industry benefited from the shortfall in imported manufactures, landowners secured good prices for their produce, and contractors cheerfully fleeced the military commissariat. Egyptian bank deposits tripled as the number of millionaires rose from 50 to 400; when the war ended, the British exchequer would owe Egypt £300 million.[14] Politicians, while demonstrating their nationalist credentials by criticizing the treaty and the British, had to do so without rocking the boat of wartime prosperity. This was a feat more easily performed in opposition than in government and when the war kept its distance. When Egyptian territory was invaded or when the Axis powers looked as if they might replace the British, other considerations came into play.

In June 1940, as Italy entered the war, Farouq and his then pro-Axis prime minister had prevaricated, just like Rashid Ali, about closing the Italian legation and dismissing the King's Italian retainers (the King had spent part of his childhood in Italy). Farouq quickly backed down and the prime minister was dismissed, but not before mischievous demands that, since Lady Lampson was the daughter of a well-known Italian physician, the ambassador too should dismiss his Italian retinue.

A similar situation developed in January 1942 as Egyptians again scented an Axis victory. The Germans had retaken Benghazi in Libya; on the eastern front, they continued their advance into Russia; meanwhile in the Far East the Japanese appeared to be opening up a new front every week. Cries of 'Up Rommel' echoed through the streets of Cairo; the then prime minister, far from curbing these demonstrations, seemed inclined to heed them; and the British became convinced that Mussolini's Radio Bari was being primed with Egyptian news by transmissions from one of Farouq's royal establishments. According to Grafftey-Smith, whose disinformation service was being frustrated by this leak, the evidence of 'an actively hostile Egyptian administration' was overwhelming. Lampson therefore demanded the prime minister's resignation and the reinstatement of Nahas. When this was refused, he secured London's approval for the 'forced abdication' of Farouq himself. Ironically Farouq was to be replaced as king by Muhammad Ali his elderly cousin who was the son of the khedive who had been forced to abdicate at the beginning of the previous world war.

A resignation letter was prepared ('the document, I am told, had a dingy look', says Grafftey-Smith), an audience with the King arranged, a warship readied for his reception in Alexandria and plans laid for the instant installation of Muhammad Ali. At the last minute a question arose as to what Lampson should do if the King now agreed to accept Nahas as prime minister. Farouq was not to be encouraged in this line, but if he took it, in all fairness the abdication letter would have to be withdrawn.

At 9 p.m. on the night of 4 February 1942, Lampson and the general commanding British troops in Egypt, accompanied by a bodyguard of officers 'all over six foot tall', approached Farouq's Abdin palace at the head of a column of armoured cars and tanks. The gates were locked. The lock had to be shot off, and one gate was damaged as the ambassador's car swept through. Outside, the armoured vehicles deployed in the square so as to command both its approaches and the palace. Meanwhile within, Farouq was behaving with great dignity, saying little other than to grumble about the quality of the paper he was to sign; it was as if he had rehearsed the scene.

His chamberlain and closest adviser alerted him to the possible alternative of accepting Nahas. The King stood firm. Twice he took up the pen and twice his chamberlain dissuaded him from signing. At the third attempt he simply threw down the pen and capitulated. He would, after all, call on Nahas to form a government.[15]

The abdication was off, although it was scarcely cause for celebration. Farouq was mortally wounded in the eyes of his countrymen and, despite sustained cold-shouldering and occasional defiance, would never again pose a serious challenge to the ambassador. Instead, he began to indulge interests more appropriate to a sidelined sovereign and in November 1943 appeared to emulate King Ghazi of Iraq when the car he was driving collided head-on with a British army truck outside Cairo. 'Not badly hurt, though he is bruised in some peculiar places,' reported Ranfurly. She claimed that 'his fat had saved him',[16] others that he put on weight prodigiously as a result of the accident. Whatever the case, for another ten years' tenure of the Pharoah's throne he paid a hefty price.

So, for their part in the Abdin affair, would the British. Writing five years later, Kim Roosevelt, the son of Kermit who had fought in Mesopotamia in the First World War, noted that Lampson and the British 'had not yet been forgiven by the Egyptians'. Nor had Nahas by Farouq. Roosevelt, newly arrived in 1942 as an OSS recruit, reckoned the King's hatred of Nahas and the Wafd 'unflagging'.[17] 'We earned,' wrote Grafftey-Smith, 'and duly collected, the resentment and obloquy of a nation deeply humiliated and insulted in the person of its king'; and all 'merely to impose one prime minister rather than another'. True, the Wafd was a populist party and commanded the largest bloc of seats in the Egyptian parliament. And true, Nahas rewarded Lampson by swinging this support behind the war effort. When, later in 1942, Rommel reached El Alamein and the British evacuated Alexandria and began burning sensitive documents prior to withdrawal from Cairo, Nahas held firm and Lampson was gratified by the thought that the British enjoyed the support of what passed for a representative government.

But it was not a democratic government as understood by apostles of democracy like Freya Stark. 'You can't think how beastly it is to be a propagandist just now,' she wrote from Baghdad in March 1942. In her book the recent 'Farouq crisis in Cairo', far from being a shining vindication of democracy (let alone liberty), ranked with the military setbacks in Burma and Malaya as negative news requiring prompt counter-action.[18] Democracy, as she informed a cell of her 'brothers' gathered amid the bombed-out remains of Rutba Wells, must grow from the grass roots upwards. 'It is men like yourselves who carry the seed of the little plant,' she told her audience of assorted police and tribesmen; Baghdad would yet have its own 'Mother of Parliaments', just like London's; they had only to tend the seedling so that it took root and became 'a part of your land'; it was a living thing, not a theory; 'that is the meaning of Democracy'.[19]

Among Rutba's charred blockhouses, in the midst of a howling wilderness like the Syrian desert, talk of seeds and plants may have been inappropriate. But her point was well made. As Graffey-Smith had implied, one prime minister was not much different from another. In Egypt, as in Iraq and Syria, only men had the vote and they customarily exercised it in accordance with traditional and communal loyalties. Elections themselves were multi-stage and indirect; returns were easily managed at the primary stage by local landowners, officials and tribal leaders, and at the secondary stage by power-brokers operating on behalf of the government, the court and the political parties. In Iraq 60 per cent of the candidates stood as of right (ex-ministers, ex-officials, community and tribal leaders, and so on); and 'the remainder', according to Nuri al-Said, 'depend for the most part on the will of the government in power'.[20] Instead of a majority of those elected forming a government from which the cabinet was chosen, it was more normal for cabinets to form governments and for governments then to organize their own majorities. Parties reflected personal, rather than policy, differences and were grounded on nothing more solid than the shifting sands of advantageous alliance and temporary convenience.

In short, Stark's seedlings were arriving as cut flowers, with precious little stalk and not a root to be seen. In his monumental work on Egypt in the twentieth century, the French sociologist Jacques Berque helpfully includes in his index an entry for 'Democracy'. There are just two subheadings; the first is 'various counterfeits of' (with a whole string of page references), the second '1928 government condemns' (with one page reference).[21] In the merry-go-round of ministries the same tarbooshed and moustachioed figures rose and fell and rose again with mechanical monotony. A Nahas or a Nuri might dabble with reform in opposition; in government his enactments were likely to be much more cautious, reflecting and rewarding his supporters but in no way endangering their hold on office.

The only people in the Middle East who were actually practising the grass-roots democracy advocated by Stark were Palestine's Zionists. From Europe they had brought their own traditions of communal self-government as embodied in a variety of Jewish charitable, educational and political institutions. In Palestine this same imported culture of self-reliance and representation was readily adopted by Zionism's agricultural settlements, by its organized labour and its political hierarchy. Having no army did not preclude fielding troops; just as having no state did not preclude electing representatives. British officials complained that the Zionists in Palestine were behaving as 'a state within a state'. But the would-be 'state within' enjoyed a popular legitimacy of which the mandated 'state without' had long since despaired.

THE ARAB LEAGUE

Halted at El Alamein in November 1942, Rommel withdrew west with the Allied forces in hot pursuit. Tunis fell in May 1943, Sicily in July and the landings in Italy came in September. Allied control of the Mediterranean was regained and the Middle East was no longer in danger. From Cairo the military circus moved on. 'Westward Ho!' announced Ranfurly as she trailed her current general to Algiers, then Italy. Stark had already left. Heading for the United States to deploy her skills as a propagandist on behalf of the 1939 British White Paper on Palestine, she had first driven from Baghdad to Beirut, stopping on the way at Zahle in the Lebanon.

There Iraq's Nuri al-Said, 'our' prime minister as Stark always calls him, was convalescing from a bout of pneumonia. She found him sitting in the sunshine in reminiscent mood, 'a slight figure in a grey suit, and grey at the temples, with grey eyes . . . [yet with] a certain striking, sprightly youthfulness about him'.[22] This sprightly bearing the uncharitable ascribed to his wearing a corset. Now 55 and apparently indestructible, his political views seemed correspondingly rigid.

In the cause of Arab freedom and unity, Nuri had sided with the British and fought with Lawrence in the First World War. Now, with the British back in Syria, the French on their way out, and Zionism apparently stopped in its tracks by the White Paper, the situation again approximated to that of 1918. The slate was being rubbed clean, and, as the end of the Second World War drew near, Nuri looked forward to reversing the mistakes made at the end of the First. He saw new hope in the joint interventions made by the Arab states on behalf of the Palestinians during their Revolt; and he was convinced that the solution to Zionist demands for statehood lay in Arab acceptance of an autonomous Jewish entity within some form of pan-Arab federation. Moreover he had rightly detected a British willingness to countenance such an initiative.

In fact he had just elaborated his thoughts in a long paper that he had prepared at the instigation of Richard Casey, the current British Minister of State in Cairo. The first move, according to what became known as Nuri's 'Blue Book', would be to recreate Greater Syria by the reintegration of Syria, Transjordan, Palestine and, if the Lebanese were agreeable, Lebanon; alternatively Lebanon's Maronites could constitute another autonomous enclave, like that of the Zionists. This reunited Greater Syria could then choose whether to be a republic or a monarchy. (In the unlikely event of its choosing the latter, Nuri reckoned that the Palestinians and the Syrians could be counted on to oppose the adoption of the distrusted Abdullah as king.) And finally the recreated Syria would be invited to join Iraq in an Arab league or federation.

Other Arab states, like Saudi Arabia and Egypt, were deemed incompatible with such an Arab league on economic or demographic grounds. Saudi Arabia was too backward, Egypt too populous. But Nuri told Stark that Egypt's interest in the project was encouraging, and he informed Casey that 'if such a union succeeded between Iraq and Syria, there is every likelihood that in time [the Egyptians] would wish to join it'.[23] This was vintage Nuri; for it was in fact precisely because from Saudi Arabia and Egypt alternative schemes of integration were already being floated that Nuri was pressing his own scheme. The rivalries which had beset the Arab states when they attempted to arbitrate in Palestine were, if anything, sharper than ever. Philby, while ensconced in Riyadh as Ibn Saud's adviser, had touted the idea of Saudi recognition for a Jewish state in return for British support for a Saudi-led Arab federation. Recently revived by a Saudi representative, the idea appealed to President

Roosevelt and to Churchill but had been shot down by the British Foreign Office as guaranteed to provoke the Hashemite kingdoms. More recently the Foreign Office, through Lampson in Cairo, had been exploring another proposal from Mustafa al-Nahas for an Arab federation under Egyptian leadership.

None of the Arab governments was keen to surrender any sovereignty. Association, rather than integration, with an emphasis on economic and cultural ties, therefore looked a more realistic outcome. ('Your Commonwealth is the model for the Arabian world,' Nuri told Stark.) On the other hand most Arab governments faced domestic criticism for their failure to render effective support to Palestine's Arabs. They therefore talked up integration as a sign of their intention to concert pan-Arab action to pressurize the British government over Palestine.

With so many proposals in circulation and such pressing reasons for their adoption, Arab integration was beginning to look like a running certainty. Either that or it was an almighty scam. The French, not surprisingly, suspected the latter. Clutching at any straw to explain their plight in the Levant states, they saw the new pan-Arabism of Nuri and Nahas as a straight revival of the old pan-Arabism of Husayn and Faysal. The one was as much a British ploy as the other, their purpose being to excite the Arabs of the Levant, embarrass France, and secure British influence throughout the Arab world. Consistent with this belief, France would later make common cause with the equally suspicious Zionists, support their claim to statehood at the United Nations and lend them timely support in the 1948 war.

The Arab League, as it slowly emerged, would do nothing to dispel these suspicions. As early as May 1941, in a well-flagged speech, Anthony Eden had indeed approved the strengthening of economic, cultural and 'political ties, too' between the Arab countries; and he had then, in measured words reminiscent of the Balfour Declaration, pledged his government's 'full support for any scheme which commands general approval'. At the time the British relief force in Iraq had been poised to retake Baghdad and the cavalry were saddling up for their charge into Syria. No doubt his kite-flying speech was influenced by these moves and by a more general anxiety to keep the Arabs 'on side' at a critical moment in the war. Nevertheless this was not just a casual nod to pan-Arab sentiment; it was a definite pledge in favour of some form of Arab integration. The British had no more devised pan-Arabism than they had Zionism. But in both cases they perceived advantage in lending sufficient support to encourage the implementation of such programmes.

After his meeting with Freya Stark in 1943, Nuri proceeded to Cairo for discussions with Nahas about convening an Arab conference. A year later Nahas himself took the initiative and invited the Arab governments to a meeting. It took place at Alexandria in September 1944 and resulted in a protocol setting up the Arab League. The Protocol talked of co-operation and co-ordination but not of integration; and the subsequent pact in fact affirmed the individual sovereignty of the participant states. The pact was agreed at the League's first meeting in Cairo in March 1945 when Abd al-Rahman Azzam was appointed secretary-general. Azzam was Egyptian, like Nahas, and Cairo was to remain the League's headquarters. In effect Nahas was insisting on Egypt's Arab identity and, in view of his country's economic and demographic pre-eminence, claiming Egyptian leadership of the Arab world. Whether he was doing so to bolster the flagging fortunes of his government, still tainted by the Abdin affair, or whether he acted at Lampson's instigation, is not clear. The British had certainly persuaded Nuri and the Syrians to acquiesce in Egyptian leadership;[24] with Nahas heading what was currently, from a British point of view, the most compliant and accessible government in the region (excluding Transjordan's), Egyptian leadership was preferred.

But a note of caution was sounded, even by delighted Arabists like Cornwallis in Baghdad. Nahas and Nuri al-Said had been told that, despite Palestine being the issue which had brought the Arab states together, Britain's support for the League depended on its avoiding provocative pronouncements on Palestine. Accordingly the Alexandria Protocol simply indicated acceptance of the existing White Paper. This was an improvement on the Paper's equivocal reception in 1939 and, in so far as the Paper still represented official British policy, therefore welcome. But the British government, and especially Churchill, who had never endorsed the White Paper, was already backtracking. Arab support for the Paper was therefore potentially a major embarrassment. For any deviation from the Paper was now guaranteed to incur a pan-Arab hostility from which individual Arab governments would not find it easy either to detach themselves or to be detached.

Worse still, the White Paper's pledges were becoming due at a most unfortunate moment. Its virtual moratorium on the sale of land to Jews had become effective in 1941 and been greeted with a flurry of protests. Now, in 1944, its five years of regulated Jewish immigration, after which all immigration was supposed to be subject to Arab agreement, was due to expire. Simultaneously the opening of the Mediterranean permitted a resumption of migration. The pathetic survivors of the Nazi death-camps began emerging into a Europe from which their one thought was to flee; and all the while the imperative, both moral and humanitarian, for the urgent resettlement of these European Jews was gaining international recognition.

If British policy-makers imagined that the objections of the Arab League, let alone the lobbying of Arabists like Lampson, Cornwallis and Stark, would in any way quell the Zionist demand for a rejection of the White Paper, they were about to be sorely mistaken. Cushioned by the mandate, Britain had sat on the Palestine fence for a quarter of a century, often discomforted by its thorns, shifting about uneasily, but not unseated. Briefly the war had actually provided some justification for this feat. But as the war drew to a close, and sharp new barbs thrust through the now threadbare cushion, they would squirm miserably in a ruck of policies, cast about for support, then look to get off. Too late. They were already impossibly entangled. Getting off would mean demolishing the fence.

TO CHANGE THE COURSE OF HISTORY

The Arab League, though conceived amid high expectations, was born to disappoint. The omens were adverse from the start in so far as two of its principal progenitors were immediately removed. Mustafa al-Nahas was relieved of office by King Farouq within days of the 1944 Alexandria Protocol; and Lord Moyne, who had succeeded Richard Casey as the British Minister of State in Cairo, was assassinated four weeks later.

Nahas had to go in order to make way for what the Egyptian King glibly hailed as 'a democratic ministry', one that would, he claimed, serve the national interest, abide by the constitution, root out corruption, and feed the working classes. Farouq, in other words, was simply taking his revenge on Nahas for the Abdin affair. He had himself assumed much of the credit for the Arab League and presumably felt that his position was strong enough to risk Lampson's objections. Ahmad Mahir, Nahas's replacement, was anyway acceptable to the British. Four months later, in February 1945, Mahir would actually declare war on the side of the Allies. Egypt, like Iraq, wanted a say in the post-war order, and that meant being in at the kill. Or so the argument went. But it was unacceptable to radical nationalists who, recalling the Abdin affair, saw the British as the real enemy. To them joining the Allies meant betraying the Egyptian people. Accordingly Ahmad Mahir was himself killed the moment he declared war. Farouq was once again rattling through his prime ministers.

Moyne's murder was also an expression of extremist opposition to the British, but it came from a very different quarter. The two young assassins, when overpowered as they pedalled away from the British minister's Cairo residence on bicycles, made no secret of their allegiance. They gave their names as Cohen and Saltzman, proudly admitted their responsibility, and under interrogation acknowledged that they belonged to 'LEHI'.

This was the acronym for an underground organization the name of which translated from the Hebrew as 'Fighters for the Freedom of Israel'. It was otherwise stigmatized by the British, and by most Zionists, as the Stern Gang, a radical offshoot of the Irgun Zvai Leumi (National Military Organization, NMO, Etsel, IZL, and so on), itself a paramilitary group closely connected with Vladimir Jabotinsky's Revisionist movement. The Irgun's attacks, mostly directed at British targets, had been exercising the Palestine authorities ever since the 1939 White Paper. And although neither the Irgun nor LEHI enjoyed popular support, the wave of Zionist terror unleashed by these organizations had, with Arab dissent subdued by the absence of the Mufti, come to replace the Arab Revolt as the most destabilizing factor in Palestine.

Zionism at the beginning of the war had been undergoing another of its crises. Apparently denied the statehood implicit in the 1937 Royal Commission's partition proposal, then confronted with the 1939 White Paper whose strictures, like that on immigration, amounted to a reversal of the mandate, most Zionists had yet felt obliged to render loyal support to the British in their war effort (any other attitude to Nazi Germany being unthinkable – or nearly so). Weizmann continued to look to his British friends, especially Churchill, for an equitable reward when the war was over; but Weizmann was an ageing figure and his endeavours to win British approval for a Jewish army had seemingly been rebuffed. His wheelings and dealings, diplomatic enough in London, looked high-handed from Jerusalem; similarly his gradualism, in the context of European Jewry's imminent extermination, looked woefully inappropriate.

Like a flash-flood whose usual run-off has become obstructed, the waters of Zionist struggle eddied to left and right in search of other outlets. During the war years the mainstream leftist leadership in Palestine, headed by David Ben-Gurion, began to assert itself internationally and, challenging Weizmann's Anglophile approach, sought non-British sponsors, especially in the United States. Another stream, strongly opposed to socialism and propelled by the urgent plight of Jews in east and central Europe, espoused a more strident nationalism and a more militaristic ethos. Buoyed by prophecy and desperate for sanctuary, the Zionists of the European ghettos disdained legal restraint and readily responded to Jabotinsky's maximalist rhetoric.

Jabotinsky, operating from Europe ever since his 1929 exile from Palestine, maintained that immigration should be in millions, not thousands, and that it should be now. Palestine's 'absorptive capacity' was limited only by its artificial borders and by British obstruction. That which the Revisionists would revise was the clause in the mandate that exempted Transjordan from Jewish settlement. If the whole of Palestine-Transjordan was open to immigration there need be no limit to it. Moreover, the sheer volume and determination of the immigrant invasion envisaged by Jabotinsky would of itself dictate British compliance and relegate the Arab problem to irrelevance.

Such a programme called for national discipline, military training and single-minded dedication, all of which featured prominently in the curriculum of Jabotinsky's Betar, a youth movement not unlike those of National Socialism with its uniforms and parade-ground displays. Having split with the official Zionist Organization, Jabotinsky had formed a New Zionist Organization (NZO) under whose political direction his Betar recruited widely in eastern Europe. In Poland as of 1938 the NZO even enjoyed a degree of

Polish government approval. Training-camps were set up, arms supplied, and plans laid for a mass invasion of Palestine by armed immigrants in 1940.

Meanwhile NZO-chartered ships had joined those organized by other groups in smuggling Betar recruits into Palestine. There, before and during the Palestine Revolt, they made common cause with those militant sections of the Haganah (the mainstream Zionist militia) who disapproved of the official policy of non-retaliation in the face of Arab provocation. From this union of Polish and Palestinian activists emerged the Irgun Zvai Leumi, in effect the military wing in Palestine of the NZO (although Jabotinsky himself often discountenanced it). Militarism among the Jews of Palestine, like democracy, had originated in Europe and was smuggled piecemeal into Palestine in the roped bundles and battered suitcases of desperate migrants.

Adopting 'armed struggle' at a time when Orde Wingate was inducting Haganah units into equally dubious tactics, the Irgun had begun its bombings and shootings, principally of Arab targets, in 1938. A security crackdown and the publication of the 1939 White Paper turned these attacks against the British. The first policeman was killed in May 1939 and the first British officers in August. But much of the Irgun leadership, including the charismatic Avraham Stern and David Raziel, was quickly hunted down. When in September the world war had broken out and the Irgun's Polish heartland had been overrun by the Nazis, Raziel and Stern were in detention in Palestine. In Europe Betar's commander, a young firebrand sporting the horn-rimmed glasses of a novelty-store ideologue, fell into Russian hands. His name was Menachem Begin, and he would eventually resurface in Palestine, but not until 1942. Meanwhile Jabotinsky, having urged the Irgun to cease hostilities during the war, himself died in 1940, whereupon his followers split.

Raziel headed a group who gave priority to the fight against the Nazi persecutor. It was he who, undertaking a sabotage operation against Rashid Ali and the Mufti in Baghdad, was killed near the Habbaniya base in Iraq in May 1941. Avraham Stern, a more dazzling and erratic leader, had also been released from detention but, far from collaborating with the British, formed his LEHI, the Stern Gang, to continue the struggle. 'In conventional eyes,' according to J. Bowyer Bell, an American specialist on revolutionary movements (including the IRA), the LEHI evolved 'into the most violent and unrestrained terrorist organisation in the modern era'.[25]

A campaign which, in the name of Zionism, targeted those who were fighting Jewry's prosecutors might look perverse. Stern thought otherwise. He feared that amid the exigencies of a world war the Zionist dream might go by default, scuttled between the devil of Nazism and the deep blue sea of British imperialism. Somehow it had to make its presence felt, to keep the flame burning. His sights were set on the British but his quarrel was as much with Weizmann, the Zionist establishment and all who dabbled in compromise.

Light on logic and low on realism, this stand yet derived a certain credibility from British provocation. Illegal Jewish immigrants – perhaps the first of the century's 'boat people' – fled Europe in large numbers in the first months of the war and were repeatedly turned away from Palestine's shore. In November 1940 when the *Patria*, a vessel laden with just such a cargo of deportees, sank in Haifa harbour, over 250 were drowned. The tragedy followed a bomb blast which was meant merely to disable the ship and so draw attention to the heartless conduct of the British. In this it succeded all too well, the appalling loss of life being added to the catalogue of British crimes.

Much resented, too, were the White Paper's restrictions on Arab land sales to Jews, which came into effect in 1941. The Royal Commission's proposal in favour of partition had given to Zionist land acquisition a new strategic impetus; wherever possible, settlements had been hastily established along the proposed frontiers of partition with a view to maximizing the Jewish claim. But a freeze of land transfers brought this process to an abrupt end; and it was particularly objectionable at a time when many Palestinian Jews were loyally signing up with British regiments or awaiting the chance to fight alongside them in a Jewish army. Penalties were being incurred just when rewards would have been in order. Cynically, it seemed, the international situation was indeed being exploited to compromise Zionist objectives.

In February 1942 Stern's hold-ups, bombings and run-ins with the Palestine CID ended in a Tel Aviv gutter, his body riddled with British bullets. To his associates, like the diminutive but pugnacious Yitzhak Shamir, avenging Stern's death became a priority in itself. Hermione Ranfurly, now working as personal assistant to Palestine's High Commissioner Harold MacMichael, began her 16 March diary entry with a single word: 'Trouble.' A ship called the *Struma* had just been sunk.[26] Its illegal immigrants waded ashore to instant detention, a howl of Jewish protest, and a bomb attack by 'Jewish extremists' on the Inspector-General of Police and his deputy. 'The latter was killed.' It was then found that the cemetery where the Deputy Inspector was to be buried had been mined, and that his superior's compound had been booby-trapped with sticks of dynamite. 'I think seventy were found in the Inspector-General's garden,' recalled Ranfurly. The fence round the High Commisioner's residence also contained a bomb. 'It went off while we were at dinner – made a terrific bang but did no damage.'[27]

There followed the inevitable security crack-down and the arrest, often as a result of information supplied by disenchanted Zionists, of most of the LEHI membership. Although many eventually escaped, including Shamir, their activities during 1943 were restricted to re-organization and propaganda. It was at this time that reports of Hitler's Jewish deportations and of his 'final solution' were confirmed. Again the gruesome implications failed to deflect the single-minded zealots of LEHI. On the contrary, past and present British restrictions on immigration thereby gained a retrospective notoriety. Now every would-be immigrant who had been refused the right of entry into Palestine, or merely discouraged from seeking such a right, could be seen as having been condemned to the death camps. In surreptitiously pasted bills and clandestine broadcasts LEHI's propagandists had much to work with. Complicity in the holocaust might not have been the most plausible of the myriad charges laid at London's door, but so explosive was even a hint of it that to the suspicious minds of LEHI it was tantamount to proof.

In January 1944 LEHI's vendetta with the police resumed with a vengeance. At about the same time the larger and better-armed Irgun, now under Menachem Begin's direction, abandoned its wartime truce and joined in the fray. Palestine plunged into revolutionary turmoil as bombs exploded in tax and immigration offices, police stations, broadcasting stations and defence establishments. The organs of official Zionism – the Jewish Agency, the Histadrut labour union, the Haganah militia – pleaded for restraint, then actively engaged in operations against the Irgun. LEHI, on the other hand, welcomed the Irgun's support, although it resisted an alliance; instead it looked to upstage its Revisionist rival with a definitive strike.

The obvious target was the High Commissioner. A thin and austere figure of formidable intelligence and impeccable silk tailoring, MacMichael epitomized the British ideal of strict impartiality between Arab and Jew. Ranfurly, after eighteen months at his side, still could not fathom where his true sympathies lay. But Jews saw his bloodless detachment as evidence of Arabist leanings, and Arabs vice versa. To the cold minds of LEHI, the man mattered less than the power he represented and the ineffectual Anglo-Zionist relationship he symbolized. Vengeance was almost irrelevant. What mattered to dedicated revolutionaries was the act itself and its supposed potential for changing the course of history.

Six times the ambush was laid, the last in August 1944 when MacMichael's ADC was killed. The High Commissioner somehow survived them all; then he returned to England at the end of his term of office. Undeterred, LEHI cast about for an alternative target and lit upon Lord Moyne, the new British Minister of State in Cairo. Here was an even more senior figure, a Cabinet minister, the British government's supremo for the whole of the Middle East, a member of the British aristocracy, a close friend of Churchill, and someone who, having previously served as both Colonial Secretary and deputy minister in Cairo, was clearly identified with Britain's wartime appeasement of the Arabs as well as with the new Arab League.

Cairo was obviously less convenient than Jerusalem, but the two operatives who slipped across the Palestine border in October easily blended into its cosmopolitan throng and encountered little of the oppressive security that had frustrated the attacks on MacMichael. Perhaps aware of the assassination of General Lee Stack exactly twenty years earlier, they likewise planned their strike for when Moyne habitually returned to his residence for the long afternoon break. They waited near the gates, rushed the minister's car, and succeeded at the first attempt. Moyne, like Stack, died of his wounds a few hours later. The most senior British politician to be killed in the Second World War had been assassinated in the name of Zion.

BILTMORE AND BEYOND

If our dreams for Zionism are to end in the smoke of assassins' pistols [Churchill told a horrified House of Commons], and our labours for its

> future to produce only a new set of gangsters worthy of Nazi Germany, many like myself will have to reconsider the position we have maintained so consistently in the past ...

Prior to the 6 November atrocity, the British government had been steadily edging away from the White Paper. The Jewish Brigade had at last been authorized, a Cabinet committee on Palestine had just recommended that partition (with its promise of a Jewish state) be readopted as official policy, and sufficient British troops were available, if necessary, to impose such a change on Palestine's still subdued Arabs. Weizmann was optimistic, Churchill bullish, and the US administration supportive. As the war wound down, progress towards a Palestine settlement looked both possible and imminent.

Now all was changed. In the light of Moyne's murder, the best outcome looked to be a long delay. Consideration of the Cabinet committee's favourable report on partition was postponed indefinitely; in the meantime British opponents of partition rallied; and even Weizmann wavered as the Jewish Agency held out for the more extreme demands formulated by American Zionists. Churchill, despite that threat to reconsider his position, alone remained firm; but not so his government. The Conservatives' defeat in the 1945 elections, while not in itself fatal to partition, meant further delay, which might be.

The course of history had indeed been changed. An extreme group committed to forcing the pace of Zionist settlement had derailed a process that might have conceded Zionist sovereignty. As Michael Cohen, a historian of the period, notes, there was a further irony. While it had been Revisionist lobbying in the United States that had hastened the British retreat from the White Paper, a Revisionist splinter-group 'was now responsible for the delay of Government measures that would have displaced the White Paper principles as the basis for British policy'.[28]

The American involvement in all this was becoming highly significant. Cut off by the war from its largest constituency in Europe, Zionism's leadership had begun to look increasingly to its second largest constituency, the five million Jews resident in the US. Moral and financial support had long been forthcoming from American Jewry. Political support had become the new priority; and partly for American consumption, partly in response to the unfolding tragedy in Europe, and partly because of the cogency this lent to Zionist appeals, some redefinition of Zionist objectives had been undertaken.

The 1939 White Paper had predictably roused the ire of American Zionists. When primed by Weizmann, Ben-Gurion and Jabotinsky, all of whom visited the US in the early years of the war, this sense of anti-British outrage acquired direction; and just as it was the 'gangsters' of Revisionist struggle who were making the early running in the resort to arms in Palestine, so it was the storm-troopers of Revisionist polemics who set the pace in the US. With the death of Jabotinsky himself in 1940, Hillel Kook, a dashing figure known in the US as Peter Bergson, successfully organized a succession of Revisionist pressure groups whose objectives rapidly advanced from the abandonment of the White Paper to the establishment of a Jewish army and the creation of a 'Free Palestine'.

Bergson, and then mainstream Zionists, tailored their message to the American public. European Jewry was presented as the hapless victim, British colonialism as the implacable enemy, and the liberation of Jewish Palestine as the ultimate goal. The ambiguities which Zionism posed for American Jews were skilfully played down by dissociating 'Hebrews' – by which were meant the Jews of Palestine and Europe for whom the 'Hebrew' state of Palestine was intended – from American Jews, who though 'Hebrew' by extraction and Jewish by religion were US citizens and no less American patriots than, say, Hispanic Catholics. Non-Zionist reservations about American Jewry's divided loyalties were thus lulled. Before a now receptive audience the presentation could begin.

Hollywood script-writers joined celebrated journalists and other public figures in providing arresting copy for petitions, articles, advertisements and staged extravaganzas portraying the heroic struggle of the 'Hebrews'. There was no need for exaggeration. Wrestling overwhelming odds – Nazi genocide, British colonialism, Arab terrorism, the diplomatic disadvantage of statelessness and an often cruel and unyielding terrain – the Zionist endeavour transcended romance. Here was a beacon of hope in a war-dark world; it epitomized the universal struggle for survival; deploring Zionism was tantamount to denigrating the human spirit. Righteous and compelling, the Zionist cause won a wide hearing and became embedded in the nation's psyche.

Congressmen took up the cry and congressional resolutions were canvassed. In 1944 the Revisionists would actually open a 'Hebrew

Embassy' in Washington.[29] But it was the audacity of the Revisionist approach in appealing to all sections of American Jewry and, beyond them, to the wider American public that was novel. In Britain no attempt had been made to generate mass interest in the Zionist cause. A large proportion of British Jews would have nothing to do with it; it commanded no popular support and never constituted an electoral issue. In the US it played to a much wider audience, actively engaging Christians as well as Jews, generating electoral advantage in key states like New York, commanding support in influential sectors of the economy and the media, and generally winning the sympathetic attention of a caring people excited by the pioneering spirit of Zionist settlement, ever alert to the injustices of colonialism, and appalled by the reports of Nazi atrocities. The British would never understand this. The American Zionist lobby was either underestimated as a vociferous distraction or overestimated as a pervasive subversion.

Amid the Zionist clamour, it was hardly surprising that the reservations of the US State Department and the pleas of British apologists like Freya Stark attracted little popular sympathy; or that the American public remained largely ignorant of the prior rights, even the existence, of Palestine's Arab majority. Heckled by passionate Zionists at every stage of her coast-to-coast tour in 1943–4, Stark likened her situation to that of 'an unarmed Christian with no particular method for dealing with lions'. The lions, hypnotized perhaps by her hats, nevertheless heard her out. Her audiences learnt about Palestine's demography and were apprised that the Balfour Declaration had afforded guarantees to the Arabs as well as the Jews. Meanwhile she herself learnt a truth no less inconvenient and easily forgotten – that in the USA the words 'liberal and pro-Zionist seem to be considered synonymous'.[30]

Where the Revisionists of New Zionism led, mainstream Zionism followed. Only by echoing the militancy, maximalism and mass tactics of its rivals could it retain control of Zionist institutions and organs. Weizmann's legendary charm and his carefully chosen phrases were relentlessly upstaged by the more aggressive and outspoken Ben-Gurion. Similarly the craggy and convivial Rabbi Stephen Wise, the main spokesman of American Zionism, was challenged by the younger and more fiery Rabbi Abba Hillel Silver. 'Put not your trust in princes' quoted Silver in what amounted to a veiled criticism of Weizmann's dealings with Churchill and Wise's with Roosevelt.

The personality clashes both prompted and mirrored the policy changes. Weizmann was prepared to wait on the British government over the authorization of a Jewish army. The Revisionists were not, and so nor was Ben-Gurion. With the US becoming an active participant in the war, the Roosevelt administration had a legitimate interest in the deployment of all available troops, not excluding a purely Jewish army. The campaign for the recruitment of such a force was therefore carried to Washington, and advertisements in the press proclaimed support on Capitol Hill. This brought protests from both the British government and Nuri al-Said on behalf of the Arabs. The Roosevelt administration backed off. Palestine was a British responsibility and, in so far as it was also an insoluble problem, Roosevelt was generally happy for it to remain British. Until the end of the war, official American involvement in the contortions of British policy in Palestine was limited to a few rather utopian suggestions and such 'soothing private and public declarations of sympathy' as would mollify Zionist petitioners.[31]

The Zionist leadership was unimpressed. In an article published in the January 1942 issue of the US magazine *Foreign Affairs* Weizmann himself for the first time publicly espoused a self-governing 'state of their own' for the Jews of Palestine. He was looking ahead to a still distant post-war period and was not flattered when, four months later, Ben-Gurion tabled this rosy-tinted vision as a black-on-white resolution for the consideration of an 'Extraordinary Zionist Conference' at the Biltmore Hotel in New York. Ben-Gurion preferred the less controversial 'commonwealth' but he meant the same thing: a sovereign state. 'A home for the Jewish people' of Balfour had long since become 'the Jewish national home' of the mandate and was now being reformulated as 'a Jewish Commonwealth integrated in the structure of the new democratic world'. This new Palestinian state was not geographically defined and so could refer to a partitioned part of Palestine, all Palestine, or all Palestine-including-Transjordan. However one interpreted it, its 'gates' were to 'be opened' for Jewish immigration and, crucially, 'the Jewish Agency [was to] be vested with control of immigration'.[32] Weizmann had once dreamt of a Palestine as Jewish as England was English; Ben-Gurion now proclaimed 'a Palestine . . . as Jewish as the Jews will make it'.[33]

To an American audience, an emergent commonwealth's right to carve out its own destiny and control its own immigration seemed entirely reasonable. In the final resolution adopted by the Biltmore conference there was much nostalgic evocation of the frontier spirit; the new settlers were repopulating a wilderness while their 'pioneering achievements in agriculture and industry . . . made the waste places to bear fruit and the desert to blossom'. Their 'Arab neighbors' within and beyond Palestine were sharing in these 'new values'; indeed 'the Jewish people in its own work of national redemption' welcomed the development of this native population. It did so in much the same paternalistic spirit as Americans had welcomed the development of their own, pre-Columbian, native population.

In a world divided between the colonial 'haves' and the colonized 'have-nots', Zionism was a curious hybrid. Here was a people struggling against colonialism while itself undertaking a colonizing, even colonializing, enterprise of its own. At their trial the LEHI men who had killed Moyne were defended by two of Egypt's most eminent barristers. There was no question of acquittal; the men had confessed. But the two lawyers made out an interesting case for clemency on the basis that the assassins had acted in the name of a woefully oppressed people driven to desperation by British duplicity. In other words they appealed to the Egyptian judges in the name of anti-colonialism and on the assumption that Egyptians engaged in their own freedom struggle would appreciate the lengths to which Zionists, similarly engaged, might be driven. The appeal failed and the men were hanged, but even the Hebrew press praised this defence.[34] It was not only Zionists who acknowledged that the Irgun and LEHI were freedom fighters; yet these same freedom fighters denied to Palestinian Arabs any equivalent recognition.

The contradiction inherent in both opposing colonialism and practising it, though rare, was not unknown; nor, to those so positioned, was it a contradiction. In the late nineteenth century Afrikaners had derived strength and brotherhood from its ambiguities; and so, in the late eighteenth century, had the white colonists of America. It was not surprising that Zionism resonated in the US as perhaps nowhere else in the world.

The Biltmore resolution said nothing about Palestinian Arabs still outnumbering Palestinian Jews by two to one because this imbalance was seen as the result of purely artificial restrictions on Jewish settlement. Nor were the Jewish settlers obligated to accord the Arab natives political recognition. The mandate had been silent on the subject, and in his Biltmore speech Ben-Gurion offered an explanation: four hundred years of Turkish rule had left Palestine with no Turkish population or culture; therefore 'it was a country to all intents and purposes unclaimed, except by the Jewish people, which [had] never . . . ceased to regard it as the Land of Israel'.[35]

Warming to Ben-Gurion's passionate advocacy, the largely Zionist audience at the Biltmore conference gave near unanimous approval to what became the 'Biltmore Program'. Carefully phrased so as to be acceptable to the widest possible spectrum of Jewish opinion, the Biltmore Program was in 1943 adopted both by the executive of the Jewish Agency in Palestine and by the American Jewish Committee, the senior forum of American Jewry. Outright rejection of the White Paper, the establishment of a Jewish state in Palestine, and exclusively Jewish control of immigration were now official Zionist policy.

The political campaign in the US was then taken up by an American Zionist Emergency Council. In early 1944 it organized congressional support for the introduction of a Palestine resolution in both the House of Representatives and the Senate. The hope was that, if such a resolution were adopted, the administration would, at the very least, oppose any British implementation of the White Paper's threatened stoppage of immigration. Roosevelt appeared to go one better, authorizing an announcement to the effect that he (just like Churchill) had never approved the White Paper. But he also arranged for the congressional resolution to be shelved and then reassured the British and the Arabs that no decision would be taken on Palestine 'without full consultation with both Arabs and Jews'.

The American Zionist Emergency Council then turned its attention to the 1944 elections and successfully interested both Republicans and Democrats in vying for Zionist support. The former duly endorsed a 'free and democratic Commonwealth' in Palestine and the latter a 'free and democratic Jewish Commonwealth'. Thus committed, Roosevelt might have been expected to welcome the Palestine resolution when it was reintroduced into Congress in November. But against the background of Moyne's murder it was again aborted; and again the President backtracked, assuring Ibn Saud in February 1945 that he would 'do nothing to assist the Jews against the Arabs'.

Two months later, when the President died, his true sentiments towards a Jewish Palestine remained a mystery, and the political efforts of American Zionists remained largely unrewarded. Sharp divisions reopened in the Zionist camp as disillusionment set in. The incoming President Truman had an ambiguous record on Palestine. His administration seemed unlikely to adopt a more favourable attitude than Roosevelt's. His dramatic interventions of 1947–8 could in no way be anticipated. Zionism's first major political initiative in the US looked to have failed.

Yet Truman, a president unnominated by his party and unelected by his country, was understandably alert to public opinion. In sowing the seeds across the country of what now became known as America's Zionist lobby, Bergson, Silver and Wise had not laboured in vain. It was as if the ground had been carefully prepared for the new eventuality of an unelected president in pursuit of a mandate.

Part Four

1945–1960

13

Cold War, Hot Tempers

ARABIAN OIL AND AMERICAN SECURITY

DURING HIS FORTY-YEAR rule in the Arabian peninsula King Abd al-Aziz Ibn Saud made only two foreign trips: one to Iraq courtesy of the Royal Navy in 1915, the other to Egypt courtesy of the US Navy in 1945. The first had resulted in a long-lasting treaty with the British; the second produced no treaty but inaugurated an even longer-lasting relationship with the United States.

The 1945 trip began at the port of Jidda in February when, with an entourage of fifty including his prime minister, his astrologer, two of his thirty-nine sons, and a flock of sheep by way of rations, the septuagenarian sovereign boarded a US destroyer. Cooking fires and coffee parties instantly disfigured the decks; but as the destroyer steamed up the Red Sea and into the Gulf of Suez, safety regulations were enforced and the sheep grew fewer. With order restored, the ship finally entered the lower section of the Suez Canal *en route* to a rendezvous with the cruiser USS *Quincy* in the Great Bitter Lake.

There waited President Franklin D. Roosevelt. Homeward-bound from the Yalta conference on the last of his own foreign trips, the ailing President of the world's greatest democracy duly entertained the arthritic scion of the world's most absolute monarchy on a warship moored in the desert. The symbolism was appropriate; and the contrast between the genial but chair-bound President and the black-robed 'desert colossus' could scarcely have been greater. They spent five hours closeted together; but, as Roosevelt later told Congress, five minutes sufficed to teach him 'more about the whole problem of Arabia – the Moslems – the Jewish problem' than could have been gleaned from any amount of correspondence.[1] Across the chasm of culture, religion, conflicting interests and steel decking, minds evidently met.

What prompted this unlikely meeting was a new American perception of the Middle East. Before the war *Harper's* magazine had seen fit to publish a survey of Washington's international interests that skipped over the entire region with a dismissive 'our relations with these people are not important'. 'Nothing ever happens there' confirmed a State Department official when commiserating over the penitential posting of a colleague, Loy Henderson, as US ambassador to Baghdad in 1943.[2] Roosevelt's big idea that Ibn Saud, as keeper of Islam's holy places, might exert his influence to reconcile Muslim Palestinians to Zionist settlement was a shot in the dark. Dictated by humanitarian concern and domestic pressures, it was repeatedly and emphatically rejected by the King himself and necessitated American assurances that US policy in respect of Zionism would not be changed without Arab consultation. In effect the President was confirmed in his belief that Palestine was a British problem to which the British were welcome.

Nor was Roosevelt much exercised over Saudi Arabia's strategic value. Its potential as an air corridor and staging-post between the theatres of war in the Mediterranean and the Far East was of declining interest in early 1945, and its value as a post-war regional base was only dimly perceived. Like Palestine, Saudi Arabia was still considered a British responsibility. London had been subsidizing Ibn Saud ever since the First World War and continued to do so throughout the Second.

Jack Philby, returning to Riyadh in 1945 aboard a Dakota presented to the King by Roosevelt, testified to the 'excellent' relationship with Washington yet insisted that the King 'scarcely regards [the United States] as being likely to be a permanent factor in the politics of the Middle East'. Ibn Saud was well aware of the changing world order; still 'his fast-reaching imagination cannot but picture Britain standing alone as a barrier to the expanding imperialism of Soviet Russia'.[3] 'The big question', thought the ebullient Philby, was would the British, their pretensions exposed by the war, now have the sense to follow his own thirty-year example of 'endeavour in the service of humanity' by forswearing empire, championing 'principles of virtue', doling out freedom, and opting for that 'dominion of the spirit' that was the only defence against Soviet hegemony?

Such language would have appealed to Woodrow Wilson in 1918; and though too woolly and self-serving for the fastidious gentlemen of the British Foreign Office, it conformed to the Atlantic Charter and resonated in the US State Department. There Loy Wesley Henderson, rescued from his Baghdad exile in 1945 and made director of the Department's Office for Near Eastern and African Affairs, had already slated the Arab states as potential bulwarks against the expansion of Russian influence.

The architect, if rarely the builder, of US policy in the Middle East, Loy Henderson viewed the region in its global context and never lost sight of this wider picture. Never, though, did he acquire the domestic perspective from which the executive was obliged to view international relations. He held no brief for Jew or Arab, but while Arab nationalism fitted neatly into his global vision, Zionism with its potential for alienating the Arabs did not. He therefore resented and resisted it. Here was an Arabist without Arabic, a Kirkbride without a *keffiyeh*. Saturnine and balding, with the sharp pencil-moustache of a matinée idol and the even sharper mind of a consummate diplomatic impresario, Henderson had earlier served in Moscow where he sat through Stalin's show-trials. This insight into the Soviet system had made him less than deferential to the man then perceived as stalwart 'Uncle Joe' and disqualified him as a wartime intermediary with a vital ally.

In Baghdad, convinced that Moscow's totalitarianism was as menacing and insidious as Berlin's, Henderson had planned for a possible third world war while the second yet raged. British management of Iraq impressed him; the French manhandling of Syria/Lebanon did not. As for Saudi Arabia, its importance lay not in the King's Islamic credentials nor in his territory's strategic potential but in his possession of that ultimate 'prize' that Churchill had once equated with world mastery.[4] For what mattered about Saudi Arabia, what slewed the whole US perspective on the Middle East, and what lay beneath Roosevelt's rendezvous with Ibn Saud on the Great Bitter Lake, was Arabian oil.

Just as the First World War had been fought with an eye to oil reserves in Persia and Mesopotamia whose potential was only realized in the post-war era, so in the Second World War the new reserves in Arabia and the Gulf figured hugely, though the huge figures remained projections and the oil stayed mainly under ground. Not until the 1950s would Saudi oil reach world markets in any quantity. Yet for twenty years before that, in the manner of an inheritance long anticipated and heavily traded upon, it excited an industry, exercised policy-makers, and obsessed statesmen.

Philby, as usual, claimed some credit in the matter. Back in 1931, during an afternoon drive in the desert, Ibn Saud had confided in him about his financial plight. *Hajji* (pilgrim) numbers were down because of the world recession, and with them had plummeted the revenues on which the kingdom depended. The House of Saud was broke, the tribal subsidies which held the kingdom together in arrears; what to do? Philby told him to stop whining and start digging. 'You are like a man sleeping over a buried treasure and complaining of poverty,' he claims to have said. Ibn Saud, overlooking the impudence, enquired what he had in mind. Gold, as well as oil, said Philby; and something in excess of £1 million just for the concessionary rights.

Even allowing for Philby's loose talk, and despite his own reservations about admitting infidels into his hallowed land, Ibn Saud was persuaded. Armed with the royal assent Philby, as a British renegade, immediately cabled an American friend in Cairo. And that, says Philby, 'was how Charles Crane came to Jidda in May 1931, and, in return for the King's hospitality, placed a well-known mining engineer . . . at the disposal of Ibn Saud's government'.[5]

Charles Crane, erstwhile member of the King-Crane commission, patron of George Antonius, and long-time friend of the Arabs, owed his personal fortune to a family business that made sanitary ware. On a previous visit to Jidda he had given to its then ruler, the *sharif* Husayn, a magnificent rose-red bathtub equipped with sixteen different taps and levers for the delivery of waves, jets, showers and what Grafftey-Smith called 'other refinements of ablution'. It lacked only water, Jidda being then innocent of pipes or pressure.[6] On a later visit, Crane had addressed this problem with a scheme for water storage and irrigation. But the 1931 trip was much more productive. Crane at last got to meet Ibn Saud and establish bonds of trust. His

endorsement of the King as 'the most important man who has
appeared in Arabia since the time of Mohammed' was taken up by
the State Department and impressed even Roosevelt.[7] A few months
later Karl S. Twitchell, the Vermont mining engineer supplied by
Crane, confirmed that Arabia not only had oil but very probably vast
quantities of it. And it was thanks to Crane's involvement and
Twitchell's reports that American companies came to head the queue
of prospective concessionaires.

They were not the first. That honour belonged to Major Frank
Holmes, a fast-talking New Zealander who, like the bus-running
Nairn brothers, had opted to stay on in the Middle East after the
First World War. During the 1920s Holmes had interested several
Gulf potentates in trading mineral concessions for cash advances
and had then hawked the concessions round the oil companies. In
1923 he had actually secured rights in the al-Hasa region of Saudi
Arabia. But in what must surely rank as one of history's crueller
jokes, the concession lapsed following a damning report by an
incompetent Swiss geologist to the effect that Arabia did 'not present
any decided promise' and must be 'classified as pure gamble'.[8]

Holmes fared better with Bahrain, where Standard Oil of
California bought out his option, and Kuwait, where the interested
party was Gulf Oil, another American company. But complications
then arose, partly from Britain's ambivalence about foreign concessions in shaykhdoms under its protection, and partly from the
restrictions placed on Middle Eastern exploration by members of
the Iraq Petroleum consortium under their infamously obscure 'Red
Line' agreement. Not until 1936 did seismic studies in Kuwait get
under way, by when Gulf Oil had been forced into partnership with
the Anglo-Iranian Oil Company (AIOC; the 'I' had replaced the 'P'
of APOC when 'Persia' became 'Iran' in 1935). Two years later the
first strike surprised even the optimists. Kuwait's days as a run-down
haven for pearl-divers and smugglers would soon be over.

Bahrain was quicker off the mark. Drilling began in 1931, and oil
gushed forth in 1932. The much put-upon Holmes at last walked tall.
It was the first strike in the Gulf; moreover Bahrain island was only
twenty miles from the al-Hasa coast of Saudi Arabia where Twitchell,
contradicting the 'pure gamble' of Holmes's Swiss expert, had just
reported highly favourable geology. Armed with these reports and
buoyed by the news from Bahrain, Twitchell was deputed by Ibn

Saud to find an oil company. He did not have far to look. By the spring of 1933 Standard Oil of California (SOCAL), the parent company of the Bahrain operator, was locked in negotiations with Ibn Saud's finance minister. To this battle of the bids came others, including Stephen Longrigg, a British colonel (and later historian of Iraq and Syria), on behalf of the AIOC-dominated Iraq Petroleum Company.

Present too, hovering conspicuously, was the meddlesome Philby. While advising the Saudis and passing information to Longrigg, Philby was secretly in receipt of a fat retainer from SOCAL. Neither it, though, nor he, was decisive. The Americans were offering substantial payments in gold; Longrigg's British backers were offering considerably less in Indian rupees. There was never much doubt as to the winner. The British, confident of their existing position in Saudi Arabia and unconvinced by its oil potential, hung back; the Americans were more forthcoming as well as generous; and Ibn Saud was predisposed to any bid which, innocent of political ties, might yet offset his dependence on the British.

The United States government had extended diplomatic recognition to Saudi Arabia only three years previously; at the time it had neither embassy nor consulate in the country. It had no other interests in the region, nor, like the British government in AIOC, did it have any proprietary role in either SOCAL, CASOC (the California Arabian Standard Oil Company, SOCAL's Saudi subsidiary) or ARAMCO (the Arabian American Oil Company, CASOC's post-1944 designation).

As drilling got under way in 1934, it looked as if the British had been right to be wary. There was no quick strike as in Bahrain, and the physical and logistical difficulties of working in the Arabian hinterland proved awesome. Like D'Arcy's Burmah Oil backers, SOCAL began having second thoughts. Not until 1938, by when a drilling bit had penetrated to a depth of nearly a mile, were the riggers finally rewarded. A pipeline to Ras Tanura on the coast had still to be laid, a Dhahran township fit for Americans to live in built, and markets for Saudi oil found. The first tanker, after Ibn Saud himself had opened the pipeline valve, loaded in April 1939. Six months later the world was at war. Closure of the Mediterranean and an Italian attempt to bomb Dhahran (they apparently mistook it for Bahrain) brought operations to a near standstill. Saudi-produced oil thus played practically no part in the war; and Ibn Saud remained chronically in debt as his lavish expenditure raced ahead of declining receipts from the war-stalled *hajj* and the sluggish flow of royalties from Saudi crude.

But Saudi reserves were a different matter. The surveys and strikes of 1938–40 were more productive of elation than oil in that they proved beyond reasonable doubt that Ibn Saud and CASOC were indeed sitting on 'a liquid goldmine'. Estimates varied wildly. In 1941 it was reckoned that the existing wells could produce up to 200,000 barrels per day, nearly three times the current output from Iraq but still less than that of Iran and barely 4 per cent of US production. Proven and probable reserves, on the other hand, soared to galactic proportions with 1945 projections ranging anywhere from a billion barrels to a hundred billion. Taken in conjunction with the reserves elsewhere in the Gulf, plus those in Iraq and Iran, the Middle East looked to have more oil even than the USA; and it was not being depleted at anything like the same rate.

As CASOC increasingly emphasized in its dealings with the US administration, the new discoveries represented more than just a commercial bonanza. In the twentieth century oil was power; and no country understood this equation better than the USA whose ever-expanding economy was in 1945 still supplying two-thirds of the world demand for oil. But with this demand expected to continue growing exponentially, America's ability to sustain its percentage contribution without prejudice to its existing reservoir was thought highly doubtful. The prospect of the US actually becoming a net importer of oil was exaggerated. Yet during the war the acquisition of foreign reserves as an insurance against the depletion of domestic reserves came to be accounted a national priority.

US domestic producers who, on the grounds of unfair competition, objected to government support for overseas operators, made little headway. Nor did it matter that the pretexts for government support were often far-fetched. Japan's supposed designs on the Gulf, for instance, were as preposterous as the sinister motives imputed by US oilmen to a team of British bug-hunters and desert-lovers (including the explorer Wilfrid Thesiger) who were engaged in locust control in southern Arabia. But however unappetizing these titbits served up by CASOC and the State Department, the US government simply could not afford to stay away from the table. In

- US provides subsidy to Ibn Saud 1943

1939 it appointed a minister (that is, an ambassador) to Saudi Arabia, in 1941 funds supplied by the US to the British were earmarked for an increase in Ibn Saud's subsidy, and in 1943 direct aid was made available to Ibn Saud under lend-lease legislation. Six months later a currency crisis in Saudi Arabia was averted by the US supplying the Saudi mint with 2,500 tons of silver under this arrangement. Lend-lease terms were available only for purposes deemed 'vital to the defense of the United States'. The connection between Saudi oil and America's national security had finally been made.

If an element of fortune had been present in the US acquisition of Gulf reserves, nothing could be left to fortune in their defence. Arguably both world wars had been fought over oil; demonstrably both world wars had been won by oil. Supporting the oil companies and their patrons, especially the House of Saud, had a geopolitical logic that transcended both commercial and economic considerations. Any global power with holdings in the Gulf must expect to defend them for the simple reason that any power with global ambitions could be expected to challenge them.

No doubt such thoughts were aired when Roosevelt and Ibn Saud addressed what the former called 'the problem of Arabia' during their historic meeting on the Great Bitter Lake. Unfortunately what was actually said on that occasion went largely unrecorded; and two months later Roosevelt was dead. Apart from that pledge restating that there would be no change in US policy towards Palestine without prior consultation, the meeting was most notable just for having taken place. Though hastily arranged, it was sufficiently momentous to bring Churchill racing out from Cairo to match the President's hospitality with a 'cloth of gold' luncheon on the shores of the lake. The British, too, had interests in the Gulf and Arabia; Ibn Saud was not to imagine that London was deferring to Washington or in any way derogating its responsibilities. Here, as throughout the Middle East, the British were to be seen simply as inviting US collaboration in the face of a new global peril.

SCUFFLES ON THE FRONTIER

Six months after Franklin D. Roosevelt's meeting with Ibn Saud, the war was over. But as remarked by another member of the Roosevelt family, the victorious Allies thereby exchanged a well-defined and always winnable confrontation for a more insidious and less winnable one. The military might of the Axis had been handicapped by the limited appeal of an ideology that amounted to little more than Nazi supremacism; the Soviet threat, on the other hand, was greatly enhanced by an egalitarian ideology full of encouraging Marxist-Leninist certainties. Ubiquitous and persuasive, communism already had a global constituency. The disadvantaged and discontented were especially susceptible to it, and Western intellectuals especially sympathetic to it. Its international status was attested by the establishment of communist parties in practically every country, all directed by the Comintern in Moscow. Rare were the beds that did not conceal Reds; and with western Europe lying ravaged and exhausted in a whole dormitory of them, it appeared that 'the only power which could effectively block [the Soviets] was the United States'.[9]

This gloomy reading came from the 25-year-old Archie Roosevelt, grandson (like Kim, his Cairo-based cousin) of President Theodore Roosevelt but more closely related to First Lady Eleanor than to FDR. Like Kim, Archie was serving with the OSS and had spent the last years of the war as a junior military attaché in Baghdad under Loy Henderson. Henderson was 'one of the most brilliant American diplomats of his time', thought Archie, who was himself tempted by diplomacy. But Archie, toothy, bespectacled and a first-class linguist, looked destined for a peace-time career in academia.

What changed his mind was the eruption on Iraq's doorstep of a Soviet challenge that Henderson and his State Department colleagues instantly identified as posing a clear and present danger to the whole Middle East, especially its oilfields. Suddenly young Roosevelt realized that he was, as he put it, 'part of something new, something exciting'. The revelation was vouchsafed to him in a blinding flash during an excursion from Baghdad in early 1946 – not on the road to Damascus but on a plane to Tehran. Taking off from Abadan on the second leg of the flight, the plane climbed over the Zagros mountains, their ridges snow-flecked, sharp and excitingly lit by the early morning light. 'At that moment a thought came to my mind,' he later wrote. It was as if the challenging spectacle below mirrored his awareness of the new political landscape. He saw them both with the same clarity, the same sense of privileged insight. How could he deny such inviting prospects in order 'to study dead languages and old civilisations' in some university? 'At that moment I started the process of becoming a committed intelligence officer.'

This first post-war crisis in the Middle East – 'the first scene of the first act of the Cold War' as Archie called it[10] – originated in Iran. That country had been occupied by the Allies during the war as a supply corridor to the eastern (Russian) front and to protect the Anglo-Iranian oilfields, whose output was then the largest in the Middle East (the Abadan refinery then being the largest in the world). Soviet troops had moved into the northern half of Iran, British troops into the southern half. Both undertook to withdraw within six months of peace being signed.

But the Soviet government took this parity of occupation a stage further by demanding from the Iranians oil concessions in the north equivalent to those of the British in the south. The demand threatened to delay withdrawal; and the withdrawal itself looked to be prejudiced by Soviet support for separatist movements among Iran's Kurdish and Azerbaijani minorities. In November 1945 a Soviet-backed puppet state of Azerbaijan was set up in north-western Iran while an embryonic Kurdish entity was being constituted in the mountains between it and Iraq. Archie Roosevelt, whose intelligence-gathering in Iraq had brought him into close contact with the Kurds, noted that the border of this Soviet-sponsored Kurdistan would be only a hundred miles from the Iraqi oilfields and that the putative state was already a base for outlawed Iraqi Kurds.

As the March 1946 deadline for Anglo-Soviet withdrawal from Iran drew near, the Middle East's first post-war crisis deepened. Monitored from the air, Russian troop and tank movements in Iranian Azerbaijan suggested an imminent advance rather than a retreat. Meanwhile in Fulton, Missouri, Churchill was delivering his speech about the descent of an 'iron curtain' across the continent of Europe. The Cold War was polarizing the globe; and with another confrontation similar to that in Iran threatening over control of the Bosporus, the Iron Curtain appeared to be clanking ominously eastwards.

The British, whose forces in Iran were hopelessly outnumbered by the Russians, favoured an accommodation. They had no interest in more Iranian oil concessions and, for guarantees in respect of their existing installations in the south, they were willing to accept a Russian concession in the north, along with negotiations over some form of autonomy for Iranian Azerbaijan. But whether that would satisfy Soviet ambitions was uncertain. Ernest Bevin, British Foreign Secretary in Clement Attlee's new government, saw oil as the only possible Russian incentive. Most others agreed, but while the charitably minded accepted Soviet protestations that they were only trying to augment and protect their own oilfields around Baku, the alarmists detected a Soviet resumption of the nineteenth-century Tsarist drive towards the Indian Ocean, its warm-water ports and its busy sea-lanes. They thought the oil on Moscow's mind was not that of Baku nor even of northern Iran but of Abadan, Iraq and the Gulf.

This was how the US embassy in Moscow read the situation when in early 1946 it fired off the longest telegram in State Department history. The telegram prompted Loy Henderson in Washington to draw up a map showing recent Soviet troop movements in Iran, whence three arrows of probable advance pointed west into Turkey, south-west into Iraq, and south to the Gulf. In a forceful presentation to James Byrnes, Truman's Secretary of State at the time, Henderson hammered home the perils of a Soviet presence in the Gulf and the imperative of keeping Soviet troops and influence 'removed as far as possible' from the region. This went down well, and it brought from the Secretary of State a pounding of fists and a gung-ho 'Now we'll give it to them with both barrels.'[11]

At the time the United States had the atomic bomb while the Soviet Union did not. It was unnecessary to 'give it to them' with any barrels. A stiff note from Truman, plus some equivocal noises from the Iranians themselves, did the trick. The Soviet troops withdrew from Iran in April 1946 with a better understanding of the balance of power in the Middle East, plus the promise of an oil concession, which never materialized. The concession was significant only to the extent that its terms foresaw joint Russo-Iranian ownership of any discoveries and a fifty-fifty sharing of any profits. Here was a novel arrangement, one which ARAMCO would eventually adopt in Saudi Arabia but which AIOC would stoutly resist in Iran. By thus digging its heels into the soft sand of D'Arcy's forty-year-old concession, the British AIOC would find itself ineluctably dragged towards the precipice of Iranian nationalization in 1951.

The Iran crisis of 1946 was rapidly succeeded by similar scares in Turkey and Greece. In both countries, as in Iran, the British had assumed wartime commitments – financial in the case of Turkey, financial and military in Greece – which, although they were now unable to sustain because of their own indebtedness, they were unwilling to relinquish lest the Soviet Union move in. In effect what was at stake was the southern alignment of the Cold War frontier and so the security of the Middle East. Would Soviet expansion be halted along a rugged chain of checkpoints running through the Balkans, the Caucasus and the Himalayas? Or would the Iron Curtain fall much further south, with its filigreed fringes dangling in the eastern Mediterranean, the Gulf and the Indian Ocean?

Soviet pressure on Turkey focused on the demand for a right of Russian passage into the Mediterranean through the Bosporus/ Dardanelles Straits and for a military base in their vicinity. Churchill had shown some sympathy for these requirements during the war when Russia was an ally. No such indulgence was now extended, although London still angled for a negotiated settlement. Washington was much more emphatic. As in Iran, the US administration saw a Soviet presence in Turkey as leading to Soviet control of the entire country which in turn, according to a State Department memo endorsed by the President, would threaten 'the whole Near East and Middle East'.[12] In August 1946 a US naval task-force was therefore rushed to the area. Meanwhile Truman issued another firm statement in support of the principles, now being transferred from the Atlantic Charter to that of the United Nations, in favour of the independence and integrity of all established states. Moscow again backed off. But subsequent alarms kept Turkey in turmoil and obliged Ankara to uphold a level of military deployment that relied heavily on British aid.

Money, plus a sentimental regard for the cradle of democracy, also featured prominently in the Greek crisis. There an on-off civil war between communists, nationalists and monarchists confronted British troops with a peacekeeping task as thankless as that in Palestine. When a new flare-up occurred in early 1947, London's decision in favour of a staged withdrawal was widely anticipated. Less expected, in Washington anyway, was the February announcement that all British financial aid to Greece and Turkey would also cease within a matter of weeks. For a hopelessly indebted Britain, belt-tightening was essential; an ally willing to take up the slack was the ideal solution; and when better to raise the matter than during a long British winter of deep snow and deeper discontent with the country paralysed by rationing, coal shortages, power cuts and sub-zero temperatures?

Washington duly obliged, indeed it had little choice if the Greek and Turkish governments were to stand any chance of resisting communist insurgency and pressure. Much to British satisfaction, the Truman administration pulled out all the stops and a massive aid subvention was rushed through Congress. It passed scrutiny on the grounds not of propping up the dubious regimes in Athens and Ankara but of averting, in the words of Loy Henderson, 'the consequences of a widespread collapse of resistance to Soviet pressure throughout the Near and Middle East and in large parts of Western Europe'. The President himself, formulating his Truman Doctrine for the occasion, generalized still further. The US must support 'free peoples attempting to resist subjugation' throughout the world, a commitment that was readily interpreted as authorizing the containment of communism whenever and wherever.[13]

Not unreasonably Washington had accepted London's word over the Greek and Turkish subsidies. At the time Britain seemed to have completely lost its imperial nerve and to be baling out all over the globe. On New Year's Day 1946, Britannia ruled more of the world than in the Victorian heyday of her empire. This was especially so in Asia where the occupying British and British Indian troops had set up administrations in Indonesia and southern Vietnam as well as Malaya, Burma, Ceylon and, of course, India itself. But a year later they had pulled out of Vietnam and Indonesia; London had managed to antagonize the normally obliging Malays; and within the next fourteen months India/Pakistan, Burma and Ceylon all achieved complete independence. Almost incidentally the services of the Indian Army, one of the world's largest, were also lost to Great Britain. The jewel had gone, and with it most of the crown. All that remained of British might in the Far East were the naval bases of Singapore and Hong Kong. It was possibly the most dramatic derogation of power by an undefeated empire in history.

'There is no reasonable basis for doubting that the same considerations are operating to terminate [British] expenditures in Greece and Turkey,' concluded General George C. Marshall, the new US Secretary of State who was then working on his Marshall Aid plan for Europe's economic recovery. The League of Nations had been superseded by the United Nations, to which most Middle Eastern states belonged; the mandates were now obsolete; the French, with much prompting from Loy Henderson, had finally pulled out of

Syria/Lebanon; and the British looked to be following suit elsewhere. But in citing as evidence of this trend the liquidation of the British positions in 'Burma, India, Palestine and Egypt', Marshall misread British intentions.[14] In the Middle East the British were not bent on liquidation. On the contrary, it has been convincingly argued that, with the loss of India, the Middle East came to be regarded as 'the principal pillar of Britain's position in the world'.[15] By inveigling Washington into assuming responsibility for the peripheral states of Greece and Turkey, London had merely freed itself to concentrate its admittedly dwindling resources on the Middle Eastern core.

Here, while Washington obligingly kept the Soviet threat at bay along what became known as 'the northern tier' (Greece, Turkey, Iran and Afghanistan), the British now busied themselves with shoring up their position in ways which they understood best – like treaty-making. The war had provided an excuse for suspending political negotiations with the Arab states; peace instantly reactivated them. Nationalist resentment in Egypt over the Abdin affair, in Iraq over the suppression of the Rashid Ali revolt, and everywhere over the failure of the British government to implement the 1939 White Paper on Palestine resurfaced with a vengeance. Transjordan had been promised its independence, although Abdullah still had his sights set on heading a Greater Syria. Palestinians demanded the end of Jewish immigration and progress towards self-government. And Egypt and Iraq clamoured for the redefinition, and preferably the revocation, of existing treaties, while as host nations they insisted on the withdrawal of British troops and advisers even more vehemently than did the home nation and its impoverished exchequer.

At the end of the war there were around 200,000 British troops in Egypt (compared with 20,000 in Iran and only slightly more in Greece). Palestine accounted for another 40,000 – and rising. Transjordan's Arab Legion, which had quadrupled in size during the war and was now the most effective Arab force in the region, was still funded by Britain and commanded by the tongue-tied Glubb. In civil matters Transjordan was equally malleable, Amir Abdullah confiding in Kirkbride, his towering *éminence grise*, 'with a frankness which is sometimes startling'.[16] Likewise, Iraq post-Rashid Ali was as much under British direction as Alan MacDonald had found it pre-Rashid Ali. The Habbaniya and Shaiba (Basra) bases supposedly provided an airborne shield for the oilfields in both Iraq and Iran, while internally, in the guise of liaison and intelligence operatives, British officers and civilians retained a strong hold on the administration. RAF 'Area Liaison Officers' were distributed throughout the country, while 'tribal Iraq [which was most of it] was largely under the control of British political officers who, despite their modest ranks, were really kinglets in their own domains'. Archie Roosevelt, who relied heavily on the latter's insights and hospitality, went on to note that these foreigners were not supposed to interfere in local politics but 'in fact they often played an important local role, sometimes virtually as proconsuls'.[17]

The new Labour government in London was sensitive to nationalist sentiment and committed to troop reductions. The withdrawal from Iran in early 1946 was partly intended to impress the Arab states with Britain's good faith in the matter. But military economies and nationalist concessions were not meant to signify the liquidation of the British position. Ernest Bevin, once a shrewd union boss and now a forceful Foreign Secretary, aimed at co-operation rather than confrontation. A good socialist, he saw the need to broaden the base of Arab collaboration and to reach out beyond the old guard of Hashemite and Saudi sovereigns, of shaykhs and pashas (like Nuri and Nahas), to the Arab people. Ideally he would harness the strength of Arab nationalism in joint schemes of defence, perhaps through the Arab League, which would preserve British influence (by the usual monopoly of military instruction and supply) and make of the Arab world a convincing bastion against communism, so earning the all-important approval and support of the United States.

TREATIES GOOD, BAD AND UGLY

Of all the Arab states, Transjordan posed the least problems and so received the earliest attention in the post-war round of British treatymaking. Its population was still well short of half a million; its elected assembly habitually and unanimously approved whatever was put before it. Within his amirate Abdullah reigned unopposed. But without, he was almost friendless. Ibn Saud distrusted him as a Hashemite and still disputed the incorporation into Transjordan of Ma'an and Aqaba; the Syrians and Iraqis, along with Ibn Saud, saw his promotion of a Greater Syria as a poorly disguised bid for a throne in Damascus; the Palestinians rightly suspected his dealings with the Zionists; and the Egyptians rightly suspected his subservience to the British.

By necessity as well as choice, this last troubled Abdullah least. Isolated and impoverished, he needed the British more than they needed him. He had loyally supported them throughout the war; and despite disappointment over Britain's failure to promote his candidature in Damascus following the defeat of the Vichy French, he had no illusions about managing without their subsidy and support. Safeguarding both of these was his main concern when he was invited to London in early 1946.

The purpose of the visit being to formalize the end of the mandate, British recognition of Transjordan's sovereign 'independence', plus his own elevation to 'king', could be taken for granted. Anything less than the former would have been unacceptable to the United Nations, anything less than the latter insulting to himself. Recognition nevertheless marked the crowning moment in a prolonged endeavour as creditable to the unfancied Hashemite as to the British. Twenty-five years after alighting from the Hijaz railway, Abdullah had succeeded in consolidating the desert scraps of his family's lost kingdoms in Syria and the Hijaz into a stable and militarily respected state whose separation from Palestine was now formalized.

More controversially, for the now £2 million per annum British subsidy which financed the Arab Legion and constituted his country's main source of revenue, and for the mutual defence pact which guaranteed Transjordan's integrity, he was obliged to accept the presence of British troops, of RAF airbases and of some proposed naval and communications installations. None of these did he resent. On the contrary, he welcomed them. They demonstrated Britain's commitment to Transjordan and they provided him with useful leverage should he require further British favours.

Critics, though, saw them differently. Transjordan's independence was fundamentally flawed, its 'king' no better than a British lackey who was a militarized menace to his neighbours and a colonial stooge within the Arab League. What Iran's Azerbaijan might have become to the Soviets, Arabia's Transjordan was to the British. The Anglo-Transjordan treaty was welcomed by none but its signatories. At Abdullah's May enthronement as king, British uniforms were much in evidence and the ceremonial was faultless; but the only Arab deputations were those from Iraq, Lebanon and Yemen. The Yemenis arrived a day late; the Syrians closed their frontier, inconveniencing the Lebanese and embargoing even the fruit ordered for the occasion; and although Abd al-Rahman Azzam of the Arab League turned up, he did so uninvited. Internationally Transjordan's independence went largely unrecognized. The United States, alert to Zionist anger over the break-up of mandated Palestine, refused recognition until 1949. The United Nations, reflecting the hostility of the Soviet bloc as well as most Arab countries, only admitted the new state in 1955.

For as the ever candid Kirkbride noted, nothing had changed. Instead of being British Resident in Amman, Kirkbride was now British Minister; but the new job description, like his knighthood, came 'without causing any drastic modifications in my activities'.[18] These still included lending an ear to the royal confidences and denying any responsibility for the royal rants about reconstituting Greater Syria. Far from assuaging his ambition, Abdullah's elevation seemed to have emboldened him. Now in his late sixties, he let his dreams of reclaiming Damascus for the Hashemites become an obsession and, from behind the wire-mesh of his British playground, took what Kirkbride called an 'impish' delight in taunting the likes of Ibn Saud with his plans of aggrandisement.

Kim Roosevelt, in charge of the Middle Eastern branch of what was about to become the CIA, took the King's ambition only slightly more seriously. A Greater Syrian federation, within which a Zionist state might somehow be accommodated, might yet provide a Palestine solution. But its championship by Abdullah was counterproductive. Though 'a cheery fellow . . . plump [and] expansive', he was 'glib rather than sound on international affairs' and was so distrusted by other Arabs that they automatically discounted any initiative he espoused. Kim Roosevelt illustrated his point by repeating the gossip about Abdullah being so passionate a chess-player that he would rather cheat than lose.[19] But chess is a game in which cheating is possible only against a woefully inattentive opponent. Kirkbride, Glubb and the British attended closely. If, as the Palestine crisis unfolded, Abdullah was about to interfere with the board, they would know – and he would know they knew. Such was the level of mutual understanding implied by the 'full and frank discussion' of Transjordan's international relations as enshrined in the 1946 treaty.

No such understanding informed the post-war British treaty-making with Egypt and Iraq. In both cases the British Labour government attached enormous importance to the negotiations but were ambivalent about their objective. Was it to uphold Britain's waning prestige as a world power by concentrating military and political resources in a region of indisputable strategic and psychological moment? Was it, more modestly, to provide for the security of specific British interests, like the oilfields, pipelines, sea-lanes and air routes? Was it to register a claim to being a major player in the Cold War with responsibility for a vital sector in the global defence shield against communism? Or was it to create a local environment conducive to the political reforms, economic development and social provision so dear to Attlee's socialist government? Loth to relinquish imperial responsibilities but keen to exercise them for the benefit of fellow-nations and an equitable world order, the new British government could not decide.

Nor, in the end, would any decision have made much difference. It was the Egyptians and the Iraqis who decided the matter. In both cases the treaty negotiations succeeded, but only for the Arab negotiators to be repudiated by those on whose behalf they negotiated. The terms of agreement, in other words, although in themselves objectionable to most Egyptians and Iraqis, were no more so than the regimes that countenanced them. As Gerald de Gaury would observe of the Iraqi talks, 'attempts to put through a treaty with an unrepresentative government . . . only led to failure'. The British were detested but respected, the Arab power-brokers simply detested.[20] The ground was already being prepared for the revolutions of 1952 in Egypt and 1958 in Iraq.

After the Second World War, as after the First, the Egyptians were quickest out of the blocks. Mustafa al-Nahas and his Wafd, having served the British well during the most crucial years of the war and acquired a reputation for exceptional venality in the process, had been prised from office by King Farouq in 1944. From the safety of opposition, in August 1945 they began calling for the withdrawal of all British troops and the revision of the existing treaty. Students echoed the cry, and massive demonstrations in Cairo and Alexandria chanted it *ad nauseam*. In December 1945 the Egyptian government itself formally took up the matter. But the turmoil continued with Egyptian communists being rounded up as scapegoats even after the

British Foreign Secretary Ernest Bevin had responded by sending a Cabinet Mission to Cairo in April 1946.

Both sides had high expectations of the Mission. Encouraged by the departure of the overbearing Lampson as British ambassador, the Egyptians supposed a Labour government to be more sympathetic to nationalist sentiment and to their demands for equality of status. The British, for their part, expected that an Egyptian government headed by Ismail Sidqi, a doughty nationalist, entrepreneur and 'the strongest man in Egypt',[21] would be keen to do business and capable of carrrying the country with them. Both sides were wrong.

Bevin's notion that the withdrawal of British troops to the Canal Zone and some face-saving fudge over the status of the Sudan would meet Egyptian requirements was instantly rebuffed. Sidqi demanded complete withdrawal (including from the Canal Zone) and unconditional recognition of Egyptian sovereignty in the Sudan. Bevin responded with a May announcement in parliament that all troops would indeed be withdrawn from the whole of Egypt. This would, though, be a protracted business; at the time they had still to be pulled back to the Canal Zone as per the 1936 treaty. Perhaps, too, by way of compensation, the bases could be temporarily leased back; and perhaps favourable terms for the return of British troops in the event of war could be secured. If the worst came to the worst, the British government supposed that troops still in Syria and Lebanon might be retained there and the Egyptian bases relocated in Palestine, Transjordan, Iraq, Cyprus and even East Africa. Thus an overwhelming strength in the region could be preserved with Egypt and its canal being contained within a ring of steel.

From Cairo the negotiations moved to London. There they finally resulted in a protocol of agreement in October 1946. All troops were to be withdrawn to the Canal Zone over the next five months, and from there within three years. A defence pact provided for their return in the event of war but only following joint consultation. And a much-argued statement on the Sudan conceded sovereignty to the extent of a 'union' of Egypt and the Sudan 'under a common [that is, Egyptian] crown', yet safeguarded the rights of the Sudanese to decide their eventual status for themselves.

It was this last that proved to be the undoing of the whole agreement. Sudanese nationalists who opposed Egyptian union interpreted the agreement as prejudicial to their country's prospects of independence and, not without Egyptian suspicions of British collusion, protested vigorously. This resulted in the British military presence in the Sudan, about which no undertakings had been given, having to be reinforced. Meanwhile Egyptian nationalists, having been given to understand that sovereignty over the Sudan had been conceded, were bitterly disillusioned by British assurances to the Sudanese that in fact nothing had changed. The Wafd, still the largest party in Egypt, promptly condemned the protocol, as did King Farouq. Sidqi needed the support of both for ratification. Far from well, the man once described by Grafftey-Smith as *'capable de tout'* proved *capable* of persuading neither King nor country. He promptly resigned.

His successor reverted to the absolutist demands of immediate evacuation and unconditional sovereignty in the Sudan. Bevin in despair abandoned negotiation. But, no Lampson, he drew the line at armed intervention in the manner of the Abdin affair. Consoling himself with the thought that the old treaty still stood, he chose instead to 'stick with 1936', as he put it. Six months later the Egyptians made good on their threat to take the matter to the United Nations. But with the United States awarding a higher priority to containing communism than to the pleas of 'free people attempting to resist subjugation', this appeal was to no avail.

The treaty issue was still unresolved when in 1948 Egyptian troops entered Palestine at the beginning of the first Arab-Israeli war. The advance involved crossing the still British-garrisoned Canal Zone. As Nasser would recall with disgust, the would-be liberators of Arab Palestine had first, like prisoners being let out for exercise, to be checked across their own occupied territory by officers of an alien army.

The Anglo-Egyptian dealings had been closely watched throughout the Arab world and nowhere more so than in Iraq. There too post-war renegotiation of the existing (1930) treaty was deemed desirable. With Nuri al-Said, the godfather of Iraqi politics, weaving his way through his eighth and ninth cabinets, the British hoped to take advantage of a still amenable regime, just as in Transjordan. Iraq's more radical elements, on the other hand, whether nationalist or communist, demanded an end to one-sided treaties and complete evacuation, just as in Egypt. A party system of sorts had been introduced by the occasionally reform-minded Regent Abd al-Ilah to give some expression to these views. But obstructive parties were soon banned and the press muzzled. The Regent, like Nuri, was in no hurry to ditch the existing treaty. Both men preferred to watch and wait on the machinations in Cairo. The pressure came from the streets and, as the Anglo-Egyptian negotiations foundered and the difficulties of endorsing an agreement became apparent, from the British.

Happily the outcome of Iraq's early 1947 elections boded well. A conventional parliament looked susceptible to the usual pressures from the palace while a prime minister with a difference deflected accusations of the British dealing only with their cronies. Aged 47, Salih Jabr could not be said to belong the old guard of collaborationist politicians; as the first Shi'ite to lead the country, his appointment gratified its largest and least privileged community; and as a redoubtable and pragmatic nationalist he enjoyed something like popular support. Like Sidqi in Egypt, he was perceived as Iraq's new strongman, a worthy successor to Nuri but untainted by the latter's record of complacency in domestic affairs. Indeed so ambitious was Salih Jabr's programme for economic and social reform that it 'made the goals of the Labour government in England seem modest' according to W.R. Louis's magisterial analysis.[22]

Better still, the new prime minister's political commitments included renegotiation of the 1930 treaty. From a British point of view he was just the man to grasp that nettle. Secret discussions quickly got under way in Baghdad in an atmosphere untainted by acrimony, and a basis for agreement was laid. In January 1948 Salih Jabr, accompanied by his formidable wife, several members of his cabinet and the ubiquitous Nuri, arrived in Britain to consummate the process. It took just under a week.

Signed somewhat tactlessly aboard Nelson's flagship HMS *Victory*, the new 'treaty of Portsmouth' appeared generous. Bevin, no less than Salih Jabr, had insisted on 'complete independence' and 'full equality' of status. The airbases were to be returned to Iraq and all remaining British troops withdrawn. But the defence of an oil-rich country so close to the Soviet Union obviously required some safeguarding. A Joint Defence Board was therefore to be set up, under which the Habbaniya and Shaiba airbases would be temporarily shared and other arrangements made for a continued British say in the training and equipment of Iraq's armed forces. There was also a clause about the return of British forces in the event of war.

Meanwhile, back in Iraq a bread crisis had brought near-famine conditions; and the resultant criticism of the government immediately extended to suspicions about the new treaty. The Anglo-Egyptian negotiations had taken nearly a year; the Anglo-Iraqi deal seemed to have been hatched in a week. In their anxiety for secrecy, the signatories had done nothing to prepare the country for the actual terms, nor did they now hasten to explain them. No Arabic text of the treaty was available. No member of the delegation sped back to Iraq to explain it. Instead Salih Jabr lingered in London, a hostage to his wife's demand for more shopping time.

'From the 16th to the 21st of January agitations and demonstrations by the people of Baghdad and students continued,' observed Gerald de Gaury who was the Regent's British minder and later the author of a cloying palace narrative. The trouble, which had begun even before the delegation left Iraq, now intensified with a general strike, massive protests by the more radical parties, outbreaks of mob violence, and 'ugly clashes' with the police. 'The number killed will never be known,' says de Gaury. He put it at about a hundred, but the climax had yet to come. The Regent, who along with the acting prime minister was bearing the brunt of the obloquy, now shrugged off his habitual indecision and summoned all parties to a meeting. He listened for five hours and then, whether panicked into capitulation or, as de Gaury would have it, 'obliged' to act by the 'almost complete disorder', he officially disclaimed the treaty.[23]

The British were taken completely by surprise. 'There must', explained Bevin to a perplexed House of Commons, 'be some misunderstanding in Baghdad.'[24] There de Gaury, whose suave demeanour seems to have irritated British mandarins as much his suede shoes had offended the guardsmen of the Rashid Ali expedition, now advised against the return of Salih Jabr. He was ignored. In London the Iraqi prime minister was ushered aboard the first flight home on the strength of his own conviction that he had but to reappear in Baghdad to quell the chaos.

But he was wrong, and his attempts to justify the treaty only made matters worse. What the British called the 'Portsmouth Riots' and the Iraqis *al-wathba* ('the Leap') climaxed on 26–27 January 1948. Two protest marches converged on one of the city's bridges and were mown down by rifle and machine-gun fire from police marksmen, then engaged by armoured vehicles. The death-toll this time was put at 'several hundred'. Next day, Salih Jabr tendered his resignation and fled into exile in Transjordan. The Anglo-Iraqi treaty thus shared the fate of its Egyptian equivalent; the British government were left, in this case, to 'stick with 1930'; and within a year it was business as usual as Nuri formed his tenth cabinet.

'It may be', wrote de Gaury with the benefit of hindsight, 'that it was during these days of rioting that the more malevolent opposition and mob leaders first felt the nature of their power and realised the weakness of the Iraqi throne and of British authority.'[25] The throne and the British would last another ten precarious years. But the writing was on the wall, and little of it had to do with the treaty. The British were habitually disparaged, the monarchy ridiculed, but those condemned outright were the old-guard politicians. 'Salih Jabr and Nuri al-Said to the Gallows!' bellowed the crowds in grim anticipation of future events.[26] More than liberation from foreign interference, or Arab solidarity, or justice for the Palestinians, or even bread, the cry was for the overthrow of a collaborationist élite. Revolution was indeed in the air.

14

Palestine Partitioned

Two years before the breakdown of the Anglo-Iraqi negotiations, a distinguished witness had explored the nature of colonial collaboration when giving evidence to an Anglo-American Committee of Enquiry on Palestine. The 'difficulties' in Palestine, he declared, had been 'artificially created by the English'. In attempting to dominate subject territories without deploying excessive manpower, the British invariably entered into 'a passive alliance' with the local landowning interests who, in turn, exploited this arrangement to keep the masses subservient.

A degree of enmity between rulers and ruled, oppressors and oppressed, was inevitable under such circumstances and not uncongenial to the colonial power. This was the root cause of the conflict in Palestine. 'National trouble-making is a British enterprise,' the witness insisted. It was the British presence that perpetuated the troubles, not, as received opinion had it, the troubles that perpetuated the need for a British presence. Only if Palestine's landowning interests, which included the Zionists, united with the masses against the British, or if an impartial international body took over Britain's role, would the cycle be broken.[1]

This was standard anti-colonialist rhetoric. It roused the twelve members of the Anglo-American Committee of Enquiry as they sat in a packed chamber in the State Department's Washington head-quarters only because the witness, a white-haired dignitary speaking in the gentlest of tones, was the renowned relativitist Albert Einstein. 'Professor Einstein came to the stand with adoring women gazing up at him like Gandhi, flashlights, movie-cameras and so on,' sneered Richard Crossman, a British member of the committee who took strong exception to this 'expected' attack on British imperialism.

Less expected was the rest of Einstein's testimony. He was supposed to be appearing on behalf of the Zionists but in fact averred that a Jewish majority in Palestine was 'unimportant'. Disapproving of all nationalisms, including that of the Jews, he thought that Palestinian society, undistorted by the British need for collaborators and undisturbed by the Balfour Declaration, would have developed its own social momentum and devised it own means of accommodating any incomers.

Quite logically, then, the Anglo-American Committee of Enquiry was, in Einstein's words, 'a waste of time' – or rather a way to gain time while the British tried to decide what to do about Palestine.[2] In this the professor was certainly right. But the enquiry – by one reckoning it was the eighteenth since the mandate was handed to the British – proceeded with its deliberations regardless. Buoyed by the full support of both the British and the US administrations, and assured that their recommendations, if unanimous, would be fully implemented, the committee members went about their business with the self-conscious solemnity of adjudicators resolving an old anomaly for the benefit of a brave new world. For perhaps the last time, there seemed room for some genuine optimism about a Palestine solution.

When in London the Labour government came to power in mid-1945, the Palestine mandate was still operative, Britain was still the responsible power, and her official policy was still that enshrined in the 1939 White Paper. Jewish immigration was thereby curtailed and would imminently be subject to Arab veto; land sales to Jews were virtually at a standstill; and the political groundwork for a single Arab-dominated successor state was supposed to be under way. Churchill's 1944 initiative for the partition of Palestine into Jewish and Arab entities (as originally recommended by the 1937 Royal Commission) had come to nothing after being stalled by the murder of Lord Moyne and then overtaken by the defeat of the Conservative Party at the polls.

Official policy nevertheless looked likely to change. The mandate would be subject to review by the United Nations and presumably replaced with some new form of trusteeship. The White Paper's five-year immigration quota of 75,000 was nearly exhausted. More obviously, the anti-Zionism of a Paper drafted in the aftermath of Palestine's Arab Revolt had become unsustainable in the aftermath of the Nazi holocaust. The enormity of that crime, its individual tragedies, its obscene intent and its implications for humanity were only now beginning to be comprehended. Revulsion and compassion were universal. The holocaust had horrifically substantiated Jewish forebodings, making the Zionist case for a Jewish state hard to refute and redoubling the determination of those bent on achieving it. In makeshift centres throughout Europe over half a million displaced survivors of the Nazi death camps were, as the Anglo-American Commission of Enquiry would confirm, almost unanimous in demanding resettlement in a Jewish Palestine. It was seen as their only chance of rebuilding their shattered lives and their best guarantee against further persecution. It was also the least that an outraged humanity could offer by way of reparation.

The US government in the person of President Truman was genuinely concerned by the humanitarian aspects of the problem, as well as being alert to American opinion and under siege from American Zionists. Likewise the British Labour Party was committed to addressing the problem and thereby fulfilling the Balfour pledge. A resolution adopted at its party conference in December 1944 was just the latest of many statements in favour of Jews being permitted to 'enter this tiny land [of Palestine] in such numbers as to become a majority' even to the extent of 'Arabs [being] encouraged to move out as the Jews move in'.

The memo from President Truman which Prime Minister Attlee had found on his desk the day he took office should therefore have been encouraging. It asked for early consultation on the Palestine problem and supported a lifting of the White Paper restrictions on immigration. In August it was followed by a report on the plight of Jewish Displaced Persons (DPs) in Europe compiled with presidential approval by Earl Harrison. This recommended treating the Jewish DPs as a special case, despite their accounting for under 5 per cent of the estimated 10.5 million total of DPs, and urged the granting of 100,000 Palestine immigration certificates immediately. When the President publicly espoused this figure, Loy Henderson and his colleagues at the State Department were taken by surprise. It was the first of many occasions on which the new president would sideline what he called 'the striped pants boys' at the State Department with their oil-related concerns and their pro-Arab sympathies; and they in no way approved, of either the procedure or the policy.

Nor did the British Foreign Office or the British military. Inviting Arab hostility at a time of troop reductions was the last thing they wanted. The President insisted that he was not trying to influence Palestine policy, merely responding to the humanitarian crisis. But to the British his proposal appeared to break an earlier understanding whereby the US had agreed not to press for the admission of DPs into Palestine in return for the British not pressing for their admission into the US. Bevin, as Foreign Secretary, found the President's betrayal of this understanding 'thoroughly dishonest' and suspected him of angling for the Zionist vote. In a long telegram to the British ambassador in Washington he articulated an accusation that would become something of a British refrain: 'To play on racial feelings for the purpose of winning an election is to make a farce of [the Americans'] insistence on free elections in other countries,' he wrote.[3]

Yet the irresponsibility occasionally imputed to Truman, and more freely to Arab and Jewish leaders, was not unknown in perfidious Albion. Within a year of the Labour Party pledging a green light to Jewish immigration, the Labour government had switched to a cautious amber and Bevin himself to an adamant red. Failing to grasp the political imperative behind Zionism or to fathom the depths of its appeal, Bevin more readily responded to the Arab priorities advanced by his Foreign Office, the regional defence concerns voiced by the military, the security issues raised by the Colonial Office (still in charge of Palestine), and the exigencies of Britain's crippled economy. The last necessitated US loans and US collaboration in defence matters. Bevin, no less than Churchill, believed passionately in Anglo-American co-operation. If there was anything to be salvaged from Truman's unwelcome championship of Jewish immigration, it was the chance of involving the US in the Palestine problem. The rancour, the expenditure and the military burden that it invariably occasioned might thus be shared, and time gained for the formulation of a long-term policy.

—1946 Study

Hence Bevin's November 1945 proposal for an Anglo-American Committee of Enquiry. It would stall the President's demand for immigration on a scale previously espoused only by Jabotinsky, it would distract Arab attention from the extension (contrary to the White Paper) of the existing level of immigration, it would give the British military time to reinforce their Palestine presence in the face of a new Irgun offensive, and it would delay the presentation to the UN of British proposals for the future of Palestine. Truman was aware of this delaying tactic. He endorsed the idea of the enquiry as a step towards admitting the 100,000 but insisted that the committee make its report within 120 days. Bevin, on the other hand, emphasized the need for a unanimous report, promised to 'do everything in his power to put it into effect' and, with misplaced optimism, staked his political future on 'solving the problem'.

The problem, as finally defined by Truman in the enquiry's terms of reference, was not about resettling DPs, or even just Jewish DPs, but about assessing the latter's preference for Palestine, examining the ability of Palestine and the unspecified 'peoples now living therein' to absorb them, hearing all relevant schools of opinion, and making recommendations for future policy. Twelve honest men, six American, six British, none of whom had much prior knowledge of the problem, were appointed to the committee. Its hearings commenced in Washington in January 1946, proceeded to London and various parts of Europe, then Cairo, other Arab capitals, and Jerusalem, with the final report being drawn up in Switzerland.

Most notable was the spectrum of witnesses testifying to the committee. In Washington they were predominantly Jewish and, besides Einstein, included several non-Zionists as well as Zionists like Rabbi Wise and the Revisionist Peter Bergson. The fiery Rabbi Silver, suspecting the exercise to be a British trap to ensnare Washington in the Labour Party's betrayal of Zionism, was one of the few to boycott it. Nevertheless Richard Crossman, an MP, don, and later diarist, found that the surfeit of Zionist propaganda in Washington brought on an attack of British cynicism. Half the people of America 'don't care two hoots', he noted, 'while the other half, either for Zionist reasons or because they don't want any more Jews [in America], back the Jewish case . . . By shouting for a Jewish state . . . they are diverting attention from the fact that their own immigration laws are the basic cause of the problem.'[4]

The hearings in London brought a wider range of opinions and suggestions. Hubert Young, the man who had once rafted down the Tigris, then played Sancho Panza to Lawrence's Quixote in the Arab Revolt, and had since risen to dizzy heights in the Colonial Office, dusted down an old and complicated scheme for provincial autonomy in Palestine. Under it, the country would be divided into four units, one overwhelmingly Arab, a second with a narrow Jewish majority, a third comprising the mostly desert Negev, and the fourth a directly administered enclave covering Jerusalem; the second entity would be open to as many Jewish immigrants as it chose to admit; and for all four the British would accept responsibility as UN trustees and exercise authority for shared concerns, such as defence and communications. These concerns would correspond to the *intérêts communes* by which the French had perpetuated their hold on the Levant states. Indeed the whole provincial autonomy proposal was redolent of France's fragmentation of Syria/Lebanon in the 1920s.

Next to the witness stand came Leo Amery, a Conservative MP of crypto-Jewish descent who claimed to have been responsible for the final wording of the Balfour Declaration and had lately spearheaded Churchill's 1944 proposal for partition. He duly resurrected the same as the only scheme that had commended itself to the 1937 Royal Commission to the extent that it satisfied both Zionist and Arab demands for statehood, however irreconcilable these demands might be in practice.

He was followed by Louis Spears, the outspoken British minister for Syria and Lebanon. Spears vouchsafed the committee the benefit of his thoughts on the urgent need to outlaw and disarm the Zionist militias (Haganah as well as Irgun and LEHI). Alone among the committee's respondents, according to Crossman, Spears 'did not bother to conceal a clearly unsympathetic point of view about the Jews'; even the Arabs were more careful in their choice of words. According to Bartley Crum, a young California lawyer who was Crossman's American counterpart in age and eager engagement, Spears accused the Zionists of espousing a rabid nationalism indistinguishable from Nazism and ridiculed the whole idea of a people as racially mixed as contemporary Jewry laying claim to the heritage of the biblical Jews.[5]

These three solutions – a crackdown on Zionist militias, provincial autonomy, and partition – were all quickly dismissed by the committee. They are notable only for being the options which, *pace* the committee, would in practice be successively pursued over the next eighteen months. Bevin's promise to implement the committee's preference, however sincere at the time, would be frustrated by the committee's failure to produce an elaborated proposal, by his own ambivalence and by US reaction. The Foreign Secretary had staked his future on a loser. He would not, though, feel obliged to resign.

In Europe the committee members were predictably appalled at the plight of the Jewish DPs and impressed, despite suspicions of Zionist orchestration, by their insistence on settlement in Palestine. Just as predictably, in Cairo they were shocked by the dusty odours and the glaring inequalities of the Arab East, while in Palestine they were reassured by the cheery smiles and the spring-time sprouting in the Zionist settlements. Each drew his own conclusion. Bart Crum was unashamedly 'sickened' by Egypt. Taking the measure of Islam during a jaunt to downtown Cairo, he fought off beggars, tripped over bundles that turned out to be 'Arab women crouched with their young', and castigated the well-heeled clientele of Shepheard's Hotel as he sipped coffee on the famous terrace. The 'human degradation' was beyond belief; 'disease stalked me as I walked.'[6] Crum saw a clear case for encouraging the spread of Western notions of democratic accountability, social decency and public health; and how better than through the settlement in neighbouring Palestine of the determinedly democratic, socialist and progressive Zionists?

Crosssman, although also persuaded by the Zionist case and discomfited by Cairo, paid close heed to the 'moving' testimony of Abd al-Rahman Azzam of the Arab League. Azzam claimed that most returning Jews had become so Europeanized as to be now unrecognizable to Arabs as their one-time Semitic 'cousins'. They were returning not as the familiar and submissive Ottoman Jews but as Polish, Russian or German Jews imbued with the European will to impose their own 'imperialistic . . . materialistic . . . reactionary or revolutionary ideas and trying to implement them first by British pressure, then by American pressure, and then by terrorism on their own part'. This 'civilising mission' of the Zionists was as insidious as that of the French or the British, and just as objectionable. Crossman, a great admirer of Antonius's *Arab Awakening*, knew all about the resurgence of Arab identity, and how, as Azzam put it, 'the difference between knowledge and ignorance is just ten years in school'. The Arabs would decide their own rate of advance. They were not, in the name of progress, going to allow themselves to be controlled 'either by great nations or small nations or dispersed nations', insisted the Secretary-General of the Arab League.[7]

It was an argument which, thought Crossman, 'cut away at a single stroke the whole Jewish case'. And it was heard again, in more measured tones, in Jerusalem where Albert Hourani, a young British-born and Oxford-educated Christian of Lebanese parentage, was being groomed by Katy Antonius for her late husband's mantle as the acceptable spokesman of the Arab cause. The West, with enormous undeveloped colonial territories at its disposal, had no right to impose the solution of the Jewish problem on the Arab world, reiterated Hourani.

Yet the Jews, on both humanitarian and legal grounds, had an overwhelming case for expecting the West to do just that; and either way, one party would be wronged. The whole question, as Weizmann himself put it during a long and typically persuasive deposition in Jerusalem, therefore boiled down to choosing between two injustices. But how to assess which was the greater and which the lesser? The exercise threw open the doors to all manner of practical considerations and personal prejudices.

Faced with this conundrum, and desperate to deliver the unanimous report requested by Bevin, the Anglo-American committee could bring itself neither to endorse a Jewish state nor to uphold the White Paper. Instead, it proposed a bi-national state under British trusteeship in which Arabs and Jews would be equally represented. Few concrete suggestions were offered as to how this might be made acceptable to either party, how it might be implemented, or how it would actually operate. But to achieve something closer to the parity of numbers that bi-nationalism supposed, as well as to answer the crying humanitarian need, the committee urged speedy admission of President Truman's 100,000 DPs.

This was not the outcome that Ernest Bevin had expected. In the week in which the committee delivered its report, seven British soldiers were killed by Zionist operations in Palestine. The recommendation about immediate admission of the 100,000 was bad enough, but without some rider about the Zionist militias being first disarmed and illegal immigration curtailed, it was viewed in London with what Martin Jones in his forensic *Failure in Palestine* calls 'something approaching apoplexy'.

Worse was to follow. On the day the report was published Truman made another of his unilateral pronouncements. This time he cheerfully·hailed the committee's endorsement of his 100,000 and its implied abrogation of the White Paper but pointedly reserved the rest of the report for further consideration. In effect, he was cherry-picking the document for domestic (principally Zionist) consumption without regard either to its less palatable items or to the preferences of its British co-sponsor. Loy Henderson made another valiant attempt at damage limitation, but in London the blow to Bevin's policy of involving the US in Palestine was regarded as severe. It led him, according to a friend, 'into one of the blackest rages I ever saw him in'.[8]

THE WALLS COME TUMBLING DOWN

Enquiries generate reports, reports generate discussions, discussions recommendations, and recommendations may, in due course, invite executive consideration. Just so, the Anglo-American Committee of Enquiry led to an Anglo-American conference, and the conference to a new set of recommendations, the so-called Morrison-Grady proposals. The bureaucratic capacity for procrastination was seemingly infinite. Like the cock that crows at dead of night rather than adjust to winter's shortened days, the men in dark suits filed into their ministries and prepared their papers strangely immune to the growing urgency of the Palestine situation.

London's delaying tactics – 'stunts' as he called them – undoubtedly tested the US President's patience. But they also provided him with ready-made excuses – to the Zionists for the lack of action and to the Arabs for the lack of consultation. Palestine remained a British responsibility; the US could effect nothing on its own. Its policy, in so far as it had one, remained that of co-operating with the British, in so far as they had one. The US could not therefore be said to have changed its policy sufficiently to warrant Arab consultation. Likewise it could not be held responsible for achieving so little for Zionism. The British were to blame.

London retorted by accusing Washington of incautious pronouncements, of cultivating expectations over Palestine which it could not satisfy and of seeking influence without responsibility.

There was always someone to blame. That was the beauty of a joint policy. A conspiracist might have added that a US commitment that kept the Jews on side while upholding a British commitment that kept the Arabs on side was also a wondrous creation. It would have been, had it worked. Sincerity was not lacking on either side, but both governments were also in the business of managing matters to their joint and individual advantage.

This transatlantic ping-pong of pronouncement and protestation was more than matched by the tit-for-rat-a-tat-tat of outrage and reprisal between the British and the Zionists in Palestine. Whose was the outrage and whose the reprisal depended on one's allegiance; so did the degree of restraint or brutality with which they were allegedly conducted. Menachem Begin's Irgun (though not of course its LEHI, or Stern Gang, splinter-group) had suspended military operations during the war. It had resumed its campaign in August 1945 when the war's end brought no relaxation of the White Paper policy. Illegal immigration gathered pace at the same time, and the heartless British treatment of apprehended immigrants persuaded Ben-Gurion and others in the Jewish Agency to countenance retaliatory action against the authorities and installations involved. This brought the Haganah, the official Zionist militia, into action. As the violence steadily escalated, the British recruited more police and deployed more troops. When the Anglo-American Committee of Enquiry visited Palestine, its members found enough barbed wire, sandbags, gun emplacements and security checks to convince them that Palestine was in a state of near war.

But they witnessed no incidents. While the committee was in the field, the opposing sides supposed their cases were best served by a cessation of violence. When the committee reported, the violence resumed. Taking the report itself as a provocation, the Zionist 'resistance' hit back. Eight of the country's main bridges were blown up by the Haganah on a single night in June 1946. The next day LEHI attacked the railway workshops in Haifa. A day later six British officers were kidnapped with a view to their being exchanged for commutation of the death sentences passed on two convicted Zionists. The rate at which illegal immigrants were being arrested stood at around 1,500 a month. And instead of the surge in legal Jewish immigration as requested by Truman, it was the number of British 'immigrants' – all either troops or police – that was approaching the magic figure of 100,000.

Backed by Louis Spears, the military estabishment advocated a countrywide sweep of Jewish settlements, including the headquarters of the Jewish Agency whose leadership was thought to be implicated in the violence. Such an offensive had long been planned and widely leaked, though repeatedly postponed. The June incidents finally triggered it. In the early hours of the 29th the crackdown began. Troops stormed the headquarters of the Jewish Agency, armoured vehicles rolled into twenty-five settlements, roads were blocked, telephones cut, and a curfew imposed. Evidence of Jewish Agency collusion in the recent violence was not found, but senior leaders were arrested anyway along with thousands of other 'suspects'. The British called their operation 'Agatha'. To the Zionists it was barely distinguishable from the latest round of Polish pogroms which, a week after Agatha, left forty-two dead in the town of Kielce. In the tradition of resistance movements the world over, the British offensive became known as Black Saturday.

Retaliation was a near certainty. In the absence of Ben-Gurion, the now nearly blind Weizmann pleaded for restraint on the part of the Zionist militias and demanded of the British that they release the detained Jewish leaders. He failed to shift the Palestine authorities but he left for London confident in the assurances of no immediate retaliation by the Haganah. In fact, joint operations by all three Zionist militias had already been agreed. The Haganah and LEHI operations were now postponed; and so, twice, was that by the Irgun. But a third stand-down proved too much for Menachem Begin. He ignored it. The Irgun's carefully laid plan for the most daring and devastating 'terrorist' action in the history of British Palestine slid into gear.

The King David Hotel, a vast six-storey H-plan block, stood in the heart of the business and administrative district of Jerusalem, the country's capital. As well as being a renowned watering-hole second only to Cairo's Shepheard's, the hotel housed the British military secretariat. The army had taken over several floors during the low occupancy years of the war and the place had in effect become Britain's military and intelligence HQ. Here the most senior officials had their offices; here too worked, in addition to all the hotel staff, hundreds of secretaries, telephonists, cleaners and messengers. Some were Jewish, some Arab, some neither. The King David symbolized British rule like no other building in Jerusalem. Literally as well as figuratively it was the highest-profile target in Palestine. That was why it had been chosen.

The heavy security was evaded and seven milk churns each packed with 50 kilograms of explosives were safely delivered to the basement kitchens and manhandled into position round the main supporting piers of the building's south wing. Then they were primed with thirty-minute fuses. It was mid-morning on 22 July 1946, a working weekday. Telephoned warnings were received in the hotel, at the French consulate and at a local newspaper office. But they failed to ensure evacuation. Too many previous calls had turned out to be hoaxes; some thought the calls referred to the diversionary device that had already exploded in the street outside; an exchange of fire with the retreating saboteurs persuaded others that the hotel staff were safer inside than out; anyway, it was probably too late. The bombs went off prematurely. At 12.37 the 350 kilograms of TNT blew away a third of the building.

The blast, writes Thurston Clarke in his painstaking reconstruction, 'ripped off clothes, tore rings from fingers and watches from wrists. It sucked the window panes out of nearby buildings . . . Automobiles rolled over, small trees were uprooted . . . women's stockings burst open at their seams, drinking glasses rattled and then shattered in hands.'[9] Bodies and bits thereof, along with glass, chunks of masonry, office safes and typewriters, were propelled down the adjacent street ahead of a wall of dust. Fires spurted all over the building; the six storeys of the south wing concertinaed into a single storey of smoking rubble.

The scene has since become familiar. Only the TV footage was missing. 'We actually provided the example of what the urban guerrilla is,' claimed the unrepentant Menachem Begin. A future Israeli prime minister, he was confiding in another, Golda Meir. 'We created', he insisted, 'the method of the urban guerrilla.'[10] But 'guerrilla', or 'terrorist'? That too depended on one's allegiance. The final count gave 91 dead, most of them clerical staff and hotel workers: 41 were Arabs, 28 British, 17 Jews.

All shades of Zionist opinion quickly condemned the outrage. But the perpetrators, having eluded the British, also went unpunished by the Zionist authorities, and Begin himself remained at his command. Fresh from the scene, the General commanding British troops in Palestine obligingly played into his hands by issuing an order designed to penalize not the saboteurs but the race to which they belonged. In forbidding British troops to enter any Jewish shop or restaurant, General Barker declared his intention to be that of punishing Jews 'in a way the race dislikes as much as any, namely by striking at their pockets and showing our contempt for them'. Like Allenby's vindictive response to the murder of General Lee Stack, this casual jibe betrayed the very prejudice that Irgun propaganda laboured to emphasize in justification of its operations.

BITING THE BULLET

No sooner had the King David Hotel erupted than Ernest Bevin's dream of a joint Anglo-American policy on Palestine also fell apart. In July 1946 a British team led by Lord Morrison entertained in London a US delegation headed by Henry F. Grady. But instead of making proposals based on the admittedly vague recommendations of the Anglo-American Committee of Enquiry, the Morrison-Grady talks focused on the provincial autonomy scheme lately advocated by Hubert Young and heavily favoured by the British Colonial Office. Its chief commendation was that it would preserve British defence interests in Palestine, a vital consideration in the light of Bevin's May decision to kick-start his negotiations over the Anglo-Egyptian treaty by announcing the withdrawal of all troops from Egypt.

Anxious to ensure admission for the President's 100,000, Grady and his colleagues went along with this. Provincial autonomy could, after all, develop into the bi-national state favoured by the enquiry. Alternatively it could develop into the outright partition now being championed by moderate Zionists. Seen as a short-term solution, it precluded nothing. On that basis agreement was amicably reached just two days after the King David explosion.

But the fall-out was not what was expected. From Washington's perspective, it was bad enough that Grady had allowed the admission of the 100,000 to be contingent on the implementation of the new scheme. Worse still, the scheme itself, by awarding the Jews only a small, defenceless and unsovereign province, precluded both the balm of statehood and the tonic of further large-scale immigration. The US State Department still thought the plan viable, but when the Secretary of State himself virtually disowned it, and when horrified senators characterized the Jewish province as no better than an 'oriental ghetto', the President threw in his hand. 'Jesus Christ couldn't please them,' he reportedly said, '. . . so how could anyone expect that I would have any luck.'[11]

The British continued to promote provincial autonomy as the nearest thing to a practicable solution; and with a view to presenting it to all the parties involved, they had already scheduled another round-table conference in London for September 1946. But so far as the US President was concerned, provincial autonomy was dead.

The final parting of the ways came in October when the first session of the London conference had already adjourned without agreement. By then mainstream Zionists had rallied round a plan for a generous scheme of partition that would concede the principle of a Jewish state in part of Palestine while eclipsing the more extreme demands of radicals like Silver (for a Jewish state in the whole of Palestine) or of the Revisionists (for a state that included Transjordan as well). Partition as a long-term solution might yet be reconcilable with provincial autonomy as a transitional stage; and it was with the idea of bridging this gap between the partitionists and the provincial proposal that Loy Henderson backed the idea of a statement by the President.

The President was persuaded of the need to speak out in order to clarify US policy in the light of the Morrison-Grady débâcle and because of the forthcoming congressional elections in New York. The newspapers at the time were carrying advertisements demanding that he honour his party's past pledges to Zionism and the 100,000; the Democratic Party itself was pleading for a pro-Zionist statement in the light of adverse poll predictions; and Republican opponents were threatening to steal the Democrats' thunder with promises of not just 100,000 DP immigrants but 'several' hundred thousand.

The President's statement, as finally issued, did mention the desirability of a compromise with 'the proposals which have been put forward' (in other words, the Morrison-Grady version of provincial autonomy). But more significantly, it also insisted that partition – and thus, for the first time, a Jewish state – would be welcomed by the American people. The British Prime Minister, informed of the statement's contents at midnight British time, immediately requested a postponement. He was refused. Intended for maximum electoral effect, Truman's bombshell made the news that day and was in the papers the next, the feast of Yom Kippur. According to Rabbi Silver, it was Bart Crum and presidential adviser David Niles who persuaded the President to issue the statement 'as a smart pre-election move'.[12]

Once again British hopes of a settlement acceptable to Arab opinion had been torpedoed by what they considered US electioneering, or 'playing on racial feelings for the purpose of winning an election'. It was Truman who went in for 'stunts'. In handwriting dripping with sarcasm, Attlee drafted a telegram decrying the President's 'precipitancy' and expressing icy 'regret' over his refusing 'even a few hours' grace to the Prime Minister of the country which has actual responsibility for . . . Palestine'.[13]

Yet the President's Yom Kippur statement did not in fact torpedo the provincial autonomy scheme or the London conference. Both were already doomed. The conference which was supposed to decide the fate of Palestine had opened without a single representative from Palestine, both the Zionists and the Arabs having also rejected provincial autonomy as a basis for agreement. Nor were those representatives of the Arab states who did attend any more enthusiastic. The British still hoped to salvage something, if only by dropping hints about their willingness, failing an agreement, to abandon the mandate altogether and hand it over to the United Nations. Referral to the UN had until recently been regarded as a counsel of depair, a drastic threat and a last unthinkable resort. Now, in the light of the Yom Kippur statement and the US Zionist move towards partition, it began to look a distinct possibility.

Reassembling in early 1947 the London (or Lancaster House) conference at last welcomed representatives of the Palestinian Arabs. Zionist representatives, although still refusing to take part, were also in London. The discussions were therefore separate. Yet their outcome was depressingly uniform. Provincial autonomy was again rejected by both; so was the bi-national formula of the Anglo-American Committee of Enquiry. In a final throw of the dice, even partition along the lines of the 1937 Royal Commission was vehemently opposed on principle by the Arabs and in practice (as falling well short of their territorial expectations) by the Zionists. There now seemed nowhere to go. On 18 February 1947 the British government announced that, the Palestine mandate having proved

The first Palestinian riots to be directed at the British broke out in 1933 when twenty-six Arabs were killed by police gunfire in Jaffa and Jerusalem (*above*). The protests anticipated the 1936–9 Palestine Revolt in expressing 'the wrath of the Palestinian Arab Nation . . . suffering from British imperialism and the British government's violations of the rights of the owners of the country'.

At Rutba in the Syrian desert, buses made an overnight halt on the Damascus– Baghdad run. In 1941, during the bleakest weeks of the Second World War, Rutba was occupied by the nationalist forces of Rashid Ali's pro-Axis regime in Baghdad. Bombed (*as here*) by the Royal Air Force, it was recaptured by a column of Buckingham Palace guardsmen and Arab Legion bedouin *en route* to the relief of Baghdad.

3In 1941, seeking sanctuary from Iraqi insurgents, Baghdad's expatriates barricaded themselves in the British embassy. The 'siege' lasted five weeks; but no one was hurt. The bodies strewn about the lawns were sleeping. From the roof Freya Stark noted 'a horrible beauty about a fire in a town' as Baghdad sustained the first of its aerial bombardments.

'Our troops advancing into Syria are prepared for all emergencies and wear their steel helmets.' The caption provided by the British War Office belied the ferocity of the fighting as Allied forces swept into Syria in 1941. To deny Nazi Germany the services of the French 'Army of the Levant' and its Syrian bases, General de Gaulle had urged the advance.

(*Above*) De Gaulle quickly regretted the Allied victory in Syria/Lebanon when General Louis Spears, the new British Minister (*centre*), championed Syrian opposition to French rule and sidelined General Georges Catroux (*extreme right*).

(*Below*) The Anglo-French *entente* in Syria was patched up at this 1943 meeting in Alexandria. But de Gaulle remained resentful and would take his revenge seventeen years later when Britain applied to join the European Community. *Left to right seated:* Catroux, de Gaulle, Churchill, General Giraud, Anthony Eden.

Jerusalem's King David Hotel also served as the headquarters of the British administration. Its 1946 bombing by Menachem Begin's ultra-Zionist Irgun was the worst single incident in Britain's thirty-year rule in Palestine. Of the 91 killed only 28 were British, the rest being Arabs and Jews. 'We created the method of the urban guerrilla,' boasted Begin.

Shadowed by the Royal Navy and rammed as she approached Palestine, the *Exodus 1947* was escorted into Haifa harbour. There her 4,500 Jewish immigrants from refugee camps in Europe were bundled aboard a prison ship by the British and taken back to France. Refusing to disembark, they would be finally and forcibly landed in Germany after an appalling and heavily publicized odyssey.

On 29 November 1947 the UN General Assembly voted in favour of the partition of Palestine into a Jewish state, an Arab state and an internationalized Jerusalem. Throughout the Arab world, as here in Cairo, demonstrators instantly protested against the alienation of Arab land and the arm-twisting employed at the UN, principally by the United States.

The state of Israel was declared at midnight on 14 May 1948. Though often at loggerheads during the Zionist struggle, Dr Chaim Weizmann (*left*) and David Ben-Gurion (*right*) agreed to serve together as respectively president and prime minister.

Menachem Begin addresses an Irgun rally in 1948. The poster shows a gun to symbolize the Irgun's military ethos and a map outlining how Zionist Revisionists would 'revise' the mandate to include (Trans) Jordan in the Israeli state. The framed photograph of Vladimir Jabotinsky, the Revisionists' founder, would accompany Begin into the Prime Minister's office in 1977.

(*Above*) Amir Abdullah inspects troops of Transjordan's Arab Legion commanded by Glubb Pasha (*extreme left*). The Legion, although the most effective of the Arab armies in the 1948 Arab-Israeli war, was bound by Abdullah's secret agreement with the Israelis not to enter the new Jewish state.

(*Below*) No such agreement bound the volunteers serving in the Arab 'Salvation Army' commanded by the veteran Fawzi al-Qawuqji (*foreground*). Fawzi, though, was at odds with other Palestinian units and 'a menace to his own side . . . in spite of his bombastic claims to the contrary'.

Prised from his throne by the Nasserist revolution of 1952, Egypt's King Farouq retired into exile in Italy. His favourite haunt was the pool-side restaurant of singer Gracie Fields on the island of Capri.

(*Above*) Celebrating the fifth anniversary of the Egyptian Revolution, President Gamal Abd-al Nasser seemed unassailable; he was about to head the new United Arab Republic (UAR) of Egypt and Syria. But in the context of the Cold War, his Soviet arms purchases had condemned him as a crypto-communist.

(*Right*) A safer bet in Western eyes was Nuri al-Said, the long-serving Iraqi premier. Here Nuri condemns the subversive activities of the UAR in Lebanon and demands international intervention. Three weeks later Nuri's dismembered body decorated the streets of Baghdad as Iraq underwent its own revolution.

As US ambassador in Baghdad, Loy Henderson anticipated a Third World War while the Second yet raged. Later, at the State Department in Washington and then in Iran, he successfully orchestrated US attempts to blunt Soviet ambitions in the Middle East; but he signally failed to dissuade President Truman from supporting Israel.

'Disinformation was the cloak to his dagger.' Miles Copeland of the CIA freely claimed, and as freely disclaimed, numerous political initiatives. He probably did mastermind the region's first military coup, that in Syria in 1949. With Kim Roosevelt he also cultivated the 'Free Officers', Nasser among them, who overthrew Farouq in Egypt.

Nasser's 1956 nationalization of the Suez Canal Company was the last straw for Prime Minister Sir Anthony Eden. In November the British and French, in secret alliance with the Israelis, attacked Egyptian installations including Port Said's fuel dumps (*above*) and naval headquarters (*below*). A week later the invasion was called off. Without US support, the British and French economies could no longer sustain a Middle Eastern adventure.

Brits invite failure; want out

unworkable, they must refer the problem to the United Nations. As if to emphasize this washing of hands, they offered no trace of any recommendation as to its future solution.

Whether this was really a gesture of despair, or whether it was part of some Machiavellian scheme to bring all parties to their senses and so find a new basis for the British position in Palestine, has been much argued. The British seemed all along to have been inviting failure. Opportunities for informal discussion with individual Arab states had been ignored. The Egyptians, possibly the Lebanese and certainly Abdullah of Transjordan might have been amenable to unilateral deals over partition. Instead, the Foreign Office had persisted in upholding the Arab League, addressing itself to the Arab states as a whole, and providing them with a round-table forum in which, as at the 1939 St James's conference, competitive rhetoric was sure to triumph over realism. Acutely conscious of its continuing negotiations with Egypt, its forthcoming ones with Iraq, and the Saudi claims in Transjordan, the Foreign Office was not unhappy to be seen siding with the Arabs and supporting Arab unanimity.

If that meant a stalemate and referral to the UN, all might still not be lost. So uncertain was the outcome of a UN referral that neither the Zionists, the Arabs nor the US government welcomed it. A reprieve, so the argument goes, was thus possible. Perhaps the other parties would come to their senses and accept some version of the existing proposals. In the last analysis, the UN itself might throw its weight behind such a solution; it would surely not adopt a policy so unacceptable to the British that they would be unable to support its implementation. And all the while the British Foreign Office would have kept faith with the Arabs on whose oil and military facilities Great Britain's existence as a global power depended. As in Egypt and Iraq, and as events would indeed reveal in Palestine, military withdrawal and political disengagement need not mean an end to British influence.

But decisions are taken not in the Foreign Office but in the Cabinet, and there the attitude appears to have been very different. The government genuinely wanted out. The disappointing results of Operation Agatha/Black Saturday, the tragedy of the King David Hotel, the embarrassment of General Barker's outburst, and the disastrous publicity that attended every measure against illegal immigration had turned Palestine into a liability. It could only get worse. The morale of the security forces was crumbling, the expense was crippling, and the defence dividends were diminishing.

February 1947, the month in which the London conference broke up and the mandate was referred to the UN, was also that in which the British government abruptly announced an end to its aid to Greece and Turkey. In Cairo the Anglo-Egyptian treaty terms had just been rejected, in Delhi an August deadline for India's independence was about to be set, and at home the worst winter of the century was accompanied by dire evidence of economic recession. Any recovery depended on Arab oil, just as hopes of salvaging a global role depended on Arab friendship. Palestine had become expendable.

The counter-argument that referral to the UN was all about calling the Americans' bluff 'appears to be utterly unsubstantiated by anything in the British documents, instructions, memoranda or in the minutes of officials', concludes Dr Jones after exhaustive investigation. On the contrary, the documents 'show plainly that all of the British government's concerns at this time revolved around speedy liquidation of the burdens of the Mandate, if necessary by leaving Palestine, while aiming to accomplish this with the minimum damage to Anglo-Arab relations'. 'The crucial and conscious turning point' in British policy towards Palestine was reached during the 1946–7 winter of deepest discontent, not months later when the UN ground out a policy of its own.[14]

This being the case, there would be no going back. After failing to accompany its referral with any recommendation, the British government made a virtue of what its representative at the UN gamely called 'manful neutrality'. In accordance with this posture the British would decline to give evidence to the United Nations Special Commission on Palestine (UNSCOP) which convened in June, would reject the commission's majority report in favour of partition in September, would abstain from the crucial General Assembly vote on partition in November, would refuse to participate in the UN Commission set up to implement this, and would do its utmost, regardless of the developing civil war in Palestine, to keep the commission out of the country until all British personnel had been safely withdrawn in May 1948.

Some found this conduct incomprehensible, others merely shameful. To a Zionist like Arthur Koestler it was rather more – not simply 'muddled, short-sighted or pseudo-Machiavellian . . . [but] plainly surrealistic'. A Hungarian Jew, like Herzl, Koestler had joined the Betar as a schoolboy and in the 1920s had briefly served the Revisionist cause in Palestine. Subsequently winning fame as an author and intellectual prize-fighter, he now laid into British policy with a flurry of damaging paradoxes. Bevin had claimed that the British had no right to impose immigration on Palestine by force; yet they had taken for granted the right to exclude immigration by force. The UN's recommendations had been rejected on the grounds that Britain could not carry them out alone; yet when international assistance was offered, Britain refused to shoulder her share of the burden. She had renounced the mandate on the grounds that the claims of Jews and Arabs were irreconcilable; yet she now insisted that she would only support an agreement that did reconcile them.

> To appeal for the judgement of an international body in order to stop two parties from quarrelling, and then to reject the judgement because it meant enforcing peace between them, was no longer diplomacy but sheer Harpo Marx logics.[15]

Koestler was more at home with Karl Marx than Harpo, with controversy than whimsy. From Palestine and Revisionist Zionism his intellectual odyssey had taken him to Russia and Soviet communism, then Spain and international socialism. An insatiable activist, he took up ideologies and then demolished them much as he did women. Even his Zionism, to which, like countless other Jews, he was about to make a public 'return', was more pugnacious than pragmatic. It thus beggared his comprehension that the British government might have sought no 'judgement' from the UN, merely conceded defeat. Or that it had refrained from undertaking to impose such a 'judgement' lest, like partition, it mean exciting a war. Arab opinion was still what mattered to the British and, as a Palestinian delegate had put it at the London conference, 'it is a foregone conclusion that the Arabs of Palestine are determined to reject partition, and resist it with all the means at their disposal'.[16]

ENTER *EXODUS*

Events both in Palestine and at the UN did nothing to dent this determined British neutrality. The United States had long aspired to influence events in Palestine; now, instead of leaning on the British, it could do so by leading at the UN. The UN being an American-born and American-based organization, Washington was ideally placed to provide the guidance that London declined to offer. And although initially UNSCOP was allowed to pursue its enquiries with minimal supervision, once its report was out this guidance would come to look more like propulsion.

Not all of it was in the same direction. On the one hand the State Department advised against endorsing UNSCOP's majority decision in favour of partition. Loy Henderson in particular feared that partition, if enforced, would involve a US deployment in Palestine as thankless as that of the British, and if not enforced, would mean civil war and intervention by the other Arab states, possibly with Soviet support. This would eventually engage the US anyway. Henderson, backed by the US Joint Chiefs of Staff, therefore mounted a strong rearguard action against partition which, in the final months of the mandate, would very nearly succeed.

The President, though, heeded other concerns, and once again his well-attested humanitarian sympathy for those still languishing in the DP camps found support from the exigencies of domestic politics. Throughout the second half of 1947, petitions and telegrams were arriving at the White House at the rate of 600 a day. Most of them were from, or on behalf of, pro-partition Zionists. Advisers simultaneously reminded the President of his party's debt to Jewish American donors and of its funding requirements for the next year's presidential elections. Failure to honour his Yom Kippur statement in favour of partition could prejudice his chances of finally winning an electoral mandate. Moreover, were the US, as well as Britain, to reject the majority decision of the United Nations, that infant body might itself be fatally weakened.

In the final showdown within the US administration in October it took a last-minute intervention by the ever persuasive Dr Chaim Weizmann to ensure that the President supported not only the principle of partition but also a generous application of it. At issue was the status of the Negev, the long and largely uninhabited blade of Palestinian territory between Sinai and Transjordan whose point pricked the Red Sea coast near Aqaba. It already contained a few Zionist kibbutzim; and settlement being, as ever, the key to sovereignty, more were being hastily constructed. For possession of the

Negev would double the size of the new Jewish state. It would also give it access to the Indian Ocean, thereby reducing its vulnerability to Mediterranean blockade and closure of the Suez Canal. Additionally it would slice apart the crescent of encircling Arab states by severing Egyptian from Transjordanian territory.

US support for a territorial conformation so rich in strategic potential for the Jewish state was correspondingly disastrous for its would-be Arab counterpart. But with the Arabs boycotting UNSCOP and reluctant to engage with the UN's subsequent deliberations, a rare protest from the British was easily brushed aside and US backing of the Zionist claim to the Negev carried the day.

Less predictably, the world's other superpower also threw its weight behind partition. Instead of opposing, on Cold War principles, any measure supported by the US, the Soviet Union and her satellites chose to see the creation of a Jewish state as the culmination of an anti-imperialist freedom struggle and announced active support for it. US and British observers were taken by surprise. They suspected that the Soviet decision must be a cynical ploy to destabilize the Middle East and so embarrass the Western powers. But in Palestine Zionists wisely hailed Moscow's decision as energetically as they had Washington's. Without it, the required two-thirds majority in the UN General Assembly would have been unattainable.

Even with it, the outcome of the final vote on partition on 29 November 1947 hung in the balance. Officially no US pressure was to be brought to bear, but in fact numerous senators, congressmen and Supreme Court justices, encouraged by the President himself, leant heavily on vulnerable nations like Liberia, the Philippines, Greece, (Nationalist) China, and numerous Central and South American republics. Zionist pressure also played a crucial part; so, to some extent, did British indifference in that some Commonwealth nations felt at liberty to support what was now seen as essentially 'America's' partition plan. Amid scenes of partisan enthusiam more appropriate to a great sporting occasion, the final voting tally just delivered the necessary two-thirds majority: 33 for, 13 against, 10 abstentions.

Zionism was deliriously vindicated. The dreams of Herzl would be fulfilled, the patient suasions of Weizmann had paid off. So had Silver's lobbying, Ben-Gurion's bullying, Begin's bombs. The Balfour pledge, at least in respect of the Jews, would be redeemed; and against all odds, a 3,000-year-old prophecy was coming to fruition. Even to one as scientifically minded as Arthur Koestler it was nothing short of a 'miracle'. The Chief Rabbi had offered prayers at the Wailing Wall, he reported. 'That seemed to work'; the delegate from Haiti promptly switched his vote from no to yes.[17] God moved, as ever, in mysterious ways.

But the evidence indicated a triumph for management over miracles, muscle over mystery. And the impression thus given of an infant Jewish state, fathered on Palestine by the brute imperatives of US electoral practice and delivered by the rough manipulation of a compliant UN, filled Jeremiahs like Loy Henderson with the deepest foreboding. 'The policy we are following in New York at the present time', he wrote in the week before the final vote, 'is contrary to the interests of the United States and will eventually involve us in international difficulties of so grave a character that the reaction throughout the world . . . will be very strong.'[18]

The British greeted the 29 November vote with more sour grapes and what many construed as an ultimatum. Unwilling to be seen by the Arab states as facilitating partition in any way, they announced plans for a phased withdrawal to begin imminently; no responsibility would be accepted for law and order in areas once they had been evacuated; and this process of retraction would enable the mandate to be surrendered on 15 May 1948. There were less than five months to go.

The decision to pull out was not new. It had been announced in principle after the UNSCOP report in September. But the deadline had now been considerably advanced. This echoed a similar decision taken ahead of the exodus from India in the previous August. There too, once partition was accepted as inevitable, the handover had been brought forward so as to stress British resolve and secure a more amicable (if not peaceful) transfer of power.

But in Palestine, as in India, the security situation itself also dictated precipitate action. As Arabs and Jews squared up for war, British lives were being lost, British loyalties tested, and British public opinion enraged. Even the old strategic argument for retaining military facilities in Palestine as part of the wider region's defence became untenable. As one minister put it, 'you cannot . . . have a secure base on top of a wasps' nest'.[19] The wasps belonged principally to Irgun and, much sat upon, they retaliated. In 1946 the judicial flogging of

Zionist 'terrorists' was matched, lash for lash, by the Irgun's flogging of kidnapped British soldiers. A year later the booby-trapped bodies of two British sergeants were found hanging from a eucalyptus tree soon after a similar sentence had been executed on convicted Irgun saboteurs.

Between these notorious outrages the thump of bombs and mines claimed dozens of lives, many of them British, and brought the country to a standstill. The provocation commonly lay offshore. There a new armada of immigrant ships, often unseaworthy and always overcrowded, was being determinedly intercepted and forcibly boarded, sometimes with loss of life. As of August 1946, the desperate passengers had been denied even the consolation of internment in their Promised Land; instead, they were escorted to camps in Cyprus or still further afield. The heartrending cries of those turned away were matched by the rage of friends and relatives watching from the shore.

Zionist fund-raisers, principally in the United States, were the only beneficiaries of this trafficking in humanity. The publicity generated by each such incident yielded the donations needed to fund the next, or to arm its sponsors. In an open 'Letter to the Terrorists' at which even Begin might have flinched, the American publicist Ben Hecht informed the Zionist militias that 'every time you blow up a British arsenal . . . or let go with your guns and bombs at the British betrayers and invaders of your homeland, the Jews of America make a little holiday in their hearts'.[20]

To stem the flow of rhetoric and funds the British protested to the US government; and to stop the immigrant traffic they reserved the right to return refugees to their place of embarkation while leaning particularly on the French, at whose ports many of the immigrant ships loaded. Thus was the scene set for two seafaring sagas of tragic but very different memory. The first, later fictionalised, concerned the *Exodus*; the second, less publicized, the *Altalena*.

Specially so named for the voyage, the *Exodus 1947* dwarfed all previous immigrant vessels. Once an American cruise ship, she had been offered for sale as scrap in Baltimore, purchased by a Haganah agent, sailed across the Atlantic under Haganah direction, and then moored off the Languedoc resort of Sète. There 4,500 refugees, gathered mainly from camps in Germany and brandishing visas for Columbia, trooped aboard. There was no secret about their identity, nor about their real destination. In effect the Haganah was courting a trial of strength with the mandatory authority. The British duly obliged, first by repeatedly lodging vigorous protests with the French government. All were to no avail. Barely a year after the last French troops had been ignominiously shepherded out of the Levant, Paris owed London no favours. The *Exodus* was allowed to sail.

Shadowed by the Royal Navy, it was finally rammed as it neared Palestine's territorial waters, then boarded. Against fierce resistance in which two Jews were killed, His Majesty's men finally gained the bridge. The ship was then sailed into Haifa while a wireless operator, broadcasting live to a Zionist radio station, regaled the world with its plight. It was July 1947, the month in which, not incidentally, the members of UNSCOP were conducting their enquiries in Palestine. The spectacle of several thousand ragged and destitute Jews being herded like cattle from the now sinking *Exodus* on to three prison ships, and there packed into the cages stacked high on their decks, was duly noted by the international team. It did nothing to convince them that the number of Jews desirous of living in Palestine was not being forcibly depressed. Nor did it foster regard for the British authorities. Short of goose-stepping, it was hard to see how they could have devised a more painful experience for survivors of the Nazi death camps.

This linkage between the plight of European Jewry and the aspirations of Palestine's Zionists was reinforced by what followed. While the three floating prisons drifted aimlessly about the Mediterranean, the British elicited from the French an undertaking to take back the migrants. But when returned to Sète, the now sick, sun-frazzled and stinking passengers refused to disembark. Instead they advertised their defiance to the waiting media. For three weeks the prison ships rode at anchor while an August heatwave, then heavy rains, beat down on their unshaded cages. A hunger strike was staged, four babies were born. Finally the 'floating Auschwitzes' headed back to sea, this time making for Hamburg. Again the world's press was tipped off. Again it dutifully reported the pitiful spectacle of women and children armed with sticks and cans being pressure-hosed out of their wretched cages and returned to a land steeped in their relatives' blood.[21]

No doubt the tragedy had been partly contrived; certainly the legend would be heavily embellished. For the 4,500 whose hopes had been so cruelly dashed, posterity's plaudits could never make amends. But the episode had served its purpose. British immigration policy was utterly discredited, and the UN Special Committee on Palestine profoundly impressed. More than any other experience, the *Exodus* affair had edged UNSCOP towards its majority decision in favour of partition.[22]

DAYLIGHT AT MIDNIGHT

Sailing a year later, the *Altalena* set an identical course to the *Exodus*. A smaller, faster vessel of 4,000 tons, she too had been purchased in the United States, renamed and reflagged, sailed across the Atlantic, and then positioned off Sète. But there, instead of immigrants, she was to load armaments and crack recruits. By 1948 Zionism's immediate requirements had changed. The name 'Altalena' was an alias once used by Vladimir Jabotinsky; the men and the guns belonged exclusively to the Irgun; and their arrival in Israel would prove to be both nemesis and salvation for the infant state.

As of December 1947, while the partition scheme was being finely ground in the UN's mill of committees, subcommittees and commissions, and while the evacuating British forces were methodically executing their withdrawal from prepared positions to final bridgeheads, Arabs and Jews throughout the rest of Palestine went to war. Until the mandate actually expired – and to the extent that none of the Arab states was as yet officially engaged in military intervention – this was a 'civil war'. But it was otherwise indistinguishable from the international conflict, known as the first Arab-Israeli war, which it duly became when on 15 May the mandate ended, partition took effect, and the Arab states launched their first strikes.

Hence in early 1948 the UN, while wrestling with the minutiae of the impending partition, was already being distracted by the prior and far more pressing need to resolve the conflict in Palestine. The gloomy forebodings of Loy Henderson and the State Department had proved all too prescient. Partition was totally unacceptable to the Arabs; it could only be imposed by the international community intervening militarily; and since it was perceived as America's brainchild, and since, above all else, any Soviet participation in a UN enforcement policy must be forestalled, it fell to America to provide the military personnel required.

A figure of 80,000–160,000 men, plus naval and air support, was suggested, then firmly ruled out. Washington was no more willing than London to deploy troops in Palestine to enforce partition, least of all in an election year. Such a move risked stirring up American anti-Semitism which could be as fatal to the President's re-election prospects as alienating the Zionists. Moreover, if Arab solidarity meant anything, US intervention would invite retaliation against American interests throughout the Middle East, possibly culminating in an Arab request for Soviet assistance. This could precipitate a superpower showdown as serious as that currently taking place over Berlin. If some limited Arab-Israeli 'blood-letting' (as one British observer put it) was unavoidable, then so be it. Through arms embargoes, economic sanctions and diplomatic pressure, such a conflict was probably manageable; if it reconciled the participants to partition, it could even be seen as desirable. 'Third World' wars in other words were one thing, a Third World War quite another.

Faced with the quandary over enforcing partition, President Truman beat a tactical retreat from Palestine policy and looked to the State Department to find a way out. Loy Henderson saw his chance. With the support of Kim Roosevelt and other Middle Eastern stalwarts, Henderson and the State Department set about reversing the commitment to partition. They duly came up with a plan whereby, the UN having confessed itself unable to impose partition, the US would pledge support for a form of temporary trusteeship until peace was restored and the Arabs reconciled.

The President approved this new idea, although still insisting that partition remained the ultimate objective. But to most others – presidential advisers, fellow Democrats, Republican critics, Zionists, anti-Zionists, the British, the French and the entire UN – it appeared that the US had performed a complete volte-face. A presidential policy aimed at underpinning partition had suddenly turned into a State Department one aimed at frustrating it. Like a punch-bag, Washington's duplicity positively invited the jabbed paradoxes visited by Koestler on the British, or the table-thumping accusations habitually administered by Rabbi Silver. Instead, the President was treated to another of Chaim Weizmann's gentle and apparently conclusive presentations. Weizmann left the White House convinced that partition was still on. Next day the senior US delegate at the UN officially advocated its suspension. A twin-track approach, far from reassuring the travelling public, had led to a head-on collision.

In the creation of a Jewish state Truman's role is generally reckoned to have been decisive. But he was not, and never had been, a Zionist. He shared neither Lloyd George's enthusiasm for biblical prophecy nor Churchill's for fashioning history. A shrewd and caring patriot rather than a visionary, he esteemed homelier values, such as respect, loyalty, honesty. Endorsing trusteeship left him exposed to accusations of having forfeited all three. And as an unelected president, he feared failure in the forthcoming poll not just as a political defeat but as a peculiarly personal rejection. It was not a question of 'playing on racial prejudices for electoral advantage', more one of salvaging his endangered integrity.

Whether he fully mastered the intricacies of the Palestine problem is doubtful, but of the perils it posed for his political survival he could now be in no doubt. Words such as 'traitor', 'appeaser', 'capitulation' and 'surrender' greeted the statement on trusteeship in the UN. Former First Lady Eleanor Roosevelt, on whose endorsement Truman was counting for his presidential campaign, threatened to resign her post on America's UN delegation. With his popularity ratings at a new low, Truman was told by other Democratic stalwarts to forget about election as they cast about for an alternative candidate. The only consolation was that trusteeship quickly proved as impracticable as partition. Rejected by the Arabs as well as the Zionists, it too could only be imposed by force and thus ran up against identical objections.

In a lucid and scrupulously balanced account of the administration's heart-searchings,[23] Michael J. Cohen cites as crucial a letter of 5 May, just ten days before the mandate was to end. It came from the chairman of New York's main pro-Zionist Christian lobby and formulated an idea which, readily adopted by the President's advisers, would transform the whole situation. As things stood, said the writer, Truman could not hope to win the state of New York in the November elections. 'The Jewish vote against him would be overwhelming.' Only 'a dramatic move' on the President's part could change the situation. And assuming that the Zionists in Palestine declared their independence as soon as the mandate expired, 'such a move might well be the recognition of the Jewish state'. Trusteeship had been aborted 'by events', not by the President. 'Logically', therefore, the US should respect the UN's earlier decision in favour of partition by according the Jewish state instant recognition.[24]

This would undoubtedly prejudice the UN's concurrent efforts to broker a peace in Palestine, efforts in which the US was a prime mover. But the domestic dividend could not be doubted, and the scheme was duly put into effect. On 12 May, amid the usual storm of petitions, the President summoned his closest (largely pro-Zionist) advisers and accepted their recommendation for immediate recognition of the Jewish state. The State Department's warnings were once again rejected and its trusteeship proposal heavily criticized. Henderson, the man held accountable for recent policy, was not invited to the meeting. His views about global priorities taking precedence over Palestine preferences, and national considerations over electoral requirements, were well known. Too ready with such inconvenient reflections, he had to go. Siberia beckoned, but India actually needed an ambassador. A broken man, Henderson was soon packing for New Delhi. He was later shunted to Tehran, where a more congenial challenge would present itself.

Two days after the White House meeting, on the eve of the mandate expiring, David Ben-Gurion in Tel Aviv duly proclaimed the independent state of Israel. It would become effective at midnight Israeli time. That was 6 p.m. in Washington. At eleven minutes past six, the President announced America's de facto recognition of the new Jewish state.

The US delegation at the UN was among those taken completely by surprise. A mass resignation was only narrowly averted. Other UN representatives were equally disgusted. Anglo-American relations plummeted to an all-time low. Those states dragooned into supporting partition, then invited to prefer trusteeship, felt 'double-crossed' (if not triple-tricked). Even Eleanor Roosevelt, a keen Zionist, was appalled that a government she represented could display such an arrogant contempt for the feelings of its allies and the repute of the UN.

It was not the last of the President's about-turns; a greater one was yet to come. But it would be as naïve to see either as scandalous as it would be to see Zionist lobbying as subversive. Even Loy Henderson never ventured such comments. Zionist tactics were no different from those of other special-interest groups, such as the armaments industry or the oil companies. That was how representational politics worked. Likewise, timely and advantageous accommodation with influential sections of the electorate was the way to win votes. That was how democracy worked.

Any other president would probably have done the same; and especially so if, as now – and indeed ever after – he found that support for Israel was quickly justified by events. America's national interests were not being prejudiced; the Arab states did not retaliate against the US; and the Soviet Union, having trumped America's instant de facto recognition with its own speedy *de jure* recognition, remained too closely identified with the Jewish state to interest Arab leaders. Moreover the Israel so hastily recognized by the two superpowers quickly proved viable, even assertive, and thus more than worthy of their confidence. While London and Washington had shied away from the military burden of imposing partition, Tel Aviv embraced the task with determination, defying arms embargoes, outdistancing UN peace efforts, and thus rewarding overseas supporters with a 'holiday in the heart' that would last, on and off, for the best part of a year.

One who rejoiced was Arthur Koestler. Having exhausted Europe's intellectual pastures, Koestler had arrived in New York in February 1948. He witnessed at close quarters the twists and turns of American policy over partition and he shared in the mounting Zionist excitement. When on the night of 14–15 May the state of Israel came into being, the man best known for the novel *Darkness at Noon* sensed daylight at midnight. 'Israel's citizens are rubbing their eyes,' he wrote. 'It does not often happen that a dream comes true.' But could it last? With the Arab League mobilizing its members for an all-out assault, it looked to Koestler as if the newborn state might 'share the fate of the infants under Herod whose tender bodies were put to the sword'.[25] As a Jew he must bear witness; as an ex-Irgunist he must act. Pausing only to organize a clutch of journalistic assignments, within a matter of days he was in Paris collecting from the Jewish Agency's headquarters only the fifth Israeli visa ever issued. Two days later he landed in Haifa, hard on the heels of Count Fulke Bernadotte, the UN's specially appointed mediator.

DAVID AND GOLIATH

In Palestine the night of 14–15 May had in fact been dark, though fine. As midnight approached, King Abdullah and his personal staff

Abdullah advances into Palestine [handwritten annotation in top margin]

stood at the east end of the Allenby bridge, by which the main road to Jerusalem crossed the Jordan river. Alec Kirkbride, now in his tenth year as Britain's representative in Amman, wondered why the king bothered to wait. The border was unmanned; all British personnel had already departed.

> At twelve o'clock precisely the King drew his revolver, fired a symbolical shot into the air and shouted the word 'forward'. The long column of Jordanian troops, which stretched down the road behind the bridge, already had the engines of their cars ticking over and, as they moved off at the word of command, the hum of their motors rose to a roar.[26]

To the north, more of Abdullah's troops advanced into Palestinian Samaria. Further north still, an Iraqi detachment headed for Nablus, while Syrian and Lebanese units moved to their respective borders with Galilee. Egyptian ground troops were still negotiating their way across the British Canal Zone *en route* to Sinai and the Negev, but three Egyptian aircraft were quickly off the ground and by dawn on the 15th were buzzing Tel Aviv's power plant. Like Herod's sword, they flashed as they went about their business in the early morning light.

Yet appearances were deceptive. The aircraft over Tel Aviv were fighters, not bombers; and Egypt's invading troops, though numbering 10,000 and advancing almost to Jerusalem, were wretchedly equipped, decidedly battle-shy and soon hopelessly extended. The Syrian, Lebanese and Iraqi forces, all equally ill-prepared, were very much fewer. Token units of no more than 3,000 men apiece, they operated independently and were capable only of diversionary action. The highly motivated and disciplined Haganah, aided by Irgun and LEHI, could field about the same number of men (perhaps 30,000) and, as predicted by some British military observers, were more than a match for their opponents. Instead of an infant Israeli state being sliced up by the sword-slashing Herod, the biblical analogy that sprang to most minds, including eventually Koestler's, was that of a small but resourceful David squaring up to a crazed and ungainly Goliath.

In the charismatic person of Ben-Gurion, Israel was indeed led by a defiant, if balding, David. But the Arabs' Goliath was less obvious. 'Red-headed, strongly and well built, a soldier first and foremost',

Fawzi al-Qawuqji would have been Gerald de Gaury's candidate. De Gaury had come to know Fawzi well in Baghdad and admired him. He was no fanatic and reminded de Gaury of 'the soldiers of fortune under the Ottomans who carved out kingdoms for themselves'.[27]

Fawzi led a force raised and paid for by the Arab League which was variously known in English as 'the Army of Deliverance', 'the Liberation Army', or more quaintly 'the Salvation Army'. It had been operating inside Palestine since the previous December, when the war was still a 'civil' one. To its incursion and its occasional assaults on Zionist settlements the British had turned a blind eye, being anxious neither to antagonize the League nor unnecessarily to expose their homeward-bound troops. But Fawzi al-Qawuqji, the veteran of more campaigns than there are variant spellings of his name, had found glory hard to come by. Kirkbride, another survivor of Lawrence's Arab Revolt, had no regard for the military prowess of his old comrade-in-arms. Fawzi was 'a menace to his own side', and his raids were 'invariably unsuccessful in spite of his bombastic claims to the contrary'.[28] With a nod to de Gaury, Kirkbride believed that Fawzi's operations were indeed designed to carve out a personal fief for himself; and to abort this, he persuaded King Abdullah to stop reinforcements from reaching 'the Salvation Army' through Transjordan.

There was, though, another contender for the role of Goliath. Fawzi rarely managed to field more than 2,000 men, mostly Syrian and Iraqi irregulars who were soon as unpopular with the Palestinians they were supposedly liberating as were the Jews. For within Palestine the Arabs were as divided as they had been in the 1930s. Many still clung to the rejectionist nationalism of ex-Mufti Hajj Amin al-Husayni who, after miraculously escaping trial for associating with the Nazis, now attempted to orchestrate Palestinian resistance from his sanctuary in Cairo. But the Mufti's relations with the Arab League were strained; and since he was still as hostile to Fawzi as he had been in 1938, his own guerrilla bands in Palestine refused to co-operate with 'the Salvation Army'. The strength of these pro-Mufti bands was uncertain, but among their leaders Abd al-Qadir al-Husayni, a kinsman of the Mufti who operated in the Jerusalem-Ramallah area, had rapidly eclipsed Fawzi as a military commander.

Respected by all sides, Abd al-Qadir's forces held the the main road from the coast to Jerusalem, so placing that city's Jewish community in a state of siege. But on the same road, during some of the most desperate engagements of the civil war, Abd al-Qadir was killed in early April 1948. Days later, Irgun forces followed up this triumph with a massacre of possibly 250 inhabitants in the village of Dayr Yassin. Even the ex-Irgunist Koestler found it hard to excuse this 'worst atrocity committed by the terrorists [*sic*] in their whole career'. But he thought it 'an isolated episode', and if it triggered a mass exodus of Arabs, that was because the Arab media chose to report the butchery of women and children with 'the lurid detail of oriental imagination'.[29] An Arab massacre of a Jewish medical convoy in Jerusalem followed. As ever, retaliation established not an equilibrium of atrocity but a momentum of murder. Soldiers and civilians killed and were killed in a frenzy of 'blood-letting' as if, for all the world, Arab and Jew were genetically incompatible and the war was of their own sole making.

Fawzi's dismal record and Abd al-Qadir's untimely death left one other contender for the role of an Arab Goliath. Nearing seventy, knee-high to a small camel and more gamesman than general, Abdullah scarcely looked the part; from his only recorded battle, that of Turaba against Ibn Saud's tribal supporters, he had fled across the desert in his nightshirt. Yet it was he who, after Glubb had declined the honour, chosen as the Arab commander-in-chief. This recognized the fact that, of all the units poised to operate in Palestine, Jewish as well as Arab, his Arab Legion was both the most formidable and the least hampered by domestic disturbances. If Transjordan had begun life as an amirate strung together by a railway line, it was now a kingdom predicated on an army. Well-equipped by the British, commanded by the taciturn Glubb and trained by his mainly British officers, the Legion had lately served under the British in Palestine as an auxiliary unit. Then as 15 May approached, most of its personnel hastily exited that country as peacekeepers to re-enter across the Allenby Bridge, like overworked extras in a theatrical production, as belligerents.

The Legion's potential was blunted only by doubts about who it was actually fighting for. Abdullah, of course, claimed to be acting on behalf of the Arab League and at the urgent request of his Palestinian neighbours. But the League rightly suspected him of colluding with the Israelis to promote his own territorial ambitions in Palestine; the Mufti rightly supposed that these ambitions precluded his own; and all, both Israelis and Arabs, wondered whether he was not in fact being used by the British to further their own plans for rediscovering a role in Palestine.

Kirkbride, when describing the Arab legionaries trundling over the Allenby Bridge, had called them 'Jordanian' forces. It was no slip of the pen. Largely unnoticed at the time – or since – in 1947 constitutional adjustments in Amman had for the first time referred to the Hashemite kingdom as 'Jordan' rather than 'Transjordan'.[30] The implication was clear. Passionate chess-player that he was, Abdullah had spied an opening: the end of the mandate could be taken to expose that document's territorial definition of his 'Across-the-Jordan' bit of Palestine. The logic, if not the legality, of the river constituting his realm's immutable frontier might now be questioned; and by renaming the country as Jordan, he was preparing the ground for a state that might soon embrace the river's west bank as well as its east. If a 'Greater Syria' was still his ultimate goal, a 'Greater Jordan' incorporating Arab Palestine was a long step in the right direction.

To this end, Abdullah had probed both British and Zionist reaction. Golda Meir (then Meyerson) had been authorized to speak for the Jewish Agency, and in November 1947 she returned from Amman with a vague understanding that Abdullah's forces would not invade those parts of Palestine awarded by the UN's partition experts to the Zionists in return for the Zionists not opposing Abdullah's occupation of the parts awarded to the Arabs. The arrangement seems to have been reconfirmed in early May 1948. It was not, needless to say, divulged to the Arab League, whose plans to reclaim the whole of Palestine Abdullah continued publicly to endorse.

Kirkbride had been privy to this deal, although cautious. The British officers serving in the Legion were in a potentially embarrassing situation; and on no account must London be seen as supporting an arrangement that would be anathema to the other Arab states, especially Saudi Arabia and Iraq. Nevertheless, in January 1948 Abdullah's prime minister, accompanied by Glubb of the Legion, had gone to London to sign a revised treaty with the British. The new treaty, only two years after the previous one and not significantly different from it, was largely window-dressing. It was supposed to reassure other members of the Arab League that (Trans)Jordan was no British puppet and its relations with London were on a par with those of Egypt and Iraq. It therefore replicated the arrangements offered to, but just rejected by, the Iraqis.

Much more significant was a private interview with Ernest Bevin at which Abdullah's plan for invading Palestine and occupying 'that part . . . awarded by the UN to the Arabs which was contiguous with the frontier of Transjordan' was duly revealed. Bevin, probably prepared, did not demur. 'It seems the obvious thing to do,' he retorted, '. . . but do not go and invade the areas alotted to the Jews.'[31] The US government was also informed and it too concurred. A proposed Trans-Arabian Pipeline (TAPLine) from ARAMCO's Saudi wells to the Mediterranean would run through Transjordan. Keeping on good terms with Abdullah was the obvious course for Washington, as it was for London.

Other Arab forces, especially those of Fawzi and the Palestinian irregulars, did operate within what now became Israel. But for the most part Abdullah respected his arrangement with Golda Meir and to that extent the Arabs' most effective fighting force was neutralized as an instrument of aggression against the Zionists. The exception was Jerusalem which, designated by the UN as an international zone, did not fall within territory allotted either to the Jews or the Arabs. It was therefore considered fair game by both. With a view to impressing suspicious members of the Arab League while securing a capital worthy of his enlarged kingdom, Abdullah ordered the Arab Legion into the Old City and captured its Jewish quarter. But much of the larger New City remained under Zionist control, although besieged more closely than ever.

Elsewhere in Palestine both sides made good their occupation of the zones allotted to them by the UN partition. The demographic flaw in any such division was immediately apparent. Well populated and mainly coastal, the Jewish zone included far more Arabs than the less populated and mainly inland Arab zone did Jews. Regardless of the fortunes of war, the Arab loss was always going to be much the more acute; and whether moved by force or fear, as major cities like Haifa and Jaffa were taken over by the Jews, hundreds of thousands of Arabs hastily vacated their homes to seek temporary refuge in the Arab zone or beyond Palestine's borders. In this exodus they followed the lead of the Arab Higher Committee, whose members habitually looked outside Palestine for redress. Resting their hopes on the intervention of the states of the Arab League rather than on their own nation-building efforts, the Palestinian leaders seemed more concerned for those landed rights and privileges noted by Einstein

and now endangered by the departure of the British than they did for
the national aspirations of their own people as challenged by Jewish
exclusivity and Jordanian expansionism.

THE FIRST ARAB-ISRAELI WAR

The war itself was on a scale commensurate with a country no bigger
than Wales. Glubb called it 'an imitation war', Koestler 'a phony war'.
The fighting, as observed by Koestler, involved 'small and hopelessly
inefficient bands of Levantine mercenaries skirmishing against
improvised Jewish home-guard units, with a great amount of brag-
ging and bombast on both sides'.[32] It claimed several thousand lives,
a heavy toll for so small a country though less than the Iraqi and
Syrian revolts of the 1920s and a mere fraction of the several
hundred thousand victims of India/Pakistan's partition.

Although spread over a year, it anticipated the pattern of later
Arab-Israeli conflicts to the extent that the actual hostilities lasted
only days. How many it is hard to say. There is no accepted date for
the outbreak of the civil war, and its elevation to international status
brought immediate pressure for a ceasefire. Stuttering and often
localized, the first round of the Arab-Israeli conflict lasted a month
(15 May–11 June). There then followed a month's truce, a second
round of ten days (9–18 July), a second truce of three months, and
finally a third round that mainly involved the Egyptians and the
Israelis and was divided into two short campaigns of a week in
October and two weeks in December–January.

This erratic performance was partly due to the tireless efforts of
the UN to mediate, partly to the pressures directly exerted by the
great powers, and substantially to the participants' inability to sustain
prolonged conflict. The UN's efforts were led by Count Bernadotte
of the Swedish Red Cross, whose appointment as mediator was
backed by an immediate UN move for a ceasefire. Among those who
initially objected were the British, presumably to win time for
Abdullah to effect occupation of the 'West Bank'. Three weeks later
they relented, the Arabs were pressured into acceptance, and the first
ceasefire came into effect.

During the four-week truce Bernadotte exceeded his role as mediator by proposing a settlement plan. This involved a retreat from

partition and a return to something like the bi-national state proposed by the 1946 Anglo-American Committee of Enquiry in which Israel and 'Greater Jordan' would be merged. The scheme was roundly rejected by all parties, including the British, who deemed its negation of a Jewish state too good to be true. It was then quickly rendered obsolete when in the next short burst of hostilities the Israelis made substantial gains. These were possible thanks to an infusion of troops and armaments during the truce. Some of the arms came by air from the countries of the Soviet bloc, especially Czechoslovakia, so belying State Department fears about the Arabs turning to communism though increasing British fears that it was Israel that was 'going communist'. Additionally, on the night of the 20 June the *Altalena* finally slipped into Israeli waters.

Ceasefires, though sometimes reluctantly accepted, were necessities to both sides as an opportunity to rearm, upgrade and recruit. Because of the international embargo on arms sales and reinforcements, all units remained chronically short of troops and ammunition for most of the war. The Arab states were largely dependent on the British for military *matériel* and lacked the overseas funds and contacts to acquire arms elsewhere. Israel, on the other hand, commanded ample overseas funds and contacts courtesy of international Jewry; but it was more vulnerable to the embargo because its only open border was its short and closely watched coastline. Thus even modest acquisitions, like a single arms shipment, could make a significant difference to the balance of advantage.

The *Altalena* carried 900 men, some of them munitions specialists and engineers, all of them recruited and trained by the Irgun in Europe. As well as their equipment, the ship's French-supplied cargo comprised 5,000 rifles, 300 bren-guns, 150 mortars, 5 tank-tracked armoured cars, and countless bombs and rounds of ammunition. Menachem Begin believed it was enough to win the war. Accordingly he was prepared to make some of it available to the Israeli High Command with whom he had lately reached agreement about merging Irgun troops and weaponry with those of the Haganah. But this arrangement, like that between Abdullah and the Israelis, did not apply to the proposed international zone of Jerusalem. There Irgun and LEHI retained their separate identities. Begin therefore had some grounds for insisting that part of the *Altalena*'s hoard be reserved exclusively for Irgun units serving in Jerusalem, if not for insisting that ex-Irgun units now under Israeli command should also benefit.

Arthur Koestler may himself have been involved in the ticklish negotiations over the *Altalena*'s cargo. As an ex-Irgunist, he certainly took a lively interest in the matter and followed the ship's progress closely. But the share-out of the arms was still unsettled when, under cover of darkness at a small port north of Tel Aviv, the recruits were safely landed and the Irgunists began unloading the crates. First light revealed the unloading to be still far from complete. Moreover the whole shoreline was found to be ringed by troops and artillery of the regular Israeli army. Worse still, a UN spotter plane flew low overhead.

What ensued, though carefully chronicled by Koestler, remains far from clear. Shooting broke out between the Israeli regulars and the Irgunists, an attempt at mediation failed, and the ship sailed away, still with a large part of its precious cargo on board. It put into Tel Aviv. The Irgun evidently believed that its supporters there would rise to the occasion and rescue the cargo. But communications broke down and the ship was clumsily beached right in front of the UN headquarters.

The Israeli government was now faced with a dilemma. If it claimed the remaining cargo, it would invite dire international condemnation and further sanctions. If the Irgun got the guns, the government could disclaim responsibility but would have a civil war on its hands. And if neither got them, it would be a tragedy for the war effort. The last option was nevertheless preferred. Government artillery opened fire on the ship, and amid a sensational display of pyrotechnics the ill-fated *Altalena* along with much of her precious cargo was finally blown up. 'About forty people had been killed in the fighting . . .' reported Koestler. 'Begin was the last man to leave the ship.'

There followed a round-up of Irgun activists. But there were no trials, Begin remained at liberty, and the peaceful incorporation of the Irgun into the regular forces resumed. Koestler thought Ben-Gurion's government had showed great political maturity. The young state had survived its hour of crisis; and as 'tempers gradually calmed down, the renewal of the war, a fortnight later, did the rest'.[33] But Tel Aviv's willingness to countenance a flagrant breach of the UN embargo did not go unnoticed, nor was it the end for the hard men of Zionist Revisionism.

The second phase of the war lasted only ten days and was followed by another truce, then another Bernadotte plan. Announced in September, this fared better than the first. It accepted the principle of partition but with adjustments to recognize the military situation. Hence the state of Israel was now to be denied the Negev, into which its forces had scarcely penetrated, but compensated with territory in Galilee which, previously awarded to the Arabs, had been overrun by the Israelis. Britain and the US were consulted and approved the plan. But Israel was by no means reconciled to the loss of the Negev, and the ire of its supporters in the US clearly posed a potential embarrassment to President Truman on the eve of elections.

In fact, the issue provoked an exact repeat of the pressure tactics and the presidential about-turn occasioned by the trusteeship proposal six months earlier. A UN Security Council resolution censuring Israel for flouting the ceasefire in order to improve its position in the Negev looked to have the necessary US support, then was suddenly aborted on the President's orders. His instructions were perfectly candid and applied only until election day on 2 November; 'thereafter proceed on understanding of American position [as] previously taken', concluded this most un-presidential of directives. 'It is doubtful', comments Michael Cohen, 'if there has ever been, before or since, such a direct interplay between domestic politics and foreign affairs.'[34] Ironically, when, against all predictions, Truman duly secured his first popular mandate, he won less of the Jewish vote than had Roosevelt. Evidently Zionist gratitude for past favours was offset by a realistic appreciation of the President's vacillating motivation.

Meanwhile the second Bernadotte plan had run into trouble of a more sensational nature. Forty-eight hours after submitting it, Bernadotte had shared the fate of Lord Moyne when he was assassinated by a LEHI hit-squad in Jerusalem. The Israelis had always regarded him as a pro-British stooge, if not an ex-Nazi; and Irgun/LEHI had construed his peacemaking as a direct challenge to the Jewish state.

Again the crime was universally condemned, again the perpetrators were spared retribution. Yitzhak Shamir, still one of LEHI's leaders, was swiftly rehabilitated and subsequently joined Begin in the Herut Party. As the later Likud, the same party would provide both men with a platform from which to launch legitimate political careers and eventually form governments. To few liberationist causes was tactical terrorism anathema. Israel would not be the last emergent state to embrace its practitioners. Shamir and Begin, who on his own admission 'provided the example', may have bequeathed to Israel's leaders a higher than average tolerance of political criminality but they scarcely inspired the Arab and Islamist excesses of later years. Traumatizing opponents was an ancient trade. To the dictum, so beloved of the ideology-eating Koestler, about all 'isms' degenerating into 'wasms', terrorism proved a notable exception.

Deprived of its champion and denied the wholehearted endorsement of the US administration, the second Bernadotte plan, like the first, was ultimately scuttled by battlefield realities. With a newly improvised air force and vastly augmented ground forces, in October and December 1948 Israel successfully challenged the plan's basic premise by routing the Egyptian troops in the south. It thus effectively occupied the Negev which Bernadotte had sought to deny it. British objections and even some British troop deployments on behalf of the Arabs were ignored. Only American pressure finally halted Israeli incursions into Egypt itself and secured a Cairo-Tel Aviv armistice.

By then, January 1949, Fawzi's forces had been dispersed and the Syrians repelled. The Iraqis were about to head home, and Abdullah held as much of Arab Palestine as he could hope to retain – plus rather more Palestinian Arabs than he could easily manage. The challenge of organizing and assimilating his gains made him an early candidate for peace, even if it meant surrendering some Palestinian territory to achieve it. Israel also favoured disengagement. It would clear the path to UN membership and Washington's *de jure* recognition. On the latter hinged a promised US government loan, the first of many, for $100 million. Such a dividend alone made peace desirable.

London and Washington, for their part, were again edging towards consensus. Freed of the mandate and still on reasonable terms with most of the Arab states, the British had become reconciled to Israel's existence and to its intimate relationship with the US. The US reciprocated by accepting the principle of Abdullah's 'Greater Jordan'. It meant that Arab Palestine was now, by extension, subject to the Anglo-Jordanian treaty, and it would tidy up the political geography of the region, clear the way for Aramco's TAPLine, and absorb the troublesome residue of Palestinian identity.

Seemingly peace promised something for nearly everyone. The one obvious exception was the Palestinians themselves, otherwise the unregarded 'non-Jewish communities' of Balfour and the unspecified 'peoples living therein' of the Anglo-American Committee of Enquiry. Their wishes should, by the standards of the League of Nations, the UN, the US, Great Britain and every other nation wedded to the principles of democracy, have been paramount. In fact they had not even been ascertained; and at least 750,000 of these spectral denizens of a land renowned for its crucifixions had lost everything.

Less obviously the ruling élites of all the Arab states who had failed to prevent this disaster found themselves fatally discredited in the eyes of their own people. Henceforth, with the loss of Palestine 'pinned to their robes and frock coats' (as Mary Wilson puts it),[35] the kings, shaykhs and pashas of the existing order were seen to be peddling a brand of nationalism as embarrassing and self-serving as it was unresponsive. More protests in Baghdad, a coup in Damascus, plots in Amman and another assassination in Cairo would set the alarm bells ringing. Revolution, long in the air, had now entered the bloodstream.

15

Coup and Countercoup

THE MAN WITH THE IRON BRAIN

IN THEIR MANAGEMENT of the Middle East, the British and the French had usually enjoyed the luxury of international legitimation. They had exercised rights in their respective territories either on behalf on the League of Nations or in accordance with bilateral treaties which, however unequal, were not illegal. This paperwork was important. Besides giving their rhetoric a righteous ring, it had defined the moral and physical limits within which they might openly deploy the trappings of power and enforce local compliance.

It was otherwise for the United States. Washington's assumption of ever greater responsibilities in the region was matched neither by an international consensus as to its role there nor by a domestic consensus in favour of risking American lives there. Monitored by both the Kremlin and Congress, direct military intervention was as yet rarely an acceptable option. On the other hand, the lack of paperwork, and so of definition, did encourage a more flexible approach both in the exercise of influence and in the area to which it applied. The region itself was now perceived in a truly global context, not principally in that of North Africa, as by the French, or of India and empire, as by the British. This led to some redefinition, with Iran and the Gulf states being firmly reinstated in the 'Middle Eastern' arena. More significantly, in the exercise of power it called for subtler

methods with preference being given to diplomatic and economic
pressure, plus a ready recourse to covert operations. If, in the normal
conduct of their business, the British and the French dispensations
had relied on civil commissioners, military liaison officers and *conseillers techniques*, the US would perforce look more to global fixers, corporate and financial executives, and the assorted operatives, agents
and spies who constituted the intelligence community.

The latter enjoyed something of a golden age in the 1950s. But
for historians, as for politicians, the murky world of espionage
poses major problems of interpretation. Burning to tell but sworn
to secrecy, the intelligence officer who would write his memoirs had
either to withhold the facts or disguise them. Archie Roosevelt, the
younger, slighter and more academic-looking of the Roosevelt
cousins, chose the first option. After a plausible account of his conversion to 'committed intelligence officer' in the course of that
dawn flight to Tehran in 1946, it is as if his text encounters heavy
turbulence. For the next three decades the narrative lurches erratically from minor personal crises to descriptions of scenery and
meetings with famous people until, quite suddenly, it is 1975 'when
I joined the Chase Manhattan Bank'.[1] Subtitled *The Memoirs of an
Intelligence Officer*, the book in fact memorializes no intelligence-
gathering; its main title, *For Lust of Knowing*, invites a '*But Not of
Telling*'.

Miles Copeland, by contrast, told too much. To the spare, professional 'Stan Laurel' of Archie (and later Kim) Roosevelt, the
Alabama-born Copeland would play a robust and earthy 'Hardy'.
Becoming fast friends and close associates during two of Archie's
missing years, Copeland and the younger Roosevelt made an unlikely
duo for the sensitive task of managing an Arab state in accordance
with Truman's doctrine of containing communism. Copeland, 'a brilliant, talented extrovert' in Archie's bespectacled eyes and an outstanding jazz musician in his own, characterized their antics as
'crypto-diplomacy'. In a succession of racy works purporting to
contain 'the confessions of the CIA's original political operative' he
would trot out the psycho-babble, spill the beans and dish the dirt so
freely that even the credulous reader must smell a rat. Where Archie
Roosevelt is evasive, Copeland is effusive, covering his tracks with so
much garrulous chatter that the truth is hard to discern, let alone
credit. Which was, of course, the intention.

No ARAb-Amer. lobby

'If any of you readers are writing Ph.D. theses on post-war Syria you should use your Freedom of Information rights to check out the WEEKAs [weekly intelligence bulletins] coming from Damascus between 1947 and 1950,' booms Copeland in a helpful aside. 'In them you will find history you can *use*.'[2] But the bulletins, on his own admission, comprise edited reports from local agents to whom he had fed the information that Washington liked to hear, then appraised it in the bureaucratic gobbledygook that Washington liked to read. Conversely, the history that the Ph.D. student could *not* use was that provided by Copeland's own technicolour narrative. In writing books, as in crypto-diplomacy, disinformation was the cloak to his dagger.

The dagger, though, was real enough. Archie Roosevelt had been in military intelligence during the Second World War, Copeland with the OSS. After the war both were recruited and trained by the Washington-based Central Intelligence Group, a successor to the OSS which adapted that organization's wartime method of intelligence, propaganda and subversion for Cold War eventualities. Then in September 1947 both men flew together to the Middle East, Roosevelt being accredited to the US embassy in Beirut and Copeland to that in Damascus. Loy Henderson, while still at the State Department in Washington, knew of their role but did not direct the covert operations that it envisaged. By way of various anodyne-sounding offices (of 'Special Operations', 'Policy Co-ordination' and so on) both came under the umbrella of the emerging Central Intelligence Agency (CIA).

Since there was no American-Arab equivalent to the vociferous American Jewish vote, Washington's policy-makers had a freer hand in relations with the Arab world than they did with the Zionists. But initially they showed forbearance, hoping that the Arab states had only to savour representative government and cash in on the bonanza of Arab oil in order to appreciate the values of 'the free world' and spontaneously reject the blandishments of communism. In this connection, Syria's July 1947 elections had been seen as something of a test-case. Rid at last of both British and French troops, the politically alert and largely republican Syrians had gone to the polls with every chance of exercising their vote freely and returning a representative and reform-minded government. To ensure that this would in fact be the case, the US embassy in Damascus supplied the latest in voting machines while US oil companies, much interested in trans-Syrian pipelines, plastered the cities with posters urging the electorate to resist the customary mix of incentives and intimidation and vote as conscience dictated.

The result embarrassed President Shukri al-Quwwatli's ruling National Party (which had succeeded the National Bloc of the French period) by reducing its deputies to 24 while boosting the representation of the reformist opposition parties to 53. But American observers were not impressed by the street battles, the vote-rigging and the blatant venality. Nor were they reassured to find that the balance of power still rested with some 50 independent deputies, all of them devoid of party or programme allegiance and eager only to recoup the expense of election from the rewards of office.

The National Party duly cobbled together another government. Its only notable piece of legislation was a constitutional amendment enabling Shukri al-Quwwatli to stand for another five-year term as president. 'Profiteers rejoiced and scrambled for their share of the loot,' writes Patrick Seale in *The Struggle for Syria*. The old guard, its credentials and policies still founded on the struggle with the French, was back in charge of the spoils. 'Quwwatli himself . . . sat on top of an edifice of nepotism and mismanagement eroded at the base by price inflation, by crop failures . . . and by rumblings of discontent from the emerging labour unions.'[3] Far from making Syrian society immune to leftist ideology, the democratic process was only making it more vulnerable. 'A serious political explosion was looming,' judged Copeland. Clearly, other methods were called for.

Targeting Syria as a test ground, first for spontaneous democratic change, then for covert intervention, seems to have been a conscious decision. According to Copeland, other options, like Iraq and Egypt, were considered but then rejected lest the British cry foul. Unencumbered by an alliance with any of the European powers, Syria was the ideal candidate. Additionally, Damascus's outspoken championship of Palestinian Arab rights and of the Arab League were winning it no friends in the White House, while its acrimonious relationship with neighbouring Turkey, now on the US payroll, supposedly made it receptive to Soviet overtures.

But if the idea of targeting Syria was deliberate, the opportunity for intervention came courtesy of the 1948 Arab-Israeli war. Like other Arab governments, Syria's had excelled in anti-Zionist rhetoric but not, when 15 May dawned, in military commitment. The Syrian army, comprised mainly of the *Troupes Speciales* recruited by the French from the country's Circassian, Armenian, Kurdish, Alawi and Druze minorities, conformed to Koestler's description of 'Levantine mercenaries'. Its sympathies were not closely engaged in the plight of Palestine's Arabs, and it was generally distrusted by the landowning power-brokers of the Syrian political establishment. Accordingly it had of late been starved of equipment and its numbers reduced. The 3,000 men sent to the front were in no shape to take on the Israelis and, apart from a few cross-border acquisitions of no significance, they failed to make any greater impression than Fawzi's Syrian-backed 'Salvation Army'.

Defeat by the Zionists was compounded by a less obvious reverse at the hands of the (Trans)Jordanians. At the time King Abdullah's dealings with the Zionist leadership were merely suspected by the Syrians. But his plans for a Hashemite 'Greater Syria' and his encouragement of secessionist tendencies among the ever restive Druze were well known and induced as much Syrian paranoia as they had French. Arguably the Syrian support given to Fawzi before 15 May, and the commitment of regular Syrian forces thereafter, had little to do with furthering the Arab League's policy of regaining all Palestine and everything to do with frustrating Abdullah's ambitions in the part of Palestine awarded to the Arabs.

In this reading of the war, Arab Palestine is seen as carrion, a juicy carcase no less fiercely contested between the encircling Arab states than by the Zionists. The Egyptians, coveting the Negev, ultimately scavenged a protecting role over the strip that was Gaza. Abdullah's talons clutched the more substantial morsel now known as the West Bank. And in the north, although Syria's posturing, plus Fawzi's squawking, kept Abdullah's Arab Legion out of Galilee, the stand-off only played into Zionist hands. While the Arabs bickered, the Israeli jackal made off with the Galilean titbit. Syria emerged with nothing.

In early 1949, as Egypt and (Trans)Jordan responded to the UN-sponsored armistice and consolidated their Palestine gains, Syria glowered from the sidelines. The government's failure to maintain and equip adequate forces came in for heavy criticism and prompted the increasingly unpopular al-Quwwatli to shuffle portfolios. As chief of staff he appointed Colonel Husni al-Za'im.

'A burly Kurd . . . known for his will of iron and brain to match', according to Copeland, al-Za'im had already been identified by the Americans as a strong but amenable contender for power. Indeed Copeland claims to have engineered al-Za'im's recall to Damascus and, through paid agents within the Syrian defence ministry, to have secured his appointment as military supremo. However this may be, Archie Roosevelt in Beirut and Jim Keeley, the new American ambassador in Damascus, preferred not to expose the ebullient Copeland any further. Instead the Beirut-based Colonel Steve Meade arrived as al-Za'im's handler; and it was Meade, prompted by Copeland, who 'suggested to [al-Za'im] the idea of a coup d'état, advised him how to go about it, and guided him through the intricate preparations in laying the ground work for it'.[4]

Copeland retreated into 'crypto-diplomacy'. In a classic 'sting' he claims to have planted information incriminating himself as a spy in the eyes of the al-Quwwatli government. A night raid on his home by the Syrian *sécurité* followed. Copeland and colleagues were waiting behind the furniture. The ensuing shoot-out lasted twenty-two minutes. In the best Hollywood tradition, no one was hurt, and a subsequent search of the house revealed nothing incriminating. With Copeland loudly protesting his innocence, a stiff US protest was lodged with the government. Meanwhile al-Za'im gratefully added to his catalogue of grievances against the al-Quwwatli regime its inability to afford even basic protection to foreign diplomats.

Whether all this actually happened (and if it did, whether it made any difference) depends on whether one accepts Copeland's 1969 claim that the imminent coup was an all-American affair, or his 1989 claim that, barring the promise of US recognition, 'it was Husni [al-Za'im]'s show all the way'. Suffice it to say that, following extensive US contacts and confident of US support, on the night of 30 March 1949 al-Za'im made his move. In what would become a classic of the CIA training manuals, the Syrian president and prime minister were summarily arrested, all key installations and offices were secured, and next morning Damascus awoke to the national anthem followed by al-Za'im's announcement of a military take-over. It was not 'the first intervention of the army in politics in the Middle East'.[5] The Iraqi army had already intervened repeatedly. But it did set new standards of efficiency, not so say unconstitutionality, in the seizure of power; and al-Za'im was indeed the first military dictator of an independent

Arab state. Both precedents would be much imitated. Within a decade, army coups and military dictators were so commonplace as to be the rule, and not just in the Middle East.

Copeland and his colleagues, for whom failure would have meant being disowned by their own government, now basked in the credit of a job well done. Two years earlier the Truman Doctrine, in justifying support for Greece and Turkey, had declared that 'totalitarian regimes imposed on free peoples by direct or indirect aggression undermine the foundations of international peace and hence the security of the United States'. Now, seemingly, 'free peoples' did not include Arabs, aggression did not include subversion, and Moscow's dirty tricks could usefully be countered in kind. After all, this first attempt at 'interfering in the internal affairs of a sovereign nation', as Copeland nicely puts it, seemed to have been a dazzling success. Meade was soon helping al-Za'im with the selection of his ambassadors; approval for the Syrian section of ARAMCO's TAPline was forthcoming; and an armistice with Israel was signed.

But the satisfaction proved short-lived. As affairs of state pressed upon him, al-Za'im cooled to the buddying of Meade and Copeland and absented himself behind the bullet-proof glass of his motorcade. Self-promoted to general, then marshal and head of state, he had his own ideas about a dictator's responsibilities and energetically embarked on policies of social, electoral and economic reform, alienating and outlawing the political parties in the process while strengthening and re-equipping the army with French assistance. His regime, 'brief, spirited and energetic' according to Seale, 'lay somewhere between political gangsterism and musical comedy'.[6]

What it was not was puppetry. 'Certain *sine qua nons* had been left out of our plans,' noted a rueful Copeland when the man with the iron brain failed to respond to direction. Encased in gold braid and twirling a green and gold baton the size of a rolling pin, al-Za'im stomped the Arab world, wooing then antagonizing Baghdad, insulting Amman by claiming Jordan as a Syrian province, and cultivating the friendship of the Saudi and Egyptian kings, while at home preferring the French ambassador's company to that of the American. It was 'time to be thinking about a replacement', writes Copeland within a paragraph of the congratulatory back-slapping.[7]

The 'replacements' followed thick and fast. Barely twenty weeks after the first coup came the second, and barely eighteen weeks after the second came the third. That was three in a year (1949). A fourth in November 1951 elevated to sole control Adib Shishakli, long the confidant of Archie Roosevelt and Copeland and invariably the brains behind the braid. He lasted a creditable twenty-six months. Since then, says Copeland, for once without exaggeration, 'coups and counter-coups have occurred so frequently in [Syria] that even those of us who know it well are unable to keep track . . .'[8]

Although al-Za'im was shot and then buried in the French cemetery – a favour to the US in that it marked him as a French agent rather than an American one – little blood was shed in these upheavals and political activity sporadically resumed. But the politicians, no less than the dictators, sought legitimation and funds outside Syria as much as within it. Parties, like regimes, were identified with particular foreign alignments. For quite apart from the rivalries between the two superpowers and the two European powers, Damascus was burdened with peculiarly Syrian expectations of reconstituting a supra-national Arab federation or union.

Copeland seems to have been barely aware of these stresses, or indeed of the ethnic and confessional divisions operating within Syrian society. Like other foreign observers, he dismissed such hairsplitting as typical of the sophisticated but volatile and ineffectual nature of the Syrian psyche. That a nation of such modest size and limited capabilities could aspire to Arab centrality, let alone leadership, seemed preposterous. But Syria, as the focus of pan-Arab sentiment since the days of King Faysal, and as the first Arab state (along with the Lebanon) to cut loose from its European apronstrings, could in fact be defined in terms of such ambitions. Itself triumphantly recreated from the mini-states of the French mandate, it looked to the day when the rest of the Arab world would likewise reject colonialism's artificial boundaries and again acknowledge Damascus's leadership.

Of the various constructs on offer, a 'Greater Syria' under Hashemite dominion was probably the least acceptable to most Syrians. But a republican 'Greater Syria' (including Jordan and Lebanon), an 'Arab Fertile Crescent' (with the addition of Iraq), or a pan-Arab federation (including Egypt and/or Saudi Arabia) was confidently expected, actively canvassed, and rarely missing from any political initiative. If Syria seemed a wayward and incomprehensible maverick to outsiders, within the Arab world it epitomized an

orthodox Arabism with which other Arab states, and most notably —
Nasser's Egypt, would willingly associate themselves.

To this revival of the pan-Arab 'dream palace', as Lawrence had
once called it, the Arab-Israeli war and the plight of Palestine had
lent a new logic and a pressing urgency. In every construct of Arab
union, Palestine was a constant. It was the heart of a 'Greater Syria',
the horn of a 'Fertile Crescent' and the axis of any wider federation.
If the Arab states agreed on anything, it was that Palestine must be —
liberated and that this could only be achieved if the Arab world sank —
its rivalries, pooled its military resources, and concerted its diplo- —
matic and economic leverage. —

That, of course, had been the co-ordinating role expected of the
Arab League. But the Cairo-based League, ineffectual in the war, had
become closely associated with Egypt's anti-British and anti-
Hashemite agenda, thus provoking more dissent than consensus.
The 'dream palace' awaited a less compromised prince. And among
those soon actively engaged in the search for such a paragon were
Copeland and his colleagues. With the blueprint of their Syrian coup
discreetly under their belt, by early 1952, writes Copeland, 'we
thought ourselves ready for a major operation and . . . it was finally
decided that Egypt was the place to start'.[9]

OUR MAN IN EGYPT

The Arab-Israeli war was to Arabs simply *al-Nakba*, 'the Disaster'.
The shame of defeat, heightened by the ignominy of utter disarray,
traumatized the whole Arab world. In Iraq, Nuri al-Said responded
in character, cracking down hard on radical pan-Arabists and communists alike, while refusing to conclude an armistice with Israel and
making what capital he could out of Syrian approaches over a union
of the 'Fertile Crescent'. In the Lebanon, by contrast, Riad Solh, the
nationalist prime minister of al-Quwwatli's generation, saw all such
pan-Arab constructs as a threat to his country's still fragile identity.
In 1950, faced with border incursions by the radical Syrian
Nationalist Party, he had Antun Sa-ada, the party's inspirational
leader, executed. Vengeance came the following July when, during
a visit to King Abdullah, Riad Solh was gunned down outside
Amman.

Six days later, on 20 July 1951, while Jordan still reeled over this breach of both security and etiquette, Abdullah attended the al-Aqsa mosque in Jerusalem for Friday prayers and was himself there shot dead at point-blank range. Appropriately, the chess-player's last move had been a visit to the grave of his father, the *sharif* Husayn. Another Husayn, his 16-year-old grandson and eventual successor, was at his side when the shots rang out; the young prince only narrowly avoided accidental death as guards of the Arab Legion fired indiscriminately at the assassin.

Alec Kirkbride, nearing the end of his long term as British minister in Amman, was one of several who claimed to have sensed the danger. Security at the al-Aqsa, he had warned, was impossible to guarantee; the Arab Legion, its ranks swollen by new recruits, was not the compact and dependable force it had once been; Glubb was being openly accused of having betrayed the war effort and Abdullah of having sold out to the Zionists; Palestinians on both sides of the Jordan river were not as enthusiastic about rule from Amman as the King liked to think; in short, 'the atmosphere seemed to reek of murder and violence'. But at the time Kirkbride was on leave in England, and his warnings had gone unheeded.[10]

Among the twenty killed by retaliatory fire in the al-Aqsa mosque was the presumed assassin. His backers supposedly included a disaffected Legion commander, now living in Cairo, plus a member of the Mufti's al-Husayni clan and various lesser agents. Four men were duly tried, convicted and executed; but it was Kirkbride's conviction that Abdullah had been killed less for his Palestinian ambitions than for his pro-British sympathies, and that the real culprit was the fiercely anti-British government in Cairo.

— Of all the Arab states Egypt had suffered the most from *al-Nakba*. As principal sponsor of the Arab League, as the largest contributor of troops and the loudest in its triumphalist rhetoric, Cairo's investment in the war had been commensurate with its ambitions of Arab leadership. But at the end of the war, when Egyptian forces were ignominiously expelled from southern Palestine by the Israelis and when Egyptian territory was itself invaded, the other Arab states had stood by. A series of humiliating defeats then exposed the Egyptian forces as no better equipped or supported than the Syrians. The subsequent recriminations in Cairo duly mirrored those in Damascus. As in Damascus the government bore the brunt of the criticism; but unlike in Damascus the Egyptian government had someone else to blame. The British, it claimed, had hampered operations, supplied defective arms, reneged on the mutual defence clause of the 1936 treaty, and withheld the 'sterling balance' owing to the Egyptian government since the Second World War.

Years later, Gawain Bell, himself once a colonel in the Arab Legion, particularly cherished the account given by an Egyptian major of his part in Egypt's defeat. At the October 1948 siege of Faluja (where units of the Egyptian army had been cut off inside Palestine) there were many desertions; the Israeli bombardment was relentless, the Egyptian ammunition all but exhausted. 'After a great deal of thought', the Egyptian Major judged the situation hopeless and himself slipped away in the dead of night. Making for Gaza, he passed through the Israeli lines and, as day dawned, spied a Bedouin woman sitting on a rock. Still in his uniform and coveting her long dark robes by way of disguise, he approached the woman and offered to buy them. She said nothing and turned away. He doubled his offer. The woman again shook her head. As she did so, her veil slipped. 'Imagine my discomfiture', concluded the Major with a flourish, 'to find myself looking into the harassed face of my own Commanding Officer.'[11]

The Major told his story well and Bell delighted in its self-deprecating drift. Faluja had been the moment of truth for the Egyptian army. The defenders had felt themselves betrayed not only by their allies but by their own government. Yet the surrenders and desertions had been more than matched by extraordinary heroics, among them those of another major, Gamal Abd al-Nasser. Since the humiliation of King Farouq in the Abdin affair, Nasser had become a key figure in an association of 'Free Officers' dedicated to working for the removal of Egypt's constitutional and political structure. Only a change of regime could spare the army from again being sabotaged by the politicians; and this change could only be effected by the army itself.

To Gawain Bell, too, the heroism, the crumbling morale and even the Major's sense of humour had a wider significance. All were 'a symptom of the *fin de siècle* through which Egypt was passing'. Military defeat was being compounded by scandals over the misappropriation of war funds; the British were merely scapegoats. Inflation and profiteering were rampant. 'The poor grew poorer and the rich richer,' wrote Bell; 'if ever a country was ripe for revolution it was Egypt'.[12]

Farouq's amours and eccentricities had become as notorious as his obesity, and the royal debauch seemed to symbolize that of the nation. Parliamentary democracy, such as it was, wilted in the conflagrations and bombings conducted by Marxist cells and the Muslim Brotherhood. The Brothers had been outlawed and responded by assassinating another prime minister. Someone, presumably a government agent, then gunned down Hassan al-Banna, the Brotherhood's founder. Domestic politics were getting out of hand. The traditional parties were being sidelined, their intricate manoeuvres ignored. The game was turning sour. As the historian John Marlowe saw it, 'the spectators were swarming onto the pitch'.[13]

Into this mêlée now boldly blundered the British government. In January 1950, elections in Egypt had produced the usual majority for the Wafd. Farouq, prompted partly by the British, partly by his own belief that a closing of ranks was vital to his survival, invited Mustafa al-Nahas to form his fourth government. Nahas in power was a man the British could deal with. Bevin sounded him out; negotiations over the revision of the 1936 Anglo-Egyptian treaty resumed that summer. As ever, the twin bones of contention were the future of the Sudan and of the occupying British troops in Egypt.

The latter topped the agenda for the British. Trawling through the records to select salient documents for the official history of British disengagement in the Middle East, John Kent would reach the conclusion that '[British] policy was less geared to the ending of informal empire . . . than to preserving it at all costs' and that this had little to do with economic interests or strategic goals and everything to do with 'an emotive or irrational commitment to preserve prestige and status'.[14] Americans suspected as much at the time; indeed imperial hubris was precisely the attitude of which the British had accused the French over the Levant and latterly Indo-China. But to the British, as to the French, 'this fundamental truth' in respect of their own policies was lost beneath a variety of arguments, some commendable and all weighty, yet whose basic dishonesty went unrecognized by either government. It would take the tragedies of Dien Bien Phu in 1954, Suez in 1956 and Iraq in 1958 to undeceive them.

With India lost to the British, oil had replaced empire in these arguments as the proverbial lifeblood of the Canal. Western Europe depended on it; the defence of the oilfields, pipelines and sea-lanes remained paramount; and with military facilities in Israel/Palestine no longer available, the Canal Zone bases were more vital than ever. Never mind the 1936 commitment to reduce British troop numbers to 10,000 (they currently stood at nearly 40,000), never mind Bevin's 1946 offer to evacuate altogether. Surrender of the bases was unthinkable. But if Egypt was adamant, perhaps the British presence could be disguised as an international presence with an overwhelmingly British component. The North Atlantic Treaty Organization (NATO) had lately been set up for the defence of western Europe; and in Korea communism was being contained by UN forces led and largely manned by the US. Perhaps the Canal Zone could be incorporated into a Middle Eastern equivalent of NATO (METO or, as wishful-thinking wits pronounced it, 'Me too'); and perhaps, like the Americans in the Far East, the British in the Middle East could stand forth as the region's international supervisors.

But to Nahas, the Wafd and the Egyptian people, this was all window-dressing. In opposition and now in government, the Wafd was committed to getting the British out and making good on union with the Sudan. There was no room for manoeuvre; by November 1950 the talks had reached deadlock. When Nahas declared the 1936 treaty 'null and void', Jefferson Caffery, the highly regarded US ambassador in Cairo, urged the British to compromise, perhaps by concessions over the Sudan in return for further negotiation over the Canal Zone. The Canal Zone bases (10 airfields, 2 naval dockyards, 34 'military stations', and so on) were, after all, crucial to the defence against communism. But the British refused. Self-determination for the Sudanese lent a righteous gloss to Britain's insistence on retaining her position in the Sudan. The Egyptians were given to understand that guardianship of the Sudanese, like management of the Canal Zone's installations, required skills that they did not possess. It was getting personal.

The talking continued throughout 1951 but to little purpose. Nahas, well past his prime and with a wife who was heavily implicated in the war funds scandal, spent four hours a day closeted in his bathroom; Bevin, who was dying, stood down as Foreign Secretary; and the British Labour government limped towards its defeat in the October elections. In the same month Nahas formally abrogated the 1936 treaty and repeated his demand for complete and instant evacuation.

The British presence was now illegal under Egyptian law. Over 60,000 Egyptian workers in the Canal Zone withdrew their labour; some volunteered for guerrilla training before undertaking acts of sabotage. Against these saboteurs British units pushed out from the Canal Zone in pre-emptive or retaliatory strikes. One such mission on 25 January 1952 surrounded an Egyptian police barracks in Ismailia and demanded that all guns be surrendered. When answered with shots, the British stormed the place, killing at least thirty. The news quickly spread to Cairo.

Next morning was a Saturday, otherwise 'Black Saturday', 'the Day that Cairo Burned'. By 7 a.m. an unprecedented combination of student demonstrators and incensed policemen was surging, arm in arm, through the streets. A government minister endorsed their 'day of vengeance'; radical elements from the political underworld – Brothers with jerrycans and Comrades with Molotov cocktails – infiltrated the demonstrators. At Madame Badia's gambling and belly-dancing establishment an altercation with a mid-morning drinker led to the striking of the first match. The place went up in flames; no one interfered.

This set the pattern for the rest of the day. The preferred targets were symbols either of the British presence, like the offices of BOAC, Thomas Cook, W. H. Smith, Barclays Bank, the British Council, and various showrooms and department stores, or of Western 'culture', like the cinemas, the night-clubs, the tea rooms and the dance halls. Places redolent of both received exceptional attention. Shepheard's Hotel was burnt to the ground, never to rise again; above the smouldering rubble 'the great lift-shafts stood like towers filled with hanging cords and wires', recalled a witness.[15] At the Turf Club escaping members were pushed back into the inferno or beaten to death by the mob. Fire engines had their hoses cut; the flames went uncontrolled, turning the sky red as a pall of smoke trailed away to the south. The seventy-odd fatalities included nine Britons; the damage is said to have cost 15,000 jobs. Yet at the Abdin palace Farouq's luncheon party for 600, including the top military brass, went ahead as scheduled. Not until the evening was the Egyptian army called out to disperse the crowds and restore order.[16]

Nahas immediately declared martial law but was then sacked. His ministry was replaced by one more amenable to the palace, then another and another. Farouq was clutching at straws, treading water in a sea of corruption and intrigue as he swopped charge for counter-charge with the political establishment. The British protested but, rejecting direct military intervention, continued to trot out schemes of regional defence designed to perpetuate their presence. Meanwhile the Free Officers, keen to capitalize on the popular resentment and yet pre-empt a bloodbath, planned their big move.

Into this explosive situation flew Kim Roosevelt, closely followed by Miles Copeland. Kim, christened Kermit, was Archie's first cousin and the son of that other Kermit who had joined the British forces in the First World War (and had tried to do the same in the Second before alcohol led to his suicide). No less of an adventurer than his father, young Kim had spent part of the Second World War in Cairo, there striking up a close relationship with Farouq in the aftermath of the Abdin affair. Courteous, thoughtful, soft-spoken and the perfect gentleman, Kim was universally liked, impeccably connected and 'the last person you would expect to be up to his neck in dirty tricks'. This was the verdict of another Kim, the son of the pro-Saudi 'Jack' Philby; already a Soviet double agent inside British intelligence, Kim Philby knew a dirty trick when he saw one.

Kim Roosevelt, having since pipped cousin Archie to the directorship of CIA operations in the Middle East, revisited Cairo immediately after the Black Saturday riots. The US embassy there had already arranged for a few Egyptian army officers to receive training in the US. Roosevelt's idea was to persuade Farouq to cultivate such military contacts with a view to asserting his authority over the politicians. But this alignment between the palace and the army was stillborn. Farouq, no longer the youthful and charismatic figure whom Roosevelt remembered, was pursuing his own contacts with radical elements such as the Muslim Brotherhood.

Roosevelt returned to Washington; Copeland stayed on in Cairo. Nothing if not resourceful, Copeland's first idea was to manage the King's interest in Islamic revivalism by identifying and promoting an evangelical figure who could play the part of what he called 'the Moslem Billy Graham'. Putting aside his trumpet (he claimed to have once played, and probably had, with the Glenn Miller orchestra), Copeland frequented crowded mosques and late-night prayer meetings. Doubtless the plan had seemed a stroke of genius in Washington; but in Cairo it quickly proved a non-starter. Instead Copeland, with prompting from the US embassy's political staff, was alerted to the existence of the Free Officers movement. The CIA had agreed on a 'conscious though perhaps covert' strategy to cultivate potential pro-Western leaders 'even when they are not in power'.[17] Copeland was doing just that when he held exploratory talks with three of the Free Officers in early March. Later in the month Kim Roosevelt returned to take over the negotiations and for the first time met Nasser.

Copeland's account of these contacts has been questioned by Arab nationalists, especially by the journalist Mohamed Hassanein Heikal, a close associate of Nasser and later editor of the newspaper *Al-Ahram*. Heikal disapproved of Copeland. He had no time for the Alabaman's endless stories, his psychological insights and his back-slapping bonhomie.[18] He resented the suggestion that Nasser, the champion of Arab nationalism and non-alignment, might have owed his elevation to the CIA. And he rightly pounced on the bewildering inconsistencies in Copeland's published account; he 'automatically denies everything I have to say', complained Copeland. In a later book Copeland was therefore at pains to emphasize that he personally did not meet Nasser, that Roosevelt was not present at his first meeting with the Free Officers, and that no coup was discussed there. Copeland merely expressed his government's concern at the turn of events and its willingness to discuss with 'representative and trustworthy army officers . . . what, if anything, we might do to assist in halting a further deterioration of the situation'.[19]

It was Kim Roosevelt who reached an understanding with the Free Officers during the three subsequent meetings – meetings that were, as Copeland puts it, 'prototypical of those preceding political action of the *coup d'état* variety'. In the course of these meetings both sides agreed that it would be a mistake to pin their hopes on a popular revolution that might never materialize. It was therefore, says Copeland, 'understood from the start that the Egyptian army would take control of the country'. The US government, for its part, would not object. Presumably it would recognize and support the new regime while, as one witness suggests, using its good offices to restrain the British from intervention.[20] Additionally it was agreed that phrases like 're-establishing representative government', although employed in public statements, were not to be taken literally. No pressure would be brought to bear for the restoration of 'democratic processes' since the preconditions 'did not exist and wouldn't exist for many years'.

Coup and Countercoup

On three issues agreement proved impossible: Israel, Farouq and the British. But Copeland judged that, despite appearances, defending Palestinian rights was not an overwhelming priority for most Egyptians. He also reckoned that if the Free Officers insisted on the removal of Farouq, it would not be in US interests to oppose it. As for the British, if the Officers also insisted on their removal, the US would be well placed to advise caution and could only gain from acting as arbiter. Officially it was not to be America's coup any more than al-Za'im's had been; but there was some satisfaction in the fact that it was more America's than Britain's. Finally, lest the Syrian experience prejudice Washington's support, Roosevelt emphasized that the Free Officers professed only 'standard' motivations, not outsize ones like al-Za'im. Once in power, they should therefore be both more acceptable to the Egyptians and more 'reasonable and flexible'.

This confidence was not misplaced. Contacts with Nasser and his Free Officers continued for the next three months as they laid their plans. The US embassy was informed when the coup was imminent, and the ambassador Caffery then issued a statement ('the policy of the US is not to interfere in the domestic politics of another country') that could be read either as a disclaimer or as an encouragement but not as a coincidence.

A week later the coup was staged amid rumours of a counterstroke against the Free Officers. In a carbon copy of al-Za'im's putsch, overnight on 22–23 July 1952 army units rolled up to the Abdin palace, to the military headquarters, radio station, telephone exchange and airports. Other members of the Officers' inner circle took over command of different sections of the Egyptian armed forces. By breakfast time Anwar Sadat, the Officer in charge of communications, was informing the nation that the army had seized power to purge the country of 'traitors and weaklings'. Farouq, who qualified as both, was passing the hot weather in his Alexandria palace. There he was surrounded. Meanwhile approach roads from the Canal Zone were being carefully watched lest the British try to interfere.

In fact the British, unlike the Americans, were taken completely by surprise. But the coup having apparently passed off without hitch or bloodshed, and reassurances having been received from the new regime, London saw no cause to object. Sadat's announcement had been made in the name of a respected figure, the pipe-smoking

General Mohamed Neguib. The Revolutionary Command Council (RCC), which Neguib headed, promptly reinstated a reform-minded prime minister at the head of a civilian government. Even the monarchy was not actually abolished. Farouq was obliged to sail off into the sunset in the royal yacht, aboard which he had stashed a considerable quantity of the nation's gold, but a regency council was set up in the name of his son, the young Prince Fuad.

For a revolution this was not particularly revolutionary. The army returned to barracks, and Nasser maintained a low profile. The British hoped that they might yet get to stay on in the Canal Zone, 'the free world' that it might yet get an Egyptian 'bulwark' against communism, and the US that it had at last secured the goodwill of the most important Arab state. British treaty negotiations were soon resumed; Washington pored over Egypt's military and economic requirements. There was much to be gained, it seemed, and little to be feared, from the new regime.

FIFTY-FIFTY

History locates the 1952 Egyptian revolution in the foreground of a short perspective down which the eye is quickly led, past Soviet weapons deals and Western protests, to the 1956 showdown of the Suez war. It did not appear that way at the time. Contemporary observers scanned the existing geopolitical horizon and looked to their maps. China had fallen to the communists. India, Burma and Indonesia were independent, Indo-China rapidly becoming so; even Africa was stirring. All the signs indicated an ineluctable retreat from colonialism. The colonial powers might try to manage this process to their own and the free world's advantage, but a concerted effort to reverse the trend seemed most unlikely.

The Egyptian revolution neither altered this perception nor upset the East-West balance of power. It also happened to coincide with a more protracted and, to the Western powers, a much more menacing Middle Eastern crisis that involved Iran and the fate of the Anglo-Iranian Oil Corporation (AIOC). In Iran between 1951 and 1953 all that was unthinkable in terms of the British economy and unacceptable in terms of superpower rivalry looked to be coming to pass. If British negotiators in Cairo dragged their feet over troop evacuations it was because a repeat of the Iranian situation must at all costs be avoided. Likewise, if Nasser eventually came to regard the national-ization of the Suez Canal as a feasible proposition it was because of the Iranian precedent in seizing Abadan and the oilfields. As for the CIA's involvement in the Egyptian revolution, it seemed to be con-firmed beyond doubt when the Cairo coup, preceded by the Syrian test-run, was promptly followed by the CIA's triumphant 'counter-coup' in Tehran. The juicy yarns retailed by Miles Copeland acquired substance, 'crypto-diplomacy' seemed vindicated. The reinstated Shah of Iran would confirm as much in August 1953. Raising a glass to Kim Roosevelt, he reportedly declared that he owed his throne 'to God, my people, my army – and to you'.[21]

Unmuddied by Anglo-Arab ties or American-Jewish voting pat-terns, the Iranian affair revealed the stark realities of British decline and American ascendancy. In effect, the CIA's reinstatement of the Shah meant the replacement of British influence with American. The US would retain this paramount position in Iran for a quarter of a century, so rendering the country a buttress to 'the northern tier' of front-line states – Greece, Turkey and Iraq – ranged along commu-nism's southern flank.

In this respect Iran/Persia fulfilled the role in south-west Asia that Siam/Thailand played in south-east Asia. The two countries had much in common. Both had been spared colonial rule in the nine-teenth century thanks to their buffer locations between rival imperi-alisms – French and British in the case of Thailand, Russian and British in the case of Iran. With some success their respective sover-eigns had continued to play off one colonial suitor against the other until the Second World War, thus substantially preserving their terri-torial integrity while perpetuating their economic, political and mili-tary vulnerability. The Azerbaijan crisis of 1946 and concurrent Soviet moves in eastern Europe demonstrated the dangers of repris-ing this independent role in a new, ideologically polarized world. Passive neutrality and buffer status were no longer options. In the Tudeh (or People's Party), Iran, like Thailand, had its communists; and, as elsewhere, the communists found a ready target in ruling élites unsecured by either a powerful state apparatus or a popular mandate. Conservative regimes founded on patronage and privilege needed the support of the West as much as the West needed their concurrence in the containment of communism.

But where Iran differed from Thailand was in its oil reserves. Not only was the Abadan refinery now the largest in the world but the AIOC's Iranian installations represented Britain's greatest overseas investment. This might have made for excellent relations founded on an identity of interests. The impoverished Iranian economy was being primed with oil royalties, while Britain's petroleum concerns in Iran neatly underpinned America's strategic concerns. But any such complacency ignored two crucial factors: the highly competitive nature of the oil business and the appeal of Iranian nationalism as an outlet for social discontent.

Oil set the ball rolling. Mexico had nationalized its oil industry in 1938, Venezuela had negotiated the first 50:50 division of profits with the oil companies in 1943, and the Soviet government had endorsed this principle in the Middle East during its abortive negotiations for an Iranian concession in 1946. Saudi Arabia, following a blip in demand and so in its revenues, requested a similar division of the spoils in 1949. In that year ARAMCO, while paying $39 million in royalties to Riyadh, had paid $43 million into the US Treasury in tax. King Saud's advisers thought this unfair. But anxious not to disturb the goose, merely to secure more of the golden eggs, they sought the services of an adviser on US tax law and so fortuitously discovered the potential of the 'foreign tax credit'.

This arrangement permitted US companies to deduct the amount they paid in overseas taxes from their tax liability in the US. It was not immediately clear whether the arrangement would apply to the rents ARAMCO paid to the Saudi government; but under pressure from the US State Department and after consultation with the Treasury Department, ARAMCO agreed to the 50:50 deal. The threat of nationalization had not been raised by the Saudis. The State Department was simply mindful of US interests in the region and anxious to provide a good client with the means to develop his country, subsidize his wayward tribes, acquire American arms and generally maintain his authority. In that the foreign tax credit was indeed eventually approved, the new arrangement cost ARAMCO nothing and had no effect on the competitive price of its Saudi crude. The only losers were the US Treasury and the tax-paying American public.

The administration was not unhappy about this. By foregoing revenue which now went straight to Riyadh, the US became in effect the Saudi kingdom's paymaster and guarantor on a grand scale. Moreover, it had achieved this desirable position without antagonizing the oil companies, without embarrassing King Saud in the eyes of his subjects, and without submitting the matter to the scrutiny of Congress, whose approval and supervision were essential to conventional aid packages.

According to the Assistant Secretary of State (as paraphrased by Daniel Yergin in his epic history of the oil industry), the deal 'was not a sleight of hand'.[22] After all, US national interests were very much at stake. Saudi oil was 'probably the richest economic prize in the world in the field of foreign investment', said the State Department's Petroleum Division; the Dhahran airfield, already upgraded for military use and with its lease just renewed, was America's only base in the Middle East; and Saudi Arabia, according to a military analyst, was 'strategically the most important nation in the Arabian peninsula, and the Arabian peninsula the most important area in the Middle East-Mediterranean region'.[23] As for the foreign tax credit, the discovery that it might apply to oil rents was certainly timely, even surprising. But it was not new, it was a necessary incentive for US companies operating overseas, and it was perfectly legitimate.

Congress would nevertheless take a dim view of the affair in later discussions. And London was appalled the moment it got wind of the deal. The AIOC took it as a hostile bid by the US oil industry to discredit, and eventually muscle in on, its Iranian operations. The Prime Minister, Attlee, actually compared the Saudi 50:50 arrangement to the trauma of Indian independence in its implications for the British position in the Middle East.[24] At the time, late 1950, the AIOC was in the midst of complicated negotiations of its own over a supplemental oil agreement with the Tehran government. This offered improved royalties for the Iranians that fell well short of a 50:50 profits share-out and certainly did not commit the British government to foregoing its own tax receipts. But the supplemental agreement, although accepted by the Iranian government, was stalled in the Majlis, the national assembly. There a committee headed by Muhammad Musaddiq, leader of the populist National Front, opposed the agreement on principle and demanded the cancellation of the AIOC's concession and the nationalization of all its facilities.

News of the Saudi-ARAMCO deal came after these demands had been formulated; it did not precipitate them. Musaddiq was a fervent and incorruptible nationalist. He saw the AIOC's pervasive presence as detrimental to Iran's sovereignty and a baneful influence in domestic politics. Oil receipts were not for him the basic issue. But news of the Saudi-ARAMCO deal did lend substance to his accusations of British exploitation while doing nothing to blunt his rhetoric. It is possible that, had the AIOC promptly matched ARAMCO's 50:50 share-out, Musaddiq would have felt obliged to capitulate. The US government urged the British to make such a concession, but by the time the AIOC reluctantly did so, it was too late. In March 1951 the then prime minister was assassinated by a member of the Iranian equivalent of the Muslim Brotherhood. Musaddiq succeeded him in April and on 1 May the Shah signed a bill, just passed by the Majlis, that nationalized the Iranian oil industry.

Where this left the world's third largest crude supplier was at first unclear. A US mission, then a British mission, descended on Tehran during 1951 but failed to find a compromise acceptable to Musaddiq. Celebrating crowds surged down the city's boulevards; in Abadan sheep were ritually slaughtered and the AIOC's signboards overpainted. Six months ahead of their Canal Zone cousins, 12,000 Iranian oil workers walked out on the company. Refining operations were scaled down as holding tanks filled to their brims. The head of the British mission sought to highlight the dereliction by declaring that 'grass was growing in the streets of Abadan', an emotive notion but a horticultural impossibility. Meanwhile the British government imposed economic sanctions; tanker traffic was stopped, Iranian assets frozen and military action threatened. In London 'Mossy' was variously demonized as a rabble-rousing 'lunatic' or a paranoid charlatan. Bent, bald and with a nose like a stalactite ever adrip, he was a gift to the cartoonists and, often seen in olive pyjamas, attracted the popular ridicule once reserved for the *dhoti*-clad Gandhi.

But in Iran as in Egypt Attlee shrank from 'the splutter of musketry' advocated by Churchill and the Conservatives. Military moves were planned but never executed. When in September 1951 the AIOC's British staff were abruptly expelled, the cruiser HMS *Mauritius* steamed into Abadan not to support them but to evacuate them. Nationalization, after all, was not in itself objectionable. In fact it was the British Labour government's own panacea for economic recovery. Among the UK's industrial and infrastructural assets lately acquired by Whitehall were the coal mines, the country's principal energy resource. Musaddiq could claim to be doing for Iran's oil precisely what Attlee had done for Britain's coal. For the latter now to insist on denationalization at the point of a gun was scarcely a palatable option, particularly when the beneficiaries would be the quintessentially capitalist AIOC and its mainly corporate shareholders (among whom the British government was the principal). Attlee was hoist on his own socialist petard.

Additionally, American warnings that precipitate action might edge Iran towards the Soviet camp held out little promise of US support. Nor, as the crisis dragged on, did armed intervention seem quite so imperative. With the US, the UN and then the Court of International Justice in The Hague all becoming involved, a negotiated settlement was still possible. The loss of Iranian oil production was being made good from other sources under an Anglo-American deal. And Musaddiq's intransigence, though ecstatically hailed by his supporters, had yet to pay off. Mass rallies and theatrical speeches pumped no oil, filled no mouths, built no schools, created no jobs. Musaddiq's back was bent beneath the weight of national expectation, his paranoia dictated by the knowledge that, as in Damascus, governments could be toppled by other than gunboats.

SHOWDOWN IN TEHRAN

In London as early as June 1951 the Foreign Office had been in touch with Dr Ann Lambton, a Persian scholar whose long residence in Iran made her a leading authority on the country. No fan of Musaddiq, she advised against making any concessions. Support of Musaddiq was not as unanimous as it appeared and might, thought Lambton, be eroded 'by covert means'. The AIOC was being used as a scapegoat for a wounded nation's pride and as a focus for all manner of social, economic and political grievances. Redirect these grievances and Musaddiq would be isolated. Many Iranians, including the young Shah, accepted that the reforms desired by the aggrieved (like land redistribution, industrialization and social provision) ultimately depended on Western aid and so on a settlement of the oil dispute. In the climate of anti-British hysteria such 'moderates' hesitated to speak out; but a discreet exercise in public relations would encourage them; and according to Miss Lambton, the man to conduct it was another academic, currently at Oxford, called Robin Zaehner. Zaehner had been in Tehran during the 1940s conducting covert propaganda against the Russian presence in Azerbaijan. To Tehran he now speedily returned.

He arrived in the late summer of 1951, just ahead of Christopher Montague Woodhouse, another experienced British practitioner in the arts of espionage. During the Second World War the decidedly dashing 'Monty' Woodhouse had served with distinction in SOE as a saboteur and resistance leader in mainland Greece. In 1949, 'when the Cold War looked like becoming hot', he was approached about heading a section of MI6, Britain's equivalent of the CIA. He accepted and promptly identified Iran 'as the likeliest target for the next round of Soviet expansion'. The AIOC crisis confirmed his judgement. He claims to have been convinced that Musaddiq's support depended heavily on the communist Tudeh party and that his government, if not toppled by a pro-Western coup, would be supplanted by a pro-Soviet one.

Building on Zaehner's contacts while himself remaining undercover, Woodhouse recruited a network of agents. They included a highly placed official who fed him 'intimate details from within the Iranian administration', several tribal leaders and military figures outside Tehran, and within the city an influential mercantile family, two of whom, 'the brothers', controlled their own network of officials, opinion-makers and mobsters. Woodhouse supplied them all with funds – £10,000 a week in the case of 'the brothers' – and on at least one occasion he organized arms shipments, flying the guns in from Iraq and then surreptitiously stashing them in the desert.[25]

Following the change of government in London in late 1951, the new Foreign Secretary pulled the plug on Zaehner's propaganda operation. Woodhouse and MI6 continued in the field alone. Indeed by mid-1952 they were ready to move; by then 'we had the means to overthrow Musaddiq and forestall a revolution by the Tudeh party', says Woodhouse. But the Shah, a young, untried figure at the time, was reluctant to commit himself without a clear sign from the new British government; and the British in turn hesitated to move without an assurance of support from Washington.

Meanwhile the Soviet-sensitive Loy Henderson had arrived as US ambassador to Iran; Musaddiq had amassed more powers following a bloody trial of strength with the Shah; the Court of International

Justice had declared the oil dispute beyond its competence; and the Egyptian revolution had come and gone. In October Woodhouse's informants reported plans for an imminent break in diplomatic relations. The entire British embassy staff, Woodhouse and Zaehner included, were given ten days to clear out. With MI6's operation thrown into jeopardy, Woodhouse desperately contrived new channels for the outward flow of intelligence and the inward flow of cash using colleagues in the CIA. He then flew to London for consultations with Eden, the Foreign Secretary, then back to the Middle East to set up a communications centre in Cyprus for handling contacts with Iran, then on to Washington. General Eisenhower had just won a Republican victory in the November presidential elections. Though Eden was cool to the idea of an Iranian coup, Woodhouse, possibly primed by Loy Henderson, hoped for better things from Eisenhower and his Secretary of State designate, John Foster Dulles.

Like Copeland and the Roosevelts, Woodhouse would later write an account of his Iranian activities which ran up against the usual constraints of confidentiality. But as an Oxford prodigy with a peer for a father and a countess for a wife, he solved the problem of censorship by liberally indulging the upper-class Englishman's penchant for understatement and allusion. The result, though urbane and entertaining, is no more generous with names, dates and details than the memoirs of his CIA colleagues. 'The brothers' on whom he principally depended (although he claims never knowingly to have met them) were subsequently identified as the immensely wealthy Rashidians; but of contacts with Loy Henderson, who 'changed the atmosphere in the US embassy towards sympathy with the British', there is barely mention; nor of when, where and to what extent he was already colluding with 'James F. Lochridge', otherwise the ubiquitous Kim Roosevelt.

Roosevelt, still head of the CIA in the Middle East, had begun taking an interest in Iran immediately after the July 1952 coup in Cairo. During several visits in the second half of that year he assessed the situation and expanded the CIA's own network of agents; like MI6's operation, it depended heavily on two influential but unnamed brothers. In November, while Woodhouse was testing the waters in Washington, Roosevelt *en route* from Tehran stopped in London and was approached by MI6. 'What they had in mind was nothing less than the overthrow of [Musaddiq],' he reports with a sharp intake of breath, tongue somehow firmly in cheek. His family name, his pro-British sympathies and his professional status recommended him to MI6 as the ideal person to champion the Woodhouse plan in Washington. More to the point, with Woodhouse unable to return to Tehran, Roosevelt's part in the Cairo coup made him the ideal person to execute the Iranian coup, should it be approved.

Roosevelt would always insist that the Iranian coup was in fact a 'counter-coup', a move to restore the legitimate government, represented by the Shah and the Majlis, which Musaddiq and his communist 'allies' were endeavouring to usurp. He had originally been recruited into military intelligence, and thence the CIA, on the strength of a paper he had written about clandestine state security services which, he claims, was itself based on his postgraduate doctoral thesis on the propaganda techniques used during the English Civil War. The young Kim Roosevelt evidently knew his Stuarts, his Cromwell and his Milton; a throne abolished might be restored, a revolution accomplished might be discredited, a paradise lost regained.

In Tehran, as in Cairo, while analysing the political landscape in terms of its component power groups, he found familiar parallels. The Shah and the Majlis, the one as indecisive and the other as unrepresentative as their seventeenth-century English equivalents, were being challenged by an unholy alliance of social levellers (the communists), religious fanatics (the ayatollahs), tract-waving intellectuals (journalists and academics), burgers (the mercantile classes), squires (Musaddiq was himself a landowner), the army and the urban proletariat. Some of these elements, especially in the army and among the squirearchy and the money-men, needed little persuading to turn against Musaddiq, just timely encouragement. Others could be bought with cash, like the mob and the intellectuals. Yet others could be detached by subterfuge; desecrating a few mosques in the name of the communist Tudeh and publicizing Musaddiq's supposed dealings with that ungodly party duly won over the ayatollahs. Methodically Roosevelt ticked them off in his mind as to each element he assigned its operatives and its budget.

MI6 favoured an agreed plan of action; Roosevelt wanted a free hand. With the British Foreign Office (as opposed to MI6) still reluctant, the Americans had their way. The British were to mobilize the tribes, the Americans to work on the armed forces, and both through their respective 'brothers' (who were fortunately not the same) to exercise all the influence they could in Tehran. Agreement was also reached on the general who was to replace Musaddiq as prime minister and on the outline of the post-coup settlement.

But the Eisenhower administration did not take office until late January 1953. It then needed some convincing that the operation was not being undertaken simply for the AIOC's benefit, that it would actually succeed, and that the outcome was worth the risks. Among the British there was some well-founded scepticism about whether the Soviets really had designs on Iran and whether Musaddiq would ever be eased aside by the Tudeh. Such doubts, though, were not allowed to cloud their presentation. In Washington, Monty Woodhouse 'decided to emphasise the Communist threat to Iran rather than the need to recover control of the oil industry';[26] likewise his British colleagues played on the anti-communist hysteria currently being whipped up in the US by Senator Joe McCarthy. Seemingly neither the British nor the Americans were troubled by the prospect of overturning a government which, for all its faults, was popular, legitimate, comparatively liberal, and now itself committed to an ambitious programme of reforms.

As chronicled in Kim Roosevelt's *Countercoup*, it was the influence of a third set of brothers, Allen Dulles as head of the CIA and John Foster Dulles as Secretary of State, that finally prevailed in Washington. The go-ahead for what MI6 had called 'Operation Boot' but which the CIA now honoured with the title of 'Ajax' was agreed in principle in March and confirmed in June. But unmentioned by Roosevelt and outside the administration's smoke-filled chambers, another meeting of minds may also have been decisive. It seems to have been at about this time that, at the instigation of their respective governments, representatives of the AIOC and of various US oil companies reached an understanding about the future of Iranian oil. Once the coup had succeeded, the AIOC was to surrender its monopoly and retain only a 40 per cent share; another 20 per cent was to go to Royal Dutch Shell and a French company; the remaining 40 per cent was to go to US companies. The deal was complicated by an anti-trust suit pending against the US oil companies and by the compensation terms demanded by the AIOC. But at governmental level the whole arrangement now looks suspiciously like a *quid pro quo*. London was forgoing part of its oil concession in return for Washington's adoption and funding of the originally British scheme now known as Operation Ajax.

CIA, oil, Republicans

It was perfectly normal for Republican administrations to recognize their responsibilities to big business. Moreover individual members of the Eisenhower administration, including the Dulles brothers, had close links with the oil companies. So too did Herbert Hoover, Junior, a noted oil-man who was also a close friend of the Roosevelts and himself the son of a president. As chairman of the National Security Council board that approved all funds for covert operations, Hoover is credited with having forged an alliance between the CIA and the oil companies. In Iran, as in Saudi Arabia, this combination would now spearhead US policy and challenge even the State Department as its effective agent.[27]

With the deals done, the responsibilities allocated, and a war-chest of $1 million waiting in Tehran, in July 1953 Kim Roosevelt flew to Beirut and headed east by road. 'My nerves tingled, my spirits soared as we moved up the mountain road to Damascus,' he would recall. Thence to Baghdad along Brooks-Murdoch's highway he drove through the night, stopping for a dawn stretch at 'Rutbah Wells'. A sentence from one of his father's books came back to him: 'it was a great adventure and all the world was young'. He grabbed a good night's sleep in Baghdad, left in the early hours of the following morning, crossed the Iranian border undetected by the dozy officials, and slipped unnoticed into Tehran on the evening of the 20th. Exactly a month later he would be the toast of the town.

Yet it was far from plain sailing. Bugged by alarms and complications, the coup – or counter-coup – fell short of the copy-book affair of later myth. Much of the blame lay with the Shah who, cautious, canny or plain scared, hung back until the last moment. At the instigation of Steve Meade of the Damascus coup, Princess Ashraf, the Shah's twin sister who was in exile in Switzerland, risked a visit to Tehran; she was followed by General Norman Schwarzkopf who had commanded the local gendarmerie during the war. Both were thought to have influence with the Shah but neither was able to get a firm commitment from him. In early August, therefore, Roosevelt himself had to break cover for a series of highly dangerous excursions to the royal palace at dead of night. As the grandson of a president and the 'personal emissary' of Eisenhower, Roosevelt was trusted. But the Shah still insisted on confirmation of British support. It eventually came via a coded message over the BBC.

Then on 16 August, at the height of the operation, the Shah suddenly flew to Baghdad, then Rome. Putting the best possible gloss on this move, Roosevelt made out that he had been forced into exile. In fact he had fled, and not without reason. The coup had misfired. Brandishing an imperial order for the dismissal of Musaddiq, Colonel Nasiri of the Imperial Palace Guard had presented himself at the prime minister's residence with the idea of taking Musaddiq into custody but had promptly been himself overpowered and arrested. Musaddiq had evidently received prior warning. Further arrests followed; thousands of mainly Tudeh supporters took to the streets to revile the Shah and denounce the US.

The reports forwarded via Cyprus prompted doom and despondency in Washington. 'We now have to . . . snuggle up to [Musaddiq],' advised the Assistant Secretary of State. Ambassador Loy Henderson, who for form's sake had been keeping out of the way, rushed back to Tehran on a damage-limitation mission. Only Roosevelt stayed calm. In what was surely his finest hour, he moved into a bunker with a radio set and from there organized a city-wide distribution of the imperial orders dismissing Musaddiq and orchestrated the network of agents painstakingly built up by MI6 and the CIA. On the 18th, following his urgent requests, troops loyal to the Shah were reported moving on the capital. 'We had what we needed,' wrote Roosevelt with a long sigh of relief. The news was spread throughout the city. To capitalize on it, the various 'brothers' were ordered to bring out their hired support on the following day.[28]

'This was, to be sure, the showdown,' says Roosevelt. But it was a confused affair, and as much about show business as politics. The 'brothers' had hired every juggler, wrestler, tumbler and fire-eater they could find. At the head of a well-armed, well-paid mob these bazaar celebrities took to the streets, proclaiming loyalty to the Shah and death to his godless opponents. The police joined them; Tudeh supporters were attacked. Musaddiq, forced to flee, was captured and detained. By midday the struggle was over. As Roosevelt put it, 'the Shah was in'. His picture, hastily printed by CIA agents, decked the city. Roosevelt, Henderson and the four other Americans in the know quietly celebrated.

The Shah returned in triumph on the 23rd. He was met at the airport by his new prime minister and cheered all the way to the palace. As foreseen, most Iranians probably did welcome an end to the confrontation and hardship of the Musaddiq years. Two days later, Kim Roosevelt was himself at the airport. He left as unobtrusively as he had arrived, but warmed now by the gratitude of the Shah and the satisfaction of having masterminded the most ambitious coup on record.

Estimates of the cost vary. Perhaps two hundred lives were lost in the street battles, and anything up to $10 million of British and US funds expended. But this was little compared to the subventions and aid that followed; and the dividends were at least commensurate. British face was saved. The AIOC was renamed British Petroleum (or BP) and its oil interests, if not its market share, were secured. Arguably, if less creditably, it was the success of the Iranian 'counter-coup' that would embolden Anthony Eden to attempt his own master-stroke over Suez.

More certainly, 'with the establishment of the Iranian [oil] consortium,' writes Daniel Yergin, 'the United States was now *the* major player in the oil, and the volatile politics, of the Middle East'.[29] Among those US advisers who were soon pouring into Iran was Colonal Steve Meade. His task was to organize for the Shah an internal intelligence service, the notorious Savak. For the next twenty-five years, until the Iranian revolution, Savak and the Shah's lavishly re-equipped armed forces would indeed make of Iran the desired bulwark against communism. But public acknowledgement of the CIA's role in overturning a genuinely nationalist government, and the extent of subsequent US involvement in the Shah's rapacious regime, invited popular hostility. When in 1978–9 the crowds again took to the streets and the Shah to his heels, the flag that was burnt for the benefit of every news bulletin was the Stars and Stripes.

16

Game Up

SCUTTLING EGYPT

SIR HUMPHREY TREVELYAN credits Arabic with a saying to the effect that when, in the depths of the ocean, two fish fight, the British are behind it. Arriving as Her Majesty's ambassador to Egypt in August 1955, Trevelyan was at first inclined to think the adage unfair and the British no more devious than anyone else. In the subaquatic world of Middle Eastern affairs nothing was quite as it seemed. Dark deals and long-line intrigues lay behind every development and made a nonsense of conventional diplomacy. Americans and Russians, Arabs and Israelis, French as well as British were all, as he puts it, 'widely believed to be not wholly averse from some of the fashionable methods of influencing policy'. After postings in India and China, Trevelyan found that it was the Middle East that was a 'jungle'. 'Bribery, subversion, revolutionary conspiracy were common and no government which had the means, was innocent of these expediences in the conduct of international relations.'[1]

Just how bad the situation was dawned on him slowly. On 27 September, seven weeks after his arrival, he was instructed to pay an after-hours call on Colonel Gamal Abd al-Nasser. The West's honeymoon with the Egyptian revolution was coming to an acrimonious end amid news of a massive Egyptian arms purchase from the Soviet

Union. Trevelyan was to ask Nasser for the facts and warn him of the consequences if the deal went ahead.

Hastening across the Nile to the headquarters of the Revolution Command Council, he found the lights still burning. Nasser received him briskly. The deal was already done, he was told. It did not mean that Egypt had become a Soviet satellite, merely that, denied the means of defending herself by the Western powers, she had been obliged to look elsewhere. Full details would be made public shortly; the West had only itself to blame. Trevelyan was back in his black limousine within five minutes. The Colonel was obviously busy.

In fact he had company. 'I learnt afterwards', says a frosty Trevelyan, that 'he was entertaining two Americans, not members of the [US] embassy'.[2] He was indeed. Upstairs in the same building, observing the ambassador's arrival, Kim Roosevelt and Miles Copeland paused in their efforts to draft Nasser's announcement of the arms deal and helped themselves to a whisky as they waited for their host's return. How would it be, they joked, if one of them popped downstairs to ask Gamal where he kept the soda? At this defining moment in the West's relations with Egypt, when arguably the security of the Middle East and so of the whole 'free world' lay in tatters, London would not have been amused to learn that senior members of the CIA were enjoying a convivial evening with the Egyptian leader.

The US ambassador in Cairo was no better informed. He was unaware even that Roosevelt and Copeland were in town. Ambassador Henry ('Hank') Byroade had replaced Jefferson Caffery earlier in the year and was that evening attending a dinner party. When, hours late and still mightily pleased with themselves, Nasser and his advisers swept into the room arm-in-arm with Roosevelt and Copeland, Byroade was 'stunned'. Already smarting over the weapons deal, he took his feelings out on the Egyptians. According to Copeland, 'he launched into a tirade' about Egypt being a police state and the Revolution Command Council (RCC) 'behaving like a lot of juvenile delinquents'.[3] Next day he apologized. Fortunately Nasser bore no grudge and Byroade was 'most easy-going'. The fault lay elsewhere. As Copeland saw it, this short-circuiting of diplomacy was just 'the sort of thing which happened under Secretary [of State John Foster] Dulles'.[4] To Byroade as to Trevelyan the continual crossing of wires, the unheralded antics of the CIA (not to mention

MI6), and the ambiguities in both policy and direction which they betrayed, boded ill for crisis management.

After seizing power in the July 1952 coup, the Free Officers of the RCC had used the past three years to consolidate their revolution. Political parties had been banned, the post-coup ministry dismissed, and the old political hierarchy superseded. While Roosevelt was busy organizing the Iranian coup, Copeland claims to have been entrusted with the task of setting up Egypt's internal intelligence service. A crackdown on the communists was launched in 1952; the Muslim Brotherhood was banned and its adherents arrested in January 1954. Meanwhile, in June 1953, the regency council had been disbanded, the monarchy abolished, and a republic declared. Briefly the affable General Neguib served as both president and prime minister, but in February 1954 he resigned as the latter and in December was dismissed as the former. Nasser, as chairman of the RCC, succeeded him in both posts.

In accordance with Kim Roosevelt's pre-coup undertaking, little US pressure was brought to bear for the early restoration of democracy. Having established what Copeland calls 'a repressive base', the RCC's priority was social and economic reform. A ceiling on land ownership was imposed, royal estates requisitioned, the resulting acreage redistributed to the *fellahin*, and co-operatives encouraged. Titles such as pasha and bey were summarily abolished. To balance the budget, expenditure was cut, imports controlled and the cotton trade regulated. Private enterprise and foreign investment were encouraged, while the government investigated more ambitious schemes of desert reclamation, irrigation and industrialization. The state was becoming intimately involved in economic management. But the reforms stopped well short of the command economy and the collectivized production typical of the Soviet system. As revolutions go, it was overdue, popular and internationally acceptable.

So was Nasser's settlement with the British. The negotiations over the 1936 treaty – essentially about the status of the Sudan and the Canal Zone – had resumed in 1952 and, belying their intractable reputation, been successfully concluded in 1954. A new era of Anglo-Egyptian 'co-operation and mutual understanding' was dawning, according to the agreement. This was all the more surprising in that the contracting party in London was the arch-imperialist Winston Churchill at the head of a Conservative government in which

Anthony Eden, architect of the 1936 treaty, was Foreign Secretary. But it helped that the RCC, unlike the Sidqi ministry with which Bevin had dealt, was not vulnerable to domestic criticism or, like the Wafd, wedded to an unnegotiable position. The removal of Farouq and eventual abolition of the monarchy also helped in so far as the union of Egypt and the Sudan 'under the Egyptian crown' thereby lost both its logic and its most ardent supporter. Agreement over a three-year transition period in the Sudan, at the end of which the Sudanese would decide between union with Egypt and independence, had been reached in February 1953.

The future of the Canal Zone had been less easily resolved. Evicting foreign troops, ending British influence and redeeming Egypt from its seventy years of imperialist domination lay at the heart of the revolution. Attacks on British installations had continued after the 1952 coup, and from powerful new transmitters Radio Cairo bombarded the Arab world with anti-British invective. London responded more subtly through MI6-controlled outlets like the Cyprus-based Near East Broadcasting Service. When either broadcaster devoted air time to two fish fighting, the news lay neither in the fish nor the fight but in the fact of it being reported.

The pressure for an Anglo-Egyptian settlement had come mainly from Washington. But following John Foster Dulles's May 1953 visit to the region, US policy had veered away from the British-backed idea of making Egypt the linchpin of a Middle East Defence Organization (METO or MEDO) that would complement NATO and SEATO (the South-East Asia Treaty Organization). Dulles, no fan of European colonialism, readily sympathized with Nasser's objections. Why should Egypt be dragooned into the defence of a 'free world' which was substantially composed of colonial powers unsympathetic to Arab aspirations? To the Egyptian people the positioning of foreign troops on Egyptian soil, howsoever presented, would appear as a 'perpetuation of occupation'. Egypt, Nasser insisted, did need defending, did need rearming, but against an immediate and aggressive neighbour in erstwhile Palestine, not against a remote and unknown foe in upper Asia.

To replace an Egypt-based defence-in-depth, Dulles revived the idea of spanning the 5,000-mile gap between NATO in Europe and SEATO in the Far East with a narrower mesh involving the more forward front-line states. The genesis of this 'Northern Tier' lay in

Truman's 1947 undertakings to Greece and Turkey and in a proposed understanding between Turkey and Iraq, for whom Dulles now earmarked substantial military aid. Similar inducements would tie Pakistan, and possibly Syria and Afghanistan, into the defensive basketry. But it was Iran and the unexpected chance of enrolling that country following Roosevelt's recent 'counter-coup' against Musaddiq that made the Northern Tier so attractive. Iran virtually completed the encradlement of communism in southern central Asia. Better still, it shifted the global defence of 'the free world' away from the contentious ambit of Arab-Israeli relations, so rendering Egyptian territory redundant and the Canal Zone bases expendable.

Copeland, with a quote for every occasion, awards Dulles 'a mind which, once made up, couldn't be opened with a crowbar'.[5] Released from the embarrassments of upholding colonial intransigence and inviting Egyptian obloquy, the Dulles mechanism had snapped shut; Washington would no longer support London in its negotiations with Nasser. The British stood alone; and, deprived of their best argument as well as their most powerful supporter, they found the Egyptian carpet slipping inexorably from under their boots.

The final negotiations in 1953–4 still owed much to the US, but as intermediary rather than joint plaintiff. The State Department's insights into the British position were pooled with the CIA's into Nasser's position, so creating a situation tailor-made for cryptodiplomacy. Supposedly orchestrating the whole exchange, Copeland cheerfully brags not only of drafting Nasser's responses but of doing so in reply to demands from London which London had yet to formulate. The British, suspecting some such collusion, grumbled and protested, but to little effect. In July 1954 outline agreement was reached on a package which involved the withdrawal of all British forces from the Canal Zone within twenty months, the mothballing of their bases with no more than 1,200 civilian technicians retained for maintenance purposes, and their reactivation only in the event of war, or the threat of war, against one of the Arab states or Turkey. The agreement was confirmed in October.

Eden now sought consolation in the idea of a British redoubt in the Middle East based on a new 'Iraqi-Jordanian axis'. This was intended partly by way of response to the US's Northern Tier initiative, partly to provide airfields and barracks in which to relocate the ex-Suez forces. But Churchill, on whom age and alcohol were taking their toll, was not reassured. A harrumph about his being unaware that 'Munich was situated on the Nile' had already consigned Eden's Sudan settlement to the pariah status of Hitlerian appeasement. Now he grunted encouragement to imperially minded backbenchers who were waging a press campaign against his Foreign Secretary's 'scuttling' of Egypt. Shedding an empire could be a painful process.

Eden himself had won international esteem (though not that of John Foster Dulles) by championing the Geneva conference that had just ended the French agony in Indo-China. A polished performer, Britain's impeccably groomed Foreign Secretary and about-to-be Prime Minister (following Churchill's retirement) saw himself as epitomizing his country's post-imperial destiny as the world's favourite older statesman. Like him, Great Britain, generously dispensing her authority from a great height of experience, might yet regulate the affairs of nations and so 'find a new role' not dissimilar to her old one. But for the British people all this looked like a conceit too far. To anyone with a map and a memory, the pageantry of Elizabeth II's 1953 coronation evoked nostalgia, not optimism. The second Elizabethan era, far from resurrecting the first, could only be its antithesis.

ARMS AND THE MAN

In Anglo-Egyptian relations the new era of 'co-operation and mutual understanding' soon succumbed to incomprehension, then mutual detestation. In February 1955 Eden visited Cairo where he famously entertained Nasser. Making allowances for the chasm of age, education and background, Eden discerned across the embassy's silver tableware an able protagonist and declared himself 'impressed'. Nasser was less complimentary. He found the Foreign Secretary patronizing and he damned as 'a crime' his support for the just announced Turkish-Iraqi pact.

This alignment, which with Britain's imminent adherence would become 'the Baghdad Pact', was a variation on the American Northern Tier. But whereas Washington's scheme envisaged bilateral agreements (underpinned by aid) with each of the states concerned, London's version favoured the creation of a bloc, mainly Arab and based on Iraq and Jordan, through which British influence in the region might be perpetuated. Washington was intent on its ring-fencing of communism, in other words, London on repairing its status in the Arab world.

The prime mover in the Baghdad Pact was Nuri al-Said who in 1955 embarked on his twelfth term as Iraq's prime minister. Nuri saw the pact as a way of reconciling Iraqis to a continuation of the British presence, on which his personal ascendancy depended, and of confounding his Arab rivals in Cairo and Riyadh. For similar reasons Jordan looked a likely recruit, and Syria too if al-Quwwatli, also reinstated in 1955, could again be toppled by a coup (on which the CIA and MI6 were already working). Ironically the United States, though warm to the concept, would not join the Baghdad Pact. Israeli objections to the arming of a predominantly Arab bloc communicated themselves to sympathizers in the US and promised a tussle with Congress which the administration declined. The Northern Tier might be sufficiently removed from the Arab-Israeli arena but the Baghdad Pact was not.

Nasser also stood aloof. Nuri's gentle nudging and some Anglo-American arm-twisting made no impression on him. The Arabs, he insisted, already had a defensive alliance in the Arab League's Mutual Defence Pact against Israel. Come the consequent 'battle of the pacts', as Heikal calls it, the Egyptian leader could count on the support of the anti-Hashemite Saudis and – coups permitting – of Syria's al-Quwwatli (whose best chance of survival was seen to lie in an ever closer relationship with Cairo). Nasser had yet to espouse an aggressive pan-Arabism, but his anti-imperialism burned brightly and had lately been stoked by fraternal contacts with India's Jawaharlal Nehru and Yugoslavia's Josip Broz Tito. He recognized the Baghdad Pact for what it largely was – an attempt to perpetuate Britain's role in the region by promoting the ambitions of the pro-British Nuri over his own, so splitting the Arab world and prejudicing its chances of redressing Israeli aggression.

Vicariously, London and Cairo thus prolonged their struggle for Arab hegemony through the rivalries ramifying from the Baghdad Pact. 'The manoeuvres over the Pact were the main cause of the real deterioration in Anglo-Egyptian relations which now set in,' recalled Trevelyan.[6] Nasser's outrage over this festering 'crime', and Eden's satisfaction, would be consistent throughout the looming crisis, informing and inflaming the more obvious disputes over arms procurement, the financing of the Aswan Dam and the Suez Canal itself.

The arms issue had been triggered by Israel. Nasser held the fate of the Palestinians dear but feared the might of the Israelis more. Wounded as well as shamed in the 1948 war, he had since resisted Anglo-American pressures for a détente with Israel and in June 1954 had frustrated an Israeli Intelligence operation to discredit his regime. This was the Lavon affair (so-called after the then Israeli defence minister) in which Jewish saboteurs directed from Tel Aviv attempted to blow up British and US properties in Cairo. One of the culprits was caught red-handed when his device ignited prematurely; two more were eventually executed by the Egyptians. The executions provoked a cabinet crisis in Israel and a retaliatory strike on the Egyptian military headquarters in Gaza. Thirty-eight Egyptians were killed.

Coinciding with Eden's February 1955 visit and the launch of the Baghdad Pact, the Gaza raid 'was a turning point in Arab-Israeli relations'. In a scrupulous account of Anglo-American attitudes to the Suez crisis, W. Scott Lucas sees the Gaza raid as leading to the reinstatement of a hawkish Ben-Gurion, the resumption of Israeli arms purchases from France, the organization of Egyptian commando units (*fedayin*) for raids into Israel, and the supersession of the Arab League's Mutual Defence Pact by a military alliance of Egypt, Syria and Saudi Arabia. 'From this point,' says Lucas, 'Anglo-Egyptian compromise was almost impossible.'[7] Additionally Nasser was personally devastated by the Gaza raid. He had just reassured the Gaza troops that there would be no attack. Worse still, he had yet to provide them with the military hardware to repel aggression.

The main arms suppliers to the region, Britain, France and the US, had agreed in the aftermath of the 1948 war to uphold the existing military balance. Arabs and Israelis were to be supplied *pari passu* with the weapons and spare parts necessary for their defence but not for renewed offensives. More substantial military aid had been promised to Egypt in return for the treaty settlement with the British but, save for a few tanks, it had not materialized. Arming a country that declined to fall in with Anglo-American defence arrangements did not recommend itself to Congress or Parliament, quite apart from Israeli objections. Nasser's repeated requests were therefore being stalled when the Gaza raid, then rumours of the Franco-Israeli arms deal, made the matter urgent.

Game Up

In April 1955, in pursuit of a possible solution, the Egyptian leader flew to Indonesia on his first-ever excursion outside the Middle East. The inaugural Asia-Africa conference was assembling in Bandung, a sprightly hill resort in west Java. Conceived as a riposte to the 'Europe-America' get-togethers of the transatlantic allies, the Asia-Africa conference aired the grievances of once colonialized peoples against the still colonializing powers. Rarely seen flags bedecked the streets of Bandung as little-known leaders like Hanoi's Pham Van Dong blinked in the blaze of publicity. The Philippines' Raul Manglapus brought along his saxophone, India's Nehru brought his daughter, Indira. Liberian delegates in outrageous ties and co-respondent shoes chased the local girls; Burma's U Nu wore national dress, Nasser a crisp safari suit. The average age was under 50.

Having just expelled the British and being the only country with a foot in both Asia (Sinai) and Africa, Egypt was especially welcome in Bandung, and its leader became the star attraction. Supposedly isolated within the Arab world by the Baghdad Pact, Nasser found himself anything but isolated in the wider world. Indonesia's Sukarno swapped anti-colonial slogans, Nehru expounded his vision of a neutralism that would spawn the non-aligned movement, and China's Zhou Enlai listened sympathetically to the plight of Egypt's armed forces. Beijing, said Zhou, looked to Moscow for weaponry. If Nasser wished, he would pass the word to his Russian comrades.

A month later, back in Cairo, Nasser was advised by the Soviet ambassador that arms were indeed available. Moreover they might be paid for, not in dollars which Egypt did not possess or in concessions over Palestine which Egypt was unwilling to make, but in Egyptian cotton, a product which was unacceptable in the US because of objections from its own cotton-growers. Anglo-American weaponry was still preferable on the grounds of familiarity. But another US brush-off in July prompted substantive discussions with a Soviet emissary and in late August the order was placed. Egypt was to receive $100 millions'-worth, later increased to $300 millions'-worth, of guns, tanks, submarines, MIG fighters and Ilyushin bombers plus the Soviet personnel necessary for installation and retraining.

It was word of this deal that brought Kim Roosevelt and Miles Copeland dashing back to Cairo and that prompted Trevelyan's night visit to the headquarters of the RCC. London and Washington were horrified. Soviet communism appeared to have escaped its containment and, hurdling both the Northern Tier's ring-fence and the Baghdad Pact's blockhouse, to have landed astride the most strategically sensitive crossroads in the world. Oilfields, pipelines and sealanes were exposed; Israel was in jeopardy, Africa wide open. The only hope of rescuing the situation lay in the personal rapport between Nasser and the CIA.

Without informing either the President or his Cairo embassy, John Foster Dulles had ordered Roosevelt and Copeland to Cairo. They found that it was too late to change Nasser's mind. The deal was done. They could only limit the damage – or, more ingeniously, persuade Nasser that there was none. After all, no treaty had been broken, no relationship severed. Why then, they hinted, did Nasser not retain US goodwill by combining the announcement of the weapons deal with an offer of Israeli negotiation? Nasser agreed. In fact Copeland was in the midst of drafting a suitable text for him when Humphrey Trevelyan drove up in his limousine. Why not tell Trevelyan that the arms were in fact Czech, suggested Roosevelt. Again Nasser agreed. He duly mumbled something to Trevelyan about 'Brag' (that is, Prague). Although a Soviet satellite, Czechoslovakia sounded much less alarming than Russia and, in so far as the Czechs had previously supplied the Israeli defence forces, was definitely less objectionable.

But soft-talking Nasser was only half the battle. It was also essential to shield him from the righteous anger of regular US diplomats. Ambassador Hank Byroade was silenced after his first unfortunate outburst. Then an incoming Assistant Secretary of State was waylaid at Cairo airport and talked into defusing what amounted to an ultimatum from Dulles. Unfortunately Associated Press had already picked up on the 'ultimatum' word. When it made the next day's newspapers, Nasser thundered his contempt and took revenge by removing all mention of peaceful intent from his announcement of the arms deal. Copeland, crediting Nasser with his own brand of gamesmanship, nevertheless thought that in reality the Egyptian leader was not displeased. In fact he was probably 'delighted' – 'with the chance to respond to the ultimatum, with his public's reaction to his response, and with the fact that in the end there was no ultimatum'.[8]

Game Up

Nasser had gained immense prestige throughout the Arab world by defying the Americans. But America was still in the game, and Egypt appeared to have settled for an aggressive neutrality rather than Soviet alignment. Roosevelt and Copeland congratulated themselves on having chalked up a modest success. Their crisis management had averted a complete rupture; the door remained ajar; and as they reminded Nasser, it needed to remain ajar. How else, they emphasized, was Egypt to receive its share of US aid – let alone the funding required for the most ambitious civil engineering project of the mid-twentieth century?

FROM DAM TO CANAL

Feasibility studies for the construction of a high-level dam across the Nile had been under way since 1947. To be located at Aswan, just north of the Sudanese border, the dam would provide irrigation for 2 million acres and generate the electricity needed to power the country's ambitious industrialization programme. Nasser rated the dam's symbolic significance as equivalent to that of the pyramids. It was Egypt's only hope of feeding its ever-expanding population; it would provide a model for the whole developing world; the prestige would be incalculable.

But if Nasser saw the dam as a triumphant vindication, the West saw it as a way to rein in Nasser. It 'could be a trump card,' thought Dulles.[9] 'The Russians were giving arms,' wrote Trevelyan. 'This [the dam] was the best way for us to stay in the picture.'[10] To both men it seemed peculiarly appropriate that, while the communist world doled out death-dealing weaponry to the military, the 'free world' would be dispensing life-giving water to the peasantry. Construction could well take a decade with progress on each phase dependent on Cairo's collaboration, including guarantees about Egyptian public spending. Additionally, substantial teams of Western technical and liaison personnel would require protection and freedom of movement throughout the country. Cairo was going to have to pay dearly. Its inflammatory rhetoric would have to be curbed, its military adventures on behalf of the Palestinians suspended, and its support for other freedom fighters in, for instance, Algeria curtailed. The Nile was not the only flood that the dam was designed to divert.

— financing the dam

Not to be outdone, within weeks of their arms deal the Soviets were also expressing an interest in financing the dam. But Nasser gave them little encouragement. The technical studies had been conducted by Western engineers, a European consortium had tendered for the work, and the support of the World Bank was reckoned essential. Of the estimated cost of $1 billion, $400 million would need to be in hard currency. The Bank was willing to provide half that sum if the American and British governments would provide the other half. They agreed in principle, and in November 1955 Egypt's finance minister visited Washington to finalize the arrangements.

The negotiations were complicated and the terms, in so far as they limited Egypt's freedom of action, hotly contested. In particular, the World Bank's insistence on inspection of Egypt's financial administration was resented. It reminded the Egyptian leadership of the international control of the economy that had resulted from the construction of the Suez Canal. Once again Kim Roosevelt had to respond to an urgent call from Dulles and fly to Cairo to reassure Nasser. Once again the Roosevelt charm did the trick; the deal with the Bank was agreed in February 1956. But the Bank's contribution depended on Washington and London approving the other $200 million; and for quite separate reasons, both were by now inclined to renege.

London's misgivings were prompted by a bombshell from Amman. There 'Jack' Glubb, the chinless enigma who as 'Glubb Pasha' had commanded Jordan's Arab legion for a quarter of a century, was suddenly dismissed. Summoned to the prime minister's office, he was told that he 'needed a rest' and was given two hours to leave the country. He took it well. 'I felt no particular emotion,' he says. Like a sudden bereavement, the news that one's life's work was over was hard to grasp. 'There was a box of cigarettes on the table. I took one and lit it.' It was 29 February but, overlooking the leap year in his confusion, Glubb made it 1 March.[11] He asked for a few hours' grace and was told to be ready at dawn.

'We'll have some tea,' said Mrs Glubb when he arrived home unexpectedly. Then she put the children to bed early and helped the living legend with his packing. Back in 1924 the man hailed as the 'second Lawrence of Arabia' had made his entry into what was then Transjordania on a camel. Thirty-two years later he left by air with a single suitcase. From a village with a station on the Hijaz railway,

Amman had grown to a city of a quarter of a million; from a handful of policemen on camels he had built up the Arab Legion into a force which, with the Jordanian National Guard, numbered nearly 60,000 men. As the plane rose above the scene of his labours, bitterness overwhelmed him. 'Now, in a few hours, twenty-six years of work had been destroyed.'[12]

In No. 10 Downing Street Anthony Eden rued a greater loss. As an Englishman at the head of an Arab army Glubb, more than any other officer or official, had become the embodiment of Britain's ambitions in the Middle East. He had worked with Cox and Bell in Iraq, 'relieved' Baghdad from Rashid Ali in the darkest days of the war, and won Jerusalem, or part of it, for the Arabs in 1948. He epitomized all that the British regarded as romantic and noble in their long Arab affair; and like no other event, his going signified its demise. Eden was flabbergasted. Normally contemptuous of the diehard imperialists and their right-wing newspapers, he suddenly became more Churchillian than Churchill.

The Prime Minister's mood swings had lately become notorious. They were attributed to the cocktail of drugs that he was taking to combat the effects of a ruptured bile duct. But the analgesic properties of pethidin, Benzedrine and possibly amphetamines did nothing to dull the pain of the news from Amman. Not so much embittered as demented, Eden raved that Nasser was behind it all, Nasser was to blame. Britain's good name and his own Olympian endeavours in the cause of international understanding were being undermined by a colonel in Cairo. The world was not big enough to hold both of them, he reportedly spluttered. Anthony Nutting, a Foreign Office Minister, pointed out that the decision to dismiss Glubb had been King Husayn's. Eden was having none of it. Was Nutting 'in love with Nasser'? Any fool could see that the Egyptian leader was 'the incarnation of all the evils of Arabia who would destroy every British interest in the Middle East, unless he himself were speedily destroyed.' 'Can't you understand?' he later told Nutting, 'I want him murdered . . .'[13]

Behind the hysteria there lay some logic. Had there been no Nasser to expose Britain's post-imperial manoeuvres, Jordan would by now have joined the Baghdad Pact and Glubb's job would have been secured. Husayn was a hostage to forces beyond his control. Barely 20, British-educated, short even by Hashemite standards, and only three years into his reign, the boy-king was caught up in 'the battle of the pacts'. His kingdom included nearly as many Palestinians as Jordanians. Its border was impossible to police; and the Palestinians' unfinished business in what was now Israel brought devastating Israeli commando raids on Jordanian villages. His treaty with Britain represented his one security. But this sheet-anchor was also a millstone. Because of it, the British and Nuri wanted him in the Pact; yet legislation to that effect in December 1955 had brought Jordan's first serious riots, the resignation of the government, and a torrent of abuse and intrigue from Cairo. Husayn, fearing for his own survival, had quickly backed down.

That left Glubb, who had been repeatedly singled out by Radio Cairo as a British agent and the real ruler of Jordan, highly vulnerable. But the crisis had since blown over. Glubb's dismissal two months later originated with the King and had more to do with Glubb being an anomaly than a liability. At 58, the 'Pasha' was nearing retirement anyway. Kirkbride had left for the limbo which was pre-Gaddafi Libya immediately after Abdullah's assassination; Glubb's departure had been under consideration for over a year. There had been recent misunderstandings and differences of opinion; by dismissing him the King genuinely sought to assert his own authority and proclaim his nationalist credentials. Kirkbride, investigating the affair later, confirmed this. So did Trevelyan in Cairo, Nutting in London and Glubb himself in retirement. Selwyn Lloyd, Eden's Foreign Secretary, who happened to be in Cairo on 29 February, soon realized that his account of Nasser gloating over the news was based on a misapprehension. At the time Nasser was ignorant of events in Amman. Lloyd, too, then conceded that Nasser was not to blame.

Seemingly only Eden, backed by much of the tub-thumping British press, held the Egyptian leader directly responsible. But that was sufficient to end British interest in the Aswan dam. As Selwyn Lloyd put it, the British offer of part-finance was now 'allowed to wither on the vine'. It was also enough to persuade the Prime Minister that, Cabinet support being unlikely, the only way to rid himself of the turbulent colonel was by subterfuge. With the Musaddiq precedent much in mind, he turned to gung-ho elements in MI6 and in effect issued them carte blanche to 'get Nasser'.

Washington's change of heart over the dam came two months later. In April the Egyptian government, grateful for Beijing's earlier assistance and keen to open another possible channel for arms supplies, officially recognized the communist People's Republic of China. The British had long since done so; so had Israel. But US indulgence to London and Tel Aviv did not extend to Cairo, especially at a time when Chinese support of the communist government in Hanoi was rattling the dominoes of south-east Asia, including that which America was now shoring up in Saigon. The Egyptian recognition of communist China was not what was expected of a would-be recipient of substantial aid. It was also peculiarly maladroit in what was an election year in the US. Cotton-producing states in the American south, hydro dam-building interests in the Rockies and Zionist supporters in the major cities all had reason to oppose the wisdom of directing US aid to a competitive and hostile Egypt. With the presidential election due in four months, they could not be ignored.

Thus the chances of getting the grant for the dam approved were already negligible when in July Nasser capitulated to US demands in respect of all outstanding issues on the actual terms. Armed with these concessions, the Egyptian ambassador met Dulles on 19 July. Expecting confirmation, he was rewarded with cancellation. The offer was withdrawn. Dulles may have been riled by mention of the Soviet counter-offer; more certainly he said nothing about the lack of American political will and much about the Egyptian economy being unequal to such a project.

The slur was resented almost as much as the rebuff itself. When Britain followed suit two days later, *Time* magazine celebrated 'a victory for the West' with a cartoon showing the chess-playing Dulles checkmating an apoplectic Nasser.[14] Wiser heads waited. Retaliation was wholly predictable, and Eden, mindful of the Musaddiq coup when demanding Nasser's destruction, should surely have recalled the Iranian move against the AIOC. Yet when on the evening of 29 July, before a crowd of a quarter of a million in Alexandria, Nasser announced the nationalization of the Suez Canal Company, London like Washington was taken completely by surprise. Not even Kim Roosevelt or the all-knowing Miles Copeland would claim to have foreseen so devastating a response.

Nasser's speech lasted ninety minutes. He reviewed Egypt's history of colonial exploitation, recalled the heavy price paid for Ferdinand de Lesseps's cutting of the Suez Canal, and demanded that earnings from the Canal should henceforth benefit Egypt by providing the finance to build the Aswan dam. By the time he ended to delirious applause, the Company's palatial Port Said offices, its Ismailia communications centre and its Cairo headquarters were already in Egyptian hands. Mentioned thirteen times in all, 'de Lesseps' had been the code-word for activating the take-over. It duly passed off without a hitch and almost without a shot being fired. Elsewhere pandemonium reigned. 'All Alexandria jumped for joy around us,' wrote a French reporter;[15] the jubilation whirled across the delta like a dust-storm; 'nobody in Egypt slept that night', recalled Heikal;[16] Nasser was a national hero not just to his people but to the whole Arab world.

THE WORST POSSIBLE MOVE

That night in London Eden happened to be hosting a dinner party in honour of the Iraqi royal family. The lately crowned Faysal II, son of the unfortunate Ghazi and grandson of the original Faysal, was another bright-eyed, English-schooled Hashemite in his early twenties. It was his first state visit to London, and it would be his last. He was accompanied by his uncle Abd al-Ilah who, now that the regency had ended, rejoiced in the title of 'Crown Prince', and by the tightly corseted prime minister *ad nauseam*, Nuri al-Said.

'Hit him,' urged Nuri when an ashen-faced Eden read out the slip of paper just passed to him, 'hit him hard and hit him now.'[17] Eden needed no encouragement. Cars were quickly called and the stiff-shirts departed; less formally dressed dignitaries took their place. Under the chairmanship of an incensed Eden, senior Cabinet colleagues and military Chiefs of Staff went into closed session with the French ambassador, the US chargé d'affaires and the Director-General of the Canal Company.

The British and French governments were the major shareholders in the Canal Company. A third of the shipping using the Canal was British; two-thirds of Europe's oil came via the Canal. Both governments, according to the historian Hugh Thomas, had a feeling about oil supplies 'comparable to the fear of castration'.[18] Additionally the British were still smarting from Nasser's attacks on the Baghdad Pact while the French, fighting the most savage of all colonial wars in

Algeria, held Nasser responsible for encouraging, arming and occasionally training the North African Arabs. 'Hit him' both governments must, the sooner and the harder the better. But the last British troops had left the Canal Zone in June. Assembling the necessary paratroops, aircraft, transports and warships for a full-scale invasion of Egypt would take weeks. Plans were nevertheless to be drawn up, and troop movements to begin, immediately.

Nasser had foreseen this response. He calculated that during the long military build-up international hostility might be disarmed by demonstrating that Egyptians could themselves operate the Canal without prejudice to British shipping or European masculinity. Oil supplies were not in fact interrupted. Despite the withdrawal of foreign pilots, Egyptians confidently shepherded ships through the waterway and saw to its dredging. Vessels which refused to pay transit dues to the Egyptian government were allowed passage. There was talk of compensation being paid to the Company's shareholders.

Eden was unimpressed. In a cable to Eisenhower, he wrote of using force only as a last resort to 'bring Nasser to his senses'. The implication was that negotiations would be given a chance, but the reality was that assassination would be given a chance. Destroying the man whom Eden now called 'a Muslim Mussolini', not 'bringing him to his senses', was the objective. While Dulles, with a view to a peaceful settlement, tirelessly encouraged talking between the Canal Company, the Canal users and the British and French governments, Eden endorsed negotiations only for as long it took to explore other options and to mobilize.

The other options failed to materialize. MI6, despite what its historian calls 'some of the riskiest special operations of its existence',[19] found Nasser an elusive target, and Egypt a much tougher proposition than Iran. In August MI6's main operations centre in Cairo (otherwise the 'Arab News Agency') was raided by the Egyptian security police whom Copeland had trained. Two Britons were among the thirty arrested; additionally two members of the British embassy staff were implicated, then expelled. The director of the news agency was left at liberty; under the impression that he enjoyed Nasser's confidence, he regaled MI6 with disinformation fed to him by the Egyptian leadership; Copeland's pupils were proving a credit to their master. Despite this set-back, MI6's intrigues with assorted Egyptian malcontents continued, though to little purpose. Desultory attempts to give Nasser a box of spiked chocolates or to get someone to put strychnine in his food or release nerve gas into his ventilation system either failed or were abandoned.

French and Israeli agents also tried their hand. But the CIA kept out of it. Nasser, after all, was their man; 'our first mission was to keep him in power', says Copeland;[20] toppling him made no sense and rarely played any part in official American policy. Though personally fond of the British, Copeland was scathing of their crypto-diplomacy. If the Syrian and Iranian coups had proved anything it was that covert political action might facilitate change but could not initiate it. There had to be a credible alternative leader and a pre-existing locus of opposition in the army, the palace or the political élite. In Nasser's Egypt, as even the British eventually accepted, no such things existed. Irresponsible efforts to remove Nasser promised only chaos and a triumph for more extreme elements, like the Muslim Brotherhood or the communists.

Outrageously arrogant as to political ends, Copeland was a stickler as to acceptable means. To his mind a good clean coup was essentially orderly, bloodless and unattributable. MI6's ill-conceived endeavours disgusted him. So too did the CIA's growing preference for paramilitary operations and bureaucratic proliferation. He played little part in the plans for another Syrian coup which were being laid by the CIA in the person of Archie Roosevelt, aided by MI6 with encouragement from Nuri. In early July the Syrian government, which had already followed the Egyptian example of buying Soviet arms, had pledged itself to converting its military alliance with Egypt into a union of the two countries. The coup was on. But three weeks later the nationalization of the Canal Company had relegated Syria to the sidelines. The coup was off. In October more Soviet arms purchases by the Syrian government and closer ties with Moscow reactivated it. The outback of the war over Suez again stalled it.

While the sudden flurry of Anglo-French troop movements in the Mediterranean clearly threatened Egypt, and while Guy Mollet's government in France no less than Eden's in London was clearly set on intervention, it was unclear on what grounds an attack might be mounted. Since the Canal Company was registered in Egypt, Nasser's action was not obviously illegal; so long as the Canal traffic was uninterrupted, reference to the International Court of Justice looked unpromising. British actions designed to provoke Nasser into some further outrage also failed. The call-up of British reservists, the freezing of Egypt's UK assets and the loss of the Canal's foreign pilots elicited little response from the noticeably restrained Egyptian leader. Nor did a demand, formulated by the international maritime community at the instigation of Dulles, for an international consortium to take over the Canal. Nasser refused to have anything to do with it, but Eisenhower then confirmed that the object of the proposal was 'a peaceful settlement . . . *nothing else*'.[21] With US elections now only weeks away, Washington was not in favour of war.

A similar outcome awaited the 'Suez Canal Users Association' (SCUA). This was Dulles's September negotiating gambit. The newly established SCUA, rather than the old Canal Company or the Egyptian government, was to be empowered to accept the shipping companies' Canal dues pending a solution to the crisis. An Anglo-French proposal that all dues must be paid exclusively to SCUA would have deprived Egypt of any Canal revenue, rendered nationalization worthless, and might well have provoked Nasser into action, if only to wipe the egg from his face. But to British fury the proposal was rejected. SCUA, too, was to have 'no teeth', as Dulles put it. Another possible pretext for invasion had eluded the bellicose Europeans; and Washington's opposition to the use of force was as clear-cut as ever.

October brought in the United Nations. Under pressure from Nehru and some Arab states, Nasser responded positively; indeed he was becoming unexpectedly co-operative. Much to Eden's dismay, though to the relief of many of his colleagues, a settlement looked to be looming. It was then, at a late-night rendezvous on 14 October, that a French delegation presented Eden with what Copeland, like countless others with the benefit of hindsight, would call 'easily the worst move that could possibly have been made'.[22]

By introducing a top-secret ingredient this French plan nevertheless owed much to what Trevelyan calls the 'fashionable methods of influencing policy' pioneered by Copeland's school of 'covert political action'. MI6 was heavily involved, and the plan had more layers of deception than an onion. The secret ingredient was Israel. By prior arrangement Israel would invade Egyptian Sinai. Never short of a pretext and militarily superior, the Israelis would advance towards the Canal. The French and British would then quickly condemn the action, demand a cease-fire, and order the warring parties to withdraw ten miles either side of the Canal. The Israelis would comply; Egypt would not. The ten-mile wide corridor would therefore be occupied by Anglo-French forces to ensure the security of the Canal. As a preliminary to occupation, Nasser's air force would be eliminated and his ground forces speedily expelled. Defeat on such a scale must discredit his leadership and lead to his downfall and replacement.

Eden was delighted with the plan. He had called the Canal 'Britain's windpipe'; here was a chance to intubate it with a swift surgical strike whose happy outcome should silence any objections. The Franco-Israeli 'alliance', forged by illegal arms deals and normally regarded with the deepest suspicion by the British, had saved the day.

Eden was the more disposed towards the plan because Israel's involvement, though disastrous for Britain's standing in the Arab world if it ever became public, would have the bonus of relieving pressure on Jordan. Israeli raids into a Glubb-less Jordan had recently intensified. The British, still keen to corral Jordan into the Baghdad Pact, supported King Husayn's request for Iraqi military assistance. And Israel, supposing the advent of Iraqi troops to presage the break-up of Jordan, then threatened a full-scale invasion. In October 1956 the British thus found themselves obliged to prepare for a war which could as well be with Israel as with Egypt. In fact Washington was inclined to interpret recent British military manoeuvres in the eastern Mediterranean in this Jordanian context.

But the new plan changed everything. The Israelis could hardly challenge the British in Jordan when actively colluding with them in Egypt, nor would they choose to be engaged on two fronts simultaneously. The plan, in effect, neatly disposed of the threat to Jordan. Possibly it did so a little too neatly. For there is evidence to suggest that Israeli bellicosity towards Jordan had in fact been contrived. Its intent was precisely its outcome: to ensure Eden's agreement to British military participation in a Franco-Israeli attack on Egypt.

The details of the Suez plan were speedily concerted through highly secret contacts. One involved the Foreign Secretary Selwyn Lloyd donning a false moustache for a trip to France to meet Ben-Gurion and Moshe Dayan. The tentacles of subterfuge had found their way to the pinnacles of government. Trevelyan in Cairo was given no inkling of the plan. The Foreign Office in London was equally in the dark. Even the British Cabinet was invited simply to endorse intervention in the event of an Israeli advance threatening the Canal. It duly did so, but with profound misgivings and unaware that Eden and his closest advisers had in fact condoned the Israeli action. The plotters consoled themselves with the thought that they had not actually instigated it. Responding to a contingency of which they had foreknowledge was not the same as contriving it. The charge, should it come to that, would be one of complicity, of being an accessory not an agent. Such were the quibbling contortions to which an empire in its death throes was reduced.

At one point the operation was off, then it was on. Two frantic weeks after it was first mooted, on 29 October the Israelis began their advance. All seemed to go according to plan. Next day a twelve-hour ultimatum was issued to the Egyptians to withdraw from the Canal. When it expired, Egyptian airports and installations were bombed. The bombing lasted nearly a week during which time the ships carrying the landing forces steamed into position. On 5 November, paratroops poured from the sky, troops swarmed up the beaches and tanks rumbled on to the streets of Port Said.

Ingenious may be too kind a word, but it was the plan's ingenuity which had made it so seductive. The same ingenuity now proved its undoing. Necessitating haste and the strictest secrecy, especially if word of the collusion with the Israelis was not to leak out, it had precluded the most elementary precautions. Public opinion in Britain was unprepared, Parliament unprimed, the Foreign Office unsympathetic and the country deeply divided. Closely questioned in the House of Commons, even the government failed to offer a consistent explanation of what it was trying to achieve or whether it was actually at war. Meanwhile the military operation was bedevilled by the same uncertainty. The Royal Air Force was deeply puzzled about how its supposed French allies could be operating from the airfields of its supposed Israeli foes, indeed supporting their advance. The Royal Navy somehow became entangled with the US Sixth Fleet. Neither fully understood the need for urgency. And by the time the ground forces made their belated entry, the political retreat was under way. Their presence was now represented as a trail-blazing exercise for a UN Emergency Force; already the challenge was not occupation but extrication.

Worse still, secrecy had precluded all the more obvious economic and diplomatic precautions. Oil was in short supply, the government's finances in a mess, and the currency unprotected. Likewise there had been no consultation with either Arab friends, Commonwealth partners or treaty allies, most especially the United States. Harold Macmillan, currently the Chancellor, got on well with John Foster Dulles and had reassured his Cabinet colleagues that American support would indeed be forthcoming. 'My judgement was wrong,' he would later admit. As the man who would imminently succeed the disgraced Eden as Prime Minister, Macmillan had less cause to regret this 'mistake' than most.[23]

In fact Eisenhower, though deeply suspicious of the Anglo-French action, had initially reserved judgement on its morality and was happy to refer it to the UN. Had the action resulted in the instant occupation of the Canal corridor, the preservation of the Canal itself and the overthrow of Nasser, he might have accepted it as a *fait accompli*. But when a week dragged by with no such outcome, and when that week happened to be the last before the US elections, his resentment mounted. Allies were supposed to be more considerate of one another's domestic circumstances. John Foster Dulles had just suffered a heart attack and the Russians were being challenged in Hungary. At such a juncture, for trusted allies to set light to the Middle East without consultation or warning was politically inexcusable. They could expect no further favours from him.

Fortunately any danger of Soviet intervention was averted by the coincidence of Soviet retaliation in Hungary. British tanks on the streets of Port Said did nothing for the West's case against Soviet tanks on the streets of Budapest, but at least Soviet support for the Egyptians was now limited to protests and skirmishes at the UN. Not much else went right. The Israelis, from whom the Anglo-French forces were supposed to be protecting the Canal, never got within thirty miles of it. The order for a ten-mile-wide *cordon sanitaire* along the Canal was therefore a nonsense in that it rewarded the aggressor while penalizing the victim of aggression. Worse still, such partiality strongly hinted at the collusion that was supposed to be so secret.

This absurdity was exceeded only by the Anglo-French claim that intervention, as well as separating the combatants, would secure the Canal as an international waterway. For in reality the Canal was now no one's waterway. A ship hit by the aerial bombardment had sunk in mid-channel, and the Egyptians had then completed the job by scuttling hulks filled with concrete. The attempted intubation, instead of saving 'Britain's windpipe', had blocked it. Simultaneously Nasser's Syrian allies knocked out the Iraq Petroleum Company's pipeline to the Mediterranean. Not unforeseeably, military intervention had precipitated the catastrophic interruption of oil supplies that months of politicking had been designed to avert.

A blockage might of course be cleared, and the Canal eventually reopened, if only Nasser would withdraw his forces from it. But he chose not to; and when, in the face of Egyptian resistance, Soviet rumblings and a far more damaging barrage of international condemnation, the Anglo-French 'liberators' boldly advanced down the Canal, they were immediately stopped in their tracks. For it was then that, in the ultimate indignity for any so-called 'great power', the war chest was found to be bare. Britain's Chancellor Harold Macmillan, hitherto so hawkish, had suddenly begun to coo; sterling was on the verge of collapse, he reported, and Britain's oil-starved economy about to go into free-fall. Without an immediate cease-fire in compliance with UN demands, the American 'support', of which he had so recently assured his Cabinet colleagues, would extend neither to defending the pound, nor to approving a bridging loan from the International Monetary Fund, nor to substituting oil from the western hemisphere for that bottled up in the east. Barely thirty-six hours after the landings, ruination beckoned.

The French were for carrying on regardless. The British dared not delay for even a day. On the night of 6 November, eight days into the adventure but barely thirty-six hours into the advance, the operation was aborted and the cease-fire accepted: 33 British and French lives had been lost, 171 Israeli, and well over a thousand Egyptian, mostly civilians. In a final convulsion, mercifully brief but typically bloody, colonial-style management of the Middle East had expired. Only the obsequies remained.

By Christmas the troops were home. On 9 January 1957 Eden, now sore as well as sick, stepped down from office with but the gentlest of shoves. And in March the US Congress approved the 'Eisenhower Doctrine'. A refinement of Truman's doctrine, this applied exclusively to the Middle East and provided for economic and military assistance, not excluding the dispatch of US troops, to any Middle Eastern nation or group of nations who believed their independence was under threat of aggression from 'international communism'. The US, in effect, was assuming the responsibility of managing the region. Britain's interests, especially in relation to oil, would be respected, but any notion of Britain supervising the defence of the Middle East or policing its internal affairs was now unsustainable. To restore Anglo-American relations in the aftermath of Suez, Macmillan had been obliged to settle for a subservient role in the Middle East.

NEITHER DREAM NOR PALACE

For the French the 'Suez Affair' was a failure, nothing worse; their credibility in the Arab world had already been lost by arms shipments to Israel and oppression in Algeria. For the British, Suez was a catastrophe. Quite apart from the domestic repercussions and the damage to Anglo-American relations, it had soured moderate Arab opinion and discredited all the old and cherished pretensions to being the friend of the Arabs. Even a trusted ally like Iraq had lent its voice to the demand for a Suez cease-fire.

Worst of all from a British point of view, Suez vindicated the construction placed on the policies of the European powers by Nasser. Far from silencing him, it enhanced his reputation, exaggerated his revolutionary rhetoric, amplified its appeal. Already idolized, the now president of Egypt was idealized. His picture, says Nutting, 'hung in souks, cafés, taxis and shops from the Atlantic to the Indian Ocean'; he was compared to Saladin who had repulsed the Crusaders. But unlike the military adventurers and high-born dynasts of history, Nasser's dynamic owed little to Islamic fervour, nothing to family pride and everything to the Arab people. He was one of them; they identified with him and they saw in him what they could be. Young, shrewd, reserved, incorruptible and inspirational, this postman's son was all that other Arab leaders were not. Over the airwaves his words hissed a defiance to which the masses responded spontaneously. He was saying what they felt, not by design but from empathy.

Emotionally if not constitutionally, Suez had handed the leadership of the Arab world to Nasser. Pan-Arabism was no longer a

Hashemite prerogative, a Damascene pipe dream or a pro-Palestine blueprint. Inseparable from Nasserism, it shared its revolutionary dynamism and populist appeal. The 'dream palace' was neither dream nor palace; it was something much more attainable – a crowded street with a portrait and a radio anywhere in the Middle East.

In Beirut, Baghdad, Amman and Riyadh existing regimes could not ignore the clamour. Threatened and edgy, they paid lip-service to Nasserist triumphalism while curbing domestic enthusiasm as best they could. The Saudis, formally in alliance with Cairo against the Hashemite-based Baghdad Pact, backed away as Nasser became more dependent on the Soviet bloc. Any accommodation with communism was as objectionable to the Saudi kingdom's purist brand of Islam as it was to the Saudis' American paymasters. Jordan followed suit. King Husayn briefly indulged his pro-Nasserist ministry by rejecting Britain's annual subsidy in favour of one from Egypt, Syria and Saudi Arabia. But as expected, only the Saudis actually paid up. In the confidence born of Saudi and Anglo-American support, during the summer of 1957 King Husayn engineered the overthrow of his Nasserist politicians and reaffirmed Jordan's Western alignment.

Syria, on the other hand, drew ever closer to Nasser. A joint military programme, carefully orchestrated by the Soviets, and a political programme designed to integrate the two countries in an Arab union, had already handed control of Syria's foreign policy to Cairo. In Baghdad Nuri and his British advisers regarded Syria as an Egyptian satellite; in the bars of Beirut's better hotels CIA operatives gloomily foresaw it becoming a Soviet satellite. The last intended coup, instigated by MI6 at the time of the Suez invasion, had ended in disaster when a consignment of arms for the Druze had been discovered. Show trials had followed. A CIA operation in July 1957 met an identical fate. Licking their wounds, London and Washington then set up a 'Syrian Working Group' to concert intelligence on Soviet activities in the country.

In Syria's 1955 presidential elections the Egyptian journalist Mohamed Heikal quoted the going rate for a deputy's vote as 100,000 Syrian pounds 'rising to £S500,000 on election day'.[24] With the Saudis, the Iraqis, the Lebanese and the Egyptians, not to mention the CIA and MI6, all bidding heavily, the political parties in Damascus enjoyed lavish funds but little credibility and less cohesion. They were easily overawed by the Syrian military and outmanoeuvred by the Arab socialist ideologues of the rising Ba'th ('Renaissance') Party. In alliance, the army and the Ba'thists resolved to cut the Gordian knot of foreign intrigues by bouncing Syria into union with Egypt. Nasser, wary of Syrian factionalism, was not particularly enthusiastic, but eventually he agreed on condition that Syria's political parties were all disbanded.

The 'United Arab Republic' (UAR) was duly proclaimed in February 1958 to an ecstatic welcome in both Egypt and Syria. On paper, in the eyes of their respective generals and to the satisfaction of their Soviet supporters, the two countries (plus the maverick Yemen) were now one. Under Nasserist direction, pan-Arabism appeared to have chalked up its most significant triumph since Faysal's entry into Damascus forty years earlier. Yet Nasser himself knew little of Syria and had yet to set foot in the country. It was the triumph of an idea.

The formation of the UAR, followed by a rapturous visit to the Soviet Union by Nasser, its president, spread near panic among Syria's neighbours. In the Lebanon, the simmering rivalry between the country's Muslim community, headed by the prime minister, and its Christian community, headed by the president, now assumed pan-Arabist proportions. Having already subscribed to the Eisenhower Doctrine about accepting US support for opposing 'international communism', the Maronite president found himself opposed by a Muslim prime minister wedded to the pan-Arab ideals of Soviet-backed Nasserism. Propaganda and arms for the mostly Muslim pro-Nasserists poured into the country across the Syrian border while the mostly Christian anti-Nasserists sought assistance from the US. The Lebanese army, being as divided as the country, stayed in its barracks; but armed groups fought it out in the hills and a situation approaching civil war developed.

The same fears prompted King Husayn of Jordan to turn to his Hashemite cousins in Iraq for support. Iraq, equally threatened by the Nasserist regime in Syria and especially worried about the Iraq Petroleum Company's pipeline through Syria, responded positively. Just two weeks after the United Arab Republic was proclaimed, Amman and Baghdad matched it with their own federal 'Arab' or 'Hashemite Union'. The British had finally got their Iraqi-Jordanian axis and Jordan was thus effectively co-opted into the Baghdad Pact.

From Cairo and Damascus, Nasser poured scorn on the new Union as a concoction of the West and its Hashemite 'lackeys'. The Arabs of Iraq and Jordan would not, he declared, be fobbed off with such ersatz Arabism.

This propaganda had its effect. The Hashemite Union was popular neither in Jordan nor in Iraq. In Baghdad 'there was perfect indifference', according to a British observer; 'under the coloured lights which the government hung out there were no signs of gaiety'.[25] Yet it does not appear that Nasser had any direct hand in the blood bath that was about to engulf Baghdad. In fact the Iraqi revolution seems to have taken him as much by surprise as it did everyone else. In the best traditions of Western diplomacy in the Middle East, the British and US embassies knew no more of it than they had of Rashid al-Kaylani's revolt in 1941 or would of the Iranian revolution in 1978–9. It was as if Western diplomats, hard pushed to keep track of upheavals for which their own government agencies were responsible, could scarcely be expected to anticipate those engineered by others.

FULL-BLOODED REVOLUTION

Five years earlier Gerald de Gaury, the long-serving British liaison officer with the Iraqi royal family, had recorded with deep satisfaction Faysal II's coming-of-age ceremonies. Coinciding almost exactly with Elizabeth II's coronation, the celebrations in Baghdad mirrored those in London. De Gaury's court circular noted the ecstatic crowds, the guards of honour and the endless processions. 'The float of the Ministry of Works and Communications received particularly loud cheers as connoting technical progress, something most modern,' wrote the unctuous de Gaury. 'The people of Baghdad were in a seventh heaven of happiness.'[26]

Three years later, in 1956, the new king paid his one and only state visit to London. As well as more processions, it included a dinner at Buckingham Palace and another at Downing Street, the same that was interrupted by the news of the nationalization of the Canal company. In her welcoming speech Queen Elizabeth also touched on modernity, hailing Iraq as 'the model of a modern state'. Heartily approving, de Gaury would later produce a tabulated checklist to show just how modern it had become under the Anglo-Hashemite dispensation. A few examples will serve:

1921	1958	
Religion:	Muslim	Little-practising except for Ramadhan ...
Means of Eating:	Fingers	Knife, fork and spoon ...
Number of Wives:	Up to four ...	One, emancipated, or none.

There were now fifty Arabic newspapers, cinemas, radio and, as of 1957, television. Instead of camels, people rode on buses; and instead of baggy night-shirts, they wore 'close-fitting European clothes, comparatively expensive'. Secular education was offered by schools, technical colleges and law schools. 'Leisure and Pleasure', which in 1921 meant 'boy female impersonators', now included 'half-Westernised cabarets' with copious alcohol, 'only female dancers', and 'some Western dancing'. Iraq was not, of course, perfect. In fairness, de Gaury felt bound to mention that the history books used in the schools were 'prejudiced' and that 'the way of life of youth was different'. But on the whole it was still, he thought, a splendid record and one for which the Iraqi people were now displaying their gratitude by unstinting support support for the King, the Crown Prince and the faithful Nuri al-Said.

The 1948 'Portsmouth riots' over the Anglo-Iraq treaty, which de Gaury himself had witnessed, were evidently forgotten. Indeed those 'malevolent opposition and mob leaders' whom he had held responsible were no longer in evidence. Four of them had been seen dangling from gibbets outside popular institutions in Baghdad, including a government secondary school and a private school 'for middle class children of all denominations run by the Sisters of the Presentation'. But these four were all communists. Others – teachers, army officers, lawyers – had simply disappeared, presumably into some form of detention; yet others, mostly students and often for no obvious reason, were still disappearing, sometimes *en masse*. There was a price to be paid for being the 'model of a modern state'. De Gaury called it social discipline. But Nuri's intelligence agents and their myriad informers displayed such vigilance that less optimistic observers overlooked the modernity and saw only a corrupt and repressive police state whose 'popularity' stemmed from the brutal and indiscriminate suppression of all but its supporters.

As a result, 'by 1958 a great change had come over Iraq', says the highly critical 'Caractacus' (the pseudonym belonged to someone who clearly knew the country well, witnessed the revolution at first hand and, writing only a year after it, deemed anonymity advisable; he looks to have been a teacher, perhaps Scottish). 'Terror and corruption', he continues, 'had between them done their job.' The young king was not unpopular; but his uncle Abd al-Ilah, the ex-Regent, now Crown Prince, and still the power behind the throne, was 'to the ordinary man in the street the symbol of evil living'. Nuri, the power behind the dynasty, was even more cordially detested as, for the fourteenth time, he assumed the prime ministership of what was about to become the Hashemite Union. And the British, the power behind the regime, though increasingly excluded from Iraqi politics by Nuri's machinations, were scarcely less 'unpopular, positively disliked, even hated' than in the 1930s. It was ironic that, just when their presence was about to end, they had discovered a new logic for it in the Baghdad Pact and the containment of communism.

Yet with any protest by the Iraqi people being accounted disorder and so instantly punishable, all remained quiet in Baghdad. The police and the army 'were believed to be loyal' says 'Caractacus', and 'there seemed less immediate likelihood of revolution than there had for years'.[27] Then in March 1958 came the union with Jordan and the closing of Hashemite ranks. Like a Damascene sword, the perceived threat from Cairo's propaganda and from the Soviet-backed UAR dangled menacingly over all Syria's neighbours. The worsening situation in Lebanon was the chief concern. It both invited Hashemite intervention and presaged similar disturbances in Jordan. Accordingly, at Amman's request, Iraqi troops were ordered forward into Jordan in July 1958.

For the 3rd Division of the Iraqi army this posting meant passing through Baghdad *en route* to Rutba by Brooks-Murdoch's road. On the night of 13 July a brigade of this division commanded by Brigadier Abd al-Salam Arif and supported by another under Brigadier Abd al-Karim Qasem, duly marched into the city but did not emerge on the desert road next morning. Instead, in a series of carefully pre-planned manoeuvres, the brigadiers took over the radio station, surrounded the police headquarters, and by 6 a.m. were disarming the palace guard.

Crown Prince Abd al-Ilah was being shaved when he heard the shots. The young king, who had learnt of the revolt over his radio, burst into his uncle's apartments and confirmed his worst suspicions. With the palace surrounded, they had little choice but to surrender. The royal party, including womenfolk and servants, mustered at the palace doors. Then they stepped out into the sunshine of the palace gardens and were instantly shot down.

In a different part of the town Nuri al-Said donned female disguise and for twenty-four hours went on the run. Discovered or betrayed, he too was instantly dispatched. His body, like that of Abd al-Ilah, was then dragged through the streets, repeatedly run over, dismembered and partially exhibited to universal approval. He 'had failed to adapt himself to the political needs of the time', wrote the always diplomatic Humphrey Trevelyan. One of the few Britons to have come out of the Suez crisis with his reputation unsullied, Trevelyan was about to be posted from the frying-pan of Nasser's Cairo to the fire that was post-coup Baghdad.

But it was not actually a *coup d'état*, insisted 'Caractacus'; it was an extremely popular revolution. On 14 July, and for days thereafter, the streets rang with joy as Iraq celebrated its own Bastille Day. Statues associated with the old regime were spontaneously demolished. The five foreigners (two Jordanian, two American and one German) who were also hacked to bits just happened to fall foul of a lynch-mob. It was regrettable but not typical. When the British embassy from whose roof Freya Stark had watched the city burn in 1941 was itself burnt beyond repair, the culprits were supposedly the British themselves who had been incinerating their paperwork. Its staff, though robbed and threatened, were eventually protected by the army. The Iraqi people, like the British ambassador Trevelyan, saw the embassy's destruction as symbolizing that of the forty-year-long Anglo-Arab relationship associated with the names of Townshend, Wilson, Bell, Cox and Lawrence. Trevelyan was saddened, of course, but he understood the Iraqis' delight. 'When [Brigadier Arif and others] spoke of "this blessed day" and "holy day" they expressed what all felt,' wrote 'Caractacus'. Then, with the humourless innocence of the righteous, he added a quotation: 'Bliss was it in that dawn to be alive.'[28]

Game Up

The return from his seventeen years in Saudi exile of Rashid Ali al-Kaylani, the leader of the 1941 revolt, occasioned more rejoicing. 'Lorries filled with cheerful youths and improvised banners drove up and down,' observed 'Caractacus'; in the best traditions of socialist realism, 'groups, often family gatherings', lined the streets 'with the air of holiday-makers'.[29] Simultaneously, in a reversal of 1941 fortunes, British nationals were queueing up for air tickets. 'The old links with Iraq were severed, never to be restored,' wrote Trevelyan.[30]

British intervention on behalf of the toppled regime had been considered but rejected. It was too soon after the Suez fiasco; the revolution was too obviously welcome, and the old regime too quickly liquidated. At first, portraits of the royal family were replaced with ones showing Nasser. But these in turn were hastily removed as Qasem, the new ruler, arrested Nasserists, including his colleague Abd al-Salam Arif, and veered towards the communists. Qasem's ideological convictions would keep the country guessing for some years but clearly they did not coincide with those of the Baghdad Pact. When Iraq formally withdrew, the Pact was dissolved and replaced by the US-backed Central Treaty Organization (CENTO), a variation on the Northern Tier.

The realities of power in the region could no longer be disguised. The Cold War freeze tightened its grip, the US stood forth as the undisputed protector of Western interests, and Israel awaited the summons to act as its agent. Panicked by the revolution in Iraq, Lebanon had immediately asked for and received US support. As the Marines landed in Beirut in August 1958, the British began an airlift of troops into an equally jittery Amman. This action was approved and paid for by the US who also secured the necessary rights to overfly Israeli territory and henceforth shared the burden of subsidizing the Jordanian kingdom. Likewise, when in 1961 Iraq's Qasem revived Iraqi claims to Kuwait, it was only after US approval that British troops were landed to protect the shaykhdom. Britain's forty-year imperium in the Middle East was over. Its ambitions now scarcely extended beyond the protection of oil supplies; and to that end its role scarcely extended beyond providing loyal support for US policies.

At about the same time dispossessed Palestinians were alerted to the existence of al-Fatah, an organization headed by the young Yasser Arafat and dedicated to reviving a sense of the Palestinian nation and securing its return to Palestine. In 1964 Arab leaders officially endorsed this move to the extent of setting up the Palestine Liberation Organization (PLO). Meanwhile in 1962 the Kennedy administration in Washington had agreed to supply Israel with its first ground-to-air missiles. To old injuries new urgency was being added, for old injustices new agonies were being devised. By the early 1960s the transition from colonial-style management of the Middle East to superpower subordination of it could be said to be complete.

EPILOGUE

Reaping the Whirlwind

A SPECIAL RELATIONSHIP

SOMEWHERE IN THE course of the twentieth century, history abruptly slips out of the class-room to join the rough-and-tumble of current affairs. The names begin to have faces; the events stir memories. We recognize them as belonging to the playground of our own experience. A new dimension is added to the record, that of remembered reaction, even engagement.

For the present writer this cognitive puberty came during the late 1950s. The 'Suez Affair' roused the first pricklings of schoolboy awareness; the Iraqi revolution induced a vivid shudder of revulsion. Then Kennedy got elected, just. Three years later he was killed; the clock stopped and we all remembered where we were. It restarted when B-52s began bombing the North Vietnamese cities of Haiphong and Hanoi.

Primed on headlines and newsreels, this sort of personal perception of the past has a seductive immediacy. It is also highly selective, often inconsequential, and not necessarily objective. The headlines owe too much to deadlines; the pictures portray not everything which was worthy of record but something of what was capable of record and congenial to the news provider. For the writer after the event it poses a whole new set of problems. A rapid changing of gears is called for. Instead of grinding across largely dead and unremembered desert, one must address a pool of shared experience. The pool is mired in prejudice and its surface snapping with still lively saurians. Ideally one would change vehicles and start a new book. What follows here is little more than an *aide-mémoire* to the events of the next forty years, an emergency tow-rope to the new century.

In the 1960s a trip to the Middle East usually meant buying a ticket to either Beirut or Tehran. They were the places where the 707s and the VC10s landed on the long haul to the Far East. Air crews usually changed there, and those coming off duty hastened into town for the bars and the poolside. Hilton had hotels there, American Express had offices. In a region churning with Arab-Israeli resentment, within a continent rent by the Cold War, these neon-lit oases welcomed the Westerner to the East with the obliging smiles and the favourable exchange rates he expected. By contrast, Damascus was dirty, Baghdad dangerous, Cairo chaotic, Amman boring, and Jerusalem divided. But Beirut and Tehran were agreeable, colourful, even modern. Their governments were aligned with the West, their economies safe enough to tempt investors. They were the twin show-places of 'the Free World' in the Middle East.

So they remained until the late 1970s, windows on the region for the well-heeled visitor if plate-glass affronts to the unshod resident. Iran under the Shah seemed not only a model of stability but also a beacon of progress. Ambitious development plans got under way; schools, highways and hospitals were built; the armed forces were among the best-equipped in Asia. Lebanon in the 1960s, though less stable and less crucial to the containment of communism, espoused more liberal values and boasted a more representative government. Such attributes, laudable in themselves, were rare enough among the West's clients to be worth upholding. Sandbagged by the presence of US Marines, in 1958 Lebanon's intricate system of confessional power-sharing had withstood the threat of civil war, survived the fall-out from the Iraqi revolution, and continued to weather the blasts of contempt emanating from the United Arab Republic. It helped that the US Marines did not overstay their welcome and that the revolutionaries in Iraq obligingly turned against Nasser's Arabism. The momentum towards a pan-Arab super-state seemed to have stalled.

Then Pan-Arabism went into reverse. In 1961 it was not Lebanon which fell a casualty to the chronic feuding of Levantine politics but

Syria. Capitalizing on the widespread resentment of Cairo's management of the Syrian economy, a military faction declared Syria's secession from the UAR and set up a new government in Damascus. Syria was conforming to its reputation for being ungovernable just as Iraq had lived up to its reputation for what Freya Stark called 'notorious savagery' in its 1958 revolution. If anywhere seemed to be living on borrowed time, it was not Tehran and Beirut but Damascus and Baghdad.

Prominent in the latter cities, as in Cairo, were East European 'engineers' toasting Soviet-Arab friendship while their wives courted sunburn in capacious floral swimsuits. Nasser might crack down on his own communists, and Qasem in Baghdad use his as storm-troopers, but Moscow was learning to live with the ideological inconsistencies of the Arab world. So was Washington. Clearly Nasser was far from the crypto-communist of British demonology. Islam abhorred the godless doctrines of Marxism, and Egypt's Arabism was as wary of the imperialism of the East as of the West. The CIA and the State Department maintained close links with Cairo; limited US aid to Egypt resumed; and in 1960 Nasser met Eisenhower in New York. Rapprochement was in the air. The election of John F. Kennedy, Nasser's equal in both age and charisma, produced a friendly exchange of letters between the two leaders and a new three-year aid programme.

In the post-Suez decade even the Arab-Israeli confrontation appeared more manageable. The Eisenhower administration, perhaps the least sympathetic of any to Israeli anxieties, had accompanied its condemnation of the 1956 Suez war by demanding a complete withdrawal of Israel's forces from Sinai and Gaza. Tel Aviv prevaricated, but eventually concurred on two conditions: the UN Emergency Force must establish its *cordon sanitaire* on the Egyptian side of the 1949 armistice line; and Israel's handing back of Sharm el Sheikh, a place at the southern tip of the Sinai peninsula which commanded the Straits of Tiran into the Gulf of Aqaba, should not entitle Egypt to claim the straits as within its territorial waters and close them to international shipping. With the Suez Canal closed to Israel-bound shipping, this last mattered most; for only through the Straits of Tiran to the port of Elat (Eilat) at the head of the Gulf of Aqaba could Israel conveniently import eastern commodities, like oil.

Epilogue

Egypt resented both these conditions as contrary to the principle of restoring the pre-1956 borders and unwarranted infringements of its national sovereignty. But for ten years it did not challenge them and for ten years Israel avoided provoking such a challenge. Egyptian forces became involved in a civil war in Yemen; Israel was more exercised over attacks across and within its existing borders by Palestinian guerrillas. Meanwhile the US and the USSR indulged their respective clients with the military hardware and the diplomatic sweet-talk that would make further war feasible.

In the Middle East, as in south-east Asia, Kennedy created precedents for his successor Lyndon Johnson to adopt as principles. Despite his regard for Nasser, Kennedy aired the idea of 'a special relationship' with Israel and authorized the $21 million sale of largely defensive Hawk missiles. Johnson, already a staunch friend to Israel, took the special relationship for granted and provided an offensive arsenal of top-of-the-range tanks and fighter-bombers worth over $100 million.

There were always cogent reasons for such a radical departure from Washington's avowed aim of limiting arms sales to the region. The tanks were needed to offset the US weaponry being supplied to Saudi Arabia for its Cold War defence but which might, nevertheless, be used against Israel; the planes were needed to pre-empt a pro-Israeli outcry on Capitol Hill over arms supplied to Jordan to discourage it from buying from the Soviets; as for the ancillary equipment, the spare parts and the ammunition, they were essential to match continuing Soviet shipments to Syria, Iraq and Egypt. Inexorably Cold War rivalry was combining with divisions inside the Arab world and the imperatives of American domestic politics to propel the United States into becoming Israel's main backer. It followed that Israel enjoyed the status of America's protégé. But there was no alliance. A treaty would have invited the ire of both the Soviets and the Arabs. And it was unnecessary. To so special a relationship an unstated understanding was more appropriate.

With the Israelis and the Egyptians well primed with both guns and grievances, the 1967 conflagration should not have taken the international community by surprise. Wars elsewhere, especially in Indo-China, were marginalizing the squabbles of Arabs and Israelis and distracting the superpowers. Israeli plans to divert the waters of the Jordan river for irrigation purposes, Palestinian attacks on Israeli

— 6 day war

citizens, a devastating Israeli raid into Jordanian territory as retaliation, and artillery exchanges along the Israeli-Syrian border occasioned considerable alarm. But such matters looked manageable and were not seen as preludes to war.

To the fragile regimes in Damascus and Amman, however, as to Israel's embattled Labour government, these incidents were a matter of life and death. Arab ranks were the first to close as the hitherto inactive Nasser entered into a mutual defence pact with Syria, then Jordan. Goaded into further action by his allies, in May 1967 Nasser responded to new Syrian-Israeli clashes and the perceived danger of an Israeli invasion of Syria by moving troops up to his Sinai border. More ominously the UN removed its Emergency Force from Egyptian territory at Nasser's request, and Egypt reasserted its right to close the Straits of Tiran.

Supported by the US and Britain, Israel protested vigorously over the closure of the Straits, demanded international action, and then went on to a war footing. The formation of a government of national unity in which the still fire-breathing Menachem Begin became a minister and Moshe Dayan, the one-eyed darling of the military, took charge of defence, boded ill for any compliance with the UN's continuing deliberations. Nasser was insisting that Egypt would not fire first, but no such undertaking was explicitly forthcoming from Tel Aviv; and though Washington assumed that the Israelis would at least wait for the UN's ruling, it assumed wrong.

Without warning on 5 June 1967 Israel launched a massive air attack that effectively wiped out the air forces of Egypt, Jordan and Syria before they could become airborne. There followed a rapid Israeli advance across Sinai towards and beyond the Suez Canal, the simultaneous seizure of Jerusalem's Old City and the military occupation of Gaza, of Jordan's West Bank territories, and of Syria's Golan Heights. It was all over within a week. Instead of the roughly 50 per cent of mandated Palestine awarded to the Zionists by the UN's 1947 partition, or the roughly 75 per cent achieved as a result of the 1948–9 Arab-Israeli war, Israel now controlled 100 per cent, plus substantial chunks of Egyptian and Syrian territory.

Washington could not but be impressed. Though taken by surprise, though unpersuaded by mendacious Israeli claims that Egypt had made the first move, and though enfuriated by an Israeli attack on the intelligence-gathering USS *Liberty* that left 34 Americans dead, it did not censure the aggressor. Such a course was unthinkable in a US domestic climate overwhelmingly disposed in favour of Israel and would long remain so. Technically the US had declared itself neutral; but neutrality was not to be construed as indifference, least of all by the Soviets whose feared intervention was vigorously discouraged. This the Israelis interpreted as meaning that they had at least tacit US support. The Arabs were convinced of it, crediting claims even of active US involvement in the war. US diplomats in Cairo were therefore sent packing, and Washington found itself the whipping boy of the Arab world. The 1967 war had in fact exploded the fiction of US neutrality. Israel was now acknowledged as America's most favoured client and America as Israel's exclusive patron.

As in 1948, an Israeli reverse would have severely embarrassed Washington. So would an Israeli advance as laboured as that of the British and French in 1956. A whirlwind victory, though, was cause for barely suppressed satisfaction. US weaponry had proved effective, Washington's leverage in the region was enhanced, and the American public's pro-Israeli leanings were vindicated. The Soviets had been wrong-footed and found wanting by their Arab clients. Arab leaders had in turn been discredited in the eyes of their own people; and the Arab states had been discredited in the eyes of the luckless, still stateless and now largely homeless Palestinians.

Ill and demoralized, Nasser was dissuaded from resigning; but he died in 1970 with defeat still unavenged. He was succeeded by Anwar Sadat, his underrated vice-president who nevertheless took to the reins of power with relish. In the same year in Damascus, Hafez Assad, a wily Alawi air force officer, elbowed a path to power past disputatious Ba'thist colleagues hoist with the stigma of the 1967 defeat. In Iraq, too, defeat had compounded the unpopularity of the incumbent regime. Ineffectually led by the brother of one of the 1958 revolutionaries, it was eased from power in an unusually bloodless revolution staged by Iraqi Ba'thists in 1968. Already estranged from their Syrian brethren, Iraq's Ba'thists were much beholden for their success to Saddam Husayn, now a clean-cut, industrious and scruple-free 30-year-old who was about to become security chief and vice-president.

Only in Amman was there no change; King Husayn, the last of the reigning Hashemites, clung on in Jordan. But it was a Jordan whose territory, without the West Bank, was pruned back to the Transjordan of old and whose population included nearly as many Palestinians as Jordanians. From the occupied West Bank at least another 250,000 refugees had crossed the river during and after the 1967 war. Jordan found itself accommodating more Palestinians than what was once – and must, they vowed, again be – Palestine.

That Gaza and the West Bank should indeed be returned to Arab rule, and Sinai and the Golan to the Egyptians and Syrians, was the evident intent of UN Resolution 242 of November 1967. Accepted by all parties with the exception of Syria and the Palestinians themselves, this resolution was rightly seen as a milestone. But the price of a limited consensus was a woeful caution of wording. In calling for 'the withdrawal of Israeli armed forces from territories occupied in the recent conflict' Resolution 242 shied away from actually identifying the territories and further obscured its intent by linking withdrawal to a host of less assessable requirements – such as an end to 'claims' of belligerence or 'threats' of force, and the recognition of the integrity and independence of all existing states (including Israel). Israel contended that even its partial withdrawal was contingent on the prior and complete fulfilment of these latter requirements; the Arabs claimed that fulfilment of the latter requirements, in so far as they could be fulfilled, was contingent on a complete and prior Israeli withdrawal.

In a bid to close the gap between these interpretations – and so halt a new and escalating Egypto-Israeli 'war of attrition' along the Suez Canal – in 1970 William Rogers, US Secretary of State in the first Nixon administration, advanced a settlement plan. Cairo indicated acceptance; so did Husayn of Jordan. But the plan, based on Resolution 242, was anathema to rejectionists on both sides – to Begin and his Zionist Revisionists (who had withdrawn from government over Israel's earlier acceptance of Resolution 242) and to Syria and the various Palestinian guerrilla groupings who were now massed in Jordan. The latter included Yasser Arafat's mainly Muslim al-Fatah, George Habash's Maoist-leaning and Christian-led Popular Front for the Liberation of Palestine (PFLP) and the umbrella Palestine Liberation Organization (PLO).

As US support for the Rogers plan wavered, and as tension between King Husayn and these radical Palestinian groups grew, a multiple hijacking of civilian airliners by the PFLP grabbed the world's attention. One of the planes was landed in Cairo and there stormed, three others were grounded and eventually blown up in Jordan. There was little loss of life but much photogenic pistol-waving. By inviting international opprobrium the Palestinians sought to advertise their desperation and to nail the responsibility for it not just on Israel but on the Western powers as a whole.

Western outrage quickly choked on a still greater crisis when, in early September 1970, Jordan plunged into civil war. In real danger of being overthrown, King Husayn had ordered his forces to engage and expel the Palestinian militias. Syrian tanks then rolled south in support of the Palestinians, Israeli forces readied to intervene in support of Husayn, and the US Sixth Fleet manoeuvred to support the Israelis. It remained only for Moscow to make good on its threatened intervention on behalf of the Syrians for the 'global flashpoint' to ignite and Armageddon to begin. That it did not was largely thanks to the Jordanian military, whose attacks on the invading Syrians secured their retreat and whose ferocious treatment of the Palestinians effected Husayn's expulsion of the armed guerrilla groups. Most of them relocated to Lebanon, some under the banner of 'Black September', that being the month of massacres and intimidation during which Husayn had betrayed the Palestinian fighters and driven them into a second exile.

The Jordanian crisis satisfactorily demonstrated Nixon's contention that Israel, once deemed a quasi-socialist republic and an embarrassment to US relations with the Arab world, might now be regarded as a Cold War asset with a strategic utility of proven potential. In this enhanced role the Tel Aviv government joined the ranks of other stalwarts, like Iran's Shah and Indonesia's Suharto, whose willingness to share the burden of the 'Free World's' defence entitled them to generous supplies of the latest US weaponry.

Egypt, naturally, objected. Still counting on the Rogers plan, Sadat had taken little part in the Jordanian scare and in 1972 signalled his hopes for the future by expelling Soviet military advisers. But as Israel acquired more Phantom jets, as its 1971 US arms bill was revealed to have topped $600 million (mostly on credit or low-interest loans), and as US pressure for an Israeli retreat from Sinai fizzled out amid Nixon's 1972 electioneering requirements, Sadat despaired of wooing Washington and resolved to force the issue by other means. Operations to reclaim the occupied territories were concerted with Assad in Damascus; and having this time reserved for themselves the option of striking first, in October 1973 Egyptian and Syrian troops mounted a simultaneous offensive.

The 1967 war, known to Arabs as 'the June War' and to Israelis as 'the Six-Day War', had clarified the region's political allegiances but confounded its geographical divisions. The 1973 war, known to Arabs as 'the October War' and to Israelis as 'the Yom Kippur War', failed to redress the geographical imbalance but greatly complicated the pattern of regional alignments. It lasted eighteen days, three times as long as the '67 war; and the Arabs again lost. After early successes which did much to restore Arab morale, the Syrians were driven back in the Golan and the Egyptians from Sinai. Arab territories occupied in '67 remained occupied; further Israeli acquisitions were halted only by the superpowers tinkering with the flow of arms and concerting peace moves.

Waged against the new background of Soviet-American détente, the '73 war wrung from the superpowers less of rhetoric and more of management. A clash between them did threaten, but over Soviet demands for a role in future peace-keeping rather than over the war itself. Any untoward escalation seemed more likely to come from the actual belligerents. Israel was by now widely supposed to possess a nuclear capability, a contention which mercifully remained unproven. And the Arab states, though they lacked anything of comparable enormity, were reassured to discover an entirely legitimate, but no less effective, instrument of power in their oil exports.

Herein lay the real novelty of the '73 war. Instead of blowing up airliners like the PFLP, the Arab world could nail its grievances on the doors of the West and expect redress simply by withholding oil. The superpowers might control the flow of arms but the Arabs controlled the flow of crude; and with even the US now importing a third of its total oil requirement, the West was peculiarly vulnerable. Ten days into the '73 war, Arab members of the Organization of Petroleum Exporting Countries (OPEC) announced a production cut of 5 per cent per month until such time as Israel should withdraw from the territories occupied in 1967. This was quickly followed by a complete embargo on all oil sales to the US when Nixon approached Congress for the $2 billion needed to fund military replacements for the Israeli armed forces. The shortfall in oil deliveries, not to mention the war itself, had the inevitable effect of bidding up prices, which quadrupled in the space of a year. This in turn panicked buyers, inflated costs, pushed up interest rates and threatened to provoke world recession.

None of which endeared the Arabs to the West or undermined US sympathy for Israel. Neither did it last. Fearful of losing their market share, the Arab states lifted their embargo in March 1974. But the embargo, while it lasted, had concentrated Western minds, most notably that of US Secretary of State Henry Kissinger who began protracted negotiations between Israel and Egypt, and Israel and Syria. These produced grudging agreement from Assad to the disengagement of his forces in the Golan and two much more encouraging agreements with Sadat over staged Israeli withdrawals from part of Sinai. In return, Israel got from Washington financial compensation, more weaponry and various pledges (including one about the US not dealing with the PLO). Cairo also got limited US aid and pledges, the latter including a commitment to full implementation of Resolution 242. But the Palestinian territories of Gaza and the West Bank, as also much of Sinai and the Golan, remained under Israeli occupation. Indeed, they now became subject to Revisionist Zionism's programme for their colonization by Jewish settlers with a view to eventual annexation. To many Arabs, especially Palestinians and Syrians, Sadat's unilateralism seemed ineffectual, neglectful of the Palestinian cause, fatal to Arab unity, and designed to secure purely Egyptian objectives, like the 1975 reopening of the Suez Canal.

These suspicions were confirmed when in 1977, to the delight of the new Carter administration in Washington, Sadat flew to Jerusalem to address the Israeli Knesset. His offer – of peace plus recognition of the state of Israel in return for the gradual handover of the occupied territories – was less significant than the fact that it was being made to a just-installed right-wing coalition government led by Menachem Begin. A portrait of Vladimir Jabotinsky, the embodiment of Revisionism, now hung in the Israeli prime minister's office. No administration headed by one for whom even trans-Jordan formed part of Israel's historic 'Promised Land' was going to relinquish the cis-Jordan West Bank ('Judaea' and 'Samaria' in Revisionist-speak), or Gaza, or any part of Jerusalem.

The only occupied territory which was disposable, and the one which Sadat most coveted, was Sinai. Anciently, as recently, it had been part of Egypt, never of Zion. Otherwise a howling wilderness with a couple of oilfields (for which the US would compensate Israel) and some strategic potential (which would be negated by peaceful coexistence), Sinai duly became the centrepiece of the Begin-Sadat negotiations orchestrated at Camp David in Maryland by the painfully well-intentioned Jimmy Carter.

The significance of the Camp David accords, reached in 1978 and ratified in 1979, was grossly inflated in the West. They did include a 'Framework for Peace in the Middle East' which dutifully reaffirmed Resolution 242 with provision for Jordan and even 'representatives of the Palestinian people' to join Egypt and Israel in further negotiations. But given that the sole Palestinian body with any representative credentials was the PLO, and given that the PLO was now chaired by Arafat, wedded to terror tactics, still in denial of Resolution 242, and totally unacceptable to the Israeli people (let alone Begin) as a negotiating partner, the 'Framework for Peace' carried little conviction.

The only Camp David accord with substance was that by which Israel, in return for a peace treaty with Egypt recognizing its existence, withdrew from all of Sinai. The principle of trading territory for peace in unilateral negotiations with individual Arab states was thus established. So was that of both parties being handsomely rewarded with more US arms and aid packages. As for the US itself, it had neutralized one volatile Middle Eastern frontier and gained a significant new recruit to the congress of 'freedom-loving peoples'. Egypt, in short, had defected – from Palestinian activism, from Arab socialism and from the Soviet ambit. For that, Camp David rejoiced American hearts. And for that, Sadat, now the revered statesman, Nobel laureate and increasingly autocratic darling of the West, paid the price. In 1981 he was gunned down by Egypt's habitual executioners, a cell of 'Islamic fanatics'.

HOSTAGES AND MARTYRS

The pyramids were now back on the international 'must-see' list. Cameleers brushed up their English; Cairo's 'open door' beckoned. But almost simultaneously the lights began flickering in Beirut and Tehran. The twin showrooms of the Western alliance were suddenly 'inadvisable', and stop-overs in their five-star hotels hard to organize. Carter's Camp David euphoria had lasted less than a year. His administration, from a zenith of Middle Eastern achievement, was plunging to its nadir.

Strife in Lebanon had been predicted. The influx of 400,000 Palestinian refugees had already upset the country's delicate confessional balance. With the arrival from Jordan of armed and strife-ridden Palestinian guerrillas, militancy became endemic. Internationally the Black Septembrists were excelling themselves with assassinations, hijackings and a particularly heinous massacre of Israeli athletes at the 1972 Munich Olympics. Two years later an unabashed Yasser Arafat attended the UN to offer the world a choice between, as he put it, the olive branch and the gun. Partial UN recognition and Arab League endorsement followed. The PLO was sufficiently encouraged to act in the manner of the Zionist Agency under the British mandate and set up a skeleton administration-in-waiting, or 'national authority', based in southern Lebanon. Raids thence into Israel were mounted and duly reciprocated, bringing grief to the mainly Shi'ite Lebanese of the area as much as to the Palestinians.

In 1975–6 the situation deteriorated into civil war, initially between the militias of Lebanon's right-wing Christians and left-wing Druze but soon involving the Palestinians and the Syrians as well as most of Lebanon's myriad sects. If the reported death toll of 50,000 may be credited, little Lebanon's blood-letting exceeded that of any Arab-Israeli conflict to date. Peace, as brokered by the Arab states and enforced by the presence of Syrian troops, proved patchy and not altogether popular. It was shattered in 1978 when, following Palestinian raids into Israel that left 37 civilians dead, the Begin government unleashed the first major Israeli incursion into southern Lebanon.

International outrage secured an early withdrawal. But the Israelis left the border area in the hands of a friendly Lebanese warlord to keep the pressure on the Palestinians; the UN International Force in Lebanon proved an irrelevance; and with the PLO's 'administration-in-waiting' anything but patient, the next Israeli incursion was not long in materializing. It came in 1982, a full-scale invasion rather than an incursion. Beirut itself was heavily bombed, then besieged by Israeli ground forces. Tanks now replaced tourist buses on the famous corniche. The show-place had become a war zone.

Tehran's demise – redemption according to most Iranians – was less expected. The CIA may have saved the Shah in 1953 but seemingly neither it nor any other intelligence agency anticipated being called on to do so in 1978. Détente or not, the Pentagon's suspicious eyes were still on the Soviets, whose imminent adventure into the medieval world of neighbouring Afghanistan would justify such vigilance. Iran, on the other hand, had long since embraced the twentieth century and shown itself proof against Marxist revolution and random regicide. Carter marvelled at the people's 'respect, admiration and love' for their Shah; their country he called 'an island of stability in one of the most troubled regions of the world'. That what the West regarded as the most proudly progressive of states might be on the verge of succumbing to the most inordinately retrograde of revolutions was, in the US ambassador's judgement, 'unthinkable'.

But progress – in terms of mass education, conspicuous consumption and rapid urbanization – had brought its drawbacks. The clerical establishment, a much more influential body in Shi'ite Iran than in the mainly Sunni Arab countries, condemned the new climate of intellectual, material and sexual entitlement as un-Islamic and attributed it to what many Muslims regarded as the West's irreligion and vulgarity. From the comparative safety of an Iraqi and then French exile, the outspoken Ayatollah Khomeini was particularly critical of the Shah, a now imperious figure in whom Western adulation, declining health and unlimited petro-dollars had induced a bespangled megalomania. Under his Savak-ridden rule the constitution offered an outlet for only the most anodyne dissent. Khomeini's fearless messianic challenge, relayed by radio and audio-cassettes, struck a chord of wonder. To rich and poor, right and left, religious and secular, it carried irresistible conviction. Whether all understood, let alone endorsed, the finer points of Islamic revolution and theocratic rule was beside the point. Demonology came before ideology. The US was 'the Great Satan', the Shah his despicable creature; and both must go.

Disbelieving as well as indecisive, the Shah hung on throughout 1978. Paralysing strikes, massive demonstrations and sporadically draconian repression climaxed in December. The Shah made way for a cabinet composed of his more moderate opponents. But Khomeini disowned them, and with the ferment unabated in early 1979 the Shah fled the country. Khomeini's followers took power. Amid the burning of US flags and a welcome verging on a stampede, the Ayatollah returned to enact his revolution.

The Carter administration, bathed in Camp David smiles throughout these dramatic events, still expected to salvage something from the ruins. After all, Khomeini had no love for the godless Soviets; Iran still needed Western markets for its oil and Western spare parts for its armed forces; and if a conservative Islamic monarchy like that of the Saudis could enjoy excellent relations with Washington, why not a revolutionary Islamic republic?

But for Khomeini, compromise with 'the Great Satan' was out of the question. If there was still a role for the Stars and Stripes, it was merely as fuel for the furnace in which his revolutionary support was to be cauterized. Carter obligingly provided a pretext by admitting the now dying Shah to the US in November 1979 for medical treatment. Khomeini railed at this harbouring of a criminal and, ostensibly to provide bargaining counters for the Shah's extradition but more realistically to sustain the white heat of revolution and burn off less combustible moderates (like the incumbent prime minister), first condoned and then upheld an attack on the US embassy in Tehran. Flouting diplomatic convention, his revolutionary activists took some 70 hostages, most of them US citizens.

The hostages would remain in custody for over a year, their release only coming on 20 January 1981. Not perhaps coincidentally, that was also the day on which in Washington Ronald Reagan was sworn into office as President. In the US, as in Iran, the hostages had become political fodder. Khomeini was happy to hold on to them only for as long as the international advantages to be gained from their release were outweighed by the domestic advantages to be gained from their retention. Carter, on the other hand, with the 1980 elections looming, wanted them back fast. When sanctions failed (not to mention negotiations, adjudications and deportations), the US military got the nod. Its rescue attempt, dogged by technical failures, proved an unmitigated disaster with incriminating evidence left strewn about the desert and its casualties all self-inflicted. Even the death of the Shah in July 1980 made no difference to the plight of the hostages. Meanwhile Reagan, though not unhappy to see his presidential opponent repeatedly smeared with failure, was deeply worried that an eve-of-poll release of the hostages might yet torpedo otherwise certain victory.

The hostage issue preyed on American minds throughout 1980. When it slipped from the headlines, it was only to make room for worse tidings. Oil prices were again being inflated by panic buying, initially because of the Iranian situation, then because of war: the Soviets had invaded Afghanistan in the dying days of 1979; nine months later Iraq invaded Iran. The spectre of Loy Henderson flourishing maps and foretelling an apocalypse in the Gulf returned to haunt US policy-makers. Khomeini's revolution had torn a hole in the basketwork of the communism-containing 'Northern Tier'. As a result, the Soviets were streaming into Afghanistan from where they scented warm Arabian waters across a mere 300 miles of undefended desert. The Gulf was already being destabilized by Iran's attempts to export its Islamic revolution to the oil-producing emirates. And now Iraq, under a Ba'thist regime which was heavily indebted to the Soviets, still technically at war with Israel, and allegedly bent on developing nuclear weapons, threatened to overrun the Iranian oil-fields and so challenge the Saudis' clout in the oil business and the Gulf.

Against this deteriorating situation, Carter's chances of securing a second term looked bleak. Smiling hostages deplaning on to American tarmac might have helped the Democrats' chances, but probably not decisively. On the other hand, any hint that Republican party aides were exploring contacts with representatives of the Khomeini government to delay a hostage release would have been disastrous for Reagan. Such a deal – whereby Iran would postpone the hostage release until after the election in return for the supply of much-needed military spares – simply beggared belief. It was also treasonable. Yet an airlift of spares to Tehran did indeed take place, albeit from Israel. The Israelis would later admit that this operation was co-ordinated with US officials. And five years later precisely the same ruse would be adopted when Reagan again endeavoured to negotiate with Tehran over a new hostage crisis.

The new hostages were chained to radiators and immured in basements not in Tehran but in Beirut. Israel's 1982 invasion of Lebanon, though roundly condemned by most Western countries as a flagrant breach of Lebanese sovereignty, had elicited an ambiguous response from the Reagan administration. Obsessed by 'the evil empire' of the Soviet Union, hawks in the new administration applauded the Israeli destruction of Soviet missiles positioned in

Lebanon by the Syrians. They also sympathized with Israeli bombardments of the PLO aimed at forcing its fighters to surrender or evacuate.

After considerable carnage, the PLO chose the latter. The US operated as honest broker, securing a cease-fire and providing troops to ensure safe conduct for 1,300 PLO guerrillas. They sailed away to Algeria and Tunisia; the US troops were in turn withdrawn; and Beirut's Palestinian refugees were left to the tender mercies of Lebanon's Christian militia groups plus the Israeli forces, some of which promptly moved into West Beirut, supposedly to keep the peace. Following the September 1982 assassination of their leader, the Christian militias descended on Beirut's Sabra and Shatila refugee camps. The camps had already been sealed off by Israeli troops whose observation posts overlooked them. Yet the militiamen entered the camps unchallenged by the Israelis and for two days went about their business unmolested, if not actively assisted, by the Israelis. Between 800 and 2,000 unarmed Palestinians, many of them women and children, were massacred.

Perpetrated in a city well served by newsmen and aid workers, this was one atrocity which did not go unnoticed. As well as discrediting in Israeli eyes Prime Minister Begin, his deputy Yitzhak Shamir, and his Defence Minister Ariel Sharon (who was forced to resign), it scandalized the international community and exposed the US to accusations of having abandoned the Palestinians to their fate. In response, a multi-national peace-keeping force, including US Marines, was quickly reinstated in Beirut. But the Israeli invasion, the massacres and the US 'betrayal' had also provoked radical Islamist groups. Hizbollah and Islamic Jihad, though sympathetic to the Palestinians, were ensconced in Lebanon under Syrian protection and inspired and directed by revolutionary Iran. To recruits thirsting for revenge, whether Palestinian or Lebanese Shi'ites, the mullahs handed round the chalice of martyrdom.

In April 1983 a suicide bomber detonated himself in the US embassy in Beirut, killing 17 Americans including two senior CIA officers. US clashes with the Islamist guerrillas then escalated, and six months later a bomber in a truck drove into the US lines at Beirut airport. The explosion of his load claimed the lives of over 300 servicemen, the majority of them US Marines. Reagan's face-saving response was to deny the enemy further triumphs by redeploying the

US contingent off-shore. Hizbollah and the other guerrilla groups responded by targeting individual Westerners who were either taken hostage, killed, or both.

Massacres, though they made the headlines, soon became history. Hostages stayed in the news; loved ones, employers and the hostage-takers themselves saw to it. As the US would discover in bombing raids over Libya in 1987, taking the fight to the 'terrorists' raised all manner of domestic and international complications. But hatching deals with hostage-takers could always be denied; and a hostage freed was pure political gain. So reasoned members of Reagan's National Security Council as they opened – or reopened – contacts with revolutionary Iran when in 1985 Israeli troops were finally withdrawn from most of Lebanon.

Colossal losses and a virtual stalemate in their continuing war found both Iran and Iraq badly in need of new weaponry, with the Iranians particularly desirous of anti-tank and anti-aircraft missiles. Apropos the Beirut hostages Reagan loftily proclaimed 'no concessions . . . no deals'. But he could not speak for others. Israel had long supported distant and distracted Iran against still hostile Arab Iraq and in 1981 had launched a pre-emptive strike to obliterate Baghdad's French-supplied nuclear reactor. Additionally Israel was in a position to supply Iran with the required missiles and to obtain, without undue scrutiny, replacements from the US. If Iran, in exchange for missiles, could get its protégés in Lebanon to release the hostages, America could only be grateful.

George Schultz and Caspar Weinberger, the US Secretaries of State and Defense, opposed any such deal and were kept in ignorance of its progress. Reagan, whether honestly or wilfully, would not be able to remember how much he knew of it. And others, who did know of it, would claim ignorance of its even more controversial refinement whereby the proceeds of the arms sales to Iran, after hefty commissions to the go-betweens, were used to finance the operations of right-wing guerrillas in Nicaragua, the so-called Contras. Whether or not the missiles were supplied via Israel, the deal with Iran shattered an international embargo on arms sales to that country which the US itself was vigorously enforcing on its allies. And similarly, funding the Contras ran decidedly contra to a recent congressional amendment blocking US support for them. Notwithstanding any of these objections, the operation went ahead.

Epilogue

In 1985 it took 500 missiles to produce one hostage. The Iranians persistently reneged, while in the US National Security Council Oliver North simply persisted. In 1986 missiles by the thousand were supplied direct from the US, plus some strategic data gained from aerial surveillance. This produced two hostages. They were the last. A Lebanese journal had pieced together what was happening, and publication brought too much corroboration for the official denials to be accepted. The subsequent investigation claimed the scalp of Oliver North, among others. Reagan, saved by amnesia, now wanted nothing more to do with Tehran. He reasserted his public denunciations of its regime and looked with greater favour on the war still being waged against it by Saddam Husayn's Iraq.

The Iran-Iraq War, known as 'the Gulf War' until that title was appropriated by the international community for its own 1991 reckoning with Saddam Husayn, was indeed spilling into the Gulf. One of the century's longer wars (1980–8), it was also one of its bloodiest with casualties far exceeding those suffered during any other purely Middle Eastern conflict. Yet until 1986 the wider world took scant account of it. The belligerents enjoyed little international sympathy. The best the West could hope for was that neither should gain a decisive advantage and both eventually lose. Tactically retrograde, the fighting was an ill-reported affair of tanks and trenches, of mustard gas and Maginot lines, like the First World War. Human waves of kamikaze conscripts advanced to their death in fruitless endeavour; fronts shifted little from one year to the next. Meanwhile a 'battle of the cities' claimed thousands of civilian lives as Baghdad and Tehran exchanged bombing raids and missiles.

Iraq had started the conflict. Saddam Husayn, President of Iraq since 1979 but effective leader since 1969, had resented the Shah's support of Iraq's ever-fractious Kurds in the north of his country and now feared Khomeini's influence among Iraq's Shi'ite majority in the south. As since the days of its inception, Iraq had the look of a state at odds with itself. But an enemy was a useful distraction, and failing the British (who were gone) and the Israelis (who were too formidable), Iran would serve. The turmoil of the Khomeini revolution coupled with Iran's loss of US patronage and weaponry provided an opportunity.

At first all went well for Saddam. Then in 1982 the Iranians hit back, pushing the Iraqis on to their own soil. Saddam offered peace but refused the terms on offer. Interestingly it was Khomeini's Iran which first insisted that, in any reckoning, the *sine qua non* was that Saddam must go. Instead of Iraq grabbing Iran's oil, on which the West had ceased to count, Iran now looked set to grab Iraq's oil, which after long years of low production due to disputes over rights was being pumped for all it was worth. Each side attacked the other's installations and tried to prevent tankers sailing. But Iran's interdiction was the more effective and it obliged Iraq to turn to its Arab neighbours for financial support, especially Saudi Arabia and Kuwait.

The Gulf states, so long of little consequence, had by now come to loom large in Western thinking. Thanks in part to the hike in oil prices in the 1970s but equally to a combination of more advantageous deals with the oil companies, more locally added value through refining operations, and vastly increased production, receipts from petro-sales had rocketed. The sleepy Gulf creeks of the 1940s had become the gleaming city-states of the 1980s. They attracted labour and expertise from all over the Arab world and the Far East while, in the West, purchasing heavily and investing handsomely. Sales to the Gulf states, especially of the weaponry now commonly designated as 'defence systems', filled Western order books; Saudi Arabia was said to have currency reserves that exceeded those of the US and Japan combined. Even economies, like Britain's, which were now less dependent on the Gulf's exports thanks to recent oil and gas discoveries nearer home, could ill afford to forgo the Gulf's imports.

Kuwait's $7 billion war loan to Baghdad did not go unnoticed in Tehran. The Iranian forces edging into Iraq were now on Kuwait's doorstep and its oil exports were exposed to Iranian attack. Kuwait therefore appealed for international protection and was answered by the Soviet Union, whose bid was hastily trumped by the US. As of early 1987 Kuwaiti tankers were reflagged with the Stars and Stripes and were afforded protection through the Gulf from US warships, later aided by British and French vessels.

The resultant confrontation never quite lived up to its billing as 'the Tanker War'. Numerous incidents involving Iranian mines and gunboats nearly ignited it; but the most deadly action, the destruction by a US Navy missile of an Iranian airliner and its 290 passengers, apparently as a result of misidentification, came in July 1988 when Iran had indicated acceptance of a UN cease-fire. The cease-fire held, and the US Navy's explanation of the disaster appeared to

Epilogue

have been accepted. But what many Muslims still reckoned a flagrant act of terrorism was not forgotten. Four days before Christmas 1988, the bomb which pulverized Pan Am 103 over Lockerbie in Scotland killing all 243 passengers, most of them Americans, was widely seen as a settling of scores.

GROUND TO ZERO

In the late 1980s, as the West looked ever more anxiously towards the Gulf, the Middle East was turning ever more readily to radical Islam. It was thus somewhat ironic that the regime with which the world, instigated by the West, went to war in early 1991 was one of the most secular in the region. Saddam Husayn had fought the fanaticism of Islamic revolution for eight years. His regime was grounded in Ba'thism, a resurgent brand of Arab Socialism that owed more to Moscow than to Mecca. Indeed Ba'thism's co-founder and ideologue, a Christian, had been made welcome in Saddam's Iraq whose social climate was markedly more liberal than that of the Gulf states, including Kuwait, and especially Saudi Arabia. Saddam was no religious bigot; and neither was he a crazed tyrant impervious to the aspirations of his people. His use of chemical weapons in 1988 against those Kurdish districts that had welcomed the Iranian invader certainly ranks high among international obscenities; but, as noted, it was not without precedent; nor was it, to many Arab Iraqis, irrational.

The same could be said of the action that brought down on him the wrath of 'Desert Storm'. In fact Saddam's 1990 invasion and annexation of Kuwait was a logical move calculated to popularize and so, he hoped, legitimize his rule. Even those Iraqis whom he drove into exile largely supported it. Since the 1930s Baghdad's claim to Kuwait, however doubtful in international law, had been promoted by Iraqis of every persuasion, from the unfortunate King Ghazi to the ultra-conservative Nuri al-Said and the revolutionary Brigadier Qasem. Geographically, the Kuwaiti emirate was lodged in Iraq's narrow Gulf frontage, its only maritime outlet for oil, like a cork in a bottle. The war with Iran had demonstrated how vulnerable this outlet was. And, making the inevitable linkage, Iraqis saw the cork's removal by fellow Arabs as rather less objectionable than the unremitting and unredressed appropriation of Arab Palestine by Jewish Israel.

Epilogue

Quite rightly, none of this impressed UN signatories sworn to uphold the sovereignty and integrity of existing states, especially when the same signatories had interests, mainly oil-related, which in Kuwait were now endangered and which in Saudi Arabia might become so. UN resolutions about Israel and the Palestinians were one thing; essential international interests – strategic and domestic – argued against over-zealous enforcement of them. But the string of UN resolutions passed on Iraq in 1990 were quite another matter. They were supported by West and East, and by most Arab states as well as Israel; they were specific and unambiguous; and their enforcement carried no risks other than those of the battlefield. Given Saddam's intransigence, the Gulf War was inevitable; and given the firepower ranged against him, so was the outcome.

More significant for the future management of the Middle East were two developments, both dating from the late 1980s, which would govern perceptions of the region into the twenty-first century. The first, the end of the Cold War, looked to augur well for the settlement of outstanding differences. Washington had long argued that the main threat to stability in the region came from the Soviets. Their retreat from Afghanistan in 1989, closely followed by the USSR's economic collapse, the end of Moscow's hegemony in central Asia and eastern Europe, and the repudiation of communism, undermined Russian influence in the region and orphaned those regimes, like Syria's, that had relied on Soviet subventions. The consequences were soon obvious. Of Saddam Husayn's several miscalculations over Kuwait, that in respect of Moscow exercising its UN veto to frustrate international action was the most disastrous. In a world with only one superpower, the UN could bite as well as bark.

Logically the removal of the main threat to the region should have heralded a whole new game in which the pieces fell neatly into place. Conflicts would be resolved, representative government would triumph, and every Middle Eastern metropolis would become as market-orientated, tourist-friendly, franchise-welcoming and pro-Western as Beirut or Tehran in the 1960s. But this assumed that the pieces did actually fit, that the states of the Middle East conformed to geographical, historical and social realities, and that their governments accepted these conformations. It took no account of the fact that the pieces had been cut by the colonial powers to suit their own requirements – principally of imperial prestige, strategic advantage,

Marxism replaced by Islam

economic reward and collaborative governance; nor of their then having been mauled by Washington for similar purposes, plus that of assuaging a powerful domestic preference in favour of Israel.

Thus it was that the end of the Cold War failed to deliver. Although raising Western expectations, the removal of the main threat to stability soon came to be seen as itself a destabilizing factor. Superpower rivalry had run along predictable lines and imposed a certain discipline on client states. Without it, they might strike out on their own. Would Washington be able to rein in an Israel no longer constrained by its neighbours' access to Soviet weaponry and diplomatic support? How now, without the heavy hand of Moscow behind and before them, would autocratic regimes like those of Syria, Iraq and the PLO survive? To retain power, would they succumb to extremism and double their defiance of the West? Or would they submit to the new world order and compete with Egypt and the Gulf states for Western favour? Whence now would come their soft loans, their military hardware and their ideological rationale?

One answer was soon apparent. Ideology could defer to theology; the discredited certainties of Marxism might be replaced by the eternal certainties of Islam. Building mosques, proclaiming Islamist rhetoric, harbouring Islamist fighters, and subscribing to the idea that Islamic values were superior to those of the West attracted financial support from wealthy sources in the devout states of the Gulf and in Saudi Arabia. It also put the fear of God, literally, into Jewish Israel and the Christian West. US installations and personnel anywhere in the world became acceptable targets as what the West called 'Islamic fundamentalism' fired up all manner of sub-national grievances. Additionally, Islamic sanction appealed strongly to the downtrodden, disenfranchised and perpetually desperate peoples of the Middle East, especially the Palestinians.

In a spontaneous eruption of popular protest among Palestinian civilians in the occupied territories lay the second far-reaching development of the 1990s. The Intifada (Uprising) had begun and been so named in the late 1980s when Palestinian youths in occupied Gaza and the West Bank engaged Israeli settlers and supporting troops with stones and petrol bombs. To a catalogue of existing grievances too long for recapitulation, and to a sense of desertion by their dispersed leaders and of betrayal by the Arab states, had been added the increasingly discriminatory and annexationist policies of the Israeli

government. For the new generation of Palestinians, home was just a
fading photograph and Palestine a name on a mandate map. Better
educated, they sensed the loss less and the injustice more. And unlike
the older generation they looked for redress not from others but
from themselves.

As civil disobedience escalated, so did the litany of killings, reprisals and detentions. By 1995 the Intifada had claimed the lives of
thousands of Palestinians and hundreds of Israelis. The arithmetic
was less important than the visual effect. Acts of brutal Israeli repression captured on film left no doubt that this was a popular mass
uprising. The scenes brought to mind the anti-colonial struggles of
an earlier generation of freedom fighters in Africa and Asia. So did
the paraphernalia of occupation – fortified settlements, checkpoints,
identity cards, search-and-destroy tactics. The repression in fact
owed much to the methods and legal sanctions employed by the
British against the Arabs in the 1930s and against the Zionists in the
1940s. But this was the 1990s. It was no good the Intifada looking to
Marxism or even Maoism for revolutionary inspiration. That could
now only come from Islam.

Long sustained, the Intifada challenged Israelis to reflect on the
political wisdom of the occupation and to calculate the moral cost of
retaining the occupied territories and denying the Palestinians some
form of statehood. It also challenged the Palestinian leadership, the
Arab world and the whole international community. With the end of
the Cold War, an international consensus had become possible; and
in the afterglow of 'Desert Storm', the US and its new Arab allies discovered a common resolve to readdress the issue of Palestine.

The peace moves, which would run throughout the 1990s,
involved hefty compromises and endangered both the Israeli and the
Palestinian leadership. Dubbed a 'process', the negotiations duly processed, from Madrid to Geneva to Oslo, Washington, Taba, Sharm el-
Sheikh and so on. But they made only erratic progess. Resolution 242
was dusted down and at last accepted by the PLO. A Palestinian
Authority assumed responsibility for some urban enclaves in the
occupied territories, then larger pockets as and when Israel handed
them over. Meanwhile the construction of Israeli settlements within
the occupied territories, including East Jerusalem, actually accelerated. The US, while issuing occasional rebukes, consistently vetoed
UN censure of this settlement programme which was largely funded

473

from the US. Israel's supposedly endangered security required ever more sophisticated US weaponry. And on the ground the killings continued. Bombs replaced stones in Arab preference as shells replaced bullets in Israeli preference. Arab assassins indiscriminately targeted Israeli civilians; Israeli troops no less callously rocketed Arab suspects.

The peace envisaged by the 1993 Oslo Accords found no favour with dogmatic Zionists unwilling to trade any 'promised' land for an uncertain peace or with Palestinian nationalists unwilling to trade any long-cherished sovereignty for the trappings of a vitiated statehood. The terms on offer to the Palestinian entity presumed neither parity of status with Israel nor economic independence nor territorial homogeneity. Prejudiced and subordinate, the proffered 'independence' brought to mind only the helpless plight of South Africa's 'Bantustans'. To Arab rejectionists wanting the clock put back to 1947, as also to Quranic fundamentalists bent on restoring a seventh-century theocracy or Revisionist Zionists who would settle for nothing later than 2000 BC, this was not so much compromise as betrayal.

Among those less engaged, the twenty-first century nevertheless dawned with a flush of real hope. Yet the sun was barely up before a woefully provocative stroll in the precincts of the al-Aqsa mosque by Israel's now Prime Minister Ariel Sharon triggered a new and even more explosive Intifada. Suicide bombers swarmed from the West Bank towns. Israeli troops reoccupied what their tanks and helicopter gunships had not already destroyed.

Elsewhere, in acts of revenge sanctioned in the minds of their perpetrators by a century of injustice in the Middle East, US embassies, bases and warships were targeted. Out of clear American skies airliners descended as missiles in September 2001. Again the clock stopped. Again we remembered where we were. But from this massacre of innocents no lesson of redress was drawn, only a licence for aggression. Hope itself was hijacked, then ground to zero.

Notes

CHAPTER 1: STRAWS IN THE WIND

1. Unpublished letter to *Blackwoods Magazine*, courtesy of Mrs Marjorie Quarton.
2. *The Times*, 28 June 1906.
3. *Egyptian Gazette*, 29 June 1906; quoted in Adelson, *London and the Invention of the Middle East*, p. 78.
4. Marlowe, *Cromer in Egypt*, p. 266.
5. Elgood, *Egypt and the Army*, p. 24.
6. Mansfield, *The British in Egypt*, p. 169.
7. Lutfi al-Sayyid, *Egypt and Cromer*, p. 173.
8. Lacouture, *Egypt in Transition*, p. 81; and Berque, *Egypt: Imperialism and Revolution*, p. 238.
9. Storrs, *Orientations*, p. 121.
10. Eldon Gorst, quoted in Marlowe, *Cromer in Egypt*, p. 271.
11. Gertrude Bell, letter of 1 January 1900 in *The Letters of Gertrude Bell*.
12. Copeland, *The Game of Nations*, p. 32.
13. Stein, *The Balfour Declaration*, p. 82.
14. Quoted in Vital, *The Origins of Zionism*, p. 295.
15. Meinertzhagen, *Middle East Diary 1917–56*, p. 2.
16. Quoted in Suny, 'A Journeyman for the Revolution', p. 373.
17. Yergin, *The Prize*, p. 135.
18. Ferrier, *The History of the British Petroleum Company*, vol. 1, p. 86.
19. Wilson, *South West Persia*, pp. 41–2.
20. Ibid., p. 42.

CHAPTER 2: GETTING UP STEAM

1. Quoted in Antonius, *The Arab Awakening*, p. 73.
2. Young, *The Independent Arab*, p. 15.
3. Burgoyne, *Gertrude Bell*, vol. 1, p. 278.
4. Woolley, in *T.E. Lawrence, By his Friends*, p. 90.
5. Ibid., p. 89.
6. Antonius, *The Arab Awakening*, p. 101.
7. Ibid., p. 18.

8. Young, *The Independent Arab*, pp. 10–11.
9. Storrs, *Orientations*, p. 142.
10. Ibid., p. 143.
11. Shakespear, letter of 19 January 1915, quoted in Westrate, *The Arab Bureau*, pp. 13–14.
12. Quoted in part in Kedourie, *England and the Middle East*, p. 52, and in full in Monroe, *Britain's Moment*, p. 27.
13. Byron, *The Road to Oxiana*, p. 46.
14. Winstone, *Gertrude Bell*, p. 153.
15. Millar, *Kut*, p. 55.
16. Lawrence, *Seven Pillars*, p. 58.
17. Gertrude Bell, letter of 16 April, 1916, quoted in Burgoyne, *Gertrude Bell*, vol. 2, p. 38.
18. Millar, *Kut*, p. 276.
19. Young, *The Independent Arab*, p. 78.
20. Ibid., p. 126.
21. Gertrude Bell, letter of 22 February, 1918, quoted in Burgoyne, *Gertrude Bell*, p. 78.
22. Young, *The Independent Arab*, p. 72.
23. Ibid., p. 73.

CHAPTER 3: SOMETHING CONNECTED WITH A CAMEL

1. Quoted in Hoffman, *Our Arabian Nights*, p. 113.
2. Memorandum by A.J. Balfour as quoted by Kedourie, *England and the Middle East*, p. 41.
3. Quoted in Nevakivi, *Britain, France and the Middle East*, p. 17.
4. Fromkin, *A Peace to End All Peace*, p. 190.
5. Westrate, *The Arab Bureau*, p. 26.
6. Lawrence, *Seven Pillars*, pp. 56 and 58.
7. Ibid., p. 57.
8. Ibid., p. 65.
9. Storrs, *Orientations*, p. 200.
10. Lawrence, *Seven Pillars*, p. 113.
11. Ronald Storrs, in *T.E. Lawrence, by His Friends*, p. 178.
12. Lawrence, *Secret Despatches*, p. 60.
13. Ibid., p. 66.
14. Lawrence, *Seven Pillars*, p. 23.
15. Lawrence, *Secret Despatches*, p. 61.
16. Ibid., pp. 107–8.
17. Ibid., p. 108.
18. *The Letters of T.E. Lawrence*, p. 291.
19. Quoted in Westrate, *The Arab Bureau*, p. 60.
20. Lawrence, *Seven Pillars*, p. 282.
21. Ibid., p. 24.
22. Ibid., p. 306.
23. Ibid., p. 283.

CHAPTER 4: A TALE OF TWO CITIES

1. Lawrence, *Seven Pillars*, pp. 327–30.
2. Fromkin, *A Peace to End All Peace*, p. 238.
3. Kedourie, *England and the Middle East*, p. 108.
4. Ibid., p. 112.
5. Sykes, *Crossroads to Israel*, p. 16.
6. Roosevelt, *Arabs, Oil and History*, p. 174.

Notes

7. Monroe, *Britain's Moment*, p. 43.
8. Burgoyne, *Gertrude Bell*, p. 75.
9. Kirkbride, *An Awakening*, p. 28.
10. Wavell, *Allenby*, p. 229.
11. Antonius, *The Arab Awakening*, pp. 268–9.
12. Quoted in Ingrams, *Palestine Papers*, pp. 51–2.
13. Young, *The Independent Arab*, p. 142.
14. Yale Papers, quoted in Kedourie, *England and the Middle East*, p. 114.
15. Quoted in Kedourie, *England and the Middle East*, p. 113.
16. Yale Papers, quoted in Nevakivi, *Britain, France and the Arab Middle East*, pp. 65–6.
17. Pichon, *Sur La Route des Indes*, pp. 121–2, quoted in Kedourie, *England and the Middle East*, pp. 119–20.
18. Lawrence, *Seven Pillars*, pp. 664–6.
19. Kirkbride, *An Awakening*, p. 92.
20. Lawrence, *Seven Pillars*, pp. 683–4.

CHAPTER 5: CAIRO ROSE

1. As quoted from the *Morning Post*, 8 November 1918, in Lyell, *The Ins and Outs of Mesopotamia*, p. 237. For another version see Antonius, *The Arab Awakening*, pp. 435–6.
2. Quoted in Lloyd, *Egypt since Cromer*, vol. 1, p. 290.
3. Storrs, *Orientations*, p. 167.
4. Ibid., p. 54.
5. Grafftey-Smith, *Bright Levant*, p. 62.
6. Roosevelt, *War in the Garden of Eden*, p. 199.
7. Thomas Rapp and J. de V. Loder in Hopwood, *Tales of Empire*, pp. 16 and 90.
8. Forster, *Alexandria*, pp. xix–xxv.
9. Grafftey-Smith, *Bright Levant*, pp. 55–6.
10. Thomas Russell, quoted in Berque, *Egypt, Imperialism and Revolution*, p. 277.
11. Quoted in Hopwood, *Tales of Empire*, p. 100.
12. Gilbert Clayton, quoted in Kedourie, *The Chatham House Version*, p. 147.
13. Grafftey-Smith, *Bright Levant*, p. 83.
14. Mansfield, *The British in Egypt*, p. 235.
15. Marlowe, *Anglo-Egyptian Relations*, p. 264.
16. Husayn Haikal, *Mudhakkirat*, vol. 1, p. 216, quoted in Berque, *Egypt: Imperialism and Revolution*, p. 390.
17. Grafftey-Smith, *Bright Levant*, pp. 86–8.
18. Ibid., p. 96.
19. Quoted in Adam, *Life of Lloyd*, p. 198, and Mansfield, *The British in Egypt*, p. 256.
20. Grafftey-Smith, *Bright Levant*, p. 137.

CHAPTER 6: UNCHARTED TERRITORY

1. Hill, *The Baghdad Air Mail*, pp. 19–25.
2. Arthur Hirtzel, quoted in Marlowe, *Late Victorian*, p. 165.
3. Variously related; see Nevakivi, *Britain, France and the Arab Middle East*, p. 91; Monroe, *Britain's Moment in the Middle East*, pp. 50–1; and Kedourie, *England and the Middle East*, p. 133.
4. Kent, *Oil and Empire*, p. 134.
5. Wilson, *A Clash of Loyalties*, p. 22.
6. Sluglett, *Britain in Iraq*, p. 103.
7. Quoted in Marlowe, *Late Victorian*, p. 235.
8. Quoted in Sluglett, *Britain in Iraq*, p. 111.

9. Yale, *The Near East*, p. 283.
10. Ibid., p. 322.
11. Wilson, *A Clash of Loyalties*, pp. 302 and 307–8.
12. Marlowe, *Late Victorian*.
13. Wilson, *South West Persia*, p. x.
14. Young, *The Independent Arab*, pp. 44–5 and 75–6.
15. Burgoyne, *Gertrude Bell*, vol. 2, p. 110.
16. Quoted in Winstone, *Gertrude Bell*, p. 210.
17. A.T. Wilson in *Central Asian Society Journal*, Vol. XIV, 1927, Part III, p. 284.
18. Wilson, *A Clash of Loyalties*, p. 227.
19. Catroux, *Deux Missions au Moyen Orient (1919–22)*, Paris, 1958, p. 15.
20. Quoted in Andrew and Kanya-Forstner, *France Overseas*, p. 195.
21. Quoted in Zeine, *The Struggle for Arab Independence*, p. 94.
22. Ibid., p. 101.
23. See Gelvin, *Divided Loyalties, passim*.
24. Lyautey, *Le Drame Oriental*, Paris, 1924, pp. 163–4, quoted in Kedourie, *England and the Middle East*, p. 170.
25. Storrs, *Orientations*, p. 506.

CHAPTER 7: THREE WEE KINGS OF ORIENT ARE

1. Yale, *The Near East*, p. 316.
2. Wilson, *A Clash of Loyalties*, p. 115.
3. Quoted in Wilson, *A Clash of Loyalties*, pp. 330–41.
4. Quoted in Winstone, *Gertrude Bell*, pp. 214–15.
5. Quoted in ibid., p. 215.
6. Wilson to his parents, quoted in Marlowe, *Late Victorian*, p. 184.
7. Wilson, *A Clash of Loyalties*, p. 252.
8. Burgoyne, *Gertrude Bell*, p. 135.
9. See especially Vinogradov, 'The 1920 Revolt in Iraq Reconsidered', pp. 123–39.
10. Burgoyne, *Gertrude Bell*, pp. 140–1.
11. Quoted in Marlowe, *Late Victorian*, p. 196.
12. Young, *The Independent Arab*, p. 317.
13. Quoted in Marlowe, *Late Victorian*, p. 236.
14. Burgoyne, *Gertrude Bell*, p. 210.
15. Philby, *Arabian Days*, p. 192.
16. Wilson, *King Abdullah, Britain and the Making of Jordan*, p. 37.
17. Ibid., p. 58.
18. Burgoyne, *Gertrude Bell*, p. 211.
19. Ibid., p. 214.
20. Ibid., pp. 213–19.
21. Philby, *Arabian Days*, p. 201.
22. See Knightley and Simpson, *The Secret Lives of Lawrence of Arabia*, pp. 138–9.
23. Sluglett, *Britain in Iraq*, p. 97.
24. Royle, *Glubb Pasha*, p. 101; and Sluglett, *Britain in Iraq*, pp. 266–8.
25. Kedourie, *England and the Middle East*, p. 211.
26. Burgoyne, *Gertrude Bell*, p. 382.
27. Sluglett, *Britain in Iraq*, p. 131.

CHAPTER 8: STIFLING SYRIA

1. Grafftey-Smith, *Bright Levant*, p. 160.
2. *The Letters of T.E. Lawrence*, p. 245.
3. Burgoyne, *Gertrude Bell*, p. 376.

4. Kirkbride, *A Crackle of Thorns*, pp. 18–28.
5. Lyautey, *Paroles d'Action*, p. 472, quoted in Williams, *Britain and France in the Middle East and North Africa*, p. 70.
6. Andrew and Kanya-Forstner, *France Overseas*, pp. 7 and 24.
7. Yale, *The Near East*, pp. 330–1.
8. Catroux, *Deux Missions en Moyen Orient*, p. 58.
9. Hourani, *Syria and Lebanon*, p. 121.
10. Khoury, *Syria and the French Mandate*, pp. 119–25.
11. Catroux dates the attempted assassination to June 1922, although most other sources give May or June 1921.
12. Catroux, *Deux Missions en Moyen Orient*, pp. 107–10.
13. Graves, *The Land of Three Faiths*, p. 224.
14. Philby, *Arabian Days*, p. 212.
15. Catroux, *Deux Missions en Moyen Orient*, p. 116.
16. Ibid., pp. 87–8.
17. Ibid., pp. 44–9.
18. Quoted in Khoury, *Syria and the French Mandate*, p. 156.
19. Longrigg, *Syria and Lebanon under French Mandate*, p. 152.
20. Khoury, *Syria and the French Mandate*, p. 178
21. Ibid., pp. 227–39.
22. Quoted in ibid., p. 486.

CHAPTER 9: STRANGER THAN HISTORY
1. Graves, *The Land of Three Faiths*, p. 13.
2. Quoted in Storrs, *Orientations*, pp. 442–3.
3. Quoted in Hopwood, *Tales of Empire*, pp. 131 and 141–2.
4. Storrs, *Lawrence of Arabia, Zionism and Britain*, p. 53.
5. Marlowe, *The Seat of Pilate*, pp. 69–70.
6. Storrs, *Orientations*, pp. 383–4.
7. Ibid., pp. 386–7.
8. Graves, *The Land of Three Faiths*, p. 60.
9. Storrs, *Orientations*, p. 438.
10. Wasserstein, *The British in Palestine*, p. 89.
11. Storrs, *Orientations*, p. 394.
12. Tibawi, *Anglo-Arab Relations and the Question of Palestine*, p. 434.
13. Ibid., pp. 413–14 and 426–7.
14. Quoted in Wasserstein, *The British in Palestine*, p. 90.
15. Graves, *The Land of Three Faiths*, p. 64.
16. Storrs, *Orientations*, pp. 457–8.
17. Wasserstein, *The British in Palestine*, p. 109.
18. Quoted in ibid., p. 110.
19. Hopwood, *Tales of Empire*, p. 121.
20. Storrs, *Orientations*, pp. 506–7.
21. Quoted in Wilson, *King Abdullah, Britain and the Making of Jordan*, p. 104.
22. Kirkbride, *A Crackle of Thorns*, p. 19.
23. Philby, *Arabian Days*, pp. 206–12.
24. Wilson, *King Abdullah, Britain and the Making of Jordan*, p. 90–1.
25. Kirkbride, *A Crackle of Thorns*, p. 41.
26. Wilson, *King Abdullah, Britain and the Making of Jordan*, p. 85.
27. E. Keith-Roach, quoted in Wasserstein, *The British in Palestine*, p. 222.
28. Wasserstein, *The British in Palestine*, p. 131.
29. Sykes, *Crossroads to Israel*, p. 130.

30. Ibid., p. 151.
31. Wasserstein, *The British in Palestine*, p. 139.
32. Porath, *The Palestinian Arab National Movement*, vol. 2, pp. 22–3 and 27–8.
33. Quoted in ibid., p. 21.
34. Quoted in Marlowe, *The Seat of Pilate*, pp. 120–3.
35. Wilson, *King Abdullah, Britain and the Making of Jordan*, p. 114.

CHAPTER 10: THE ARAB REAWAKENING

1. MacDonald, A.D., *Euphrates Exile*, pp. 105–7.
2. Ibid. Intriguingly, the London Library's copy of this book was presented by A.T. Wilson.
3. Ibid., pp. 118–24.
4. Porath, *The Palestinian Arab Nationalist Movement*, vol. 2, p. 44.
5. MacDonald, *Euphrates Exile*, p. 298.
6. Ibid., p. 96.
7. Yale, *The Near East*, p. 326.
8. Ibid., p. 324.
9. Sluglett, *Britain in Iraq*, p. 289.
10. Simon, *Iraq between the Two World Wars*, pp. 173–7.
11. Aburish, *A Brutal Friendship*, pp. 118–19.
12. *New York Times*, 14 July 1923.
13. *Near East*, 5 June 1924, quoted in Munro, *The Nairn Way*, p. 61.
14. Byron, *The Road to Oxiana*, pp. 45–6.
15. Munro, *The Nairn Way*, pp. 94–5.
16. Stark, *Baghdad Sketches*, p. 4.
17. Graffey-Smith, *Bright Levant*, p. 163.
18. Hoffman, *We Married an Englishman*, London, 1937.
19. Hoffman, *Our Arabian Nights*, pp. 157–60.
20. Stark, *Dust in the Lion's Paw*, pp. 7–8.
21. Marlowe, *Rebellion in Palestine*, p. 139.
22. See Sykes, *Crossroads to Israel*, pp. 159–60.
23. Marlowe, *Rebellion in Palestine*, p. 171.
24. Edward Keith-Roach, quoted in Hopwood, *Tales of Empire*, p. 143.
25. Cohen, *Palestine*, p. 23.
26. Ibid., p. 29.
27. Porath, *The Palestinian National Movement*, p. 227.
28. Sykes, *Crossroads to Israel*, p. 203.
29. Quoted in Marlowe, *The Seat of Pilate*, p. 146.
30. Quoted in Porath, *The Palestinian Arab National Movement*, p. 232.
31. Shepherd, *Ploughing Sand*, pp. 117, 191.
32. Kirkbride, *A Crackle of Thorns*, p. 99.
33. Ibid., pp. 98–108.
34. Bierman and Smith, *Fire in the Night*, p. 63.
35. Kirkbride, *A Crackle of Thorns*, p. 103.
36. Bierman, *Fire in the Night*, pp. 108–9.
37. Kirkbride, *A Crackle of Thorns*, p. 106.
38. Porath, *The Palestinian Arab National Movement*, pp. 254–6.
39. Quoted in Cohen, *Palestine*, p. 84.
40. Sykes, *Crossroads to Israel*, p. 240.
41. Variously quoted. See, for example, Shlaim, *Collusion Across the Jordan*.

Notes

CHAPTER 11: SIDESHOWS OF WAR

1. Stark, *Dust in the Lion's Paw*, p. 76.
2. Churchill, *The Second World War*, vol. 3, p. 433.
3. Gaunson, *The Anglo-French Clash in Lebanon and Syria*, p. 24.
4. Stark, *Dust in the Lion's Paw*, p. 77.
5. Ibid., p. 83.
6. Khadduri, *Independent Iraq*, pp. 210–15.
7. Churchill, *The Second World War*, vol. 3, p. 201.
8. Ibid., p. 226.
9. Stark, *Dust in the Lion's Paw*, p. 97.
10. Ibid., p. 97–8.
11. Cecil Hope-Gill, quoted in Hopwood, *Tales of Empire*, pp. 194–6.
12. Churchill, *The Second World War*, vol. 3, p. 227.
13. Kirkbride, *A Crackle of Thorns*, p. 132.
14. De Chair, *The Golden Carpet*, p. 26.
15. Ibid., p. 48.
16. Ibid., p. 50.
17. Ibid., p. 7.
18. De Gaury, *Three Kings in Baghdad*, p. 128.
19. Stark, *Dust in the Lion's Paw*, p. 114.
20. Moorehead, *African Trilogy*, p. 168.
21. Ranfurly, *To War with Whitaker*, p. 123.
22. Gaunson, *The Anglo-French Clash in Lebanon and Syria*, p. 16.
23. Spears, *Fulfilment of a Mission*, p. 38.
24. Gaunson, *The Anglo-French Clash in Lebanon and Syria*, p. 35.
25. Stark, *Dust in the Lion's Paw*, p. 117.
26. Mockler, *Our Enemies the French*, p. 176.
27. Spears, *Fulfilment of a Mission*, p. 138.
28. Bell, *Shadows on the Sand*, pp. 130–1.
29. Kirkbride, *Crackle of Thorns*, pp. 148–9.
30. Spears, *Fulfilment of a Mission*, p. 171.
31. Ibid., pp. 170–3.
32. Gaunson, *The Anglo-French Clash in Lebanon and Syria*, pp. 80–3.
33. Quoted in ibid., p. 147.
34. Churchill, *The Second World War*, vol. 4, pp. 218–20.
35. Gaunson, *The Anglo-French Clash in Lebanon and Syria*, p. 172.
36. Khoury, *Syria and the French Mandate*, p. 617.
37. Spears, *Fulfilment of a Mission*, p. 298.

CHAPTER 12: TAKING SIDES

1. Ranfurly, *To War with Whitaker*, pp. 38–9.
2. Spears, *Fulfilment of a Mission*, p. 90.
3. Ranfurly, *To War with Whitaker*, pp. 67–9.
4. Quoted in Cohen, *Palestine: Retreat from the Mandate*, pp. 98–104.
5. Moorehead, *African Trilogy*, p. 4.
6. Quoted in Cooper, *Cairo in the War 1939–45*, p. 254.
7. Ranfurly, *To War with Whitaker*, pp. 202–8.
8. Ibid., pp. 120–2 and 128–30.
9. Moorehead, *African Trilogy*, p. 200.
10. Ranfurly, *To War with Whitaker*, pp. 106 and 112–13.
11. Quoted in Nutting, *Nasser*, p. 20.
12. Grafftey-Smith, *Bright Levant*, pp. 232–3.

13. Stark, *East is West*, p. 64.
14. Lacouture, *Egypt in Transition*, p. 99.
15. Grafftey-Smith, *Bright Levant*, pp. 233–5.
16. Ranfurly, *To War with Whitaker*, p. 198.
17. Roosevelt, *Arabs, Oil and History*, p. 89.
18. Stark, *Dust in the Lion's Paw*, p. 131.
19. Stark, *East is West*, pp. 192–3.
20. Quoted in Birdwood, *Nuri es-Said*, p. 212.
21. Berque, *Egypt: Imperialism and Revolution*, p. 719.
22. Stark, *East is West*, pp. 194–5.
23. 'Arab Independence and Unity', quoted in Birdwood, *Nuri es-Said*, p. 205.
24. Seale, *The Struggle for Syria*, p. 22.
25. Bell, *Terror out of Zion*, p. 63.
26. The *Struma* was torpedoed in the Black Sea and there was only one survivor. Ranfurly seems to have confused it with another vessel that sank off the coast of Palestine at about the same time.
27. Ranfurly, *To War with Whitaker*, p. 125.
28. Cohen, *Palestine: Retreat from the Mandate*, p. 179.
29. See Ganin, *Truman, American Jewry and Israel*, pp. 5–6.
30. Stark, *Dust in the Lion's Paw*, p. 177.
31. Ganin, *Truman, American Jewry and Israel*, pp. 6–7.
32. 'The Biltmore Program (1942)', in Laqueur and Rubin (eds), *The Israel-Arab Reader*, pp. 66–7.
33. Ben-Gurion, *Rebirth and Destiny of Israel*, p. 132.
34. Doran, *Pan-Arabism before Nasser*, pp. 94–5.
35. Ben-Gurion, *Rebirth and Destiny of Israel*, p. 114.

CHAPTER 13: COLD WAR, HOT TEMPERS
1. Quoted in Ganin, *Truman, American Jewry and Israel*, pp. 16–17.
2. Brands, *Into the Labyrinth*, p. xi.
3. Philby, *Arabian Days*, p. 329.
4. Yergin, *The Prize*, p. 12.
5. Philby, *Arabian Days*, pp. 290–1.
6. Grafftey-Smith, *Bright Levant*, p. 167.
7. Quoted in Miller, *Search for Security*, p. 226.
8. Quoted in Yergin, *The Prize*, p. 281.
9. Roosevelt, *For Lust of Knowing*, pp. 208–9.
10. Ibid., p. 224.
11. Quoted in Brands, *Into the Labyrinth*, pp. 10–11.
12. Quoted in Louis, *The British Empire in the Middle East*, p. 81.
13. Miller, *Search for Security*, p. 175.
14. Louis, *The British Empire in the Middle East*, pp. 98–9.
15. Ibid., p. 5.
16. Quoted in Wilson, *King Abdullah, Britain and the Making of Jordan*, p. 149.
17. Roosevelt, *For Lust of Knowing*, pp. 169 and 204.
18. Kirkbride, *A Crackle of Thorns*, p. 2.
19. Roosevelt, *Arabs, Oil and History*, pp. 118–28.
20. De Gaury, *Three Kings in Baghdad*, p. 153.
21. R.J. Bowker, quoted in Louis, *The British Empire in the Middle East*, p. 235.
22. Ibid., p. 321.
23. De Gaury, *Three Kings of Baghdad*, pp. 151–3.
24. Quoted in Khadduri, *Independent Iraq*, p. 269.

25. De Gaury, *Three Kings of Baghdad*, p. 155.
26. Quoted in Louis, *The British Empire in the Middle East*, p. 340.

CHAPTER 14: PALESTINE: PARTITIONED

1. Crum, *The Silken Curtain*, pp. 28–30.
2. Crossman, *Palestine Mission*, p. 47.
3. Quoted in Jones, *Failure in Palestine*, p. 64.
4. Crossman, *Palestine Mission*, p. 46.
5. Crum, *The Silken Curtain*, p. 53.
6. Ibid., pp. 111–15.
7. Crossman, *Palestine Mission*, pp. 118–19.
8. Jones, *Failure in Palestine*, pp. 102–4.
9. Clarke, *By Blood and Fire*, pp. 220–3.
10. Meir, *My Life*, p. 188.
11. Henry A. Wallace, quoted in Louis, *The British Empire in the Middle East*, p. 436.
12. Quoted in Cohen, *Truman and Israel*, p. 65.
13. Louis, *The British Empire in the Middle East*, p. 441.
14. Jones, *Failure in Palestine*, pp. 264–5 and 296.
15. Koestler, *Promise and Fulfilment*, p. 143.
16. Quoted in Jones, *The British Empire in the Middle East*, p. 221.
17. Koestler, *Promise and Fulfilment*, p. 145.
18. Quoted in Jones, *The British Empire in the Middle East*, p. 306.
19. Ibid., p. 285.
20. Quoted in ibid., p. 287.
21. Bell, *Terror out of Zion*, pp. 229–34.
22. Pappé, *The Making of the Arab-Israeli Conflict*, p. 25.
23. Cohen, *Truman and Israel*, *passim*.
24. Quoted in ibid., p. 209.
25. Koestler, *Promise and Fulfilment*, pp. 187 and 192.
26. Kirkbride, *From the Wings*, pp. 28–9.
27. De Gaury, *Three Kings in Baghdad*, p. 156.
28. Kirkbride, *From the Wings*, p. 7.
29. Koestler, *Promise and Fulfilment*, p. 160.
30. Wilson, *King Abdullah, Britain and the Making of Jordan*, p. 190.
31. Glubb, *A Soldier with the Arabs*, p. 66.
32. Koestler, *Promise and Fulfilment*, p. 232.
33. Ibid., pp. 245–54.
34. Cohen, *Truman and Israel*, p. 256.
35. Wilson, *King Abdullah, Britain and the Making of Jordan*, p. 199.

CHAPTER 15: COUP AND COUNTERCOUP

1. Roosevelt, *For Lust of Knowing*, p. 378.
2. Copeland, *The Game Player*, p. 106.
3. Seale, *The Struggle for Syria*, p. 32.
4. Copeland, Miles, *The Game of Nations*, p. 42.
5. Seale, *The Struggle for Syria*, p. 45.
6. Ibid., p. 118.
7. Copeland, *The Game of Nations*, p. 44.
8. Ibid., p. 45.
9. Ibid., p. 51.
10. Kirkbride, *From the Wings*, pp. 127–31.
11. Bell, *Shadows on the Sand*, pp. 187–8.

12. Ibid., p. 191.
13. Marlowe, *Anglo-Egyptian Relations*, p. 378.
14. Kent, Introduction to 'Egypt and the Defence of the Middle East', pp. xl–xli.
15. Dorothea Russell, quoted in Hopwood, *Tales of Empire*, p. 112.
16. Cooper, *Cairo in the War*, pp. 330–5.
17. Quoted in Lucas, *Divided We Stand*, pp. 13–14.
18. Heikal, *Cutting the Lion's Tail*, p. 41.
19. Copeland, *The Game Player*, pp. 152–4.
20. Mohi El Din, *Memories of a Revolution*, p. 79.
21. Roosevelt, *Countercoup*, p. 199.
22. Yergin, *The Prize*, pp. 445–9.
23. Miller, *The Search for Security*, pp. 201–2.
24. Louis, *The British Empire in the Middle East*, p. 647.
25. Woodhouse, *Something Ventured*, pp. 104–19.
26. Ibid., p. 117.
27. Dorril, *MI6*, pp. 581 and 583.
28. Roosevelt, *Countercoup*, pp. 181–99.
29. Yergin, *The Prize*, p. 477.

CHAPTER 16: GAME UP

1. Trevelyan, *The Middle East in Revolution*, pp. 10–11.
2. Ibid., pp. 29–30.
3. Copeland, *The Game of Nations*, pp. 134–9.
4. Ibid., p. 137.
5. Copeland, *The Game Player*, p. 168.
6. Trevelyan, *The Middle East in Revolution*, p. 69.
7. Lucas, *Divided We Stand*, pp. 44–5.
8. Copeland, *The Game of Nations*, p. 143.
9. Quoted in Lucas, *Divided We Stand*, p. 68.
10. Trevelyan, *The Middle East in Revolution*, p. 49.
11. Heikal also has 1 March, but Nutting and Trevelyan 29 February.
12. Glubb, *A Soldier with the Arabs*, pp. 422–8.
13. Lucas, *The Middle East in Revolution*, p. 95; Dorril, *MI6*, pp. 612–13; Nutting, *Nasser*, pp. 122–3.
14. Thomas, *The Suez Affair*, p. 25.
15. Lacouture, *Nasser*, p. 170.
16. Heikal, *Cutting the Lion's Tail*, p. 127.
17. Thomas, *The Suez Affair*, p. 31.
18. Ibid., p. 32.
19. Dorril, *MI6*, p. 626.
20. Copeland, *The Game Player*, p. 200.
21. Quoted in Lapping, *End of Empire*, p. 268.
22. Copeland, *The Game Player*, p. 202.
23. Lucas, *The Middle East in Revolution*, pp. 250–1.
24. Heikal, *Cutting the Lion's Tail*, p. 74.
25. 'Caractacus', *Revolution in Iraq*, p. 70.
26. De Gaury, *Three Kings in Baghdad*, p. 170.
27. 'Caractacus', *Revolution in Iraq*, pp. 55–6.
28. Ibid., p. 126.
29. Ibid., p. 138.
30. Trevelyan, *The Middle East in Revolution*, p. 135.

Bibliography

All titles were published in London unless otherwise specified.

Abu-Lugod, I. (ed.), *The Transformation of Palestine: Essays on the Origin and Development of The Arab-Israeli Conflict*, Evanston, 1971.

Aburish, Said K., *A Brutal Friendship: The West and the Arab Elite*, New York, 1988.

—— *Saddam Hussein: The Politics of Revenge*, 2000.

Adam, C. Forbes, *Life of Lord Lloyd*, 1948.

Adelson, R., *Mark Sykes: Portrait of an Amateur*, 1975.

—— *London and the Invention of the Middle East*, 1995.

Andrew, Christopher, and Kanya-Forstner, A.S., *France Overseas: The Great War and the Climax of French Imperial Expansion, 1914–1924*, Stanford, 1981.

Antonious, George, *The Arab Awakening*, 1938.

Arakie, Margaret, *The Broken Sword of Justice: America, Israel and the Palestine Tragedy*, 1973.

Begin, Menachem, *The Revolt*, 1951.

Bell, Gawain, *Shadows on the Sand*, 1983.

Bell, Gertrude, *The Desert and the Sown*, 1907.

—— *The Letters of Gertrude Bell*, 1930.

Bell, J. Bowyer, *Terror out of Zion: The Fight for Israeli Independence, 1929–1949*, Dublin, 1979.

Ben-Gurion, David, *The Rebirth and Destiny of Israel*, 1959.

Bentwich, N. and H., *Mandate Memories, 1914–1948*, 1985.

Berque, Jacques, *Egypt: Imperialism and Revolution*, 1972.

Bierman, J., and Smith, C., *Fire in the Night: Wingate of Burma, Ethiopia and Zion*, 1999.

Birdwood, Lord, *Nuri es-Said*, 1970.

Brands, H.W., *Inside the Cold War: Loy Henderson and the Rise of American Empire, 1918–1961*, 1991.

—— *Into the Labyrinth: The United States and the Middle East, 1945–1993*, New York, 1994.

Brémond, F., *Le Hedjaz dans la Guerre Mondiale*, Paris, 1931.

Brown, Carl L., *International Relations and the Middle East*, Princeton, 1984.

Burgoyne, E., *Gertrude Bell: From her Personal Papers, 1889–1926*, 2 vols., 1958 and 1960.

Butt, Gerald, *The Lion in the Sand: The British in the Middle East*, 1995.

Bibliography

Byron, Robert, *The Road to Oxiana*, 1937; reprint, 1950.

Cambridge Encyclopedia of the Middle East and North Africa, eds. Trevor Mostyn and Albert Hourani, Cambridge, 1988.

Candler, Edmund, *The Long Road to Baghdad*, 1919.

'Caractacus' (pseudo), *Revolution in Iraq*, 1959.

Catroux, Georges, *Deux Missions au Moyen Orient, 1919–1922*, Paris, 1958.

Cecil, Edward, *The Leisure of an Egyptian Official*, 1921.

Childers, Erskine B., *The Road to Suez*, 1962.

Churchill, W.S., *The Second World War*, 1948–53.

Clarke, Thurston, *By Blood and Fire: The Attack on the King David Hotel*, New York, 1981.

Cohen, Michael, *Palestine: Retreat from the Mandate. The Making of British Policy, 1936–1945*, 1978.

—— *Truman and Israel*, Berkeley, 1990.

Collier, Peter, *The Roosevelts: An American Saga*, 1993.

Collins, Larry, and Lapierre, Dominique, *O Jerusalem*, 1972.

Cooper, Artemis, *Cairo in the War, 1939–1945*, 1989.

Copeland, Miles, *The Game of Nations*, 1970.

—— *The Game Player: Confessions of the CIA's Original Political Operative*, 1989.

Crossman, R.H., *Palestine Mission: A Personal Record*, 1947.

Crum, Bartley, *The Silken Curtain*, 1947.

Dann, Uriel (ed.), *The Great Powers in the Middle East, 1919–1939*, New York, 1988.

Darwin, John, *Britain, Egypt and the Middle East: Imperial Policy in the Aftermath of War 1918–1922*, 1981.

De Chair, Somerset, *The Golden Carpet*, 1944.

De Gaury, Gerald, *Three Kings in Baghdad, 1921–1958*, 1961.

Doran, Michael, *Pan-Arabism before Nasser: Egyptian Power Politics and the Palestine Question*, New York, 1999.

Dorril, Stephen, *MI6: Fifty Years of Special Operations*, 2000.

Elgood, P.G., *Egypt and the Army*, Oxford, 1924.

Elliot, Matthew, '*Independent Iraq': The Monarchy and British Influence, 1941–1958*, 1996.

Ferrier, R.W., *The History of the British Petroleum Company*, Cambridge, 1982.

Forster, E.M., *Alexandria: A History and a Guide*, 1922; reprint, 1983.

Fromkin, David, *A Peace to End All Peace: Creating the Modern Middle East, 1914–1922*, 1989.

Ganin, Zvi, *Truman, American Jewry and Israel, 1945–1948*, New York, 1979.

Gaunson, A.B., *The Anglo-French Clash in Lebanon and Syria, 1940–1945*, 1987.

Gelvin, James, *Divided Loyalties: Nationalism and Mass Politics in Syria at the Close of Empire*, Berkeley, 1988.

Glubb, J.B., *A Soldier with the Arabs*, 1959.

—— *War in the Desert*, 1960.

—— *Arabian Adventures*, 1978.

Grafftey-Smith, Lawrence, *Bright Levant*, 1970.

Graves, Philip, *The Land of Three Faiths*, 1923.

Grose, P., *Israel in the Mind of America*, New York, 1983.

Haldane, A.L., *The Insurrection in Mesopotamia*, Edinburgh, 1922.

Heikal, Mohamed H., *Cutting the Lion's Tail: Suez through Egyptian Eyes*, 1986.

Higham, R., *Britain's Imperial Air Routes, 1918–1939*, 1961.

Hill, Roderic, *The Baghdad Air Mail*, 1929.

Hirst, David, *The Gun and the Olive Branch: The Roots of Violence in the Middle East*, 1978.

Hoffman, Ruth and Helen, *We Married an Englishman*, 1939.

—— *Our Arabian Nights*, 1941.

Hogarth, D.G., *Wandering Scholar in the Levant*, 1925.

Bibliography

Holland, Matthew F., *America and Egypt: From Roosevelt to Eisenhower*, Westport, 1996.
Hopwood, Derek, *Tales of Empire: The British in the Middle East, 1880–1952*, 1978.
Hourani, Albert, *Europe and the Middle East*, 1980.
—— *Syria and Lebanon: A Political Essay*, 1946.
Hurewitz, J.C., *The Struggle for Palestine*, New York, 1950.
Ingrams, Doreen (ed.), *Palestine Papers, 1917–1923*, 1972.
Jones, Martin, *Failure in Palestine: Britain and United States Policy after the Second World War*, 1986.
Kaplan, Robert D., *The Arabists: The Romance of an American Elite*, New York, 1955.
Kedourie, Elie, *England and the Middle East: The Destruction of the Ottoman Empire, 1914–1921*, 1956.
—— *The Chatham House Version and Other Middle East Studies*, Hanover, 1980; reprint 1984.
Keith-Roach, E., *Pasha of Jerusalem: Memoirs of a British Commissioner under the British Mandate*, 1994.
Kent, John (ed.), 'Egypt and the Defence of the Middle East', in *British Documents on the End of Empire: Part 1, 1945–1949*, 1998.
Kent, Marian, *Oil and Empire: British Policy and Mesopotamian Oil, 1900–1920*, 1976.
Khadduri, Majid, *Independent Iraq, 1932–1958*, 1960.
Khoury, Philip S., *Syria and the French Mandate: The Politics of Arab Nationalism, 1920–1945*, Princeton, 1987.
Kimche, Jon, *Seven Fallen Pillars*, 1950.
—— *Palestine or Israel: The Untold Story of Why We Failed, 1917–1923: 1967–73*, 1973.
Kimche, Jon and David, *Both Sides of the Hill*, 1960.
Kirkbride, Alec, *A Crackle of Thorns*, 1956.
—— *An Awakening: The Arab Campaign, 1917–1918*, Tavistock, 1971.
—— *From the Wings: Amman Memoirs, 1947–1951*, 1976.
Knightley, Philip, and Simpson, C., *The Secret Lives of Lawrence of Arabia*, 1969/76.
Koestler, Arthur, *Promise and Fulfilment*, 1949.
Lacouture, Jean, *Nasser*, 1973.
Lacouture, J. and S., *Egypt in Transition*, 1958.
Lapping, Brian, *End of Empire*, 1985.
Laquer, W.Z., *Communism and Nationalism in the Middle East*, 1956.
Laquer, Walter and Rubin, Barry (eds.), *The Israel-Arab Reader*, 1970.
Lawrence, T.E., *Seven Pillars of Wisdom*, 1935; reprint 1940.
—— *T.E. Lawrence, by His Friends*, ed. A.W. Lawrence, 1937.
—— *The Letters of T.E. Lawrence*, ed. D. Garrett, 1938.
—— *Secret Despatches from Arabia and Other Writings*, ed. M. Brown, 1991.
Leslie, Shane, *Mark Sykes: His Life and Letters*, 1923.
Lewis, Bernard, *The Middle East and the West*, 1964.
Lloyd, George, *Egypt since Cromer*, 1933.
Longrigg, S.H., *Iraq, 1900–1950*, 1953.
—— *Syria and Lebanon under French Mandate*, London, 1958.
—— *Oil in the Middle East*, 1968.
Louis, William Roger, *The British Empire in the Middle East*, Oxford, 1984.
Louis, William Roger, and Owen, R., *Suez, 1956*, 1989.
Lucas, W.S., *Divided We Stand: Britain, the US and the Suez Canal*, 1991.
Lutfi al-Sayyid, Afaf, *Egypt and Cromer*, 1971.
Lyell, Thomas, *The Ins and Outs of Mesopotamia*, 1923.
MacCallum, E.P., *The Nationalist Crusade in Syria*, New York, 1928.
MacDonald, A.D., *Euphrates Exile*, 1936.
MacDonald, J.G., *My Mission in Israel, 1948–1951*, New York, 1951.

Bibliography

Mansfield, Peter, *The British in Egypt*, 1971.
—— *The Ottoman Empire and Its Successors*, 1973.
—— *A History of the Middle East*, 1991.
Marlowe, John, *Rebellion in Palestine*, 1946.
—— *The Seat of Pilate: An Account of the Palestine Mandate*, 1959.
—— *Late Victorian: The Life of Sir Arnold Talbot Wilson*, 1967.
—— *Cromer in Egypt*, 1970.
—— *Perfidious Albion: The Origin of Anglo-French Rivalry in the Levant*, 1971.
—— *Anglo-Egyptian Relations, 1800–1953*, 1953.
Mattar, Philip, *The Mufti of Jerusalem: Al-Hajj Amin al-Husayni and the Palestine National Movement*, New York, 1988.
Meir, Golda, *My Life, 1917–1956*, 1975.
Meinertzhagen, R., *Middle East Diary*, 1959.
Meyers, Jeffrey (ed.), *T.E. Lawrence: Soldier, Writer, Legend*, 1989.
Millar, Ronald, *Kut: The Death of an Army*, 1969.
Miller, Aaron David, *The Search for Security: Saudi Arabian Oil and American Foreign Policy, 1939–1949*, Chapel Hill, 1980.
Mockler, Anthony, *Our Enemies the French . . . Syria, 1941*, 1976.
Mohi El Din, Khaled, *Memories of a Revolution: Egypt, 1952*, Cairo, 1995.
Morris, James, *The Hashemite Kings*, 1959.
Monroe, Elizabeth, *Britain's Moment in the Middle East, 1914–1956*, 1963.
Moorehead, Alan, *African Trilogy: The North African Campaign, 1940–1943*, 1944; reprint, 1998.
Moorehead, Caroline, *Freya Stark*, 1985.
Munro, J.M., *The Nairn Way: Desert Bus to Baghdad*, New York, 1980.
Nasser, Gemal Abdul, *Egypt's Liberation: The Philosophy of the Revolution*, Buffalo, 1959.
Nevakivi, Jukka, *Britain, France and the Arab Middle East, 1914–1920*, New York, 1969.
Nutting, A., *Nasser*, 1971.
O'Balance, Edgar, *The Arab-Israeli War, 1948*, 1956.
Omissi, David E., *Air Power and Colonial Control: The Royal Air Force, 1919–1939*, Manchester, 1990.
Ovendale, Ritchie, *The Middle East since 1914*, 1992.
—— *Britain, the United States and the Transfer of Power in the Middle East, 1945–1962*, 1996.
Pappé, Ilan, *Britain and the Arab-Israeli Conflict*, 1988.
—— *The Making of the Arab-Israeli Conflict, 1947–1951*, 1994.
Perlmutter, Amos, *The Life and Times of Menachem Begin*, New York, 1987.
Philby, H. St J., *Arabian Days*, 1948.
—— *Forty Years in the Wilderness*, 1957.
Pipes, Daniel, *Greater Syria*, 1990.
Porath, Y., *The Emergence of the Palestine-Arab National Movement, 1918–1929*, 1974.
—— *The Palestinian Arab National Movement: From Riots to Rebellion, 1929–1939*, 1977.
Ranfurly, Hermione, Countess of, *To War With Whitaker: The Wartime Diaries of the Countess of Ranfurly, 1939–1945*, 1994.
Rogan, Eugene L., and Shlaim, Avi (eds), *The War for Palestine: Rewriting the History of 1948*, Cambridge, 2001.
Roosevelt, Archie, *For Lust of Knowing: Memoirs of an Intelligence Officer*, 1988.
Roosevelt, Kermit, sen., *War in the Garden of Eden*, 1919.
Roosevelt, Kermit, jun., *Arabs, Oil and History*, 1949.
—— *Countercoup: The Struggle for the Control of Iran*, New York, 1979.
Rose, N.A., *The Gentile Zionists*, 1973.
Royle, Trevor, *Glubb Pasha*, 1992.
Rubin, Barry, *Paved with Good Intentions: The American Experience and Iran*, New York, 1980.

Bibliography

Salibi, Kamal S., *The Modern History of Lebanon*, 1958.

Samuel, Horace, *Memoirs*, 1945.

Sattin, Anthony, *British Society in Egypt, 1768–1956*, 1988.

Seale, Patrick, *The Struggle for Syria: A Study of Post-War Arab Politics, 1945–1958*, 1986.

Shepherd, Naomi, *Ploughing Sand: British Rule in Palestine, 1917–1948*, 1999.

Shlaim, Avi, *Collusion across the Jordan: King Abdullah, the Zionist Movement, and the Partition of Palestine*, Oxford, 1988.

Shuckburgh, E., *Descent to Suez: Diaries, 1951–1956*, 1986.

Silverfarb, Daniel, *Britain's Informal Empire in the Middle East: A Case Study of Iraq*, Oxford, 1986.

Simon, Reeva S., *Iraq between the Two World Wars*, New York, 1986.

Sluglett, Peter, *Britain in Iraq, 1914–1932*, 1976.

Spears, E.L., *Fulfilment of a Mission: The Spears Mission to Syria and Lebanon, 1941–1944*, 1977.

Stark, Freya, *Baghdad Sketches*, 1937.

—— *Letters from Syria*, 1942.

—— *East Is West*, 1945.

—— *Dust in the Lion's Paw*, 1961.

Stein, Leonard, *The Balfour Declaration*, 1961.

Storrs, Ronald, *Orientations*, 1937.

Storrs, Ronald, *Lawrence of Arabia, Zionism and Britain*, 1940.

Suny, Ronald G., 'A Journeyman for the Revolution: Stalin and the Labour Movement in Baku', in *Soviet Studies*, 23 (January 1972).

Sykes, Christopher, *Crossroads to Israel*, Bloomington, 1973.

Temperley, H.W.V. (ed.), *History of the Peace Conference of Paris*, 6 vols., 1920–4.

Tibawi, A.L., *A History of Modern Syria*, 1969.

—— *Anglo-Arab Relations and the Question of Palestine, 1914–1924*, 1977.

Thomas, Hugh, *The Suez Affair*, 1967.

Trevelyan, Humphrey, *The Middle East in Revolution*, 1970.

Vatikiotis, P.J., *The Modern History of Egypt*, 1969.

Vinogradov, Amal, 'The 1920 Revolt in Iraq Reconsidered', in *International Journal of Middle Eastern Studies*, 3 (1972).

Vital, David, *The Origins of Zionism*, 1975.

Wasserstein, Bernard, *Herbert Samuel*, reprint Oxford, 1992.

—— *The British in Palestine: The Mandatory Government and the Arab-Jewish Conflict, 1917–1929*, 1978.

Wavell, A.P., *The Palestinian Campaigns*, 1928.

—— *Allenby: A Study in Greatness*, 1940.

Weisgal, M.W., and Carmichael, J. (eds), *Chaim Weizmann: A Biography by Several Hands*, 1962.

Weizmann, Chaim, *Trial and Error*, 1949.

Westrate, Bruce, *The Arab Bureau: British Policy in the Middle East, 1916–1920*, Pennsylvania, 1992.

Williams, Ann, *Britain and France in the Middle East and North Africa*, 1968.

Wilson, A.T., *Journal of the Central Asian Society*, vol. xiv, 1927, Part III.

—— *Loyalties: Mesopotamia, 1914–1917*, 1930.

—— *A Clash of Loyalties: Mesopotamia, 1917–1920*, 1931.

—— *Thoughts and Talks*, 1938.

—— *South West Persia: A Political Officer's Diary, 1907–1914*, 1941.

Wilson, Mary C., *King Abdullah, Britain and the Making of Jordan*, Cambridge, 1987.

Winstone, H.V.F., *Gertrude Bell*, 1978.

—— *The Illicit Adventure*, 1982.

Woodhouse, C.M., *Something Ventured*, 1982.

Bibliography

Yale, W., *The Near East: A Modern History*, Ann Arbor, 1958.

Yapp, M.E., *The Near East since the First World War*, 1991.

—— *The Making of the Modern Near East, 1792–1923*, 1987.

Yergin, Daniel, *The Prize: The Epic Quest for Oil, Money and Power*, 1991.

Young, Hubert, *The Independent Arab*, 1933.

Zeine, Z.N., *The Struggle for Arab Independence: Western Diplomacy and the Rise and Fall of Faisal's Kingdom in Syria*, Beirut, 1960.

—— *The Emergence of Arab Nationalism*, Beirut, 1966.

Ziadeh, N.A., *Syria and Lebanon*, 1957.

Index

Index

Index

Index

Index

I; Syria/Iraq agreement bet. UK + Fr.

conf; brits pull out of Syria leaving Faysal alone in Damascus;

—March: Faysal declared King; French march on Damascus in July,
creation of Lebanese state in Aug w/ expanded territory
—under French rule; Samuel High Commissioner in Israel

1921 —creation of Jordan w/ Abdullah as King; Faysal King of Iraq in July
Fragmentation of Syria by France - 1924

1922 - Egypt independence - Feb; King Faud; Palestinian mandate
confirms Jewish homeland and excludes Arabs

1923 - mandates confirmed

1924 —druze & damascus unite in revolt; Ibn Saud conquers Hija
1926   —All Saudi Arabia

1925   Iraq's borders confirmed;

1926 24 May: Lebanese republic proclaimed

1928 - Syrian election a constituent assembly under mandate
- constitution called for a united Syria + was thus refused by France
1929

1929 - Riots in Jerusalem

1932 - Iraq joins league of nations as an independent state
35 - persia becomes Iran
1936-39 - palestine revolt, 36 - Egypt independ.

1940

1941

1941 - unification of Syria; w/out Palestine, Leb, or Jordan

1943 - Syrian independence; US subsidizes Ibn Saud for oil

- bombing of King David hotel
1946 - UK + France pull troops out of Syria & Leb.; ends Jordan mandate